D1567979

PROJECT
OBERON

ACM PRESS BOOKS

Editor-in-Chief **Peter Wegner** Brown University
International Editor **Dines Bjørner** Technical University of
(Europe) Denmark

SELECTED TITLES

Object-Oriented Reuse, Concurrency and Distribution *Colin Atkinson*

Advances in Database Programming Languages *Francois Bançilhon
and Peter Buneman (Eds)*

Algebraic Specification *J.A. Bergstra, J. Heering and P. Klint (Eds)*

Software Reusability (Volume 1: Concepts and Models) *Ted
Biggerstaff and Alan Perlis (Eds)*

Software Reusability (Volume 2: Applications and Experience) *Ted
Biggerstaff and Alan Perlis (Eds)*

Object-Oriented Software Engineering: A Use CASE Driven
Approach *Ivar Jacobson, Magnus Christerson, Patrik Jonsson and
Gunnar Övergaard*

Object-Oriented Concepts, Databases and Applications *Won Kim and
Frederick H. Lochovsky (Eds)*

Distributed Systems *Sape Mullender (Ed)*

Computing: A Human Activity *Peter Naur*

The Oberon System: User Guide and Programmer's Manual *Martin
Reiser*

Programming in Oberon: Steps Beyond Pascal and Modula *Martin
Reiser and Niklaus Wirth*

The Programmer's Apprentice *Charles Rich and Richard C. Waters*

User Interface Design *Harold Thimbleby*

PROJECT OBERON

The Design of an Operating System and Compiler

Niklaus Wirth
Jürg Gutknecht

Institut fur Computersysteme
ETH Zentrum
8092 Zürich

ACM Press
New York, New York

Addison-Wesley Publishing Company
Wokingham, England · Reading, Massachusetts · Menlo Park, California · New York
Don Mills, Ontario · Amsterdam · Bonn · Sydney · Singapore
Tokyo · Madrid · San Juan · Milan · Paris · Mexico City · Seoul · Taipei

Cover designed by Hybert Design and Type, Maidenhead
and printed by The Riverside Printing Co. (Reading) Ltd.
Typeset by Keyword Publishing Services Ltd.
Printed in Great Britain at the University Press, Cambridge

ISBN 0-201-54428-8

First printed 1992.

British Library Cataloguing in Publication Data
A catalogue record for this book is available from the British Library

Library of Congress Cataloging in Publication Data
Available from the publisher

Preface

This book presents the results of Project Oberon, an entire software environment for a modern workstation. The project was undertaken by the authors during 1986–89. Its primary goal was to design and implement an entire system from scratch, and to structure it in such a way that it can be described, explained, and understood as a whole.

In order to address all aspects, problems, design decisions and details, the authors not only conceived but also programmed the entire system described in this book, and more. Although there are numerous books explaining principles and structures of operating systems, there are few which give descriptions of systems actually implemented and used. We wished not only to give advice on how a system might be built, but to demonstrate how one was built. Program listings, therefore, play a key role in this text, because they alone contain the ultimate explanations. The choice of a suitable formalism, therefore, assumed great importance, and we designed the language Oberon as not only an effective vehicle for implementation, but also as a publication medium for algorithms in the spirit in which Algol 60 was created three decades ago.

Because of its structure, the language Oberon is equally well suited to exhibit global, modular structures of programmed systems. Despite the small number of man-years spent on realizing the Oberon System, and the compactness of its description in a single book, it is not an academic toy, but rather a versatile workstation system that has found many satisfied and even enthusiastic users in academia and industry.

The core system described here, comprising storage, file, display, text, and viewer managers, program loader and device drivers, draws its major power from a suitably chosen, flexible set of basic facilities offering, most importantly, effective extensibility in many directions and for many applications. This extensibility is enhanced both by the language Oberon and the efficiency of the basic core. It is rooted in the application of the object-oriented paradigm which is employed wherever extensibility appears advantageous.

In addition to the core system, we describe in detail the compiler for the language Oberon and a graphics system, both of which may be regarded as applications. The former reveals how a compact compiler is designed to achieve both fast compilation and efficient, dense code. The latter stands as an example of extensible design based on object-oriented techniques, and shows how proper integration with an existing text system is possible. Another addition to the core system is a network module, allowing many workstations to be interconnected. We also show how the Oberon System conveniently serves as the basis for a multi-server station, accommodating facilities for file distribution, printing, and electronic-mail. Compactness and regular structure, together with attention to efficient implementation of important details, appear to be the key to economical software engineering.

With the Oberon System, we wish to refute Reiser's Law, which has been confirmed by virtually all recent releases of operating systems. That is, despite great leaps forward, hardware is becoming faster more slowly than software is becoming slower. The Oberon System has required a tiny fraction of the manpower used in the construction of widely-used commercial operating systems, and a small fraction of their demands on computing power and storage capacity, while providing equal power and flexibility to the user, albeit without certain bells and whistles. The reader is invited to study how this was possible. But, most importantly, we hope to present a worthwhile case study of a substantial piece of programming for the benefit of all those who are eager to learn from the experiences of others.

Acknowledgements

We wish to thank the many anonymous contributors of suggestions, advice, and encouragement. In particular we wish to thank our colleagues, H. Moessenboeck and B. Sanders, and our associates at the Institut für Computersysteme for reading all or parts of the draft of this book. We are grateful to M. Brandis, R. Crelier, A. Disteli, M. Franz, and J. Templ for their work in importing the Oberon System successfully to various commercially available computers, thus making the book more worthwhile for many readers. And we gratefully acknowledge the contribution of our school, ETH, for providing the environment and support which made it possible for us to pursue and complete this project.

N. Wirth and J. Gutknecht
Zurich, February 1992

Free Oberon Implementations

Oberon is available without fee from Institut für Computersysteme, ETH. Currently there are implementations for Apple Macintosh II, Digital Equipment DECstation, IBM RS6000 and Sun SPARCStation and IBM PC (MS/DOS). These implementations are completely source-code compatible with each other and share the same document architecture.

Language

- Strong type checking.
- Modules with type-checked interfaces and separate compilation.
- Type extension which provides for object-oriented programming.
- Support for run-time tests.
- Compatibility between all numeric types (mixed expressions).
- String operations.

Compiler

- Generates native code; no separate linking necessary.
- Very fast compilation.
- Can compile directly from edit window.

System

- Single-process multitasking.
- Automatic garbage collection.
- Commands: procedures that can be called like programs.
- Dynamic loading (adding modules to a running program).
- Text as a built-in abstract data type.
- Tools for text and graphics editing, and for program development.

How to get Oberon

Oberon can be obtained via anonymous internet file transfer ftp (at no charge) or on floppy disks (for a fee of 50 Swiss Francs per implementation, which is about 35 US Dollars). We accept payment via Eurocard/Mastercard or VISA. To order by credit card, specify your credit card number, expiry date and your name exactly as it appears on the card. Please remember to specify your type of machine when ordering.

Source Text Electronic Form
The source text for the module in this book is also available without
fee from ETH via anonymous internet file transfer.

FTF Hostname: neptune.inf.ethz.ch
Internet Address: 129.132.101.33
FTP Director: Oberon

For further information, please contact

The Secretary, Institut für Computersysteme ETH, 8092 Zurich, Switzer-
land. Telephone (+41-1) 254 7311. Facsimile (+41-1) 261 5389.

Contents

1 Historical background and motivation

How could anyone diligently concentrate on his work on an afternoon with such warmth, splendid sunshine and blue sky. This rhetorical question was one I asked many times while spending a sabbatical leave in California in 1985. Back home everyone would feel compelled to profit from the sunny spells to enjoy life at leisure in the countryside, wandering or engaging in one's favourite sport. But here, every day was like that, and giving in to such temptations would have meant the end of all work. And, had I not chosen this location in the world because of its inviting, enjoyable climate?

Fortunately, my work was also enticing, making it easier to buckle down. I had the privilege of sitting in front of the most advanced and powerful workstation anywhere, learning the secrets of perhaps the newest fad in our fast-developing trade, pushing colored rectangles from one place of the screen to another. This all had to happen under strict observance of rules imposed by physical laws and by the newest technology. Fortunately, the advanced computer would complain immediately if such a rule was violated, it was a rule checker and acted like your big brother, preventing you from making steps towards disaster. And it did what would have been impossible for oneself, keeping track of thousands of constraints among the thousands of rectangles laid out. This was called computer-aided design. 'Aided' is rather a euphemism, but the computer did not complain about the degradation of its role.

While my eyes were glued to the colorful display, and while I was confronted with the evidence of my latest inadequacy, in through the always-open door stepped my colleague (JG). He also happened to spend a leave from duties at home at the same laboratory, yet his face did not exactly express happiness, but rather frustration. The chocolate bar in his hand did for him what the coffee cup or the pipe does for others, providing temporary relaxation and distraction. It was not the first time he appeared in this mood, and without words I guessed its cause. And the episode would reoccur many times.

His days were not filled with the great fun of rectangle-pushing; he had an assignment. He was charged with the design of a compiler for the same advanced computer. Therefore he was forced to deal much more closely, if not intimately, with the underlying software system. Its rather frequent failures had to be understood in his case, for he was programming, whereas I was only using it through an application; in short, I was an end-user! These failures had to be understood not for purposes of correction, but in order to find ways to avoid them. How was the necessary insight to be obtained? I realized at this moment that I had so far avoided this question; I had limited familiarization with this novel system to the bare necessities that sufficed for the task on my mind.

It soon became clear that a study of the system was nearly impossible. Its dimensions were simply awesome, and documentation accordingly sparse. Answers to questions that were momentarily pressing could best be obtained by interviewing the system's designers, who all were in-house. In doing so, we made the shocking discovery that often we could not understand their language. Explanations were fraught with jargon and references to other parts of the system that had remained equally enigmatic to us.

So, our frustration-triggered breaks from compiler construction and chip design became devoted to attempts to identify the essence, the foundations of the system's novel aspects. What made it different from conventional operating systems? Which of these concepts were essential, which ones could be improved, simplified, or even discarded? And where were they rooted? Could the system's essence be distilled and extracted, as in a chemical process?

During the ensuing discussions, the idea emerged slowly to undertake our own design. And suddenly it had become concrete. 'Crazy' was my first reaction, and 'impossible'. The sheer amount of work appeared as overwhelming. After all, we both had to carry our share of teaching duties back home. But the thought was implanted and continued to occupy our minds.

Sometime thereafter, events back home suggested that I should take over the important course about System Software. As it was the unwritten rule that it should primarily deal with operating system principles, I hesitated. My scruples were easily justified: after all, I had never designed such a system nor a part of it. And how can one teach an engineering subject without *first-hand* experience!

Impossible? Had we not designed compilers, operating systems and document editors in small teams? And had I not repeatedly experienced that an inadequate and frustrating program could be programmed from scratch in a fraction of source code used by the original design? Our brain-storming continued, with many intermissions, over several weeks, and certain shapes of a system structure slowly emerged through the haze. After some time, the preposterous decision was made: we would embark on the design of an operating system for our workstation (which happened to be much less powerful than the one used for my rectangle-pushing) from scratch.

The primary goal, to personally obtain first-hand experience, and to reach full understanding of every detail, inherently determined our manpower: two part-time programmers. We tentatively set our time-limit for completion to three years. As it later turned out, this had been a good estimate; programming was begun in early 1986, and a first version of the system was released in the fall of 1988.

Although the search for an appropriate name for a project is usually a minor problem and often left to chance and the whim of the designers, this may be the place to recount how Oberon entered the picture in our case. It happened that around the time of the beginning of our effort, the space probe Voyager made headlines with a series of spectacular pictures taken of the planet Uranus and of its moons, the largest of which is named *Oberon*. Since its launch, I had considered the Voyager project as a singularly well-planned and successful endeavour, and as a small tribute to it I picked the name of its latest object of investigation. There are indeed very few engineering projects whose products perform way beyond expectations and beyond their anticipated lifetime; mostly they fail much earlier, particularly in the domain of software. And, last but not least, we recall that Oberon is famous as the king of elfs.

The consciously planned shortage of manpower enforced a single, but healthy, guideline: concentrate on essential functions and omit embellishments that merely cater to established conventions and passing tastes. Of course, the essential core had first to be recognized and crystallized. But the basis had been laid. The ground rule became even more crucial when we decided that the result should be able to be used as teaching material. I remembered C.A.R. Hoare's plea that books should be written presenting actually operational systems rather than half-baked, abstract principles. He had complained in the early 1970s that in our field engineers were told to constantly create new artefacts without being given the chance to study previous works that had proven their worth in the field. How right he was, even to the present day!

The emerging goal to publish the result with all its details let the choice of *programming language* appear in a new light: it became crucial. Modula-2 which we had planned to use, appeared as not quite satisfactory. First, it lacked a facility to express extensibility in an adequate way. And we had put extensibility among the principal properties of the new system. By 'adequate' we include machine-independence. Our programs should be expressed in a manner that makes no reference to machine peculiarities and low-level programming facilities, perhaps with the exception of device interfaces, where dependence is inherent.

Hence Modula-2 was extended with a feature that is now known as *type extension*. We also recognized that Modula-2 contained several facilities that we would not need, that do not genuinely contribute to its power of expression, but at the same time increase the complexity of the compiler. But the compiler would not only have to be implemented, but also to be described, studied and understood. This led to the decision to start from a clean slate also in the domain of language design, and to apply the same principle to it: concentrate on the essential, purge the rest. The new language, which still bears much resemblance to Modula-2, was given the same name as the system: Oberon (Wirth, 1988; Reiser and Wirth, 1992). In contrast to its ancestor, it is terser and, above all, a significant step towards expressing programs on a high level of abstraction without reference to machine-specific features.

We started designing the system in late fall 1985, and programming in early 1986. As a vehicle we used our workstation Lilith and its language Modula-2. First, a cross-compiler was developed, then followed the modules of the inner core together with the necessary testing and down-loading facilities. The development of the display and the text system proceeded simultaneously, without the possibility of testing, of course. We learned how the absence of a debugger, and even more so the absence of a compiler, can contribute to careful programming.

Thereafter followed the translation of the compiler into Oberon. This was swiftly done, because the original had been written with anticipation of the later translation. After its availability on the target computer Ceres, together with the operability of the text editing facility, the umbilical cord to Lilith could be cut off. The Oberon System had become real, at least its draft version. This happened around mid-1987; its description was published thereafter (Wirth and Gutknecht, 1989).

The system's completion took another year, and concentrated on connecting the workstations in a network for file transfer (Wirth, 1990), on a central printing facility, and on maintenance tools. The goal of completing the system within three years had been met. The system was introduced in mid-1988 to a wider user community, and work on applications could start. A service for electronic mail was developed, a graphics system was added, and various efforts for general document preparation systems proceeded. The display facility was extended to accommodate two screens, including color. At the same time, feedback from experience in its use was incorporated by improving existing parts. Since 1989, Oberon has replaced Modula-2 in our introductory programming courses.

At this point, a word about the underlying hardware is perhaps in order. The Ceres workstation had also been developed at the Institute for Computer Systems of ETH, and it provided an ideal platform for implanting the Oberon System on a bare machine. It offered the immensely valuable opportunity to design without regard to established constraints and to avoid compromises enforced by an incompatible environment.

Ceres-1 was built around a National Semiconductor 32032 microprocessor, which was in 1985 the first commercially available processor using a 32-bit wide bus. It appeared as particularly attractive to the compiler builder because of its regular instruction set. The computer was equipped with 2 Mbytes of main memory, a 40 Mbyte disk, a diskette, a 1024 × 800 pixel display, and of course keyboard and mouse. These resources were more than adequate for the Oberon System.

Ceres-2 was introduced in 1988, and replaced the processor by its faster version, the NS 32532, which increased its computing power by a factor of at least 5 over its predecessor. Memory was extended to 4–8 Mbyte and the disk to 80 Mbyte. In order to install the software, only a few modules had to be adapted, the kernel because of different page structure, and device drivers because of different device addresses.

In 1990, a low-cost version, Ceres-3, was designed, and 100 computers were built and installed in laboratories. This single-board computer is based on the NS 32GX32 processor without virtual addressing unit, and includes a 4–8 Mbyte memory. The distinctive feature is that the file system is implemented in one (protected) half of memory instead of a disk, increasing operating speed dramatically. Ceres-3 is free from mechanically moving parts (no fan) and therefore is completely noiseless. It is primarily used in laboratories for students. The usefulness of a central server for system file distribution is evident.

Because of its success and flexibility in use, a project was started in 1989 to transport the system to a number of commercially available workstations. The plan to install it on bare machines, as on Ceres, was quickly discarded; nobody would even give it a try, if one had to buy another computer or even only to exchange ROMs in order to experiment with Oberon. The drawback of building on top of an existing system had to be accepted; it implies the cost of some rarely used software occupying part of memory, sometimes even occupying a sizeable part. At the time of this writing, implementations exist on Apple's Macintosh II, Sun Microsystem's Sparcstation, DEC's DECstation 3100 and 5000, and IBM's RISC System/6000 and MS/DOS. These implementations each took about half a man-year of effort. The solution to build on top of an existing system carries the invaluable advantage that applications designed under the base system are accessible from Oberon. All these systems comply with their published description in a user manual (Reiser, 1991), all have exactly the same user interface, and every program operating on one of these computers can be executed on any of the others without change. Evidently, this is an important advantage that can only be gained by programming at a higher level of abstraction, such as in the language Oberon.

1.1   References

Wirth, N. (1988). The programming language Oberon. *Software – Practice and Experience*, **18**(7), 671–690.

Reiser, M. and Wirth, N. (1992). *Programming in Oberon: Steps beyond Pascal and Modula*. Wokingham, England: Addison-Wesley.

Wirth, N. and Gutknecht, J. (1989). The Oberon System. *Software – Practice and Experience*, **19**(9), 857–893.

Wirth, N. (1990). Ceres-Net: A low-cost computer network. *Software – Practice and Experience*, **20**(1), 13–24.

Reiser, M. (1991). *The Oberon System: User Guide and Programmer's Manual*. Wokingham, England: Addison-Wesley.

2 Basic concepts and structure of the system

2.1 Introduction

In order to warrant the sizeable effort of designing and constructing an entire operating system from scratch, a number of basic concepts need to be novel. We start this chapter with a discussion of the principal concepts underlying the Oberon System and of the dominant design decisions. On this basis, a presentation of the system's structure follows. It will be restricted to its coarsest level, namely the composition and interdependence of the largest building blocks, the modules. The chapter ends with an overview of the remainder of the book. It should help the reader to understand the role, place and significance of the parts described in the individual chapters.

The fundamental objective of an operating system is to present the computer to the user and to the programmer at a certain level of abstraction. For example, the store is presented in terms of requestable pieces or variables of a specified data type, the disk is presented in terms of sequences of characters (or bytes) called *files*, the display is presented as rectangular areas called *viewers*, the keyboard is presented as an input stream of characters, and the mouse appears as a pair of coordinates and a set of key states. Every abstraction is characterized by certain properties and governed by a set of operations. It is the task of the system to implement these operations and to manage them, constrained by the available resources of the underlying computer. This is commonly called *resource management*.

Every abstraction inherently hides details, namely those from which it abstracts. Hiding may occur at different levels. For example, the computer may allow certain parts of the store or certain devices to be made inaccessible according to its mode of operation (user/supervisor mode), or the programming language may make certain parts inaccessible through a hiding facility inherent in its visibility rules. The latter is of course much more flexible and powerful, and the former indeed plays an almost negligible role in our system. Hiding is important because it allows maintenance of certain properties (called *invariants*) of an abstraction to be guaranteed. Abstraction is indeed the key of any modularization, and without modularization every hope of being able to guarantee reliability and correctness vanishes. Clearly, the Oberon System was designed with the goal of establishing a modular structure on the basis of purpose-oriented abstractions. The availability of an appropriate programming language is an indispensible prerequisite, and the importance of its choice cannot be over-emphasized.

2.2 Concepts

2.2.1 Viewers

Whereas the abstractions of individual variables representing parts of the primary store, and of files representing parts of the disk store, are well-established notions and have significance in every computer system, abstractions regarding input and output devices became important with the advent of high *interactivity* between user and computer. High interactivity requires high bandwidth, and the only channel of human users with high bandwidth is the eye. Consequently, the computer's visual output unit must be properly matched with the human eye. This occurred with the advent of the high-resolution display in the mid-1970s, which in turn had become feasible due to faster and cheaper electronic memory components. The high-resolution display marked one of the few very significant breakthroughs in the history of computer development. The typical bandwidth of a modern display is of the order of 100 MHz. Primarily the high-resolution display made visual output a subject of abstraction and resource management. In the Oberon System, the display is partitioned into *viewers*, also called

Frames   *windows*, or more precisely into *frames*, rectangular areas of the screen(s). A viewer typically consists of two frames, a title bar containing a subject name and a menu of commands, and a main frame containing some text, graphic, picture or other object. A viewer itself is a frame; frames can be nested, in principle to any depth.

The system provides routines for generating a frame (viewer), for moving and for closing it. It allocates a new viewer at a specified place, and upon request delivers hints as to where it might best be placed. It keeps track of the set of opened viewers. This is what is called *viewer management*, in contrast to the handling of their displayed contents.

But high interactivity requires not only a high bandwidth for visual output, it also demands flexibility of input. Surely, there is no

Mouse

need for an equally large bandwidth, but a keyboard limited by the speed of typing to about 100 Hz is not good enough. The breakthrough on this front was achieved by the so-called *mouse*, a pointing device that appeared at roughly the same time as the high-resolution display.

Cursor

This was by no means just a lucky coincidence. The mouse comes to fruition only through appropriate software and the high-resolution display. It is itself a conceptually very simple device, delivering signals when moved on the table. These signals allow the computer to update the position of a mark – the *cursor* – on the display. Since feedback occurs through the human eye, no great precision is required from the mouse. For example, when the user wishes to identify a certain object on the screen, such as a letter, he or she moves the mouse as long as required until the mapped cursor reaches the object. This stands in marked contrast to a digitizer, which is supposed to deliver exact coordinates. The Oberon System relies very much on the availability of a mouse.

Handler

Perhaps the cleverest idea was to equip mice with buttons. By being able to signal a request with the same hand that determines the cursor position, the user obtains the direct impression of issuing *position-dependent* requests. Position dependence is realized in software by delegating interpretation of the signal to a procedure – a so-called *handler or interpreter* – which is local to the viewer in whose area the cursor momentarily appears. A surprising flexibility of command activation can be achieved in this manner by appropriate software. Various techniques have emerged in this connection, for example pop-up menus and pull-down-menus, which are powerful even under the presence of a single button only. For many applications, a mouse with several keys is far superior, and the Oberon System basically assumes three buttons to be available. The assignment of different functions to the keys may of course easily lead to confusion when every application prescribes different key assignments. This is, however, easily avoided by the adherence to certain 'global' conventions. In the Oberon System, the left button is primarily used for *marking* a position (setting a caret),

Command

the middle button for issuing general *commands* (see below), and the right button for *selecting* displayed objects.

Recently, it has become fashionable to use overlapping windows mirroring documents being piled up on one's desk. We have found this metaphor not entirely convincing. Partially hidden windows are typically brought to the top and made fully visible before any operation is applied to their contents. In contrast to the insignificant advantage stands the substantial effort necessary to implement this scheme. It is a good example of a case where the benefit of a complication is incommensurate with its cost. Therefore, we have chosen a solution that is much simpler to realize, yet has no genuine disadvantages compared to overlapping windows: *tiled* viewers as shown in Figure 2.1.

2.2.2 Commands

Position-dependent commands with fixed meaning (fixed for each type of viewer) must be supplemented by *general commands*. Conventionally, such commands are issued through the keyboard by typing the program's name that is to be executed into a special command text. In this respect, the Oberon System offers a novel and much more flexible solution, which is presented in the following paragraphs.

First of all we remark that a program in the common sense of a text compiled as a unit is mostly far too large a unit of action to serve as a command. Compare it, for example, with the insertion of a piece of text through a mouse command. In Oberon, the notion of a *unit of action* is separated from the notion of *unit of compilation*. The former is a *command* represented by a (exported) procedure, the latter is a *module*. Hence a module may, and typically does, define several (even many) commands. Such a (general) command may be invoked at any time by pointing at its name *in any text* visible in any viewer on the display, and by clicking the middle mouse button. The command name has the form *M.P*, where P is the procedure's identifier and M that of the module in which P is declared. As a consequence, any command click may cause the loading of one or several modules, if M is not already present in main store. The next invocation of M.P occurs instantaneously, since M is already loaded. A further consequence is that modules are never (automatically) removed, because a next command may well refer to the same module.

Every command has the purpose to alter the state of some operands. Typically, they are denoted by text following the command identification, and Oberon follows this convention. Strictly speaking, commands are denoted as parameterless procedures; but the system provides a way for the procedure to identify the text position of its origin, and hence to read and interpret the text following the command, that is the actual parameters. Both reading and interpretation must, however, be programmed explicitly.

The parameter text must refer to objects that exist before command execution starts and are quite likely the result of a previous command interpretation. In most operating systems, these objects are *files* registered in the directory, and they act as interfaces between commands. The Oberon System broadens this notion; the links between consecutive commands are not restricted to files, but can be any global variable,

Module

M.P.

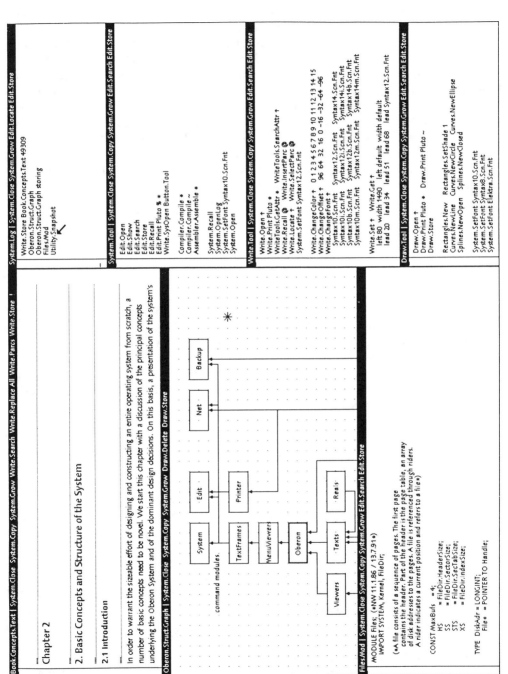

Figure 2.1 Oberon display with tiled viewers.

because modules do not disappear from storage after command termination, as mentioned above.

This tremendous flexibility seems to open Pandora's box, and indeed it does when misused. The reason is that global variables' states may completely determine and alter the effect of a command. The

Hidden state   variables represent *hidden states* – hidden in the sense that the user is in general unaware of them and has no easy way to determine their value. The positive aspect of using global variables as interfaces between commands is that some of them may well be visible on the display. All viewers – and with them also their contents – are organized in a data structure that is rooted in a global variable (in module *Viewers*). Parts

Visible state   of this variable therefore constitute *visible states*, and it is highly appropriate to refer to them as command parameters.

One of the rules of what may be called the Oberon Programming Style is therefore to *avoid hidden states*, and to reduce the introduction of global variables. We do not, however, raise this rule to the rank of a dogma. There exist genuinely useful exceptions, even if the variables have no visible parts.

There remains the question of how to denote visible objects as command parameters. An obvious case is the use of the most recent selection as parameter. A procedure for locating that selection is provided by module *Oberon* (it is restricted to text selections). Another possibility is the use of the caret position in a text. This is used in the case of inserting new text; the pressing of a key on the keyboard is also considered to be a command, and it causes the character's insertion at the caret position.

A special facility is introduced for designating viewers as operands: the star pointer. It is placed at the cursor position when the keyboard's mark key (SETUP) is pressed. The procedure *Oberon.Marked-Viewer* identifies the viewer in whose area the star lies. Commands that take it as their parameter are typically followed by an asterisk in the text. Whether the text contained in a text viewer, a graph contained in a graphic viewer, or any other part of the marked viewer is taken as the actual parameter depends on how the command procedure is programmed.

Finally, a most welcome property of the system should not remain unmentioned. It is a direct consequence of the persistent nature of global variables, and becomes manifest when a command fails. Detected failures result in a trap. Such a trap should be regarded as an abnormal command termination. In the worst case, global data may be left in an inconsistent state, but they are *not lost*, and a next command can be initiated based on their current state. A trap opens a small viewer and lists the sequence of invoked procedures with their local variables and current values. This information helps a programmer to identify the cause of the trap.

2.2.3 Tasks

From the presentations above, it follows that the Oberon System is distinguished by a highly flexible scheme of command activation. The notion of a command extends from the insertion of a single character and the setting of a marker to computations that may take hours or days. It is, moreover, distinguished by a highly flexible notion of operand selection not restricted to registered, named files. And most importantly, it is distinguished by the virtual absence of hidden states. The state of the system is practically determined by what is visible to the user.

Multitasking

This makes it unnecessary to remember a long history of previously activated commands, started programs, entered modes and so on. Modes are in our view the hallmark of user-unfriendly systems. It should at this point have become obvious that the system allows a user to pursue *several different tasks* concurrently. They are manifest in the form of viewers containing texts, graphics or other displayable objects. The user switches between tasks implicitly when choosing a different viewer as operand for the next command. The characteristic of this concept is that task-switching is under explicit control of the user, and the atomic units of action are the commands.

Single process

At the same time, we classify Oberon as a *single-process* (or single-thread) system. How is this apparent paradox to be understood? Perhaps it is best explained by considering the basic mode of operation. Unless engaged in the interpretation of a command, the processor is engaged in a loop continuously polling event sources. This loop is called the

Central loop

central loop; it is contained in module *Oberon*, which may be regarded as the system's heart. The two fixed event sources are the mouse and the keyboard. If a keyboard event is sensed, control is dispatched to the handler installed in the so-called *focus viewer*, designated as the one holding the caret. If a mouse event (key) is sensed, control is

Focus

dispatched to the handler in which the cursor currently lies. This is all possible under the paradigm of a single, uninterruptible process.

The notion of a single process implies non-preemption, and therefore also that commands cannot interact with the user. Interaction is confined to the selection of commands *before* their execution. Hence there exists no input statement in typical Oberon programs. Inputs are given by parameters supplied and designated *before* command invocation.

This scheme at first appears as gravely restrictive. In practice, it is not, if one considers single-user operation. It is this single user who carries out a dialog with the computer. A human might be capable of engaging in simultaneous dialogs with several processes only if the commands issued are very time-consuming. We suggest that execution of time-consuming computations might better be delegated to loosely coupled compute-servers in a distributed system.

The primary advantage of a system dealing with a single process is that task switches occur at user-defined points only, where no local process state has to be preserved until resumption. Furthermore, because the switches are user-chosen, the tasks cannot interfere in unexpected and uncontrollable ways by accessing common variables. The system designer can therefore omit all kinds of protection mechanisms that exclude such interference. This is a significant simplification.

The essential difference between Oberon and multiprocess systems is that in the former task switches occur between commands only, whereas in the latter a switch may be invoked after any single instruction. Evidently, the difference is one of *granularity of action*. Oberon's granularity is coarse, which is entirely acceptable for a single-user system.

The system offers the possibility to insert further polling commands in the central loop. This is necessary if additional event sources are to be introduced. The prominent example is a network, where commands may be sent from other workstations. The central loop scans a list of so-called *task descriptors*. Each descriptor refers to a command procedure. The two standard events are selected only if their guard permits, that is, if either keyboard input is present or if a mouse event occurs. Inserted tasks must provide their own guard in the beginning of the installed procedure.

The example of a network inserting commands, called *requests*, raises a question: what happens if the processor is engaged in the execution of another command when the request arrives? Evidently, the request would be lost unless measures are taken. The problem is easily remedied by buffering the input. This is done in every driver of an input device, in the keyboard driver as well as the network driver. The incoming signal triggers an interrupt, and the invoked interrupt handler accepts the input and buffers it. We emphasize that such interrupt handling is confined to drivers, system components at the lowest level. An interrupt does not evoke a task selection and a task switch. Control simply returns to the point of interruption, and the interrupt remains unnoticeable to programs. There exists, as with every rule, an exception: an interrupt due to keyboard input of the abort character returns control to the central loop.

2.2.4 Tool texts as configurable menus

Certainly, the concepts of viewers specifying their own interpretation of mouse clicks, of commands invokable from any text on the display, of any displayed object being selectable as an interface between commands, and of commands being dialog-free, uninterruptible units of action, have considerable influence on the style of programming in Oberon, and they thoroughly change the style of using the computer. The ease and flexibility in the way pieces of text can be selected, moved, copied, and designated as command and as command parameters, drastically reduces the need for typing. The mouse becomes the dominant input device: the keyboard merely serves to input textual data. This is accentuated by the use of so-called *tool texts*, compositions of frequently used commands, which are typically displayed in the narrower system track of viewers. One simply doesn't type commands! They are usually visible somewhere already. Typically, the user composes a tool text for every project pursued. Tool texts can be regarded as individually configurable private menus.

Tool text

The rarity of issuing commands by typing them has the most agreeable benefit that their names can be meaningful words. For example, the copy operation is denoted by *Copy* instead of *cp*, rename by *Rename* instead of *rn*, the call for a file directory excerpt is named *Directory* instead of *ls*. The need for memorizing an infinite list of cryptic abbreviations, which is another hallmark of user-unfriendly systems, vanishes.

But the influence of the Oberon concept is not restricted to the style in which the computer is used. It extends also to the way programs are designed to communicate with the environment. The definition of the abstract type *Text* in the system's core suggests the replacement of files by texts as carrier of input and output data in very many cases. The advantage to be gained lies in the text's immediate editability. For example, the output of the command *System.Directory* produces the desired excerpt of the file directory in the form of a (displayed) text. Parts of it or the whole may be selected and copied into other texts by regular editing commands (mouse clicks). Alternatively, the compiler accepts texts as input. It is therefore possible to compile a text, execute the program, and to recompile the re-edited text without storing it on disk between compilations and tests. The ubiquitous editability of text together with the persistence of global data (in particular viewers) allows many steps that do not contribute to the progress of the task actually pursued to be avoided.

2.2.5   Extensibility

An important objective in the design of the Oberon System was *extensibility*. It should be easy to extend the system with new facilities by adding modules that make use of the already-existing resources. Equally important, it should also reduce the system to those facilities that are currently and actually used. For example, a document editor processing documents free of graphics should not require the loading of an extensive graphics editor, a workstation operating as a standalone system should not require the loading of extensive network software, and a system used for clerical purposes need include neither compiler nor assembler. Also, a system introducing a new kind of display frame should not include procedures for managing viewers containing such frames. Instead, it should make use of existing viewer management. The staggering consumption of memory space by many widely used systems is due to violation of such fundamental rules of engineering. The requirement of many megabytes of store for an operating system is, albeit commonly tolerated, absurd and another hallmark of user-unfriendliness, or perhaps manufacturer-friendliness. Its reason is none other than inadequate extensibility.

We do not restrict this notion to procedural extensibility, which is easy to realize. The important point is that extensions may not only add further procedures and functions, but introduce their own data types built on the basis of those prtpided by the system: *data extensibility*. For example, a graphics system should be able to define its graphics frames based on frames provided by the basic display module and by extending them with attributes appropriate for graphics.

Type extension   This requires an adequate language feature. The language Oberon provides precisely this facility in the form of *type extensions*. The language was designed for this reason; Modula-2 would have been the choice, had it not been for the lack of a type extension feature. Its influence on system structure was profound, and the results have been most encouraging. In the meantime, many additions have been created with surprising ease. One of them is described at the end of this book. The basic system is nevertheless quite modest in its resource requirements (see Table 2.1 at the end of Section 2.3).

2.2.6   Dynamic loading

Activation of commands residing in modules that are not present in the store implies the loading of the modules and, of course, all their imports. Invoking the loader is, however, not restricted to command activation; it may also occur through programmed procedure calls.

This facility is indispensible for a successful realization of genuine extensibility. Modules must be loadable on demand. For example, a document editor loads a graphics package when a graphic element appears in the processed document, but not otherwise.

The Oberon System features no separate linker. A module is linked with its imports when it is loaded, and never before. As a consequence, every module is present only once, in main store (linked) as well as on backing store (unlinked, as file). Avoiding the generation of multiple copies in different, linked object files is the key to storage economy. Prelinked mega-files do not occur in the Oberon System, and every module is freely reusable.

2.3 The system's structure

The largest identifiable units of the system are its modules. It is therefore most appropriate to describe a system's structure in terms of its modules. As their interfaces are explicitly declared, it is also easy to exhibit their interdependence in the form of a directed graph. The edges indicate imports.

The module graph of a system programmed in Oberon is hierarchical, that is, it has no cycles. The lowest members of the

Driver module hierarchy effectively import hardware only. We refer here to modules that contain device drivers. But module *Kernel* also belongs to this class; it 'imports memory' and includes the disk driver. The modules on the top of the hierarchy effectively export to the user. As the user has direct

Command access to command procedures, we call these top members *command*
module *modules* or tool modules.

The hierarchy of the basic system is shown in Figure 2.2. The picture is simplified by omitting direct import edges if an indirect path also leads from the source to the destination. For example, *Files* imports *Kernel*; the direct import is not shown, because a path form *Kernel* leads to *Files* via *FileDir*. Module names in the plural form typically indicate the definition of an abstract data type in the module. The type is exported together with the pertinent operations. Examples are *Files*, *Modules*, *Fonts*, *Texts*, *Viewers*, *MenuViewers*, and *TextFrames*. (The exception is *Reals*, which is an auxiliary module to *Texts* containing conversion operations for floating-point numbers programmed in assembler code.) Modules whose names are in singular form typically denote a resource that the module manages, be it a global variable or a device. The variable or the device is itself hidden (not exported) and becomes accessible through the module's exported procedures. Examples are all device drivers, *Input* for keyboard and mouse, *Kernel* for the store and disk, *Display*, and *SCC* (communication controller). Exceptions

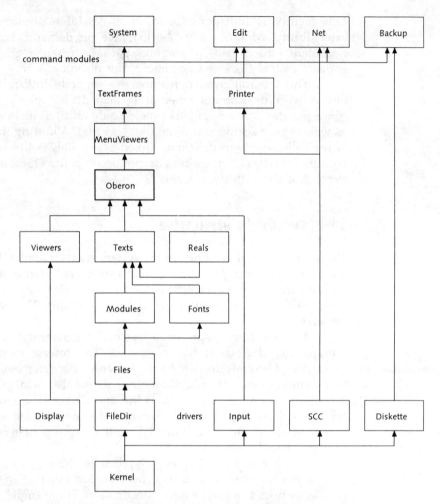

Figure 2.2 Structure of the Oberon core.

are the command modules whose name is mostly chosen according to the activity they primarily represent, like *Edit* and *Backup*.

Module *Oberon* is, as already mentioned, the heart of the system containing the central loop to which control returns after each command interpretation, independently of whether it terminates normally or abnormally. *Oberon* exports several procedures of auxiliary nature, but primarily also the one allowing the invocation of commands (*Call*) and access to the command's parameter text through variable *Oberon.Par*. Furthermore, it contains the log text and exports this variable. The log text typically serves to issue prompts and short failure reports of commands. The text is displayed in a log viewer that is automatically opened when module *System* is initialized. Module *Oberon* furthermore contains the two cursors used globally on the display, the *mouse cursor* and the *star pointer*. It exports procedures to draw and to erase them, and allows the installation of different patterns for them.

No frills

The system shown in Figure 2.2 basically contains facilities for generating and editing texts, and for storing them in the file system and for backing them up on diskettes. All other functions are performed by modules that must be added in the usual way by module loading on demand. This includes, notably, the compiler, network communication, document editors, and all sorts of programs designed by users. The high priority given in the system's conception to modularity, to avoiding unnecessary frills and to concentrate on the indispensible in the core has resulted in a system of remarkable compactness. Although this property may be regarded as of little importance in this era of falling costs of large memories, we consider it to be highly essential. We merely should like to draw the reader's attention to the correlation between a system's size and its reliability. Also, we do not consider it good engineering practice to consume a resource lavishly just because it happens to be cheap. Table 2.1 lists the core's modules and the major application modules, and it indicates the number of bytes used for their code, their constants, and their static variables and, lastly, the number of source code lines.

2.4   A tour through the chapters

Implementation of a system proceeds bottom-up. This is natural, because modules on higher levels are clients of those on the lower levels and cannot function without the availability of their imports. Description of a system, on the other hand, is better ordered in the top-down direction. This is because a system is designed with its expected applications and functions in mind. Decomposition into a hierarchy of modules is justified by the use of auxiliary functions and abstractions and by postponing their more detailed explanation to a later time when their need has been fully motivated. For this reason, we shall proceed essentially in the top-down direction.

Outer core

Chapters 3–5 describe the *outer core* of the system. Chapter 3 focuses on the dynamic aspects. In particular, this chapter introduces the fundamental operational units of *task* and *command*. Oberon's tasking

Interactive task

model distinguishes the categories of interactive tasks and background tasks. Interactive tasks are represented on the display screen by *viewers*.

Background task

Background tasks need not be connected with any displayed object. They are scheduled with low priority when interactions are absent. A good example of a background task is the memory garbage collector.

Table 2.1

Module name lines	Code (bytes)	Constants	Variables	Source
Kernel	1 896	144	108	*
FileDir	4 324	56	0	368
Files	3 640	24	4	450
Modules	2 356	32	48	299
Input	452	4	48	73
Display	2 284	392	52	*
Fonts	1 204	44	8	117
Viewers	1 836	12	20	248
Reals	484	104	0	*
Texts	9 388	176	8	666
Oberon	3 836	48	120	495
MenuViewers	2 776	8	4	226
TextFrames	10 148	152	112	868
System	6 820	688	76	617
	51 444	1 884	608	4 357
SCC	1 144	8	2 056	161
V24	340	4	516	71
Diskette	2 812	40	1 504	382
Printer	1 512	36	1 072	175
Edit	4 668	240	596	458
Backup	1 428	280	48	147
Net	5 868	548	88	610
Total	17 772	1 156	5 880	2 004

Both interactive tasks and background tasks are mapped to a single process by the task scheduler. Commands in Oberon are explicit atomic units of interactive operations. They are realized in the form of exported parameterless procedures and replace the heavier-weight notion of program known from more conventional operating systems. The chapter continues with the definition of a software toolbox as a logically connected collection of commands. It terminates with an outline of the system management toolbox.

Display system

Chapter 4 explains Oberon's display system. It starts with a discussion of our choice of a hierarchical tiling strategy for the allocation of viewers. A detailed study of the exact role of Oberon viewers follows. Type *Viewer* is presented as an object class with an open message interface providing a conceptual basis for far-reaching extensibility.

Table 2.1 Continued

Module name lines	Code (bytes)	Constants	Variables	Source
Compiler	8 988	144	84	967
OCS	3 600	448	944	314
OCT	5 000	504	260	583
OCC	6 252	140	22 540	611
OCE	12 212	320	48	972
OCH	5 804	48	36	553
	41 856	1 604	23 912	4 000
Graphics	7 124	232	116	728
GraphicFrames	5 648	60	60	566
Draw	2 876	268	44	265
Rectangles	1 508	16	8	128
Curves	3 572	12	4	229
	20 728	588	232	1 916
Total	131 800	5 232	30 632	12 277

*Written in assembler code

Viewers are then recognized as just a special case of so-called *frames* that may be nested. A category of standard viewers containing a menu frame and a frame of contents is investigated. The next topic is cursor handling. A cursor in Oberon is a marked path. Both viewer manager and cursor handler operate on an abstract logical display area rather than on individual physical monitors. This allows a unified handling of display requests, independent of number and types of monitors assigned. For example, smooth transitions of the cursor across screen boundaries are conceptually guaranteed. The chapter continues with the presentation of a concise and complete set of raster operations that is used to place textual and graphical elements in the display area. An overview of the system display toolbox concludes the chapter.

Text system   Chapter 5 introduces text. Oberon distinguishes itself by treating *Text* as an abstract data type that is integrated in the central system. Numerous fundamental consequences are discussed. For example, a text can be produced by one command, edited by a user, and then consumed by a next command. Commands themselves can be represented textually in the form M.P, followed by a textual parameter list. Consequently, any command can be called directly from within a text (so-called *tool* text) simply by pointing at it with the mouse. However, the core of this chapter is a presentation of Oberon's text system as a case study in program modularization. The concerns of managing a text and displaying it are nicely separated. Both the text manager and the text display feature an abstract public interface as well as an internally hidden data structure. Finally in this chapter, Oberon's type-font management and the toolbox for editing are discussed and, in particular, an abstract printer interface is defined.

Module loader

Chapters 6–9 describe the *inner core*, still in a top-down path. Chapter 6 explains the loader of program modules and motivates the introduction of the data type *Module*. The chapter includes the management of the memory part holding program code and defines the format in which compiled modules are stored as object files. Furthermore, it discusses the problems of binding separately compiled modules together and of referencing objects defined in other modules. It is explained how the processor's addressing modes support this objective in the case of the Ceres computer.

File system

Chapter 7 is devoted to the file system, a part of crucial importance, because files are involved in almost every program and computation. The chapter consist of two distinct parts, the first describing the structure of files, that is, their representation on disk storage with its sequential characteristics, the second describing the directory of file names and its organisation as a B-tree for obtaining fast searches.

Storage management

The management of memory is the subject of Chapter 8. A single, central storage management was one of the key design decisions, guaranteeing an efficient and economical use of storage. The chapter explains the store's partitioning into specific areas. Its central concern, however, is the discussion of dynamic storage management in the partition called the *heap*. As an exception, the algorithm for allocation (corresponding to the intrinsic procedure NEW) and for retrieval (called garbage collection) are explained in their principles rather than through concrete program listings. The reason for this is that they are programmed in assembler code rather than in the language Oberon, and therefore their details are of less general interest to the readership.

Device drivers

At the lowest level of the module hierarchy we find device drivers. They are described in Chapter 9, which contains drivers for some widely accepted interface standards: an RS-232 line driver used in module *Input* for the keyboard, and in module V24 for data links, an RS-485 line driver (module SCC) used for the network connecting workstations, and a SCSI driver usable for interfaces to disks and possibly other devices via a 8-bit parallel bus.

The second part of the book, consisting of Chapters 10–14, is devoted to what may be called first applications of the basic Oberon

System. These chapters are therefore independent of each other, making reference to Chapters 3–9 only.

Network

Although the Oberon System is well suited for operating stand-alone workstations, a facility for connecting a set of computers should be considered as fundamental. Module *Net*, which makes transmission of files among workstations connected by a bus-like network possible, is the subject of Chapter 10. It presents not only the problems of network access, of transmission failures and collisions, but also those of naming partners. The solutions are implemented in a surprisingly compact module, which uses the network driver presented in Chapter 9.

Central server

When a set of workstations is connected in a network, the desire for a central server appears. A central facility serving as a file distribution service, as a printing station, and as a storage for electronic mail is presented in Chapter 11. It emerges by extending the *Net* module of Chapter 10, and is a convincing application of the tasking facilities explained in Section 2.2. In passing, we note that the server operates on a machine that is not under observation by a user. This circumstance requires an increased degree of robustness, not only against transmission failures, but also against data that do not conform to defined formats.

The presented system of servers demonstrates that Oberon's single-thread scheme need not be restricted to single-user systems. It is acceptable that every command or request, once accepted, is processed until completion if the request does not occupy the processor for too long, which is mostly the case in the presented server applications. Requests arriving when the processor is engaged are queued. Hence the processor handles requests one at a time instead of interleaving them, which, in general, results in faster overall performance due to the absence of frequent task-switching.

Compiler

Chapter 12 describes the *Oberon compiler*. Although here it appears as an application module, it naturally plays a distinguished role, because the system (and the compiler itself) is formulated in the language that the compiler translates into code. Together with the text editor, it was the principal tool in the system's development. The use of straightforward algorithms for parsing and symbol table organization led to a reasonably compact piece of software (see Section 2.3). A main contributor to this result is the language's definition: the language is devoid of complicated structures and rarely used embellishments. Its structure is regular and its syntax compact.

The compiler and thus the chapter are partitioned into three main parts. The first is language-specific, but does not refer to any particular target computer. This part is therefore of most general interest to the readership. The second part is, essentially, language-independent, but is specifically tailored to the instruction set of the target computer; it discusses the selection of instructions. The third part describes the module that puts instructions into the particular format defined by the target machine.

Although the algorithms and details decribed in the latter two parts are machine-specific, much would remain similar for other target computers with similar architectures. Our choice of the National Semiconductor 32000 processor (eight years ago) may appear mistaken, because it happens to be not widely known. In contrast to similar architectures (like Motorola 680x0 and Intel 80x86) it is distinguished by a much more regular instruction set. This is the most attractive property for compiler designers, and it is even more so for the compiler's description. Every irregularity is a source of additional complexity. Even in retrospect, the 32000 was by far the best choice from the point of view of description. And we presume that our readers wish to not merely copy, but also understand our programs.

Graphics editor

Texts play a predominant role in the Oberon System. Their preparation is supported by the system's major tool, the editor. In Chapter 13 we describe another editor, one that handles graphic objects. At first, only horizontal and vertical lines and short captions are introduced as objects. The major difference from texts lies in the fact that their coordinates in the drawing plane do not follow from those of their predecessor automatically, because they form a set rather than a sequence. Each object carries its own, independent coordinates. The influence of this seemingly small difference upon an editor is far-reaching and permeates the entire design. There exist hardly any similarities between a text and a graphics editor. Perhaps one should be mentioned: the partitioning into three parts. The bottom module defines the respective abstract data structure for texts or graphics, together with, of course, the procedures handling the structure, such as searches, insertions, and deletions. The middle module in the hierarchy defines a respective frame and contains all procedures concerned with displaying the respective objects including the frame handler defining interpretation of mouse and keyboard events. The top modules are the respective tool modules (*Edit*, *Draw*). The presented graphics editor is particularly interesting in so far as it constitutes a convincing example of Oberon's extensibility. The graphics editor is integrated into the entire system; it embeds its graphic frames into menu-viewers and uses the facilities of the text system for its caption elements. And lastly, new kinds of elements can be incorporated by the mere addition of new modules, that is, without expanding, even without recompiling the existing ones. Three examples are shown in Chapter 13 itself: rectangles, circles and ellipses.

The *Draw* system has been extensively used for the preparation of diagrams of electronic circuits. This application suggests a concept that is useful elsewhere too, namely a recursive definition of the notion of object. A set of objects may be regarded as an object itself and be given a name. Such an object is called a *macro*. It is a challenge to the designer to implement a macro facility such that it is also extensible, that is, in no way refers to the type of its elements, not even in its input operations of files on which macros are stored.

At this point, the reader may have become aware that our presented applications are those that were actually required by our own project. This at least bears the guarantee that they were not only designed but *used*. In fact, many have been used by hundreds of people, and many daily over several years. Chapter 14 indeed presents two other such tools, namely one used for installing an Oberon System on a new, bare machine, and two used to recover from failures of the disk. Although rarely employed, the first was indispensible for the development of the system. The maintenance or recovery tools are invaluable assets when failures occur. And they do! Chapter 14 covers material that is rarely presented in the literature.

3 The tasking system

Eventually, it is its generic ability to perform customized tasks orderly that turns a rigid computing device into a versatile universal tool. Consequently, modelling and scheduling of tasks are principal and crucial issues in the design of any operating system. Of course, we cannot expect a single fixed tasking metaphor to be the ideal solution for all possible modes of use. For example, different metaphors are probably appropriate in the cases of a closed central system serving a large set of users in time-sharing mode on the one hand, and of a personal workstation that is operated by a single user with a high degree of interactivity on the other.

In the case of Oberon, we have consciously concentrated on personal workstations. More precisely, we have directed Oberon's tasking facilities towards a single-user interactive personal workstation that is possibly integrated into a local area network. We start the presentation in Section 3.1 with a clarification of the notion of *task*. In Section 3.2, we continue with a detailed explanation of the scheduling strategy. Then, in Section 3.3, we introduce the concept of *command*. Finally, Section 3.4 provides an overview of predefined system-oriented *toolboxes*. A toolbox is a coherent collection of commands that are devoted to a specific topic. Example topics are system control and diagnosis, display management and file management.

3.1 The concept of task

In principle, we distinguish two categories of tasks in Oberon: *interactive tasks* and *background tasks*. Roughly said, interactive tasks are bound to local regions on the display screen and to interactions with their contents. In contrast, background tasks are global. They are not necessarily related to any specific displayed entity.

Interactive tasks

Every interactive task is represented by a so-called *viewer*. Viewers constitute the interface to Oberon's display system and embody a variety of roles that are collected in an abstract data type *Viewer*. We shall give a deeper insight into the display system in Chapter 4. For the moment, it suffices to know that viewers are representable graphically as rectangles on the display screen and that they are implicit carriers of interactive tasks. Figure 3.1 shows a typical Oberon display screen that is divided up into seven viewers corresponding to seven simultaneously active interactive tasks.

In order to get firmer ground under our feet, we give the programmed declaration of type *Viewer* in a slightly abstracted form:

Viewer = POINTER TO ViewerDesc;

ViewerDesc = RECORD
  X, Y, W, H: INTEGER;
  state: INTEGER;
  handle: Handler
END;

X, Y, W, H define the viewer's rectangle on the screen, that is, location X, Y of the lower left corner relative to the display origin, width W and height H. The variable *state* informs about the current state of visibility

Handlers

(visible, closed, covered), and *handle* represents the functional interface of viewers. The type of the handler is

Handler = PROCEDURE (V: Viewer; VAR M: ViewerMsg);

where *ViewerMsg* is some base type of messages whose exact declaration is of minor importance for the moment:

ViewerMsg = RECORD ... (*basic parameter fields*) END;

However, we should point out the use of object-oriented terminology. It is justified because *handle* is a procedure variable whose identity depends on the specific viewer. A call *V.handle(V, M)* can therefore be interpreted as the sending of a *message* M to be handled individually by a method of the receiving viewer V.

We recognize an important difference between the standard object-oriented model and our handler paradigm. The standard model is *closed* in the sense that only a fixed set of messages is understood by a given class of objects. In contrast, the handler paradigm is *open* because it defines just the root (*ViewerMsg*) of a potentially unlimited

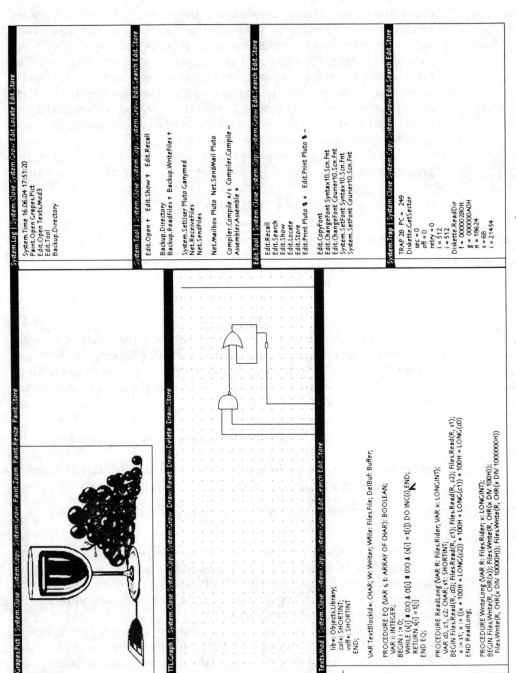

Figure 3.1 Typical Oberon display configuration consisting of seven viewers.

tree of extending message types. For example, a concrete handler might be able to handle messages of type *MyViewerMsg*, where

```
MyViewerMsg = RECORD (ViewerMsg)
   mypar: MyParameters
END;
```

is an extended type of *ViewerMsg*.

Coming back now to the role of viewers as tasks, we should note that the primitive operation of *activation* (or *reactivation*) is expressed in this model by the sending of an appropriate message to the viewer object. The exact request that is transmitted with an activation is determined by the type and value of the message.

Background tasks

Oberon background tasks are not connected a priori with any specific aggregate in the system. Seen technically, they are instances of an abstract data type consisting of type declarations *Task* and *TaskDesc* together with intrinsic operations *Install* and *Remove*:

```
Task = POINTER TO TaskDesc;

TaskDesc = RECORD
   safe: BOOLEAN;
   handle: PROCEDURE
END;

PROCEDURE Install (T: Task);
PROCEDURE Remove (T: Task);
```

The procedures *Install* and *Remove* are called explicitly in order to transfer the state of the specified task from *not ready* to *ready* and from *ready* to *not ready* respectively. The field named *safe* in *TaskDesc* distinguishes so-called *safe* tasks. In contrast to potentially unsafe tasks, they are not cancelled automatically after a program trap. The procedure variable *handle* is again used for the activation of the task. We should view a call of the parameterless procedure *handle* as the sending of an implicit message *continue*.

A concrete background task is normally a type-extension of the abstract type *Task*. Typically, the extending part refers to the object(s) on which this task is operating:

```
MyTask = POINTER TO MyTaskDesc;

MyTaskDesc = RECORD (TaskDesc)
   myobj: MyObjType
END;
```

Table 3.1

Task type	Create	To ready	(Re)Activate	Passivate	To not ready
Interactive	Create viewer	Open viewer	Send message	Terminate handling	Close viewer
Background	Create task	Install	Send continue	Terminate handling	Remove

It may contribute to an improved understanding, if we give two realistic examples of concrete background tasks. The first one is a system-wide *garbage collector* collecting unused memory. The second example is a *network monitor* monitoring incoming traffic on a local area network. In both examples the state of the task is captured by global system variables. We shall come back to these topics in Chapters 8 and 10 respectively.

Summary
Table 3.1 now summarizes Oberon's tasking model. We should not end this section without drawing an important conclusion. Transfers of control between tasks are implemented in Oberon as ordinary calls and returns of ordinary procedures (procedure variables, actually). Preemption is not possible. From that we imply that active periods of tasks are sequentially ordered and can be controlled by a *single flow* (thread, process). This simplification pays well: locks of common resources are completely dispensable and deadlocks are not a topic at all.

3.2   The task scheduler

We start from the general assumption that, at any given time, a number of well-determined tasks are ready in the system to be serviced. Remember that two categories of tasks exist: interactive tasks and background tasks. They differ substantially in the criteria of activation or reactivation and in the priority of dispatching. Interactive tasks are (re)activated exclusively upon interactions by the user and are dispatched with high priority. In contrast, background tasks are polled with low priority.

Input messages
We already know that interactive tasks are activated by sending messages. The types of messages used for this purpose are *InputMsg* and *ControlMsg*, reporting on keyboard events and mouse events respectively. Slightly simplified, they are declared as

```
InputMsg = RECORD (ViewerMsg)
    id: INTEGER;
```

```
      X, Y: INTEGER;
      keys: SET;
      ch: CHAR
END;

ControlMsg = RECORD (ViewerMsg)
   id: INTEGER;
   X, Y: INTEGER
END;
```

The field *id* specifies the exact request transmitted with this activation. In the case of *InputMsg*, the possible requests are *consume* (the character specified by field *ch*) and *track* (mouse, starting from state given by *keys* and X, Y). In the case of *ControlMsg*, the choice is *mark* (the viewer at position X, Y) or *neutralize*. *Marking* means moving the global *system pointer* (typically represented as a star-shaped mark) to the current position of the mouse. *Neutralizing* a viewer is equivalent to removing all marks and graphical attributes from this viewer.

All tasking facilities are collected in one module, called *Oberon*. In particular, the module's definition exposes the declarations of the abstract data type *Task* and of the message types *InputMsg* and *ControlMsg*. The module's most important contribution, however, is the *task scheduler* that can be regarded as the system's dynamic center.

Focus viewer
Before we can study the scheduler in detail, we need some more preparation. We start with the institution of the *focus viewer*. By definition, this is a distinguished viewer that applied for consuming subsequent keyboard input. Note that the focus *viewer* is actually a focus *task*. However, recalling our definition of tasks, we regard the terms *viewer* and *interactive task* as interchangeable.

Module Oberon provides the following facilities in connection with the focus viewer: a global variable *FocusViewer*, a procedure *PassFocus* to transfer the role of focus to a new viewer, and a *defocus* variant of *ControlMsg* to notify the old focus viewer of such a transfer.

Next, we reveal the implementation of the abstract type *Task* that is hidden from the clients. It is based on a ring of task descriptors and on a pointer to the previously activated task in the ring. The ring is guaranteed never to be empty, because the above mentioned garbage collector is installed as a safe task at system loading time.

Scheduling strategy
We can now scrutinize the following version of the task scheduler. The reader should relate this to procedure *Loop* in module *Oberon* listed in detail at the end of this chapter.

```
get mouse position and state of keys;
LOOP
   IF keyboard input available THEN read character
      IF character is escape THEN
```

broadcast *neutralize* message to viewers
ELSIF character is *setup* THEN
   send *mark* message to viewer containing mouse
ELSE send *consume* message to focus viewer
END;
get mouse position and state of keys
ELSIF at least one key pressed THEN
  REPEAT
    send *track* message to viewer containing mouse;
    get mouse position and state of keys
  UNTIL all keys released
ELSE (*no key pressed*)
  send *track* message to viewer containing mouse;
  get mouse position and state of keys;
  WHILE mouse unmoved and no keyboard input DO
    take next task in ring as current task;
    IF current task is unsafe THEN remove it from ring
      END;
    send *continue* message to current task;
    assure current task in ring again;
    get mouse position and state of keys
  END
END
END

Program traps   It is fair to add some conceptual remarks about the way of continuation in case of a *program trap* or, in other words, in case of a failing task. Of course, the handling of such a case can be pursued on many different levels of abstraction. In accordance with our general top-down approach, we focus our current attention to the level of our tasking model.

We can identify three sequential actions of recovery after a program failure:

recovery after program failure = BEGIN
  save current system state;
  call installed trap handler;
  roll back to start of task scheduler
END

Essentially, the *system state* is determined by the values of all global and local variables at the given time. The trap handler typically opens an extra viewer displaying the cause of the trap and the saved system state. Figure 3.1 shows a trap viewer at the lower right corner of the display screen.

Remember from the program fragment above that unsafe background tasks are removed from the ring of ready tasks before reactivation, and are installed again only after successful return. Consequently, unsafe tasks are eliminated automatically after failing. This is an effective precaution against cascades of repeated failures. Obviously, no such precaution is necessary in the case of interactive tasks, because their reactivation is under control of the system user.

Summary
In summary, Oberon is a *multitasking system* based on a two-category model. Interactive tasks are interfacing with the display system and are scheduled with high priority upon user interactions. Background tasks are stand-alone and are scheduled with low priority. Task activations are modelled as message passing and eventually as calls of procedures assigned to variables. They are sequentially ordered and controlled by a *single process*.

3.3　The concept of command

Essentially an operating system constitutes a general purpose *platform* on which specialized application software packages can build. The platform appears to software designers as interface to 'the system' and (in particular) to the underlying hardware resources. Unfortunately, interfaces defined by more conventional operating systems suffer from an all too primitive access mechanism that is based solely on the concept of so-called *supervisor call* and on files taking the role of 'connecting pipes'. The situation is especially ironic in comparison with the development of high-level programming languages towards abstraction.

We have put greatest emphasis in Oberon to close the semantic gap between application software packages and the system platform. The result of our effort is a highly expressive and consistent interface in the form of an explicit hierarchy of module definitions. Perhaps the **Abstract** most significant and most conspicuous outcome of this approach is a **data types** collection of very powerful abstract data types like *Task, Frame, Viewer, File, Font, Text, Module, Reader, Scanner* and *Writer*.

The most important (because most generic) function of any operating system is *calling programs*. Our next step is therefore a clarification of the term *program*, as it is used in Oberon. We should consider a *static aspect* as well as a *dynamic aspect*. Statically, an Oberon program is simply a package of software together with an entry point. More formally, it is a pair (M*, P), where M is an arbitrary module, P is an exported parameterless procedure of M, and M* denotes the hierarchy consisting of M itself and of all directly and indirectly imported modules. Notice that two hierarchies M* and N* are not disjoint in

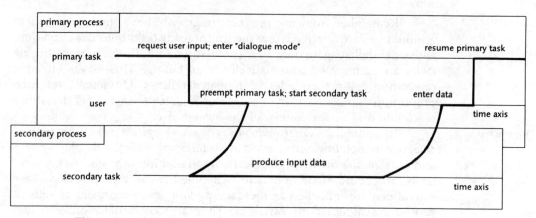

Figure 3.2　Typical trace of processing in a classical interactive system.

general, even if M and N are different modules. Rather, their intersection is a superset of the operating system.

Atomic actions　　Viewed dynamically, an Oberon program is defined as an *atomic action* operating on the global system state, where *atomic* means 'without user interaction'. In essence this definition is just a compelling consequence of our model of non-preemptive task scheduling with the benefit of a single carrier process. We can argument like this: when a traditional interactive program requires some input from the user in order to be able to proceed, there is no justification whatsoever not to allow the user to preempt the current task and to start another task with the aim of producing the required input data. Figures 3.2 and 3.3 visualize this argumentation by opposing possible traces of processing in a more traditional interactive system and in the Oberon system respectively.

Program calls　　Quintessentially, Oberon programs are represented in the form of exported parameterless procedures that do not interact with the user of the system. In honour of these distinguishing properties, such procedures are called *commands*.

Returning to the calling of programs, we now arrive at the following refinement:

```
call program (M*, P) = BEGIN
  load module hierarchy M*; call command P
END
```

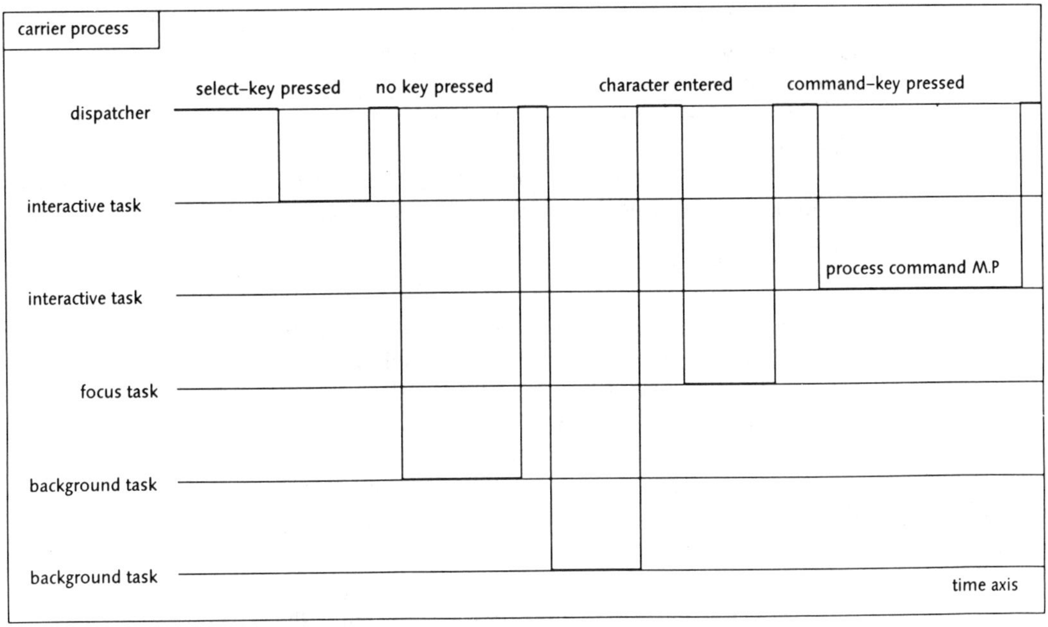

Figure 3.3 Typical trace of processing in the Oberon system.

The system interface to the command mechanism itself is again provided by module Oberon. Its primary operation can be paraphrased as 'call a command by its name and pass a list of actual parameters':

PROCEDURE Call (VAR name: ARRAY OF CHAR; par: ParList; new: BOOLEAN; VAR res: INTEGER);

Parameter record

name is the name of the desired command in the form *M.P*, *par* is the list of actual parameters, *new* is an option guaranteeing preliminary loading of a new version of M*, and *res* is a result code.

Type *ParList* is declared essentially as

ParList = POINTER TO ParRec;
ParRec = RECORD
    vwr: Viewers.Viewer;
    text: Texts.Text;
    pos: LONGINT
END;

Parameter *vwr* indicates the calling viewer (task) and the pair (*text, pos*) of parameters specifies the starting position *pos* of a textual parameter list within *text*. Notice the occurrence of another abstract data type with name *Text* that is exported by module *Texts*. We shall devote the entire Chapter 5 to a thorough presentation of Oberon's text system. For the moment, we can simply look at a text as a sequence of characters.

The list of actual parameters is put at the disposal of the called command by module Oberon in the form of an exported global variable

Par: ParList;

The actual list of parameters may well be an extension of the standard parameter list *ParList*. In such a case, the extending fields represent non-standard and customized parameters.

In principle, commands operate on the entire system and can access the current global state via the system's powerful modular interface, of which the list of actual parameters is just one component.

System log Another one is the so-called *system log*, which is a system-wide protocol reporting on progress of command execution and on exceptional events in chronological order.

The log is represented as a global variable of type *Text*:

Log: Texts.Text;

It should have become clear by now that implementors of versatile and adaptable commands rely on a rich arsenal of global facilities reflecting the current system state and making it accessible. In other

System integration words, they rely on a high degree of *system integration*. Therefore we find in Oberon an extraordinarily broad spectrum of integrated notions. For example, the system distinguishes itself by a complete integration of the abstract data types *Viewer* and *Text* that we encountered above. They will be the subjects of Chapters 4 and 5.

Module Oberon assists the integration of these types with the following conceptual features, of which the first two are familiar to us already: standard parameter list for commands, system log, generic text selection, generic copy-over for text, and generic copy viewer. At this point, we should perhaps add a word of clarification to our use of the term *generic*. It is synonymous with 'interpretable by any viewer (interactive task)', and is typically used in connection with messages or orders whose receiver's exact identity is unknown.

We now go into a brief discussion of the generic facilities, without, however, leaving the level of our current abstraction and understanding.

Generic text selection Textual selections are characterized by a text, a stretch of characters within that text, and a time stamp. Without further qualification, 'the text selection' always means 'the most recent text selection'. It can be obtained by calling procedure *GetSelection*:

```
PROCEDURE GetSelection (VAR text: Texts.Text;
    VAR beg, end, time: LONGINT);
```

The parameters specify the desired stretch of text starting at position *beg* and ending at *end – 1* as well as the associated time stamp. The procedure is implemented by a broadcast of a so-called *selection* message to all viewers. The declaration of this message is

```
SelectionMsg = RECORD (ViewerMsg)
    time: LONGINT;
    text: Texts.Text;
    beg, end: LONGINT
END;
```

Generic copy-over text

The aim is an integrated 'copy-over text'. A variant of type *ViewerMsg* is defined the purpose of transmitting such requests:

```
CopyOverMsg = RECORD (ViewerMsg)
    text: Texts.Text;
    beg, end: LONGINT
END;
```

Typically, receivers of a copy-over message copy the specified stretch of text to their local focus.

Generic copy viewer

Generic copy is synonymous to reproducing and to *cloning*. It is the most elementary generic operation possible. Again, a variant of type *ViewerMsg* is used to the purpose of transmitting requests of the desired type:

```
CopyMsg = RECORD (ViewerMsg)
    vwr: Viewers.Viewer
END;
```

Receivers of a copy message generate a clone of themselves and return it to the sender via field *vwr*.

Summary

We summarize this section as follows. Oberon is an operating system presenting itself to its clients in the form of a highly expressive modular interface exporting many powerful abstract data types like, for

Table 3.2

Form of module	Role of definition	Role of implementation
Declaration cluster	Declare data and objects	Void
Abstract data type	Define interface	Implement operations
Object class	Define object generator	Implement methods
Service package	Define procedures	Implement procedures
Toolbox	Define command names	Implement commands

example, *Viewer* and *Text*. A rich arsenal of global and generic facilities serve the purpose of system integration. Programs in Oberon are modelled as so-called commands, that is, as exported parameterless procedures that do not interact with the user. The collection of commands provided by a module appears as interface to its run-time clients. Parameters are claimed by the commands from a global parameter list registered by the calling task in the central module Oberon. Commands operate on the global state of the system.

3.4 Toolboxes

In a modular programming environment software modules may appear in many different forms. Some familiar examples are listed in Table 3.2: a collection of logically connected declarations of data and of types, a capsule representing an abstract data type, a framework for the implementation of an object class, and a library of service procedures.

Toolbox   Oberon adds another form: the *toolbox*. By definition, this is a pure collection of commands in the sense of the previous section.

Toolboxes distinguish themselves principally from the other forms of modules by the fact that they lie on top of the modular hierarchy. Toolbox modules are 'imported' by system users at run-time. In other

Command interface words, their definitions define the *command interface*.

As a rule of thumb, there exists a toolbox to every topic or application. Table 3.3 lists system-oriented topics together with the name of the associated toolbox and a reference to the chapters explaining the commands.

As an example of a toolbox definition, we quote an annotated version of module *System*:

DEFINITION System;

(*System management*)
  PROCEDURE SetUser; (*identification*)
  PROCEDURE SetFont; (*for typed text*)
  PROCEDURE SetColor; (*for typed text and graphics*)
  PROCEDURE Time; (*set or display*)
  PROCEDURE Collect; (*garbage*)

(*Display management*)
  PROCEDURE Open; (*viewer*)
  PROCEDURE OpenLog; (*viewer*)
  PROCEDURE Close; (*viewer*)
  PROCEDURE CloseTrack;
  PROCEDURE Recall; (*most recently closed viewer*)
  PROCEDURE Copy; (*viewer*)
  PROCEDURE Grow; (*viewer*)

(*Module management*)
  PROCEDURE Free; (*specified modules*)
  PROCEDURE ShowCommands; (*of specified module*)
  PROCEDURE ShowModules; (*loaded*)

(*File management*)
  PROCEDURE Directory;
  PROCEDURE CopyFiles;
  PROCEDURE RenameFiles;
  PROCEDURE DeleteFiles;

(*System inspection*)
  PROCEDURE Watch; (*memory and disk storage*)
  PROCEDURE State; (*of global module variables*)

END System;

In principle, generic commands of type "do it" can be interpreted by an interactive task in an arbitrary and individual way. However, if the task is represented by a textual viewer, we obtain an attractive universal command interpreter simply by interpreting the underlying text. If the text is a list of command names followed by parameters, we

Tools call it a *tool*.

More precisely, a tool is a text obeying the following syntax in EBNF notation (Extended Backus–Naur formalism):

tool = { [Comment] CommandName [ParameterList] }.

If present, the textual parameter list is made available to the called command via fields *text* and *pos* in the global parameter list *Par* that is exported by module Oberon. Because this parameter list is interpreted individually by every command, its format is completely open. However, we fixed some conventions and rules for the purpose of a standardized user interface:

Parameter conventions

(1) The elements of a textual parameter list are universal syntactical tokens like *name, literal string, integer, real number, long real number* and *special character*.

(2) A *reference-character* " ↑ " in the textual parameter list refers to the current text selection for continuation. In the special case of the reference character following the command name immediately, the entire parameter list is represented by the text selection.

(3) A *mark-character* "*" in the textual parameter list refers to the currently marked viewer. Typically, the mark-character replaces the name of a file. In such a case the contents of the viewer marked by the system pointer is processed by the command interpreter instead of the contents of a file.

(4) An *at-character* "@" in the textual parameter list indicates that the selection marks the (beginning of the) text which is taken as operand.

(5) A *terminator-character* "~" terminates the textual parameter list in case of a variable number of parameters.

Typical display layout

Because tools are ordinary and editable texts (in contrast to conventional *menus*), they can be customized interactively. We refer again to Figure 3.1 showing a typical Oberon screen layout consisting

Table 3.3

Topic	Toolbox	Chapters
System management	System	3
Display management	System	4
Text editing	Edit	5
Module management	System	6
File management	System	7
System inspection	System	8, 12
Network management	Net	10
Compiling	Compiler	12
Graphics editing	Draw	13

```
System.SetUser { type user/password }
System.Time { dd mo yy hh mm ss }
System.SetFont Syntax10i.Scn.Fnt
System.SetFont ↑
System.SetColor @
System.Collect
```

Figure 3.4   An excerpt of a system management tool.

of two vertical tracks, a wider *user track* on the left and a narrow *system track* on the right. Three documents are displayed in the user track: a text, a graphic and a picture. In the system track, we find one *log-viewer* displaying the system log, two *tool-viewers* making available the standard *system tool* and a customized private tool respectively, and one *trap viewer* at the bottom.

System toolbox   We want to exemplify the concepts of command and tool by the *system management section* of the *System* toolbox. Consisting of the commands *SetUser*, *Time*, *SetFont*, *SetColor* and *Collect*, it is used to control system-wide facilities. In detail, their function is installing the user's identification, displaying or setting the system time, presetting the system type-font for typed text, setting the system color, and activating the garbage collector. The implementations are included in Section 3.5 at the end of this Chapter. Figure 3.4 presents a possible excerpt of a textual tool consisting of system management commands.

Summary   And this concludes the section. In summary, toolbox is a special form of an Oberon module. It is defined as a collection of commands. Appearing at the top of the modular hierarchy, the toolboxes in their entirety fix the command interface to the system. Tools are sequences of textually represented command calls. They are editable and customizable. In a typical Oberon screen layout, the tools are displayed in viewers within the system track.

3.5 Detailed implementations

MODULE Oberon; (*JG 6.9.90*)

IMPORT Kernel, Modules, Input, Display, Fonts, Viewers, Texts;

CONST
    consume* = 0; **track*** = 1; (*input message id*)
    defocus* = 0; **neutralize*** = 1; **mark*** = 2; (*control message id*)

```
    BasicCycle = 20;


    ESC = 1BX; SETUP = 0A4X;


TYPE
    Painter* = PROCEDURE (x, y: INTEGER);
    Marker* = RECORD
      Fade*, Draw*: Painter
    END;


    Cursor* = RECORD
      marker*: Marker; on*: BOOLEAN; X*, Y*: INTEGER
    END;


    ParList* = POINTER TO ParRec;


    ParRec* = RECORD
      vwr*: Viewers.Viewer;
      frame*: Display.Frame;
      text*: Texts.Text;
      pos*: LONGINT
    END;


    InputMsg* = RECORD (Display.FrameMsg)
      id*: INTEGER;
      keys*: SET;
      X*, Y*: INTEGER;
      ch*: CHAR;
      fnt*: Fonts.Font;
      col*, voff*: SHORTINT
    END;


    SelectionMsg* = RECORD (Display.FrameMsg)
      time*: LONGINT;
      text*: Texts.Text;
      beg*, end*: LONGINT
    END;


    ControlMsg* = RECORD (Display.FrameMsg)
      id*, X*, Y*: INTEGER
    END;


    CopyOverMsg* = RECORD (Display.FrameMsg)
      text*: Texts.Text;
      beg*, end*: LONGINT
    END;


    CopyMsg* = RECORD (Display.FrameMsg)
      F*: Display.Frame
    END;


    Task* = POINTER TO TaskDesc;
```

```
    TaskDesc* = RECORD
      next: Task;
      safe*: BOOLEAN;
      handle*: PROCEDURE
    END;

VAR
    User*: ARRAY 8 OF CHAR;
    Password*: LONGINT;

    Arrow*, Star*: Marker;
    Mouse*, Pointer*: Cursor;

    FocusViewer*: Viewers.Viewer;

    Log*: Texts.Text;
    Par*: ParList; (*actual parameters*)

    CurTask*, PrevTask: Task;

    CurFnt*: Fonts.Font; CurCol*, CurOff*: SHORTINT;

    DW, DH, CL, H0, H1, H2, H3: INTEGER;

    ActCnt: INTEGER; (*action count for GC*)
    Mod: Modules.Module;

    PROCEDURE Min (i, j: INTEGER): INTEGER;
    BEGIN IF i <= j THEN RETURN i ELSE RETURN j END
    END Min;

(*user identification*)

    PROCEDURE Code(VAR s: ARRAY OF CHAR): LONGINT; <BEGIN RETURN calculated
        code
    END Code;

    PROCEDURE SetUser* (VAR user, password: ARRAY OF CHAR);
    BEGIN COPY(user, User); Password := Code(password)
    END SetUser;

(*clocks*)

    PROCEDURE GetClock* (VAR t, d: LONGINT);
    BEGIN Kernel.GetClock(t, d)
    END GetClock;

    PROCEDURE SetClock* (t, d: LONGINT);
    BEGIN Kernel.SetClock(t, d)
    END SetClock;

    PROCEDURE Time* (): LONGINT;
    BEGIN RETURN Input.Time()
```

```
        END Time;

(*cursor handling*)


    PROCEDURE* FlipArrow (X, Y: INTEGER);
    BEGIN
        IF X < CL THEN
            IF X > DW - 15 THEN X := DW - 15 END
        ELSE
            IF X > CL + DW - 15 THEN X := CL + DW - 15 END
        END;
        IF Y < 15 THEN Y := 15 ELSIF Y > DH THEN Y := DH END;
        Display.CopyPattern(Display.white, Display.arrow, X, Y - 15, 2)
    END FlipArrow;


    PROCEDURE* FlipStar (X, Y: INTEGER);
    BEGIN
        IF X < CL THEN
            IF X < 7 THEN X := 7 ELSIF X > DW - 8 THEN X := DW - 8 END
        ELSE
            IF X < CL + 7 THEN X := CL + 7
            ELSIF X > CL + DW - 8 THEN X := CL + DW - 8
            END
        END ;
        IF Y < 7 THEN Y := 7 ELSIF Y > DH - 8 THEN Y := DH - 8 END;
        Display.CopyPattern(Display.white, Display.star, X - 7, Y - 7, 2)
    END FlipStar;


    PROCEDURE OpenCursor* (VAR c: Cursor);
    BEGIN c.on := FALSE; c.X := 0; c.Y := 0
    END OpenCursor;


    PROCEDURE FadeCursor* (VAR c: Cursor);
    BEGIN IF c.on THEN c.marker.Fade(c.X, c.Y); c.on := FALSE END
    END FadeCursor;


    PROCEDURE DrawCursor* (VAR c: Cursor; VAR m: Marker; X, Y: INTEGER);
    BEGIN
        IF c.on & ((X # c.X) OR (Y # c.Y) OR (m.Draw # c.marker.Draw)) THEN
            c.marker.Fade(c.X, c.Y); c.on := FALSE
        END;
        IF ~c.on THEN
            m.Draw(X, Y); c.marker := m; c.X := X; c.Y := Y; c.on := TRUE
        END
    END DrawCursor;

(*display management*)


    PROCEDURE RemoveMarks* (X, Y, W, H: INTEGER);
    BEGIN
        IF (Mouse.X > X - 16) & (Mouse.X < X + W + 16) & (Mouse.Y > Y - 16) &
            (Mouse.Y < Y + H + 16) THEN
            FadeCursor(Mouse)
        END;
        IF (Pointer.X > X - 8) & (Pointer.X < X + W + 8) & (Pointer.Y > Y - 8) &
            (Pointer.Y < Y + H + 8) THEN
```

```
            FadeCursor(Pointer)
        END
    END RemoveMarks;


    PROCEDURE* HandleFiller (V: Display.Frame; VAR M: Display.FrameMsg);
    BEGIN
        WITH V: Viewers.Viewer DO
            IF M IS InputMsg THEN
                WITH M: InputMsg DO
                    IF M.id = track THEN DrawCursor(Mouse, Arrow, M.X, M.Y) END
                END;
            ELSIF M IS ControlMsg THEN
                WITH M: ControlMsg DO
                    IF M.id = mark THEN DrawCursor(Pointer, Star, M.X, M.Y) END
                END
            ELSIF M IS Viewers.ViewerMsg THEN
                WITH M: Viewers.ViewerMsg DO
                    IF (M.id = Viewers.restore) & (V.W > 0) & (V.H > 0) THEN
                        RemoveMarks(V.X, V.Y, V.W, V.H);
                        Display.ReplConst(Display.black, V.X, V.Y, V.W, V.H, 0)
                    ELSIF (M.id = Viewers.modify) & (M.Y < V.Y) THEN
                        RemoveMarks(V.X, M.Y, V.W, V.Y − M.Y);
                        Display.ReplConst(Display.black, V.X, M.Y, V.W, V.Y − M.Y, 0)
                    END
                END
            END
        END
    END HandleFiller;


    PROCEDURE OpenDisplay* (UW, SW, H: INTEGER);
        VAR Filler: Viewers.Viewer;
    BEGIN
        Input.SetMouseLimits(Viewers.curW + UW + SW, H);
        Display.ReplConst(Display.black, Viewers.curW, 0, UW + SW, H, 0);
        NEW(Filler); Filler.handle := HandleFiller;
        Viewers.InitTrack(UW, H, Filler); (*init user track*)
        NEW(Filler); Filler.handle := HandleFiller;
        Viewers.InitTrack(SW, H, Filler) (*init system track*)
    END OpenDisplay;


    PROCEDURE DisplayWidth* (X: INTEGER): INTEGER;
    BEGIN RETURN DW
    END DisplayWidth;


    PROCEDURE DisplayHeight* (X: INTEGER): INTEGER;
    BEGIN RETURN DH
    END DisplayHeight;


    PROCEDURE OpenTrack* (X, W: INTEGER);
        VAR Filler: Viewers.Viewer;
    BEGIN
        NEW(Filler); Filler.handle := HandleFiller;
        Viewers.OpenTrack(X, W, Filler)
    END OpenTrack;


    PROCEDURE UserTrack* (X: INTEGER): INTEGER;
```

```
        BEGIN RETURN X DIV DW * DW
        END UserTrack;


    PROCEDURE SystemTrack* (X: INTEGER): INTEGER;
        BEGIN RETURN X DIV DW * DW + DW DIV 8 * 5
        END SystemTrack;


    PROCEDURE UY (X: INTEGER): INTEGER;
        VAR fil, bot, alt, max: Display.Frame;
    BEGIN
        Viewers.Locate(X, 0, fil, bot, alt, max);
        IF fil.H >= DH DIV 8 THEN RETURN DH END;
        RETURN max.Y + max.H DIV 2
    END UY;


    PROCEDURE AllocateUserViewer* (DX: INTEGER; VAR X, Y: INTEGER);
    BEGIN
        IF Pointer.on THEN X := Pointer.X; Y := Pointer.Y
        ELSE X := DX DIV DW * DW; Y := UY(X)
        END
    END AllocateUserViewer;


    PROCEDURE SY (X: INTEGER): INTEGER;
        VAR fil, bot, alt, max: Display.Frame;
    BEGIN
        Viewers.Locate(X, DH, fil, bot, alt, max);
        IF fil.H >= DH DIV 8 THEN RETURN DH END;
        IF max.H >= DH − H0 THEN RETURN max.Y + H3 END;
        IF max.H >= H3 − H0 THEN RETURN max.Y + H2 END;
        IF max.H >= H2 − H0 THEN RETURN max.Y + H1 END;
        IF max # bot THEN RETURN max.Y + max.H DIV 2 END;
        IF bot.H >= H1 THEN RETURN bot.H DIV 2 END;
        RETURN alt.Y + alt.H DIV 2
    END SY;


    PROCEDURE AllocateSystemViewer* (DX: INTEGER; VAR X, Y: INTEGER);
    BEGIN
        IF Pointer.on THEN X := Pointer.X; Y := Pointer.Y
        ELSE X := DX DIV DW * DW + DW DIV 8 * 5; Y := SY(X)
        END
    END AllocateSystemViewer;


    PROCEDURE MarkedViewer* (): Viewers.Viewer;
    BEGIN RETURN Viewers.This(Pointer.X, Pointer.Y)
    END MarkedViewer;


    PROCEDURE PassFocus* (V: Viewers.Viewer);
        VAR M: ControlMsg;
    BEGIN M.id := defocus; FocusViewer.handle(FocusViewer, M); FocusViewer := V
    END PassFocus;


(*command interpretation*)


    PROCEDURE Call* (VAR name: ARRAY OF CHAR; par: ParList; new: BOOLEAN;
        VAR res: INTEGER);
```

```
    VAR Mod: Modules.Module; P: Modules.Command; i, j: INTEGER;
BEGIN res := 1;
    i := 0; j := 0;
    WHILE name[j] # 0X DO
        IF name[j] = "." THEN i := j END;
        INC(j)
    END;
    IF i > 0 THEN
        name[i] := 0X;
        IF new THEN Modules.Free(name, FALSE) END;
        Mod := Modules.ThisMod(name);
        IF Modules.res = 0 THEN
            INC(i); j := i;
            WHILE name[j] # 0X DO name[j - i] := name[j]; INC(j) END;
            name[j - i] := 0X;
            P := Modules.ThisCommand(Mod, name);
            IF Modules.res = 0 THEN
                Par := par; Par.vwr := Viewers.This(par.frame.X, par.frame.Y); P; res := 0
            END
        ELSE res := Modules.res
        END
    END
END Call;


PROCEDURE GetSelection* (VAR text: Texts.Text; VAR beg, end, time: LONGINT);
    VAR M: SelectionMsg;
BEGIN
    M.time := -1; Viewers.Broadcast(M);
    text := M.text; beg := M.beg; end := M.end; time := M.time
END GetSelection;


PROCEDURE* GC;
    VAR x: LONGINT;
BEGIN IF ActCnt <= 0 THEN Kernel.GC; ActCnt := BasicCycle END
END GC;


PROCEDURE Install* (T: Task);
    VAR t: Task;
BEGIN t := PrevTask;
    WHILE (t.next # PrevTask) & (t.next # T) DO t := t.next END;
    IF t.next = PrevTask THEN T.next := PrevTask; t.next := T END
END Install;


PROCEDURE Remove* (T: Task);
    VAR t: Task;
BEGIN t := PrevTask;
    WHILE (t.next # T) & (t.next # PrevTask) DO t := t.next END;
    IF t.next = T THEN t.next := t.next.next; PrevTask := t.next END;
    IF CurTask = T THEN CurTask := PrevTask.next END
END Remove;


PROCEDURE Collect* (count: INTEGER);
BEGIN ActCnt := count
END Collect;


PROCEDURE SetFont* (fnt: Fonts.Font);
```

```
        BEGIN CurFnt := fnt
        END SetFont;

        PROCEDURE SetColor* (col: SHORTINT);
        BEGIN CurCol := col
        END SetColor;

        PROCEDURE SetOffset* (voff: SHORTINT);
        BEGIN CurOff := voff
        END SetOffset;

        PROCEDURE Loop*;
            VAR V: Viewers.Viewer; M: InputMsg; N: ControlMsg;
                prevX, prevY, X, Y: INTEGER; keys: SET; ch: CHAR;
        BEGIN
            LOOP
                Input.Mouse(keys, X, Y);
                IF Input.Available() > 0 THEN Input.Read(ch);
                    IF ch < 0F0X THEN
                        IF ch = ESC THEN
                            N.id := neutralize; Viewers.Broadcast(N); FadeCursor(Pointer)
                        ELSIF ch = SETUP THEN
                            N.id := mark; N.X := X; N.Y := Y; V := Viewers.This(X, Y); V.handle(V,
                                N)
                        ELSE
                            IF ch < " " THEN
                                IF ch = 1X THEN ch := 83X (*ä*)
                                ELSIF ch = 0FX THEN ch := 84X (*ö*)
                                ELSIF ch = 15X THEN ch := 85X (*ü*)
                                END
                            ELSIF ch > "~" THEN
                                IF ch = 81X THEN ch := 80X (*Ä*)
                                ELSIF ch = 8FX THEN ch := 81X (*Ö*)
                                ELSIF ch = 95X THEN ch := 82X (*Ü*)
                                END
                            END;
                            M.id := consume; M.ch := ch; M.fnt := CurFnt; M.col := CurCol; M.voff
                                := CurOff;
                            FocusViewer.handle(FocusViewer, M);
                            DEC(ActCnt)
                        END
                    ELSIF ch = 0F1X THEN Display.SetMode(0, {}) (*on*)
                    ELSIF ch = 0F2X THEN Display.SetMode(0, {0}) (*off*)
                    ELSIF ch = 0F3X THEN Display.SetMode(0, {2}) (*inv*)
                    END
                ELSIF keys # {} THEN
                    M.id := track; M.X := X; M.Y := Y; M.keys := keys;
                    REPEAT
                        V := Viewers.This(M.X, M.Y); V.handle(V, M);
                        Input.Mouse(M.keys, M.X, M.Y)
                    UNTIL M.keys = {};
                    DEC(ActCnt)
                ELSE
                    IF (X # prevX) OR (Y # prevY) OR ~Mouse.on THEN
                        M.id := track; M.X := X; M.Y := Y; M.keys := keys; V := Viewers.This(X, Y);
                            V.handle(V, M);
                        prevX := X; prevY := Y
                    END;
                    CurTask := PrevTask.next;
```

```
               IF ~CurTask.safe THEN PrevTask.next := CurTask.next END;
               CurTask.handle; PrevTask.next := CurTask; PrevTask := CurTask
            END
         END
      END Loop;

BEGIN User[0] := 0X;
   Arrow.Fade := FlipArrow; Arrow.Draw := FlipArrow;
   Star.Fade := FlipStar; Star.Draw := FlipStar;
   OpenCursor(Mouse); OpenCursor(Pointer);

   DW := Display.Width; DH := Display.Height; CL := Display.ColLeft;
   H3 := DH - DH DIV 3;
   H2 := H3 - H3 DIV 2;
   H1 := DH DIV 5;
   H0 := DH DIV 10;

   OpenDisplay(DW DIV 8 * 5, DW DIV 8 * 3, DH);
   FocusViewer := Viewers.This(0, 0);

   CurFnt := Fonts.Default;
   CurCol := Display.white;
   CurOff := 0;

   Collect(BasicCycle);
   NEW(PrevTask);
   PrevTask.handle := GC;
   PrevTask.safe := TRUE;
   PrevTask.next := PrevTask;

   Mod := Modules.ThisMod("System");
   Display.SetMode(0, {})

END Oberon.

MODULE System; (* JG 11.11.90*)
   IMPORT Kernel, Input, Oberon, Fonts, Texts;

   CONST
      StandardMenu = "System.Close System.Copy System.Grow Edit.Search Edit.Store";
      LogMenu = "System.Close System.Grow Edit.Locate Edit.Store";

   VAR W: Texts.Writer;

   PROCEDURE Max (i, j: LONGINT): LONGINT;
   BEGIN IF i >= j THEN RETURN i ELSE RETURN j END
   END Max;

   (* ------------- Toolbox for system management --------------*)

   PROCEDURE SetUser*;
      VAR i: INTEGER; ch: CHAR;
         user: ARRAY 8 OF CHAR;
         password: ARRAY 16 OF CHAR;
      BEGIN
```

```
            i := 0; Input.Read(ch);
            WHILE (ch # "/") & (i < 7) DO user[i] := ch; INC(i); Input.Read(ch) END;
            user[i] := 0X; i := 0; Input.Read(ch);
            WHILE (ch > " ") & (i < 15) DO password[i] := ch; INC(i); Input.Read(ch) END;
            password[i] := 0X;
            Oberon.SetUser(user, password)
        END SetUser;

        PROCEDURE SetFont*;
            VAR beg, end, time: LONGINT;
                T: Texts.Text; S: Texts.Scanner;
        BEGIN Texts.OpenScanner(S, Oberon.Par.text, Oberon.Par.pos); Texts.Scan(S);
            IF (S.class = Texts.Char) & (S.c = "@") THEN
                Oberon.GetSelection(T, beg, end, time);
                IF time >= 0 THEN
                    Texts.OpenScanner(S, T, beg); Texts.Scan(S);
                    IF S.class = Texts.Name THEN Oberon.SetFont(Fonts.This(S.s)) END
                END
            ELSIF S.class = Texts.Name THEN Oberon.SetFont(Fonts.This(S.s))END
        END SetFont;

        PROCEDURE SetColor*;
            VAR beg, end, time: LONGINT;
                T: Texts.Text; S: Texts.Scanner; ch: CHAR;
        BEGIN Texts.OpenScanner(S, Oberon.Par.text, Oberon.Par.pos); Texts.Scan(S);
            IF (S.class = Texts.Char) & (S.c = "@a") THEN
                Oberon.GetSelection(T, beg, end, time);
                IF time >= 0 THEN
                    Texts.OpenReader(S, T, beg); Texts.Read(S, ch); Oberon.SetColor(S.col)
                END
            ELSIF S.class = Texts.Int THEN Oberon.SetColor(SHORT(SHORT(S.i)))
            END
        END SetColor;

        PROCEDURE SetOffset*;
            VAR beg, end, time: LONGINT;
                T: Texts.Text;S: Texts.Scanner; ch: CHAR;
        BEGIN Texts.OpenScanner(S, Oberon.Par.text, Oberon.Par.pos); Texts.Scan(S);
            IF (S.class = Texts.Char) & (S.c = "@") THEN
                Oberon.GetSelection(T, beg, end, time);
                IF time >= 0 THEN
                    Texts.OpenReader(S, T, beg); Texts.Read(S, ch); Oberon.SetColor(S.voff)
                END
            ELSIF S.class = Texts.Int THEN Oberon.SetOffset(SHORT(SHORT(S.i)))
            END
        END SetOffset;

        PROCEDURE Time*;
            VAR par: Oberon.ParList;
                S: Texts.Scanner;
                t, d, hr, min, sec, yr, mo, day: LONGINT;
        BEGIN par := Oberon.Par;
            Texts.OpenScanner(S, par.text, par.pos); Texts.Scan(S);
            IF S.class = Texts.Int THEN (*set date*)
                day := S.i; Texts.Scan(S); mo := S.i; Texts.Scan(S); yr := S.i; Texts.Scan(S);
                hr := S.i; Texts.Scan(S); min := S.i; Texts.Scan(S); sec := S.i;
                t := (hr*64 + min)*64 + sec; d := (yr*16 + mo)*32 + day;
                Kernel.SetClock(t, d)
            ELSE (*read date*)
                Texts.WriteString(W, "System.Time");
```

```
        Oberon.GetClock(t, d); Texts.WriteDate(W, t, d); Texts.WriteLn(W);
        Texts.Append(Oberon.Log, W.buf)
    END
END Time;


PROCEDURE Collect*;
BEGIN Oberon.Collect(0)
END Collect;


BEGIN Texts.OpenWriter(W)
END System.
```

4 The display system

The display screen is the most important part of the interface presented by a personal workstation to its users. At first sight, it simply represents a rectangular output area. However, in combination with the mouse, it quickly develops into a complex interactive input/output platform of almost unlimited flexibility. It is mainly its Janus-faced characteristic that makes the display screen stand out from ordinary external devices to be managed by the operating system. In the current Chapter we shall give more detailed insight into the reasons for the central position the display system takes within the operating system, and for its determining influence on the entire Oberon architecture. In particular, we shall show that the display system is a natural basis or anchor for functional extensibility.

4.1 Screen layout model

In the early 1970s, Xerox PARC in California launched the Smalltalk project with the goal of conceiving and developing new and more natural ways to communicate with personal computers (Goldberg, 1984). Perhaps the most conspicuous among several significant achievements of this endeavour is the idea of applying the *desktop metaphor* to the display screen. This metaphor comprises a desktop and a collection of possibly overlapping pages of paper that are laid out on the desktop. By projecting such a configuration onto the surface of a screen, we get the (today) familiar picture of Figure 4.1(a), showing a collection of partially or totally visible rectangular areas on a background – so-called *windows* or *viewers*.

Desktop metaphors

The desktop metaphor is used by many modern operating systems and user interface shells, both as a natural model for the system to separate displayed data belonging to different tasks and as a powerful tool for users to organize the display screen interactively, according to individual taste and preference. However, there are inherent drawbacks

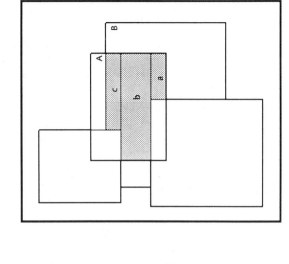

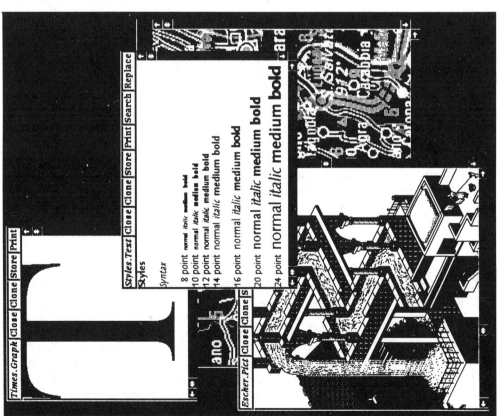

Figure 4.1 (a) Simulated desktop, showing overlapping viewers. (b) Partial overlappings in the desktop model.

in the metaphor. They are primarily connected with *overlapping*. First, any efficient management of overlapping viewers must rely on a subordinate management of (arbitrary) subrectangles and on sophisticated clipping operations. This is so because partially overlapped viewers must be partially restored under control of the viewer manager. For example, in Figure 4.1(b), rectangles a, b and c of viewer B ought to be restored individually after closing of viewer A. Secondly, there is a significant danger of covering viewers completely and losing them forever. And thirdly, no canonical heuristic algorithms exist for automatic allocation of screen space to newly opened viewers.

Tiling

Experience has shown that partial overlapping is desirable and beneficial in rare cases only, and so the additional complexity of its management (Binding, 1985; Wille, 1988) is hard to justify. Therefore alternative strategies to structure a display screen have been looked for. An interesting class of established solutions can be titled as *tiling*. There are several variants of tiling (Cohen *et al.*, 1985). Perhaps the most obvious (because the most unconstrained) one is based on iterated horizontal or vertical splitting of existing viewers. Starting with the full screen and successively opening viewers A, B, C, D, E and F, we get to a configuration as in Figure 4.2. A second variant is *hierarchic tiling*. Again the hierarchy starts with a full screen that is now decomposed into a number of vertical tracks, each of which is further decomposed into a number of horizontal viewers. Figure 4.3 shows a snapshot of a hierarchically tiled display screen. We decided in favor of this kind of tiling in Oberon, mainly because the algorithm of reusing the area of a closed viewer is simpler and more uniform. For example, assume that in Figure 4.2(b) viewer F has been closed. Then, it is straightforward to reverse the previous opening operation by extending viewer E at its bottom end. However, if the closed viewer is B, no such simple procedure exists. For example, the freed area can be shared between viewers C and D by making them extend to their left. Clearly, no such complicated situations can occur in the case of hierarchic tiling.

Hierarchic tiling

Hierarchic tiling is also used in Xerox PARC's *Cedar* system (Teitelman, 1984). However, the Oberon variant differs from the Cedar variant in some respects. First, Oberon supports quick temporary context switching by overlaying one track or any contiguous sequence of tracks with new layers. In Figure 4.4, a snapshot of a standard Oberon display screen is represented graphically. It suggests two original tracks and two levels of overlay, where the top layer is screen-filling. Secondly, unlike Cedar display screens, Oberon displays do not provide reserved areas for system-wide facilities. As depicted in Figure 4.5, standard Cedar screens feature a *command row* at the top and an *icon row* at their bottom. And thirdly, Oberon is based on a different heuristic strategy for the automatic placement of new viewers. As a Cedar default

Viewer allocation

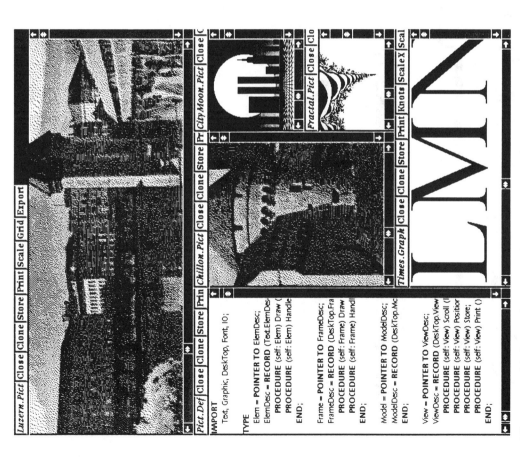

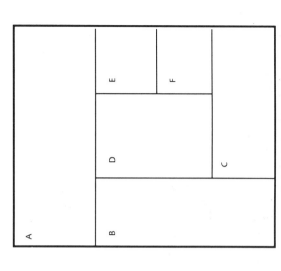

Figure 4.2 (a) Screen layout produced by unconstrained tiling. (b) Viewer configuration resulting from unconstrained tiling.

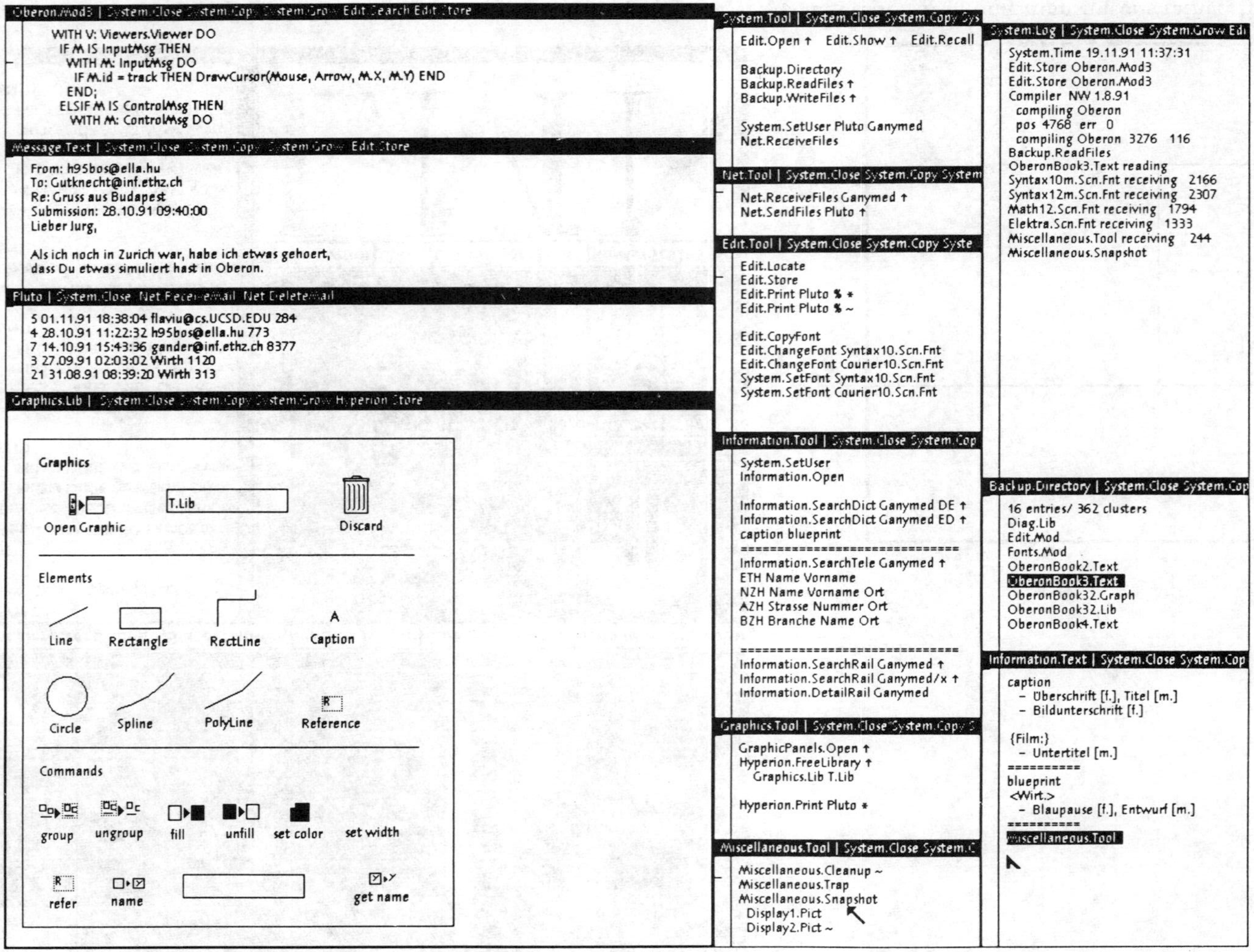

Figure 4.3 Screen layout produced by hierarchic tiling.

Oberon.Mod3 | System.Close System.Copy System.Grow Edit.Search Edit.Store
```
WITH V: Viewers.Viewer DO
IF M IS InputMsg THEN
  WITH M: InputMsg DO
  IF M.id = track THEN DrawCursor(Mouse, Arrow, M.X, M.Y) END;
  END;
ELSIF M IS ControlMsg THEN
  WITH M: ControlMsg DO
```

Message.Text | System.Close System.Copy System.Grow Edit.Store
```
From: h95bos@ella.hu
To: Gutknecht@inf.ethz.ch
Re: Gruss aus Budapest
Submission: 28.10.91 09:40:00
Lieber Jurg,

Als ich noch in Zurich war, habe ich etwas gehoert,
dass Du etwas simuliert hast in Oberon.
```

Pluto | System.Close Net.Fetch Net.Recall Net.Delete Recall
```
5 01.11.91 18:38:04 flaviu@cs.UCSD.EDU 294
4 28.10.91 11:22:32 h95bos@ella.hu 773
7 14.10.91 15:43:36 gander@inf.ethz.ch 8377
3 27.09.91 02:03:02 Wirth 1120
21 31.08.91 08:39:20 Wirth 313
```

Graphics.Lib | System.Close System.Copy System.Grow Hyperion.Store

```
Graphics
 [icon] Open Graphic    [ T.Lib ]    [icon] Discard

Elements
 Line  Rectangle  RectLine           A
 Circle  Spline  PolyLine         Caption
                                  Reference

Commands
 group  ungroup  fill  unfill  set color  set width
 refer  name                              get name
```

System.Tool | System.Close System.Copy.Sys   Edit.Open ↑ Edit.Show ↑ Edit.Recall
```
Backup.Directory
Backup.ReadFiles ↑
Backup.WriteFiles ↑

System.SetUser Pluto Ganymed
Net.ReceiveFiles
```

Net.Tool | System.Close System.Copy System
```
Net.ReceiveFiles Ganymed ↑
Net.SendFiles Pluto ↑
```

Edit.Tool | System.Close System.Copy Syste
```
Edit.Locate
Edit.Store
Edit.Print Pluto % *
Edit.Print Pluto % ~

Edit.CopyFont
Edit.ChangeFont Syntax10.Scn.Fnt
Edit.ChangeFont Courier10.Scn.Fnt
System.SetFont Syntax10.Scn.Fnt
System.SetFont Courier10.Scn.Fnt
```

Information.Tool | System.Close System.Cop
```
System.SetUser
Information.Open

Information.SearchDict Ganymed DE ↑
Information.SearchDict Ganymed ED ↑
caption blueprint

Information.SearchTele Ganymed ↑
ETH Name Vorname
NZH Name Vorname
AZH Strasse Nummer Ort
BZH Branche Name Ort

Information.SearchRail Ganymed ↑
Information.SearchRail Ganymed/x ↑
Information.DetailRail Ganymed
```

GraphicsTool | System.Close System.Copy S
```
GraphicPanels.Open ↑
Hyperion.FreeLibrary ↑
Graphics.Lib T.Lib

Hyperion.Print Pluto *
```

Miscellaneous.Tool | System.Cleanup System.C
```
Miscellaneous.Cleanup ~
Miscellaneous.Trap
Miscellaneous.Snapshot
Display1.Pict
Display2.Pict ~
```

System.Log | System.Close System.Grow Edi
```
System.Time 19.11.91 11:37:31
Edit.Store Oberon.Mod3
Edit.Store Oberon.Mod3
Compiler NW 1.8.91
  compiling Oberon
  pos 4768 err 0
compiling Oberon 3276 116
Backup.ReadFiles
OberonBook3.Text reading
Syntax10m.Scn.Fnt receiving 2166
Syntax12m.Scn.Fnt receiving 2307
Math12.Scn.Fnt receiving 1794
Elektra.Scn.Fnt receiving 1333
Miscellaneous.Tool receiving 244
Miscellaneous.Snapshot
```

Backup.Directory | System.Close System.Cop
```
16 entries/ 362 clusters
Diag.Lib
Edit.Mod
Fonts.Mod
OberonBook2.Text
OberonBook3.Text
OberonBook32.Graph
OberonBook32.Lib
OberonBook4.Text
```

Information.Text | System.Close System.Cop
```
caption
 - Oberschrift [l.], Titel [m].
 - Bildunterschrift [f.]

(Film:)
 - Untertitel [m]
blueprint
<Wirt.>
 - Blaupause [f.], Entwurf [m]
Miscellaneous.Tool
```

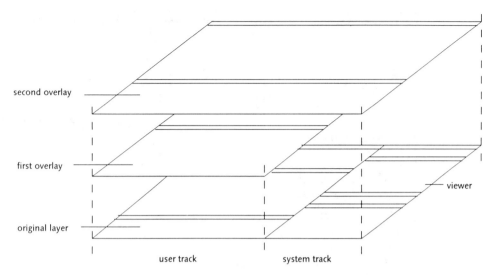

second overlay

first overlay

viewer

original layer

user track   system track

Figure 4.4   Overlays of tracks and of sequences of tracks.

invariant, the area of every track is divided up evenly among the viewers in this track. When a new viewer is to be placed, the existing viewers in the track are requested to reduce their size and move up appropriately. The newly opened viewer is then allocated in the freed spot at the bottom. In contrast, Oberon normally splits the largest existing viewer in a given track into two halves of equal size. As an advantage of this latter allocation strategy, we note that existing contents are kept stable.

4.2 Viewers as objects

Although everybody seems to agree on the meaning of the term *viewer*, no two different system designers actually do. The original role of a viewer as merely a separate display area has meanwhile become heavily overloaded with additional functionality. Depending on the underlying system are viewers individual *views* on a certain configuration of objects, carriers of tasks, processes, applications and so on. Therefore we first need to define our own precise understanding of the concept of viewer.

Abstract type viewer   The best guide to this aim is the abstract data type *Viewer* that we introduced in Chapter 3. We recapitulate: type *Viewer* serves as a template describing viewers by a *state of visibility*, a *rectangle* on the display screen and a *message handler*. The exact functional interface provided by a given variant of viewer is determined by the set of

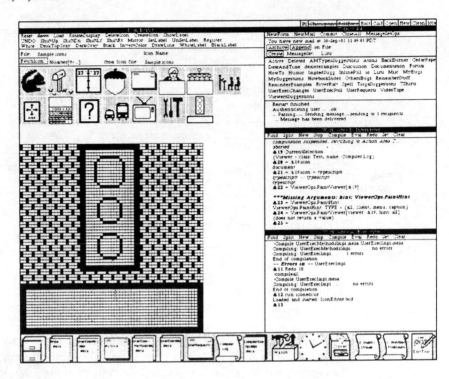

Figure 4.5   The layout of a standard Cedar screen showing command row and icon row.

messages accepted. This set is structured as a customized hierarchy of type extensions.

We can now obtain a more concrete specification of the role of **Universal messages** viewer by identifying some basic categories of *universal messages* that are expected to be accepted by all variants of viewer. For example, we know that messages reporting about user interactions as well as messages specifying a generic operation are universal. These two categories of universal messages document the roles of viewers as interactive tasks and as parts of an integrated system respectively.

In total, there are four such categories. They are listed in Table 4.1, together with the corresponding topics and message dispatchers.

These topics together essentially define the role of Oberon viewers. In short, we may look at an Oberon viewer as a non-overlapped rectangular field on the screen, both acting as an integrated display area for some objects of a document and representing an interactive task in the form of a sensitive editing area.

Shifting emphasis is often a key to illuminating new views of old facts. Applying this principle to our current case and regarding the

Table 4.1

Dispatcher	Topic	Message
Task scheduler	Dispatching interactive tasks	Report user interaction
Command interpreter	Processing of integrated commands	Define generic operation
Viewer manager	Organizing the display area	Request change of location or size
Document manager	Operating on documents	Report change of contents or format

Subsystems various message dispatchers as *subsystems*, we recognize immediately the importance of viewers as elements connecting the different subsystems via message-based interfaces. In this light, the object type *Viewer* appears as a common basis of Oberon's subsystems.

Before we continue our explanations, we want to give a rough map of the sections treating in detail the topics that are emphasized by Table 4.1. Task scheduling and command interpreting are already familiar to us from Sections 3.2 and 3.3. Viewer management and text management are the topics of Sections 4.4 and 5.2 respectively. Because *text* is the only built-in type of document, it will act as a prime example. Taking the view of a receiver of messages, we shall discuss message handling in the cases of an abstract class of standard viewers and of a concrete class of viewers displaying standard text in Sections 4.4 and 5.3 respectively.

The following summaries may serve as a rough guide on the way to a complete understanding of the message traffic between dispatchers and viewers.

Task scheduler In the case of a keyboard stroke, a message with the typed character is sent to the focus viewer by the task scheduler. In the case of a mouse movement, the scheduler sends a message specifying the new state of the mouse to the viewer containing the mouse position.

Command interpreter Generic operations are an important tool for system integration. In our case, they allow viewers to interpret universal operations individually. Familiar examples are 'return current textual selection', 'copy-over stretch of text' and 'produce a copy (clone)'.

Viewer manager In a tiling viewer environment, every opening of a new viewer and every change of size or location of an existing viewer has an obvious effect on neighbouring viewers. The viewer manager therefore issues a message for every affected viewer requesting it to adjust its size appropriately.

Document manager
Whenever the contents or the format of a document have changed, a message notifying all visible viewers of the change is broadcast to the display space.

4.3 Frames as basic display entities

When we introduced viewers in Chapter 3 and in the previous section, we simplified with the aim of abstraction. We know already that viewers appear as elements of second order in the tiling hierarchy. Having treated them as *black boxes* so far, we have not revealed anything about the continuation of the hierarchy. As a matter of fact, viewers are
Display frames
neither terminal objects nor elementary display units. They are just a special case of so-called *display frames*. Display frames or frames, in short, are arbitrary rectangles displaying a collection of objects or an excerpt of a document. In particular, frames may recursively contain other frames, a capability that makes them an extremely powerful tool for any display organizer.

The type *Frame* is declared as

Frame = POINTER TO FrameDesc;

FrameDesc = RECORD
   next, dsc: Frame;
  X, Y, W, H: INTEGER;
  handle: Handler
END;

Frame hierarchy
The components *next* and *dsc* are connections to further frames. Their names suggest a multilevel recursive hierarchical structure: *next* points to the next frame on the same level, while *dsc* points to the (first) descendant, that is, to the next lower level of the hierarchy of nested frames. X, Y, W, H and the handler serve the original purpose to that we introduced them. In particular, the handler allows frames to react individually on the receipt of messages. Its type is

Handler = PROCEDURE (F: Frame; VAR M: FrameMsg);

where *FrameMsg* represents the root of a potentially unlimited tree hierarchy of possible messages to frames:

FrameMsg = RECORD END;

Having now introduced the concept of frames, we can reveal the whole truth about viewers. As a matter of fact, type *Viewer* is a derived type, it is a type extension of *Frame*:

Viewer = POINTER TO ViewerDesc;

ViewerDesc = RECORD (FrameDesc)
    state: INTEGER
END;

These declarations express formally the fact that viewers are nothing but a special case (or *variant* or *subclass*) of general frames, additionally featuring a state of visibility. In particular, viewers inherit the hierarchical structure of frames. This is an extremely useful property, immediately opening an unlimited spectrum of possibilities for designers of a specific subclass of viewers to organize the representing rectangular area. For example, the area of viewers of, say, class *Desktop* may take the role of a background being covered by an arbitrary collection of possibly mutually overlapping frames. See Figure 4.6 for an example. In other words, our decision of using a tiling viewer scheme *globally* can easily be overwritten *locally*.

Menu viewers

An even more important example of a predefined structure is provided by the abstract class of so-called *menu viewers*, whose shape is familiar from most snapshots taken of the standard Oberon display screen. A menu viewer consists of a thin rectangular boundary line and of an interior area being vertically decomposed into a *menu region* at the top and a *contents region* at the bottom (see Figure 4.7).

In terms of data structures, the class of menu viewers is defined as a type extension of *Viewer*, with an additional component *menuH* specifying the height of the menu frame:

MenuViewer = POINTER TO MenuViewerDesc;

MenuViewerDesc = RECORD (ViewerDesc)
    menuH: INTEGER
END;

Each menu viewer V specifies exactly two descendants: the menu frame *V.dsc* and the *frame of main contents* or *main frame V.dsc.next*. Absolutely nothing is fixed about the contents of the two descendant frames. In the standard case, however, the menu frame is a *text frame*, displaying a line of commands in inverse video mode. By definition, the nature of the main frame specifies the type of the viewer. If it is a text frame

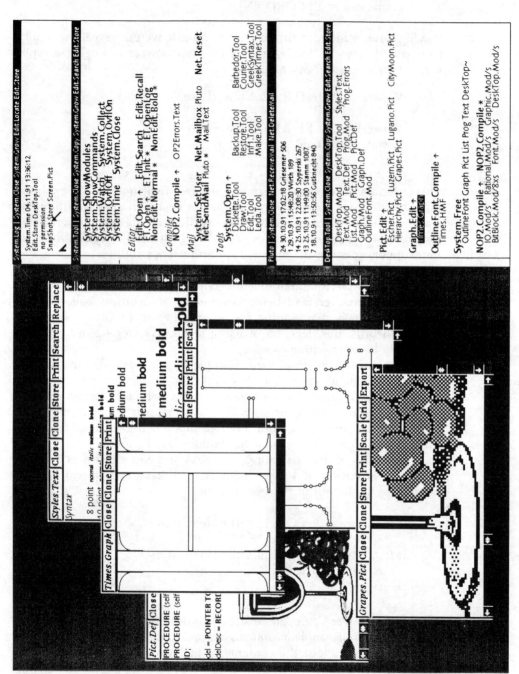

Figure 4.6 A viewer class desktop organizing overlapping frames.

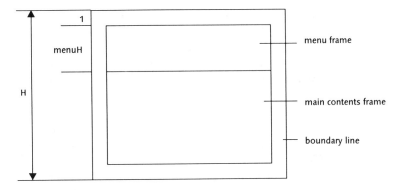

Figure 4.7   The compositional structure of a menu viewer.

Table 4.2

Module	Objects	Service
MenuViewers	Viewer	Message handling for menu viewers
↑	↑	
Viewers	Viewer	Tiling viewer management
↑	↑	
Display	Frame	Block-oriented raster operations

as well then we call the viewer a *text viewer*; if it is a *graphics frame* then we call it a *graphics viewer*, and so on.

4.4   Display management

Oberon's display system comprises two main areas: *Viewer management* and *cursor handling*. Let us first turn to the much more involved topic of viewer management, and postpone cursor handling to the end of this section. Before we can actually begin our presentation, we need to introduce the concept of the so-called *logical display area*. It is modelled as two-dimensional Cartesian plane housing the totality of objects to be displayed. The essential point of this abstraction is a rigorous decoupling of any aspects of physical display devices. As a matter of fact, any concrete assignment of display monitors to certain finite regions of the display area is a pure matter of configuring the system.

Modular hierarchy   Being a subsystem of a system with a clear modular structure, the display system appears in the form of a small hierarchy of modules. Its core is a linearly ordered set consisting of three modules: *Display,*

Viewers and *MenuViewers*, the latter building upon the former. Conceptually, each module contributes an associated class of display-oriented objects and a collection of related service routines.

Table 4.2 provides an overview of the subsystem *viewer management*. Recall that the operator " ↑ " means *import* if applied to modules and *type extension* if applied to data types.

Inspecting the column titled *Objects* in Table 4.2, we recognize precisely our familiar types *Frame*, *Viewer* and *MenuViewer* respectively, where the latter type is abbreviated (*MenuViewers.Viewer* instead of *MenuViewers.MenuViewer*).

In addition to the modules of the display system core, there exists a section on viewer management in module Oberon. This section provides a specialized interface to application oriented programs. A collection of highly self-contained functions is included with the aim of simplifying the use of the viewer management package in the case of standard Oberon display configurations. We shall come back to this topic in Section 4.6.

For the moment, we concentrate on the core of the viewer management. We shall devote the remaining part of the current section primarily to the presentation of modules *Viewers* and *MenuViewers*, saving the discussion of module *Display* for the next section. Typically, we start the presentation of a module by listing and commenting on its definition, and we end it by revealing its implementation.

4.4.1   Viewers

Focusing first on module *Viewers*, we can roughly define the domain of its responsibility as 'initializing and maintaining the global layout of the display area'. From the previous discussions, we are well acquainted already with the structure of the global layout as well as with its building blocks: the display area is hierarchically tiled with display frames. The first two levels in the frame hierarchy correspond precisely to tracks and viewers respectively.

Now we are ready to understand the following definition:

DEFINITION Viewers;

   IMPORT Display;

   CONST restore = 0; modify = 1; suspend = 2; (*message
      ids*)

```
TYPE
    Viewer = POINTER TO ViewerDesc;

    ViewerDesc = RECORD (Display.FrameDesc)
        state: INTEGER
    END;
    ViewerMsg = RECORD (Display.FrameMsg)
        id: INTEGER;
        X, Y, W, H: INTEGER;
        state: INTEGER
    END;

VAR curW: INTEGER;

(*track handling*)
PROCEDURE InitTrack (W, H: INTEGER; Filler: Viewer);
PROCEDURE OpenTrack (X, W: INTEGER; Filler: Viewer);
PROCEDURE CloseTrack (X: INTEGER);

(*viewer handling*)
PROCEDURE Open (V: Viewer; X, Y: INTEGER);
PROCEDURE Change (V: Viewer; Y: INTEGER);
PROCEDURE Close (V: Viewer);

(*miscellaneous*)
PROCEDURE This (X, Y: INTEGER): Viewer;
PROCEDURE Next (V: Viewer): Viewer;

PROCEDURE Recall (VAR V: Viewer);
PROCEDURE Locate (X, H: INTEGER; VAR fil, bot, alt, max:
        Viewer);

PROCEDURE Broadcast (VAR M: Display.FrameMsg);

END Viewers.
```

In order to complete the functional description of this module, some additional comments are probably necessary.

Track management   Let us start our explanation with a group of procedures supporting the track structure of the display area: *InitTrack*, *OpenTrack*, and *CloseTrack*. *InitTrack* creates a new track of width W and height H by partitioning off a vertical strip of width W from the infinite display area. In addition, *InitTrack* initializes the newly created track with the *filler viewer* that is supplied as parameter. The filler viewer essentially serves as background filling up the track at its top end. It reduces to height 0 if the track is covered completely by productive viewers.

Configuring the display area is part of system initialization after startup. It amounts to a sequence of steps of the form

NEW(Filler); Filler.handle := HandleFiller; InitTrack(W, H,
   Filler)

where *HandleFiller* is supposed to handle messages requiring modifications of size and cursor drawing.

The global variable *curW* indicates the width of the already configured part of the display area. Note that configuring starts with x = 0 and is non-reversible in the sense that the grid defined by the initialized tracks cannot be refined later. However, remember that it can be made coarser at any time by overlaying a contiguous sequence of existing tracks by a single new track.

OpenTrack serves exactly this purpose. The track (or sequence of tracks) to be overlaid in the display area must be spanned by the segment [X, X + W]. *CloseTrack* is inverse to *OpenTrack*. It is called to close the (topmost) track located at X in the display area, and to restore the previously covered track (or sequence of tracks).

Viewer management   The next three procedures are used to organize viewers within individual tracks. *Open* allocates a given viewer at a given position. More precisely, *Open* locates the viewer containing the point (X, Y), splits it horizontally at height Y, and opens the viewer V in the lower part of the area. In the special case of Y coinciding with the upper boundary line of the located viewer, this is closed automatically. Procedure *Change* allows to change the height of a given viewer V by moving its upper boundary line to a new location Y (within the limits of its neighbours). *Close* removes the given viewer V from the display area. Figure 4.8 makes these operations clear.

The last group of procedures provides miscellaneous services. Procedure *This* identifies the viewer displayed at (X, Y). Procedure *Next* returns the next upper neighbour of a given displayed viewer V. Procedure *Recall* allows recalling and restoring the most recently closed viewer. *Locate* is a procedure to assist heuristic allocation of new viewers. For any given track and desired minimum height, *Locate* offers a choice consisting of some distinguished viewers in the track: the filler viewer, the viewer at the bottom, an alternative choice and the viewer of maximum height. Finally, procedure *Broadcast* broadcasts a message to the display space, that is, it sends the given message to all viewers that are currently displayed.

Having gained a functional understanding of module *Viewers* in quite some detail, it is now time to throw a glance behind the scenes. We begin by revealing its internal data structure. Remember that,

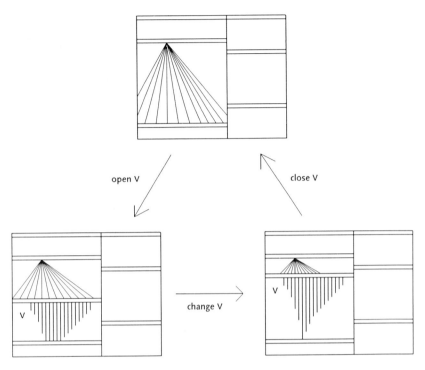

Figure 4.8 The basic operations on viewers.

according to the principle of information hiding, a module's internal data structure is typically fully private and accessible through its procedural interface only. Figure 4.9 shows a data structure view of the snapshot taken in Figure 4.4. Note that the overlaid tracks and viewers are still part of the internal data structure.

Viewer data structure

In the data structure, we recognize an anchor representing the display area and pointing to a list of tracks, each of them pointing to a list of viewers, each of them pointing to a list of arbitrary subframes. The list of tracks and the list of viewers are each closed to a ring, where the filler track (filling up the display area) and the filler viewers (filling up the tracks) act as anchors. Additionally, each track points to a (possibly empty) list of tracks lying underneath.

Technically, *TrackDesc* descriptor is a private extension of type *Viewer Desc*. Repeating the declarations of viewer descriptors and frame descriptors, we obtain the following hierarchy of types:

TrackDesc = RECORD (ViewerDesc)
    under: Display.Frame
END;

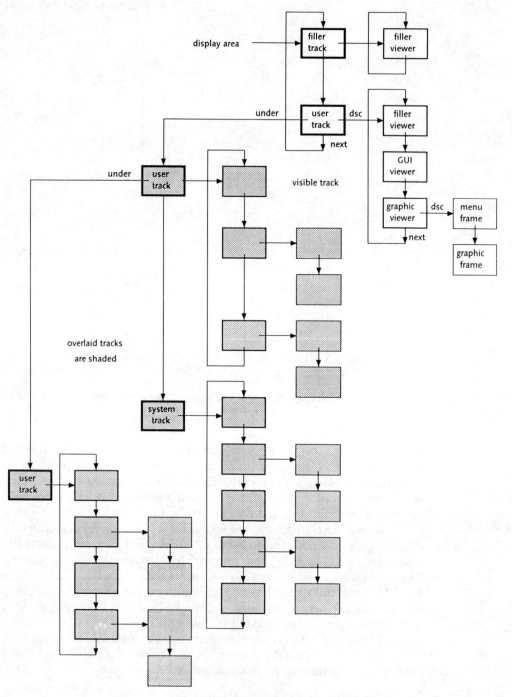

Figure 4.9 A snapshot of the internal display data structure corresponding to the display layout of Figure 4.4.

```
ViewerDesc = RECORD (FrameDesc)
    state: INTEGER
END;

FrameDesc = RECORD
    next, dsc: Frame;
    X, Y, W, H: INTEGER;
    handle: Handler
END;
```

Here we should point out that the data structure of the viewer manager is *heterogeneous*, with *Frame* as base type. It provides a nice example of a nested hierarchy of frames, with the additional property that its first two levels correspond exactly to the first two levels in the type hierarchy defined by *Track*, *Viewer* and *Frame*.

Bound objects

In an object-oriented environment, objects are *autonomous* entities in principle. However, they may be *bound* to a higher instance (other than the system) temporarily. For example, we can look at the objects belonging to a module's private data structure as bound to this module. Deciding if an object is bound is then a fundamental problem. In the case of viewers, this information is contained in an extra instance variable called *state*.

As a system invariant we have for every viewer V

V is bound to module *Viewers* $\Leftrightarrow$ *V.state # 0*

If we call *visible* any displayed viewer and *suspended* any viewer that is covered by an overlaying track, we can refine this invariant to

(V is visible $\Leftrightarrow$ V.state > 0) and (V is suspended $\Leftrightarrow$ V.state < 0)

In addition, more detailed information about the kind of viewer V is given by the magnitude */V.state/*:

$|V.state|$	Kind of viewer
0	Closed
1	Filler
>1	Productive

(1) The magnitude |V.state| is kept invariant by module *Viewers*. It could be used, for example, to distinguish different levels of importance or preference, with the aim of supporting a smarter algorithm for heuristic allocation of new viewers.

(2) Although there is no language facility to enforce it, the variable *state* is to be treated as read-only by every module other than *Viewers*.

Operations

We are well prepared now to understand how the exported procedures of module *Viewers* work behind the scenes. All of them operate on the internal dynamic data structure just explained. Some use the structure as a reference only or operate on individual elements (procedures *This, Next, Locate, Change*), others add new elements to the structure (procedures *InitTrack, OpenTrack, Open*), and still others remove elements (procedures *CloseTrack, Close*). Most of them have side-effects on the size or state of existing elements.

We want to concentrate our explanations on the handling of such side-effects, because this leads us to an important conceptual aspect of implementation. We start with a characterization of module *Viewers* as a general and low-level manager for viewers whose exact contents are unknown to it (and whose controlling software might only have been developed years later). In short, we let module *Viewers* treat viewers as *black boxes*. Such an abstraction immediately makes it impossible for the implementation to call fixed procedures for, say, changing a viewer's size or state. The facility needed is a message-oriented interface of viewers.

Viewer messages

Module *Viewer*'s contribution to this message interface corresponds exactly to the third category of messages listed in Table 4.1. Their common type is

```
ViewerMsg = RECORD (Display.FrameMsg)
    id: INTEGER;
    X, Y, W, H: INTEGER;
    state: INTEGER
END;
```

There exist three variants of this type: *Restore contents, modify height* (extend or reduce at bottom), and *suspend* or *close*. The field *id* specifies the variant and the additional components of the message inform about the desired new location, size, and state.

Table 4.3 lists originators, messages and recipients of viewer messages.

Table 4.3

Originator	Message	Receivers
OpenTrack	Suspend	Viewers covered by opening track
CloseTrack	Close	Viewers in closing track
	Restore	Viewers covered by closing track
Open	Modify or close	Upper neighbour of opening viewer
Change	Modify	Upper neighbour of changing viewer
Close	Close	Closing viewer
	Modify	Upper neighbour of closing viewer

4.4.2 Menu viewers

Let us now zoom in from the global context of the display area to a
more local context of the area of individual viewers. More concretely,
let us turn our attention to the management of *menu viewers*. Remembering the definition, we see that every black box representing a menu
viewer can now be resolved into a pair of black boxes, the first
Subframes representing the *menu frame* and the second the *frame of main contents*.
We can therefore repeat our argument of above to conclude that the
handling of menu viewers is also to be based on the message paradigm,
this time on messages sent by the menu viewer to its subframes.
However, the situation is slightly more general than before, because a
menu viewer is both a sender and a receiver of messages.

Again, we start our more detailed discussion with a module
definition:

```
DEFINITION MenuViewers;

  IMPORT Viewers, Display;

  CONST extend = 0; reduce = 1; move = 2; (*message ids*)

  TYPE
    Viewer = POINTER TO ViewerDesc;

    ViewerDesc = RECORD (Viewers.ViewerDesc)
      menuH: INTEGER
    END;

    ModifyMsg = RECORD (Display.FrameMsg)
      id: INTEGER;
      dY, Y, H: INTEGER
    END;
```

```
PROCEDURE Handle (V: Display.Frame;
    VAR M: Display.FrameMsg);
PROCEDURE New (Menu, Main: Display.Frame;
    menuH, X, Y: INTEGER): Viewer;

END MenuViewers.
```

The interface represented by this definition is conspicuously narrow. There are just two procedures: a generator procedure *New* and a standard message handler *Handle*. The generator returns a newly created and opened menu viewer displaying the two (arbitrary) frames that are passed as parameters. The message handler implements a standard scheme of reaction to the receipt of messages.

Object generating   Remember that, according to our object-oriented paradigm, the actual 'intelligence' of an object is borne by its message handler while its state is represented by the remaining record components. Therefore we regard the creation of an object as an atomic action consisting of three basic steps:

> allocate memory block; install message handler; initialize state variables

In the case of a standard menu viewer V, it can be expressed as

> NEW(V); V.handle := Handle; V.dsc := Menu; V.dsc.next := Main; V.menuH := menuH

With that, calling *New* is equivalent to

> create V; open V at X, Y

where opening V needs assistance by module *Viewers*.

The implementation of procedure *Handle* embodies the standard strategy of message handling by menu viewers. We now present a coarse view of it.

Message handler for menu viewers

```
IF message reports about user interaction THEN
    IF variant is mouse tracking THEN
        IF mouse is in menu region THEN
            IF mouse is in upper menu region and left key is
                    pressed THEN
                handle changing of viewer
            ELSE delegate handling to menu-frame
            END
```

```
        ELSE
            IF mouse is in main-frame THEN delegate handling to
                main-frame
            END
        END
    ELSIF variant is keyboard input THEN
        delegate handling to menu frame;
        delegate handling to main frame
    END
ELSIF message defines generic operation THEN
    IF message requests copy (clone) THEN
        send copy message to menu frame to get a copy (clone);
        send copy message to main frame to get a copy (clone);
        create menu viewer clone from copies
    ELSE
        delegate handling to menu frame;
        delegate handling to main frame
    END
ELSIF message reports about change of contents THEN
    delegate handling to menu frame;
    delegate handling to main frame
ELSIF message requests change of location or size THEN
    IF operation is restore THEN
        draw viewer area and border;
        send modify message to menu frame to make it extend
            from height 0;
        send modify message to main frame to make it extend
            from height 0
    ELSIF operation is modify THEN
        IF operation is extend THEN
            extend viewer area and border;
            send modify message to menu frame to make it extend;
            send modify message to main frame to make it extend
        ELSE (*reduce*)
            send modify message to main frame to make it reduce;
            send modify message to menu frame to make it reduce;
            reduce viewer area and border
        END
    ELSIF operation is suspend THEN
        send modify message to main frame to make it reduce to
            height 0;
        send modify message to menu frame to make it reduce to
            height 0
    END
END
```

In principle, the handler acts as a *filter* immediately processing or preprocessing messages of selected types and delegating the processing of others to its descendant frames. Note that the handler's main alternative statement discriminates precisely among the four basic categories of messages identified by Table 4.1.

Cloning

From the above algorithm for generating a copy or clone of a menu viewer, we can derive a general recursive scheme for the creation of a clone of an arbitrary frame:

send copy message to every element in the list of descendants;
compile new list of descendants from copies;
generate copy of original frame descriptor;
attach new list of descendants

The essential point here is the use of new outgoing messages in order to process a given incoming message. As a general matter of fact, we can regard message processing as a *transformation* mapping incoming messages into sequences of outgoing messages, possibly under side-effects. The simplest case of such a transformation is known as *delegation*. Here the input message is simply passed on to the descendant(s).

Modify message

A more intricate example is a mouse tracking message received by a menu viewer while the mouse is located in the upper part of its menu frame and the left mouse key is pressed. This means 'change viewer's height by vertically moving its top line'. No message to express the required transformation of the subframes yet exists. Consequently, module *MenuViewers* needs to introduce an appropriate message type *ModifyMsg:*

ModifyMsg = RECORD (Display.FrameMsg)
  id: INTEGER;
  dY, Y, H: INTEGER
END;

The field *id* specifies one of two variants: *extend or reduce*. The first variant of the message requests the receiving frame to move by the vertical translation vector dY and then to extend to height H at bottom. The second variant requests the frame to reduce to height H at bottom and then to move by dY. In both cases Y indicates the Y coordinate of the new lower left corner. Figure 4.10 summarizes this graphically.

We should perhaps mention here that messages arriving from the viewer manager and requesting the receiving viewer to extend or reduce at its bottom are mapped into messages of type *ModifyMsg* as well. Of course, no translation is needed in these cases, and dY is 0.

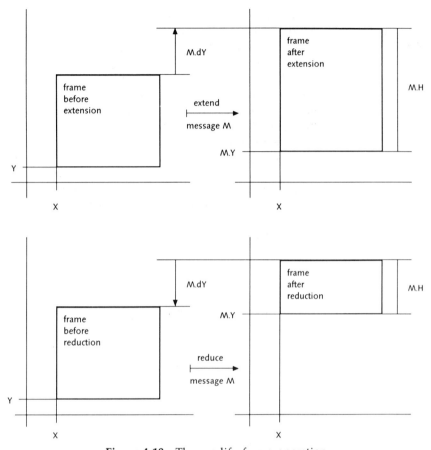

Figure 4.10   The modify frame operation.

The attentive reader might perhaps have asked why the standard handler is exported by module *MenuViewers* at all. The thought behind this is reusability of code. More concretely, a message handler for a subclass of menu viewers could be implemented effectively by reusing menu viewer's standard handler. After having handled all new or differing cases first, it would simply call the standard handler subsequently.

4.4.3   Cursor management

Traditionally, a *cursor* indicates and visualizes on the screen the current location of the caret in a text or, more generally, the current *focus* of editing. A small arrow or similar graphic symbol is typically used for that purpose. We have slightly generalized and abstracted this concept. In Oberon, a cursor is a path in the logical display area whose current position can be made visible by a *marker*.

The viewer manager and the cursor handler are two separate users of the same display area. Actually, we should imagine two parallel planes, one displaying viewers and the other displaying cursors. If there is just one physical plane, we take care of painting markers non-destructively, for example in inverse video mode. Then no precondition must be established before drawing a marker. However, in the case of a viewer task painting destructively in its viewer's area, the area must be *monopolized* first by turning invisible all markers in the area.

The technical support of cursor management is also contained in module Oberon. Its interface to the programmer is

```
DEFINITION Oberon;
  . . .

TYPE
  Marker = RECORD
    Fade, Draw: PROCEDURE (x, y: INTEGER)
  END;

  Cursor = RECORD
    marker: Marker; on: BOOLEAN; X, Y: INTEGER
  END;

VAR
  Arrow, Star: Marker;
  Mouse, Pointer: Cursor;

  PROCEDURE OpenCursor (VAR c: Cursor);
  PROCEDURE FadeCursor (VAR c: Cursor);
  PROCEDURE DrawCursor (VAR c: Cursor; VAR m: Marker;
      X, Y: INTEGER);

  PROCEDURE MarkedViewer (): Viewers.Viewer;
  PROCEDURE RemoveMarks (X, Y, W, H: INTEGER);
  . . .

END Oberon.
```

The state of a cursor is given by its *mode of visibility* (*on*), its position (X, Y) in the display area, and the current *marker. Marker* is an abstract data type with an interface consisting of two operations

Fade and *Draw*. The main benefit we can draw from this abstraction is once more conceptual independence of the underlying hardware. For example, *Fade* and *Draw* can adapt to a given monitor hardware with built-in cursor support or, in the absence of such support, they can be implemented as identical involutory procedures drawing the marker pattern in inverse video mode.

The functional interface to cursors consists of three operations: *OpenCursor* to open a new cursor, *FadeCursor* to switch off the marker of an open cursor, and *DrawCursor* to extend the path of a cursor to a new position and mark it with the given marker. We emphasize that the marker representing a given cursor can change its shape dynamically on the fly.

Predefined cursors

Two cursors, *Mouse* and *Pointer*, are predefined. They represent the mouse and the interactively controlled global *system pointer* respectively. Typically (but not necessarily) these cursors are visualized by the built-in markers *Arrow* (a small arrow pointing to north-west) and *Star* (a star symbol) respectively. The pointer can be used to mark any displayed object. It serves primarily as an implicit parameter of commands.

Two assisting service procedures *MarkedViewer* and *RemoveMarks* are added in connection with the predefined cursors. *MarkedViewer* returns the viewer that is currently marked by the pointer. Its resulting value is equivalent to *Viewers.This(Pointer.X, Pointer.Y)*. *RemoveMarks* turns invisible the predefined cursors within a given rectangle in the display area. This procedure is used to monopolize the rectangle for its caller.

Let us recapitulate the essential points and characteristics of Oberon's concept of cursor handling.

Summary

(1) By virtue of the use of abstract markers and of the logical display area, any hardware dependence is encapsulated in system modules and is therefore hidden from the application programmer. Cursors are moving uniformly within the whole of the display area, *even across screen boundaries*.

(2) Cursor handling is decentralized and left to the individual handlers that are installed in viewers. Typically, a handler reacts on the receipt of a mouse tracking message by drawing the mouse cursor at the indicated new location. The benefit of such individualized handling is flexibility. For example, a smart local handler might choose the shape of the visualizing marker depending on the exact location, or it might force the cursor to a grid point.

(3) Even though cursor handling is decentralized, there is some intrinsic support for cursor drawing built into the declaration of

type *Cursor*. Cursors are objects of full value and, as such, can 'memorize' their current state. Consequently, the interface operations *FadeCursor* and *DrawCursor* need to refer to the desired future state only.

(4) Looking at the viewer manager as one user of the display area, the cursor handler is a second user of the same resource. If there is just one physical plane implementing the display area, any region must be monopolized by a current user before destructive painting. Therefore markers are usually painted non-destructively in inverse video mode.

Let us now summarize this section. The central resource managed by the display subsystem is the logical display area whose purpose is abstraction from the underlying display monitor hardware. The display area is primarily used by the viewer manager for accomodation of tracks and viewers. They are just the first two levels of a potentially unlimited nested hierarchy of display frames. For example, standard menu viewers contain two subordinate frames: a menu frame and a main frame of contents. Viewers are treated as black boxes by the viewer manager and are operated via messages. In addition, they are used as elements of message-based interfaces connecting the display subsystem with other subsystems like the task scheduler and the various document managers. Finally, the display area also provides a base space for the movements of cursors. In Oberon, a cursor is a marked path. Two standard cursors *Mouse* and *Pointer* are predefined.

4.5 Raster operations

In Section 4.4 we introduced the display area as an abstract concept. We learnt that it is modelled as a two-dimensional Cartesian plane. So far, this information has been sufficient because we have been interested in its global structure only and have ignored contents completely. However, concentrating our interests on contents now, we need to reveal more details about the model.

The Cartesian plane representing the display area is *discrete*. We shall consider points in the display area as *grid points* or *picture elements* (*pixels*). We assume that contents are generated by assigning colors to the pixels. For the moment, the number of possible colors a pixel can attain is irrelevant. In the binary case of two colors we think of one color representing *background* and the other color representing *foreground*.

The most elementary operation generating contents in a discrete plane is 'set color of pixel' or 'set pixel' for short. However, there are few algorithms actually building directly on this atomic operation. Much more important in practice are block-oriented operations, traditionally called *raster operations*. By a *block* we mean a rectangular area of pixels whose bounding lines are parallel to the axes of the coordinate system.

Principle of operation

Raster operations are based on a common principle of operation: a block of width W and height H of source pixels is placed at a given point of destination (DX, DY) in the display area. In the simplest case, the destination block (DX, DY, W, H) is simply overwritten by the source block. In general, the new value of a pixel in the destination block is a combination of its old value and the value of the corresponding source pixel: d := f(s, d). f is sometimes called the *mode of combination* of the raster operation.

In the binary case we have the following modes:

Mode	f
replace	s
paint	s OR d
invert	s XOR d

Note that *invert* is equivalent to inverse video mode with mask s.

There are many different variants of raster operations. Some refer to a source block in the display area, others specify a constant *pattern* to be taken as source block. Some variants require *replication* of the source block within an explicitly given destination block (DX, DY, DW, DH) rather than simple placement.

Unification of concepts on all levels was one of the most important and most challenging mottos guiding the Oberon project. Related to our current topic, the challenge was to define a small and complete set of raster operations covering all needs, including in particular writing characters.

Basic raster operations

The amazingly compact resulting set of raster operations is exported by module *Display*:

DEFINITION Display;
  . . .

  CONST
    black = 0; white = 15; (*colors*)
    replace = 0; paint = 1; invert = 2; (*operation modes*)

  PROCEDURE CopyBlock (SX, SY, W, H, DX, DY, mode:
    INTEGER);

```
PROCEDURE CopyPattern (col: INTEGER; pat: Pattern;
    DX, DY, mode: INTEGER);

PROCEDURE Dot (col: INTEGER; DX, DY: LONGINT;
    mode: INTEGER);

PROCEDURE ReplPattern (col: INTEGER; pat: Pattern;
    DX, DY, DW, DH, mode: INTEGER);
PROCEDURE ReplConst (col: INTEGER;
    DX, DY, DW, DH, mode: INTEGER);
    . . .
END Display.
```

In the parameter lists, *mode* is the mode of combination (*replace*, *paint*, or *invert*). *CopyBlock* copies the source block (SX, SY, W, H) to location (DX, DY) and uses *mode* to combine new contents in the destination block (DX, DY, W, H). It is assumed tacitly that the numbers of colors per pixel in the source block and in the destination area are identical. It is perhaps informative to know that *CopyBlock* is essentially equivalent to the famous *BitBlt* (bit block transfer) in the *SmallTalk* project (Goldberg, 1984). In Oberon, *CopyBlock* is primarily used for scrolling contents in a viewer.

Patterns   The remaining raster operations use a constant pattern. Conceptually, we should regard type *Pattern* as a pointer:

```
Pattern = POINTER TO PatternDesc;

PatternDesc = RECORD
    w, h: SHORTINT;
    raster: ARRAY (w + 7) DIV 8 * h OF SYSTEM.BYTE
END;
```

w and h are the width and height of a block containing the binary pattern data defined by raster. The pattern data are given as a linear sequence of bytes to be poured into the block from left to right and from bottom to top.

There are two non-conceptual problems with this declaration. First, arrays of variable length are not allowed in Oberon. The second problem concerns economy of memory usage. Looking at fonts as large collections of character patterns, it would be extremely wasteful to allocate a separate record for every single pattern. We shall see in Chapter 5 how sequences of character patterns are packed. As a way

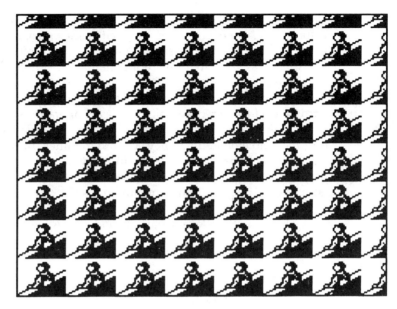

Figure 4.11 Visualization of the replicate pattern operation.

out, we decided to define type *Pattern* as LONGINT (in the sense of memory address), together with a pattern constructor

PROCEDURE SetPattern (VAR image: ARRAY OF
    SYSTEM.BYTE; W, H: INTEGER; VAR pat: Pattern);

Some standard patterns are predefined in module *Display* and exported as global variables of type *Pattern*. Among them are patterns *arrow*, *star* and *cross* intended to represent markers, a *hook* representing the caret, and a *downArrow*. A second group of predefined patterns supports drawing graphics. It includes several grey tone patterns and a grid pattern.

The parameter *col* in the pattern-oriented raster operations specifies the pattern's foreground color. Colors *black* and *white* are predefined. *CopyPattern* copies the colored pattern to location (DX, DY) in the display area, using the given combination mode. It is probably the most frequently used operation of all, because it is needed to write text. *Rep/Pattern* replicates the given pattern to the given destination block. It starts at bottom left and proceeds from left to right and from bottom to top. Figure 4.11 exemplifies the way this operation works.

Dot and *Rep/Const* are special cases of *CopyPattern* and *Rep/Pattern* respectively, taking a fixed implicit pattern consisting of a single foreground pixel. *Dot* is exactly our previously mentioned 'set pixel'. *Rep/Const* is used to draw horizontal and vertical lines as well as rectangles.

Display monitors So far, we have carefully avoided any reference to the underlying hardware. However, eventually, the raster operations operate on concrete *bitmaps* mirroring the contents of concrete display monitors. In our original implementation, they are programmed in assembler code for efficiency reasons. We decided to include the necessary support directly in place. For this reason, we loaded module *Display* with two more domains of responsibility: mapping display monitors to the display area and acting as device driver.

Here is the relevant part of module *Display*'s definition:

DEFINITION Display;
  . . .

    VAR (*map*)
      Unit: LONGINT;
      Width, Height: INTEGER;
      Bottom, UBottom: INTEGER;
      Left, ColLeft: INTEGER;

    PROCEDURE Map (X: INTEGER): LONGINT;

    (*device drivers*)
    PROCEDURE SetMode (X: INTEGER; s: SET);

    (*color table*)
    PROCEDURE SetColor (col, red, green, blue: INTEGER);
    PROCEDURE GetColor (col: INTEGER; VAR red, green,
      blue: INTEGER);

    (*hardware cursor*)
    PROCEDURE SetCursor (mode: SET);
    PROCEDURE DrawCX (X, Y: INTEGER);
    PROCEDURE FadeCX (X, Y: INTEGER);
    . . .

    END Display.

Supported configurations This definition (and even more so its implementation) provides support for a restricted class of possible configurations only. Any

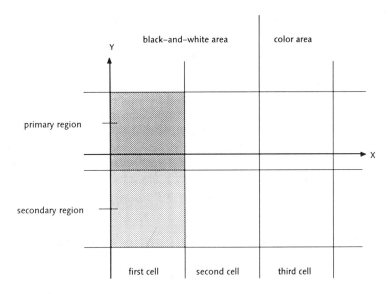

Figure 4.12 The standard regular cell structure of the display area.

number of display monitors is theoretically possible. However, they must be mapped to a regular horizontal array of predefined *cells* in the display area. Each cell is vertically split into two congruent displayable regions. The corresponding monitor is supposed to be able to select and display one of the two regions alternatively. Finally, it is assumed that all cells of black-and-white monitors are allocated to the left of all cells of color monitors. Figure 4.12 gives a good impression of a general such configuration.

Under these restrictions, any concrete configuration can be parametrized by the variables of the definition above. *Unit*, *Width* and *Height* specify the extent of a displayable region, where *Width* and *Height* are width and height in pixel units, and *Unit* is the size of a pixel in units of 1/36 000 mm. 1/36 000 mm is a common divisor of all of the standard metric units used by the typesetting community like mm, inch, Pica point and point size of usual printing devices. *Bottom* and *UBottom* specify the bottom y coordinate of the primary region and the secondary region respectively. Finally, *Left* and *ColLeft* give the left x coordinate of the area of black-and-white monitors and of color monitors respectively.

Functional description   We conclude these explanations with a short functional description of the procedures listed in the above definition: to a given x coordinate, procedure *Map* returns the starting address of the (primary) bitmap corresponding to the display monitor at this position. This procedure allows a client to transform any given pair (X, Y) of coordinates into a memory address and thus to implement private raster operations. The remaining procedures are driver procedures. Obviously, they are tailored to certain concrete types of monitors.

SetMode sets the display mode of the monitor at position X. Typically, the mode selects among normal, inverse video and display screen off. Also, it specifies the region to be displayed (primary or secondary). *SetColor* and *GetColor* maintain the (common) color table of the color screens. This table maps color numbers to concrete colors that are composed of intensities of *red*, *green* and *blue*. The remaining procedures support hardware cursor management. *SetCursor* selects among two possible cursor classes: crosshair or pattern. Finally, *DrawCX* and *FadeCX* draw and erase the selected cursor at the given position.

4.6　Standard display configurations and toolbox

Let us now take up again our earlier topic of configuring the display area. We have seen that no specific layout of the display area is distinguished by the general viewer management itself. However, some support of the familiar standard Oberon display look is provided by module Oberon.

**User track
system track**　　In the terminology of this module, a standard configuration consists of one or several horizontally adjacent *displays*, where a display is a pair consisting of two tracks of equal height, a *user track* on the left and a *system track* on the right. Figure 4.13 shows a standard configuration featuring two displays of equal size: one black-and-white and one colored. Note that even though no reference to any physical monitor is made, a display is typically associated with a monitor in reality.

This is the relevant excerpt of the definition:

DEFINITION Oberon;
　　. . .

　　　PROCEDURE OpenDisplay (UW, SW, H: INTEGER);
　　　PROCEDURE OpenTrack (X, W: INTEGER);

　　　PROCEDURE DisplayWidth (X: INTEGER): INTEGER;
　　　PROCEDURE DisplayHeight (X: INTEGER): INTEGER;
　　　PROCEDURE UserTrack (X: INTEGER): INTEGER;
　　　PROCEDURE SystemTrack (X: INTEGER): INTEGER;

　　　PROCEDURE AllocateUserViewer (DX: INTEGER;
　　　　　VAR X, Y: INTEGER);

Figure 4.13 Standard Oberon configuration featuring two logically adjacent displays of equal size and structure.

        PROCEDURE AllocateSystemViewer (DX: INTEGER; VAR X,
            Y: INTEGER);

    . . .

    END Oberon.

OpenDisplay initializes and opens a new display of the dimensions H (height), UW (width of user track) and SW (width of system track). *OpenTrack* overlays the sequence of existing tracks spanned by the segment [X, X + W) by a new track. Both *OpenDisplay* and *OpenTrack* take the burden of creating a filler viewer from the client.

The next block of procedures *DisplayWidth*, *DisplayHeight*, *User-Track*, *SystemTrack* return width or height of the respective structural entity located at position X in the display area.

Standard allocation   *AllocateUserViewer* and *AllocateSystemViewer* make proposals for the allocation of a new viewer in the desired track of the display located at DX. In first priority, the location is determined by the system pointer that can be set manually. If the pointer is not set, a location is calculated on the basis of some heuristics whose exact details are of minor importance. We only mention that strategies relying on different splitting fractions are applied in the user track and in the system track with the aim of generating aesthetically satisfactory layouts.

Standard commands

In addition to the programming support of standard display layouts provided by module Oberon, there is a *display management section* in the *System toolbox* supporting interactive users:

DEFINITION System;

```
(*Display management*)
    PROCEDURE Open; (*viewer*)
    PROCEDURE OpenLog; (*viewer*)
    PROCEDURE Close; (*viewer*)
    PROCEDURE CloseTrack;
    PROCEDURE Recall; (*most recently closed viewer*)
    PROCEDURE Copy; (*viewer*)
    PROCEDURE Grow; (*viewer*)

END System.
```

In turn, these commands are called to open a text viewer in the system track, open a viewer displaying the log text, close a viewer, close a track, recall the most recently closed viewer, copy a viewer, and grow a viewer. The commands *Close, CloseTrack, Recall, Copy* and *Grow* are generic. *Close, Copy* and *Grow* are typically included in the title bar of a menu viewer. Their detailed implementations follow in Section 4.8.

4.7 References

Binding, C. (1985). *User Interface Components Based on a Multiple Window Package.* University of Washington, Seattle, Technical Report 85-08-07.

Cohen, E. S., Smith, E. T. and Iverson, L. A. (1985). *Constraint-Based Tiled Windows.* New York: IEEE.

Goldberg, A. (1984). *Smalltalk-80: The Interactive Programming Environment.* Wokingham, England: Addison-Wesley.

Teitelman, W. (1984). A tour through Cedar. *IEEE Software,* **1**(2), 44–73.

Wille, M. (1988). *Overview: Entwurf und Realisierung eines Fenstersystems für Arbeitsplatzrechner.* Dissertation, ETH Nr. 8771.

4.8 Detailed implementations

MODULE Viewers; (*JG 14.9.90*)

    IMPORT Display;

    CONST
      restore* = 0; *modify** = 1; *suspend** = 2; (*message ids*)
      inf = MAX(INTEGER);

    TYPE
      Viewer* = POINTER TO ViewerDesc;

      ViewerDesc* = RECORD (Display.FrameDesc)
        state*: INTEGER
      END;

      (*state > 1: displayed
        state = 1: filler
        state = 0: closed
        state < 0: suspended*)

      ViewerMsg* = RECORD (Display.FrameMsg)
        id*: INTEGER;
        X*, **Y***, **W***, **H***: INTEGER;
        state*: INTEGER
      END;

      Track = POINTER TO TrackDesc;

      TrackDesc = RECORD (ViewerDesc)
        under: Display.Frame
      END;

    VAR
      curW*, **minH***, DW, DH: INTEGER;
      FillerTrack: Track; FillerViewer, buf: Viewer; (*for closed viewers*)

    PROCEDURE **Open*** (V: Viewer; X, Y: INTEGER);
      VAR T, u, v: Display.Frame; M: ViewerMsg;
    BEGIN
      IF (V.state = 0) & (X < inf) THEN
        IF Y > DH THEN Y := DH END;
        T := FillerTrack.next;
        WHILE X >= T.X + T.W DO T := T.next END;
        u := T.dsc; v := u.next;
        WHILE Y > v.Y + v.H DO u := v; v := u.next END;
        IF Y < v.Y + minH THEN Y := v.Y + minH END;
        IF (v.next.Y # 0) & (Y > v.Y + v.H − minH) THEN
          WITH v: Viewer DO
            V.X := T.X; V.W := T.W; V.Y := v.Y; V.H := v.H;
            M.id := suspend; M.state := 0;

```
                    v.handle(v, M); v.state := 0; buf := v;
                    V.next := v.next; u.next := V;
                    V.state := 2
                END
            ELSE
                V.X := T.X; V.W := T.W; V.Y := v.Y; V.H := Y − v.Y;
                M.id := modify; M.Y := Y; M.H := v.Y + v.H − Y;
                v.handle(v, M); v.Y := M.Y; v.H := M.H;
                V.next := v; u.next := V;
                V.state := 2
            END
        END
END Open;


PROCEDURE Change* (V: Viewer; Y: INTEGER);
    VAR v: Display.Frame; M: ViewerMsg;
BEGIN
    IF V.state > 1 THEN
        IF Y > DH THEN Y := DH END;
        v := V.next;
        IF (v.next.Y # 0) & (Y > v.Y + v.H − minH) THEN
            Y := v.Y + v.H − minH
        END;
        IF Y >= V.Y + minH THEN
            M.id := modify; M.Y := Y; M.H := v.Y + v.H − Y;
            v.handle(v, M); v.Y := M.Y; v.H := M.H;
            V.H := Y − V.Y
        END
    END
END Change;


PROCEDURE RestoreTrack (S: Display.Frame);
    VAR T, t, v: Display.Frame; M: ViewerMsg;
BEGIN
    WITH S: Track DO
        t := S.next;
        WHILE t.next.X # S.X DO t := t.next END;
        T := S.under;
        WHILE T.next # NIL DO T := T.next END;
        t.next := S.under; T.next := S.next;
        M.id := restore;
        REPEAT t := t.next;
            v := t.dsc;
            REPEAT v := v.next; v.handle(v, M);
                WITH v: Viewer DO v.state := − v.state END
            UNTIL v = t.dsc
        UNTIL t = T
    END
END RestoreTrack;


PROCEDURE Close* (V: Viewer);
    VAR T, U: Display.Frame; M: ViewerMsg;
BEGIN
    IF V.state > 1 THEN
        U := V.next; T := FillerTrack;
        REPEAT T := T.next UNTIL V.X < T.X + T.W;
        IF (T(Track).under = NIL) OR (U.next # V) THEN
```

```
            M.id := suspend; M.state := 0;
            V.handle(V, M); V.state := 0; buf := V;
            M.id := modify; M.Y := V.Y; M.H := V.H + U.H;
            U.handle(U, M); U.Y := M.Y; U.H := M.H;
            WHILE U.next # V DO U := U.next END;
            U.next := V.next
        ELSE (*close track*)
            M.id := suspend; M.state := 0;
            V.handle(V, M); V.state := 0; buf := V;
            U.handle(U, M); U(Viewer).state := 0;
            RestoreTrack(T)
        END
    END
END Close;

PROCEDURE Recall* ( VAR V: Viewer);
BEGIN V := buf
END Recall;

PROCEDURE This* (X, Y: INTEGER): Viewer;
    VAR T, V: Display.Frame;
BEGIN
    IF (X < inf) & (Y < DH) THEN
        T := FillerTrack;
        REPEAT T := T.next UNTIL X < T.X + T.W;
        V := T.dsc;
        REPEAT V := V.next UNTIL Y < V.Y + V.H;
        RETURN V(Viewer)
    ELSE RETURN NIL
    END
END This;

PROCEDURE Next* (V: Viewer): Viewer;
BEGIN RETURN V.next(Viewer)
END Next;

PROCEDURE Locate* (X, H: INTEGER; VAR fil, bot, alt, max: Display.Frame);
    VAR T, V: Display.Frame;
BEGIN
    IF X < inf THEN
        T := FillerTrack;
        REPEAT T := T.next UNTIL X < T.X + T.W;
        fil := T.dsc; bot := fil.next;
        IF bot.next # fil THEN
            alt := bot.next; V := alt.next;
            WHILE (V # fil) & (alt.H < H) DO
                IF V.H > alt.H THEN alt := V END; V := V.next
            END
        ELSE alt := bot
        END;
        max := T.dsc; V := max.next;
        WHILE V # fil DO
            IF V.H > max.H THEN max := V END; V := V.next
        END
    END
END Locate;

PROCEDURE InitTrack* (W, H: INTEGER; Filler: Viewer);
```

```
        VAR S: Display.Frame; T: Track;
    BEGIN
        IF Filler.state = 0 THEN
            Filler.X := curW; Filler.W := W; Filler.Y := 0; Filler.H := H;
            Filler.state := 1;
            Filler.next := Filler;
            NEW(T);
            T.X := curW; T.W := W; T.Y := 0; T.H := H;
            T.dsc := Filler; T.under := NIL;
            FillerViewer.X := curW + W; FillerViewer.W := inf − FillerViewer.X;
            FillerTrack.X := FillerViewer.X; FillerTrack.W := FillerViewer.W;
            S := FillerTrack;
            WHILE S.next # FillerTrack DO S := S.next END;
            S.next := T; T.next := FillerTrack;
            curW := curW + W
        END
    END InitTrack;

    PROCEDURE OpenTrack* (X, W: INTEGER; Filler: Viewer);
        VAR newT: Track; S, T, t, v: Display.Frame; M: ViewerMsg;
    BEGIN
        IF (X < inf) & (Filler.state = 0) THEN
            S := FillerTrack; T := S.next;
            WHILE X >= T.X + T.W DO S := T; T := S.next END;
            WHILE X + W > T.X + T.W DO T := T.next END;
            M.id := suspend;
            t := S;
            REPEAT t := t.next; v := t.dsc;
                REPEAT v := v.next;
                    WITH v: Viewer DO
                        M.state := −v.state; v.handle(v, M); v.state := M.state
                    END
                UNTIL v = t.dsc
            UNTIL t = T;
            Filler.X := S.next.X; Filler.W := T.X + T.W − S.next.X; Filler.Y := 0; Filler.H := DH;
            Filler.state := 1;
            Filler.next := Filler;
            NEW(newT);
            newT.X := Filler.X; newT.W := Filler.W; newT.Y := 0; newT.H := DH;
            newT.dsc := Filler; newT.under := S.next; S.next := newT;
            newT.next := T.next; T.next := NIL
        END
    END OpenTrack;

    PROCEDURE CloseTrack* (X: INTEGER);
        VAR T, V: Display.Frame; M: ViewerMsg;
    BEGIN
        IF X < inf THEN
            T := FillerTrack;
            REPEAT T := T.next UNTIL X < T.X + T.W;
            IF T(Track).under # NIL THEN
                M.id := suspend; M.state := 0; V := T.dsc;
                REPEAT V := V.next; V.handle(V, M); V(Viewer).state := 0 UNTIL V = T.dsc;
                RestoreTrack(T)
            END
        END
    END CloseTrack;

    PROCEDURE Broadcast* (VAR M: Display.FrameMsg);
```

```
      VAR T, V: Display.Frame;
   BEGIN
      T := FillerTrack.next;
      WHILE T # FillerTrack DO
         V := T.dsc;
         REPEAT V := V.next; V.handle(V, M) UNTIL V = T.dsc;
         T := T.next
      END
   END Broadcast;


BEGIN buf := NIL;
   NEW(FillerViewer);
   FillerViewer.X := 0; FillerViewer.W := inf; FillerViewer.Y := 0; FillerViewer.H := DH;
   FillerViewer.next := FillerViewer;
   NEW(FillerTrack);
   FillerTrack.X := 0; FillerTrack.W := inf; FillerTrack.Y := 0; FillerTrack.H := DH;
   FillerTrack.dsc := FillerViewer;
   FillerTrack.next := FillerTrack;
   curW := 0; minH := 1;
   DW := Display.Width; DH := Display.Height
END Viewers.


MODULE MenuViewers; (*JG 26.8.90*)

   IMPORT Input, Display, Texts, Viewers, Oberon;

   CONST extend* = 0; reduce* = 1; move* = 2;

   TYPE
      Viewer* = POINTER TO ViewerDesc;

      ViewerDesc* = RECORD (Viewers.ViewerDesc)
         menuH*: INTEGER
      END;

      ModifyMsg* = RECORD (Display.FrameMsg)
         id*: INTEGER;
         dY*, Y*, H*: INTEGER
      END;

   PROCEDURE Copy (V: Viewer; VAR V1: Viewer);
      VAR Menu, Main: Display.Frame; M: Oberon.CopyMsg;
   BEGIN
      Menu := V.dsc; Main := V.dsc.next;
      NEW(V1); V1↑ := V↑ ; V1.state := 0;
      Menu.handle(Menu, M); V1.dsc := M.F;
      Main.handle(Main, M); V1.dsc.next := M.F
   END Copy;

   PROCEDURE Draw (V: Viewers.Viewer);
   BEGIN
      Display.ReplConst(Display.white, V.X, V.Y, 1, V.H, 0);
      Display.ReplConst(Display.white, V.X + V.W − 1, V.Y, 1, V.H, 0);
      Display.ReplConst(Display.white, V.X + 1, V.Y, V.W − 2, 1, 0);
      Display.ReplConst(Display.white, V.X + 1, V.Y + V.H − 1, V.W − 2, 1, 0)
```

```
    END Draw;

    PROCEDURE Extend (V: Viewer; newY: INTEGER);
        VAR dH: INTEGER;
    BEGIN dH := V.Y − newY;
        IF dH > 0 THEN
            Display.ReplConst(Display.black, V.X + 1, newY + 1, V.W − 2, dH, 0);
            Display.ReplConst(Display.white, V.X, newY, 1, dH, 0);
            Display.ReplConst(Display.white, V.X + V.W − 1, newY, 1, dH, 0);
            Display.ReplConst(Display.white, V.X + 1, newY, V.W − 2, 1, 0)
        END
    END Extend;


    PROCEDURE Reduce (V: Viewer; newY: INTEGER);
    BEGIN Display.ReplConst(Display.white, V.X + 1, newY, V.W − 2, 1, 0)
    END Reduce;


    PROCEDURE Grow (V: Viewer; oldH: INTEGER);
        VAR dH: INTEGER;
    BEGIN dH := V.H − oldH;
        IF dH > 0 THEN
            Display.ReplConst(Display.white, V.X, V.Y + oldH, 1, dH, 0);
            Display.ReplConst(Display.white, V.X + V.W − 1, V.Y + oldH, 1, dH, 0);
            Display.ReplConst(Display.white, V.X + 1, V.Y + V.H − 1, V.W − 2, 1, 0)
        END
    END Grow;


    PROCEDURE Shrink (V: Viewer; newH: INTEGER);
    BEGIN Display.ReplConst(Display.white, V.X + 1, V.Y + newH − 1, V.W − 2, 1, 0)
    END Shrink;


    PROCEDURE Adjust (F: Display.Frame; id, dY, Y, H: INTEGER);
        VAR M: ModifyMsg;
    BEGIN M.id := id; M.dY := dY; M.Y := Y; M.H := H; F.handle(F, M); F.Y := Y; F.H := H
    END Adjust;


    PROCEDURE Restore (V: Viewer);
        VAR Menu, Main: Display.Frame;
    BEGIN
        Menu := V.dsc; Main := V.dsc.next;
        Oberon.RemoveMarks(V.X, V.Y, V.W, V.H);
        Draw(V);
        Menu.X := V.X + 1; Menu.Y := V.Y + V.H − 1; Menu.W := V.W − 2; Menu.H := 0;
        Main.X := V.X + 1; Main.Y := V.Y + V.H − V.menuH; Main.W := V.W − 2; Main.H :=
            0;
        IF V.H > V.menuH + 1 THEN
            Adjust(Menu, extend, 0, V.Y + V.H − V.menuH, V.menuH − 1);
            Adjust( Main, extend, 0, V.Y + 1, V.H − V.menuH − 1)
        ELSE Adjust(Menu, extend, 0, V.Y + 1, V.H − 2)
        END
    END Restore;


    PROCEDURE Modify (V: Viewer; Y, H: INTEGER);
        VAR Menu, Main: Display.Frame;
    BEGIN
        Menu := V.dsc; Main := V.dsc.next;
```

```
        IF Y < V.Y THEN (*extend*)
            Oberon.RemoveMarks(V.X, Y, V.W, V.Y − Y);
            Extend(V, Y);
            IF H > V.menuH + 1 THEN
                Adjust(Menu, extend, 0, Y + H − V.menuH, V.menuH − 1);
                Adjust(Main, extend, 0, Y + 1, H − V.menuH − 1)
            ELSE Adjust(Menu, extend, 0, Y + 1, H − 2)
            END
        ELSIF Y > V.Y THEN (*reduce*)
            Oberon.RemoveMarks(V.X, V.Y, V.W, V.H);
            IF H > V.menuH + 1 THEN
                Adjust(Main, reduce, 0, Y + 1, H − V.menuH − 1);
                Adjust(Menu, reduce, 0, Y + H − V.menuH, V.menuH − 1)
            ELSE
                Adjust(Main, reduce, 0, Y + H − V.menuH, 0);
                Adjust(Menu, reduce, 0, Y + 1, H − 2)
            END;
            Reduce(V, Y)
        END
END Modify;


PROCEDURE Change (V: Viewer; X, Y: INTEGER; Keys: SET);
    VAR Menu, Main: Display.Frame;
        V1: Viewers.Viewer; keysum: SET; Y0, dY, H: INTEGER;
BEGIN (*Keys # {}*)
    Menu := V.dsc; Main := V.dsc.next;
    Oberon.DrawCursor(Oberon.Mouse, Oberon.Arrow, X, Y);
    Display.ReplConst(Display.white, V.X + 1, V.Y + V.H − 1 − V.dsc.H, V.W − 2, V.dsc.H,
        2);
    Y0 := Y;
    keysum := Keys;
    LOOP
        Input.Mouse(Keys, X, Y);
        IF Keys = {} THEN EXIT END;
        keysum := keysum + Keys;
        Oberon.DrawCursor(Oberon.Mouse, Oberon.Arrow, X, Y)
    END;
    Display.ReplConst(Display.white, V.X + 1, V.Y + V.H − 1 − V.dsc.H, V.W − 2, V.dsc.H,
        2);
    IF ~(0 IN keysum) THEN
        If 1 in keysum theN V1 := Viewers.This(X, Y);
        IF Y < V1.Y + V.menuH + 2 THEN Y := V1.Y + V.menuH + 2 END;
        Viewers.Close(V); Viewers.Open(V, X, Y); Restore(V)
        ELSE
        IF Y > Y0 THEN (*extend*) dY := Y − Y0;
            V1 := Viewers.Next(V);
            IF V1.state > 1 THEN
                IF (V1 IS Viewer) & (V1.H >= V1(Viewer).menuH + 2) THEN
                    IF dY > V1.H − V1(Viewer).menuH − 2 THEN dY := V1.H −
                            V1(Viewer).menuH − 2
                    END
                ELSIF dY > V1.H − Viewers.minH THEN dY := V1.H − Viewers.minH
                END
            ELSIF dY > V1.H THEN dY := V1.H
            END;
            Viewers.Change(V, V.Y + V.H + dY);
            Oberon.RemoveMarks(V.X, V.Y, V.W, V.H);
            Grow(V, V.H − dY);
            IF V.H > V.menuH + 1 THEN
```

```
                    Adjust(Menu, extend, dY, V.Y + V.H − V.menuH, V.menuH − 1);
                    Adjust(Main, extend, dY, V.Y + 1, V.H − V.menuH − 1)
                ELSE Adjust(Menu, extend, dY, V.Y + 1, V.H − 2)
                END
            ELSIF Y < Y0 THEN (*reduce*) dY := Y0 − Y;
                IF dY > V.H − V(Viewer).menuH − 2 THEN dY := V.H − V(Viewer).menuH − 2
                    END;
                Oberon.RemoveMarks(V.X, V.Y, V.W, V.H);
                H := V.H − dY;
                IF H > V.menuH + 1 THEN
                    Adjust(Main, reduce, dY, V.Y + 1, H − V.menuH − 1);
                    Adjust(Menu, reduce, dY, V.Y + H − V.menuH, V.menuH − 1)
                ELSE
                    Adjust(Main, reduce, dY, V.Y + H − V.menuH, 0);
                    Adjust(Menu, reduce, dY, V.Y + 1, H − 2)
                END;
                Shrink(V, H);
                Viewers.Change(V, V.Y + H)
            END
        END
    END
END Change;


PROCEDURE Suspend (V: Viewer);
    VAR Menu, Main: Display.Frame;
BEGIN
    Menu := V.dsc; Main := V.dsc.next;
    Adjust(Main, reduce, 0, V.Y + V.H − V.menuH, 0);
    Adjust(Menu, reduce, 0, V.Y + V.H − 1, 0)
END Suspend;

PROCEDURE Handle* (V: Display.Frame; VAR M: Display.FrameMsg);
    VAR Menu, Main: Display.Frame; V1: Viewer;
BEGIN
    WITH V: Viewer DO
        Menu := V.dsc; Main := V.dsc.next;
        IF M IS Oberon.InputMsg THEN
            WITH M: Oberon.InputMsg DO
                IF M.id = Oberon.track THEN
                    IF M.Y < V.Y + 1 THEN Oberon.DrawCursor(Oberon.Mouse, Oberon.Arrow,
                        M.X, M.Y)
                    ELSIF M.Y < V.Y + V.H − V.menuH THEN Main.handle(Main, M)
                    ELSIF M.Y < V.Y + V.H − V.menuH + 2 THEN Menu.handle
                        (Menu, M)
                    ELSIF M.Y < V.Y + V.H − 1 THEN
                        IF 2 IN M.keys THEN Change(V, M.X, M.Y, M.keys)
                        ELSE Menu.handle(Menu, M)
                        END
                    ELSE Oberon.DrawCursor(Oberon.Mouse, Oberon.Arrow, M.X, M.Y)
                    END
                ELSE Menu.handle(Menu, M); Main.handle(Main, M)
                END
            END
        ELSIF M IS Oberon.ControlMsg THEN
            WITH M: Oberon.ControlMsg DO
                IF M.id = Oberon.mark THEN
                    Oberon.DrawCursor(Oberon.Mouse, Oberon.Arrow, M.X, M.Y);
                    Oberon.DrawCursor(Oberon.Pointer, Oberon.Star, M.X, M.Y)
```

```
                    ELSE Menu.handle(Menu, M); Main.handle(Main, M)
                    END
                END
            ELSIF M IS Oberon.CopyMsg THEN
                WITH M: Oberon.CopyMsg DO Copy(V(Viewer), V1); M.F := V1 END
            ELSIF M IS Viewers.ViewerMsg THEN
                WITH M: Viewers.ViewerMsg DO
                    IF M.id = Viewers.restore THEN Restore(V)
                    ELSIF M.id = Viewers.modify THEN Modify(V, M.Y, M.H)
                    ELSIF M.id = Viewers.suspend THEN Suspend(V)
                    END
                END
            ELSE Menu.handle(Menu, M); Main.handle(Main, M)
            END
        END
    END Handle;


    PROCEDURE New* (Menu, Main: Display.Frame; menuH, X, Y: INTEGER): Viewer;
        VAR V: Viewer;
    BEGIN NEW(V);
        V.handle := Handle; V.dsc := Menu; V.dsc.next := Main; V.menuH := menuH;
        Viewers.Open(V, X, Y); Restore(V);
        RETURN V
    END New;

END MenuViewers.


MODULE System; (*JG 3.10.90*)

    IMPORT Viewers, MenuViewers, Oberon, Texts, TextFrames;

    CONST
        StandardMenu ="System.Close System.Copy System.Grow Edit.Search Edit.Store";
        LogMenu ="System.Close System.Grow Edit.Locate Edit.Store";


    VAR W: Texts.Writer;


    PROCEDURE Max (i, j: LONGINT): LONGINT;
    BEGIN IF i >= j THEN RETURN i ELSE RETURN j END
    END Max;

(* ------------ Toolbox for standard display --------------*)

    PROCEDURE Open*;
        VAR par: Oberon.ParList;
            T: Texts.Text;
            S: Texts.Scanner;
            V: Viewers.Viewer;
            X, Y: INTEGER;
            beg, end, time: LONGINT;
    BEGIN
        par := Oberon.Par;
        Texts.OpenScanner(S, par.text, par.pos); Texts.Scan(S);
        IF (S.class = Texts.Char) & (S.c =" ↑ ") OR (S.line # 0) THEN
            Oberon.GetSelection(T, beg, end, time);
```

```
        IF time >= 0 THEN Texts.OpenScanner(S, T, beg); Texts.Scan(S) END
    END;
    IF S.class = Texts.Name THEN
        Oberon.AllocateSystemViewer(par.vwr.X, X, Y);
        V := MenuViewers.New(
        TextFrames.NewMenu(S.s, StandardMenu),
        TextFrames.NewText(TextFrames.Text(S.s), 0),
        TextFrames.menuH,
        X, Y)
    END
END Open;


PROCEDURE OpenLog*;
    VAR V: Viewers.Viewer; X, Y: INTEGER;
BEGIN
    Oberon.AllocateSystemViewer(Oberon.Par.vwr.X, X, Y);
    V := MenuViewers.New(
        TextFrames.NewMenu("System.Log", LogMenu),
        TextFrames.NewText(Oberon.Log, Max(0, Oberon.Log.len - 200)),
        TextFrames.menuH,
        X, Y)
END OpenLog;


PROCEDURE Close*;
    VAR par: Oberon.ParList; V: Viewers.Viewer;
BEGIN par := Oberon.Par;
    IF par.frame = par.vwr.dsc THEN V := par.vwr
    ELSE V := Oberon.MarkedViewer()
    END;
    Viewers.Close(V)
END Close;


PROCEDURE CloseTrack*;
    VAR V: Viewers.Viewer;
BEGIN V := Oberon.MarkedViewer(); Viewers.CloseTrack(V.X)
END CloseTrack;


PROCEDURE Recall*;
    VAR V: Viewers.Viewer; M: Viewers.ViewerMsg;
BEGIN
    Viewers.Recall(V);
    IF V.state = 0 THEN
        Viewers.Open(V, V.X, V.Y + V.H); M.id := Viewers.restore; V.handle(V, M)
    END
END Recall;


PROCEDURE Copy*;
    VAR V, V1: Viewers.Viewer; M: Oberon.CopyMsg; N: Viewers.ViewerMsg;
BEGIN
    V := Oberon.Par.vwr; V.handle(V, M); V1 := M.F(Viewers.Viewer);
    Viewers.Open(V1, V.X, V.Y + V.H DIV 2);
    N.id := Viewers.restore; V1.handle(V1, N)
END Copy;


PROCEDURE Grow*;
    VAR V, V1: Viewers.Viewer; M: Oberon.CopyMsg; N: Viewers.ViewerMsg;
```

```
            DW, DH: INTEGER;
BEGIN V := Oberon.Par.vwr;
    DW :4 Oberon.DisplayWidth(V.X); DH := Oberon.DisplayHeight(V.X);
    IF V.H < DH − Viewers.minH THEN Oberon.OpenTrack(V.X, V.W)
    ELSIF V.W < DW THEN Oberon.OpenTrack(Oberon.UserTrack(V.X), DW)
    END;
    IF (V.H < DH − Viewers.minH) OR (V.W < DW) THEN
        V.handle(V, M); V1 := M.F(Viewers.Viewer);
        Viewers.Open(V1, V.X, DH);
        N.id := Viewers.restore; V1.handle(V1, N)
    END
END Grow;


PROCEDURE OpenViewers;
    VAR V: Viewers.Viewer; t, d: LONGINT; X, Y: INTEGER;
BEGIN
    Oberon.GetClock(t, d); Texts.WriteString(W,"System.Time");
    Texts.WriteDate(W, t, d); Texts.WriteLn(W); Texts.Append(Oberon.Log, W.buf);
    Oberon.AllocateSystemViewer(0, X, Y);
    V := MenuViewers.New(
        TextFrames.NewMenu("System.Log", LogMenu),
        TextFrames.NewText(Oberon.Log, 0),
        TextFrames.menuH,
        X, Y);
    Oberon.AllocateSystemViewer(0, X, Y);
    V := MenuViewers.New(
        TextFrames.NewMenu("System.Tool", StandardMenu),
        TextFrames.NewText(TextFrames.Text("System.Tool"), 0),
        TextFrames.menuH,
        X, Y)
    END OpenViewers;


BEGIN
    Texts.OpenWriter(W);
    Oberon.Log := TextFrames.Text("");
    OpenViewers
END System.
```

5 The text system

At the beginning of the computing era, *text* was the only medium mediating information between users and computers. A textual notation was used not only for most diverse kinds of data like names and numbers (represented by sequences of digits), but also for the specification of programs and processes (based on the notions of formal language and syntax) and of commands and objects (by their name). Actually, not even the most modern and most sophisticated computing environments have been able to make the dominating role of text falter substantially. At most, they have introduced alternative models like *graphical user interfaces* (*GUI*) for the last two points mentioned.

There are many reasons for the popularity of texts in general and in connection with computers in particular. To name but a few, texts containing an arbitrary amount of information can be built from a small alphabet of widely standardized elements (characters), their building pattern is extremely simple (lining up elements), and the resulting structure is most elementary (a sequence).

Text files

In computing terminology, sequences of elements are called *files* and, in particular, sequences of characters are *text files*. Looking at their binary representation, we find them excellently suited to be stored in computer memories and on external media. Remember that individual characters are usually encoded in one byte each (ASCII code). We can therefore identify the binary structure of text files with sequences of bytes, matching perfectly the structure of any underlying computer storage. We should recall at this point that, with the possible exception of line-break control characters, rendering information is not part of ordinary text files. For example, the choices of type font and of paragraph formatting parameters are left entirely to the rendering interpreter.

Non-reusability

However, there exists a much more serious problem with texts in conventional computing environments. We can describe it in a word as non-reusability. Texts and their handling are assigned to local and temporary parts of a program instead of to the global system. Input texts are typically read from the keyboard under control of an individual editor and are discarded once they are interpreted. Output texts are volatile. They are displayed on screen directly and are not available to any other parts of the program. We can easily locate the root of the defect: there is no central text management in conventional environments.

Of course, such a poor integration of texts on the level of programming must reflect itself on the user surface. More often than not, users are forced to retype a certain string of text instead of simply getting it from elsewhere on the screen. Investigations have shown that, in time average, up to 80% of required input text is displayed somewhere already.

Integrated text

Prompted by our positive experiences with integrated text in the Cedar system (Teitelman, 1984), we decided to provide a central text management in Oberon at a sufficiently low system level. However, remembering our primary motivation of reusability, we recognize quickly that merely centralizing the management of static texts is insufficient. Because reusing is intimately coupled with editing, we need an abstract data type *Text* together with a complete set of intrinsic operations. We shall devote Section 5.1 to the presentation of the rationale behind this. In Section 5.2, we take a closer look at the basic text management in Oberon, including data structures and algorithms used for the implementation.

Text frames

Text frames are a special class of display frames. They appear typically (but not necessarily) as frames of main contents within a menu viewer (see Section 4.4.2). Their role is actually a polar pair of roles: rendering text on the display screen and interpreting editing commands. Section 5.3 will reveal the details.

With the aim of exploiting the power of modern bitmap displays, and also of using the results of earlier projects in the field of digital font design, we decided to include type-font specifications in Oberon texts. In Section 5.4, we shall explain the font machinery, starting from some rather far-reaching abstraction and pursuing it all the way down to the level of raster data.

5.1 Text as an abstract data type

The concept of *abstraction* is the most important achievement of programming language development. It provides a powerful tool to create simplified views on complicated program components. Expressive examples are provided by the notions of *module definition* and of *abstract data type*. These notions embody *public* views on a certain well-bounded piece of program and on objects of a well-determined type respectively.

We shall now give a precise definition of the notion of text in

Oberon by presenting it as an abstract data type. We shall see that text is a far more powerful institution than the usual type *string* as it is perhaps supported by more advanced programming languages. We emphasize that we shall consciously avoid to reveal any aspects of implementation in this section. Our viewpoint is purely that of a user or client.

Attributed characters

Before we begin with our actual presentation of type *Text*, we want to get a refined understanding of *characters*. We know that they represent textual elements of information. However, every character also refers to some specific graphical pattern. In Oberon, we do justice to both aspects by thinking of the ASCII code as an integral range indexing type-fonts. More concretely, we let characters be represented as pairs (*font, code*), where *font* designates a type-font and *code* is the character's ASCII code. We shall treat the topic of fonts and character patterns thoroughly in Section 5.4. Adding two more attributes *color* and *vertical offset*, we get to a quadruple representation of characters (*font, code, col, voff*). The components font, color, and vertical offset together are often referred to as *looks*.

Text descriptions

Now, we can roughly define a text as a sequence of attributed characters. It is described by a handle of type

Text = POINTER TO TextDesc;

TextDesc = RECORD
    len: LONGINT;
    notify: Notifier
END;

There is only one state variable and one method. The variable *len* represents the current length of the described text (that is the number of characters in the sequence). *notify* is included as a method (occasionally called *after-method*) to enable context-sensitive postprocessing after an operation on this text has been performed. Before we come to the details, we must further develop the construction of the abstract data type *Text*. Our eventual aim is it to define a reasonably complete set of associated *intrinsic operations*.

We can identify three different groups of intrinsic operations on texts. They correspond to the topics of *loading* and *storing*, *editing* and *accessing* respectively.

5.1.1   Loading and storing

Let us start with the file topic. Following document preparation terminology, we introduce a pair of mutually inverse operations

Internalizing and externalizing

internalize and *externalize*. Their meaning is 'load from file and build up an internal data structure' and 'sequentialize the internal data structure and store on file'. There are three procedures supporting internalizing and externalizing of texts:

PROCEDURE Open (T: Text; name: ARRAY OF CHAR);
PROCEDURE Load (T: Text; f: Files.File; pos: LONGINT;
    VAR len: LONGINT);
PROCEDURE Store (T: Text; f: Files.File; pos: LONGINT;
    VAR len: LONGINT);

We ought to say in advance that logical entities like texts are stored in Oberon on external media in form of *blocks*. A block is specified by a pair (file, pos) consisting of a file descriptor and a starting position. In general, the structure of blocks obeys the following syntax:

block = identification type length contents.

Open internalizes a named text file (consisting of a single text block), *Load* internalizes an arbitrary text block (f, pos), and *Store* externalizes a text block (f, pos). The parameter T always designates the internalized text. *len* returns the length of the block. Note that in the case of *Load*, the identification part of the block must have been read and consumed before the loader is called.

5.1.2 Editing

Our next group of intrinsic operations on texts supports editing. It comprises four procedures:

Basic operations

PROCEDURE Delete (T: Text; beg, end: LONGINT);
PROCEDURE Insert (T: Text; pos: LONGINT; B: Buffer);
PROCEDURE Append (T: Text; B: Buffer);

PROCEDURE ChangeLooks (T: Text; beg, end: LONGINT;
    sel: SET; fnt: Fonts.Font; col, voff: SHORTINT);

Again, we should first explain the types of parameters. Procedures *Delete* and *ChangeLooks* each take a *stretch of text* as an argument that, by definition, is an interval [beg, end) within the given text. In the parameter lists of *Insert* and *Append*, we recognize a new data type *Buffer*.

Buffers

Buffers are a facility to hold anonymous sequences of characters. Type *Buffer* presents itself as another abstract data type:

Buffer = POINTER TO BufDesc;

BufDesc = RECORD
    len: LONGINT
END;

len specifies the current length of the buffered sequence. The following procedures represent the intrinsic operations on buffers:

PROCEDURE OpenBuf (B: Buffer);
PROCEDURE Copy (SB, DB: Buffer);
PROCEDURE Save (T: Text; beg, end: LONGINT; B: Buffer);
PROCEDURE Recall (VAR B: Buffer);

Their function is in turn opening a given buffer B, copying a buffer SB to DB, saving a stretch [beg, end) of text in a given buffer, and recalling the most recently deleted stretch of text and putting it into buffer B.

We are now prepared to explain the editing operations on texts. Procedure *Delete* deletes the given stretch [beg, end) within text T, *Insert* inserts the buffer's contents at position *pos* within text T, and *Append*(T, B) is a shorthand form for *Insert*(T, T.len, B). Note that, as a side-effect of *Insert* and *Append*, the buffer involved is emptied. Finally, *ChangeLooks* allows a change of selected looks within the given stretch [beg, end) of text T. *sel* is a mask selecting a subset of the set of looks consisting of font, color, and vertical offset.

Notifier   It is now time to return to the notifier concept. Recapitulate that *notify* is an after-method of texts. It must be installed by the client opening the text and is called at the end of every editing operation. Its procedural type is

Notifier = PROCEDURE (T: Text; op: INTEGER; beg, end:
    LONGINT);

The parameters *op*, *beg* and *end* report about the operation (*op*) calling the notifier and on the affected stretch [beg, end) of the text. There are three different possible variants of *op* corresponding to the three different editing operations: *op* = *delete*, *insert* and *replace* correspond to *Delete*, *Insert* (and *Append*) and *ChangeLooks* respectively. By far the most important application of the notifier for displayed texts is updating the display, that is, adjusting all affected views that are currently displayed. We shall come back to this important point when we discuss text frames in Section 5.3.

5.1.3 Accessing

Readers

We now turn our attention to the third and last group of intrinsic operations on texts, which is concerned with *accessing*. According to our guiding principle of separation of concerns, the access mechanism operates on extra aggregates called *readers* and *writers* rather than on texts themselves. Readers are used to read texts sequentially. Their type is declared as

```
Reader = RECORD
    eot: BOOLEAN; (*end of text*)
    fnt: Fonts.Font;
    col: SHORTINT;
    voff: SHORTINT
END;
```

A reader must first be set up at any given position in the text and can then be moved forward incrementally by reading characterwise. Its state variables indicate end-of-text and expose the looks of the previously read character.

The corresponding operators are

```
PROCEDURE OpenReader (VAR R: Reader; T: Text;
pos: LONGINT);
PROCEDURE Read (VAR R: Reader; VAR ch: CHAR);
```

OpenReader sets up a reader R at position *pos* in text T. *Read* returns the character at the current position of R and makes R move to the next position.

The current position of reader R is returned by a call to the function *Pos*:

```
PROCEDURE Pos (VAR R: Reader): LONGINT;
```

Scanner

We learnt in Chapter 3 that texts are often used as parameter lists of commands. To a command interpreter, however, a text appears as sequence of *tokens* much rather than as sequence of characters. Therefore we adopted the well-known concepts of *syntax* and *scanner* from the discipline of compiler construction. The Oberon scanner recognizes tokens of some universal classes. They are *name, string, integer, real, longreal* and *special character*.

Standard syntax

The exact syntax of universal Oberon tokens is

token = name | string | integer | real | longreal | spexchar.

name = ident { "." ident }.

ident = letter { letter | digit }.
string = "''" { char } "''" | '''' { char } ''''.
integer = ["+"|"−"] number.
real = ["+"|"−"] number "." number ["E" ["+"|"−"] number].
longreal = ["+"|"−"] number "." number ["D" ["+"|"−"]
    number].
number = digit { digit }.
spexchar = any character except letters, digits, space, tabulator,
    and carriage-return.

Type *Scanner* is defined as

```
Scanner = RECORD (Reader)
    nextCh: CHAR;
    line: INTEGER;
    class: INTEGER;
    i: LONGINT;
    x: REAL;
    y: LONGREAL;
    c: CHAR;
    len: SHORTINT;
    s: ARRAY 32 OF CHAR
END;
```

This type is actually a variant record type with *class* as discriminating tag. Depending on its class, the value of the current token is stored in one of the fields i, x, y, c or s. *len* gives the length of s, *nextCh* typically exposes the character terminating the current token, and *line* counts the number of lines scanned.

The operations on scanners are

```
PROCEDURE OpenScanner (VAR S: Scanner; T: Text;
    pos: LONGINT);
PROCEDURE Scan (VAR S: Scanner);
```

They correspond exactly to their counterparts *OpenReader* and *Read* respectively.

It is important to be aware that arbitrarily many readers and scanners can coexist on one and the same text. Typically, readers and scanners are controlled by and bound to a specific activity. They are temporary in contrast to their host texts, 'living' in the system universe permanently. This fact manifests itself by the absence of any possibility to reference readers and scanners by pointers.

Writer   *Writers* are dual to readers. They serve the purpose of creating and extending texts. However, they do not operate on texts directly.

Rather, they act as self-contained aggregates continuously consuming and buffering textual data.

The formal declaration of type *Writer* resembles that of type *Reader*:

```
Writer = RECORD
    buf: Buffer;
    fnt: Fonts.Font;
    col: SHORTINT;
    voff: SHORTINT
END;
```

buf is an internal buffer containing the consumed data. *fnt*, *col* and *voff* specify the current looks for the next character consumed by this writer.

The following procedures together constitute the basic management of writers:

```
PROCEDURE OpenWriter (VAR W: Writer);
PROCEDURE SetFont (VAR W: Writer; fnt: Fonts.Font);
PROCEDURE SetColor (VAR W: Writer; col: SHORTINT);
PROCEDURE SetOffset (VAR W: Writer; voff: SHORTINT);
```

OpenWriter opens a new writer with an empty buffer. *SetFont*, *SetColor* and *SetOffset* set the respective current look. For example, *SetFont(W, fnt)* is equivalent to *W.fnt := fnt*. These procedures are included because *fnt*, *col* and *voff* are considered read-only for clients.

A question arising naturally is how data is produced and transferred to writers. The answer is a set of *write* procedures, each dedicated to an individual type of data:

```
PROCEDURE Write (VAR W: Writer; ch: CHAR);
PROCEDURE WriteLn (VAR W: Writer);
PROCEDURE WriteString (VAR W: Writer;
    s: ARRAY OF CHAR);
PROCEDURE WriteInt (VAR W: Writer; x, n: LONGINT);
PROCEDURE WriteHex (VAR W: Writer; x: LONGINT);
PROCEDURE WriteReal (VAR W: Writer; x: REAL;
    n: INTEGER);
PROCEDURE WriteRealFix (VAR W: Writer; x: REAL;
    n, k: INTEGER);
PROCEDURE WriteRealHex (VAR W: Writer; x: REAL);
PROCEDURE WriteLongReal (VAR W: Writer; x: LONGREAL;
    n: INTEGER);
PROCEDURE WriteLongRealHex (VAR W: Writer;
    x: LONGREAL);
PROCEDURE WriteDate (VAR W: Writer; t, d: LONGINT);
```

It may help to study the following schematic extract of a client program creating textual output:

```
open writer; set desired looks;
REPEAT
    process;
    write result to writer;
    append writer buffer to output text
UNTIL ended
```

Of course, writers can be reused. For example, a single global writer is typically shared by all of the procedures within a module. In this case, the writer needs to be opened at module loading time only.

Obviously, the main benefit we can draw from such a rigorous decoupling of write-type operations and editing operations on texts is the possibility to choose freely the granularity with which a text (and its displayed image) is updated.

Summary
Let us summarize. *Text* in Oberon is a powerful abstract data type with intrinsic operations from three areas: loading/storing, editing, and accessing. The latter two areas on their part introduce further abstract types called *Buffer*, *Reader*, *Scanner* and *Writer*. In combination, they guarantee a clean and rigorous separation of the notions text, editing text and accessing text. An after-method is used to allow context-dependent postprocessing of editing operations. It is used primarily for preserving consistency between texts and their displayed views.

5.2 Text management

The art and challenge of system modularization lies in finding an effective decomposition into modules with relatively thin mutual interfaces or, in other words, with a great potential for *information hiding*. Text systems provide a nice exercise to this topic. A closer analysis leads immediately to four separate tasks: font management, text management, text rendering and interactive text editing. Assigning

Modular structure
font management to module *Fonts*, text management to module *Texts*, and both text rendering and interactive text editing to module *TextFrames*, we arrive at a three-module solution. Table 5.1 gives an overview of Oberon's text subsystem appearing as a linearly ordered chain of modules.

Notice that, in contrast to the display subsystem, the associated object types are not connected hierarchically.

Sections 5.3 and 5.4 will be devoted to modules *TextFrames* and

Table 5.1

Module	Objects	Service
TextFrames ↑	Frame	Text rendering and editing
Texts ↑	Text	Text management
Fonts	Font	Font management

Fonts respectively. In this section, we direct our attention to the central module *Texts*. Regarding it as a model of the abstract data type *Text* presented in the previous section, its definition is congruent with the specification of the abstract data type itself, and we need not repeat it here.

Internal representation   The actual topics of this section are *internal representation* and *file representation* of texts. Before we start the discussion, we emphasize that the internal representation is a private matter of module *Texts*. It is encapsulated and completely hidden from clients. In particular, the representation could be changed at any time without invalidating a single client module. In principle, the same is true for the file representation. However, its stability is of paramount importance in reality because it serves the additional purposes of backing up text on external media and of porting text to other environments.

     Our choice of an internal representation of text was determined by a catalogue of requirements and desired properties. The most important points in the wish list are

(1) lean data structure

(2) closed under editing operations

(3) efficient editing operations

(4) efficient sequential reading

(5) efficient direct positioning

(6) super efficient internalizing

(7) preserving file representations

Piece chain   With the exception of point (5), we found these requirements to be met perfectly by an adequately generalized variant of the *piece chain technique* that was originally used for Xerox PARC's *Bravo* text editor and also for ETH's former document editors *Dyna* and *Lara* (Gutknecht, 1985). The original piece chain is able to describe a plain text without looks. It is based on two principles:

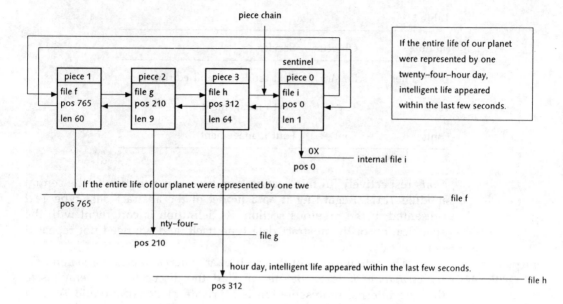

Figure 5.1   Piece chain representing a text.

(1) A text is regarded as a sequence of *pieces*, where a piece is a section of a text file consisting of a sequence of contiguous characters.

(2) Every piece is represented by a *descriptor* (f, pos, len), where the components designate a file, a starting position and a length respectively. The whole text is represented as a chain of piece descriptors (in short, *piece chain*). The editing operations operate on the chain of piece descriptors rather than on the pieces themselves.

Figure 5.1 shows a typical piece chain representing (the current state of) a text. Investigating the effects of the basic editing operations *delete* and *insert* on the piece chain we find these algorithms:

delete stretch [beg, end) of text = BEGIN
    split pieces at beg and at end;
    remove piece descriptors from beg to end from the chain
END

insert stretch of text at pos = BEGIN
    split piece at pos;
    insert piece descriptors representing the stretch at pos
END

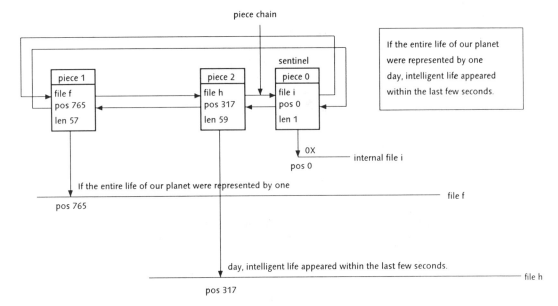

Figure 5.2 Piece chain after delete operation.

Of course, splitting is superfluous if the desired splitting point happens to coincide with the beginning of a piece. Figures 5.2 and 5.3 show the resulting piece chain after a *delete* and an *insert* operation respectively.

Checking our wish list above, we immediately recognize points (1), (2) and (3) as fulfilled. Point (4) is also met under the assumption of an efficient mechanism for *direct positioning* in files. Point (6) can be checked off because the piece list initially consists of a single piece spanning the entire text file. Finally, point (7) is fulfilled simply because the operations do not affect file representation at all.

In Oberon, we adopted the piece chain technique to texts with looks. Formally, we first define a *run* as a stretch of text whose characters show identical looks. Now, we require the piece chain to subordinate itself to the run structure. This obviously means that every piece is contained within a single run. Figure 5.4 visualizes such a piece chain representing a text with varying looks. There are only two new aspects compared to the original version of the piece chain discussed above: **Attributed piece chain** an additional operation to *change looks* and the *initial state* of the piece chain.

change looks in a stretch [beg, end) of text = BEGIN
    split pieces at beg and at end;

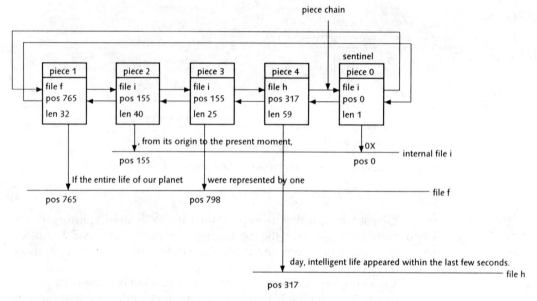

Figure 5.3   Piece chain after insert operation.

> change looks in piece descriptors from beg to end in the
>   chain
> END

This shows that points (2) and (3) in the wish list are still satisfied.
    Initially, the pieces are identical with runs, and the number of
elements in the piece chain is equal to the number of runs. Because
this number is typically small compared with the number of characters
in a text, requirement (6) is still fulfilled.
    We conclude that neither of the new aspects invalidates the
positive ratings given above to the piece chain with regard to points
(1)–(4), (6) and (7) in our wish list. However, there remains point (5).
The problem with direct positioning is the necessity to scan through
the piece list sequentially in order to locate the relevant piece. Hence

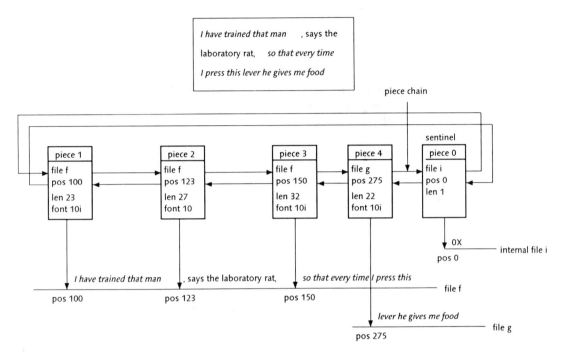

Figure 5.4 Generalized piece chain representing a text with looks.

not even a highly efficient direct positioning mechanism provided by the underlying file system helps. We investigated different solutions to this efficiency problem. They are based on different data structures connecting piece descriptors, among them the *piece tree* and a variant of the piece chain featuring an additional *long-distance link*.

Eventually, we decided for a simpler solution. In justification, we point out that the typical scenario is zooming in a local region of text for editing, that is, positioning to an arbitrary remote location once and subsequently positioning to locations in its neighbourhood many times. The appropriate solution is *caching* the most recently calculated values (*pos, piece*) of the translation map. Of course, it does not solve the problem in case of non-hitting positioning operations. Note, however, that the problem is acute only in the case of extremely long piece chains that rarely occur in ordinary texts and editing sessions.

Tour through implementation   We shall now exemplify our explanations by presenting the implementation of two important basic operations: *Insert* and *Read*. Let us first give the complete basic data types as far as they are relevant to the understanding. Up to some additional *private variables* that are marked with an arrow, the types *Text*, *Buffer* and *Reader* are familiar to us from the previous section. Type *Piece* is completely private. It is hidden from clients.

```
        Text = POINTER TO TextDesc;
        Notifier = PROCEDURE (T: Text; op: INTEGER;
            beg, end: LONGINT);
        TextDesc = RECORD
          len: LONGINT;
          notify: Notifier;
  →       trailer: Piece;
  →       org: LONGINT;
  →       pce: Piece
        END;

        Buffer = POINTER TO BufDesc;
        BufDesc = RECORD
          len: LONGINT;
  →       header, last: Piece
        END;

        Reader = RECORD
          (Files.Rider)
          eot: BOOLEAN;
          fnt: Fonts.Font;
          col: SHORTINT;
          voff: SHORTINT;
  →       ref: Piece;
  →       org: LONGINT;
  →       off: LONGINT
        END;

  →     Piece = POINTER TO PieceDesc;
  →     PieceDesc = RECORD
          f: Files.File;
          off: LONGINT;
          len: LONGINT;
          fnt: Fonts.Font;
          col: SHORTINT;
          voff: SHORTINT;
          prev, next: Piece
        END;
```

We can restrict our explanations of these types to the private fields and to type *Piece*. Before we start we should mention that, as depicted in Figure 5.1, the piece chain is implemented as a doubly linked list with a sentinel piece closing it to a ring.

Field *trailer* in type *TextDesc* points to the sentinel piece. *org* and *pce* implement a translation cache consisting of one entry (*org*, *pce*) only. It links a position *org* with a piece *pce*.

Fields *header* and *last* in type *Buffer* reveal the implementation of buffers as piece chains. They point to the first and last piece descriptors respectively.

Finally, fields *ref*, *org* and *off* in type *Reader* memorize the current piece, its origin and the current offset within this piece. We should note at this point that readers are actually type extensions of so-called *file riders*. Riders play the same role for files as readers do for texts. We shall come to the details in Chapter 7.

The fields *f*, *off* and *len* in type *Piece* specify the underlying file, starting position in the file and length of the piece. *fnt*, *col* and *voff* are its looks. Finally, *prev* and *next* are pointers to the previous piece and the next piece in the chain respectively.

Let us now turn to the two promised example procedures *Insert* and *Read*. They make use of two auxiliary procedures *FindPiece* and *SplitPiece*. We shall present pieces of source code according to a fixed scheme that is based on annotating line numbers and an added section of explanation that refers to the annotations.

```
       PROCEDURE FindPiece (T: Text; pos: LONGINT; VAR org:
          LONGINT;
          VAR p: Piece);
       VAR n: INTEGER;
       BEGIN
(1)       IF pos < T.org THEN T.org := -1; T.pce := T.trailer END;
(2)       org := T.org; p := T.pce; n := 0;
(3)       WHILE pos >= org + p.len DO org := org + p.len; p :=
             p.next; INC(n)
          END;
(4)       IF n > 50 THEN T.org := org; T.pce := p END
       END FindPiece;
```

Explanations

(1) invalidate cache if new position < position in cache

(2) use cache as starting point

(3) traverse piece chain

(4) update cache if more than 50 pieces traversed

```
(1)    PROCEDURE SplitPiece (p: Piece; off: LONGINT;
             VAR pr: Piece);
       VAR q: Piece;
       BEGIN
```

```
(2)        IF off > 0 THEN NEW(q);
           q.fnt := p.fnt; q.col := p.col; q.voff := p.voff;
           q.len := p.len − off;
           q.f := p.f; q.off := p.off + off;
           p.len := off;
(3)        q.next := p.next; p.next := q;
(4)        q.prev := p; q.next.prev := q;
           pr := q
        ELSE pr := p
        END
      END SplitPiece;
```

Explanations

(1) return right part piece *pr* after split

(2) generate new piece only if remaining length > 0

(3) insert new piece in forward chain

(4) insert new piece in backward chain

```
PROCEDURE Insert (T: Text; pos: LONGINT; B: Buffer);
VAR pl, pr, p, qb, qe: Piece; org, end: LONGINT;
BEGIN
(1) FindPiece(T, pos, org, p); SplitPiece(p, pos − org, pr);
(2) IF T.org >= org THEN
    T.org := org − p.prev.len; T.pce := p.prev
    END;
    pl := pr.prev; qb := B.header.next;
(3) IF (qb # NIL) & (qb.f = pl.f) & (qb.off = pl.off + pl.len)
    & (qb.fnt = pl.fnt) & (qb.col = pl.col) & (qb.voff = pl.voff) THEN
        pl.len := pl.len + qb.len; qb := qb.next
    END;
    IF qb # NIL THEN qe := B.last;
(4)     qb.prev := pl; pl.next := qb; qe.next := pr; pr.prev := qe
    END;
(5) T.len := T.len + B.len; end := pos + B.len;
(6) B.last := B.header; B.last.next := NIL; B.len := 0;
(7) T.notify(T, insert, pos, end)
  END Insert;
```

Explanations

(1) split piece to isolate point of insertion

(2) adjust cache if necessary

(3) merge pieces if possible

(4) insert buffer

(5) update text length

(6) empty buffer

(7) notify

```
PROCEDURE Read (VAR R: Reader; VAR ch: CHAR);
BEGIN
```
(1)
```
    Files.Read(R, ch); R.fnt := R.ref.fnt; R.col := R.ref.col;
        R.voff := R.ref.voff;
    INC(R.off);
```
(2)
```
    IF R.off = R.ref.len THEN
```
(3)
```
        IF R.ref.f = WFile THEN R.eot := TRUE END;
        R.org := R.org + R.off; R.off := 0;
```
(4)
```
        R.ref := R.ref.next; R.org := R.org + R.off; R.off := 0;
```
(5)
```
        Files.Set(R, R.ref.f, R.ref.off)
    END
END Read;
```

Explanations

(1) read character from file and update looks in reader

(2) if piece boundary reached

(3) check if sentinel piece reached

(4) move reader to next piece

(5) position file rider

Procedure *Read* serves as an elementary basis for the implementation of customized textual scanners. In particular, it is used by the built-in scanner *Scan* for the recognition of universal tokens, as they are defined in the previous section. Scanning is a much more complex procedure than perhaps expected. Typically, it includes the conversion of a sequence of digits into an internal floating-point representation. Some low-level assistance for such conversions in both directions is provided by module *Reals*, whose implementation is machine-dependent. This module is also used by *WriteReal* procedures.

```
DEFINITION Reals;

    PROCEDURE Expo (x: REAL): INTEGER;
    PROCEDURE ExpoL (x: LONGREAL): INTEGER;
    PROCEDURE SetExpo (e: INTEGER; VAR x: REAL)
    PROCEDURE SetExpoL (e: INTEGER; VAR x: LONGREAL);
    PROCEDURE Ten (e: INTEGER): REAL;
    PROCEDURE TenL (e: INTEGER): LONGREAL;
    PROCEDURE Convert (x: REAL; n: INTEGER;
        VAR d: ARRAY OF CHAR)
    PROCEDURE ConvertL (x: LONGREAL; n: INTEGER;
        VAR d: ARRAY OF CHAR);
```

```
PROCEDURE ConvertH (x: REAL;
VAR d: ARRAY OF CHAR);
PROCEDURE ConvertHL (x: LONGREAL;
VAR d: ARRAY OF CHAR);
PROCEDURE FSR (): LONGINT;
PROCEDURE SetFSR (status: LONGINT);
END Reals.
```

We emphasize that, despite its apparent simplicity, the piece chain technique is less than harmless. For example, after a period of interdocumentary editing, there are typically numerous cross-references among the documents involved. In other words, pieces of one document may refer to *foreign* files, that is, to files that were originally related to other documents. As a consequence, old file pages must not be recycled until system restart, even if a new version of a file with the same name has meanwhile been created.

A problem of another kind arises if, say, a single text line is composed of several small pieces. Then reading this line sequentially may necessitate several jumps to different positions in the underlying file(s). Depending on the quality of the file buffering mechanism, this may lead to a significantly hesitant mouse tracking.

And finally, typed characters that are to be inserted into a text need to be stored on a continuously growing file, the so-called *keyboard file*. For this file, several readers and one writer must be allowed to coexist.

In summary, we can enumerate the following qualities of the underlying file system that are necessary for the piece technique to work:

(1) Once a file page is allocated it must not be reused (unless at system restart).

(2) A versatile file buffering mechanism is required supporting multiple buffers per file.

(3) Files must be allowed to be open in read mode and write mode simultaneously.

Text file format   We devote the subsequent paragraphs to a brief description of the file format of texts. The formal syntactical specification of a *text block* in EBNF notation is

```
TextBlock = ident header {char}.
header = type offset run {run} null length.
run = font [name] color offset length.
```

In the *TextBlock* production, *ident* is an identifier for text blocks. In the *header* production, *type* is a type discriminator, *offset* is the offset to the character part, *run* is a run descriptor, *null* is a null character and *length* is the length of the character sequence. In the *run* production, *font*, *color* and *offset* are specifications of looks, and *length* is the run length. In order to save space, font names are coded as ordinal numbers within a text block. If and only if a font code appears for the first time in a text block, it is followed by the font's name.

We conclude this section with two remarks and a summary.

Remarks

(1) For compatibility reasons, pure ASCII files are accepted as text files as well. They are mapped to texts consisting of a single run with standard looks.

(2) Internalizing a text block is extremely efficient because it is obviously sufficient to read the header and translate it into the initial state of the piece chain.

Summary

The method used for the implementation of the abstract data type *Text* is completely hidden from clients. It is a generalized version of the original piece chain technique that is adopted to texts with looks. The piece chain technique is based on the principle of indirection: Operations operate on descriptors of texts rather than on texts themselves. The benefits are efficiency and non-destructive operations. However, the technique works properly only in combination with a sufficiently smart file system.

5.3 Text frames

The principal topics of this section are *text rendering* and *text editing*. They are integrated in the institution of *text frame*. Text frames build a subclass of display frames and, as such, are objects with a message interface whose characteristics are familiar to us from Chapter 4. Roughly said, a text frame represents a *clipping* of a text, a set of *rendering instructions* and an interactive *text editor*.

Geometric layout

The geometric layout of a text frame is determined by two special areas: an inner *rectangle of contents* and a vertical *scroll-bar* along the left borderline. Its type is a direct extension of type *Display.Frame*:

```
Frame = POINTER TO FrameDesc;

FrameDesc = RECORD (Display.FrameDesc)
    text: Texts.Text;
    org: LONGINT;
    col: INTEGER;
    lsp: INTEGER;
```

```
            left, right, top, bot: INTEGER;
            markH: NTEGER;
            time: LONGINT;
            mark, car, sel: INTEGER;
            carloc: Location;
            selbeg, selend: Location
          END;
```

Fields *text* and *org* specify the text part to be displayed, the former referring to the underlying text and the latter designating the starting position of the displayed part. Fields *col* and *lsp* are rendering parameters. They specify the frame's *background color* and *line spacing*. Fields *left*, *right*, *top* and *bot* are margins. They determine the rectangle of contents. *mark* represents the state of the *position marker*, which is a small horizontal bar indicating the position of the displayed part relative to the whole text. *markH* represents its location within the text frame.

Caret and selection

Caret and *selection* are two important additional features that are associated with every text frame. The caret indicates a 'point of insertion' and serves as implicit parameter for placing consumed characters (for example from the keyboard). The selection is a stretch of displayed text. It serves typically as a parameter for various operations and commands, among them *delete* and *change looks*. The state and location of the caret is given by the variables *car* and *carloc* respectively. Analogously, the state of the selection and its beginning and end are reflected by the fields *sel*, *selbeg* and *selend* in the frame descriptor. Field *time* is a time stamp on the current selection.

We should add a conceptual remark here. In principle, caret and selection could be regarded as ingredients of the underlying text equally well. However, we decided deliberately to bind these facilities to frames in order to get increased flexibility. For example, two different selections in adjacent viewers displaying the same text are normally interpreted as one extensive selection of their span.

Location

The auxiliary type *Location* summarizes information about a location in a text frame. Its definition is

```
          Location = RECORD
            org, pos: LONGINT;
            dx, x, y: INTEGER
          END;
```

x, y specifies the envisaged location relative to the text frame's origin and *dx* is the width of the character at this location. *pos* is the corresponding position in the text and *org* is the origin position of the corresponding text line.

We know that all the 'capabilities' of a frame are determined

Message handler

solely by its message handler. Thus we can get deeper insight into text frames only by studying their handler.

A rough view of it presents itself as

```
PROCEDURE Handle (F: Display.Frame;
VAR M: Display.FrameMsg);
  VAR F1: Frame;
BEGIN
  WITH F: Frame DO
    IF M IS Oberon.InputMsg THEN
      WITH M: Oberon.InputMsg DO
(1)       IF M.id = Oberon.track THEN Edit(F, M.X, M.Y,
              M.keys)
          ELSIF M.id = Oberon.consume THEN
(2)         IF F.car # 0 THEN Write(F, M.ch, M.fnt, M.col,
                M.voff)
            END
          END
      END
    ELSIF M IS Oberon.ControlMsg THEN
      WITH M: Oberon.ControlMsg DO
(3)       IF M.id = Oberon.defocus THEN Defocus(F)
(4)       ELSIF M.id = Oberon.neutralize THEN Neutralize(F)
          END
      END
    ELSIF M IS Oberon.SelectionMsg THEN
(5)     WITH M: Oberon.SelectionMsg DO
            GetSelection(F, M.text, M.beg, M.end, M.time)
        END
    ELSIF M IS Oberon.CopyOverMsg THEN
(6)     WITH M: Oberon.CopyOverMsg DO
            CopyOver(F, M.text, M.beg, M.end)
        END
    ELSIF M IS Oberon.CopyMsg THEN
(7)     WITH M: Oberon.CopyMsg DO Copy(F, F1); M.F := F1
        END
    ELSIF M IS MenuViewers.ModifyMsg THEN
(8)     WITH M: MenuViewers.ModifyMsg DO
            Modify(F, M.id, M.dY, M.Y, M.H)
        END
    ELSIF M IS UpdateMsg THEN
      WITH M: UpdateMsg DO
(9)       IF F.text = M.text THEN Update(F, M) END
      END
    END
  END
END Handle;
```

Explanations

(1) Mouse tracking message: Call built-in editor immediately.

(2) Consume-message: In case of valid caret insert character.

(3) Defocus-message: Remove caret.

(4) Neutralize-message: Remove caret and selection

(5) Selection-message: Return current selection with time stamp.

(6) Copyover-message: Copy given stretch of text to caret.

(7) Copy-message: Create a copy (clone).

(8) Modify-message: Translate and change size of frame.

(9) Update-message: If text was changed then update display.

We recognize again our categories of universal messages introduced in Chapter 4, Table 4.6: Messages in lines (1) and (2) report about user interactions. Messages (3)–(7) specify a generic operation. Messages in (8) require change of location or size. Remember that messages of this sort arrive from the ancestor menu viewer. They are generated by the handler of interactive viewer changes and by the preprocessor of original viewer messages. Finally, messages in line (9) report about changes of contents.

Update messages

The text frame handler is encapsulated in a module called *TextFrames*. This module exports the above introduced types *Frame* (text frame) and *Location*, as well as the procedure *Handle*. Furthermore, it exports type *UpdateMsg* to report on changes made to a displayable text.

```
UpdateMsg = RECORD (Display.FrameMsg)
    id: INTEGER;
    text: Texts.Text;
    beg, end: LONGINT
END;
```

id denotes one of the operations *replace*, *insert* or *delete*. The remaining fields *text*, *beg* and *end* restrict the change to a range. In addition, procedures are exported to generate a new standard menu text frame and main contents text frame respectively:

```
PROCEDURE NewMenu (name, commands: ARRAY OF
    CHAR): Frame;
PROCEDURE NewText (text: Texts.Text; pos: LONGINT):
    Frame;
```

With this, the minimum definition table of module *TextFrames* is complete. However, in reality, this module provides additional support for composing of customized handlers from elements of the standard handler for text frames. In particular, all procedures called by the above listed rough view of the standard handler are members of the export list:

```
PROCEDURE Edit (F: Frame; X, Y: INTEGER; Keys: SET);
PROCEDURE Write (F: Frame; ch: CHAR; fnt: Fonts.Font;
    col, voff: SHORTINT);
PROCEDURE Defocus (F: Frame);
PROCEDURE Neutralize (F: Frame);
PROCEDURE GetSelection (F: Frame; VAR text: Texts.Text;
    VAR beg, end, time: LONGINT);
PROCEDURE CopyOver (F: Frame; text: Texts.Text;
    beg, end: LONGINT);
PROCEDURE Copy (F: Frame; VAR F1: Frame);
PROCEDURE Modify (F: Frame; id, dY, Y, H: INTEGER);
PROCEDURE Update (F: Frame; VAR M: UpdateMsg);
```

Additionally, there are many even finer-grained service procedures in the export list. For example, some standard tracking procedures assist procedure *Edit*:

```
PROCEDURE TrackCaret (F: Frame; X, Y: INTEGER;
    VAR keysum: SET);
PROCEDURE TrackSelection (F: Frame; X, Y: INTEGER;
    VAR keysum: SET);
PROCEDURE TrackLine (F: Frame; X, Y: INTEGER;
    VAR org: LONGINT; VAR keysum: SET);
PROCEDURE TrackWord (F: Frame; X, Y: INTEGER;
    VAR pos: LONGINT; VAR keysum: SET);
```

Line destriptors

Instead of completing the enumeration of exported elements, we now want to get more insight into the module by looking behind the definition scenes of some selected operations. Before we can start, however, we must again reveal a private data structure of module *TextFrames* that is hidden from the clients. It is the *line chain* that guarantees an accelerated locating within the text frame. *Line* is a private data type:

```
Line = POINTER TO LineDesc;

LineDesc = RECORD
    len: LONGINT;
    wid: INTEGER;
    eot: BOOLEAN;
    next: Line
END;
```

Line descriptors summarize important information about the text lines: *len* is the number of characters on the line, *wid* is the line width, *eot* indicates terminating line and *next* points to the next line descriptor.

There is also a link to line descriptors in the private part of our base types *Frame* and *Location*. The complete declaration of type *Frame* is

```
Frame = POINTER TO FrameDesc;

FrameDesc = RECORD (Display.FrameDesc)
    text: Texts.Text;
    org: LONGINT;
    col: INTEGER;
    lsp: INTEGER;
    left, right, top, bot: INTEGER;
    markH: INTEGER;
    time: LONGINT;
    mark, car, sel: INTEGER;
    carloc: Location;
    selbeg, selend: Location;
→   trailer: Line
  END;
```

trailer is a pointer to a sentinel line closing the line chain to a ring and acting as a trailing sentinel.

The full declaration of type *Location* is

```
Location = RECORD
    org, pos: LONGINT;
    dx, x, y: INTEGER;
→   lin: Line
  END;
```

lin is a pointer to the relevant line.

Editor   The built-in editor *Edit* is probably the most worthwhile part to look at in some more detail. We know that it is called after a mouse interaction has been detected by the task scheduler. Scrutinizing the following piece of program is an effective way to get a deeper understanding of how the different discussed elements of the text system work together:

```
(1)    PROCEDURE Edit (F: Frame; X, Y: INTEGER; Keys: SET);
(2)    VAR
(3)      M: Oberon.CopyOverMsg;
(4)      R: Texts.Reader;
(5)      text: Texts.Text; buf: Texts.Buffer;
```

```
(6)      cmd: INTEGER;
(7)      time, pos, beg, end: LONGINT;
(8)      keysum: SET;
(9)      ch: CHAR;
(10)   BEGIN
(11)     Oberon.DrawCursor(Oberon.Mouse, Oberon.Arrow, X, Y);
(12)     IF X < F.X + Min(F.left, barW) THEN
(13)       IF (0 IN Keys) OR (1 IN Keys) THEN keysum := Keys;
(14)         REPEAT
(15)           Input.Mouse(Keys, X, Y);
(16)           keysum := keysum + Keys;
(17)           Oberon.DrawCursor(Oberon.Mouse, Oberon.Arrow,
                   X, Y)
(18)         UNTIL Keys = {};
(19)         IF ~(2 IN keysum) THEN
(20)           IF (0 IN keysum) OR (F.Y + F.H < Y) THEN
                 pos := 0
(21)         ELSE pos := (F.Y + F.H − Y) * (F.text.len)
                 DIV F.H
(22)         END;
(23)         RemoveMarks(F); Oberon.RemoveMarks(F.X, F.Y, F.W,
                 F.H);
(25)       ELSIF ~(0 IN keysum) THEN
(26)         RemoveMarks(F); Oberon.RemoveMarks(F.X, F.Y, F.W,
                 F.H);
(27)         Show(F, F.text.len)
(28)       END
(29)     ELSIF 2 IN Keys THEN
(30)       TrackLine(F, X, Y, pos, keysum);
(31)       IF (pos >= 0) & ~(0 IN keysum) THEN
(32)         RemoveMarks(F); Oberon.RemoveMarks(F.X, F.Y, F.W,
                 F.H);
(33)         Show(F, pos)
(34)       END
(35)     END
(36)   ELSE
(37)     IF 0 IN Keys THEN
(38)       TrackSelection(F, X, Y, keysum);
(39)       IF F.sel # 0 THEN
(40)         IF (2 IN keysum) & ~(1 IN keysum) THEN
(41)           Oberon.PassFocus(Viewers.This(F.X, F.Y));
(42)           Oberon.GetSelection(text, beg, end, time);
(43)           Texts.Delete(text, beg, end); SetCaret(F, beg)
(44)         ELSIF (1 IN keysum) & ~(2 IN keysum) THEN
(45)           Oberon.GetSelection(text, beg, end, time);
```

```
(46)              M.text := text; M.beg := beg; M.end := end;
(47)              Oberon.FocusViewer.handle(Oberon.FocusViewer, M)
(48)          END
(49)       END
(50)    ELSIF 1 IN Keys THEN
(51)       TrackWord(F, X, Y, pos, keysum);
(52)       IF (pos >= 0) & ~(0 IN keysum) THEN Call(F, pos,
              2 IN keysum) END
(53)    ELSIF 2 IN Keys THEN
(54)       Oberon.PassFocus(Viewers.This(F.X, F.Y));
           TrackCaret(F, X, Y, keysum);
(55)       IF F.car # 0 THEN
(56)          IF (1 IN keysum) & ~(0 IN keysum) THEN
(57)             Oberon.GetSelection(text, beg, end, time);
(58)             IF time >= 0 THEN
(59)                NEW(buf); Texts.OpenBuf(buf);
(60)                Texts.Save(text, beg, end, buf);
(61)                Texts.Insert(F.text, F.carloc.pos, buf);
(62)                SetCaret(F, F.carloc.pos + (end − beg))
(63)             END
(64)          ELSIF (0 IN keysum) & ~(1 IN keysum) THEN
(65)             Oberon.GetSelection(text, beg, end, time);
(66)             IF time >= 0 THEN
(67)                Texts.OpenReader(R, F.text, F.carloc.pos);
                    Texts.Read(R, ch);
(68)                Texts.ChangeLooks(text, beg, end, {0, 1, 2}, R.fnt,
                       R.col, R.voff)
(69)             END
(70)          END
(73)       END
(74)    END
(75)  END
(76) END Edit;
```

Structure-oriented explanations

(11) Update cursor

(12)–(35) handling of mouse within scroll bar

    (13)–(28) If right key or middle key pressed
    (14)–(18) Track mouse until all keys released
    (19)–(24) If left key was not interclicked
      (20)–(22) calculate new top origin
      (23) remove all markers to monopolize frame
      (24) jump to new top origin

(25)–(28) If right key was not pressed
  (26) remove all markers to monopolize frame
  (27) jump to the end

(29)–(35) If left key is pressed
  (30) track mouse to determine new top line
  (31)–(34) if valid then scroll to new top line

(36)–(75) handling of mouse within text area

  (37)–(49) if right key pressed ("select-key")
    (38) track mouse to determine selection
    (39)–(49) if selection valid
      (40)–(43) if left key interclicked (but not middle key)
        (41) grab focus
        (42) get selection
        (43) delete selected stretch of text
      (44)–(48) if middle key interclicked (but not left key)
        (45) get selection
        (46), (47) copy over selected stretch to focus

  (50)–(52) if middle key pressed ("execute-key")
    (51) track mouse to determine name
    (52) if valid then call command with this name

  (53)–(74) if left key pressed ("point-key")
    (54) grab focus and track mouse to determine caret
    (55)–(73) if caret valid
      (56)–(63) if middle key interclicked (but not right)
        (57) get newest selection
        (58)–(63) if existing
          (59) create and open buffer
          (60) save newest selection in buffer
          (61) insert it at caret
      (64)–(70)
        (65) get newest selection
        (66)–(69) if existing
          (67) open reader at caret and read one character
          (68) change looks of selected stretch to those of character read

Table 5.2

Scroll-bar

\ secondary key primary key	—	left	middle	right
left	scroll line to top	—	—	—
middle	jump to mouse	jump to end	—	—
right	jump to start	—	—	—

text area

\ secondary key primary key	—	left	middle	right
left	set caret	—	copy looks	—
middle	execute command	load and execute command	—	—
right	select	select and delete	select and copy	—

We see in particular that the desired operation is determined by the first key pressed (*primary key*). However, the operation can be varied by pressing a *secondary key* while holding down the primary key (*interclicking*). As a convention, interclicking both remaining keys means cancelling the operation. Note that the interpretations are different in the scroll-bar area and in the text area. Table 5.2 summarizes the two interpretations. This table can easily be derived from the above explanations.

Mouse keys   In the text area the keys are interpreted according to their universal meaning:

> left key = point key
> middle key = execute key
> right key = select key

It is perhaps instructive to zoom in to one of the editing operations. Let us choose *TrackCaret* on line (54).

```
      PROCEDURE TrackCaret (F: Frame; X, Y: INTEGER;
          VAR keysum: SET);
        VAR loc: Location; keys: SET;
      BEGIN
(1)       IF F.trailer.next # F.trailer THEN
```

```
(2)          LocateChar(F, X − F.X, Y − F.Y, F.carloc);
(3)          FlipCaret(F);
(4)          keysum := {};
        REPEAT
          Input.Mouse(keys, X, Y);
          keysum := keysum + keys;
          Oberon.DrawCursor(Oberon.Mouse,
              Oberon.Mouse.marker, X, Y);
          LocateChar(F, X − F.X, Y − F.Y, loc);
          IF loc.pos # F.carloc.pos THEN
              FlipCaret(F); F.carloc := loc; FlipCaret(F)
          END
(5)       UNTIL keys = {};
(6)        F.car := 1
        END
      END TrackCaret;
```

<table>
<tr><td>Explanations</td><td>(1)</td><td>guard guarantees non-empty chain of lines</td></tr>
<tr><td></td><td>(2)</td><td>locate the character pointed at</td></tr>
<tr><td></td><td>(3)</td><td>drag caret to new location</td></tr>
<tr><td></td><td>(4),(5)</td><td>track mouse and drag caret accordingly</td></tr>
<tr><td></td><td>(6)</td><td>set caret state</td></tr>
</table>

Let us now continue our virtual zooming tour. *TrackCaret* makes use of two auxiliary procedures *FlipCaret* and *LocateChar*. *FlipCaret* is used to turn off or on the pattern of the caret. *LocateChar* is a crucial elementary operation. It is used to locate the character at a given Cartesian position (x, y) within the frame.

```
        PROCEDURE FlipCaret (F: Frame);
        BEGIN
(1)       IF F.carloc.x < F.W THEN
(2)         IF (F.carloc.y >= 10) & (F.carloc.x + 12 < F.W) THEN
(3)           Display.CopyPattern(Display.white, Display.hook, F.X +
                  F.carloc.x, F.Y + F.carloc.y − 10, 2)
            END
          END
        END FlipCaret;
```

<table>
<tr><td>Explanations</td><td>(1), (2)</td><td>if there is room for drawing the caret</td></tr>
<tr><td></td><td>(3)</td><td>copy standard *hook*-pattern to caret location in inverse video mode</td></tr>
</table>

```
                    PROCEDURE LocateChar (F: Frame; x, y: INTEGER;
                        VAR loc: Location);
                    VAR R: Texts.Reader;
                        pat: Display.Pattern;
                        pos, lim: LONGINT;
                        ox, dx, u, v, w, h: INTEGER;
(1)                 BEGIN LocateLine(F, y, loc);
(2)                     lim := loc.org + loc.lin.len − 1;
(3)                     pos := loc.org; ox := F.left;
(4)                     Texts.OpenReader(R, F.text, loc.org);
                        Texts.Read(R, nextCh);
(5)                     LOOP
                            IF pos = lim THEN dx := eolW; EXIT END;
(6)                         Display.GetChar(R.fnt.raster, nextCh, dx, u, v, w, h,
                                pat);
                            IF ox + dx > x THEN EXIT END;
                            INC(pos); ox := ox + dx;
                            Texts.Read(R, nextCh)
(7)                     END;
(8)                     loc.pos := pos; loc.dx := dx; loc.x := ox
                    END LocateChar;
```

Explanations   (1) locate text line at y

(2) set limit to the last actual character on this line

(3) start locating loop with first character on this line

(4) setup reader and read first character of this line

(5)–(7) scan through characters of this line until limit or x is reached

(6) get character width dx of current character

(8) return found location

Proportional fonts   Notice that the need to read characters from the text (again) in *LocateChar* has its roots in the so-called *proportional fonts* in which texts are represented. We preferred this solution over an extra data structure memorizing character widths with confidence in the buffering capabilities of the underlying file system. In the case of so-called *fixed-pitch fonts*, a simple division by the character width would be sufficient, of course.

With procedure *LocateLine*, we shall conclude the zooming tour. This procedure exploits the hidden line chain and locates the desired text line without reading text at all.

```
                    PROCEDURE LocateLine (F: Frame; y: INTEGER; VAR loc:
                        Location);
                    VAR T: Texts.Text; L: Line; org: LONGINT; cury: INTEGER;
                    BEGIN T := F.text;
(1)                     org := F.org; L := F.trailer.next; cury := F.H − F.top −
                            asr;
```

(2)   WHILE (L.next # F.trailer) & (cury > y + dsr) DO
            org := org + L.len; L := L.next; cury := cury − lsp

(3)   END;

(4)   loc.org := org; loc.lin := L; loc.y := cury
        END LocateLine;

Explanations

(1) start with first line in the frame

(2),(3) traverse line chain until last line or y is reached

(4) return found line

Text rendering

Having gained enough insight into the built-in editor, we shall direct our attention to *text rendering* for the rest of this section. Let us then start a new imaginary tour after a user has pressed the point-key and then interclicked the middle key, that is, at line g556) in procedure *Edit*. We should remember the notifier that is associated with each text and is called at the end of every editing operation and in particular at the end of *Texts.Insert*. In the case of standard text frames, the notifier is equivalent to a simple broadcasting station:

```
PROCEDURE NotifyDisplay (T: Texts.Text; op: INTEGER;
    beg, end: LONGINT);
  VAR M: UpdateMsg;
  BEGIN M.id := op; M.text := T; M.beg := beg; M.end := end;
    Viewers.Broadcast(M)
  END NotifyDisplay;
```

We must now pursue the reaction of a text frame on an *update* message. Looking at line (9) in the text frame handler, we see quickly that procedure *Update* is called. It then calls procedure *Insert* in *TextFrames* immediately:

```
PROCEDURE Insert (F: Frame; beg, end: LONGINT);
  VAR R: Texts.Reader; L, L0, l: Line;
    org, len: LONGINT; curY, botY, Y0, Y1, Y2, dY, wid:
      INTEGER;
  BEGIN
    IF beg < F.org THEN F.org := F.org + (end − beg)
    ELSE
(1)     org := F.org; L := F.trailer.next; curY := F.Y + F.H −
          F.top − asr;
        WHILE (L # F.trailer) & (org + L.len <= beg) DO
          org := org + L.len; L := L.next; curY := curY − lsp
(2)     END;
(3)     IF L # F.trailer THEN
          botY := F.Y + F.bot + dsr;
(4)       Texts.OpenReader(R, F.text, org); Texts.Read(R,
            nextCh);
(5)       len := beg − org; wid := Width(R, len);
```

```
(6)              ReplConst (F.col, F, F.X + F.left + wid, curY − dsr,
                    L.wid − wid, lsp, 0);
(7)              DisplayLine(F, L, R, F.X + F.left + wid, curY, len);
(8)              org := org + L.len; curY := curY − lsp;
                 Y0 := curY; L0 := L.next;
                 WHILE (org <= end) & (curY >= botY) DO
                    NEW(l);
                    Display.ReplConst(F.col, F.X + F.left, curY − dsr,
                       F.W − F.left, lsp, 0);
                    DisplayLine(F, l, R, F.X + F.left, curY, 0);
                    L.next := l; L := l;
                    org := org + L.len; curY := curY − lsp
(9)              END;
(10)             IF L0 # L.next THEN Y1 := curY;
(11)             L.next := L0;
                 WHILE (L.next # F.trailer) & (curY >= botY) DO
                    L := L.next; curY := curY − lsp
(12)             END;
                 L.next := F.trailer;
                 dY := Y0 − Y1;
                 IF Y1 > curY + dY THEN
(13)                Display.CopyBlock
                    (F.X + F.left, curY + dY + lsp − dsr, F.W −
                       F.left, Y1 − curY − dY,
                       F.X + F.left, curY + lsp − dsr,
                       0);
                    Y2 := Y1 − dY
                 ELSE Y2 := curY
                 END;
(14)             curY := Y1; L := L0;
                 WHILE curY # Y2 DO
                    Display.ReplConst(F.col, F.X + F.left, curY −
                       dsr, F.W − F.left, lsp, 0);
                    DisplayLine(F, L, R, F.X + F.left, curY, 0);
                    L := L.next; curY := curY − lsp
(15)                END
                 END
              END
           END;
(16)             UpdateMark(F)
           END Insert;
```

Selected
explanations

(1),(2) search line where inserted part starts

(3) if it is displayed in this viewer

(4) setup reader on this line

(5) get width of unaffected part of line (avoid touching it)

(6) clear remaining part of line

(7) display new remaining part of line

(8),(9) display newly inserted text lines

(10) if it was not a one line update

(11),(12) skip overwritten text lines

(13) use fast block move to adjust reusable lines

(14),(15) redisplay previously overwritten text lines

(16) adjust position marker

Note that special care is exercised in the implementation of update of the display with regard to the concerns 'avoid flickering' and 'minimize processing time'. Concretely, the following measures are taken:

(1) Avoid writing the same data again.

(2) Keep the number of newly rendered text lines at a minimum.

(3) Use block move to adjust reusable displayed lines.

Formatting rules

Of course, the rules of rendering and formatting strongly influence the complexity of rendering procedures like the above *Insert*. For text frames, we have consciously chosen the simplest possible set of formatting rules. They can be summarized as follows:

(1) For a given text frame the distance between lines is a constant.

(2) There are no implicit line breaks.

It is exactly this set of rules that makes it possible to display a text line in *one pass*, and therefore to be super-efficient. Two passes are unavoidable, if line distances have to adjust to font sizes or if implicit line breaks have to be done at the right end of the block of contents.

The display update procedures make use of the following one-pass rendering procedures *Width* and *DisplayLine*:

```
       PROCEDURE Width (VAR R: Texts.Reader; len: LONGINT):
          INTEGER;
          VAR pat: Display.Pattern; pos: LONGINT; ox, dx, x, y, w, h:
          INTEGER;
(1)    BEGIN pos := 0; ox := 0;
          WHILE pos # len DO
             Display.GetChar(R.fnt.raster, nextCh, dx, x, y, w, h, pat);
             ox := ox + dx; INC(pos); Texts.Read(R, nextCh)
(2)       END;
(3)       RETURN ox
       END Width;
```

Explanations

(1), (2) scan through len characters of this line

(3) return accumulated width

This procedure is similar to *LocateChar*. The remark made there about buffering of character data is valid for *Width* as well.

```
                    PROCEDURE DisplayLine (F: Frame; L: Line;
                        VAR R: Texts.Reader; X, Y: INTEGER; len: LONGINT);
                        VAR pat: Display.Pattern; NX, dx, x, y, w, h: INTEGER;
(1)                 BEGIN NX := F.X + F.W;
(2)                     WHILE (nextCh # CR) & (R.fnt # NIL) DO
(3)                         Display.GetChar(R.fnt.raster, nextCh, dx, x, y, w, h, pat);
(4)                         IF (X + x + w <= NX) & (h # 0) THEN
(5)                             Display.CopyPattern(R.col, pat, X + x, Y + y, 2)
(6)                         END;
(7)                         X := X + dx; INC(len); Texts.Read(R, nextCh)
(8)                     END;
(9)                     L.len := len + 1; L.wid := X + eolW - (F.X + F.left);
(10)                    L.eot := R.fnt = NIL; Texts.Read(R, nextCh)
                    END DisplayLine;
```

Explanations   (1) set right margin

(2),(8) display characters of this line

(3) get width dx, box x, y, w, h, and pattern pat of next character

(4) if there is enough space in the rectangle of contents

(5) display pattern

(7) jump to location of next character; read next character

(9), (10) setup line descriptor

Again, this procedure is similar to *LocateChar*, and the remark made there about buffering applies for *DisplayLine* as well. The principal difference between *LocateChar* and *Width* on the one hand and *DisplayLine* on the other is the fact that the latter accesses the display screen physically. Therefore a tacit precondition for *DisplayLine* is a monopolized screen.

For the sake of completeness, we conclude the exemplary presentation of a display update operation with a listing of an auxiliary procedure to update the position marker:

```
                    PROCEDURE UpdateMark (F: Frame);
                        VAR oldH: INTEGER;
                    BEGIN
(1)                     oldH := F.markH;
                        F.markH := SHORT(F.org * F.H DIV (F.text.len + 1));
                        IF (F.mark > 0) & (F.left >= barW) & (F.markH # oldH)
                            THEN
(2)                         Display.ReplConst(Display.white, F.X + 1, F.Y + F.H − 1 −
                                oldH, markW, 1, 2);
(3)                         Display.ReplConst(Display.white, F.X + 1, F.Y + F.H − 1 −
                                F.markH, markW, 1, 2)
                        END
                    END UpdateMark;
```

Explanations (1) reveals how the marker's position is calculated. Roughly said, the invariant proportion is

$$\frac{\text{distance from top of frame}}{\text{frame height}} = \frac{\text{text position of first character in frame}}{\text{text length}}$$

(2) erase the old marker

(3) draw the new marker

Summary This concludes our section on text frames. As usual, we want to recapitulate the most important points in a quick summary. The polar tasks of text editing (input oriented) and text rendering (output oriented) are combined in a set of methods bound to text frames. They constitute a subclass of display frames and are implemented in a separate module *TextFrames*. The implementation accesses the displayed text exclusively via the official interface of module *Texts* that we discussed in Section 5.2. It hides a private data structure of line chains in order to accelerate locating. Text frames use simple formatting rules that allow super-efficient rendering of text in a single pass. In particular, line spacing is fixed for every text frame. Therefore different variations of a base font are possible within a given text frame; however, different sizes are not.

Finally, if we combine all derivations of type *Display.Frame* that we met in Chapters 4 and 5, we obtain the type hierarchy of Table 5.3.

Table 5.3

Viewers.Track	MenuViewers.Viewer
Viewers.Viewer	TextFrames.Frame
	Display.Frame

5.4 The font machinery

Attributes We have seen in the previous sections of this chapter that Oberon texts are rich enough in structure to include *attribute specifications* for characters. Remember that three different attributes are supported: *font, color* and *vertical offset*. Let us first focus on the *font* attribute. A *type-font* (or font, in short) can be regarded as a *style* in which the standard character set is designed. Typically, a whole text is typeset in a single style, that is, there is one font per text. However, sometimes, an author wants to emphasize titles or bring out some special words by changing the size of the font or by varying it to **boldface** or *italics*. Or, in specialized texts, special characters like mathematical symbols or other kinds of icons occur. In even more complex documents, whole mathematical or chemical formulae might flow with the text.

Fonts

These requirements lead us to a different interpretation of the notion of font. We can regard a font as an *indexed library* of (graphical) *objects*. In the case of ordinary characters, it is natural to use the ASCII code as index. We thus arrive at an interpretation of a text as a sequence of references (*library*, *index*). And this is exactly Oberon's view.

Character module

Before we turn to the font management, we want to get precise knowledge of the *imaging model* of characters. The model provides two levels of abstraction. On the first level, characters are black boxes given by a set of *metric data* x, y, w, h and dx. (x, y) is a vector from the current point of reference on the *base line* to the origin of the box. w and h are the width and height of the box, and dx is the distance to the point of reference of the next character on the same base line. On the second level of abstraction, a character is given by a *digital pattern* that is to be rendered into the box. Figure 5.5 visualizes this model of characters.

Color and vertical offset

The additional two character attributes *color* and *vertical* offset now appear as parameters of the character model. The *vertical offset* allows modification of the y coordinate in the vector (x, y) individually to y + voff, and the *color* attribute specifies the foreground color of the pattern.

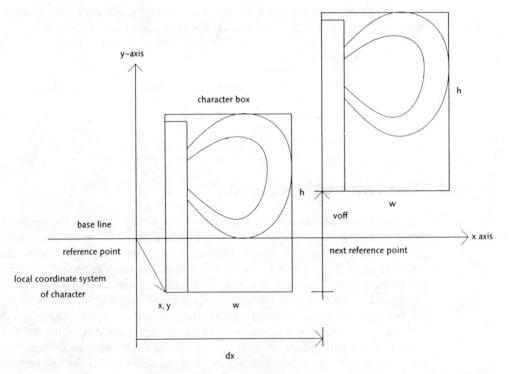

Figure 5.5 The geometric character model.

For example, procedures *LocateChar* and *Width* discussed in the previous section operate on the first level of abstraction. Another example is a text formatter for a remote printer device. In contrast, procedure *DisplayLine* operates on the second level.

Font production   At this point, we should perhaps insert a general remark about the design and production of digital type fonts. The representation of characters as digital patterns is merely the last step in the process. At the beginning is a *generic description* of the shape of each characten the form of outlines and hints. Outlines are typically composed of straight lines and spline curves. The hints are included to assist the subsequent step of automatic digitizing in the effort to preserve intrinsic properties and consistency. Examples are pronounced serifs and equal stem widths respectively. Automatic digitization produces digital patterns of sufficiently high quality for laser-printer resolutions. For screen resolutions, however, we prefer to add a hand-tuning step. This is the reason why digital patterns are not produced 'on the fly' in Oberon.

Font management   Oberon's font management is encapsulated in module *Fonts*, with a low-level extension in the module *Display* that we already know from Chapter 4. The interface to module *Fonts* is conceivably simple and narrow:

```
MODULE Fonts;
  IMPORT Display;

  TYPE
    Name = ARRAY 32 OF CHAR;
    Font = POINTER TO FontDesc;
    FontDesc = RECORD
      name: Name;
      height, minX, maxX, minY, maxY INTEGER;
      raster: Display.Font
    END;

  VAR Default: Font;

  PROCEDURE This (name: ARRAY OF CHAR): Font;
END Fonts.
```

Component *name* in type *Font* is the name of the underlying file. Components *height*, *minX*, *maxX*, *minY* and *maxY* are line height and summary metric data, and field raster refers to the mentioned low-level extension in module *Display*. *Default* is a system-wide *default font*. It is installed at system loading time. *This* is a procedure to internalize a font from a file given by its name.

The definition of the low-level extension of the font management is

```
MODULE Display;
    . . .
    TYPE
        Font = POINTER TO Bytes;
        Bytes = RECORD END;

    PROCEDURE GetChar (f: Font; ch: CHAR; VAR dx, x, y, w,
                h: INTEGER; VAR p: Pattern);
    . . .
    END Display.
```

Type *Display.Font* is a pointer to a record of open length containing the metric descriptions and patterns of all characters contained in the font. *GetChar* returns the metric data dx, x, y, w, h and the pattern p of character ch in font f.

Abstract type font

Font should be regarded as an abstract data type with two intrinsic operations *This* and *GetChar*. Its implementation does not give many problems. One is *caching*. Thinking of the static and constant nature of fonts, multiple internalizations of the same font are certainly undesired. Therefore internalized fonts are cached in a private list, manifesting itself in a private field *next* in type *FontDesc*:

```
        Font = POINTER TO FontDesc;
        FontDesc = RECORD
            name: Name;
            height, minX, maxX, minY, maxY: INTEGER;
            raster: Display.Font;
→           next: Font
        END;
```

The cache is operated by the internalizing procedure *This* according to the following scheme:

```
        search font in cache;
        IF found THEN return cached internalization
            ELSE internalize font; cache it
        END
```

Font caching

The problem mentioned arises in those cases where a certain font (or even worse, several fonts) are used for a limited time only. Because they are cached, they will never be collected by the system's garbage collector again. In extreme cases, like a print server with many and large fonts, there is a good chance for the memory to be filled up with no-longer-used fonts. The only clean way out in this and in analogous cases is making the font cache known to the garbage collector.

Font file format

We conclude this section with a precise specification of the font file format. Note that the situation is comparable to that of text files. On one hand, the file format is completely private to the managing module. On the other hand, it must be absolutely stable because it is used for long-term backup and for wide-range data exchange. The EBNF specification of Oberon font files is

FontFile = ident header contents.
header = abstraction family variant height minX maxX minY
    maxY.
contents = nofRuns { beg end } { dx x y w h } { rasterByte }.

ident, abstraction, family, and *variant* are one-byte values indicating file identification, abstraction (first level without raster bytes, second level with raster bytes), font family (*Times Roman, Syntax* and so on), and variant (boldface, italics and so on). The values *height, minX, maxX, minY* and *maxY* are two bytes long. They give line height, minimum x coordinate (of a box), maximum x coordinate, minimum y coordinate and maximum y coordinate respectively. All values in production *contents* are two bytes long. *nofRuns* specifies the number of runs within the ASCII code range (occupied intervals without gaps) and every pair [beg, end) describes one run. The tuples (dx, x, y, w, h) are the metric data of the occupied characters (in their ASCII code order), and the sequence of *rasterByte* gives the total of raster information in packed form.

Summary   In summary, fonts in Oberon are indexed libraries of objects. The objects are descriptions of character images at two levels of abstraction: as metric data of black boxes and as binary patterns. Type *Font* is an abstract data type with intrinsic operations to internalize and to get object data. Internalized fonts are cached in a private list.

5.5 The edit toolbox

Intrinsic and extrinsic commands We have seen that every text frame embodies an interactive text editor. We can regard it as an interpreter of a set of built-in commands (so-called *intrinsic* commands). Of course, we want to be able to extend this set by customized editing commands (*extrinsic* commands). It is a worthwhile exercise to test the module basis by implementing new tools operating on texts and text frames.

Module *Edit* is a toolbox of standard editing commands. Its definition is

DEFINITION Edit;

    PROCEDURE Open; (*text viewer*)
    PROCEDURE Show; (*text*)

```
                    PROCEDURE Locate; (*position*)
                    PROCEDURE Search; (*pattern*)
                    PROCEDURE Store; (*text*)

                    PROCEDURE Recall; (*deleted text*)
                    PROCEDURE CopyFont;
                    PROCEDURE ChangeFont;
                    PROCEDURE ChangeColor;
                    PROCEDURE ChangeOffset;

                    PROCEDURE Print; (*text*)

                END Edit.
```

A first group of commands in this toolbox is used to display, locate and store texts or parts of texts. In turn, they open a text file and display it, open a program text and show the declaration of a given object, locate a given position in a displayed text (main application: locating errors found by the compiler), search a pattern, and store the current state of a displayed text. Commands in the next group are related to editing. They allow restoration of the previously deleted part of text, copying a font to the current text selection, and change attributes of the current text selection. Note that *CopyFont*, *ChangeFont*, *ChangeColor* and *ChangeOffset* are extrinsic variations of the intrinsic *copy-look* operation. Finally, the *Print* command causes the specified text to be printed.

Printer

The implementations of the toolbox commands are given in Section 5.7. Note that the implementation of *Print* relies on a module called *Printer*. Consisting of a collection of procedures for accessing a printing device and printing text strings and graphical elements this module represents an *abstract printer*. It is defined as follows:

```
                DEFINITION Printer;

                VAR PageWidth, PageHeight, res: INTEGER; (*result*)

                PROCEDURE Open (VAR name, user: ARRAY OF CHAR;
                        password: LONGINT);
                    (*res = 0: opened, 1: no printer, 2: no link, 3: bad response,
                        4: no permission*)

                PROCEDURE UseListFont (VAR name: ARRAY OF CHAR);
                PROCEDURE String (x, y: INTEGER; VAR s, fname: ARRAY
                        OF CHAR);
                PROCEDURE ContString (VAR s, fname: ARRAY OF CHAR);
                        (*continuation*)
```

```
PROCEDURE Line (x0, y0, x1, y1: INTEGER);
PROCEDURE Circle (x0, y0, r: INTEGER);
PROCEDURE Ellipse (x0, y0, a, b: INTEGER);
PROCEDURE Spline (x0, y0, n, open: INTEGER;
        VAR X, Y: ARRAY OF INTEGER);
PROCEDURE Picture (x, y, w, h, mode: INTEGER;
        adr: LONGINT);
PROCEDURE ReplConst (x, y, w, h: INTEGER);
PROCEDURE ReplPattern (x, y, w, h, col: INTEGER);
PROCEDURE Page (nofcopies: INTEGER);

PROCEDURE Close;

END Printer.
```

Explanations   The printing model is page-oriented. Procedures *Open* and *Close* are used to open and close a printing session. Procedure *UseListFont* installs a suitable font for printing lists. Procedures *String, ContString, Line, Circle, Ellipse, Spline, Picture, ReplConst* and *ReplPattern* are called in order to place a string, a straight line, a circle, an ellipse, a spline, a digitized picture or a shaded rectangle onto the current page. These procedures are typically called repetitively until the desired page is laid out completely. Then procedure *Page* is called to produce the actual hard copy of this page.

The implementation of module *Printer* depends on the environment. Alternatively, it might drive a local printer or generate a program for *remote printing*. In Chapter 10, a variant is presented for a local area network with an integrated *print server*. In every printing session, a so-called *print file* is generated and subsequently sent to the server.

5.6 References

Gutknecht, J. (1985). Concept of the text editor Lara. *Communications of the ACM*, **28**(9), 942–60.
Teitelman, W. (1984). A tour through Cedar. *IEEE Software*, **1**(2), 44–73.

5.7 Detailed Implementations

```
MODULE Fonts; (*JG 18.11.90*)

  IMPORT Display, SYSTEM, Files;

  CONST FontFileId = 0DBX;
```

```
TYPE
    Name* = ARRAY 32 OF CHAR;

    Font* = POINTER TO FontDesc;
    FontDesc* = RECORD
        name*: Name;
        height*, minX*, maxX*, minY*, maxY*: INTEGER;
        raster*: Display.Font;
        next: Font
    END;


VAR Default*, First: Font; nofFonts: INTEGER;


PROCEDURE This* (name: ARRAY OF CHAR): Font;

    TYPE
        RunRec = RECORD beg, end: INTEGER END;
        BoxRec = RECORD dx, x, y, w, h: INTEGER END;


    VAR
        F: Font;
        f: Files.File; R: Files.Rider;
        NofBytes, RasterBase, A, a: LONGINT;
        NofRuns, NofBoxes: INTEGER;
        k, l, m, n: INTEGER;
        ch: CHAR;


        run: ARRAY 16 OF RunRec;
        box: ARRAY 256 OF BoxRec;


    PROCEDURE Enter (d: LONGINT);
    BEGIN
        SYSTEM.PUT(A, d MOD 256); INC(A);
        SYSTEM.PUT(A, d DIV 256); INC(A)
    END Enter;


BEGIN F := First;
    WHILE (F # NIL) & (name # F.name) DO F := F.next END;
    IF F = NIL THEN
        f := Files.Old(name);
        IF f # NIL THEN
            Files.Set(R, f, 0); Files.Read(R, ch);
            IF ch = FontFileId THEN
                Files.Read(R, ch); (*abstraction*)
                Files.Read(R, ch); (*family*)
                Files.Read(R, ch); (*variant*)
                NEW(F);
                Files.ReadBytes(R, F.height, 2);
                Files.ReadBytes(R, F.minX, 2); Files.ReadBytes(R, F.maxX, 2);
                Files.ReadBytes(R, F.minY, 2); Files.ReadBytes(R, F.maxY, 2);
                Files.ReadBytes(R, NofRuns, 2);
                NofBoxes := 0; k := 0;
                WHILE k # NofRuns DO
                    Files.ReadBytes(R, run[k].beg, 2); Files.ReadBytes(R, run[k].end, 2);
                    NofBoxes := NofBoxes + run[k].end − run[k].beg;
                    INC(k)
```

```
                END;
                NofBytes := 512 + 5; l := 0;
                WHILE l # NofBoxes DO
                    Files.ReadBytes(R, box[l].dx, 2);
                    Files.ReadBytes(R, box[l].x, 2); Files.ReadBytes(R, box[l].y, 2);
                    Files.ReadBytes(R, box[l].w, 2); Files.ReadBytes(R, box[l].h, 2);
                    NofBytes := NofBytes + 5 + (box[l].w + 7) DIV 8 * box[l].h;
                    INC(l)
                END;
                SYSTEM.NEW(F.raster, NofBytes);
                RasterBase := SYSTEM.VAL(LONGINT, F.raster);
                A := RasterBase; a := A + 512;
                SYSTEM.PUT(a, 0X); INC(a); (*dummy ch*)
                SYSTEM.PUT(a, 0X); INC(a);
                SYSTEM.PUT(a, 0X); INC(a);
                SYSTEM.PUT(a, 0X); INC(a);
                SYSTEM.PUT(a, 0X); INC(a);
                k := 0; l := 0; m := 0;
                WHILE k < NofRuns DO
                    WHILE m < run[k].beg DO Enter(515); INC(m) END;
                    WHILE m < run[k].end DO Enter(a + 3 - RasterBase);
                        SYSTEM.PUT(a, box[l].dx MOD 256); INC(a);
                        SYSTEM.PUT(a, box[l].x MOD 256); INC(a);
                        SYSTEM.PUT(a, box[l].y MOD 256); INC(a);
                        SYSTEM.PUT(a, box[l].w MOD 256); INC(a);
                        SYSTEM.PUT(a, box[l].h MOD 256); INC(a);
                        n := (box[l].w + 7) DIV 8 * box[l].h;
                        WHILE n # 0 DO
                            Files.Read(R, ch); SYSTEM.PUT(a, ch); INC(a); DEC(n)
                        END;
                        INC(l); INC(m)
                    END;
                    INC(k)
                END;
                WHILE m < 256 DO Enter(515); INC(m) END;
                COPY(name, F.name);
                IF nofFonts < 12 THEN INC(nofFonts); F.next := First; First := F END
            ELSE F := Default
            END
        ELSE F := Default
        END
    END;
    RETURN F
END This;


BEGIN Default := This("Syntax10.Scn.Fnt"); nofFonts := 1
END Fonts.


MODULE Texts; (*JG 21.11.90*)

    IMPORT Files, Fonts, Reals;

    CONST
        (*symbol classes*)
        Inval* = 0;(*invalid symbol*)
        Name* = 1;(*name s (length len)*)
        String* = 2;(*literal string s (length len)*)
```

```
        Int* = 3;(*integer i (decimal or hexadecimal)*)
        Real* = 4;(*real number x*)
        LongReal* = 5;(*long real number y*)
        Char* = 6;(*special character c*)

        TAB = 9X; CR = 0DX; maxD = 9;

        (* TextBlock = TextBlockId off run {run} 0 len {AsciiCode}.
        run = fnt [name] col voff len. *)

        TextBlockId = 1FFH;

        replace* = 0; insert* = 1; delete* = 2; (*op−codes*)

    TYPE
        Piece = POINTER TO PieceDesc;
        PieceDesc = RECORD
            f: Files.File;
            off: LONGINT;
            len: LONGINT;
            fnt: Fonts.Font;
            col: SHORTINT;
            voff: SHORTINT;
            prev, next: Piece
        END;

        Text* = POINTER TO TextDesc;

        Notifier* = PROCEDURE (T: Text; op: INTEGER; beg, end: LONGINT);

        TextDesc* = RECORD
            len*: LONGINT;
            notify*: Notifier;
            trailer: Piece;
            org: LONGINT; (*cache*)
            pce: Piece
        END;

        Reader* = RECORD (Files.Rider)
            eot*: BOOLEAN;
            fnt*: Fonts.Font;
            col*: SHORTINT;
            voff*: SHORTINT;
            ref: Piece;
            org: LONGINT;
            off: LONGINT
        END;

        Scanner* = RECORD (Reader)
            nextCh*: CHAR;
            line*: INTEGER;
            class*: INTEGER;
            i*: LONGINT;
            x*: REAL;
            y*: LONGREAL;
```

```
        c*: CHAR;
        len*: SHORTINT;
        s*: ARRAY 32 OF CHAR
    END;


    Buffer* = POINTER TO BufDesc;
    BufDesc* = RECORD
        len*: LONGINT;
        header, last: Piece
    END;


    Writer* = RECORD Files.Rider)
        buf*: Buffer;
        fnt*: Fonts.Font;
        col*: SHORTINT;
        voff*: SHORTINT
    END;


VAR W: Writer; WFile: Files.File; DelBuf: Buffer;

PROCEDURE EQ (VAR s, t: ARRAY OF CHAR): BOOLEAN;
    VAR i: INTEGER;
BEGIN i := 0;
    WHILE (s[i] # 0X) & (t[i] # 0X) & (s[i] = t[i]) DO INC(i) END;
    RETURN s[i] = t[i]
END EQ;


PROCEDURE ReadName (VAR R: Files.Rider; VAR name: ARRAY OF CHAR);
    VAR i: INTEGER; ch: CHAR;
BEGIN
    i := 0; Files.Read(R, ch);
    WHILE ch # 0X DO
        name[i] := ch; INC(i); Files.Read(R, ch)
    END;
    name[i] := 0X
END ReadName;


PROCEDURE WriteName (VAR W: Files.Rider; VAR name: ARRAY OF CHAR);
    VAR i: INTEGER; ch: CHAR;
BEGIN
    i := 0; ch := name[i];
    WHILE ch # 0X DO
        Files.Write(W, ch); INC(i); ch := name[i]
    END;
    Files.Write(W, 0X)
END WriteName;


PROCEDURE Load* (T: Text; f: Files.File; pos: LONGINT; VAR len: LONGINT);
    VAR
        R: Files.Rider;
        Q, q, p: Piece;
        off: LONGINT;
        N, fnt: SHORTINT;
        FName: ARRAY 32 OF CHAR;
        Dict: ARRAY 32 OF Fonts.Font;
BEGIN
```

```
    N := 1;
    NEW(Q); Q.f := WFile; Q.off := 0; Q.len := 1; Q.fnt := NIL; Q.col := 0; Q.voff := 0; p :=
        Q;
    Files.Set(R, f, pos); Files.ReadBytes(R, off, 4);
    LOOP
        Files.Read(R, fnt);
        IF fnt = 0 THEN EXIT END;
        IF fnt = N THEN
            ReadName(R, FName);
            Dict[N] := Fonts.This(FName);
            INC(N)
        END;
        NEW(q);
        q.fnt := Dict[fnt];
        Files.Read(R, q.col);
        Files.Read(R, q.voff);
        Files.ReadBytes(R, q.len, 4);
        q.f := f; q.off := off;
        off := off + q.len;
        p.next := q; q.prev := p; p := q
    END;
    p.next := Q; Q.prev := p;
    T.trailer := Q; Files.ReadBytes(R, T.len, 4);
    T.org := −1; T.pce := T.trailer; (*init cache*)
    len := off − pos
END Load;

PROCEDURE Open* (T: Text; name: ARRAY OF CHAR);
    VAR f: Files.File; R: Files.Rider; Q, q: Piece;
        id: INTEGER; len: LONGINT;
BEGIN
    f := Files.Old(name);
    IF f # NIL THEN
        Files.Set(R, f, 0); Files.ReadBytes(R, id, 2);
        IF id = TextBlockId THEN Load(T, f, 2, len)
        ELSE (*Ascii file*)
            len := Files.Length(f);
            NEW(Q); Q.fnt := NIL; Q.col := 0; Q.voff := 0; Q.f := WFile; Q.off := 0; Q.len :=
                1;
            NEW(q); q.fnt := Fonts.Default; q.col := 15; q.voff := 0; q.f := f; q.off := 0; q.len :=
                len;
            Q.next := q; q.prev := Q; q.next := Q; Q.prev := q;
            T.trailer := Q; T.len := len;
            T.org := −1; T.pce := T.trailer (*init cache*)
        END
    ELSE (*create new text*)
        NEW(Q); Q.fnt := NIL; Q.col := 0; Q.voff := 0; Q.f := WFile; Q.off := 0; Q.len := 1;
        Q.next := Q; Q.prev := Q;
        T.trailer := Q; T.len := 0;
        T.org := −1; T.pce := T.trailer (*init cache*)
    END
END Open;

PROCEDURE OpenBuf* (B: Buffer);
BEGIN NEW(B.header); (*null piece*)
    B.last := B.header; B.len := 0
END OpenBuf;

PROCEDURE FindPiece (T: Text; pos: LONGINT; VAR org: LONGINT; VAR p: Piece);
```

```
      VAR n: INTEGER;
BEGIN
    IF pos < T.org THEN T.org := -1; T.pce := T.trailer END;
    org := T.org; p := T.pce; (*from cache*)
    n := 0;
    WHILE pos >= org + p.len DO org := org + p.len; p := p.next; INC(n) END;
    IF n > 50 THEN T.org := org; T.pce := p END
END FindPiece;


PROCEDURE SplitPiece (p: Piece; off: LONGINT; VAR pr: Piece);
    VAR q: Piece;
BEGIN
    IF off > 0 THEN NEW(q);
        q.fnt := p.fnt; q.col := p.col; q.voff := p.voff;
        q.len := p.len - off;
        q.f := p.f; q.off := p.off + off;
        p.len := off;
        q.next := p.next; p.next := q;
        q.prev := p; q.next.prev := q;
        pr := q
    ELSE pr := p
    END
END SplitPiece;


PROCEDURE OpenReader* (VAR R: Reader; T: Text; pos: LONGINT);
    VAR p: Piece; org: LONGINT;
BEGIN
    FindPiece(T, pos, org, p);
    R.ref := p; R.org := org; R.off := pos - org;
    Files.Set(R, R.ref.f, R.ref.off + R.off); R.eot := FALSE
END OpenReader;


PROCEDURE Read* (VAR R: Reader; VAR ch: CHAR);
BEGIN
    Files.Read(R, ch); R.fnt := R.ref.fnt; R.col := R.ref.col; R.voff := R.ref.voff;
    INC(R.off);
    IF R.off = R.ref.len THEN
        IF R.ref.f = WFile THEN R.eot := TRUE END;
        R.org := R.org + R.off; R.off := 0;
        R.ref := R.ref.next; R.org := R.org + R.off; R.off := 0;
        Files.Set(R, R.ref.f, R.ref.off)
    END
END Read;


PROCEDURE Pos* (VAR R: Reader): LONGINT;
BEGIN RETURN R.org + R.off
END Pos;


PROCEDURE Store* (T: Text; f: Files.File; pos: LONGINT; VAR len: LONGINT);
    VAR
        p, q: Piece;
        R: Reader; W: Files.Rider;
        off, rlen: LONGINT; id: INTEGER;
        N, n: SHORTINT; ch: CHAR;
        Dict: ARRAY 32 OF Fonts.Name;
BEGIN
    Files.Set(W, f, pos);
```

```
      id := TextBlockId; Files.WriteBytes(W, id, 2);
      Files.WriteBytes(W, off, 4); (*place holder*)
      N := 1;
      p := T.trailer.next;
      WHILE p # T.trailer DO
        rlen := p.len; q := p.next;
        WHILE (q # T.trailer) & (q.fnt = p.fnt) & (q.col = p.col) & (q.voff = p.voff) DO
          rlen := rlen + q.len; q := q.next
        END;
        Dict[N] := p.fnt.name;
        n := 1;
        WHILE ~EQ(Dict[n], p.fnt.name) DO INC(n) END;
        Files.Write(W, n);
        IF n = N THEN WriteName(W, p.fnt.name); INC(N) END;
        Files.Write(W, p.col);
        Files.Write(W, p.voff);
        Files.WriteBytes(W, rlen, 4);
        p := q
      END;
      Files.Write(W, 0); Files.WriteBytes(W, T.len, 4);
      off := Files.Pos(W);
      OpenReader(R, T, 0); Read(R, ch);
      WHILE ~R.eot DO Files.Write(W, ch); Read(R, ch) END;
      Files.Set(W, f, pos + 2); Files.WriteBytes(W, off, 4); (*fixup*)
      len := off + T.len − pos
  END Store;


  PROCEDURE Save* (T: Text; beg, end: LONGINT; B: Buffer);
    VAR p, q, qb, qe: Piece; org: LONGINT;
  BEGIN
    IF end > T.len THEN end := T.len END;
    FindPiece(T, beg, org, p);
    NEW(qb); qb↑ := p↑;
    qb.len := qb.len − (beg − org);
    qb.off := qb.off + (beg − org);
    qe := qb;
    WHILE end > org + p.len DO
      org := org + p.len; p := p.next;
      NEW(q); q↑ := p↑; qe.next := q; q.prev := qe; qe := q
    END;
    qe.next := NIL; qe.len := qe.len − (org + p.len − end);
    B.last.next := qb; qb.prev := B.last; B.last := qe;
    B.len := B.len + (end − beg)
  END Save;


  PROCEDURE Copy* (SB, DB: Buffer);
    VAR Q, q, p: Piece;
  BEGIN
    p := SB.header; Q := DB.last;
    WHILE p # SB.last DO p := p.next;
      NEW(q); q↑ := p↑; Q.next := q; q.prev := Q; Q := q
    END;
    DB.last := Q; DB.len := DB.len + SB.len
  END Copy;


  PROCEDURE ChangeLooks* (T: Text; beg, end: LONGINT; sel: SET; fnt: Fonts.Font; col, voff:
      SHORTINT);
```

```
    VAR pb, pe, p: Piece; org: LONGINT;
BEGIN
    IF end > T.len THEN end := T.len END;
    FindPiece(T, beg, org, p); SplitPiece(p, beg − org, pb);
    FindPiece(T, end, org, p); SplitPiece(p, end − org, pe);
    p := pb;
    REPEAT
        IF 0 IN sel THEN p.fnt := fnt END;
        IF 1 IN sel THEN p.col := col END;
        IF 2 IN sel THEN p.voff := voff END;
        p := p.next
    UNTIL p = pe;
    T.notify(T, replace, beg, end)
END ChangeLooks;


PROCEDURE Insert* (T: Text; pos: LONGINT; B: Buffer);
    VAR pl, pr, p, qb, qe: Piece; org, end: LONGINT;
BEGIN
    FindPiece(T, pos, org, p); SplitPiece(p, pos − org, pr);
    IF T.org >= org THEN (*adjust cache*)
        T.org := org − p.prev.len; T.pce := p.prev
    END;
    pl := pr.prev; qb := B.header.next;
    IF (qb # NIL) & (qb.f = pl.f) & (qb.off = pl.off + pl.len)
        & (qb.fnt = pl.fnt) & (qb.col = pl.col) & (qb.voff = pl.voff) THEN
        pl.len := pl.len + qb.len; qb := qb.next
    END;
    IF qb # NIL THEN qe := B.last;
        qb.prev := pl; pl.next := qb; qe.next := pr; pr.prev := qe
    END;
        T.len := T.len + B.len; end := pos + B.len;
    B.last := B.header; B.last.next := NIL; B.len := 0;
    T.notify(T, insert, pos, end)
END Insert;


PROCEDURE Append* (T: Text; B: Buffer);
BEGIN Insert(T, T.len, B)
END Append;


PROCEDURE Delete* (T: Text; beg, end: LONGINT);
    VAR pb, pe, pbr, per: Piece; orgb, orge: LONGINT;
BEGIN
    IF end > T.len THEN end := T.len END;
    FindPiece(T, beg, orgb, pb); SplitPiece(pb, beg − orgb, pbr);
    FindPiece(T, end, orge, pe); SplitPiece(pe, end − orge, per);
    IF T.org >= orgb THEN (*adjust cache*)
        T.org := orgb − pb.prev.len; T.pce := pb.prev
    END;
    DelBuf.header.next := pbr; DelBuf.last := per.prev;
    DelBuf.last.next := NIL; DelBuf.len := end − beg;
    per.prev := pbr.prev; pbr.prev.next := per;
    T.len := T.len − DelBuf.len;
    T.notify(T, delete, beg, end)
END Delete;


PROCEDURE Recall* (VAR B: Buffer); (*deleted text*)
BEGIN B := DelBuf; NEW(DelBuf); OpenBuf(DelBuf)
```

```
END Recall;

PROCEDURE OpenScanner* (VAR S: Scanner; T: Text; pos: LONGINT);
BEGIN OpenReader(S, T, pos); S.line := 0; Read(S, S.nextCh)
END OpenScanner;

(*floating point formats:
    x = 1.m * 2 ↑ (e−127)bit 0: sign, bits 1− 8: e, bits9−31: m
    x = 1.m * 2 ↑ (e−1023)bit 0: sign, bits 1−11: e, bits 12−63: m *)

PROCEDURE Scan* (VAR S: Scanner);
    CONST maxD = 32;
    VAR ch, term: CHAR;
        neg, negE, hex: BOOLEAN;
        i, j, h: SHORTINT;
        e: INTEGER; k: LONGINT;
        x, f: REAL; y, g: LONGREAL;
        d: ARRAY maxD OF CHAR;

    PROCEDURE ReadScaleFactor;
    BEGIN Read(S, ch);
        IF ch = "−" THEN negE := TRUE; Read(S, ch)
        ELSE negE := FALSE;
            IF ch = "+" THEN Read(S, ch) END
        END;
        WHILE ("0" <= ch) & (ch <= "9") DO
            e := e*10 + ORD(ch) − 30H; Read(S, ch)
        END
    END ReadScaleFactor;

BEGIN ch := S.nextCh; i := 0;
    LOOP
        IF ch = CR THEN INC(S.line)
        ELSIF (ch # " ") & (ch # TAB) THEN EXIT
        END ;
        Read(S, ch)
    END;
    IF ("A" <= CAP(ch)) & (CAP(ch) <= "Z") THEN (*name*)
        REPEAT S.s[i] := ch; INC(i); Read(S, ch)
        UNTIL (CAP(ch) > "Z")
            OR ("A" > CAP(ch)) & (ch > "9")
            OR ("0" > ch) & (ch # ".")
            OR (i = 31);
        S.s[i] := 0X; S.len := i; S.class := 1
    ELSIF ch = 22X THEN (*literal string*)
        Read(S, ch);
        WHILE (ch # 22X) & (ch >= " ") & (i # 31) DO
            S.s[i] := ch; INC(i); Read(S, ch)
        END;
        S.s[i] := 0X; S.len := i+1; Read(S, ch); S.class := 2
    ELSE
        IF ch = "−" THEN neg := TRUE; Read(S, ch) ELSE neg := FALSE END ;
        IF ("0" <= ch) & (ch <= "9") THEN (*number*)
            hex := FALSE; j := 0;
            LOOP d[i] := ch; INC(i); Read(S, ch);
                IF ch < "0" THEN EXIT END;
                IF "9" < ch THEN
```

```
                    IF ("A" <= ch) & (ch <= "F") THEN hex := TRUE; ch := CHR(ORD(ch)−7)
                    ELSIF ("a" <= ch) & (ch <= "f") THEN hex := TRUE; ch :=
                        CHR(ORD(ch)−27H)
                  ELSE EXIT
                  END
                END
              END;
              IF ch = "H" THEN (*hex number*)
                  Read(S, ch); S.class := 3;
                  IF i−j > 8 THEN j := i−8 END ;
                  k := ORD(d[j]) − 30H; INC(j);
                  IF (i−j = 7) & (k >= 8) THEN DEC(k, 16) END ;
                  WHILE j < i DO k := k*10H + (ORD(d[j]) − 30H); INC(j) END ;
                  IF neg THEN S.i := −k ELSE S.i := k END
              ELSIF ch = "." THEN (*read real*)
                  Read(S, ch); h := i;
                  WHILE ("0" <= ch) & (ch <= "9") DO d[i] := ch; INC(i); Read(S, ch) END ;
                  IF ch = "D" THEN
                      e := 0; y := 0; g := 1;
                      REPEAT y := y*10 + (ORD(d[j]) − 30H); INC(j) UNTIL j = h;
                      WHILE j < i DO g := g/10; y := (ORD(d[j]) − 30H)*g + y; INC(j) END ;
                      ReadScaleFactor;
                      IF negE THEN
                          IF e <= 308 THEN y := y / Reals.TenL(e) ELSE y := 0 END
                      ELSIF e > 0 THEN
                          IF e <= 308 THEN y := Reals.TenL(e) * y ELSE HALT(40) END
                      END ;
                      IF neg THEN y := −y END ;
                      S.class := 5; S.y := y
                  ELSE e := 0; x := 0; f := 1;
                      REPEAT x := x*10 + (ORD(d[j]) − 30H); INC(j) UNTIL j = h;
                      WHILE j < i DO f := f/10; x := (ORD(d[j])−30H)*f + x; INC(j) END;
                      IF ch = "E" THEN ReadScaleFactor END ;
                      IF negE THEN
                          IF e <= 38 THEN x := x / Reals.Ten(e) ELSE x := 0 END
                      ELSIF e > 0 THEN
                          IF e <= 38 THEN x := Reals.Ten(e) * x ELSE HALT(40) END
                      END ;
                      IF neg THEN x := −x END ;
                      S.class := 4; S.x := x
                  END;
                  IF hex THEN S.class := 0 END
              ELSE (*decimal integer*)
                  S.class := 3; k := 0;
                  REPEAT k := k*10 + (ORD(d[j]) − 30H); INC(j) UNTIL j = i;
                  IF neg THEN S.i := −k ELSE S.i := k END;
                  IF hex THEN S.class := 0 ELSE S.class := 3 END
              END
          ELSE S.class := 6;
              IF neg THEN S.c := "−" ELSE S.c := ch; Read(S, ch) END
          END
      END;
      S.nextCh := ch
  END Scan;


  PROCEDURE OpenWriter* (VAR W: Writer);
  BEGIN
      NEW(W.buf); OpenBuf(W.buf); W.fnt := Fonts.Default; W.col := 15; W.voff := 0;
```

```
      Files.Set(W, Files.New(""), 0)
   END OpenWriter;


   PROCEDURE SetFont* (VAR W: Writer; fnt: Fonts.Font);
   BEGIN W.fnt := fnt
   END SetFont;


   PROCEDURE SetColor* (VAR W: Writer; col: SHORTINT);
   BEGIN W.col := col
   END SetColor;


   PROCEDURE SetOffset* (VAR W: Writer; voff: SHORTINT);
   BEGIN W.voff := voff
   END SetOffset;


   PROCEDURE Write* (VAR W: Writer; ch: CHAR);
      VAR p: Piece;
   BEGIN
      IF (W.buf.last.fnt # W.fnt) OR (W.buf.last.col # W.col) OR (W.buf.last.voff # W.voff) THEN
         NEW(p);
         p.f := Files.Base(W); p.off := Files.Pos(W); p.len := 0;
         p.fnt := W.fnt; p.col := W.col; p.voff:= W.voff;
         p.next := NIL; W.buf.last.next := p;
         p.prev := W.buf.last; W.buf.last := p
      END;
      Files.Write(W, ch);
      INC(W.buf.last.len); INC(W.buf.len)
   END Write;


   PROCEDURE WriteLn* (VAR W: Writer);
   BEGIN Write(W, CR)
   END WriteLn;


   PROCEDURE WriteString* (VAR W: Writer; s: ARRAY OF CHAR);
      VAR i: INTEGER;
   BEGIN i := 0;
      WHILE s[i] >= " " DO Write(W, s[i]); INC(i) END
   END WriteString;


   PROCEDURE WriteInt* (VAR W: Writer; x, n: LONGINT);
      VAR i: INTEGER; x0: LONGINT;
         a: ARRAY 11 OF CHAR;
      BEGIN i := 0;
         IF x < 0 THEN
            IF x = MIN(LONGINT) THEN WriteString(W, " −2147483648"); RETURN
            ELSE DEC(n); x0 := −x
            END
         ELSE x0 := x
         END;
         REPEAT
            a[i] := CHR(x0 MOD 10 + 30H); x0 := x0 DIV 10; INC(i)
         UNTIL x0 = 0;
         WHILE n > i DO Write(W, " "); DEC(n) END;
         IF x < 0 THEN Write(W, "−") END;
         REPEAT DEC(i); Write(W, a[i]) UNTIL i = 0
      END WriteInt;
```

```
PROCEDURE WriteHex* (VAR W: Writer; x: LONGINT);
  VAR i: INTEGER; y: LONGINT;
    a: ARRAY 10 OF CHAR;
  BEGIN i := 0; Write(W, " ");
    REPEAT y := x MOD 10H;
      IF y < 10 THEN a[i] := CHR(y + 30H) ELSE a[i] := CHR(y + 37H) END;
      x := x DIV 10H; INC(i)
    UNTIL i = 8;
    REPEAT DEC(i); Write(W, a[i]) UNTIL i = 0
  END WriteHex;


  PROCEDURE WriteReal* (VAR W: Writer; x: REAL; n: INTEGER);
    VAR e: INTEGER; x0: REAL;
      d: ARRAY maxD OF CHAR;
  BEGIN e := Reals.Expo(x);
    IF e = 0 THEN
      WriteString(W, "0");
      REPEAT Write(W, " "); DEC(n) UNTIL n <= 3
    ELSIF e = 255 THEN
      WriteString(W, "NaN");
      WHILE n > 4 DO Write(W, " "); DEC(n) END
    ELSE
      IF n <= 9 THEN n := 3 ELSE DEC(n, 6) END;
      REPEAT Write(W, " "); DEC(n) UNTIL n <= 8;
      (*there are 2 < n <= 8 digits to be written*)
      IF x < 0.0 THEN Write(W, "−"); x := −x ELSE Write(W, " ") END;
      e := (e − 127) * 77{DIV 256;
      IF e >= 0 THEN x := x / Reals.Ten(e) ELSE x := Reals.Ten(−e) * x END;
      IF x >= 10.0 THEN x := 0.1*x; INC(e) END;
      x0 := Reals.Ten(n−1); x := x0*x + 0.5;
      IF x >= 10.0*x0 THEN x := x*0.1; INC(e) END;
      Reals.Convert(x, n, d);
      DEC(n); Write(W, d[n]); Write(W, ".");
      REPEAT DEC(n); Write(W, d[n]) UNTIL n = 0;
      Write(W, "E");
      IF e < 0 THEN Write(W, "−"); e := −e ELSE Write(W, "+") END;
      Write(W, CHR(e DIV 10 + 30H)); Write(W, CHR(e MOD 10 + 30H))
    END
  END WriteReal;


  PROCEDURE WriteRealFix* (VAR W: Writer; x: REAL; n, k: INTEGER);
    VAR e, i: INTEGER; sign: CHAR; x0: REAL;
      d: ARRAY maxD OF CHAR;


    PROCEDURE seq(ch: CHAR; n: INTEGER);
    BEGIN WHILE n > 0 DO Write(W, ch); DEC(n) END
    END seq;


    PROCEDURE dig(n: INTEGER);
    BEGIN
      WHILE n > 0 DO
        DEC(i); Write(W, d[i]); DEC(n)
      END
    END dig;


  BEGIN e := Reals.Expo(x);
    IF k < 0 THEN k := 0 END;
```

```
        IF e = 0 THEN seq(" ", n−k−2); Write(W, "0"); seq(" ", k+1)
        ELSIF e = 255 THEN WriteString(W, " NaN"); seq(" ", n−4)ELSE e := (e − 127) * 77
            DIV 256;
          IF x < 0 THEN sign := "−"; x := −x ELSE sign := " " END;
          IF e >= 0 THEN{(*x >= 1.0,{77/256 = log 2*) x := x/Reals.Ten(e)
          ELSE (*x < 1.0*) x := Reals.Ten(−e) * x
        END;
          IF x >= 10.0 THEN x := 0.1*x; INC(e) END;
          (* 1 <= x < 10 *)
          IF k+e >= maxD−1 THEN k := maxD−1−e
          ELSIF k+e < 0 THEN k := −e; x := 0.0
        END;
          x0 := Reals.Ten(k+e); x := x0*x + 0.5;
          IF x >= 10.0*x0 THEN INC(e) END;
          (*e = no. of digits before decimal point*)
          INC(e); i := k+e; Reals.Convert(x, i, d);
          IF e > 0 THEN
              seq(" ", n−e−k−2); Write(W, sign); dig(e);
              Write(W, "."); dig(k)
          ELSE seq(" ", n−k−3);
              Write(W, sign); Write(W, "0"); Write(W, ".");
              seq("0", −e); dig(k+e)
          END
        END
      END WriteRealFix;


  PROCEDURE WriteRealHex* (VAR W: Writer; x: REAL);
    VAR i: INTEGER;
        d: ARRAY 8 OF CHAR;
  BEGIN Reals.ConvertH(x, d); i := 0;
    REPEAT Write(W, d[i]); INC(i) UNTIL i = 8
  END WriteRealHex;


  PROCEDURE WriteLongReal* (VAR W: Writer; x: LONGREAL; n: INTEGER);
    CONST maxD = 16;
    VAR e: INTEGER; x0: LONGREAL;
        d: ARRAY maxD OF CHAR;
  BEGIN e := Reals.ExpoL(x);
    IF e = 0 THEN
        WriteString(W, "0");
        REPEAT Write(W, " "); DEC(n) UNTIL n <= 3
    ELSIF e = 2047 THEN
        WriteString(W, "NaN");
        WHILE n > 4 DO Write(W, " "); DEC(n) END
    ELSE
        IF n <= 10 THEN n := 3 ELSE DEC(n, 7) END;
        REPEAT Write(W, " "); DEC(n) UNTIL n <= maxD;
        (*there are 2 <= n <= maxD digits to be written*)
        IF x < 0 THEN Write(W, "−"); x := −x ELSE Write(W, " ") END;
        e := SHORT(LONG(e − 1023) * 77 DIV 256);
        IF e >= 0 THEN x := x / Reals.TenL(e) ELSE x := Reals.TenL(−e) * x END ;
        IF x >= 10.0D0 THEN x := 0.1D0 * x; INC(e) END ;
        x0 := Reals.TenL(n−1); x := x0*x + 0.5D0;
        IF x >= 10.0D0*x0 THEN x := 0.1D0 * x; INC(e) END ;
        Reals.ConvertL(x, n, d);
        DEC(n); Write(W, d[n]); Write(W, ".");
        REPEAT DEC(n); Write(W, d[n]) UNTIL n = 0;
        Write(W, "D");
```

```
        IF e < 0 THEN Write(W, "-"); e := -e ELSE Write(W, "+") END;
        Write(W, CHR(e DIV 100 + 30H)); e := e MOD 100;
        Write(W, CHR(e DIV 10 + 30H));
        Write(W, CHR(e MOD 10 + 30H))
    END
END WriteLongReal;

PROCEDURE WriteLongRealHex* (VAR W: Writer; x: LONGREAL);
    VAR i: INTEGER;
        d: ARRAY 16 OF CHAR;
BEGIN Reals.ConvertHL(x, d); i := 0;
    REPEAT Write(W, d[i]); INC(i) UNTIL i = 16
END WriteLongRealHex;

PROCEDURE WriteDate* (VAR W: Writer; t, d: LONGINT);

    PROCEDURE WritePair(ch: CHAR; x: LONGINT);
    BEGIN Write(W, ch);
        Write(W, CHR(x DIV 10 + 30H)); Write(W, CHR(x MOD 10 + 30H))
    END WritePair;

BEGIN
    WritePair(" ", d MOD 32); WritePair(".", d DIV 32 MOD 16); WritePair(".", d DIV 512
        MOD 128);
    WritePair(" ", t DIV 4096 MOD 32); WritePair(":", t DIV 64 MOD 64); WritePair(":", t
        MOD 64)
END WriteDate;

BEGIN
    NEW(DelBuf); OpenBuf(DelBuf);
    OpenWriter(W); Write(W, 0X);
    WFile := Files.Base(W)
END Texts.

MODULE TextFrames; (*JG 8.10.90*)

IMPORT Input, Modules, Display, Viewers, MenuViewers, Fonts, Texts, Oberon;

CONST
    replace* = 0; insert* = 1; delete* = 2; (*message id*)
    CR = 0DX;

TYPE
    Line = POINTER TO LineDesc;

    LineDesc = RECORD
        len: LONGINT;
        wid: INTEGER;
        eot: BOOLEAN;
        next: Line
    END;

    Location* = RECORD
        org*, pos*: LONGINT;
        dx*, x*, y*: INTEGER;
```

```
      lin: Line
    END;


    Frame* = POINTER TO FrameDesc;

    FrameDesc* = RECORD (Display.FrameDesc)
      text*: Texts.Text;
      org*: LONGINT;
      col*: INTEGER;
      lsp*: INTEGER;
      left*, right*, top*, bot*: INTEGER;
      markH*: INTEGER;
      time*: LONGINT;
      mark*, car*, sel*: INTEGER;
      carloc*: Location;
      selbeg*, selend*: Location;
      trailer: Line
    END;


    (*mark < 0: arrow mark
      mark = 0: no mark
      mark > 0: position mark*)


    UpdateMsg* = RECORD (Display.FrameMsg)
      id*: INTEGER;
      text*: Texts.Text;
      beg*, end*: LONGINT
    END;

VAR
    menuH*, barW*, left*, right*, top*, bot*, lsp*: INTEGER; (*standard sizes*)
    asr, dsr, selH, markW, eolW: INTEGER;
    par: Oberon.ParList; nextCh: CHAR;
    W, KW: Texts.Writer; (*keyboard writer*)


PROCEDURE Min (i, j: INTEGER): INTEGER;
BEGIN IF i >= j THEN RETURN j ELSE RETURN i END
END Min;


(*------------------display support----------------------*)


PROCEDURE ReplConst (col: INTEGER; F: Frame; X, Y, W, H: INTEGER; mode:
      INTEGER);
BEGIN
    IF X + W <= F.X + F.W THEN Display.ReplConst(col, X, Y, W, H, mode)
    ELSIF X < F.X + F.W THEN Display.ReplConst(col, X, Y, F.X + F.W − X, H, mode)
    END
END ReplConst;

PROCEDURE FlipMark (F: Frame);
BEGIN
    IF (F.mark > 0) & (F.left >= barW) THEN
        Display.ReplConst(Display.white, F.X + 1, F.Y + F.H − 1 − F.markH, markW, 1,
            2)
    END
```

```
END FlipMark;

PROCEDURE UpdateMark (F: Frame);
   VAR oldH: INTEGER;
BEGIN
    oldH := F.markH; F.markH := SHORT(F.org * F.H DIV (F.text.len + 1));
    IF (F.mark > 0) & (F.left >= barW) & (F.markH # oldH) THEN
        Display.ReplConst(Display.white, F.X + 1, F.Y + F.H − 1 − oldH, markW, 1, 2);
        Display.ReplConst(Display.white, F.X + 1, F.Y + F.H − 1 − F.markH, markW, 1,
            2)
    END
END UpdateMark;


PROCEDURE Width (VAR R: Texts.Reader; len: LONGINT): INTEGER;
    VAR pat: Display.Pattern; pos: LONGINT; ox, dx, x, y, w, h: INTEGER;
BEGIN pos := 0; ox := 0;
    WHILE pos # len DO
        Display.GetChar(R.fnt.raster, nextCh, dx, x, y, w, h, pat);
        ox := ox + dx; INC(pos); Texts.Read(R, nextCh)
    END;
    RETURN ox
END Width;


PROCEDURE DisplayLine (F: Frame; L: Line;
    VAR R: Texts.Reader; X, Y: INTEGER; len: LONGINT);
    VAR pat: Display.Pattern; NX, dx, x, y, w, h: INTEGER;
BEGIN NX := F.X + F.W;
    WHILE (nextCh # CR) & (R.fnt # NIL) DO
        Display.GetChar(R.fnt.raster, nextCh, dx, x, y, w, h, pat);
        IF (X + x + w <= NX) & (h # 0) THEN
            Display.CopyPattern(R.col, pat, X + x, Y + y, 2)
        END;
        X := X + dx; INC(len); Texts.Read(R, nextCh)
    END;
    L.len := len + 1; L.wid := X + eolW − (F.X + F.left);
    L.eot := R.fnt = NIL; Texts.Read(R, nextCh)
END DisplayLine;


PROCEDURE Validate (T: Texts.Text; VAR pos: LONGINT);
    VAR R: Texts.Reader;
BEGIN
    IF pos > T.len THEN pos := T.len
    ELSIF pos > 0 THEN
        DEC(pos); Texts.OpenReader(R, T, pos);
        REPEAT Texts.Read(R, nextCh); INC(pos) UNTIL R.eot OR (nextCh = CR)
    ELSE pos := 0
    END
END Validate;


PROCEDURE Mark* (F: Frame; mark: INTEGER);
BEGIN
    IF ((mark >= 0) = (F.mark < 0)) & (F.H >= 16) THEN
        Display.CopyPattern(Display.white, Display.downArrow, F.X, F.Y, 2)
    END;
    IF ((mark > 0) = (F.mark <= 0)) & (F.H > 0) & (F.left >= barW) THEN
        Display.ReplConst(Display.white, F.X + 1, F.Y + F.H − 1 − F.markH, markW, 1,
            2)
```

```
      END;
      F.mark := mark
   END Mark;


   PROCEDURE Restore* (F: Frame);
      VAR R: Texts.Reader; L, l: Line; curY, botY: INTEGER;
   BEGIN (*F.mark = 0*)
      Display.ReplConst(F.col, F.X, F.Y, F.W, F.H, 0);
      IF F.left >= barW THEN
         Display.ReplConst(Display.white, F.X + barW − 1, F.Y, 1, F.H, 2)
      END;
      Validate(F.text, F.org);
      botY := F.Y + F.bot + dsr;
      Texts.OpenReader(R, F.text, F.org); Texts.Read(R, nextCh);
      L := F.trailer; curY := F.Y + F.H − F.top − asr;
      WHILE ~L.eot & (curY >= botY) DO
         NEW(l);
         DisplayLine(F, l, R, F.X + F.left, curY, 0);
         L.next := l; L := l; curY := curY − lsp
      END;
      L.next := F.trailer;
      F.markH := SHORT(F.org * F.H DIV (F.text.len + 1))
   END Restore;


   PROCEDURE Suspend* (F: Frame);
   BEGIN (*F.mark = 0*)
      F.trailer.next := F.trailer
   END Suspend;


   PROCEDURE Extend* (F: Frame; newY: INTEGER);
      VAR R: Texts.Reader; L, l: Line; org: LONGINT; curY, botY: INTEGER;
   BEGIN (*F.mark = 0*)
      Display.ReplConst(F.col, F.X, newY, F.W, F.Y − newY, 0);
      IF F.left >= barW THEN
         Display.ReplConst(Display.white, F.X + barW − 1, newY, 1, F.Y − newY, 2)
      END;
      F.H := F.H + F.Y − newY; F.Y := newY;
      IF F.trailer.next = F.trailer THEN Validate(F.text, F.org) END;
      L := F.trailer; org := F.org; curY := F.Y + F.H − F.top − asr;
      WHILE L.next # F.trailer DO
         L := L.next; org := org + L.len; curY := curY − lsp
      END;
      botY := F.Y + F.bot + dsr;
      Texts.OpenReader(R, F.text, org); Texts.Read(R, nextCh);
      WHILE ~L.eot & (curY >= botY) DO NEW(l);
         DisplayLine(F, l, R, F.X + F.left, curY, 0);
         L.next := l; L := l; curY := curY − lsp
      END;
      L.next := F.trailer;
      F.markH := SHORT(F.org * F.H DIV (F.text.len + 1))
   END Extend;


   PROCEDURE Reduce* (F: Frame; newY: INTEGER);
      VAR L: Line; curY, botY: INTEGER;
   BEGIN (*F.mark = 0*)
      F.H := F.H + F.Y − newY; F.Y := newY;
      botY := F.Y + F.bot + dsr;
```

```
      L := F.trailer; curY := F.Y + F.H − F.top − asr;
      WHILE (L.next # F.trailer) & (curY >= botY) DO
         L := L.next; curY := curY − lsp
      END;
      L.next := F.trailer;
      IF curY + asr > F.Y THEN
         Display.ReplConst(F.col, F.X + F.left, F.Y, F.W − F.left, curY + asr − F.Y, 0)
      END;
      F.markH := SHORT(F.org * F.H DIV (F.text.len + 1));
      Mark(F, 1)
   END Reduce;

   PROCEDURE Show* (F: Frame; pos: LONGINT);
      VAR R: Texts.Reader; L, l: Line;
         org: LONGINT; curY, botY, Y0: INTEGER; keys: SET;
      BEGIN
      IF F.trailer.next # F.trailer THEN
         Validate(F.text, pos);
         IF pos < F.org THEN Mark(F, 0);
            Display.ReplConst(F.col, F.X + F.left, F.Y, F.W − F.left, F.H, 0);
            botY := F.Y; F.Y := F.Y + F.H; F.H := 0;
            F.org := pos; F.trailer.next := F.trailer; Extend(F, botY);
            Mark(F, 1)
         ELSIF pos > F.org THEN
            org := F.org; L := F.trailer.next; curY := F.Y + F.H − F.top − asr;
            WHILE (L.next # F.trailer) & (org # pos) DO
               org := org + L.len; L := L.next; curY := curY − lsp;
            END;
            IF org = pos THEN
               F.org := org; F.trailer.next := L; Y0 := curY;
               WHILE L.next # F.trailer DO
                  org := org + L.len; L := L.next; curY := curY − lsp
               END;
               Display.CopyBlock
                  (F.X + F.left, curY − dsr, F.W − F.left, Y0 + asr − (curY − dsr),
                  F.X + F.left, curY − dsr + F.Y + F.H − F.top − asr − Y0, 0);
               curY := curY + F.Y + F.H − F.top − asr − Y0;
               Display.ReplConst(F.col, F.X + F.left, F.Y, F.W − F.left, curY − dsr −
                     F.Y, 0);
               botY := F.Y + F.bot + dsr;
               org := org + L.len; curY := curY − lsp;
               Texts.OpenReader(R, F.text, org); Texts.Read(R, nextCh);
               WHILE ~L.eot & (curY >= botY) DO NEW(l);
                  DisplayLine(F, l, R, F.X + F.left, curY, 0);
                  L.next := l; L := l; curY := curY − lsp
               END;
               L.next := F.trailer;
               UpdateMark(F)
            ELSE Mark(F, 0);
               Display.ReplConst(F.col, F.X + F.left, F.Y, F.W − F.left, F.H, 0);
               botY := F.Y; F.Y := F.Y + F.H; F.H := 0;
               F.org := pos; F.trailer.next := F.trailer; Extend(F, botY);
               Mark(F, 1)
            END
         END
      END
   END Show;

   PROCEDURE LocateLine (F: Frame; y: INTEGER; VAR loc: Location);
```

```
      VAR T: Texts.Text; L: Line; org: LONGINT; cury: INTEGER;
BEGIN T := F.text;
   org := F.org; L := F.trailer.next; cury := F.H − F.top − asr;
   WHILE (L.next # F.trailer) & (cury > y + dsr) DO
      org := org + L.len; L := L.next; cury := cury − lsp
   END;
   loc.org := org; loc.lin := L; loc.y := cury
END LocateLine;

PROCEDURE LocateString (F: Frame; x, y: INTEGER; VAR loc: Location);
   VAR R: Texts.Reader; pat: Display.Pattern;
      bpos, pos, lim: LONGINT; bx, ex, ox, dx, u, v, w, h: INTEGER;
   BEGIN LocateLine(F, y, loc);
      lim := loc.org + loc.lin.len − 1;
      bpos := loc.org; bx := F.left;
      pos := loc.org; ox := F.left;
      Texts.OpenReader(R, F.text, loc.org); Texts.Read(R, nextCh);
      LOOP
         LOOP (*scan string*)
            IF (pos = lim) OR (nextCh <= " ") THEN EXIT END;
            Display.GetChar(R.fnt.raster, nextCh, dx, u, v, w, h, pat);
            INC(pos); ox := ox + dx; Texts.Read(R, nextCh)
         END;
         ex := ox;
         LOOP (*scan gap*)
            IF (pos = lim) OR (nextCh > " ") THEN EXIT END;
            Display.GetChar(R.fnt.raster, nextCh, dx, u, v, w, h, pat);
            INC(pos); ox := ox + dx; Texts.Read(R, nextCh)
         END;
         IF (pos = lim) OR (ox > x) THEN EXIT END;
         Display.GetChar(R.fnt.raster, nextCh, dx, u, v, w, h, pat);
         bpos := pos; bx := ox;
         INC(pos); ox := ox + dx; Texts.Read(R, nextCh)
      END;
      loc.pos := bpos; loc.dx := ex − bx; loc.x := bx
   END LocateString;

PROCEDURE LocateChar (F: Frame; x, y: INTEGER; VAR loc: Location);
   VAR R: Texts.Reader; pat: Display.Pattern;
      pos, lim: LONGINT; ox, dx, u, v, w, h: INTEGER;
   BEGIN LocateLine(F, y, loc);
      lim := loc.org + loc.lin.len − 1;
      pos := loc.org; ox := F.left;
      Texts.OpenReader(R, F.text, loc.org); Texts.Read(R, nextCh);
      LOOP
         IF pos = lim THEN dx := eolW; EXIT END;
         Display.GetChar(R.fnt.raster, nextCh, dx, u, v, w, h, pat);
         IF ox + dx > x THEN EXIT END;
         INC(pos); ox := ox + dx; Texts.Read(R, nextCh)
      END;
      loc.pos := pos; loc.dx := dx; loc.x := ox
   END LocateChar;

PROCEDURE LocatePos (F: Frame; pos: LONGINT; VAR loc: Location);
   VAR T: Texts.Text; R: Texts.Reader; L: Line; org: LONGINT; cury: INTEGER;{
BEGIN T := F.text;
   org := F.org; L := F.trailer.next; cury := F.H − F.top − asr;
```

```
        IF pos < org THEN pos := org END;
        WHILE (L.next # F.trailer) & (pos >= org + L.len) DO
            org := org + L.len; L := L.next; cury := cury − lsp
        END;
        IF pos >= org + L.len THEN pos := org + L.len − 1 END;{
        Texts.OpenReader(R, T, org); Texts.Read(R, nextCh);
        loc.org := org; loc.pos := pos; loc.lin := L;
        loc.x := F.left + Width(R, pos − org); loc.y := cury
    END LocatePos;


    PROCEDURE Pos* (F: Frame; X, Y: INTEGER): LONGINT;
        VAR loc: Location;
    BEGIN LocateChar(F, X − F.X, Y − F.Y, loc);
        RETURN loc.pos
    END Pos;


    PROCEDURE FlipCaret (F: Frame);
    BEGIN
        IF F.carloc.x < F.W THEN
            IF (F.carloc.y >= 10) & (F.carloc.x + 12 < F.W) THEN
                Display.CopyPattern(Display.white, Display.hook, F.X + F.carloc.x, F.Y +
                    F.carloc.y − 10, 2)
            END
        END
    END FlipCaret;


    PROCEDURE SetCaret* (F: Frame; pos: LONGINT);
    BEGIN LocatePos(F, pos, F.carloc); FlipCaret(F); F.car := 1
    END SetCaret;


    PROCEDURE TrackCaret* (F: Frame; X, Y: INTEGER; VAR keysum: SET);
        VAR loc: Location; keys: SET;
    BEGIN
        IF F.trailer.next # F.trailer THEN
            LocateChar(F, X − F.X, Y − F.Y, F.carloc);
            FlipCaret(F);
            keysum := {};
            REPEAT
                Input.Mouse(keys, X, Y);
                keysum := keysum + keys;
                Oberon.DrawCursor(Oberon.Mouse, Oberon.Mouse.marker, X, Y);
                LocateChar(F, X − F.X, Y − F.Y, loc);
                IF loc.pos # F.carloc.pos THEN FlipCaret(F); F.carloc := loc; FlipCaret(F)
                END
            UNTIL keys = {};
            F.car := 1
        END
    END TrackCaret;


    PROCEDURE RemoveCaret* (F: Frame);
    BEGIN IF F.car # 0 THEN FlipCaret(F); F.car := 0 END
    END RemoveCaret;


    PROCEDURE FlipSelection (F: Frame; VAR beg, end: Location);
        VAR T: Texts.Text; L: Line; Y: INTEGER;
    BEGIN T := F.text;
```

```
        L := beg.lin; Y := F.Y + beg.y − 2;
        IF L = end.lin THEN ReplConst(Display.white, F, F.X + beg.x, Y, end.x −
            beg.x, selH, 2)
        ELSE
            ReplConst(Display.white, F, F.X + beg.x, Y, F.left + L.wid − beg.x, selH,
                2);
            LOOP
                L := L.next; Y := Y − lsp;
                IF L = end.lin THEN EXIT END;
                ReplConst(Display.white, F, F.X + F.left, Y, L.wid, selH, 2)
            END;
            ReplConst(Display.white, F, F.X + F.left, Y, end.x − F.left, selH, 2)
        END
END FlipSelection;


PROCEDURE SetSelection* (F: Frame; beg, end: LONGINT);
BEGIN
    IF F.sel # 0 THEN FlipSelection(F, F.selbeg, F.selend) END;
    LocatePos(F, beg, F.selbeg); LocatePos(F, end, F.selend);
    IF F.selbeg.pos < F.selend.pos THEN
        FlipSelection(F, F.selbeg, F.selend); F.time := Oberon.Time(); F.sel := 1
    END
END SetSelection;


PROCEDURE TrackSelection* (F: Frame; X, Y: INTEGER; VAR keysum: SET);
    VAR loc: Location; keys: SET;
BEGIN
    IF F.trailer.next # F.trailer THEN
        IF F.sel # 0 THEN FlipSelection(F, F.selbeg, F.selend) END;
        LocateChar(F, X − F.X, Y − F.Y, loc);
        IF (F.sel # 0) & (loc.pos = F.selbeg.pos) & (F.selend.pos = F.selbeg.pos + 1)
            THEN
            LocateChar(F, F.left, Y − F.Y, F.selbeg)
        ELSE F.selbeg := loc
        END;
        INC(loc.pos); loc.x := loc.x + loc.dx; F.selend := loc;
        FlipSelection(F, F.selbeg, F.selend);
        keysum := {};
        REPEAT
            Input.Mouse(keys, X, Y);
            keysum := keysum + keys;
            Oberon.DrawCursor(Oberon.Mouse, Oberon.Mouse.marker, X, Y);
            LocateChar(F, X − F.X, Y − F.Y, loc);
            IF loc.pos < F.selbeg.pos THEN loc := F.selbeg END;
            INC(loc.pos); loc.x := loc.x + loc.dx;
            IF loc.pos < F.selend.pos THEN FlipSelection(F, loc, F.selend); F.selend
                := loc
            ELSIF loc.pos > F.selend.pos THEN FlipSelection(F, F.selend, loc);
                F.selend := loc
            END
        UNTIL keys = {};
        F.time := Oberon.Time(); F.sel := 1
    END
END TrackSelection;


PROCEDURE RemoveSelection* (F: Frame);
BEGIN IF F.sel # 0 THEN FlipSelection(F, F.selbeg, F.selend); F.sel := 0 END
```

```
END RemoveSelection;

PROCEDURE TrackLine* (F: Frame; X, Y: INTEGER; VAR org: LONGINT; VAR
        keysum: SET);
    VAR T: Texts.Text; old, new: Location; keys: SET;
BEGIN
    IF F.trailer.next # F.trailer THEN T := F.text;
        LocateLine(F, Y - F.Y, old);
        ReplConst(Display.white, F, F.X + F.left, F.Y + old.y - dsr, old.lin.wid, 2,
                2);
        keysum := {};
        REPEAT
            Input.Mouse(keys, X, Y);
            keysum := keysum + keys;
            Oberon.DrawCursor(Oberon.Mouse, Oberon.Mouse.marker, X, Y);
            LocateLine(F, Y - F.Y, new);
            IF new.org 01£ old.org THEN
                ReplConst(Display.white, F, F.X + F.left, F.Y + old.y - dsr,
                        old.lin.wid, 2, 2);
                ReplConst(Display.white, F, F.X + F.left, F.Y + new.y - dsr,
                        new.lin.wid, 2, 2);
                old := new
            END
        UNTIL keys = {};
        ReplConst(Display.white, F, F.X + F.left, F.Y + new.y - dsr, new.lin.wid, 2,
                2);
        org := new.org
    ELSE org := -1
    END
END TrackLine;

PROCEDURE TrackWord* (F: Frame; X, Y: INTEGER; VAR pos: LONGINT; VAR
        keysum: SET);
    VAR T: Texts.Text; old, new: Location; keys: SET;
BEGIN
    IF F.trailer.next # F.trailer THEN T := F.text;
        LocateString(F, X - F.X, Y - F.Y, old);
        ReplConst(Display.white, F, F.X + old.x, F.Y + old.y - dsr, old.dx, 2, 2);
        keysum := {};
        REPEAT
            Input.Mouse(keys, X, Y);
            keysum := keysum + keys;
            Oberon.DrawCursor(Oberon.Mouse, Oberon.Mouse.marker, X, Y);
            LocateString(F, X - F.X, Y - F.Y, new);
            IF new.pos # old.pos THEN
                ReplConst(Display.white, F, F.X + old.x, F.Y + old.y - dsr, old.dx, 2,
                        2);
                ReplConst(Display.white, F, F.X + new.x, F.Y + new.y - dsr,
                        new.dx, 2, 2);
                old := new
            END
        UNTIL keys = {};
        ReplConst(Display.white, F, F.X + new.x, F.Y + new.y - dsr, new.dx, 2, 2);
        pos := new.pos
    ELSE pos := -1
    END
END TrackWord;

PROCEDURE Replace* (F: Frame; beg, end: LONGINT);
```

```
                    VAR R: Texts.Reader; L: Line; org, len: LONGINT; curY, wid: INTEGER;
                BEGIN
                    IF end > F.org THEN
                        IF beg < F.org THEN beg := F.org END;
                        org := F.org; L := F.trailer.next; curY := F.Y + F.H − F.top − asr;
                        WHILE (L # F.trailer) & (org + L.len <= beg) DO
                            org := org + L.len; L := L.next; curY := curY − lsp
                        END;
                        IF L # F.trailer THEN
                            Texts.OpenReader(R, F.text, org); Texts.Read(R, nextCh);
                            len := beg − org; wid := Width(R, len);
                            ReplConst(F.col, F, F.X + F.left + wid, curY − dsr, L.wid − wid, lsp, 0);
                            DisplayLine(F, L, R, F.X + F.left + wid, curY, len);
                            org := org + L.len; L := L.next; curY := curY − lsp;
                            WHILE (L # F.trailer) & (org <= end) DO
                                Display.ReplConst(F.col, F.X + F.left, curY − dsr, F.W − F.left, lsp,
                                    0);
                                DisplayLine(F, L, R, F.X + F.left, curY, 0);
                                org := org + L.len; L := L.next; curY := curY − lsp
                            END
                        END
                    END;
                    UpdateMark(F)
                END Replace;


                PROCEDURE Insert* (F: Frame; beg, end: LONGINT);
                    VAR R: Texts.Reader; L, L0, l: Line;
                        org, len: LONGINT; curY, botY, Y0, Y1, Y2, dY, wid: INTEGER;
                BEGIN
                    IF beg < F.org THEN F.org := F.org + (end − beg)
                    ELSE
                        org := F.org; L := F.trailer.next; curY := F.Y + F.H − F.top − asr;
                        WHILE (L # F.trailer) & (org + L.len <= beg) DO
                            org := org + L.len; L := L.next; curY := curY − lsp
                        END;
                        IF L # F.trailer THEN
                            botY := F.Y + F.bot + dsr;
                            Texts.OpenReader(R, F.text, org); Texts.Read(R, nextCh);
                            len := beg − org; wid := Width(R, len);
                            ReplConst (F.col, F, F.X + F.left + wid, curY − dsr, L.wid − wid, lsp,
                                0);
                            DisplayLine(F, L, R, F.X + F.left + wid, curY, len);
                            org := org + L.len; curY := curY − lsp;
                            Y0 := curY; L0 := L.next;
                            WHILE (org <= end) & (curY >= botY) DO NEW(l);
                                Display.ReplConst(F.col, F.X + F.left, curY − dsr, F.W − F.left, lsp,
                                    0);
                                DisplayLine(F, l, R, F.X + F.left, curY, 0);
                                L.next := l; L := l;
                                org := org + L.len; curY := curY − lsp
                            END;
                            IF L0 # L.next THEN Y1 := curY;
                                L.next := L0;
                                WHILE (L.next # F.trailer) & (curY >= botY) DO
                                    L := L.next; curY := curY − lsp
                                END;
                                L.next := F.trailer;
                                dY := Y0 − Y1;
```

```
                IF Y1 > curY + dY THEN
                  Display.CopyBlock
                    (F.X + F.left, curY + dY + lsp − dsr, F.W − F.left, Y1 − curY −
                      dY,
                    F.X + F.left, curY + lsp − dsr,
                    0);
                    Y2 := Y1 − dY
                ELSE Y2 := curY
                END;
                curY := Y1; L := L0;
                WHILE curY # Y2 DO
                  Display.ReplConst(F.col, F.X + F.left, curY − dsr, F.W − F.left,
                      lsp, 0);
                  DisplayLine(F, L, R, F.X + F.left, curY, 0);
                  L := L.next; curY := curY − lsp
                END
              END
            END
          END;
          UpdateMark(F)
        END Insert;


        PROCEDURE Delete* (F: Frame; beg, end: LONGINT);
          VAR R: Texts.Reader; L, L0, l: Line;
            org, org0, len: LONGINT; curY, botY, Y0, Y1, wid: INTEGER;
        BEGIN
          IF end <= F.org THEN F.org := F.org − (end − beg)
          ELSE
            IF beg < F.org THEN
              F.trailer.next.len := F.trailer.next.len + (F.org − beg);
              F.org := beg
            END;
            org := F.org; L := F.trailer.next; curY := F.Y + F.H − F.top − asr;
            WHILE (L # F.trailer) & (org + L.len <= beg) DO
              org := org + L.len; L := L.next; curY := curY − lsp
            END;
            IF L # F.trailer THEN
              botY := F.Y + F.bot + dsr;
              org0 := org; L0 := L; Y0 := curY;
              WHILE (L # F.trailer) & (org <= end) DO
                org := org + L.len; L := L.next; curY := curY − lsp
              END;
              Y1 := curY;
              Texts.OpenReader(R, F.text, org0); Texts.Read(R, nextCh);
              len := beg − org0; wid := Width(R, len);
              ReplConst (F.col, F, F.X + F.left + wid, Y0 − dsr, L0.wid − wid, lsp, 0);
              DisplayLine(F, L0, R, F.X + F.left + wid, Y0, len);
              Y0 := Y0 − lsp;
              IF L # L0.next THEN
                L0.next := L;
                L := L0; org := org0 + L0.len;
                WHILE L.next # F.trailer DO
                  L := L.next; org := org + L.len; curY := curY − lsp
                END;
                Display.CopyBlock
                    (F.X + F.left, curY + lsp − dsr, F.W − F.left, Y1 − curY,
                    F.X + F.left, curY + lsp − dsr + (Y0 − Y1), 0);
                curY := curY + (Y0 − Y1);
```

```
                            Display.ReplConst (F.col, F.X + F.left, F.Y, F.W – F.left, curY + lsp –
                                (F.Y + dsr), 0);
                            Texts.OpenReader(R, F.text, org); Texts.Read(R, nextCh);
                            WHILE ~L.eot & (curY >= botY) DO NEW(l);
                                DisplayLine(F, l, R, F.X + F.left, curY, 0);
                                L.next := l; L := l; curY := curY – lsp
                            END;
                            L.next := F.trailer
                        END
                END
            END;
        UpdateMark(F)
    END Delete;


    (*-----------------message handling----------------------*)


    PROCEDURE RemoveMarks (F: Frame);
    BEGIN RemoveCaret(F); RemoveSelection(F)
    END RemoveMarks;


    PROCEDURE NotifyDisplay* (T: Texts.Text; op: INTEGER; beg, end: LONGINT);
        VAR M: UpdateMsg;
    BEGIN M.id := op; M.text := T; M.beg := beg; M.end := end;
        Viewers.Broadcast(M)
    END NotifyDisplay;


    PROCEDURE Call* (F: Frame; pos: LONGINT; new: BOOLEAN);
        VAR S: Texts.Scanner; res: INTEGER;
    BEGIN
        Texts.OpenScanner(S, F.text, pos); Texts.Scan(S);
        IF S.class = Texts.Name THEN
            par.vwr := Viewers.This(F.X, F.Y);
            par.frame := F; par.text := F.text; par.pos := pos + S.len;
            Oberon.Call(S.s, par, new, res);
            IF res > 1 THEN
                Texts.WriteString(W, "Call error: ");
                IF res = 2 THEN
                    Texts.WriteString(W, " not an obj–file or error in file")
                ELSIF res = 3 THEN
                    Texts.WriteString(W, Modules.imported);
                    Texts.WriteString(W, " imported with bad key from ");
                    Texts.WriteString(W, Modules.importing)
                ELSIF res = 4 THEN
                    Texts.WriteString(W, " not enough space")
                END;
                Texts.WriteLn(W); Texts.Append(Oberon.Log, W.buf)
            END
        END
    END Call;


    PROCEDURE Write* (F: Frame; ch: CHAR; fnt: Fonts.Font; col, voff: SHORTINT);
    BEGIN (*F.car # 0*)
        IF ch = 7FX THEN
            IF F.carloc.pos > F.org THEN
                Texts.Delete(F.text, F.carloc.pos – 1, F.carloc.pos);
                SetCaret(F, F.carloc.pos – 1)
            END
```

```
    ELSIF (20X <= ch) & (ch < 86X) OR (ch = 0DX) OR (ch = 9X) THEN
        KW.fnt := fnt; KW.col := col; KW.voff := voff; Texts.Write(KW, ch);
        Texts.Insert(F.text, F.carloc.pos, KW.buf);
        SetCaret(F, F.carloc.pos + 1)
    END
END Write;


PROCEDURE Defocus* (F: Frame);
BEGIN RemoveCaret(F)
END Defocus;


PROCEDURE Neutralize* (F: Frame);
BEGIN RemoveMarks(F)
END Neutralize;


PROCEDURE Modify* (F: Frame; id, dY, Y, H: INTEGER);
BEGIN
    Mark(F, 0); RemoveMarks(F);
    IF id = MenuViewers.extend THEN
        IF dY > 0 THEN
            Display.CopyBlock(F.X, F.Y, F.W, F.H, F.X, F.Y + dY, 0); F.Y := F.Y +
                dY
        END;
        Extend(F, Y)
    ELSIF id = MenuViewers.reduce THEN
        Reduce(F, Y + dY);
        IF dY > 0 THEN Display.CopyBlock(F.X, F.Y, F.W, F.H, F.X, Y, 0); F.Y := Y
            END
    END;
    IF F.H > 0 THEN Mark(F, 1) END
END Modify;


PROCEDURE Open* (
    F: Frame; H: Display.Handler; T: Texts.Text; org: LONGINT;
    col, left, right, top, bot, lsp: INTEGER);
    VAR L: Line;
BEGIN NEW(L);
    L.len := 0; L.wid := 0; L.eot := FALSE; L.next := L;
    F.handle := H; F.text := T; F.org := org; F.trailer := L;
    F.left := left; F.right := right; F.top := top; F.bot := bot;
    F.lsp := lsp; F.col := col; F.mark := 0; F.car := 0; F.sel := 0
END Open;


PROCEDURE Copy* (F: Frame; VAR F1: Frame);
BEGIN NEW(F1);
    Open(F1, F.handle, F.text, F.org, F.col, F.left, F.right, F.top, F.bot, F.lsp)
END Copy;


PROCEDURE CopyOver* (F: Frame; text: Texts.Text; beg, end: LONGINT);
    VAR buf: Texts.Buffer;
BEGIN
    IF F.car > 0 THEN
        NEW(buf); Texts.OpenBuf(buf);
        Texts.Save(text, beg, end, buf);
        Texts.Insert(F.text, F.carloc.pos, buf);
        SetCaret(F, F.carloc.pos + (end - beg))
```

```
            END
        END CopyOver;


        PROCEDURE GetSelection* (F: Frame; VAR text: Texts.Text; VAR beg, end, time:
            LONGINT);
        BEGIN
            IF F.sel > 0 THEN
                IF F.time > time THEN
                    text := F.text; beg := F.selbeg.pos; end := F.selend.pos; time := F.time
                ELSIF F.text = text THEN
                    IF (F.time < time) & (F.selbeg.pos < beg) THEN beg := F.selbeg.pos
                    ELSIF (F.time > time) & (F.selend.pos > end) THEN end :=
                        F.selend.pos; time := F.time
                    END
                END
            END
        END GetSelection;


        PROCEDURE Update* (F: Frame; VAR M: UpdateMsg);
        BEGIN (*F.text = M.text*)
            RemoveMarks(F); Oberon.RemoveMarks(F.X, F.Y, F.W, F.H);
            IF M.id = replace THEN Replace(F, M.beg, M.end)
            ELSIF M.id = insert THEN Insert(F, M.beg, M.end)
            ELSIF M.id = delete THEN Delete(F, M.beg, M.end)
            END
        END Update;


        PROCEDURE Edit* (F: Frame; X, Y: INTEGER; Keys: SET);
            VAR M: Oberon.CopyOverMsg;
                T: Texts.Text; R: Texts.Reader; buf: Texts.Buffer;
                time, pos, beg, end: LONGINT; keysum: SET; ch: CHAR;
        BEGIN
            Oberon.DrawCursor(Oberon.Mouse, Oberon.Arrow, X, Y);
            IF X < F.X + Min(F.left, barW) THEN
                IF (0 IN Keys) OR (1 IN Keys) THEN keysum := Keys;
                    REPEAT
                        Input.Mouse(Keys, X, Y);
                        keysum := keysum + Keys;
                        Oberon.DrawCursor(Oberon.Mouse, Oberon.Arrow, X, Y)
                    UNTIL Keys = {};
                    IF ~(2 IN keysum) THEN
                        RemoveMarks(F); Oberon.RemoveMarks(F.X, F.Y, F.W, F.H);
                        IF (0 IN keysum) OR (F.Y + F.H < Y) THEN pos := 0
                        ELSE pos := (F.Y + F.H − Y) * (F.text.len) DIV F.H
                        END;
                        RemoveMarks(F); Oberon.RemoveMarks(F.X, F.Y, F.W, F.H);
                        Show(F, pos)
                    ELSIF ~(0 IN keysum) THEN
                        RemoveMarks(F); Oberon.RemoveMarks(F.X, F.Y, F.W, F.H);
                        Show(F, F.text.len)
                    END
                ELSIF 2 IN Keys THEN
                    TrackLine(F, X, Y, pos, keysum);
                    IF (pos >= 0) & ~(0 IN keysum) THEN
                        RemoveMarks(F); Oberon.RemoveMarks(F.X, F.Y, F.W, F.H);
                        Show(F, pos)
                    END
```

```
                END
            ELSE
                IF 0 IN Keys THEN
                    TrackSelection(F, X, Y, keysum);
                    IF F.sel # 0 THEN
                        IF (2 IN keysum) & ~(1 IN keysum) THEN (*delete text*)
                            Oberon.PassFocus(MenuViewers.Ancestor);
                            Oberon.GetSelection(T, beg, end, time);
                            Texts.Delete(T, beg, end); SetCaret(F, beg)
                        ELSIF (1 IN keysum) & ~(2 IN keysum) THEN (*copy to focus*)
                            Oberon.GetSelection(T, beg, end, time);
                            M.text := T; M.beg := beg; M.end := end;
                            Oberon.FocusViewer.handle(Oberon.FocusViewer, M)
                        END
                    END
                ELSIF 1 IN Keys THEN
                    TrackWord(F, X, Y, pos, keysum);
                    IF (pos >= 0) & ~(0 IN keysum) THEN Call(F, pos, 2 IN keysum) END
                ELSIF 2 IN Keys THEN
                    Oberon.PassFocus(Viewers.This(F.X, F.Y)); TrackCaret(F, X, Y, keysum);
                    IF F.car # 0 THEN
                        IF (1 IN keysum) & ~(0 IN keysum) THEN (*copy from selection*)
                            Oberon.GetSelection(T, beg, end, time);
                            IF time >= 0 THEN
                                NEW(buf); Texts.OpenBuf(buf);
                                Texts.Save(T, beg, end, buf);
                                Texts.Insert(F.text, F.carloc.pos, buf);
                                SetCaret(F, F.carloc.pos + (end - beg))
                            END
                        ELSIF (0 IN keysum) & ~(1 IN keysum) THEN (*copy font*)
                            Oberon.GetSelection(T, beg, end, time);
                            IF time >= 0 THEN
                                Texts.OpenReader(R, F.text, F.carloc.pos); Texts.Read(R, ch);
                                Texts.ChangeLooks(T, beg, end, {0, 1, 2}, R.fnt, R.col, R.voff)
                            END
                        END
                    END
                END
            END
        END
    END
END Edit;


PROCEDURE Handle* (F: Display.Frame; VAR M: Display.FrameMsg);
    VAR F1: Frame;
BEGIN
    WITH F: Frame DO
        IF M IS Oberon.InputMsg THEN
            WITH M: Oberon.InputMsg DO
                IF M.id = Oberon.track THEN Edit(F, M.X, M.Y, M.keys)
                ELSIF M.id = Oberon.consume THEN
                    IF F.car # 0 THEN Write(F, M.ch, M.fnt, M.col, M.voff) END
                END
            END
        ELSIF M IS Oberon.ControlMsg THEN
            WITH M: Oberon.ControlMsg DO
                IF M.id = Oberon.defocus THEN Defocus(F)
                ELSIF M.id = Oberon.neutralize THEN Neutralize(F)
                END
            END
```

```
        ELSIF M IS Oberon.SelectionMsg THEN
            WITH M: Oberon.SelectionMsg DO GetSelection(F, M.text, M.beg,
                M.end, M.time) END
        ELSIF M IS Oberon.CopyOverMsg THEN
            WITH M: Oberon.CopyOverMsg DO CopyOver(F, M.text, M.beg, M.end)
                END
        ELSIF M IS Oberon.CopyMsg THEN
            WITH M: Oberon.CopyMsg DO Copy(F, F1); M.F := F1 END
        ELSIF M IS MenuViewers.ModifyMsg THEN
            WITH M: MenuViewers.ModifyMsg DO Modify(F, M.id, M.dY, M.Y,
                M.H) END
        ELSIF M IS UpdateMsg THEN
            WITH M: UpdateMsg DO
                IF F.text = M.text THEN Update(F, M) END
            END
        END
    END
END Handle;


(*creation*)

PROCEDURE Menu (name, commands: ARRAY OF CHAR): Texts.Text;
    VAR T: Texts.Text;
BEGIN
    NEW(T); T.notify := NotifyDisplay; Texts.Open(T, "");
    Texts.WriteString(W, name); Texts.WriteString(W, " | "); Texts.WriteString(W,
        commands);
    Texts.Append(T, W.buf);
    RETURN T
END Menu;


PROCEDURE Text* (name: ARRAY OF CHAR): Texts.Text;
    VAR T: Texts.Text;
BEGIN NEW(T); T.notify := NotifyDisplay; Texts.Open(T, name); RETURN T
END Text;


PROCEDURE NewMenu* (name, commands: ARRAY OF CHAR): Frame;
    VAR F: Frame;
BEGIN NEW(F);
    Open(F, Handle, Menu(name, commands), 0, Display.white, left DIV 4, 0, 0, 0,
        lsp);
    RETURN F
END NewMenu;


PROCEDURE NewText* (text: Texts.Text; pos: LONGINT): Frame;
    VAR F: Frame;
BEGIN NEW(F);
    Open(F, Handle, text, pos, Display.black, left, right, top, bot, lsp);
    RETURN F
END NewText;


BEGIN
    menuH := Fonts.Default.height + 2; barW := menuH;
    left := barW + Fonts.Default.height DIV 2; right := Fonts.Default.height DIV 2;
    top := Fonts.Default.height DIV 2; bot := Fonts.Default.height DIV 2;
    asr := Fonts.Default.maxY; dsr := -Fonts.Default.minY; lsp :=
        Fonts.Default.height;
```

```
    selH := Fonts.Default.height; markW := Fonts.Default.height DIV 2;
    eolW := Fonts.Default.height DIV 2;
    Texts.OpenWriter(W); Texts.OpenWriter(KW);
    NEW(par)
END TextFrames.


MODULE Edit; (*JG 26.11.91*)

    IMPORT Files, Display, Viewers, MenuViewers, Oberon, Fonts, Texts, TextFrames,
        Printer;

    CONST
        CR = 0DX; maxlen = 32;
        StandardMenu = "System.Close System.Copy System.Grow Edit.Search
            Edit.Store";

    VAR
        W: Texts.Writer;
        time: LONGINT;
        M: INTEGER;
        pat: ARRAY maxlen OF CHAR;
        d: ARRAY 256 OF INTEGER;


    PROCEDURE Max (i, j: LONGINT): LONGINT;
    BEGIN IF i >= j THEN RETURN i ELSE RETURN j END
    END Max;


    PROCEDURE Open*;
        VAR par: Oberon.ParList;
        T: Texts.Text;
        S: Texts.Scanner;
        V: Viewers.Viewer;
        X, Y: INTEGER;
        beg, end, time: LONGINT;
    BEGIN
        par := Oberon.Par;
        Texts.OpenScanner(S, par.text, par.pos); Texts.Scan(S);
        IF (S.class = Texts.Char) & (S.c = " ↑ ") OR (S.line # 0) THEN
            Oberon.GetSelection(T, beg, end, time);
            IF time >= 0 THEN Texts.OpenScanner(S, T, beg); Texts.Scan(S) END
        END;
        IF S.class = Texts.Name THEN
            Oberon.AllocateUserViewer(par.vwr.X, X, Y);
            V := MenuViewers.New(
                TextFrames.NewMenu(S.s, StandardMenu),
                TextFrames.NewText(TextFrames.Text(S.s), 0),
                TextFrames.menuH,
                X, Y)
        END
    END Open;


    PROCEDURE Show*;
        VAR par: Oberon.ParList;
        T, t: Texts.Text;
        R: Texts.Reader;
        S: Texts.Scanner;
```

```
        V: Viewers.Viewer;
        X, Y, n, i, j: INTEGER;
        pos, len, beg, end, time: LONGINT;
        buf: ARRAY 32 OF CHAR;
        name: ARRAY 35 OF CHAR;
        M: INTEGER;
        pat: ARRAY maxlen OF CHAR;
        d: ARRAY 256 OF INTEGER;

    PROCEDURE Forward (n: INTEGER);
        VAR m: INTEGER; j: INTEGER;
    BEGIN m := M − n;
        j := 0;
        WHILE j # m DO buf[j] := buf[n + j]; INC(j) END;
        WHILE j # M DO Texts.Read(R, buf[j]); INC(j) END
    END Forward;

BEGIN
    par := Oberon.Par;
    Texts.OpenScanner(S, par.text, par.pos); Texts.Scan(S);
    IF (S.class = Texts.Char) & (S.c = " ↑ ") OR (S.line # 0) THEN
        Oberon.GetSelection(T, beg, end, time);
        IF time >= 0 THEN Texts.OpenScanner(S, T, beg); Texts.Scan(S) END
    END;
    IF S.class = Texts.Name THEN
        i := −1; j := 0;
        WHILE S.s[j] # 0X DO
            IF S.s[j] = "." THEN i := j END;
            name[j] := S.s[j]; j := j+1
        END;
        IF i < 0 THEN name[j] := "."; i := j END;
        name[i+1] := "M"; name[i+2] := "o"; name[i+3] := "d"; name[i+4] := 0X;
        t := TextFrames.Text(name);
        IF j > i THEN (*object name specified*)
            j := i+1; M := 0;
            WHILE (M # maxlen) & (S.s[j] # 0X) DO pat[M] := S.s[j]; j := j+1; M
                := M+1 END;
            j := 0;
            WHILE j # 256 DO d[j] := M; INC(j) END;
            j := 0;
            WHILE j # M − 1 DO d[ORD(pat[j])] := M − 1 − j; INC(j) END;
            pos := 0; len := t.len;
            Texts.OpenReader(R, t, pos);
            Forward(M); pos := pos + M;
            LOOP j := M;
                REPEAT DEC(j) UNTIL (j < 0) OR (buf[j] # pat[j]);
                IF (j < 0) OR (pos >= len) THEN EXIT END;
                n := d[ORD(buf[M−1])];
                Forward(n); pos := pos + n
            END
        ELSE pos := 0
        END;
        Oberon.AllocateUserViewer(par.vwr.X, X, Y);
        V := MenuViewers.New(
            TextFrames.NewMenu(name, StandardMenu),
            TextFrames.NewText(t, pos−200),
            TextFrames.menuH,
            X, Y)
```

```
            END
        END Show;


        PROCEDURE Store*;
            VAR par: Oberon.ParList;
                V: Viewers.Viewer;
                Text: TextFrames.Frame;
                T: Texts.Text;
                S: Texts.Scanner;
                f: Files.File;
                beg, end, time, len: LONGINT;


            PROCEDURE Backup (VAR name: ARRAY OF CHAR);
                VAR res, i: INTEGER; bak: ARRAY 32 OF CHAR;
            BEGIN i := 0;
                WHILE name[i] # 0X DO bak[i] := name[i]; INC(i) END;
                bak[i] := "."; bak[i+1] := "B"; bak[i+2] := "a"; bak[i+3] := "k"; bak[i+4]
                    := 0X;
                Files.Rename(name, bak, res)
            END Backup;


        BEGIN
            Texts.WriteString(W, "Edit.Store ");
            par := Oberon.Par;
            IF par.frame = par.vwr.dsc THEN
                V := par.vwr; Texts.OpenScanner(S, V.dsc(TextFrames.Frame).text, 0)
            ELSE V := Oberon.MarkedViewer(); Texts.OpenScanner(S, par.text, par.pos)
            END;
            Texts.Scan(S);
            IF (S.class = Texts.Char) & (S.c = " ↑ ") THEN
                Oberon.GetSelection(T, beg, end, time);
                IF time >= 0 THEN Texts.OpenScanner(S, T, beg); Texts.Scan(S) END
            END;
            IF (S.class = Texts.Name) & (V.dsc # NIL) & (V.dsc.next IS TextFrames.Frame)
                    THEN
                Text := V.dsc.next(TextFrames.Frame);
                TextFrames.Mark(Text, −1);
                Texts.WriteString(W, S.s); Texts.WriteLn(W);
                Texts.Append(Oberon.Log, W.buf);
                Backup(S.s);
                f := Files.New(S.s);
                Texts.Store(Text.text, f, 0, len);
                Files.Register(f);
                TextFrames.Mark(Text, 1)
            END
        END Store;


        PROCEDURE CopyFont*;
            VAR
                T: Texts.Text; R: Texts.Reader;
                V: Viewers.Viewer; F: Display.Frame;
                beg, end: LONGINT;
                X, Y: INTEGER;
                ch: CHAR;
        BEGIN
            V := Oberon.MarkedViewer(); F := V.dsc;
            X := Oberon.Pointer.X; Y := Oberon.Pointer.Y;
```

```
        LOOP
            IF F = NIL THEN EXIT END;
            IF (X >= F.X) & (X < F.X + F.W) & (Y >= F.Y) & (Y < F.Y + F.H) THEN
                IF F IS TextFrames.Frame THEN
                    WITH F: TextFrames.Frame DO
                        Texts.OpenReader(R, F.text, TextFrames.Pos(F, X, Y));
                        Texts.Read(R, ch);
                        Oberon.GetSelection(T, beg, end, time);
                        IF time >= 0 THEN Texts.ChangeLooks(T, beg, end, {0}, R.fnt, 0,
                            0) END
                    END
                END;
                EXIT
            END;
            F := F.next
        END
    END CopyFont;


    PROCEDURE ChangeFont*;
        VAR par: Oberon.ParList;
            T: Texts.Text; S: Texts.Scanner;
            beg, end: LONGINT;
    BEGIN
        Oberon.GetSelection(T, beg, end, time);
        IF time >= 0 THEN par := Oberon.Par;
            Texts.OpenScanner(S, par.text, par.pos); Texts.Scan(S);
            IF S.class = Texts.Name THEN
                Texts.ChangeLooks(T, beg, end, {0}, Fonts.This(S.s), 0, 0)
            END
        END
    END ChangeFont;


    PROCEDURE ChangeColor*;
        VAR par: Oberon.ParList;
            T: Texts.Text; S: Texts.Scanner;
            col: SHORTINT; ch: CHAR;
            beg, end, time: LONGINT;
    BEGIN par := Oberon.Par;
        Texts.OpenScanner(S, par.text, par.pos); Texts.Scan(S);
        IF S.class = Texts.Int THEN col := SHORT(SHORT(S.i))
        ELSIF (S.class = Texts.Char) & (S.c = " ↑ ") & (par.frame(TextFrames.Frame).sel
            > 0) THEN
            Texts.OpenReader(S, par.text, par.frame(TextFrames.Frame).selbeg.pos);
            Texts.Read(S, ch); col := S.col
        ELSE col := Oberon.CurCol
        END ;
        Oberon.GetSelection(T, beg, end, time);
        IF time >= 0 THEN Texts.ChangeLooks(T, beg, end, {1}, NIL, col, 0) END
    END ChangeColor;


    PROCEDURE ChangeOffset*;
        VAR par: Oberon.ParList;
            T: Texts.Text; S: Texts.Scanner;
            voff: SHORTINT; ch: CHAR;
            beg, end, time: LONGINT;
    BEGIN par := Oberon.Par;
        Texts.OpenScanner(S, par.text, par.pos); Texts.Scan(S);IF S.class = Texts.Int
            THEN voff := SHORT(SHORT(S.i))
```

```
        ELSIF (S.class = Texts.Char) & (S.c = " ↑ ") & (par.frame(TextFrames.Frame).sel
            > 0) THEN
            Texts.OpenReader(S, par.text, par.frame(TextFrames.Frame).selbeg.pos);
            Texts.Read(S, ch); voff := S.voff
        ELSE voff := Oberon.CurOff
        END ;
        Oberon.GetSelection(T, beg, end, time);
        IF time >= 0 THEN Texts.ChangeLooks(T, beg, end, {2}, NIL, voff, 0) END
    END ChangeOffset;


    PROCEDURE Search*;
        VAR V: Viewers.Viewer;
            Text: TextFrames.Frame;
            T: Texts.Text; R: Texts.Reader;
            pos, beg, end, prevTime, len: LONGINT; n, i, j: INTEGER;
            buf: ARRAY 32 OF CHAR;


        PROCEDURE Forward (n: INTEGER);
            VAR m: INTEGER; j: INTEGER;
        BEGIN m := M − n;
            j := 0;
            WHILE j # m DO buf[j] := buf[n + j]; INC(j) END;
            WHILE j # M DO Texts.Read(R, buf[j]); INC(j) END
        END Forward;


    BEGIN
        V := Oberon.Par.vwr;
        IF Oberon.Par.frame # V.dsc THEN V := Oberon.MarkedViewer() END;
        IF (V.dsc # NIL) & (V.dsc.next IS TextFrames.Frame) THEN
            Text := V.dsc.next(TextFrames.Frame);
            TextFrames.Mark(Text, −1);
            prevTime := time; Oberon.GetSelection(T, beg, end, time);
            IF time > prevTime THEN
                Texts.OpenReader(R, T, beg);
                i := 0; pos := beg;
                REPEAT Texts.Read(R, pat[i]); INC(i); INC(pos)
                UNTIL (i = maxlen) OR (pos = end);
                M := i;
                j := 0;
                WHILE j # 256 DO d[j] := M; INC(j) END;
                j := 0;
                WHILE j # M − 1 DO d[ORD(pat[j])] := M − 1 − j; INC(j) END
            END;
            IF Text.car > 0 THEN pos := Text.carloc.pos ELSE pos := 0 END;
            len := Text.text.len;
            Texts.OpenReader(R, Text.text, pos);
            Forward(M); pos := pos + M;
            LOOP j := M;
                REPEAT DEC(j) UNTIL (j < 0) OR (buf[j] # pat[j]);
                IF (j < 0) OR (pos >= len) THEN EXIT END;
                n := d[ORD(buf[M−1])];
                Forward(n); pos := pos + n
            END;
            IF j < 0 THEN
                TextFrames.RemoveSelection(Text);
                TextFrames.RemoveCaret(Text);
                Oberon.RemoveMarks(Text.X, Text.Y, Text.W, Text.H);
```

```
                    TextFrames.Show(Text, pos − 200);
                    Oberon.PassFocus(V);
                    TextFrames.SetCaret(Text, pos)
                END;
                TextFrames.Mark(Text, 1)
        END
    END Search;

    PROCEDURE Locate*;
        VAR V: Viewers.Viewer;
            Text: TextFrames.Frame;
            T: Texts.Text; S: Texts.Scanner;
            beg, end, time: LONGINT;
    BEGIN
        V := Oberon.MarkedViewer();
        IF (V.dsc # NIL) & (V.dsc.next IS TextFrames.Frame) THEN
            Text := V.dsc.next(TextFrames.Frame);
            Oberon.GetSelection(T, beg, end, time);
            IF time >= 0 THEN
                Texts.OpenScanner(S, T, beg);
                REPEAT Texts.Scan(S) UNTIL (S.class >= Texts.Int); (*skip names*)
                IF S.class = Texts.Int THEN
                    TextFrames.RemoveSelection(Text);
                    TextFrames.RemoveCaret(Text);
                    Oberon.RemoveMarks(Text.X, Text.Y, Text.W, Text.H);
                    TextFrames.Show(Text, Max(0, S.i − 200));
                    Oberon.PassFocus(V);
                    TextFrames.SetCaret(Text, S.i)
                END
            END
        END
    END Locate;


    PROCEDURE Recall*;
        VAR V: Viewers.Viewer;
            Menu, Main: Display.Frame;
            buf: Texts.Buffer;
            pos: LONGINT;
    BEGIN V := Oberon.FocusViewer;
        IF V IS MenuViewers.Viewer THEN
            Menu := V.dsc; Main := V.dsc.next;
            IF (Main IS TextFrames.Frame) & (Main(TextFrames.Frame).car > 0) THEN
                WITH Main: TextFrames.Frame DO
                    Texts.Recall(buf);
                    pos := Main.carloc.pos + buf.len;
                    Texts.Insert(Main.text, Main.carloc.pos, buf);
                    TextFrames.SetCaret(Main, pos)
                END
            ELSIF (Menu IS TextFrames.Frame) & (Menu(TextFrames.Frame).car > 0)
                THEN
                WITH Menu: TextFrames.Frame DO
                    Texts.Recall(buf);
                    pos := Menu.carloc.pos + buf.len;
                    Texts.Insert(Menu.text, Menu.carloc.pos, buf);
                    TextFrames.SetCaret(Menu, pos)
                END
            END
        END
```

END Recall;

PROCEDURE **Print***;

    CONST
        textX = 160; textY = 225; botY = 100;

    VAR
        par: Oberon.ParList;
        V: Viewers.Viewer;
        Menu, Text: TextFrames.Frame;
        T, source: Texts.Text;
        R: Texts.Reader; S: Texts.Scanner;
        fnt: Fonts.Font;
        id, ch: CHAR;
        pageno: SHORTINT; listing: BOOLEAN;
        nofcopies, len, lsp, Y, topY: INTEGER;
        beg, end, time: LONGINT;

    PROCEDURE SendHeader;
        VAR pno: ARRAY 4 OF CHAR;
    BEGIN Printer.String(textX, Printer.PageHeight−125, S.s, Fonts.Default.name);
        IF pageno DIV 10 = 0 THEN pno[0] := " " ELSE pno[0] := CHR(pageno
            DIV 10 + 30H) END ;
        pno[1] := CHR(pageno MOD 10 + 30H); pno[2] := 0X;
        Printer.String(Printer.PageWidth−236, Printer.PageHeight−125, pno,
            Fonts.Default.name)
    END SendHeader;

    PROCEDURE PrintUnit (source: Texts.Text; pos: LONGINT);
        VAR i: INTEGER; new: BOOLEAN;
            buf: ARRAY 200 OF CHAR;
    BEGIN Texts.WriteString(W, S.s);
      IF source.len # 0 THEN
        Texts.WriteString(W, " printing"); Texts.WriteInt(W, nofcopies, 3);
        Texts.Append(Oberon.Log, W.buf);
        lsp := Fonts.Default.height * 7 DIV 2; pageno := 0;
        SendHeader; Y := topY;
        Texts.OpenReader(R, source, pos);
        IF ~listing THEN
            REPEAT Texts.Read(R, ch);
                new := TRUE; fnt := R.fnt;
                WHILE ~R.eot & (ch # CR) DO
                    i := 0;
                    REPEAT buf[i] := ch; INC(i); Texts.Read(R, ch)
                    UNTIL R.eot OR (ch = CR) OR (R.fnt # fnt);
                    buf[i] := 0X;
                    IF new THEN Printer.String(textX, Y, buf, fnt.name)
                      ELSE Printer.ContString(buf, fnt.name)
                    END;
                    new := FALSE; fnt := R.fnt
                END;
                Y := Y − lsp;
                IF Y < botY THEN
                  Printer.Page(nofcopies); INC(pageno); SendHeader; Y := topY
                END
            UNTIL R.eot

```
            ELSE lsp := 32;
                REPEAT Texts.Read(R, ch);
                    WHILE ~R.eot & (ch # CR) DO
                        i := 0;
                        REPEAT buf[i] := ch; INC(i); Texts.Read(R, ch)
                        UNTIL R.eot OR (ch = CR);
                        buf[i] := 0X;
                        Printer.String(textX, Y, buf, Fonts.Default.name)
                    END;
                    Y := Y - lsp;
                    IF Y < botY THEN
                        Printer.Page(nofcopies); INC(pageno); SendHeader; Y := topY
                    END
                UNTIL R.eot
            END;
            IF Y < topY THEN Printer.Page(nofcopies) END
        ELSE Texts.WriteString(W, " not found")
        END;
        Texts.WriteLn(W);
        Texts.Append(Oberon.Log, W.buf)
    END PrintUnit;


    PROCEDURE Option;
        VAR ch: CHAR;
    BEGIN nofcopies := 1;
        IF S.nextCh = "/" THEN
            Texts.Read(S, ch);
            IF (ch >= "0") & (ch <= "9") THEN nofcopies := ORD(ch) - 30H END
            ;
            WHILE ch > " " DO Texts.Read(S, ch) END;
            S.nextCh := ch
        END
    END Option;


BEGIN par := Oberon.Par;
    Texts.WriteString(W, "Edit.Print"); Texts.WriteLn(W);
        Texts.Append(Oberon.Log, W.buf);
    Texts.OpenScanner(S, par.text, par.pos); Texts.Scan(S);
    IF S.class = Texts.Name THEN
        Printer.Open(S.s, Oberon.User, Oberon.Password);
        IF Printer.res = 0 THEN
            topY := Printer.PageHeight - textY; Texts.Scan(S);
            IF (S.class = Texts.Char) & (S.c = "%") THEN
                listing := TRUE; Printer.UseListFont(Fonts.Default.name);
                    Texts.Scan(S)
            ELSE listing := FALSE
            END;
            IF (S.class = Texts.Char) & (S.c = "*") THEN
                Option; V := Oberon.MarkedViewer();
                IF (V.dsc IS TextFrames.Frame) & (V.dsc.next IS TextFrames.Frame)
                    THEN
                    Menu := V.dsc(TextFrames.Frame); Text :=
                        V.dsc.next(TextFrames.Frame);
                    Texts.OpenScanner(S, Menu.text, 0); Texts.Scan(S);
                    TextFrames.Mark(Text, -1); PrintUnit(Text.text, 0);
                        TextFrames.Mark(Text, 1)
                END
            ELSE
```

```
            WHILE S.class = Texts.Name DO
               Option; NEW(source); Texts.Open(source, S.s); PrintUnit(source,
                  0);
               Texts.Scan(S)
            END;
            IF (S.class = Texts.Char) & (S.c = " ↑ ") THEN Oberon.GetSelection(T,
               beg, end, time);
               IF time >= 0 THEN Texts.OpenScanner(S, T, beg); Texts.Scan(S);
                  IF S.class = Texts.Name THEN
                     Option; NEW(source); Texts.Open(source, S.s);
                        PrintUnit(source, 0)
                  END
               END
            END
         END;
         Printer.Close
      ELSE
         IF Printer.res = 1 THEN Texts.WriteString(W, " no printer")
            ELSIF Printer.res = 2 THEN Texts.WriteString(W, " no link")
            ELSIF Printer.res = 3 THEN Texts.WriteString(W, " printer not
               ready")
            ELSIF Printer.res = 4 THEN Texts.WriteString(W, " no permission")
         END;
         Texts.WriteLn(W); Texts.Append(Oberon.Log, W.buf)
      END
   ELSE Texts.WriteString(W, " no printer specified");
      Texts.WriteLn(W); Texts.Append(Oberon.Log, W.buf)
   END
END Print;


PROCEDURE InitPattern;
   VAR j: INTEGER;
BEGIN
   pat[0] := " "; M := 1; time := −1; j := 0;
   WHILE j # 256 DO d[j] := M; INC(j) END
END InitPattern;


BEGIN Texts.OpenWriter(W); InitPattern
END Edit.
```

6 The module loader

6.1 Linking and loading

When the execution of a command M.P is requested, module M containing procedure P must be loaded, unless it is already loaded because a command of the same module had been executed earlier or the module had been imported by another module before. Modules are available in the form of so-called object files, generated by the compiler (or the assembler). The term *loading* refers to the transfer of the module code from the file into main store, from where the processor fetches individual instructions. This transfer involves also a certain amount of transformation as required by the object file format on the one hand and the storage layout on the other. A system typically consists of many modules, and hence loading modules also involves linking them together, in particular linking them with already-loaded modules. Before loading, references to another module's objects are relative to the base address of this module; the linking or binding process converts them into absolute addresses.

The linking process may require a significant amount of address computations. But they are simple enough and, if the data are organized in an appropriate way, can be executed very swiftly. Nevertheless, and surprisingly, in many operating systems linking needs more time than compilation. The remedy offered by system designers is a separation of linking from loading. A set of compiled modules is first linked; the result is a linked object file with absolute addresses. The loader then merely transfers the object file into main store.

We consider this an unfortunate proposal. Instead of trying to cure an inadequacy with the aid of an additional processing stage and an additional tool, it is wiser to cure the malady at its core, namely to speed up the linking process itself. Indeed, there is no separate linker in the Oberon system. The linker and loader are integrated and fast enough to avoid any desire for pre-linking. Furthermore, the extensibility of a system crucially depends on the possibility to link additional modules to the ones already loaded by calls from any module. This is

Dynamic loading

called *dynamic loading*. This is not possible with pre-linked object files. Newly loaded modules simply refer to the loaded ones, whereas pre-linked files lead to the presence of multiple copies of the same module code.

Evidently, the essence of linking is the conversion of relative addresses as generated by the compiler for all external references into absolute addresses as required during program execution. There exist two different strategies for this task.

Linking methods

(1) External references are directly patched in the code. The object file contains a list of the locations of all external references. It is called the *fixup list*.

(2) A separate link table is provided with external references to be converted. The actual references within the program code directly refer to these table entries, and only indirectly to the objects.

The advantage of the first strategy is execution speed, because all external references are direct during program execution. The advantage of the second strategy is an expedient linking process, because there are far fewer conversions to be performed – instead of one for every reference, only one for every referenced object. A further advantage is that no fixup list is required; the entire compiled code remains untouched. Also, code density is significantly increased: an external address in the code is an index to the table (typically 8 bits) rather than a full address (typically 32 bits). A slight disadvantage is, of course, the need for a (short) link table.

Before proceeding, we must consider an additional complication. Assume that a module B is to be compiled that is a client of (that is, it imports) module A. The interface of A – in the form of a *symbol file*

Symbol file

– does not specify the entry addresses of its exported procedures, but merely specifies a unique number (pno) for each one of them. The reason for this is that in this way the implementation of A may be modified, causing a change of entry addresses without affecting its interface specification. And this is a crucial property of the scheme of separate compilation of modules: changes of the implementation of A must not necessitate the recompilation of clients (B). The consequence is that the binding of entry addresses to procedure numbers must be performed by the linker. In order to make this possible, the object file

Entry table

must contain a list (table) of its entry addresses, one for each procedure number used as index to the table.

Import table

Similarly, the object file must contain a table of imported modules, containing their names. An external reference in the program code then appears in the form of a pair consisting of a module number (mno), used as index to the import table (of modules), and a procedure number (pno), used as index to the entry table of this module.

Such linkage information must not only be provided in each

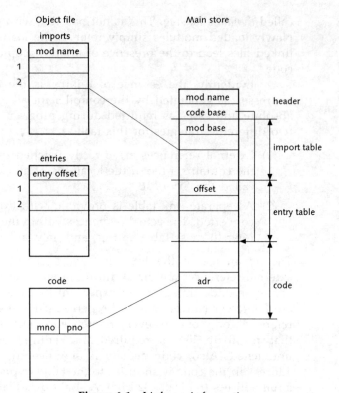

Figure 6.1 Linkage information.

object file, but also be present along with each loaded module's program code, because a module to be loaded must be linkable with modules loaded at any earlier time without reading their object files again. The linkage tables contained in the file and in main store are shown in Figure 6.1.

In the linking process, first the import table in the file (containing module names) is transformed into the internal import table containing the addresses of the respective modules. Then the entry offsets are merely copied. And finally, the code is loaded and address computations are performed either at every location of the link table (strategy 2) or at every location in the code specified by the fixup list (strategy 1). The resulting (absolute) address of a procedure specified by *mno* and *pno* is

$$adr = imptab[mno] \uparrow .codebase + imptab[mno] \uparrow .entry[pno]$$

The module name must be available for each module, because it is needed by the loader for the searches conducted during the construction of the import table. Procedure names are not needed, since they have been transformed by the compiler into numbers unique for each module.

For external references to variables, the same scheme might be used, namely identifying each exported variable by an entry number (vno). The expression for its absolute address would then be given by

$$adr = imptab[mno] \uparrow .varbase + imptab[mno] \uparrow .entry[vno].$$

However, this is usually not done. Instead, the variable's offset is directly specified in the code. The variable's absolute address is computed as

$$adr = imptab[mno] \uparrow .varbase + offset$$

The drawback is that modifications of a module that change a variable's address require recompilation of all clients (because the symbol file contains the offset). This drawback is slight in practice, since exported variables are rare and are declared at the beginning of the program text. Additions or deletions of non-exported variables have no influence on the exported information.

6.2 Module representation in the Oberon system

Our choice has been to use strategy 2 for handling external references. This can be justified only if the underlying hardware reduces the inherent loss in efficiency by adequate support in the form of addressing modes, and if thereby the gain in code density is significant. When using the NS32000 architecture, these requirements are satisfied; in particular, this architecture features a code density that is higher than most other processor's by a factor of 1.5–2.5.

Tests with an alternative compiler and loader, using strategy 1 and absolute addresses for external references, produced code that was 15% longer on the average. In extreme cases with a larger number of external calls (using 6 instead of 2 bytes of code), the length increased by as much as 20%. Surprisingly, the data about speedup remained inconclusive.

Before proceeding, we present the layout of module information as defined by the NS32000 processor's external addressing mode.

Module descriptor

Module block

Every module has an associated module descriptor. It contains three pointers (base addresses), referring respectively to the module's data section (sb), link table (lb) and code (pb), all of which are part of the *module block*. In order to accelerate cross-module access, two processor registers are provided. Register MOD points to the descriptor

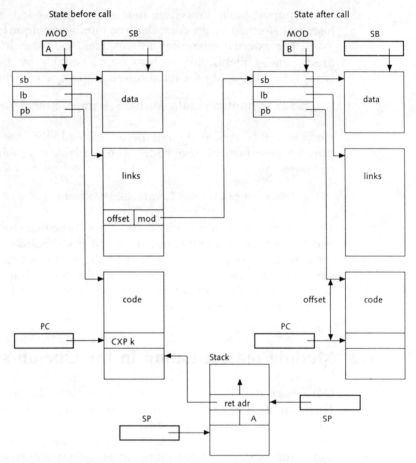

Figure 6.2 Module layout and external procedure call of the NS32000 processor.

of the module currently under control, and register SB (static base) points to its data section. These registers must be updated in every external procedure call and on its return, that is, whenever control passes from one module to another. The process of a call is shown in Figure 6.2. It is initiated by a CXP k instruction. k is the index of the link table entry of the called procedure. At the left we show the various parts of the calling module A, and at the right those of the module containing the called procedure.

The transition from the calling to the called context can be described by the following sequence of microcode statements (pd is to be considered as a temporary variable):

CXP:pd := M[M[MOD].lb + 4k];   (* procedure descriptor*)
    SP := SP-4; M[SP] := MOD;   (* stack pointer*)
    SP := SP-4; M[SP] := PC;
    MOD := pd.mod   (* module pointer*)
    PC := M[MOD].pb + pd.offset (* program counter*)
    SB := M[MOD].sb;   (* static base*)

The microcode for a procedure return is

RXP:PC := M[SP]; SP := SP + 4;
    MOD := M[SP]; SP := SP + 4;
    SB := M[MOD].sb

From these programs it can be seen that a procedure call involves 6 and a return 3 memory references, which is quite considerable. Code density, however, is also remarkable: 2 bytes for call and return each. We may compare the above program sections with the corresponding ones for the BSR and RET instructions, which are used for calls of local procedures, where no module context switch occurs. It is evident that, whenever possible, these simpler instructions should be used.

BSR: SP := SP-4; M[SP] := PC
        PC := PC + m

RET: PC := M[SP]; SP := SP+4

m is a parameter specifying the procedure's offset. Both instructions require a single memory reference only. They correspond to the typical subroutine call mechanism present in most processors.

From the preceding presentation, we conclude that a module block consists of three parts accessed during program execution – the code, the global data and the link table – and two parts accessed by the loader while linking additional modules – the import and the entry tables. Furthermore, there exists a descriptor with the addresses of the three primary parts, and it is logical to augment it with two pointers referring to the import and entry tables.

Note that the descriptor is disjoint from the block, because the MOD register has only 16 bits and hence the descriptor must be stored within the address range 0...0FFFFH.

Pointer
offset table

In fact, the module block in the Oberon System contains two additional parts, namely a table of pointer offsets and a table of

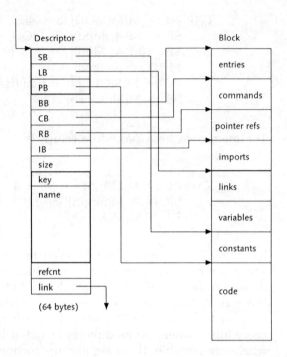

Figure 6.3   Module descriptor and associated block.

commands. The *pointer offsets* are used by the garbage collector. The table contains an entry for each global pointer variable specifying its offset in the data section. Global pointer variables are typically the roots of data structures and therefore serve as starting points of the mark phase in the garbage collection process (see Chapter 8).

Command table
The *command table* is accessed when a command is selected in some text by the user. The command's identifier must be transformed into an entry address, and this is achieved by a lookup in the module's command table. Each entry consists of the identifier followed by the offset. The same offsets also occur in the entry table.

Both the pointer offset table and the command table must have their counterparts in the object file. The loader merely copies them into the block. Pointers to both tables are added to the descriptor, which can now be described in full by the following record declaration (see also Figure 6.3).

```
ModDesc = RECORD
            SB, LB, PB, BB, CB, RB, IB, size, key:
            LONGINT;
            -name: ModName;
```

```
                 refcnt: LONGINT;
                 link: Module
       END;
    Module = POINTER TO ModDesc
```

6.3 The linking loader

The loader is represented by procedure *ThisMod* in module *Modules*. This procedure accepts a name and returns a pointer to the specified module's descriptor. It first scans the list of descriptors for the named module. If it is not present, the module is loaded and added to the list.

When loading, the header of the respective object file is read first. It specifies the required size of the block. Both descriptor and block are allocated by procedure *Kernel.AllocBlock*. First, the header indicating the lengths of the various sections of the load file and then the import section is read. For each import, procedure *ThisMod* is called recursively. Because cyclic imports are excluded, recursion always terminates. After the loading of the imports, loading of the client proceeds by allocating a descriptor and a block, and then reading the remaining sections of the file. Each module is identified by its descriptor's address.

The link section contains two kinds of elements, both denoted by two integers *mno* and *pno*. The majority stands for procedures. The loader transforms the *mno*, *pno* pairs (module and procedure numbers) of the file's entry section into the respective procedure descriptors consisting of module descriptor address and entry offset. The second kind of element denotes base addresses of a module's data section. They are identified by a special value of pno (-1).

After the module has been loaded successfully, its initialization body is executed. The corresponding procedure descriptor consist of the module (descriptor) address and an offset of zero.

```
MODULE Modules; (*NW 16.2.86 / 7.4.91*)
  IMPORT SYSTEM, Kernel, FileDir, Files;

  CONST ModNameLen* = 20; ObjMark = 0F8X; Maximps = 32;
  TYPE Module* = POINTER TO ModDesc;
    Command* = PROCEDURE;
    ModuleName* = ARRAY ModNameLen OF CHAR;

    ModDesc* = RECORD SB*, LB*, PB*, BB*, CB*, RB*, IB*, size*, key*: LONGINT;
      name*: ModuleName;
      refcnt*: LONGINT;
      link*: Module
    END;
```

```
VAR res*: INTEGER;
    importing*, imported*: ModuleName;
    loop: Command;

PROCEDURE ReadName(VAR R: Files.Rider; VAR s: ARRAY OF CHAR; n: INTEGER);
    VAR ch: CHAR; i: INTEGER;
BEGIN i := 0;
    REPEAT Files.Read(R, ch); s[i] := ch; INC(i)
    UNTIL ch = 0X;
    WHILE i < n DO Files.Read(R, ch); s[i] := 0X; INC(i) END
END ReadName;


PROCEDURE OpenFile(VAR F: Files.File; VAR name: ARRAY OF CHAR);
    VAR i: INTEGER; ch: CHAR;
        Fname: ARRAY 32 OF CHAR;
BEGIN i := 0; ch := name[0]; (*make file name*)
    WHILE ch > 0X DO Fname[i] := ch; INC(i); ch := name[i] END ;
    Fname[i] := "."; Fname[i+1] := "O"; Fname[i+2] := "b"; Fname[i+3] := "j";
    Fname[i+4] := 0X;
    F := Files.Old(Fname)
END OpenFile;


PROCEDURE PD(mod: Module; pc: LONGINT): LONGINT;
BEGIN (*procedure descriptor*)
    RETURN ASH(pc, 16) + SYSTEM.VAL(LONGINT, mod)
END PD;


PROCEDURE ThisMod*(name: ARRAY OF CHAR): Module;
    (*search module in list; if not found, load module*)


    VAR
        mod, impmod, md: Module;
        ch: CHAR; mno, pno: SHORTINT;
        i, j: INTEGER;
        nofentries, nofimps, nofptrs, comsize, noflinks, constsize, codesize: INTEGER;
        varsize, size, key, impkey, k, p, q, pos1, pos2: LONGINT;
        init: Command;
        F: Files.File; R: Files.Rider;
        modname, impname: ModuleName;
        Fname: ARRAY FileDir.FnLength OF CHAR;
        import: ARRAY 16 OF Module;


    PROCEDURE err(n: INTEGER);
    BEGIN
        IF res = 0 THEN res := n; COPY(name, imported) END
    END err;


BEGIN res := 0; mod := SYSTEM.VAL(Module, Kernel.ModList);
    LOOP
        IF name = mod.name THEN EXIT END ;
        mod := mod.link;
        IF mod = NIL THEN EXIT END
    END;
    IF mod = NIL THEN (*load*)
        OpenFile(F, name);
        IF F # NIL THEN
```

```
Files.Set(R, F, 0); Files.Read(R, ch); (*header*)
IF ch # ObjMark THEN err(2); RETURN NIL END ;
Files.Read(R, ch);
IF ch # "6" THEN err(2); RETURN NIL END ;
Files.ReadBytes(R, k, 4);   (*skip*)
Files.ReadBytes(R, nofentries, 2); Files.ReadBytes(R, comsize, 2);
Files.ReadBytes(R, nofptrs, 2); Files.ReadBytes(R, nofimps, 2);
Files.ReadBytes(R, noflinks, 2); Files.ReadBytes(R, varsize, 4);
Files.ReadBytes(R, constsize, 2); Files.ReadBytes(R, codesize, 2);
Files.ReadBytes(R, key, 4); ReadName(R, modname, ModNameLen);
i := (nofentries + nofptrs)*2 + comsize;
pos1 := Files.Pos(R); Files.Set(R, F, pos1 + i + 3);
INC(i, nofimps*2); k := (i MOD 4) + i;
(*imports*) Files.Read(R, ch); i:=0;
IF ch # 85X THEN err(4); RETURN NIL END ;
IF nofimps > maximps THEN err(6); RETURN NIL END;
WHILE (i < nofimps) & (res = 0) DO
    Files.ReadBytes(R, impkey, 4); ReadName(R, impname, 0); Files.Read(R, ch);
    impmod := ThisMod(impname);
    IF res = 0 THEN
        IF impmod.key = impkey THEN import[i] := impmod; INC(i);
            INC(impmod.refcnt)
        ELSE res := 3; imported := impname; importing := modname
        END
    END
END ;
IF res # 0 THEN
    WHILE i > 0 DO DEC(i); DEC(import[i].refcnt) END ;
    RETURN NIL
END ;


pos2 := Files.Pos(R);
size := k + noflinks*4 + constsize + codesize + varsize;
Kernel.AllocBlock(q, p, size); mod := SYSTEM.VAL(Module, q);
IF p = NIL THEN err(7); RETURN NIL END;
mod.size := size;
mod.BB := p;
mod.CB := nofentries*2 + p;
mod.RB := comsize + mod.CB;
mod.IB := nofptrs*2 + mod.RB;
mod.LB := k + p;
mod.SB := (noflinks*4 + varsize) + mod.LB;
mod.PB := constsize + mod.SB;
mod.refcnt := 0;
mod.key := key;
mod.name := modname;


(*entries*) q := mod.CB; Files.Set(R, F, pos1); Files.Read(R, ch);
IF ch # 82X THEN err(4); RETURN NIL END ;
WHILE p < q DO Files.Read(R, ch); SYSTEM.PUT(p, ch); INC(p) END ;


(*commands*) q := mod.RB; Files.Read(R, ch);
IF ch # 83X THEN err(4); RETURN NIL END ;
WHILE p < q DO Files.Read(R, ch); SYSTEM.PUT(p, ch); INC(p) END ;


(*pointer references*) q := mod.IB; Files.Read(R, ch);
IF ch # 84X THEN err(4); RETURN NIL END ;
```

```
              WHILE p < q DO Files.Read(R, ch); SYSTEM.PUT(p, ch); INC(p) END ;

              i := 0;
              WHILE i < nofimps DO SYSTEM.PUT(p, import[i]); INC(p, 2); INC(i) END ;

              (*links*) Files.Set(R, F, pos2+1); p := mod.LB; q := noflinks*4 + p;
              WHILE p < q DO
                 Files.Read(R, pno); Files.Read(R, mno);
                 IF mno > 0 THEN md := import[mno-1] ELSE md := mod END ;
                 IF pno = -1 THEN SYSTEM.PUT(p, md.SB)  (*data segment entry*)
                 ELSE SYSTEM.GET(pno*2 + md.BB, i);
                    SYSTEM.PUT(p, PD(md, i))  (*procedure entry*)
                 END ;
                 INC(p, 4)
              END ;

              (*variables*) q := mod.SB;
              WHILE p < q DO SYSTEM.PUT(p, 0); INC(p) END ;

              (*constants*) q := mod.PB; Files.Read(R, ch);
              IF ch # 87X THEN err(4); RETURN NIL END ;
              WHILE p < q DO Files.Read(R, ch); SYSTEM.PUT(p, ch); INC(p) END ;

              (*code*) q := p + codesize; Files.Read(R, ch);
              IF ch # 88X THEN err(4); RETURN NIL END ;
              WHILE p < q DO Files.Read(R, ch); SYSTEM.PUT(p, ch); INC(p) END ;

              (*type descriptors*) Files.Read(R, ch);
              IF ch # 89X THEN err(4); RETURN NIL END ;
              LOOP Files.ReadBytes(R, i, 2);
                 IF R.eof OR (i MOD 100H = 8AH) THEN EXIT END ;
                 Files.ReadBytes(R, j, 2);   (*adr*)
                 SYSTEM.NEW(md, i);
                 p := SYSTEM.VAL(LONGINT, md); q := p + i;
                 REPEAT Files.Read(R, ch); SYSTEM.PUT(p, ch); INC(p) UNTIL p = q;
                 SYSTEM.PUT(mod.SB + j, md)
              END ;

              init := SYSTEM.VAL(Command, mod); init; res := 0;

          ELSE COPY(name, imported); err(1)
          END
        END ;
        RETURN mod
     END ThisMod;

  PROCEDURE ThisCommand*(mod: Module; name: ARRAY OF CHAR): Command;
     VAR i: INTEGER; ch: CHAR;
        comadr: LONGINT; com: Command;
  BEGIN com := NIL;
     IF mod # NIL THEN
        comadr := mod.CB; res := 5;
        LOOP SYSTEM.GET(comadr, ch); INC(comadr);
           IF ch = 0X THEN (*not found*) EXIT END ;
           i := 0;
           LOOP
```

```
            IF ch # name[i] THEN EXIT END ;
            INC(i);
            IF ch = 0X THEN res := 0; EXIT END ;
            SYSTEM.GET(comadr, ch); INC(comadr)
         END ;
         IF res = 0 THEN (*match*)
            SYSTEM.GET(comadr, i); com := SYSTEM.VAL(Command, PD(mod, i)); EXIT
         ELSE
            WHILE ch > 0X DO SYSTEM.GET(comadr, ch); INC(comadr) END ;
            INC(comadr, 2)
         END
      END
   END ;
   RETURN com
END ThisCommand;


PROCEDURE unload(mod: Module; all: BOOLEAN);
   VAR p: LONGINT; k: INTEGER;
      imp: Module;
BEGIN p := mod.IB;
   WHILE p < mod.LB DO   (*scan imports*)
      SYSTEM.GET(p, k); imp := SYSTEM.VAL(Module, LONG(k));
      IF imp # NIL THEN
         DEC(imp.refcnt);
         IF all & (imp.refcnt = 0) THEN unload(imp, all) END
      END ;
      INC(p, 2)
   END ;
   Kernel.FreeBlock(SYSTEM.VAL(LONGINT, mod))
END unload;


PROCEDURE Free*(name: ARRAY OF CHAR; all: BOOLEAN);
   VAR mod: Module;
BEGIN mod := SYSTEM.VAL(Module, Kernel.ModList);
   LOOP
      IF mod = NIL THEN res := 1; EXIT END ;
      IF name = mod.name THEN
         IF mod.refcnt = 0 THEN unload(mod, all); res := 0 ELSE res := 2 END ;
         EXIT
      END ;
      mod := mod.link
   END
END Free;


BEGIN
   IF F Kernel.err = 0 THEN loop := ThisCommand(ThisMod("Oberon"), "Loop") END ;
   loop
END Modules.
```

The frequent use of the low-level procedures *SYSTEM.GET* and *SYSTEM.PUT* is easily justified in base modules such as the loader or device drivers. After all, here data are transferred into untyped main storage.

The object file consists of several sections, each of which is headed by an identification byte (see Section 6.5). These bytes are used as a check against corrupted files. A mismatch between read and expected check byte leads to an abortion of the loading process. The cause of the termination is recorded in the global variable *res* with the following values:

0 loading completed
1 object file not available
2 referenced file is not an object file or is of wrong version
3 key mismatch
4 corrupted object file
5 command not found
6 too many imports
7 no space

When an error is detected, the names of the modules involved are recorded in the (exported) variables *imported* and *importing*.

Procedure *ThisCommand* yields the procedure descriptor for the specified command by performing a linear search of the specified module's command table.

Unloading modules

When a module is no longer needed, it should be possible to unload it; and when it is to be replaced by a new, perhaps corrected version, it *must* be unloaded. Obviously, in a hierarchy of modules, no module must be removed before its clients are removed. A procedure for unloading must therefore ensure that no clients exist.

For this purpose, each module descriptor is given a reference count. The field *refcnt* is initialized to zero when a module is loaded, and incremented each time the module is imported by a newly loaded client. Procedure *Free* checks whether or not this count is zero. Its parameter *all* indicates whether only the specified module is to be unloaded, or the process is to be transitive, that is, applied to all its imports too. Hence *Free*, or rather the local procedure *unload*, is recursive. We emphasize that unloading is never automatic, but must be explicitly requested by the system's user. The global variable *res* records the result of unloading:

0 unloading completed
1 module is not loaded
2 cannot be unloaded, because clients exist

Unloading a module is a tricky operation. One must make sure that no references to the unloaded module exist in the remaining modules and data structures. Unfortunately, this is not at all easy, and is not guaranteed in the Oberon System. The violating culprits are procedure variables. If a procedure of a module A is assigned to a variable of a module B, and if A is unloaded, the procedure variable holds a dangling reference to the unloaded module's code block. In systems with virtual addressing (Ceres-1 and Ceres-2), the problem is solved by never reusing code addresses, that is, by strictly sequential allocation in virtual address space. A dangling reference then points to a not allocated page, causing an address (NIL) trap when used. The situation is unsatisfactory, however, when code space is reused (Ceres-3).

6.4 The toolbox of the loader

User commands directed to the loader are contained in module *System*. The box comprises the following three commands:

    System.ShowModules
    System.ShowCommands modname
    System.Free {modname} ~

The first command opens a viewer and provides a list of all loaded modules. The list indicates the block length and the number of clients importing a module (the reference count). *System.ShowCommands* opens a viewer and lists the commands provided by the specified module. The commands are prefixed by the module name, and hence can immediately be activated by a mouse click. *System.Free* is called in order to remove modules either to regain storage space or to replace a module by a newly compiled version.

```
PROCEDURE ShowModules*;
   VAR T: Texts.Text;
      V: Viewers.Viewer;
      M: Modules.Module;
      X, Y: INTEGER;
BEGIN T := TextFrames.Text("");
   Oberon.AllocateSystemViewer(Oberon.Par.vwr.X, X, Y);
   logV := MenuViewers.New(TextFrames.NewMenu("System.ShowModules", StandardMenu),
      TextFrames.NewText(T, 0), TextFrames.menuH, X, Y);
   M := SYSTEM.VAL(Modules.Module, Kernel.ModList);
   WHILE M # NIL DO
      Texts.WriteString(W, M.name); Texts.WriteInt(W, M.size, 8);
      Texts.WriteInt(W, M.refcnt, 4); Texts.WriteLn(W); M := M.link
   END;
   Texts.Append(T, W.buf)
END ShowModules;


PROCEDURE ShowCommands*;
   VAR M: Modules.Module;
      comadr, beg, end, time: LONGINT; ch: CHAR;
      T: Texts.Text;
      S: Texts.Scanner;
      V: Viewers.Viewer;
      X, Y: INTEGER;
BEGIN Texts.OpenScanner(S, Oberon.Par.text, Oberon.Par.pos); Texts.Scan(S);
```

```
        IF (S.class = Texts.Char) & (S.c = " ↑ ") THEN
            Oberon.GetSelection(T, beg, end, time);
            IF time >= 0 THEN Texts.OpenScanner(S, T, beg); Texts.Scan(S) END
        END ;
        IF S.class = Texts.Name THEN
            M := Modules.ThisMod(S.s);
            IF M # NIL THEN comadr := M.CB;
                Oberon.AllocateSystemViewer(Oberon.Par.vwr.X, X, Y); T := TextFrames.Text("");
                V := MenuViewers.New(TextFrames.NewMenu("System.Commands", StandardMenu),
                    TextFrames.NewText(T, 0), TextFrames.menuH, X, Y);
                LOOP SYSTEM.GET(comadr, ch); INC(comadr);
                    IF ch = 0X THEN EXIT END ;
                    Texts.WriteString(W, S.s); Texts.Write(W, ".");
                    REPEAT Texts.Write(W, ch); SYSTEM.GET(comadr, ch); INC(comadr)
                    UNTIL ch = 0X;
                    Texts.WriteLn(W); INC(comadr, 2)
                END ;
                Texts.Append(T, W.buf)
            END
        END
    END ShowCommands;


    PROCEDURE Free1(VAR S: Texts.Scanner);
    BEGIN Texts.WriteString(W, S.s); Texts.WriteString(W, " unloading");
        Texts.Append(Oberon.Log, W.buf);
        IF S.nextCh # "*" THEN Modules.Free(S.s, FALSE)
            ELSE Modules.Free(S.s, TRUE); Texts.Scan(S); Texts.WriteString(W, " all")
        END;
        IF Modules.res # 0 THEN Texts.WriteString(W, " failed") END;
        Texts.WriteLn(W); Texts.Append(Oberon.Log, W.buf)
    END Free1;


    PROCEDURE Free*;
        VAR T: Texts.Text;
            V: Viewers.Viewer;
            beg, end, time: LONGINT;
    BEGIN Texts.WriteString(W, "System.Free"); Texts.WriteLn(W); Texts.Append(Oberon.Log, W.buf);
        Texts.OpenScanner(S, Oberon.Par.text, Oberon.Par.pos); Texts.Scan(S);
        WHILE S.class = Texts.Name DO Free1(S); Texts.Scan(S) END ;
        IF (S.class = Texts.Char) & (S.c = " ↑ ") THEN
            Oberon.GetSelection(T, beg, end, time);
            IF time >= 0 THEN Texts.OpenScanner(S, T, beg); Texts.Scan(S);
                IF S.class = Texts.Name THEN Free1(S) END
            END
        END
    END Free;
```

6.5 The Oberon object file format

An object file consists of a sequence of blocks, containing the various data to be loaded as described in the preceding sections of this chapter. The file starts with an identification byte (F8), marking the file to be an object file, and each block is headed by an identification byte. The header block contains the module's name and key, and the number of items in the subsequent blocks. The syntax of object files is the following:

Object File =	HeaderBlock EntryBlock CommandBlock PointerBlock
	ImportBlock LinkBlock DataBlock CodeBlock TypeBlock [ReferenceBlock].
HeaderBlock =	0F8X versionCode refBlkPos:4 nofEntries:2 comSize:2 nofPtrs:2 nofImps:2
	nofLinks:2 varSize:4 codeSize:2 key:4 Name.
Entry Block =	82X {entryAdr:2}.
CommandBlock =	83X {Name entryAdr:2} 0X [0X].
PointerBlock =	84X {pointerOffset:2}.
ImportBlock =	85X {key:4 Name 0X}.
LinkBlock =	86X {procNumber moduleNumber}.
DataBlock =	87X {byte}.
CodeBlock =	88X {byte}.
TypeBlock =	89X {tdsize:2 tdadr:2 {byte}}.
ReferenceBlock =	8AX {ProcRef}.
ProcRef =	0F8X entryAdr:2 Name {LocalRef}.
LocalRef =	mode form adr:4 Name.
Name =	{byte} 0X.

For terminal symbols a suffix :n denotes the number of bytes used (unless it is 1).

The reference block at the end of the file is ignored by the loader, but used by the error trap routine in order to list the values of local variables at the time of the trap. For further details see procedure *Trap* in Section 12.9. The header block contains a reference to this block in order to allow the trap routine to swiftly position its reader.

7 The file system

7.1 Files

It is essential that a computer system have a facility for storing data over longer periods of time and for retrieving the stored data. Such a facility is called a *file system*. Evidently, a file system cannot accommodate all possible data types and structures that will be programmed in the future. Hence it is necessary to provide a simple yet flexible enough base structure that allows any data structure to be mapped onto this base structure (and vice versa) in a reasonably straightforward and efficient way. This base structure, called a *file*, is a sequence of bytes. As a consequence, any given structure to be transformed into a file must be sequentialized. The notion of sequence is indeed fundamental, and it requires no further explanation and theory. We recall that texts are sequences of characters, and that characters are typically represented as bytes.

The sequence is also the natural abstraction of all physically moving storage media. Among them are magnetic tapes and disks. Magnetic media have the welcome property of non-volatility and are therefore the primary choices for storing data over longer periods of time, especially over periods where the equipment is switched off.

A further advantage of the sequence is that its transmission between media is simple too. The reason is that its structural information is inherent and need not be encoded and transmitted in addition to the actual data. This implicitness of structural information is particularly convenient in the case of moving storage media, because they impose strict timing constraints on transmission of consecutive elements. Therefore the process that generates (or consumes) the data must be effectively decoupled from the transmission process that observes the timing constraints. In the case of sequences, this decoupling is simple to achieve by dividing a sequence into subsequences that are buffered. A sequence is output to the storage medium by alternately generating data (and filling the buffer holding the current subsequence) and transmitting data (fetching elements from the buffer and transmitting them). The size of the subsequences (and the buffer) depends on the storage medium under consideration: there must be no timing constraints between accesses to consecutive subsequences.

The file is not a static data structure like the array or the record, because the length may increase dynamically, that is, during program execution. On the other hand, the sequence is less flexible than general dynamic structures, because it cannot change its form, but only its length, since elements can only be appended but not inserted. It might therefore be called a semidynamic structure.

File opening

The discipline of purely sequential access to a file is enforced by restricting access to calls of specific procedures, typically read and write procedures for scanning and generating a file. In the jargon of data processing, a file must be *opened* before reading or writing is possible. The opening implies the initialization of a reading and writing mechanism, and in particular the fixing of its initial position. Hence each (opened) file not only has a value and a length, but also a position attributed to it. If reading must occur from several positions (still sequentially) in alteration, the file is 'multiply opened'; it implies that the same file is represented by several variables, each denoting a different position.

File rider

This widespread view of files is conceptually unappealing, and the Oberon file system therefore departs from it by introducing the notion of a *rider*. A file simply has a value, the sequence of bytes, and a length, the number of bytes in the sequence. Reading and writing occurs through a rider, which denotes a position. 'Multiple opening' is achieved by simply using several riders riding on the same file. Thereby the two concepts of data structure (file) and access mechanism (rider) are clearly distinct and properly disentangled.

Positioning a rider

Given a file f, a rider r is placed on a file by the call *Files.Set* (*r*, *f*, *pos*), where pos indicates the position from which reading or writing is to start. Calls of *Files.Read*(*r*, *x*) and *Files.Write*(*r*, *x*) implicitly increment the position beyond the element read or written, and the file is implicitly denoted via the explicit parameter r, which denotes a *rider*. The rider has two (visible) attributes, namely *r.eof* and *r.res*. The former is set to FALSE by *Files.Set*, and to TRUE when a read operation could not be performed, because the end of the file had been reached. *r.res* serves as a result variable in procedures *ReadBytes* and *WriteBytes* allowing one to check for correct termination.

A file system must not only provide the concept of a sequence with its accessing mechanism, but also a registry. This implies that files be identified, that they can be given a name by which they are registered and retrieved. The registry or collection of registered names is called the file system's *directory*. Here we wish to emphasize that the concepts of files as data structure with associated access facilities on the one hand, and the concept of file naming and directory management on the other, must also be considered separately and as independent notions. In fact, in the Oberon System their implementation underscores this separation by the existence of two modules: *Files* and *FileDir*. The following procedures are made available. They are summarized by the interface specification (definition) of module *Files*.

```
DEFINITION Files;
  IMPORT SYSTEM;
  TYPE File = POINTER TO Handle;
    Handle = RECORD END;
    Rider = RECORD res: INTEGER; eof: BOOLEAN END;

  PROCEDURE Old(name: ARRAY OF CHAR): File;
  PROCEDURE New(name: ARRAY OF CHAR): File;
  PROCEDURE Register(f: File);
  PROCEDURE Close(f: File);
  PROCEDURE Purge(f: File);
  PROCEDURE Length(f: File): LONGINT;
  PROCEDURE GetDate(f: File; VAR time, date: LONGINT);

  PROCEDURE Set(VAR r: Rider; f: File; pos: LONGINT);
  PROCEDURE Read(VAR r: Rider; VAR x: SYSTEM.BYTE);
  PROCEDURE ReadBytes(VAR r: Rider;
        VAR x: ARRAY OF SYSTEM.BYTE; n: LONGINT);
  PROCEDURE Write(VAR r: Rider; x: SYSTEM.BYTE);
  PROCEDURE WriteBytes(VAR r: Rider; VAR x: ARRAY OF
        SYSTEM.BYTE; n: LONGINT);
  PROCEDURE Pos(VAR r: Rider): LONGINT;
  PROCEDURE Base(VAR r: Rider): File;

  PROCEDURE Rename(old, new: ARRAY OF CHAR;
        VAR res: INTEGER);
  PROCEDURE Delete(name: ARRAY OF CHAR;
        VAR res: INTEGER);
END Files.
```

Creating files

New(name) yields a new (empty) file without registering it in the directory. *Old(name)* retrieves the file with the specified name, or yields NIL, if it is not found in the directory. *Register(f)* inserts the name of f (specified in the call of *New*) in the directory. An already-existing entry with this name is replaced. *Close(f)* must be called after writing is completed and the file is not to be registered. *Close* actually stands for

Registering and closing files

'close buffers', and is implied in the procedure *Register*. Procedure *Purge* will be explained at the end of Section 7.2.

The sequential scan of a file f is programmed as shown in the following template:

```
f := Files.Old(name);
IF f # NIL THEN
    Files.Set (r, f, 0); Files.Read (r, x);
    WHILE ~ r.eof DO . . . x . . .; Files.Read(r, x) END
END
```

The analogous template for a purely sequential writing is

```
f := Files.New(name); Files.Set(r, f, 0); . . .
WHILE . . . DO Files.Write (r, x); . . . END
Files.Register(f)
```

Deleting and removing files

There exist two further procedures; they do not change any files, but only affect the directory. *Delete(name, res)* causes the removal of the named entry from the directory. *Rename(old, new, res)* causes the replacement of the directory entry *old* by *new*.

It may surprise the reader that these two procedures, which affect the directory only, are exported from module *Files* instead of *FileDir*. The reason is that the presence of the two modules, together forming the file system, is also used for separating the interface into a public and a private (or semipublic) part. The definition (in the form of a symbol file) of *FileDir* is not intended to be freely available, but to be restricted to use by system programmers. This allows the export of certain sensitive data (such as file headers) and sensitive procedures (such as *Enumerate*) without the danger of misuse by inadvertant users.

Module *Files* constitutes a most important interface, whose stability is utterly essential, because it is used by almost every module programmed. During the entire time span of development of the Oberon System, this interface had changed only once. We also note that this interface is very terse, a factor contributing to its stability. Yet, the offered facilities have in practice over years proved to be both necessary and sufficient.

7.2 Implementation of files on a random-access store

A file cannot be allocated as a block of contiguous storage locations, because its length is not fixed. Neither can it be represented as a linked list of individual elements, because this would lead to inefficient use of storage – more might be used for the links than the elements themselves. The solution generally adopted is a compromise between the two extremes: files are represented as lists of blocks (subsequently called *sectors*) of fixed length. A block is appended when the last one is filled. On the average, each file therefore wastes half of a sector. Typical sector sizes are 0.5, 1, 2 or 4 Kbytes, depending on the device used as store.

Blocks and sectors

It immediately follows that access to an element is not as simple as in the case of an array. The primary concern in the design of a file system and access scheme must be the *efficiency of access to individual elements while scanning the sequence*, at least in the case when the next element lies within the same sector. This access must be no more complicated than a comparison of two variables followed by an indexed access to the file element and the incrementing of an address pointing to the element's successor. If the successor lies in another sector, the procedure may be more involved, since transitions to the next sector occur much less frequently.

Representation of files

The second most crucial design decision concerns the data structure in which sectors are organized; it determines how a succeeding sector is located. The simplest solution is to link sectors in a list. This is acceptable if access is to be restricted to purely sequential scans. Although this would be sufficient for most applications, it is unnecessarily restrictive for media other than purely sequential ones (tapes). After all, it is sometimes practical to position a rider at an arbitrary point in the file rather than always at its beginning. This is made possible by the use of an indexed sector table, typically stored as a header in the file. The table is an array of the addresses of the file's data sectors. Unfortunately, the length of the table needed is unknown. Choosing a fixed length for all files is controversial, because it inevitably leads to either a limitation of file length (when chosen too small) that is unacceptable in some applications, or to a large waste of file space (when chosen too large). Experience shows that in practice most files are quite short, that is, of the order of a few thousand bytes. The dilemma is avoided by a two-level table, that is by using a table of tables.

Sector table

The scheme chosen in Oberon is slightly more complex in order to favor short files (< 64 Kbytes): each file header contains a table of 64 entries, each pointing to a 1 Kbyte sector. Additionally, it contains a table of 12 entries, the so-called extensions, each pointing to an index sector containing 256 further sector pointers. The file length is thereby limited to $64 + 12 \times 256$ sectors, or 3 211 264 bytes (minus the length of the header). The chosen structure is illustrated in Figure 7.1. sec[0] always points to the sector containing the file header.

File header

The header contains some additional data, namely the length of

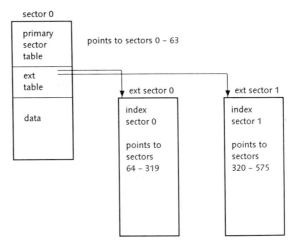

Figure 7.1 File header and extension sectors.

the file (in bytes), its name, and the date and time of its creation. The size of the header is 352 bytes; the remaining 672 bytes of the first sector are used for data. Hence truly short files occupy a single sector only. The declaration of the file header is contained in the definition of module *FileDir*. An abbreviated version containing the fields relevant so far is

```
FileHeader = RECORD
              leng: LONGINT;
              ext: ARRAY 12 OF SectorPointer;
              sec: ARRAY 64 OF SectorPointer
       END
```

Accessing files

We now turn our attention to the implementation of file access, and first present a system that uses main storage for the file data instead of a disk and therefore avoids the problems introduced by sector buffering. The key data structure in this connection is the *Rider*, represented as a record:

```
Rider = RECORD
              pos: LONGINT;
              file: File;
              adr: LONGINT
       END
```

A rider is initialized by a call *Set(r, f, pos)*, which places the rider *r* on file *f* at position *pos*. From this, it is clear that the rider record must contain fields denoting the attached file and the rider's position on it. We note that they are *not exported*. However, their values can be obtained by the function procedures *Pos(r)* and *Base(r)*. This allows a (hidden) representation most appropriate for an efficient implementation of *Read* and *Write* without being unsafe.

Consider now the call *Read(r, x)*; its task is to assign the value of the byte designated by the rider's position to x and to advance the position to the next byte. Considering the structure by which file data are represented, we easily obtain the following program, assuming that the position is legal, that is, non-negative and less than the file's length. a, b, c are local variables, HS is the size of the header (in sector 0), SS is the sector size, typically a power of 2 in order to make division efficient.

```
a := (r.pos + HS) DIV SS;   b := (r.pos + HS) MOD SS;
IF a < 64 THEN c := r.file.sec[a]
ELSE c := r.file.ext[(a − 64) DIV 256].sec[(a − 64) MOD 256]
END;
SYSTEM.GET(c + b, x); INC (r.pos)
```

In order to gain efficiency, we use the low-level procedure GET that assigns the value at address c+b to x. This program is reasonably short, but involves considerable address computations *at every access*, and in particular at positions larger than 64 × SS. Fortunately, there exists an easy remedy, namely that of caching the address of the current position. This explains the presence of the field *adr* in ·the rider record. The resulting program is shown below; note that in order to avoid the addition of HS, *pos* is defined to denote the genuine position, that is, the abstract position augmented by HS.

```
SYSTEM.GET(r.pos, x); INC(r.adr); INC(r.pos);
IF r.adr MOD SS = 0 THEN
    m := r.pos DIV SS;
    IF m < 64 THEN r.adr := r.file.sec[m]
    ELSE r.adr := r.file.ext[(m − 64) DIV 256].sec[(m − 64) MOD
        256]
    END
END
```

We emphasize that, in all but one out of 1024 cases, only three instructions and a single test are to be executed. This improvement therefore is crucial to the efficiency of file access, and to that of the entire Oberon System. We now present the entire file module:

```
MODULE MFiles; (*NW 24.8.90 / 12.10.90*)
    IMPORT SYSTEM, Kernel, FileDir;
```

(*A file consists of a sequence of sectors. The first sector contains the header.
Part of the header is the sector table, an array of addresses to the sectors.
A file is referenced through riders each of which indicates a position.*)

```
CONST
    HS = FileDir.HeaderSize;
    SS = FileDir.SectorSize;
    STS = FileDir.SecTabSize;
    XS = FileDir.IndexSize;

TYPE File* = POINTER TO Header;
    Index = POINTER TO FileDir.IndexSector;

    Rider* =
        RECORD eof*: BOOLEAN;
            res*: LONGINT;
            file: File;
            pos: LONGINT;
            unused: File;
            adr: LONGINT;
        END;
    Header =
        RECORD mark: LONGINT;
            name: FileDir.FileName;
            len, time, date: LONGINT;
            ext: ARRAY FileDir.ExTabSize OF Index;
            sec: FileDir.SectorTable
        END;


PROCEDURE Old*(name: ARRAY OF CHAR): File;
    VAR head: LONGINT;
        namebuf: FileDir.FileName;
BEGIN COPY(name, namebuf);
    FileDir.Search(namebuf, head); RETURN SYSTEM.VAL(File, head)
END Old;


PROCEDURE New*(name: ARRAY OF CHAR): File;
    VAR f: File; head: LONGINT;
BEGIN f := NIL; Kernel.AllocSector(0, head);
    IF head # 0 THEN
        f := SYSTEM.VAL(File, head); f.mark := FileDir.HeaderMark;
        f.len := HS; COPY(name, f.name);
        Kernel.GetClock(f.time, f.date); f.sec[0] := head
    END;
    RETURN f
END New;


PROCEDURE Register*(f: File);
BEGIN
    IF (f # NIL) & (f.name[0] > 0X) THEN FileDir.Insert(f.name, f.sec[0]) END;
END Register;


PROCEDURE Length*(f: File): LONGINT;
BEGIN RETURN f.len − HS
END Length;


PROCEDURE GetDate*(f: File; VAR t, d: LONGINT);
```

```
    BEGIN t := f.time; d := f.date
  END GetDate;


  PROCEDURE Set*(VAR r: Rider; f: File; pos: LONGINT);
    VAR m: INTEGER; n: LONGINT;
  BEGIN r.eof := FALSE; r.res := 0; r.unused := NIL;
    IF f # NIL THEN
      IF pos < 0 THEN r.pos := HS
      ELSIF pos > f.len-HS THEN r.pos := f.len
      ELSE r.pos := pos+HS
      END;
      r.file := f; m := SHORT(r.pos DIV SS); n := r.pos MOD SS;
      IF m < STS THEN r.adr := f.sec[m] + n
      ELSE r.adr := f.ext[(m-STS) DIV XS].x[(m-STS) MOD XS] + n
      END
    END
  END Set;


  PROCEDURE Read*(VAR r: Rider; VAR x: SYSTEM.BYTE);
    VAR m: INTEGER;
  BEGIN
    IF r.pos < r.file.len THEN
      SYSTEM.GET(r.adr, x); INC(r.adr); INC(r.pos);
      IF r.adr MOD SS = 0 THEN
        m := SHORT(r.pos DIV SS);
        IF m < STS THEN r.adr := r.file.sec[m]
        ELSE r.adr := r.file.ext[(m-STS) DIV XS].x[(m-STS) MOD XS]
        END
      END
    ELSE x := 0X; r.eof := TRUE
    END
  END Read;


  PROCEDURE ReadBytes*(VAR r: Rider; VAR x: ARRAY OF SYSTEM.BYTE; n: LONGINT);
    VAR src, dst, m: LONGINT; k: INTEGER;
  BEGIN m := r.pos − r.file.len + n;
    IF m > 0 THEN DEC(n, m); r.res := m; r.eof := TRUE END;
    src := r.adr; dst := SYSTEM.ADR(x); m := (-r.pos) MOD SS;
    LOOP
      IF n <= 0 THEN EXIT END;
      IF n <= m THEN SYSTEM.MOVE(src, dst, n); INC(r.pos, n); r.adr := src+n; EXIT END;
      SYSTEM.MOVE(src, dst, m); INC(r.pos, m); INC(dst,m); DEC(n, m);
      k := SHORT(r.pos DIV SS); m := SS;
      IF k < STS THEN src := r.file.sec[k]
      ELSE src := r.file.ext[(k-STS) DIV XS].x[(k-STS) MOD XS]
      END
    END
  END ReadBytes;


  PROCEDURE Write*(VAR r: Rider; x: SYSTEM.BYTE);
    VAR k, m, n: INTEGER; ix: LONGINT;
  BEGIN
    IF r.pos < r.file.len THEN
      m := SHORT(r.pos DIV SS); INC(r.pos);
      IF m < STS THEN r.adr := r.file.sec[m]
      ELSE r.adr := r.file.ext[(m-STS) DIV XS].x[(m-STS) MOD XS]
      END
```

```
    ELSE
      IF r.adr MOD SS = 0 THEN
        m := SHORT(r.pos DIV SS);
        IF m < STS THEN Kernel.AllocSector(0, r.adr); r.file.sec[m] := r.adr
        ELSE n := (m-STS) DIV XS; k := (m-STS) MOD XS;
          IF k = 0 THEN (*new index*)
            Kernel.AllocSector(0, ix); r.file.ext[n] := SYSTEM.VAL(Index, ix)
          END;
          Kernel.AllocSector(0, r.adr); r.file.ext[n].x[k] := r.adr
        END
      END;
      INC(r.pos); r.file.len := r.pos
    END;
    SYSTEM.PUT(r.adr, x); INC(r.adr)
  END Write;


  PROCEDURE WriteBytes*(VAR r: Rider; VAR x: ARRAY OF SYSTEM.BYTE; n: LONGINT);
    VAR src, dst, m, ix: LONGINT;
      k, lim, h0, h1: INTEGER;
  BEGIN src := SYSTEM.ADR(x); dst := r.adr; m := (-r.pos) MOD SS;
    lim := SHORT(r.file.len DIV SS);
    LOOP
      IF n <= 0 THEN EXIT END;
      IF m = 0 THEN
        k := SHORT(r.pos DIV SS); m := SS;
        IF k > lim THEN
          Kernel.AllocSector(0, dst);
          IF k < STS THEN r.file.sec[k] := dst
          ELSE h1 := (k-STS) DIV XS; h0 := (k-STS) MOD XS;
            IF h0 = 0 THEN (*new extension index*)
              Kernel.AllocSector(0, ix); r.file.ext[h1] := SYSTEM.VAL(Index, ix)
            END;
            r.file.ext[h1].x[h0] := dst
          END
        ELSIF k < STS THEN dst := r.file.sec[k]
        ELSE dst := r.file.ext[(k-STS) DIV XS].x[(k-STS) MOD XS]
        END;
      END;
      IF n < m THEN
        SYSTEM.MOVE(src, dst, n); INC(r.pos, n); r.adr := dst + n;
        IF r.pos >= r.file.len THEN r.file.len := r.pos END;
        EXIT
      END;
      SYSTEM.MOVE(src, dst, m); INC(r.pos, m);
      IF r.pos >= r.file.len THEN r.file.len := r.pos END;
      INC(src, m); DEC(n, m); m := 0
    END
  END WriteBytes;


  PROCEDURE Pos*(VAR r: Rider): LONGINT;
  BEGIN RETURN r.pos - HS
  END Pos;


  PROCEDURE Base*(VAR r: Rider): File;
  BEGIN RETURN r.file
  END Base;
END MFiles.
```

Sector allocation

Allocation of a new sector occurs upon creating a file (*Files.New*), and when writing at the end of a file after the current sector had been filled. Procedure *AllocSector* yields the address of the allocated sector. It is determined by a search in the sector reservation table for a free sector. In this table, every sector is represented by a single bit indicating whether or not the sector is allocated. Although conceptually belonging to the file system, this table resides within module *Kernel*, because for safety reasons it is write-protected in user mode.

Deallocation of a file's sectors could occur as soon as the file is no longer accessible, neither through a variable of any loaded module nor from the file directory. However this moment is difficult to determine. Therefore the method of garbage collection is used in Oberon for the deallocation of file space. In consideration of the fact that file space is large and sector garbage collection relatively time-consuming, we confine this process to system initialization. It is represented by procedure *FileDir.Init*. At that time, the only referenced files are those registered in the directory. *Init* therefore scans the entire directory and records the sectors referenced in each file in the sector reservation table (see Section 7.4).

Sector retrieval

For applications where system initialization is supposed to occur very infrequently, such as for server systems, a procedure *Files.Purge* is provided. Its effect is to return the sectors used by the specified file to the pool of free sectors. Evidently, the programmer then bears the responsibility to guarantee that no references to the purged file continue to exist. This may be possible in a closed server system, but files should not be purged under normal circumstances, since a violation of the said precondition will lead to unpredictable disaster.

The following procedures used for allocating, deallocating and marking sectors in the sector reservation table are defined in module Kernel:

```
PROCEDURE AllocSector(hint: LONGINT;
    VAR sec: LONGINT); (*used in Write*)
PROCEDURE MarkSector(sec: LONGINT); (*used in Init*)
PROCEDURE FreeSector(sec: LONGINT); (*used in Purge*)
```

Procedure *ReadBytes* and *WriteBytes* are provided for fast transfer of sequences of bytes. The increased speed is obtained through the use of block move instructions. In the case of *ReadBytes*, the result field *r.res* indicates the number of bytes requested but not delivered. It is greater than zero only if the end of the file had been reached; $r.res > 0$ implies *r.eof*. A measure of the gain in speed is indicated by the following data. A file of 32 Kbytes read sequentially by (32 000 calls of)

Read(r, ch) takes about 0.25 s (on Ceres-3 using RAM for 'disk'-sectors). The same file read in blocks of 1 Kbytes using ReadBytes(r, block, 1024) takes only about 0.013 s. This amounts to a speedup factor of 18, which is very significant.

7.3 Implementation of files on a disk

First we recall that the organization of files as sets of individually allocated blocks (sectors) is inherently required by the allocation considerations of dynamically growing sequences. However, if the storage medium is a tape or a disk, there exists an additional reason for the use of blocks. They constitute the subsequences to be individually buffered for transmission in order to overcome the timing constraints imposed by the medium. If an adequate space utilization is to be achieved, the blocks must not be too long. A typical size is 1, 2 or 4 Kbytes.

Buffering   This necessity of buffering has a profound influence on the implementation of file access. The complication arises because the abstraction of the sequence of individual bytes needs to be maintained. The increase in complexity of file access is considerable, as can be seen by comparing the program listings of the two respective implementations.

The first, obvious, measure is to copy the file's sector table into primary store when a file is 'opened' through a call of *New*() or *Old*(). The record holding this copy is the file descriptor (called *handle*), and the value f denoting the file points to this handle (instead of the actual header on disk). The descriptor also contains the remaining information stored in the header, in particular the file's length.

If a file is read (or written) in purely sequential manner, a single buffer is appropriate for the transfer of data. For reading, the buffer is filled by reading a sector from the disk, and bytes are picked up individually from the buffer. For writing, bytes are deposited individually, and the buffer is written onto disk as a whole when full. The buffer is associated with the file, and a pointer to it is contained in the descriptor.

Multiple riders   However, we recall that several riders may be placed on a file and be moved independently. It might be appealing to associate a buffer with each rider. But this proposal must quickly be rejected when we realize that several riders may be active at neighbouring positions. If these positions refer to the same sector, which is duplicated in the riders' distinct buffers, the buffers may easily become inconsistent. Obviously, buffers must not be associated with riders, but with the file itself. The descriptor therefore contains the head of a list of linked buffers. Each buffer is identified by its position in the file. An invariant of the system is that no two buffers represent the same sector.

Even with the presence of a single rider, the possibility of having several buffers associated with a file can be advantageous, if a rider is frequently repositioned. It becomes a question of strategy and heuristics when to allocate a new buffer. In the Oberon System, we have adopted the following solution:

(1) The first buffer is created when the file is opened (New, Old).

(2) Additional buffers may be allocated when a rider is placed (or repositioned) on the file.

(3) At most four buffers are connected to the same file.

(4) Purely sequential movements of riders do not cause allocation of buffers.

(5) Separate buffers are generated when extensions of the file's sector table need be accessed (rider position > 64K). Each buffers the 256 sector addresses of the respective index sector.

The outlined scheme requires and is based upon the following data structures and types:

```
File = POINTER TO Handle;
Buffer =POINTER TO BufferRecord;
Index = POINTER TO IndexRecord;
Handle = RECORD next: File;
          aleng, bleng: INTEGER;   (*file length*)
          nofbufs: INTEGER;   (*no. of buffers allocated*)
          modH: BOOLEAN;   (*header has been modified*)
          firstbuf:Buffer:  (*head of buffer chain*)
          sechint: DiskAdr;   (*sector hint*)
          name: FileDir.FileName;
          time, date: LONGINT;
          ext: ARRAY FileDir.ExTabSize OF Index;
          sec: ARRAY 64 OF DiskAdr
            END;

BufferRecord = RECORD apos, lim: INTEGER;
          (*lim = no. of bytes*)
          mod: BOOLEAN; (*buffer has been modified*)
          next: Buffer; (*buffer chain*)
          data: FileDir.DataSector
      END;

IndexRecord = RECORD adr: DiskAdr;
```

```
        mod: BOOLEAN; (*index record has been modified*)
        sec: FileDir.IndexSector
    END

Rider = RECORD eof: BOOLEAN; (*end of file reached*)
        res: LONGINT; (*no. of unread bytes*)
        file: File;
        apos, bpos: INTEGER;(*position*)
        buf: Buffer (*hint: likely buffer*)
    END;
```

In order to increase efficiency of access, riders have been provided with a field containing the address of the element of the rider's position. From the conditions stated above for the allocation of buffers, it is evident that the value of this field can be a hint only. This implies that there can be no reliance on its information. Whenever it is used, its validity has to be checked. The check consists in a comparison of the riders' position r.apos with the hinted buffer's actual position r.buf.apos. If they differ, a buffer with the desired position must be searched and, if not present, allocated. The advantage of the hint lies in the fact that the hint is correct with a very high probability. The check is included in procedures *Read*, *ReadBytes*, *Write* and *WriteBytes*.

Some fields of the record types require additional explanations:

(1) The length is stored in a 'preprocessed' form, namely by the two integers *aleng* and *bleng* such that *aleng* is a sector number and

```
length = (aleng * SS) + bleng − HS
aleng = (length + HS) DIV SS
bleng = (length + HS) MOD SS
```

The same holds for the form of the position in riders (apos, bpos).

(2) The field *nofbufs* indicates the number of buffers in the list headed by *firstbuf*:

```
1 <= nofbufs <= Maxbufs.
```

(3) Whenever data are written into a buffer, the file becomes inconsistent, that is, the data on the disk are outdated. The file is updated, that is, the buffer is copied into the corresponding disk sector, whenever the buffer is reallocated, for example during sequential writing after the buffer is full and is 'advanced'. During sequential reading, a buffer is also advanced and reused, but needs not be copied onto disk, because it is still consistent. Whether a buffer is consistent or not is indicated by its state

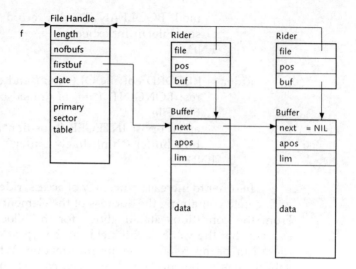

Figure 7.2   File f with two riders and two buffers.

variable *mod* (modified). Similarly, the field *modH* in the file descriptor indicates whether or not the header had been modified.

(4) The field *sechint* records the number of the last sector allocated to the file and serves as a hint to the kernel's allocation procedure, which allocates a next sector with an address larger than the hint. This is a measure to gain speed in sequential scans.

(5) The buffer's position is specified by its field *apos*. Used as index in the file header's sector table, it yields the sector corresponding to the current buffer contents. The field *lim* specifies the number of bytes stored in the buffer. Reading cannot proceed beyond this limiting index; writing beyond it implies an increase in the file's length. All buffers except the one for the last sector are filled and specify *lim* = SS.

(6) The hidden rider field *buf* is merely a hint to speed up localization of the concerned buffer. A hint is likely, but not guaranteed to be correct. Its validity must be checked before use. The buffer hint is invalidated when a buffer is reallocated and/or a rider is repositioned.

The structure of riders remains practically the same as for files using main store. The hidden field *adr* is merely replaced by a pointer to the buffer covering the rider's position. A configuration of a file f with two riders is shown in Figure 7.2.

```
MODULE Files; (*NW 11.1.86 / 22.1.91*)
  IMPORT SYSTEM, Kernel, FileDir;
```

(*A file consists of a sequence of pages. The first page contains the header.
  Part of the header is the page table, an array of disk addresses to the pages.
  A file is referenced through riders each of which indicate a position.*)
CONST MaxBufs = 4;
    HS = FileDir.HeaderSize;
    SS = FileDir.SectorSize;
    STS = FileDir.SecTabSize;
    XS = FileDir.IndexSize;

TYPE DiskAdr = LONGINT;
    File* = POINTER TO Handle;
    Buffer = POINTER TO BufferRecord;
    FileHd = POINTER TO FileDir.FileHeader;
    Index = POINTER TO IndexRecord;

    Rider* =
        RECORD eof*: BOOLEAN;
            res*: LONGINT;
            file: File;
            apos, bpos: INTEGER;
            buf: Buffer;
            unused: LONGINT
        END;

    Handle =
        RECORD next: File;
            aleng, bleng: INTEGER;
            nofbufs: INTEGER;
            modH: BOOLEAN;
            firstbuf: Buffer;
            sechint: DiskAdr;
            name: FileDir.FileName;
            time, date: LONGINT;
            unused: ARRAY 1 OF LONGINT;
            ext: ARRAY FileDir.ExTabSize OF Index;
            sec: FileDir.SectorTable
        END;

    BufferRecord =
        RECORD apos, lim: INTEGER;
            mod: BOOLEAN;
            next: Buffer;
            data: FileDir.DataSector
        END;

    IndexRecord =
        RECORD adr: DiskAdr;
            mod: BOOLEAN;
            sec: FileDir.IndexSector
        END;

    (*aleng * SS + bleng = length (including header)
        apos * SS + bpos = current position
        0 <= bpos <= lim <= SS
        0 <= apos <= aleng < PgTabSize
        (apos < aleng) & (lim = SS) OR (apos = aleng) *)

```
VAR root: File; (*list of open files*)

PROCEDURE Check(VAR s: ARRAY OF CHAR;
    . VAR name: FileDir.FileName; VAR res: INTEGER);
    VAR i: INTEGER; ch: CHAR;
BEGIN ch := s[0]; i := 0;
    IF ("A" <= CAP(ch)) & (CAP(ch) <= "Z") THEN
        LOOP name[i] := ch; INC(i); ch := s[i];
            IF ch = 0X THEN
                WHILE i < FileDir.FnLength DO name[i] := 0X; INC(i) END;
                res := 0; EXIT
            END;
            IF ~(("A" <= CAP(ch)) & (CAP(ch) <= "Z")
                OR ("0" <= ch) & (ch <= "9") OR (ch = ".")) THEN res := 3; EXIT
            END;
            IF i = FileDir.FnLength THEN res := 4; EXIT END;
        END
    ELSIF ch = 0X THEN name[0] := 0X; res := −1
    ELSE res := 3
    END
END Check;


PROCEDURE Old*(name: ARRAY OF CHAR): File;
    VAR i, k, res: INTEGER;
        f: File;
        header: DiskAdr;
        buf: Buffer;
        head: FileHd;
        namebuf: FileDir.FileName;
        inxpg: Index;
BEGIN f := NIL; Check(name, namebuf, res);
    IF res = 0 THEN
        FileDir.Search(namebuf, header);
        IF header # 0 THEN f := root;
            WHILE (f # NIL) & (f.sec[0] # header) DO f := f.next END;
            IF f = NIL THEN↳
                NEW(buf); buf.apos := 0; buf.next := buf; buf.mod := FALSE;
                head := SYSTEM.VAL(FileHd, SYSTEM.ADR(buf.data));
                Kernel.GetSector(header, head↑);
                NEW(f); f.aleng := head.aleng; f.bleng := head.bleng;
                f.time := head.time; f.date := head.date;
                IF f.aleng = 0 THEN buf.lim := f.bleng ELSE buf.lim := SS END;
                f.firstbuf := buf; f.nofbufs := 1; f.name[0] := 0X;
                f.sec := head.sec;
                k := (f.aleng + (XS-STS)) DIV XS; i := 0;
                WHILE i < k DO
                    NEW(inxpg); inxpg.adr := head.ext[i]; inxpg.mod := FALSE;
                    Kernel.GetSector(inxpg.adr, inxpg.sec); f.ext[i] := inxpg; INC(i)
                END;
                WHILE i < FileDir.ExTabSize DO f.ext[i] := NIL; INC(i) END;
                f.sechint := header; f.modH := FALSE; f.next := root; root := f
            END
        END
    END;
    RETURN f
END Old;


PROCEDURE New*(name: ARRAY OF CHAR): File;
```

```
        VAR i, res: INTEGER;
          f: File;
          header: DiskAdr;
          buf: Buffer;
          head: FileHd;
          namebuf: FileDir.FileName;
BEGIN f := NIL; Check(name, namebuf, res);
    IF res <= 0 THEN
        NEW(buf); buf.apos := 0; buf.mod := TRUE; buf.lim := HS; buf.next := buf;
        head := SYSTEM.VAL(FileHd, SYSTEM.ADR(buf.data));
        head.mark := FileDir.HeaderMark;
        head.aleng := 0; head.bleng := HS; head.name := namebuf;
        Kernel.GetClock(head.time, head.date);
        NEW(f); f.aleng := 0; f.bleng := HS; f.modH := TRUE;
        f.time := head.time; f.date := head.date;
        f.firstbuf := buf; f.nofbufs := 1; f.name := namebuf; f.sechint := 0;
        i := 0;
        REPEAT f.ext[i] := NIL; head.ext[i] := 0; INC(i) UNTIL i = FileDir.ExTabSize;
        i := 0;
        REPEAT f.sec[i] := 0; head.sec[i] := 0; INC(i) UNTIL i = STS
    END;
    RETURN f
END New;


PROCEDURE UpdateHeader(f: File; VAR h: FileDir.FileHeader);
    VAR k: INTEGER;
BEGIN h.aleng := f.aleng; h.bleng := f.bleng;
    h.sec := f.sec; k := (f.aleng + (XS-STS)) DIV XS;
    WHILE k > 0 DO DEC(k); h.ext[k] := f.ext[k].adr END
END UpdateHeader;


PROCEDURE ReadBuf(f: File; buf: Buffer; pos: INTEGER);
    VAR sec: DiskAdr;
BEGIN
    IF pos < STS THEN sec := f.sec[pos]
    ELSE sec := f.ext[(pos-STS) DIV XS].sec.x[(pos-STS) MOD XS]
    END;
    Kernel.GetSector(sec, buf.data);
    IF pos < f.aleng THEN buf.lim := SS ELSE buf.lim := f.bleng END;
    buf.apos := pos; buf.mod := FALSE
END ReadBuf;


PROCEDURE WriteBuf(f: File; buf: Buffer);
    VAR i, k: INTEGER;
        secadr: DiskAdr; inx: Index;
BEGIN
    IF buf.apos < STS THEN
        secadr := f.sec[buf.apos];
        IF secadr = 0 THEN
            Kernel.AllocSector(f.sechint, secadr);
            f.modH := TRUE; f.sec[buf.apos] := secadr; f.sechint := secadr
        END;
        IF buf.apos = 0 THEN
            UpdateHeader(f, SYSTEM.VAL(FileDir.FileHeader, buf.data)); f.modH := FALSE
        END
    ELSE i := (buf.apos - STS) DIV XS; inx := f.ext[i];
        IF inx = NIL THEN
```

```
            NEW(inx); inx.adr := 0; inx.sec.x[0] := 0; f.ext[i] := inx; f.modH := TRUE
        END;
        k := (buf.apos − STS) MOD XS; secadr := inx.sec.x[k];
        IF secadr = 0 THEN
            Kernel.AllocSector(f.sechint, secadr);
            f.modH := TRUE; inx.mod := TRUE; inx.sec.x[k] := secadr; f.sechint := secadr
        END
    END;
    Kernel.PutSector(secadr, buf.data); buf.mod := FALSE
END WriteBuf;


PROCEDURE Buf(f: File; pos: INTEGER): Buffer;
    VAR buf: Buffer;
BEGIN buf := f.firstbuf;
    LOOP
        IF buf.apos = pos THEN EXIT END;
        buf := buf.next;
        IF buf = f.firstbuf THEN buf := NIL; EXIT END
    END;
    RETURN buf
END Buf;


PROCEDURE GetBuf(f: File; pos: INTEGER): Buffer;
    VAR buf: Buffer;
BEGIN buf := f.firstbuf;
    LOOP
        IF buf.apos = pos THEN EXIT END;
        IF buf.next = f.firstbuf THEN
            IF f.nofbufs < MaxBufs THEN (*allocate new buffer*)
                NEW(buf); buf.next := f.firstbuf.next; f.firstbuf.next := buf;
                INC(f.nofbufs)
            ELSE (*take one of the buffers*) f.firstbuf := buf;
                IF buf.mod THEN WriteBuf(f, buf) END
            END;
            buf.apos := pos;
            IF pos <= f.aleng THEN ReadBuf(f, buf, pos) END;
            EXIT
        END;
        buf := buf.next
    END;
    RETURN buf
END GetBuf;


PROCEDURE Unbuffer(f: File);
    VAR i, k: INTEGER;
        buf: Buffer;
        inx: Index;
        head: FileDir.FileHeader;
BEGIN buf := f.firstbuf;
    REPEAT
        IF buf.mod THEN WriteBuf(f, buf) END;
        buf := buf.next
    UNTIL buf = f.firstbuf;
    k := (f.aleng + (XS-STS)) DIV XS; i := 0;
    WHILE i < k DO
        inx := f.ext[i]; INC(i);
        IF inx.mod THEN
```

```
            IF inx.adr = 0 THEN
                Kernel.AllocSector(f.sechint, inx.adr); f.sechint := inx.adr; f.modH := TRUE
            END;
            Kernel.PutSector(inx.adr, inx.sec); inx.mod := FALSE
        END
    END;
    IF f.modH THEN
        Kernel.GetSector(f.sec[0], head); UpdateHeader(f, head);
        Kernel.PutSector(f.sec[0], head); f.modH := FALSE
    END
END Unbuffer;


PROCEDURE Register*(f: File);
BEGIN
    IF (f # NIL) & (f.name[0] > 0X) THEN
        Unbuffer(f); FileDir.Insert(f.name, f.sec[0]); f.next := root; root := f
    END;
END Register;


PROCEDURE Close*(f: File);
BEGIN
    IF f # NIL THEN Unbuffer(f) END;
END Close;


PROCEDURE Purge*(f: File);
    VAR a, i, j, k: INTEGER;
        ind: FileDir.IndexSector;
BEGIN
    IF f # NIL THEN a := f.aleng + 1; f.aleng := 0;
        IF a <= STS THEN i := a
        ELSE i := STS; DEC(a, i);
            j := a MOD XS; k := a DIV XS;
            WHILE k >= 0 DO
                Kernel.GetSector(f.ext[k].adr, ind);
                REPEAT DEC(j); Kernel.FreeSector(ind.x[j])
                UNTIL j = 0;
                Kernel.FreeSector(f.ext[k].adr);
                j := XS; DEC(k)
            END
        END;
        REPEAT DEC(i); Kernel.FreeSector(f.sec[i])
        UNTIL i = 0
    END
END Purge;


PROCEDURE Length*(f: File): LONGINT;
BEGIN RETURN LONG(f.aleng)*SS + f.bleng − HS
END Length;


PROCEDURE GetDate*(f: File; VAR t, d: LONGINT);
BEGIN t := f.time; d := f.date
END GetDate;


PROCEDURE Set*(VAR r: Rider; f: File; pos: LONGINT);
    VAR a, b: INTEGER;
BEGIN r.eof := FALSE; r.res := 0;
```

```
        IF f # NIL THEN
            IF pos < 0 THEN a := 0; b := HS
            ELSIF pos < LONG(f.aleng)*SS + f.bleng − HS THEN
                a := SHORT((pos + HS) DIV SS); b := SHORT((pos + HS) MOD SS);
            ELSE a := f.aleng; b := f.bleng
            END;
            r.file := f; r.apos := a; r.bpos := b; r.buf := f.firstbuf
        ELSE r.file:= NIL
        END
    END Set;


    PROCEDURE Read*(VAR r: Rider; VAR x: SYSTEM.BYTE);
        VAR buf: Buffer;
    BEGIN
        IF r.apos # r.buf.apos THEN r.buf := GetBuf(r.file, r.apos) END;
        IF r.bpos < r.buf.lim THEN
            x := r.buf.data.B[r.bpos]; INC(r.bpos)
        ELSIF r.apos < r.file.aleng THEN
            INC(r.apos); buf := Buf(r.file, r.apos);
            IF buf = NIL THEN
                IF r.buf.mod THEN WriteBuf(r.file, r.buf) END;
                ReadBuf(r.file, r.buf, r.apos)
            ELSE r.buf := buf
            END;
            x := r.buf.data.B[0]; r.bpos := 1
        ELSE
            x := 0X; r.eof := TRUE
        END
    END Read;


    PROCEDURE ReadBytes*(VAR r: Rider; VAR x: ARRAY OF SYSTEM.BYTE; n: LONGINT);
        VAR src, dst, m: LONGINT; buf: Buffer;
    BEGIN dst := SYSTEM.ADR(x);
        IF LEN(x) < n THEN HALT(25) END;
        IF r.apos # r.buf.apos THEN r.buf := GetBuf(r.file, r.apos) END;
        LOOP
            IF n <= 0 THEN EXIT END;
            src := SYSTEM.ADR(r.buf.data.B) + r.bpos; m := r.bpos + n;
            IF m <= r.buf.lim THEN
                SYSTEM.MOVE(src, dst, n); r.bpos := SHORT(m); r.res := 0; EXIT
            ELSIF r.buf.lim = SS THEN
                m := r.buf.lim − r.bpos;
                IF m > 0 THEN SYSTEM.MOVE(src, dst, m); INC(dst, m); DEC(n, m) END;
                IF r.apos < r.file.aleng THEN
                    INC(r.apos); r.bpos := 0; buf := Buf(r.file, r.apos);
                    IF buf = NIL THEN
                        IF r.buf.mod THEN WriteBuf(r.file, r.buf) END;
                        ReadBuf(r.file, r.buf, r.apos)
                    ELSE r.buf := buf
                    END
                ELSE r.res := n; r.eof := TRUE; EXIT
                END
            ELSE m := r.buf.lim − r.bpos;
                IF m > 0 THEN SYSTEM.MOVE(src, dst, m); r.bpos := r.buf.lim END;
                r.res := n − m; r.eof := TRUE; EXIT
            END
        END
    END ReadBytes;
```

```
PROCEDURE NewExt(f: File);
    VAR i, k: INTEGER; ext: Index;
BEGIN k := (f.aleng - STS) DIV XS;
    IF k = FileDir.ExTabSize THEN HALT(23) END;
    NEW(ext); ext.adr := 0; ext.mod := TRUE; f.ext[k] := ext; i := XS;
    REPEAT DEC(i); ext.sec.x[i] := 0 UNTIL i = 0
END NewExt;

PROCEDURE Write*(VAR r: Rider; x: SYSTEM.BYTE);
    VAR f: File; buf: Buffer;
BEGIN
    IF r.apos # r.buf.apos THEN r.buf := GetBuf(r.file, r.apos) END;
    IF r.bpos >= r.buf.lim THEN
        IF r.bpos < SS THEN
            INC(r.buf.lim); INC(r.file.bleng); r.file.modH := TRUE
        ELSE f := r.file; WriteBuf(f, r.buf); INC(r.apos); buf := Buf(r.file, r.apos);
            IF buf = NIL THEN
                IF r.apos <= f.aleng THEN ReadBuf(f, r.buf, r.apos)
                ELSE r.buf.apos := r.apos; r.buf.lim := 1; INC(f.aleng); f.bleng := 1; f.modH
                        := TRUE;
                    IF (f.aleng - STS) MOD XS = 0 THEN NewExt(f) END
                END
            ELSE r.buf := buf
            END;
            r.bpos := 0
        END
    END;
    r.buf.data.B[r.bpos] := x; INC(r.bpos); r.buf.mod := TRUE
END Write;

PROCEDURE WriteBytes*(VAR r: Rider; VAR x: ARRAY OF SYSTEM.BYTE; n: LONGINT);
    VAR src, dst, m: LONGINT; f: File; buf: Buffer;
BEGIN src := SYSTEM.ADR(x);
    IF LEN(x) < n THEN HALT(25) END;
    IF r.apos # r.buf.apos THEN r.buf := GetBuf(r.file, r.apos) END;
    LOOP
        IF n <= 0 THEN EXIT END;
        r.buf.mod := TRUE; dst := SYSTEM.ADR(r.buf.data.B) + r.bpos; m := r.bpos + n;
        IF m <= r.buf.lim THEN
            SYSTEM.MOVE(src, dst, n); r.bpos := SHORT(m); EXIT
        ELSIF m <= SS THEN
            SYSTEM.MOVE(src, dst, n); r.bpos := SHORT(m);
            r.file.bleng := SHORT(m); r.buf.lim := SHORT(m); r.file.modH := TRUE; EXIT
        ELSE m := SS - r.bpos;
            IF m > 0 THEN SYSTEM.MOVE(src, dst, m); INC(src, m); DEC(n, m) END;
            f := r.file; WriteBuf(f, r.buf); INC(r.apos); r.bpos := 0; buf := Buf(f, r.apos);
            IF buf = NIL THEN
                IF r.apos <= f.aleng THEN ReadBuf(f, r.buf, r.apos)
                ELSE r.buf.apos := r.apos; r.buf.lim := 0; INC(f.aleng); f.bleng := 0; f.modH
                        := TRUE;
                    IF (f.aleng - STS) MOD XS = 0 THEN NewExt(f) END
                END
            ELSE r.buf := buf
            END
        END
    END
END WriteBytes;

PROCEDURE Pos*(VAR r: Rider): LONGINT;
```

```
BEGIN RETURN LONG(r.apos)*SS + r.bpos − HS
END Pos;

PROCEDURE Base*(VAR r: Rider): File;
BEGIN RETURN r.file
END Base;

PROCEDURE Delete*(name: ARRAY OF CHAR; VAR res: INTEGER);
   VAR adr: DiskAdr;
      namebuf: FileDir.FileName;
BEGIN Check(name, namebuf, res);
   IF res = 0 THEN
      FileDir.Delete(namebuf, adr);
      IF adr = 0 THEN res := 2 END
   END
END Delete;

PROCEDURE Rename*(old, new: ARRAY OF CHAR; VAR res: INTEGER);
   VAR adr: DiskAdr;
      oldbuf, newbuf: FileDir.FileName;
      head: FileDir.FileHeader;
BEGIN Check(old, oldbuf, res);
   IF res = 0 THEN
      Check(new, newbuf, res);
      IF res = 0 THEN
         FileDir.Delete(oldbuf, adr);
         IF adr # 0 THEN
            FileDir.Insert(newbuf, adr);
            Kernel.GetSector(adr, head); head.name := newbuf; Kernel.PutSector(adr, head)
         ELSE res := 2
         END
      END
   END
END Rename;

BEGIN Kernel.FileRoot := SYSTEM.ADR(root)
END Files.
```

Some comments concerning module *Files* follow.

Closing files

(1) After the writing of a file has been completed, its name is usually registered in the directory. *Register* invokes procedure *Unbuffer*. It inspects the associated buffers and copies onto disk those that have been modified. During this process, new index sectors may have to be transferred as well. If a file is to remain anonymous and local to a module or command, that is, it is not to be registered but merely to be read, the release of buffers must be specified by an explicit call to *Close* (meaning 'close buffers'), which also invokes *Unbuffer*.

(2) Procedure *Old* (and, for reasons of consistency, also *New*) deviates from the general Oberon programming rule that an object be allocated by the calling (instead of the called) module. This rule would suggest the statements

New(f); Files.Open(f, name)

instead of $f := Files.Old(name)$. The justification for the rule is that any extension of the type of f could be allocated, providing for more flexibility. And the reason for our deviation in the case of files is that, upon closer inspection, it is not a new file, but only a new descriptor that is to be allocated. The distinction becomes evident when we consider that several statements $f := Files.Old(name)$ with different f and identical *name* may occur, probably in different modules. In this case, it is necessary that the *same* descriptor be referenced by the delivered pointers in order to avoid file inconsistency. Each (opened) file must have exactly one descriptor. When a file is opened, the first action is therefore to inspect whether a descriptor of this file already exists. For this purpose, all descriptors are linked together in a list anchored by the global variable *root* and linked by the descriptor field *next*. This measure may seem to solve the problem of avoiding inconsistencies smoothly. However, there exists a pitfall that is easily overlooked: all opened files would permanently remain accessible via *root*, and the garbage collector could never remove a file descriptor nor its associated buffers. This would be unacceptable. We have found no better solution to this problem than to design the garbage collector such that it excludes this list from its mark phase.

Buffer retrieval

(3) Sector pointers are represented by sector numbers of type LONGINT. Actually, we use the numbers multiplied by 29. This implies that any single-bit error leads to a number that is not a multiple of 29, and hence can easily be detected. Thereby the crucial sector addresses are software parity checked and are safe (against single-bit errors) even on computers without hardware parity check. The check is performed by procedures *Kernel.GetSector and Kernel.PutSector*.

7.4 The file directory

A directory is a set of pairs, each pair consisting of a name (key) and an object (here, file). It serves to retrieve objects by their name. If efficiency matters, the directory is organized as an ordered set, ordered according to the keys. The most frequently used structures for ordered sets are trees and hash tables. The latter have disadvantages when the size of the set is unknown, particularly when its order of magnitude is unknown, and when deletions occur. The Oberon System therefore uses a tree structure for its file directory, more specifically a B-tree, which was developed especially for cases where not individual pairs, but only sets of pairs as a whole (placed on a disk sector) can be accessed.

B-tree

For a thorough study of B-trees, we refer the reader to Bayer and McCreight (1972) and Comer (1979). Here it must suffice to specify the B-tree's principal characteristics:

(1) In a B-tree of order N, each node (called *page*) contains m elements (pairs), where N <= m <= 2N, except the root, where 0 <= m <= 2N.

(2) A page with m elements has either 0 descendants, in which case it is called a *leaf page*, or m + 1 descendants.

(3) All leaf pages are on the same (bottom) level.

From (3) it follows that the B-tree is a *balanced tree*. Its height, and with it the longest path's length, has an upper bound of, roughly, $2 \times \log k$, where k is the number of elements and the logarithm is taken to the base N and rounded up to the next larger integer. Its minimum height is log k taken to the base 2N.

Page size

On each page, space must be available for 2N elements and for 2N + 1 references to descendants. Hence N is immediately determined by the size of a page and the size of elements. In the case of the Oberon System, names are limited to 32 characters (bytes), and the object is a reference to the associated file (4 bytes). Each descendant pointer takes 4 bytes, and the page size is given by the sector size (1024) minus the number of bytes needed to store m (2 bytes). Hence

$$N = ((1024 - 2 - 4) \text{ DIV } (32 + 4 + 4)) \text{ DIV } 2 = 12$$

A B-tree of height h and order 12 may contain the following minimum and maximum number of elements:

height	minimum	maximum
1	0	24
2	25	624
3	625	15 624
4	15 625	390 624

It follows that the height of the B-tree will never be larger than 4, if the disk has a capacity of less than about 400 Mbyte, and assuming that each file occupies a single 1K sector. It is rarely larger than 3 in practice.

The definition of module *FileDir* shows the available directory operations. Apart from the procedures *Search*, *Insert*, *Delete* and *Enumerate*, it contains some data definitions, and it should be considered as the non-public part of the file system's interface.

```
DEFINITION FileDir;
    IMPORT SYSTEM, Kernel;
    CONST
        FnLength = 32;   (*max length of file name*)
        SecTabSize = 64;   (*no. of entries in primary table*)
        ExTabSize = 12;
        SectorSize = 1024;
        IndexSize = SectorSize DIV 4;   (*no. of entries in index sector*)
        HeaderSize = 352;
        DirRootAdr = 29;
        DirPgSize = 24;   (*max no. of elements on page*)

    TYPE
        FileName = ARRAY FnLength OF CHAR;
        SectorTable = ARRAY SecTabSize OF LONGINT;
        ExtensionTable = ARRAY ExTabSize OF LONGINT;
        EntryHandler = PROCEDURE (name: FileName; sec: LONGINT; VAR continue:
                BOOLEAN);

        FileHeader = RECORD (Kernel.Sector)
            mark: LONGINT;
            name: FileName;
            aleng, bleng: INTEGER;
            date, time: LONGINT;
            ext: ExtensionTable;
            sec: SectorTable;
        END;

        IndexSector = RECORD (Kernel.Sector)
            x: ARRAY IndexSize OF LONGINT;
        END;

        DataSector = RECORD (Kernel.Sector)
            B: ARRAY SectorSize OF SYSTEM.BYTE;
        END;

        DirEntry = RECORD
            name: FileName;
            adr, p: LONGINT;
        END;

        DirPage = RECORD (Kernel.Sector)
            mark: LONGINT;
            m: INTEGER;   (*no. of elements on page*)
            p0: LONGINT;
            e: ARRAY DirPgSize OF DirEntry;
        END;
```

```
PROCEDURE Search(VAR name: FileName; VAR fad: LONGINT);
PROCEDURE Insert(VAR name: FileName; fad: LONGINT);
PROCEDURE Delete(VAR name: FileName; VAR fad: LONGINT);
PROCEDURE Enumerate(prefix: ARRAY OF CHAR; proc: EntryHandler);

END FileDir.
```

Directory operations

Procedures *Search*, *Insert* and *Delete* represent the typical operations performed on a directory. Efficiency of the first operation is of primary importance. But the B-tree structure also guarantees efficient insertion and deletion, although the code for these operations is complex. Procedure *Enumerate* is used to obtain excerpts of the directory. The programmer must guarantee that no directory changes are performed by the parametric procedure of *Enumerate*.

As in the presentation of module *Files*, we first discuss a version that uses main storage rather than a disk for the directory. This allows us to concentrate on the algorithms for handling the directory, leaving out the additional complications due to the necessity to read pages (sectors) into main store for selective updating and of restoring them onto disk. In particular, we point out the definitions of the data types for B-tree nodes, called *DirPage*, and elements, called *DirEntry*. The component $E.p$ of an entry E points to the page in which all elements (with index k) have keys $E.p.e[k].name > E.name$. The pointer $p.p0$ points to a page in which all elements have keys $p.p0.e[k].name < p.e[0].name$. We can visualize these conditions by Figure 7.3, where names have been replaced by integers as keys.

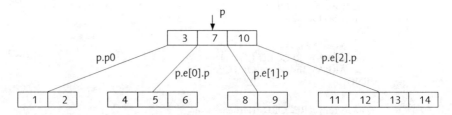

Figure 7.3 Example of a B-tree of order 2.

Directory search

Procedure *Search* starts by inspecting the root page. It performs a binary search among its elements, according to the following algorithm. Let e[0 ... m−1] be the ordered keys and x the search argument.

```
L := 0; R := m;
WHILE L < R DO
    i := (L+R) DIV 2;
    IF x <= e[i] THEN R := i ELSE L := i + 1 END
END;
IF (R < m) & (x = e[R]) THEN found END
```

The invariant is

$$e[L-1] < x <= e[R]$$

If the desired element is not found, the search continues on the appropriate descendant page, if there is one. Otherwise, the element is not contained in the tree.

Insertion and deletion

Procedures *insert* and *delete* use the same algorithm for searching an element within a page. However, they use recursion instead of iteration to proceed along the search path of pages. We recall that the depth of recursion is at most four. The reason for the use of recursion is that it facilitates the formulation of structural changes, which are performed during the 'unwinding' of recursion, that is, on the return path. First, the insertion point (respectively the position of the element to be deleted) is searched, and then the element is inserted (deleted).

Page overflow

Upon insertion, the number of elements on the insertion page may become larger than 2N, violating B-tree condition (1). This situation is called *page overflow*. The invariant must be reestablished immediately. It could be achieved by moving one element from either end of the array e onto a neighbouring page. However, we choose not to do this, and instead to split the overflowing page into two pages immediately.

Page split

The process of a *page split* is visualized by Figure 7.4, in which we distinguish between three cases, namely $R < N$, $R = N$ and $R > N$, where R marks the insertion point. *a* denotes the overflowing, *b* the new page and *u* the inserted element.

The $2N + 1$ elements (2N from the full page *a*, plus the one element *u* to be inserted) are equally distributed onto pages *a* and *b*. One element *v* is pushed up in the tree. It must be inserted in the ancestor page of *a*. Since that page obtains an additional descendant, it must also obtain an additional element in order to maintain B-tree rule (2).

A page split may thus propagate, because the insertion of element *v* in the ancestor page may require a split once again. If the root page is full, it is split too, and the emerging element *v* is inserted in a new root page containing a single element. This is the only way in which the height of a B-tree can increase.

When an element is to be deleted, it cannot simply be removed, if it resides on an internal page. In this case, it is first replaced by another element, namely one of the two neighbouring elements on a leaf page, that is, the next smaller (or next larger) element, which is always on a leaf page. In the presented solution, the replacing element is the largest on the left subtree (see procedure *del*). Hence the actual deletion always occurs on a leaf page.

Page underflow

Upon deletion, the number of elements in a page may become less than N, violating invariant (1). This event is called *page underflow*. Since restructuring the tree is a relatively complicated operation, we first try to reestablish the invariant by borrowing an element from a neighbouring page. In fact, it is reasonable to borrow several elements,

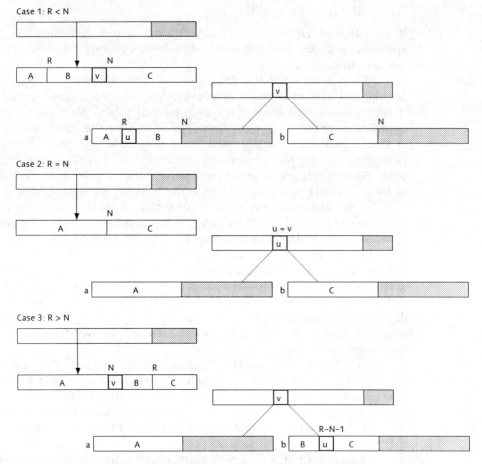

Figure 7.4   Page split when inserting element u.

and thereby to decrease the likelyhood of an underflow on the same page upon further deletions. The number of elements that could be taken from the neighbouring page b is b.m − N. Hence we shall borrow

$$k = (b.m - N + 1) \ \text{DIV} \ 2$$

Page balancing

elements. The process of *page balancing* then distributes the elements of the underflowing and its neighbouring page equally to both pages (see procedure *underflow*).

Page merge

However, if (and only if) the neighbouring page has no elements to spare, the two pages can and must be united. This action, called *page merge*, places the N−1 elements from the underflowing page, the N elements from the neighbouring page plus one element from the ancestor

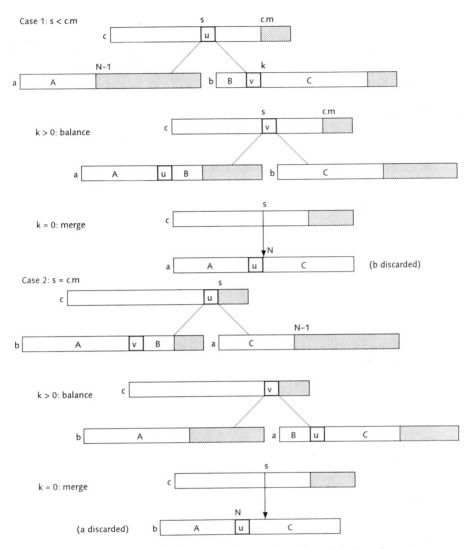

Figure 7.5 Page balancing and merging when deleting element.

page onto a single page of size 2N. One element must be taken from the ancestor page, because that page looses one descendant and invariant rule (2) must be maintained. The events of page balancing and merging are illustrated in Figure 7.5. *a* is the underflowing page, *b* its neighbouring page and *c* their ancestor; *s* is the position in the ancestor page of (the pointer to) the underflowing page *a*. Two cases are distinguished, namely whether the underflowing page is the rightmost element (s = c.m) or not (see procedure *underflow*).

Similarly to the splitting process, merging may propagate, because the removal of an element from the ancestor page may again cause an underflow, and perhaps a merge. The root page underflows only if its last element is removed. This is the only way in which the B-tree's height can decrease.

```
MODULE BTree;
  IMPORT Texts, Oberon;

  CONST N = 3;

  TYPE Page = POINTER TO PageRec;

    Entry = RECORD
                  key, data: INTEGER;
                  p: Page
              END;

    PageRec = RECORD
                  m: INTEGER;   (*no. of entries on page*)
                  p0: Page;
                  e: ARRAY 2*N OF Entry
              END;

  VAR root: Page;
      W: Texts.Writer;

  PROCEDURE search(x: INTEGER; a: Page; VAR data: INTEGER);
    VAR i, L, R: INTEGER;
  BEGIN (*a # NIL*)
    LOOP L := 0; R := a.m;   (*binary search*)
      WHILE L < R DO
        i := (L+R) DIV 2;
        IF x <= a.e[i].key THEN R := i ELSE L := i+1 END
      END;
      IF (R < a.m) & (a.e[R].key = x) THEN (*found*)
        data := a.e[R].data; EXIT
      END;
      IF R = 0 THEN a := a.p0 ELSE a := a.e[R-1].p END;
      IF a = NIL THEN (*not found*) EXIT END
    END
  END search;

  PROCEDURE insert(x: INTEGER; a: Page; VAR h: BOOLEAN; VAR v: Entry);
    (*a # NIL. Search key x in B-tree with root a; if found, increment counter.
      Otherwise insert new item with key x.  If an entry is to be passed up,
      assign it to v. h := "tree has become higher"*)
    VAR i, L, R: INTEGER;
        b: Page; u: Entry;
  BEGIN (*a # NIL & ~h*)
    L := 0; R := a.m;   (*binary search*)
    WHILE L < R DO
      i := (L+R) DIV 2;
      IF x <= a.e[i].key THEN R := i ELSE L := i+1 END
```

```
        END;
        IF (R < a.m) & (a.e[R].key = x) THEN (*found*) INC(a.e[R].data)
        ELSE (*item not on this page*)
            IF R = 0 THEN b := a.p0 ELSE b := a.e[R−1].p END;
            IF b = NIL THEN (*not in tree, insert*)
                u.p := NIL; h := TRUE; u.key := x
            ELSE insert(x, b, h, u)
            END;
            IF h THEN (*insert u to the left of a.e[R]*)
                IF a.m < 2*N THEN
                    h := FALSE; i := a.m;
                    WHILE i > R DO DEC(i); a.e[i+1] := a.e[i] END;
                    a.e[R] := u; INC(a.m)
                ELSE NEW(b); (*overflow; split a into a,b and assign the middle entry to v*)
                    IF R < N THEN (*insert in left page a*)
                        i := N−1; v := a.e[i];
                        WHILE i > R DO DEC(i); a.e[i+1] := a.e[i] END;
                        a.e[R] := u; i := 0;
                        WHILE i < N DO b.e[i] := a.e[i+N]; INC(i) END
                    ELSE (*insert in right page b*)
                        DEC(R, N); i := 0;
                        IF R = 0 THEN v := u
                        ELSE v := a.e[N];
                            WHILE i < R−1 DO b.e[i] := a.e[i+N+1]; INC(i) END;
                            b.e[i] := u; INC(i)
                        END;
                        WHILE i < N DO b.e[i] := a.e[i+N]; INC(i) END
                    END;
                    a.m := N; b.m := N; b.p0 := v.p; v.p := b
                END
            END
        END
    END insert;


PROCEDURE underflow(c, a: Page; s: INTEGER; VAR h: BOOLEAN);
    (*a = underflowing page, c = ancestor page,
      s = index of deleted entry in c*)
    VAR b: Page;
        i, k: INTEGER;
BEGIN (*h & (a.m = N−1) & (c.e[s−1].p = a) *)
    IF s < c.m THEN (*b := page to the right of a*)
        b := c.e[s].p; k := (b.m−N+1) DIV 2; (*k = nof items available on page b*)
        a.e[N−1] := c.e[s]; a.e[N−1].p := b.p0;
        IF k > 0 THEN (*balance by moving k−1 items from b to a*) i := 0;
            WHILE i < k−1 DO a.e[i+N] := b.e[i]; INC(i) END;
            c.e[s] := b.e[k−1]; b.p0 := c.e[s].p;
            c.e[s].p := b; DEC(b.m, k); i := 0;
            WHILE i < b.m DO b.e[i] := b.e[i+k]; INC(i) END;
            a.m := N−1+k; h := FALSE
        ELSE (*merge pages a and b, discard b*) i := 0;
            WHILE i < N DO a.e[i+N] := b.e[i]; INC(i) END;
            i := s; DEC(c.m);
            WHILE i < c.m DO c.e[i] := c.e[i+1]; INC(i) END;
            a.m := 2*N; h := c.m < N
        END
    ELSE (*b := page to the left of a*) DEC(s);
        IF s = 0 THEN b := c.p0 ELSE b := c.e[s−1].p END;
        k := (b.m−N+1) DIV 2; (*k = nof items available on page b*)
```

```
                    IF k > 0 THEN i := N-1;
                        WHILE i > 0 DO DEC(i); a.e[i+k] := a.e[i] END;
                        i := k-1; a.e[i] := c.e[s]; a.e[i].p := a.p0;
                        (*move k-1 items from b to a, one to c*) DEC(b.m, k);
                        WHILE i > 0 DO DEC(i); a.e[i] := b.e[i+b.m+1] END;
                        c.e[s] := b.e[b.m]; a.p0 := c.e[s].p;
                        c.e[s].p := a; a.m := N-1+k; h := FALSE
                    ELSE (*merge pages a and b, discard a*)
                        c.e[s].p := a.p0; b.e[N] := c.e[s]; i := 0;
                        WHILE i < N-1 DO b.e[i+N+1] := a.e[i]; INC(i) END;
                        b.m := 2*N; DEC(c.m); h := c.m < N
                    END
                END
        END underflow;


        PROCEDURE delete(x: INTEGER; a: Page; VAR h: BOOLEAN);
            (*search and delete key x in B-tree a; if a page underflow arises,
                balance with adjacent page or merge; h := "page a is undersize"*)
            VAR i, L, R: INTEGER; q: Page;

            PROCEDURE del(p: Page; VAR h: BOOLEAN);
                VAR k: INTEGER; q: Page;   (*global a, R*)
            BEGIN k := p.m-1; q := p.e[k].p;
                IF q # NIL THEN del(q, h);
                    IF h THEN underflow(p, q, p.m, h) END
                ELSE p.e[k].p := a.e[R].p; a.e[R] := p.e[k];
                    DEC(p.m); h := p.m < N
                END
            END del;


        BEGIN (*a # NIL*)
        L := 0; R := a.m;   (*binary search*)
        WHILE L < R DO
            i := (L+R) DIV 2;
            IF x <= a.e[i].key THEN R := i ELSE L := i+1 END
        END;
        IF R = 0 THEN q := a.p0 ELSE q := a.e[R-1].p END;
        IF (R < a.m) & (a.e[R].key = x) THEN (*found*)
            IF q = NIL THEN (*a is leaf page*)
                DEC(a.m); h := a.m < N; i := R;
                WHILE i < a.m DO a.e[i] := a.e[i+1]; INC(i) END
            ELSE del(q, h);
                IF h THEN underflow(a, q, R, h) END
            END
        ELSE delete(x, q, h);
            IF h THEN underflow(a, q, R, h) END
        END
    END delete;

PROCEDURE Search*(key: INTEGER; VAR data: INTEGER);
BEGIN search(key, root, data)
ENDSearch;.5

PROCEDURE Insert*(key: INTEGER; VAR data: INTEGER);
    VAR h: BOOLEAN; u: Entry; q: Page;
BEGIN h := FALSE; u.data := data; insert(key, root, h, u);
    IF h THEN (*insert new base page*)
```

```
        q := root; NEW(root);
        root.m := 1; root.p0 := q; root.e[0] := u
    END
END Insert;


PROCEDURE Delete*(key: INTEGER);
    VAR h: BOOLEAN;
BEGIN h := FALSE; delete(key, root, h);
    IF h THEN (*base page size underflow*)
        IF root.m = 0 THEN root := root.p0 END
    END
END Delete;


BEGIN NEW(root); root.m := 0
END BTree.
```

Directory enumeration

The B-tree is also a highly appropriate structure for enumerating its elements, because during the traversal of the tree, each page is visited exactly once, and hence needs to be read (from disk) exactly once too. The traversal is programmed by the procedure *Enumerate* and uses recursion. It calls the parametric procedure *proc* for each element of the tree. The type of proc specifies as parameters the name and the (address of) the enumerated element. The third parameter *continue* is a Boolean VAR parameter. If the procedure sets it to FALSE, the process of enumeration will be aborted.

Enumerate is used for obtaining listings of the names of registered files. For this purpose, the actual procedure substituted for *proc* merely enters the given name in a text and ignores the address (sector number) of the file, unless it requires special file information such as the file's size or creation date.

The set of visited elements can be restricted by specifying a string that is to be a prefix to all enumerated names. The least name with the specified prefix is directly searched and is the name (key) of the first element enumerated. The process then proceeds up to the first element whose name does not have the given prefix. Thereby, the process of obtaining all elements whose key has a given prefix avoids traversal of the whole tree, resulting in a significant speedup. If the prefix is the empty string, the entire tree is traversed.

The principle behind procedure *Enumerate* is shown by the following sketch, where we abstract from the B-tree structure and omit consideration of prefixes:

```
PROCEDURE Enumerate(
        proc: PROCEDURE (name: FileName; adr: INTEGER; VAR
            continue: BOOLEAN));
    VAR continue: BOOLEAN; this: DirEntry;
BEGIN continue := TRUE; this := FirstElement;
```

```
        WHILE continue & (this # NIL) DO
            proc(this.name, this.adr, continue); this := NextEntry(this)
        END
    END Enumerate
```

From this sketch, we may conclude that during the process of traversal, the tree structure must not change, because the function *NextEntry* quite evidently relies on the structural information stored in the elements of the structure itself. Hence the actions of the parametric procedure must not affect the tree structure. Enumeration must not be used, for example, to delete a given set of files. In order to prevent the misuse of the indispensible facility of element enumeration, the interface of *FileDir* is not available to users in general.

The handling of the directory stored on disk follows exactly the same algorithms. The accessed pages are fetched from the disk as a whole (each page fits onto a single disk sector) and stored in buffers of type *DirPage*, from where individual elements can be accessed. In principle, these buffers can be local to procedures *insert* and *delete*. A single buffer is allocated globally, namely the one used by procedure *Search*. The reason for this exception is not only that iterative searching requires one buffer only, but also because procedure *Files.Old* and in turn *Search* may be called when the processor is in the supervisor mode and hence uses the system (instead of the user) stack, which is small and would not accommodate sector buffers.

Naturally, an updated page needs to be stored back onto disk. Omission of sector restoration is a programming error that is very hard to diagnose, because some parts of the program are executed very rarely, and hence the error may look sporadic and mistakenly be attributed to malfunctioning hardware.

```
MODULE FileDir;(*NW 12.1.86 / 23.8.90*)
    IMPORT SYSTEM, Kernel;


    (*File Directory is a B-tree with its root page at DirRootAdr.
        Each entry contains a file name and the disk address of the file's head sector*)
    CONST FnLength* = 32;
        SecTabSize* = 64;
        ExTabSize* = 12;
        SectorSize* = 1024;
        IndexSize* = SectorSize DIV 4;
        HeaderSize* = 352;
        DirRootAdr* = 29;
        DirPgSize* = 24;
        N = DirPgSize DIV 2;
        DirMark* = 9B1EA38DH;
        HeaderMark* = 9BA71D86H;
        FillerSize = 52;
    TYPE DiskAdr = LONGINT;
```

```
FileName* = ARRAY FnLength OF CHAR;
SectorTable* = ARRAY SecTabSize OF DiskAdr;
ExtensionTable* = ARRAY ExTabSize OF DiskAdr;
EntryHandler* = PROCEDURE (name:FileName; sec: DiskAdr; VAR continue: BOOLEAN);


FileHeader* =
    RECORD (Kernel.Sector)   (*allocated in the first page of each file on disk*)
        mark*: LONGINT;
        name*: FileName;
        aleng*, bleng*: INTEGER;
        date*, time*: LONGINT;
        ext*: ExtensionTable;
        sec*: SectorTable;
        fill: ARRAY SectorSize – HeaderSize OF CHAR;
    END;


IndexSector* =
    RECORD (Kernel.Sector)
        x*: ARRAY IndexSize OF DiskAdr
    END;


DataSector* =
    RECORD (Kernel.Sector)
        B*: ARRAY SectorSize OF SYSTEM.BYTE
    END;


DirEntry* =   (*B-tree node*)
    RECORD
        name*: FileName;
        adr*: DiskAdr; (*sec no of file header*)
        p*: DiskAdr (*sec no of descendant in directory*)
    END;


DirPage* =
    RECORD (Kernel.Sector)
        mark*: LONGINT;
        m*: INTEGER;
        p0*: DiskAdr; (*sec no of left descendant in directory*)
        fill: ARRAY FillerSize OF CHAR;
        e*: ARRAY DirPgSize OF DirEntry
    END;

PROCEDURE Search*(VAR name: FileName; VAR A: DiskAdr);
    VAR i, j, L, R: INTEGER; dadr: DiskAdr;
        a: DirPage;
BEGIN dadr := DirRootAdr;
    LOOP Kernel.GetSector(dadr, a);
        L := 0; R := a.m; (*binary search*)
        WHILE L < R DO
            i := (L+R) DIV 2;
            IF name <= a.e[i].name THEN R := i ELSE L := i+1 END
        END;
        IF (R < a.m) & (name = a.e[R].name) THEN
            A := a.e[R].adr; EXIT (*found*)
        END;
        IF R = 0 THEN dadr := a.p0 ELSE dadr := a.e[R−1].p END;
```

```
                IF dadr = 0 THEN A := 0; EXIT (*not found*) END
        END
END Search;

PROCEDURE insert(VAR name: FileName;
                    dpg0: DiskAdr;
                    VAR h: BOOLEAN;
                    VAR v: DirEntry;
                    fad: DiskAdr);
    (*h = "tree has become higher and v is ascending element"*)
    VAR ch: CHAR;
        i, j, L, R: INTEGER;
        dpg1: DiskAdr;
        u: DirEntry;
        a: DirPage;


BEGIN (*~h*) Kernel.GetSector(dpg0, a);
    L := 0; R := a.m; (*binary search*)
    WHILE L < R DO
        i := (L+R) DIV 2;
        IF name <= a.e[i].name THEN R := i ELSE L := i+1 END
    END;
    IF (R < a.m) & (name = a.e[R].name) THEN
        a.e[R].adr := fad; Kernel.PutSector(dpg0, a) (*replace*)
    ELSE (*not on this page*)
        IF R = 0 THEN dpg1 := a.p0 ELSE dpg1 := a.e[R-1].p END;
        IF dpg1 = 0 THEN (*not in tree, insert*)
            u.adr := fad; u.p := 0; h := TRUE; j := 0;
            REPEAT ch := name[j]; u.name[j] := ch; INC(j)
            UNTIL ch = 0X;
            WHILE j < FnLength DO u.name[j] := 0X; INC(j) END
        ELSE
            insert(name, dpg1, h, u, fad)
        END;
        IF h THEN (*insert u to the left of e[R]*)
            IF a.m < DirPgSize THEN
                h := FALSE; i := a.m;
                WHILE i > R DO DEC(i); a.e[i+1] := a.e[i] END;
                a.e[R] := u; INC(a.m)
            ELSE (*split page and assign the middle element to v*)
                a.m := N; a.mark := DirMark;
                IF R < N THEN (*insert in left half*)
                    v := a.e[N-1]; i := N-1;
                    WHILE i > R DO DEC(i); a.e[i+1] := a.e[i] END;
                    a.e[R] := u; Kernel.PutSector(dpg0, a);
                    Kernel.AllocSector(dpg0, dpg0); i := 0;
                    WHILE i < N DO a.e[i] := a.e[i+N]; INC(i) END
                ELSE (*insert in right half*)
                    Kernel.PutSector(dpg0, a);
                    Kernel.AllocSector(dpg0, dpg0); DEC(R, N); i := 0;
                    IF R = 0 THEN v := u
                    ELSE v := a.e[N];
                        WHILE i < R-1 DO a.e[i] := a.e[N+1+i]; INC(i) END;
                        a.e[i] := u; INC(i)
                    END;
                    WHILE i < N DO a.e[i] := a.e[N+i]; INC(i) END
                END;
                a.p0 := v.p; v.p := dpg0
```

```
              END;
              Kernel.PutSector(dpg0, a)
          END
      END
  END insert;

  PROCEDURE Insert*(VAR name: FileName; fad: DiskAdr);
      VAR oldroot: DiskAdr;
          h: BOOLEAN; U: DirEntry;
          a: DirPage;
  BEGIN h := FALSE;
      insert(name, DirRootAdr, h, U, fad);
      IF h THEN (*root overflow*)
          Kernel.GetSector(DirRootAdr, a);
          Kernel.AllocSector(DirRootAdr, oldroot); Kernel.PutSector(oldroot, a);
          a.mark := DirMark; a.m := 1; a.p0 := oldroot; a.e[0] := U;
          Kernel.PutSector(DirRootAdr, a)
      END
  END Insert;

  PROCEDURE underflow(VAR c: DirPage; (*ancestor page*)
                          dpg0: DiskAdr;
                          s: INTEGER; (*insertion point in c*)
                          VAR h: BOOLEAN); (*c undersize*)
      VAR i, k: INTEGER;
          dpg1: DiskAdr;
          a, b: DirPage; (*a := underflowing page, b := neighbouring page*)
      BEGIN Kernel.GetSector(dpg0, a);
          (*h & a.m = N−1 & dpg0 = c.e[s−1].p*)
          IF s < c.m THEN (*b := page to the right of a*)
              dpg1 := c.e[s].p; Kernel.GetSector(dpg1, b);
              k := (b.m−N+1) DIV 2; (*k = no. of items available on page b*)
              a.e[N−1] := c.e[s]; a.e[N−1].p := b.p0;
              IF k > 0 THEN
                  (*move k−1 items from b to a, one to c*) i := 0;
                  WHILE i < k−1 DO a.e[i+N] := b.e[i]; INC(i) END;
                  c.e[s] := b.e[i]; b.p0 := c.e[s].p;
                  c.e[s].p := dpg1; DEC(b.m, k); i := 0;
                  WHILE i < b.m DO b.e[i] := b.e[i+k]; INC(i) END;
                  Kernel.PutSector(dpg1, b); a.m := N−1+k; h := FALSE
              ELSE (*merge pages a and b, discard b*) i := 0;
                  WHILE i < N DO a.e[i+N] := b.e[i]; INC(i) END;
                  i := s; DEC(c.m);
                  WHILE i < c.m DO c.e[i] := c.e[i+1]; INC(i) END;
                  a.m := 2*N; h := c.m < N
              END;
              Kernel.PutSector(dpg0, a)
          ELSE (*b := page to the left of a*) DEC(s);
              IF s = 0 THEN dpg1 := c.p0 ELSE dpg1 := c.e[s−1].p END;
              Kernel.GetSector(dpg1, b);
              k := (b.m−N+1) DIV 2; (*k = no. of items available on page b*)
              IF k > 0 THEN
                  i := N−1;
                  WHILE i > 0 DO DEC(i); a.e[i+k] := a.e[i] END;
                  i := k−1; a.e[i] := c.e[s]; a.e[i].p := a.p0;
                  (*move k−1 items from b to a, one to c*) DEC(b.m, k);
                  WHILE i > 0 DO DEC(i); a.e[i] := b.e[i+b.m+1] END;
                  c.e[s] := b.e[b.m]; a.p0 := c.e[s].p;
```

```
            c.e[s].p := dpg0; a.m := N−1+k; h := FALSE;
            Kernel.PutSector(dpg0, a)
        ELSE (*merge pages a and b, discard a*)
            c.e[s].p := a.p0; b.e[N] := c.e[s]; i := 0;
            WHILE i < N−1 DO b.e[i+N+1] := a.e[i]; INC(i) END;
            b.m := 2*N; DEC(c.m); h := c.m < N
        END;
        Kernel.PutSector(dpg1, b)
    END
END underflow;


PROCEDURE delete(VAR name: FileName;
                    dpg0: DiskAdr;
                    VAR h: BOOLEAN;
                    VAR fad: DiskAdr);
(*search and delete entry with key name; if a page underflow arises,
   balance with adjacent page or merge; h := "page dpg0 is undersize"*)


    VAR i, j, k, L, R: INTEGER;
        dpg1: DiskAdr;
        a: DirPage;


    PROCEDURE del(dpg1: DiskAdr; VAR h: BOOLEAN);
        VAR dpg2: DiskAdr;   (*global: a, R*)
            b: DirPage;
    BEGIN Kernel.GetSector(dpg1, b); dpg2 := b.e[b.m−1].p;
        IF dpg2 # 0 THEN del(dpg2, h);
            IF h THEN underflow(b, dpg2, b.m, h); Kernel.PutSector(dpg1, b) END
        ELSE
            b.e[b.m−1].p := a.e[R].p; a.e[R] := b.e[b.m−1];
            DEC(b.m); h := b.m < N; Kernel.PutSector(dpg1, b)
        END
    END del;


BEGIN (*~h*) Kernel.GetSector(dpg0, a);
    L := 0; R := a.m; (*binary search*)
    WHILE L < R DO
        i := (L+R) DIV 2;
        IF name <= a.e[i].name THEN R := i ELSE L := i+1 END
    END;
    IF R = 0 THEN dpg1 := a.p0 ELSE dpg1 := a.e[R−1].p END;
    IF (R < a.m) & (name = a.e[R].name) THEN
        (*found, now delete*) fad := a.e[R].adr;
        IF dpg1 = 0 THEN   (*a is a leaf page*)
            DEC(a.m); h := a.m < N; i := R;
            WHILE i < a.m DO a.e[i] := a.e[i+1]; INC(i) END
        ELSE del(dpg1, h);
            IF h THEN underflow(a, dpg1, R, h) END
        END;
        Kernel.PutSector(dpg0, a)
    ELSIF dpg1 # 0 THEN
        delete(name, dpg1, h, fad);
        IF h THEN underflow(a, dpg1, R, h); Kernel.PutSector(dpg0, a) END
    ELSE (*not in tree*) fad := 0
    END
END delete;
```

```
PROCEDURE Delete*(VAR name: FileName; VAR fad: DiskAdr);
   VAR h: BOOLEAN; newroot: DiskAdr;
      a: DirPage;
BEGIN h := FALSE;
   delete(name, DirRootAdr, h, fad);
   IF h THEN (*root underflow*)
      Kernel.GetSector(DirRootAdr, a);
      IF (a.m = 0) & (a.p0 # 0) THEN
         newroot := a.p0; Kernel.GetSector(newroot, a);
         Kernel.PutSector(DirRootAdr, a) (*discard newroot*)
      END
   END
END Delete;


PROCEDURE enumerate(VAR prefix:   ARRAY OF CHAR;
                      dpg: DiskAdr;
                      proc: EntryHandler;
                      VAR continue: BOOLEAN);
   VAR i, j, diff: INTEGER; dpg1: DiskAdr; a: DirPage;
BEGIN Kernel.GetSector(dpg, a); i := 0;
   WHILE (i < a.m) & continue DO
      j := 0;
      LOOP
         IF prefix[j] = 0X THEN diff := 0; EXIT END;
         diff := ORD(a.e[i].name[j]) - ORD(prefix[j]);
         IF diff # 0 THEN EXIT END;
         INC(j)
      END;
      IF i = 0 THEN dpg1 := a.p0 ELSE dpg1 := a.e[i-1].p END;
      IF diff >= 0 THEN (*matching prefix*)
         IF dpg1 # 0 THEN enumerate(prefix, dpg1, proc, continue) END;
         IF diff = 0 THEN
            IF continue THEN proc(a.e[i].name, a.e[i].adr, continue) END
         ELSE continue := FALSE
         END
      END;
      INC(i)
   END;
   IF continue & (i > 0) & (a.e[i-1].p # 0) THEN
      enumerate(prefix, a.e[i-1].p, proc, continue)
   END
END enumerate;


PROCEDURE Enumerate*(prefix: ARRAY OF CHAR; proc: EntryHandler);
   VAR b: BOOLEAN;
BEGIN b := TRUE; enumerate(prefix, DirRootAdr, proc, b)
END Enumerate;


PROCEDURE Init;
   VAR k: INTEGER;
      A: ARRAY 2000 OF DiskAdr;

   PROCEDURE MarkSectors;
      VAR L, R, i, j, n: INTEGER; x: DiskAdr;
         hd: FileHeader;
         B: IndexSector;
```

```
          PROCEDURE sift(L, R: INTEGER);
            VAR i, j: INTEGER; x: DiskAdr;
          BEGIN j := L; x := A[j];
            LOOP i := j; j := 2*j + 1;
              IF (j+1 < R) & (A[j] < A[j+1]) THEN INC(j) END;
              IF (j >= R) OR (x > A[j]) THEN EXIT END;
              A[i] := A[j]
            END;
            A[i] := x
          END sift;

        BEGIN L := k DIV 2; R := k; (*heapsort*)
          WHILE L > 0 DO DEC(L); sift(L, R) END;
          WHILE R > 0 DO
            DEC(R); x := A[0]; A[0] := A[R]; A[R] := x; sift(L, R)
          END;
          WHILE L < k DO
            Kernel.GetSector(A[L], hd);
            IF hd.aleng < SecTabSize THEN j := hd.aleng + 1;
              REPEAT DEC(j); Kernel.MarkSector(hd.sec[j]) UNTIL j = 0
            ELSE j := SecTabSize;
              REPEAT DEC(j); Kernel.MarkSector(hd.sec[j]) UNTIL j = 0;
              n := (hd.aleng − SecTabSize) DIV 256; i := 0;
              WHILE i <= n DO
                Kernel.MarkSector(hd.ext[i]);
                Kernel.GetSector(hd.ext[i], B); (*index sector*)
                IF i < n THEN j := 256
                ELSE j := (hd.aleng − SecTabSize) MOD 256 + 1
                END;
                REPEAT DEC(j); Kernel.MarkSector(B.x[j]) UNTIL j = 0;
                INC(i)
              END
            END;
            INC(L)
          END
        END MarkSectors;


        PROCEDURE TraverseDir(dpg: DiskAdr);
          VAR i, j: INTEGER; a: DirPage;
        BEGIN Kernel.GetSector(dpg, a); Kernel.MarkSector(dpg); i := 0;
          WHILE i < a.m DO
            A[k] := a.e[i].adr; INC(k); INC(i);
            IF k = 2000 THEN MarkSectors; k := 0 END
          END;
          IF a.p0 # 0 THEN
            TraverseDir(a.p0); i := 0;
            WHILE i < a.m DO
              TraverseDir(a.e[i].p); INC(i)
            END
          END
        END TraverseDir;


      BEGIN Kernel.ResetDisk; k := 0;
        TraverseDir(DirRootAdr); MarkSectors
      END Init;


    BEGIN Init
    END FileDir.
```

Oberon's file directory represents a single, ordered set of name–file pairs. It is therefore also called a *flat directory*. Its internal tree structure is not visible to the outside. In contrast, some file systems use a directory with a visible tree structure, notably UNIX. In a search, the name (key) guides the search path; the name itself displays structure, in fact, it is a sequence of names (usually separated by slashes or periods). The first name is then searched in the *root directory*, whose descendants are not files but *subdirectories*. The process is repeated, until the last name in the sequence has been used (and, it is hoped, denotes a file).

Since the search path length in a tree increases with the logarithm of the number of elements, any subdivision of the tree inherently decreases performance since $\log (m + n) < \log m + \log n$ for any m, $n > 1$. It is justified only if there exist sets of elements with common properties. If these property values are stored once, namely in the subdirectory referencing all elements with common property values, instead of in every element, then a gain results not only in storage economy, but possibly also in accesses that depend on those properties. The common properties are typically an owner's name, a password and access rights (read or write protection), properties that primarily have significance in a multi-user environment. Since Oberon was conceived explicitly as a single-user system, there is little need for such facilities, and hence a flat directory offers the best performance with a simple implementation.

Every directory operation starts with an access to the root page. An obvious measure for improving efficiency is to store the root page 'permanently' in main store. We have chosen not to do this for three reasons:

(1) If the hardware fails, or if the computer is switched off before the root page is copied to disk, the file directory will be inconsistent, with severe consequences.

(2) The root page has to be treated differently from other pages, making the program more complex.

(3) Directory accesses do not dominate the computing process; hence any improvement would hardly be noticeable in overall system performance. The payoff for the added complexity would be small.

(4) Procedure *Init* is called upon system initialization in order to construct the sector reservation table. Therefore this procedure (and the module) must be allowed to refer to the structure of a file's sector table(s), which is achieved by placing its definitions into the module *FileDir* (instead of *Files*). Unlike *Enumerate*, *Init* traverses the *entire* B-tree. The sector numbers of files delivered by *Traverse Dir* are entered into a buffer. When full, the entries are sorted, after which each file's head sector is read and the

sectors indicated in its sector table are marked as reserved. The sorting speeds up the reading of the header sectors considerably. Nevertheless, the initialization of the sector reservation table clearly dominates the startup time of the computer. For a file system with 10 000 files, it takes of order 15 s to record all files.

7.5 The toolbox of file utilities

We conclude this chapter with a presentation of the commands that constitute the toolbox for file handling. These commands are contained in module *System*, and they serve to copy, rename and delete files, and to obtain excerpts of the file directory.

Copy Rename Delete
Procedures *CopyFiles*, *RenameFiles* and *DeleteFiles* all follow the same pattern. The parameter text is scanned for file names, and for each operation a corresponding procedure is called. If the parameter text contains an arrow, it is interpreted as a pointer to the most recent text selection that indicates the file name. In the cases of *CopyFiles* and *RenameFiles*, which require two names for a single action, the names are separated by '=>', indicating the direction of the copy or rename actions.

```
PROCEDURE CopyFile(name: ARRAY OF CHAR; VAR S: Texts.Scanner);
    VAR f, g: Files.File; Rf, Rg: Files.Rider; ch: CHAR;
BEGIN Texts.Scan(S);
    IF (S.class = Texts.Char) & (S.c = "=") THEN Texts.Scan(S);
        IF (S.class = Texts.Char) & (S.c = ">") THEN Texts.Scan(S);
            IF S.class = Texts.Name THEN
                Texts.WriteString(W, name); Texts.WriteString(W, " => "); Texts.WriteString(W, S.s);
                Texts.WriteString(W, "copying"); Texts.Append(Oberon.Log, W.buf);
                f := Files.Old(name);
                IF f # NIL THEN g := Files.New(S.s);
                    Files.Set(Rf, f, 0); Files.Set(Rg, g, 0); Files.Read(Rf, ch);
                    WHILE ~Rf.eof DO Files.Write(Rg, ch); Files.Read(Rf, ch) END;
                    Files.Register(g)
                ELSE Texts.WriteString(W, "failed")
                END;
                Texts.WriteLn(W); Texts.Append(Oberon.Log, W.buf)
            END
        END
    END
END CopyFile;


PROCEDURE CopyFiles*;
    VAR beg, end, time: LONGINT; res: INTEGER;
        T: Texts.Text;
        S: Texts.Scanner;
BEGIN Texts.WriteString(W, "System.CopyFiles"); Texts.WriteLn(W);
    Texts.Append(Oberon.Log, W.buf);
    Texts.OpenScanner(S, Oberon.Par.text, Oberon.Par.pos); Texts.Scan(S);
    WHILE S.class = Texts.Name DO CopyFile(S.s, S); Texts.Scan(S) END;
```

```
      IF (S.class = Texts.Char) & (S.c = " ↑ ") THEN Oberon.GetSelection(T, beg, end, time);
        IF time >= 0 THEN
          Texts.OpenScanner(S, T, beg); Texts.Scan(S);
            IF S.class = Texts.Name THEN CopyFile(S.s, S) END
        END
      END
END CopyFiles;


PROCEDURE RenameFile(name: ARRAY OF CHAR; VAR S: Texts.Scanner);
    VAR res: INTEGER;
BEGIN Texts.Scan(S);
    IF (S.class = Texts.Char) & (S.c = "=") THEN Texts.Scan(S);
      IF (S.class = Texts.Char) & (S.c = ">") THEN Texts.Scan(S);
        IF S.class = Texts.Name THEN
            Texts.WriteString(W, name); Texts.WriteString(W, " => "); Texts.WriteString(W, S.s);
            Texts.WriteString(W, "renaming"); Texts.Append(Oberon.Log, W.buf);
            Files.Rename(name, S.s, res);
            IF res > 1 THEN Texts.WriteString(W, "failed") END;
            Texts.WriteLn(W); Texts.Append(Oberon.Log, W.buf)
        END
      END
    END
END RenameFile;


PROCEDURE RenameFiles*;
    VAR beg, end, time: LONGINT; res: INTEGER;
      T: Texts.Text;
      S: Texts.Scanner;
BEGIN Texts.WriteString(W, "System.RenameFiles"); Texts.WriteLn(W);
    Texts.Append(Oberon.Log, W.buf);
    Texts.OpenScanner(S, Oberon.Par.text, Oberon.Par.pos); Texts.Scan(S);
    WHILE S.class = Texts.Name DO RenameFile(S.s, S); Texts.Scan(S) END;
    IF (S.class = Texts.Char) & (S.c = " ↑ ") THEN
        Oberon.GetSelection(T, beg, end, time);
        IF time >= 0 THEN
          Texts.OpenScanner(S, T, beg); Texts.Scan(S);
            IF S.class = Texts.Name THEN RenameFile(S.s, S) END
        END
      END
END RenameFiles;


PROCEDURE DeleteFile (VAR name: ARRAY OF CHAR);
    VAR res: INTEGER;
BEGIN Texts.WriteString(W, name); Texts.WriteString(W, "deleting");
    Texts.Append(Oberon.Log, W.buf); Files.Delete(name, res);
    IF res # 0 THEN Texts.WriteString(W, "failed") END;
    Texts.WriteLn(W); Texts.Append(Oberon.Log, W.buf)
END DeleteFile;


PROCEDURE DeleteFiles*;
    VAR beg, end, time: LONGINT;
      T: Texts.Text;
      S: Texts.Scanner;
BEGIN Texts.WriteString(W, "System.DeleteFiles"); Texts.WriteLn(W);
    Texts.Append(Oberon.Log, W.buf);
    Texts.OpenScanner(S, Oberon.Par.text, Oberon.Par.pos); Texts.Scan(S);
    WHILE S.class = Texts.Name DO DeleteFile(S.s); Texts.Scan(S) END;
```

```
    IF (S.class = Texts.Char) & (S.c = " ↑ ") THEN
        Oberon.GetSelection(T, beg, end, time);
        IF time >= 0 THEN Texts.OpenScanner(S, T, beg); Texts.Scan(S);
            IF S.class = Texts.Name THEN DeleteFile(S.s) END
        END
    END
END DeleteFiles;
```

Directory   Procedure *Directory* serves to obtain excerpts of the file directory. It makes use of procedure *FileDir.Enumerate*. The parametric procedure *List* tests whether or not the delivered name matches the pattern specified by the parameter of the directory command. If it matches, the name is listed in the text of the viewer opened in the system track. Since the pattern may contain one or several asterisks (wild cards), the test consists of a sequence of searches of the pattern parts (separated by the asterisks) in the file name. In order to reduce the number of calls of *List*, *Enumerate* is called with the first part of the pattern as parameter prefix. Enumeration then starts with the least name having the specified prefix, and terminates as soon as all names with this prefix have been scanned.

If the specified pattern is followed by an option directive "/date" then not only file names are listed, but also the listed files' creation date and length. This requires not only that the directory sectors on the disk be traversed, but that additionally for each listed file its header sector must be read. The two procedures use the global variables *pat* and *diroption*.

```
PROCEDURE* List(name: FileDir.FileName; adr: LONGINT; VAR cont: BOOLEAN);
    VAR i0, i1, j0, j1: INTEGER; f: BOOLEAN; hp: FileDir.FileHeader;
BEGIN i0 := pos; j0 := pos; f := TRUE;
    LOOP
        IF pat[i0] = "*" THEN INC(i0);
            IF pat[i0] = 0X THEN EXIT END
        ELSE
            IF name[j0] # 0X THEN f := FALSE END;
            EXIT
        END;
        f := FALSE;
        LOOP
            IF name[j0] = 0X THEN EXIT END;
            i1 := i0; j1 := j0;
            LOOP
                IF pat[i1] = "*" THEN f := TRUE; EXIT END;
                IF pat[i1] # name[j1] THEN EXIT END;
                INC(i1); INC(j1);
                IF pat[i1−1] = 0X THEN f := TRUE; EXIT END
            END;
            IF f THEN j0 := j1; i0 := i1; EXIT END;
            INC(j0)
        END;
        IF ~f OR (pat[i0−1] = 0X) THEN EXIT END
    END;
```

```
IF f THEN
    Texts.WriteString(W, name);
    IF diroption = "d" THEN
        Kernel.GetSector(adr, hp);
        Texts.WriteString(W, "    "); Texts.WriteDate(W, hp.time, hp.date);
        Texts.WriteInt(W, LONG(hp.aleng)*FileDir.SectorSize + hp.bleng − FileDir.HeaderSize, 8)
    END;
    Texts.WriteLn(W)
END
END List;


PROCEDURE Directory*;
    VAR X, Y, i: INTEGER; ch: CHAR;
        R: Texts.Reader;
        T, t: Texts.Text;
        V: Viewers.Viewer;
        beg, end, time: LONGINT;
        pre: ARRAY 32 OF CHAR;
BEGIN Texts.OpenReader(R, Oberon.Par.text, Oberon.Par.pos); Texts.Read(R, ch);
    WHILE ch = " " DO Texts.Read(R, ch) END;
    IF (ch = " ↑ ") OR (ch = 0DX) THEN
        Oberon.GetSelection(T, beg, end, time);
        IF time >= 0 THEN
            Texts.OpenReader(R, T, beg); Texts.Read(R, ch);
            WHILE ch <= " " DO Texts.Read(R, ch) END
        END
    END;
    i := 0;
    WHILE (ch > " ") & (ch # "/") DO pat[i] := ch; INC(i); Texts.Read(R, ch) END;
    pat[i] := 0X;
    IF ch = "/" THEN Texts.Read(R, diroption) ELSE diroption := 0X END;
    i := 0;
    WHILE pat[i] > "*" DO pre[i] := pat[i]; INC(i) END;
    pre[i] := 0X; pos := i;
    Oberon.AllocateSystemViewer(Oberon.Par.vwr.X, X, Y); t := TextFrames.Text("");
    V := MenuViewers.New(
        TextFrames.NewMenu("System.Directory", StandardMenu),
        TextFrames.NewText(t, 0), TextFrames.menuH, X, Y);
    FileDir.Enumerate(pre, List); Texts.Append(t, W.buf)
END Directory;
```

7.6   References

Bayer R. and McCreight, E. M. (1972). Organization and maintenance of large ordered indexes. *Acta Informatica*, **1**(3), 173–189.

Comer, D. (1979). The ubiquitous B-tree. *ACM Computing Surveys*, **11**(2), 121–137.

8 Storage layout and management

8.1 Storage layout and run-time organization

A crucial property of the Oberon System is centralized resource management. Its advantage is that replication of management algorithms and premature partitioning of resources are avoided. The disadvantage is that management algorithms are fixed once and forever and remain the same for all applications. The success of a centralized resource management therefore depends crucially on its flexibility and its efficient implementation. This chapter presents the scheme and the algorithms governing main storage in the Oberon System.

The storage layout of the Oberon System is determined by the structure of code and data typical in the use of modular, high-level programming languages, and in particular of the language Oberon. It suggests the subdivision of storage into three areas.

Block space
(1) *The block space.* Every module specifies procedures (code) and global (static) variables. Its initialization part can be regarded as a procedure implicitly called after loading. Upon loading, space must be allocated for code and data. Typically, modules contain very few or no global variables; hence the size of the allocated space is primarily determined by the code. The combined code and data space is called a *block*. Blocks are allocated in the block space.

Workspace stack
(2) *The workspace (stack).* Execution of every command invokes a sequence of procedures, each of which uses (possibly zero) parameters and local variables. Since procedure calls and completions follow a strict first-in last-out order, the stack is the uniquely suited strategy for storage allocation for local data. Deallocation upon completion of a procedure is achieved by merely resetting the pointer identifying the top of the stack. Since this operation is implied in appropriate machine instructions (for returns), it costs zero execution time. Because Oberon is a

single-process system, a *single stack suffices*. Furthermore, after completion of a command, the stack is empty. This fact will be important in simplifying the scheme for reclamation of dynamically allocated space.

Heap

(3) *The dynamic space (heap)*. Apart from global (static) and local (stack-allocated) variables, a program may refer to anonymous variables referenced through pointers. Such variables are allocated truly dynamically through calls of an explicit operation (NEW). These variables are allocated in the so-called *heap*. Their deallocation is 'automatic', when free storage is needed and they are no longer referenced from any of the loaded modules. This process is called *garbage collection*.

Unfortunately, the number of distinct spaces is larger than two. If it were two, no arbitrary size limitation would be necessary; merely the sum of their sizes would be inherently limited by the size of the store. In the case of three spaces, arbitrarily determined size limits are

Address mapping

unavoidable. The presence of an address-mapping hardware alleviates the problem, however, because the virtual address space is so large that limits will hardly ever be reached.

Furthermore, we note that both the stack and the heap space must be genuinely allocated, that is, any address within the space must denote a physically present location. Hence there is no point in making the virtual address space of their sum larger than the entire physical store. The size of the virtual block space then becomes the difference between virtual and physical address space. The resulting layout is shown in Figure 8.1. The upper end of the address space is reserved for device registers.

If address mapping is unavailable, as in the case of Ceres-3, which lacks a memory management unit, the fixing of size limitations is unavoidable. The chosen layout for Ceres-3 is shown in Figure 8.2; the stack is limited to 128 Kbytes.

The area with address range 0...FFFFH contains the following:

(1) The NIL-page (0...FFFH), which remains permanently unallocated. The purpose of this measure is to let references via a NIL-pointer invoke addressing traps.

(2) The system stack (1000H...17FFH), which is used by interrupt routines executed in supervisor mode, including the trap handler.

(3) Allocation tables for pages and disk sectors.

(4) Module descriptors (4000H...7FFFH).

(5) Blocks for the permanently resident modules of the inner core, namely *Kernel*, *FileDir*, *Files* and *Modules*.

Stack organization

The workspace is organized in the usual fashion as a stack of procedure activation records. Its top is denoted by the SP-register. A

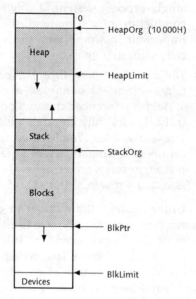

Figure 8.1 Storage layout for Ceres-1 and Ceres-2.

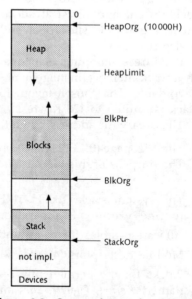

Figure 8.2 Storage layout for Ceres-3.

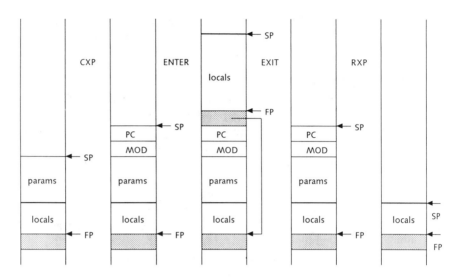

Figure 8.3 State of stack before and after procedure call and return.

Procedure activation record

second register, the so-called *frame pointer* FP is the anchor of the dynamic chain of activation records. A new element is added upon procedure call in two steps. The first step is performed after the loading of parameters by the call instruction (CXP for calls of external, BSR for calls of local procedures). The second step is performed by the ENTER instruction, which is the first instruction of every procedure body. An activation record is removed, also in two steps, upon procedure completion by the instructions EXIT and RXP for external or RET for local procedures. The state of the workspace before and after these four steps is shown in Figure 8.3.

Relative addressing

It follows that local variables are addressed relative to the FP value with negative offsets. Parameters are addressed relative to FP with positive offsets, starting at 12 for external procedures called by a CXP instruction, and at 8 for local procedures, where the MOD register is not pushed onto the stack by the call instruction.

Global variables and constants (strings) are accessed via the SB register (static base). The value of this register is automatically adjusted by the CXP and RXP instruction as well as by interrupts and traps.

8.2 Allocation of module blocks

As indicated in the preceding section, storage for global (static) variables, for constants and for the program code of modules is allocated in the block space. Every module is represented by a single block. In addition, each module is assigned a module descriptor containing various pointers into sections of the block (see Chapter 6). The separation into a descriptor and a block is imposed by the architecture of the NS32000 processor, which supports module structures through its external addressing mode. The physical separation is necessary because descriptor addresses are confined to 16 bit values and therefore cannot be managed in the same way as general, dynamic storage. This is rather unfortunate.

Block management is represented by the two procedures *Kernel.AllocBlock* and *Kernel.FreeBlock*. Implementations differ for the various models of the Ceres computer. This is because Ceres-1 and Ceres-2 incorporate the concept of virtual storage represented by an address mapping memory management unit (MMU), whereas Ceres-3 does not. In the former case, allocated (physical) pages are registered in a *page reservation table*. The store is regarded as a set of pages, and the table contains a single bit for each page, 0 signifying that the respective page has been allocated. Each block consists of an integral number of pages, whose size is as follows:

Page reservation table

Computer	Page size
Ceres-1	512
Ceres-2	4096
Ceres-3	1024

In the case of Ceres-1 and Ceres-2, the virtual address space for blocks is so large that new blocks can be given steadily increasing addresses without regard to any holes that may have arisen because of released blocks. The required physical pages are obtained by simply scanning the reservation table. Block release merely consists of marking the released pages as free in the table.

Naturally, the appropriate entries in the page tables must be marked (or reset), and possibly new page tables need to be allocated as well. We emphasize that these operations must be performed with the MMU switched off and with *all interrupts disabled*.

The NS32000 MMU architecture uses a two-stage table scheme shown in Figure 8.4. The reason is as follows. The page table must be large enough to cover the entire virtual address range. Assuming a page size of 4 Kbytes and an address space of 4 Gbytes (32-bit addresses), no less than 2^{20} elements are required, resulting in a table of 4 Mbytes, which clearly is unacceptable. Using a two-level scheme, each entry of the (primary) table points to a second-level table, which itself covers a large section of the store. In the NS32532 processor, all tables have a

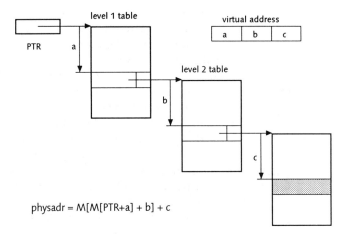

Figure 8.4 NS32000 virtual addressing scheme.

size of 4 Kbytes and consist of 1K (= 1024) entries. Hence every second-level table covers a space of 1024 × 4 Kbytes = 4 Mbytes, and therefore a first-level page of 1K entries suffices to cover the entire virtual space of 4 Gbytes.

The disadvantage of the two-stage scheme is, of course, that upon a translation-cache miss, not only two, but three memory accesses are required to access a word. (For further details, we refer the reader to the literature and the processor manual.)

The handling of the tables is concentrated in two internal Kernel routines for allocating and freeing physical pages. They consist of about 75 instructions.

Of course, the need for a triple access for every memory reference is avoided by a translation cache in the unit. Nevertheless, a decrease in performance is unavoidable for each cache miss. Furthermore, an additional subcycle is required for *every* access in order to look up the cached translation table. The Ceres-3 computer includes no MMU and address translation. As a consequence, each block must consist of an integral number of *physically adjacent* pages. Holes generated by the release of blocks must be reused. We employ the simple scheme of keeping a list of holes, and of allocating a new block in the first hole encountered that is large enough (first-fit strategy). Considering the relative infrequency of module releases, efforts to improve the strategy are not worth the resulting added complexity.

It is remarkable that the code for block allocation and release without virtual addressing is only marginally more complicated than with it (69 versus 49 instructions). If the routines for managing page tables are included, it becomes even simpler (69 versus 124 instructions).

The only remaining advantages of an MMU are better storage utilization, because no holes occur (a negligible advantage), and that inadvertent references to unloaded modules, for example via installed procedures, lead to an invalid address trap.

It is worth recalling that the concept of address mapping was introduced as a requirement for virtual memory implemented with disks as backing store, where pages could be moved into the background in order to obtain space for newly required pages, and could then be retrieved from disk on demand, that is, when access was requested. This scheme is called *demand paging*. It is not used in the Oberon System, and one may fairly state that demand paging has lost its significance with the availability of large, primary stores.

Experience in the use of Ceres leads to the conclusion that, whereas address translation through an MMU was an essential feature for multi-user operating systems, it constitutes a dispensible overkill for single-user workstations. The fact that modern semiconductor technology makes it possible to integrate the entire translation and caching scheme into a single chip, or even into the processor itself, led to the hiding (and ignoring) of the scheme's considerable complexity. Its side-effects on execution speed are essentially unpredictable. This makes systems with MMU virtually unusable for applications with tight real-time constraints.

8.3 Management of dynamic storage

The term *dynamic storage* is used here for all variables that are allocated neither statically (global variables) nor on the stack (local variables), but through invocation of the intrinsic procedure NEW. Such variables are anonymous and are referenced exclusively via pointers. The space in which they are allocated is called the *heap*.

Heap

The space allocated to such dynamic variables becomes free and reusable as soon as the last reference to it vanishes. This event is hard, and in multiprocess systems even impossible to detect. The usual remedy is to ignore it and instead to determine the accessibility of all allocated variables (records, objects) only at the time when more storage space is needed. This process is then called *garbage collection*.

Garbage collection

The Oberon System does not provide an explicit deallocation procedure allowing the programmer to signal that a variable will no longer be referenced. The first reason for this omission is that usually a programmer would not know when to call for deallocation. And secondly, this 'hint' could not be taken as trustworthy. An erroneous deallocation, that is, one occurring when there still exist references to the object in question, could lead to a multiple allocation of the same

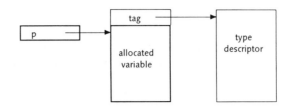

Figure 8.5 Effect of procedure NEW(p).

space with disastrous consequences. Hence it appears wise to fully rely on system management to determine which areas of the store are truly reusable.

Dynamic allocation

Before discussing the scheme for storage reclamation, which is the primary subject of dynamic storage management, we turn our attention to the problem of allocation, that is, the implementation of procedure NEW. The simplest solution is to maintain a list of free blocks and to pick the first one large enough. This strategy leads to a relatively large fragmentation of space and produces many small elements, particularly in the first part of the list. We therefore employ a somewhat more refined scheme and maintain five lists of available space. Four of them contain pieces of fixed size, namely 16, 32, 64 and 128 bytes. The fifth list contains pieces whose size is any multiple of 128. Procedure NEW rounds up the requested size to the least of these values and picks the first element of the respective list. We note that the choice of the values permits the merging of any two contiguous elements into an element of the next list. This scheme keeps fragmentation, that is, the emergence of small pieces in large numbers, reasonably low with minimal effort. The body of procedure NEW consists of only 100 instructions, and typically only a small fraction of them needs to be executed.

Lists of available pieces

Fragmentation

Type tag

The statement NEW(p) is compiled into an instruction sequence assigning the address of pointer variable p to a fixed register (R0) and the type tag to another register (R1). The type tag is a pointer to a type descriptor containing information required by the garbage collector. This includes the size of the space occupied and now to be allocated. The effect of NEW is the assignment of the address of the allocated block to p, and the assignment of the tag to a prefix of the block (see Figure 8.5). (Note that the Oberon compiler for Ceres also features a procedure SYSTEM.NEW(p, n). It allows one to allocate a block without a fixed type identified by a descriptor. Here the size n is placed in the block's prefix in place of the tag. Bit 0 indicates whether bits 0–23 represent a tag or a size. Such a facility is required because descriptors are also elements in the heap, and they lack a descriptor of the descriptor, since the system can rely on their known structure.)

In conclusion, we emphasize that this scheme makes the allocation of an object very efficient. Nevertheless, it is considerably more costly than that of a variable explicitly declared.

Storage reclamation

We now turn to the problem of storage reclamation or garbage collection. There exist two essentially different schemes: the reference counting and the mark-scan schemes. In the former, every object carries a (hidden) reference count, indicating the number of existing references.

NEW(p) initializes the reference count of p ↑ to 1.

q := p decrements the reference count of q ↑ by 1, performs the assignment, then increments the reference count of p ↑ by 1. When a reference count reaches zero, the element is linked into the free list.

There are two disadvantages inherent in this approach. The first is the non-negligible overhead in pointer assignments. The second is that circular data structures never become recognized as free, even if no external references point to their elements.

The Ceres–Oberon System employs the second scheme, which involves no hidden operations like the reference counting scheme, but relies on a process initiated when free storage has become scarce and more is needed. It consists of two phases. In the first phase, all referenced and therefore still accessible elements are marked. In the second phase, their unmarked complement is released. The first phase is called the *mark phase*, and the second the *scan phase*. Its primary disadvantage is that the process may be started at moments unpredictable to the system's user. During the process, the computer then appears to be blocked. It follows that an interactive system using mark-scan garbage collection must guarantee that the process is sufficiently fast in order to be hardly noticeable. Modern processors make this possible, even with large main stores. Nevertheless, finding all accessible nodes in an entire computer system within a second appears to be a formidable feat.

Mark phase

We recognize that the *mark phase* essentially is a tree traversal, or rather a forest traversal. The roots of the trees are all named pointer variables in existence. We shall postpone the question of how these roots are to be found, and first present a quick tutorial about tree traversal. In general, nodes of the traversed structure may contain many pointers (branches). We shall, however, first restrict our attention to a *binary tree*, because the essential problem and its solution can be explained better in this way.

Binary tree traversal

The essential problem alluded to is that of storage utilization by the traversal algorithm itself. Typically, information about the nodes already visited must be retained, be it explicitly, or implicitly as in the

Figure 8.6 Rotation of pointers.

case of use of recursion. Such a strategy is plainly unacceptable, because the amount of storage needed may become very large, and because garbage collection is typically initiated just when more storage is unavailable. The task may seem impossible, yet a solution lies in the idea of inverting pointers along the path traversed, thus keeping the return path open. It is embodied in the following procedure, whose task is to traverse the tree given by the parameter *root*, and to mark every node. Mark values are assumed to be initially 0. Let the data structure be defined by the types

```
Ptr = POINTER TO Node;
Node = RECORD m: INTEGER; L, R: Ptr END;
```

and the algorithm by the procedure

```
PROCEDURE traverse(root: Ptr);
  VAR p, q, r; Ptr;
BEGIN p := root; q := root;
  REPEAT (* p # NIL *) INC(p.m); (*mark*)
    IF p.L # NIL THEN
      r := p.L; p.L := p.R; p.R := q; q := p; p := r
    ELSE
      p.L := p.R; p.R := q; q:= NIL
    END
  UNTIL p = q
END traverse
```

We note that only three local variables are required, independent of the size of the tree to be traversed. The third, r, is in fact merely an auxiliary variable to perform the rotation of values p.L, p.R, q and p as shown in Figure 8.6. A snapshot of a tree traversal is shown in Figure 8.7.

The pair p, q of pointers marks the position of the process. The algorithm traverses the tree in a left to right, depth first fashion. When it returns to the root, all nodes have been marked.

How are these claims convincingly supported? The best way is by analysing the algorithm at an arbitrary node. We start with the

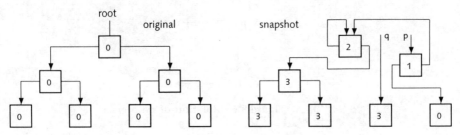

Figure 8.7   Tree traversal.

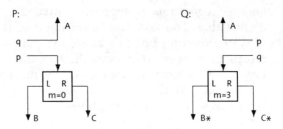

Figure 8.8   Transition from state P to state Q.

<table>
<tr><td>Postulating
hypothesis</td></tr>
</table>

Postulating hypothesis

hypothesis H that, given the initial state P, the algorithm will reach state Q (see Figure 8.8).

State Q differs from P by the node and its descendants B and C having been marked, and by an exchange of p and q. We now apply the algorithm to state P, assuming that B and C are not empty. The process is illustrated in Figure 8.9. P0 stands for P in Figure 8.8.

Transitions P0 → P1, P2 → P3 and P4 → P5 are the direct results of applying the pointer rotation as specified by the sequence of five assignments in the algorithm. Transitions P1 → P2 and P3 → P4 follow from the hypothesis H being applied to the states P1 and P3: subtrees are marked, and p and q are interchanged. We note in passing that the node is visited three times. Progress is recorded by the mark value, which is incremented from 0 to 3.

Figure 8.9 demonstrates that if H holds for steps P1 → P2 and P3 → P4, then it also holds for step P0 → P5, which visits the subtree p. Hence it also holds for the step root → root, which traverses the entire tree.

Verifying hypothesis by induction

This proof by recursion relies on the algorithm performing correct transitions also in the case of p.L being NIL, that is, B being the empty tree. In this case, state P1 is skipped; the first transition is P0 → P2 (see Figure 8.10).

If p.L is again NIL, that is also C is empty, the next transition is P2 → P4. This concludes the demonstration of the algorithm's correctness.

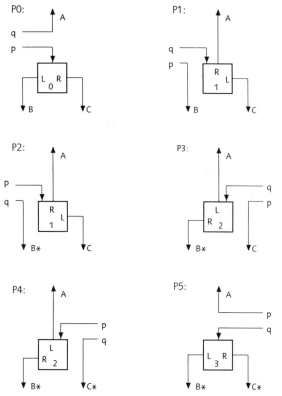

Figure 8.9 Transitions from P0 to P5, visiting node three times.

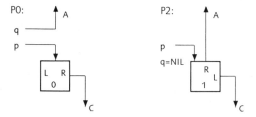

Figure 8.10 Direct transition from P0 to P2, if p.L = NIL.

We now modify the algorithm of tree traversal to the case where the structure is not confined to a binary tree, but may be a tree of any degree, that is, each node may have any number n of descendants. For practical purposes, however, we restrict n to be in the range $0 \leqslant n \leqslant N$, and therefore may represent all nodes by the type

```
Node = RECORD m, n: INTEGER;
            dsc: ARRAY N OF Node
         END
```

In principle, the binary tree traversal algorithm might be adopted almost without change, merely extending the rotation of pointers from *p.L, p.R, q, p* to *p.dsc*[0], . . . , *p.dsc*[*n*-1], *q*, *p*. However, this would be an unnecessarily inefficient solution. The following is merely a more effective variant:

```
PROCEDURE traverse(root: Ptr);
   VAR k: INTEGER; p, q, r: Ptr;
BEGIN p := root; q := root;
   LOOP (* p # NIL*) k := p.m; INC(p.m); (*mark*)
      IF k < p.n THEN
         r := p.dsc[k];
         IF r # NIL THEN p.dsc[k] := q; q := p; p := r END
      ELSIF p = q THEN EXIT
      ELSE k := q.m − 1;
         r := q.dsc[k]; q.dsc[k] := p; p := q; q := r
      END
   END
END traverse
```

We note that the mark value, starting with zero (unmarked), is used as a counter of descendants already traversed, and hence as an index to the descendant field to be processed next. The algorithm can be applied not only to trees, but to arbitrary structures, including circular ones, if the continuation condition k < p.n is extended to (k < p.n) & (r.m = 0). This causes a descendant that is already marked to be skipped.

Type descriptor prefix
    Oberon's garbage collector uses exactly this algorithm. The mark is included in each record's hidden prefix. The prefix takes 4 bytes only; 3 are used for the tag or the size, and one is reserved for the garbage collector and used as mark. It follows that no record may contain more than 255 pointers. The number n of pointers (descendants) in a record is contained in the record's type descriptor. (Records without descriptor, generated by SYSTEM.NEW, must not contain descendants.)

Format of type descriptor
    Type descriptors consist of the following fields (excluding the prefix):

size	in bytes, of the described type, (3 bytes)
n	number of descendants in the described type (1 byte)

base   a table of pointers to the descriptors of the base
              types (7 elements)

offsets   of the descendant pointers in the described type
              (2 bytes each)

Type descriptors themselves have a prefix containing a mark field and
the size of the descriptor, which is at least 36 (3 bytes for size, 1 byte
for n, 4 for the prefix and 28 for the base tag table).

We emphasize that type descriptors need to be allocated in the
heap. They cannot be placed among the module's constants in the block
space, although they are constants, because elements in the heap may
refer to a descriptor even after the module defining the type had been
unloaded. This is the case when a structure rooted in a variable of base
type T declared in a module M contains elements of an extension T'
defined in module M', after M' has been unloaded, but when M is still
present. See Figure 8.11.

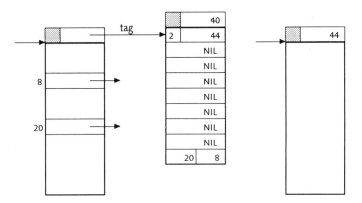

Figure 8.11 Records with and without type descriptor.

Scan phase   The scan phase is performed by a relatively straightforward
algorithm. The heap, that is, the storage area between *HeapOrg* and
HeapLimit (the latter is a variable), is scanned element by element,
starting at *HeapOrg*. Elements marked are unmarked, and unmarked
elements are freed by linking them into the appropriate list of available
space.

As the heap may always contain free elements, the scan phase
must be able to recognize them in order to skip them or merge them
with an adjacent free element. For this purpose, the free elements are
also considered as prefixed. The prefix serves to determine the element's
size and to recognize it as free due to a special (negative) mark value.
The encountered mark values and the action to be taken are as follows:

Mark value	State	Action
= 0	unmarked	collect, mark free
> 0	marked	unmark
< 0	free	skip or merge

8.4 The kernel

The NS32000 processor has two distinct modes of operation, the supervisor and the user mode. The former permits and the latter prohibits execution of certain special instructions and access to protected parts of the store. Since we wish to make use of this protection facility for certain resource allocation tables whose corruption would lead to disaster, access to them needs to be made in supervisor mode. It can **Traps** only be entered by a supervisor call instruction that causes a trap. There is, however, no facility in the language Oberon for the handling of traps. The trap handler is therefore programmed in assembler code, which also allows the expression of privileged instructions. Module *Kernel* is the collection of assembler-coded procedures executed in supervisor mode.

In passing, we note that only base modules can be assembler-coded, because the assembler purposely does not accept specification of imports. The prime justification for programming in assembler code is the need for efficiency, mostly achieved by judicious use of the few available registers. Efficiency is primarily important in leaf procedures, that is, procedures that do not call upon other procedures. Therefore it is quite appropriate to restrict the use of the assembler to leaf modules.

The procedures in the kernel can be partitioned into four groups: block management, sector management, heap management and miscellaneous. Furthermore, the kernel exports certain (read-only) variables. They reflect the state of the different managers and indicate the amounts of store already allocated.

```
MODULE Kernel; (*NW 11.4.86 / 12.4.91*)

TYPE Sector* = RECORD END;
     IntProc* = PROCEDURE;


VAR ModList*: LONGINT;
    NofPages*, NofSectors*, allocated*: LONGINT;
    StackOrg*, HeapLimit*: LONGINT;
```

```
        FileRoot*, FontRoot*: LONGINT;
        SectNo*: LONGINT;

        pc*, sb*, fp*, sp0*, sp1*, mod*, eia*: LONGINT; (*status upon trap*)
        err*, pcr*: INTEGER;

    (* Block management*)
        PROCEDURE AllocBlock(VAR dadr, blkadr: LONGINT; size: LONGINT);
        PROCEDURE FreeBlock(dadr: LONGINT);

    (* Heap management − garbage collector*)
        PROCEDURE GC;

    (* Disk sector management*)
        PROCEDURE AllocSector(hint: LONGINT; VAR sec: LONGINT);
        PROCEDURE MarkSector(sec: LONGINT);
        PROCEDURE FreeSector(sec: LONGINT);
        PROCEDURE GetSector(src: LONGINT; VAR dest: Sector);
        PROCEDURE PutSector(dest: LONGINT; VAR src: Sector);
        PROCEDURE ResetDisk;

    (* Miscellaneous*)
        PROCEDURE InstallIP(P: IntProc; chan: INTEGER);
        PROCEDURE InstallTrap(P: IntProc);
        PROCEDURE SetICU(n: CHAR);
        PROCEDURE GetClock(VAR time, date: LONGINT);
        PROCEDURE SetClock(time, date: LONGINT);

    END Kernel.
```

Procedures *GetClock* and *SetClock* represent the interface to the real-time clock. Both time and date are encoded as (long) integers as follows:

$$\text{time} = (\text{hour}*64 + \text{min})*64 + \text{sec}$$
$$\text{date} = (\text{year}*16 + \text{month})*32 + \text{day}$$

The command *Watch* in module *System* allows the user to inspect the amounts of allocated resources.

```
PROCEDURE Watch*;
BEGIN
    Texts.WriteString(W, "System.Watch"); Texts.WriteLn(W);
    Texts.WriteInt(W, Kernel.NofPages, 1); Texts.WriteString(W, "pages,");
    Texts.WriteInt(W, Kernel.NofSectors, 1); Texts.WriteString(W, "sectors,");
    Texts.WriteInt(W, Kernel.allocated, 1); Texts.WriteString(W, "bytes allocated");
    Texts.WriteLn(W); Texts.Append(Oberon.Log, W.buf)
END Watch;
```

9 Device drivers

9.1 Overview

Device drivers are procedures that constitute the immediate interface between hardware and software. They refer to those parts of the computer hardware that are usually called peripheral. Computers typically contain a system bus that transmits data among its different parts. Processor and memory are considered as its internal parts; the remaining parts, such as disk, keyboard and display, are considered as external or peripheral, notwithstanding the fact that they are often contained in the same cabinet.

Memory-mapped IO devices

Such peripheral devices are connected to the system bus via special registers (data buffers) and transceivers (switches, buffers in the sense of digital electronics). These registers and transceivers are addressed by the processor in the same way as memory locations – they are said to be *memory-mapped* – and they constitute the *hardware interface* between processor bus and device. References to them are typically confined to specific *driver procedures*, which constitute the *software interface*.

Drivers are inherently hardware-specific, and the justification for their existence is precisely that they encapsulate these specifics and present to their clients an appropriate abstraction of the device. Evidently, this abstraction must still reflect the essential characteristics of the device, but not the details (such as the addresses of its interface registers).

Simple in concepts, difficult in details

Our justification to present the drivers connecting the Oberon System with the Ceres computer in detail is on the one hand the desire for completeness. But on the other hand, it is also in recognition of the fact that their design represents an essential part of the engineering task in building a system. This part may look trivial from a conceptual point of view; it certainly is not so in practice.

Standards

In order to reduce the number of interface types, standards have been established. The Ceres computer also uses such interface standards, and we shall concentrate on them in the following presentations. The following devices are considered:

Keyboard

(1) *Keyboard.* This is considered as a serial device delivering one byte of input data per key stroke. It is connected by a serial line according to the RS-232 and ASCII (American Standard Code for Information Interchange) standards. The software is contained in module *Input* (Section 9.2).

Mouse

(2) *Mouse.* The Ceres mouse is a pointing device delivering coordinates in addition to three key states. For Ceres-1 and Ceres-2, the interface is non-standard; for Ceres-3, a serial transmission is used relying on the RS-232 standard. The software is part of module *Input.*

Display

(3) *Display.* The interface to the display is an area of memory that contains the displayed information, one bit per pixel for the monochrome and four bits per pixel for a color display. The default size is 800 lines and 1024 dots per line. The software is module *Display*, which primarily consists of operations to draw frequently occurring patterns, so-called *raster-ops* (see Chapter 4).

Disk

(4) *Disk.* The disk interface of Ceres-1 and Ceres-2 is non-standard and will not be described. The driver is contained in module *Kernel.* Ceres-3 operates without disk, but an optional hard disk can be connected through the standard SCSI interface described in Section 9.4.

Diskette

(5) *Diskette.* The 3.5 in. diskette uses the same non-standard interface as the hard disk. Software: module *Diskette.* This interface is not described in this book.

Serial line

(6) *Serial line.* This is the standard RS-232 serial interface allowing connections to be established between computers and to communicate over telephone lines via modems. The software interface is module V24 described in Section 9.2. Transmission rates go up to 19.2 Kbit/s.

Network

(7) *Network.* Ceres computers may be connected by a local area network using the RS-485 standard. It operates with a transmission rate of 230 Kbit/s, and information is sent in packets of up to 512 bytes in the SDLC standard format. The interface software is module SCC described in Section 9.3; the interface hardware is a component called Serial Communications Controller.

Real-time clock

(8) *Real-time clock.* A clock providing time and date is included in the Ceres computers and is used to record the creation time and date of files. Its interface is non-standard, hardly of general interest, and contained in module *Kernel.*

In all driver modules described below, procedures *SYSTEM.PUT*, *SYSTEM.GET* and *SYSTEM.BIT* are used to access the registers of the device interface. Their first parameter is a (long) integer specifying the address of the register.

9.2   The RS-232 ASCII Standard for keyboard and serial line

UART

All models of the Ceres computer are equipped with a component called a *Universal Asynchronous Receiver and Transmitter* (UART). It has an 8-bit parallel connection to the system bus, and two external connections – one for the transmitter and one for the receiver – resulting in a duplex transmission line. The UART performs the serialization of 8 bits upon sending and deserialization upon receiving. The 8 bits form a short packet, also called *frame*, and they are augmented by a start bit (always 1). There is no fixed time interval between consecutive packets. Transmission is called *asynchronous* because within the packet, there exists no explicit synchronization of clocks. The clock rates of the

Start bit

transmitter and the receiver must therefore be the same. The start bit is used to trigger the shift clock of the receiver. There is also a minimum time interval guaranteed between the last bit of a packet and the start bit of the next packet. It is measured in terms of bit times, and one

Stop bits

may therefore think of a number of 'stop bits' as filling this interval. Finally, the packet may be augmented by a parity bit. The format of such a packet is shown in Figure 9.1.

The Ceres computer uses the Signetics 2692 UART, which contains two (almost) independent line interfaces called channels A and B. It also makes it possible to select several parameters, such as the transmission rate, the numbers of data bits and of stop bits, and the type of parity check (none, even, odd). The chosen values are stored in the UART's parameter registers. The registers of primary importance are the data register and the status register.

Sending

When sending a byte, the processor must wait until the UART is ready. The ready state is asserted by bit 2 in the status register. Then the data byte is loaded into the data register, thereby automatically initiating transmission.

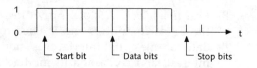

Figure 9.1   ASCII character packet.

Receiving

For receiving a byte, one might use an analogous scheme. However, this would possibly introduce undesirable timing constraints and dependencies. We must consider the act of receiving a byte as part of the act of transmission, that is, as an action intimately connected with sending a byte. Sending and receiving must be performed at the same time. The UART itself provides some decoupling through its data buffers. However, they contain only a single byte (or a small number of them), and it is highly desirable to achieve greater decoupling.

This is possible by providing larger data buffers – typically on the side of the receiver – and by letting the main processor transfer a byte into that buffer as soon as it has been received. This requires that the processor be borrowed for a brief moment, which is achieved by a

Interrupt

processor interrupt. No polling of the UART status for input is necessary in this case.

Channel A of the UART is used for the keyboard (input only). It is handled by module *Input*, whose interface is listed below:

```
DEFINITION Input;
    PROCEDURE Available(): INTEGER;
    PROCEDURE Read(VAR ch: CHAR);
    PROCEDURE Mouse(VAR keys: SET; VAR x, y: INTEGER);
    PROCEDURE SetMouseLimits(w, h: INTEGER);
    PROCEDURE Time(): LONGINT;
END Input.
```

Available
Read

The function procedure *Available* indicates the number of characters collected in the input buffer. If its value is greater than zero, *Read* delivers the next character (byte) from the buffered input stream. If no characters are available, *Read* implies a delay until a character has been received.

Module *Input* also contains the interface to the mouse (pointing device). The hardware contains two counters, one for the x direction

Mouse

and one for the y direction of movement. Procedure *Mouse* delivers the values of these counters and the state of the three buttons (keys). The latter are represented by the set element 0 for the right, 1 for the middle and 2 for the left button. *SetMouseLimits* permits determination of the limiting coordinate values of the rectangle into which the mouse position is mapped and where the cursor is drawn. The position 'wraps around' in both the horizontal and vertical directions. Changing the limits is useful when several displays are to be installed which are considered to lie in the same drawing plane, side by side.

Time

The UART component also contains an additional counter – it is truly a multipurpose chip – that is incremented every 1/300 s and may serve for measuring elapsed time. The value of this counter is delivered by procedure *Time*.

```
MODULE Input; (*NW 5.10.86 / 15.11.90 Ceres-2*)
  IMPORT SYSTEM, Kernel;
  CONST N = 32;
    MOUSE = 0FFFFB000H; UART = 0FFFFC000H; ICU = 0FFFF9000H;


  VAR MW, MH: INTEGER; (*mouse limits*)
    T: LONGINT; (*time counter*)
    n, in, out: INTEGER;
    buf: ARRAY N OF CHAR;


  PROCEDURE Available*(): INTEGER;
  BEGIN RETURN n
  END Available;


  PROCEDURE Read*(VAR ch: CHAR);
  BEGIN
    REPEAT UNTIL n > 0;
    DEC(n); ch := buf[out]; out := (out+1) MOD N
  END Read;


  PROCEDURE Mouse*(VAR keys: SET; VAR x, y: INTEGER);
    VAR u: LONGINT;
  BEGIN SYSTEM.GET(MOUSE, u);
    keys := {0,1,2} − SYSTEM.VAL(SET, u DIV 1000H MOD 8);
    x := SHORT(u MOD 1000H) MOD MW;
    y := SHORT(u DIV 10000H) MOD 819;
    IF y >= MH THEN y := 0 END
  END Mouse;


  PROCEDURE SetMouseLimits*(w, h: INTEGER);
  BEGIN MW := w; MH := h
  END SetMouseLimits;


  PROCEDURE Time*(): LONGINT;
    VAR lo, lo1, hi: CHAR; t: LONGINT;
  BEGIN
    REPEAT SYSTEM.GET(UART+28, lo); SYSTEM.GET(UART+24, hi);
      t := T − LONG(ORD(hi))*256 − ORD(lo); SYSTEM.GET(UART+28, lo1)
    UNTIL lo1 = lo;
    RETURN t
  END Time;


  PROCEDURE+ KBINT;
    VAR ch: CHAR;
  BEGIN SYSTEM.GET(UART+12, ch); (*RHRA*)
    IF ch = 0FFX THEN HALT(24) END;
    IF n < N THEN buf[in] := ch; in := (in+1) MOD N; INC(n) END
  END KBINT;


  PROCEDURE+ CTInt;
    VAR dmy: CHAR;
  BEGIN SYSTEM.GET(UART+60, dmy); (*stop timer*)
    INC(T, 0FFFFH); SYSTEM.GET(UART+56, dmy) (*restart timer*)
  END CTInt;
```

```
BEGIN MW := 1024; MH := 800;
   n := 0; in := 0; out := 0; T := 0FFFFH;
   Kernel.InstallIP(KBINT, 4); Kernel.InstallIP(CTInt, 0);
   SYSTEM.PUT(UART+16, 10X); (*ACR*)
   SYSTEM.PUT(UART+ 8, 15X); (*CRA enable*)
   SYSTEM.PUT(UART, 13X); (*MR1A, RxRdy −Int, no parity, 8 bits*)
   SYSTEM.PUT(UART, 7X); (*MR2A 1 stop bit*)
   SYSTEM.PUT(UART+ 4, 44X); (*CSRA, rate = 300 bps*)
   SYSTEM.PUT(UART+52, 14X); (*OPCR OP4 = KB and OP3 = C/T int*)
   SYSTEM.PUT(UART+28, 0FFX); (*CTLR*)
   SYSTEM.PUT(UART+24, 0FFX); (*CTUR*)
   SYSTEM.GET(UART+56, buf[0]); (*start timer*)
   SYSTEM.PUT(ICU + 4, 18X); (*clear ICU IMR and IRR bits 0*)
   SYSTEM.PUT(ICU + 4, 1CX); (*clear ICU IMR and IRR bits 4*)
END Input.
```

Comments

(1) The fact that many properties of the UART can be parametrized leads to a longer initialization sequence. We refrain from explaining all the details specific to the Signetics 2692 part and refer to the pertinent device specifications. Here it may suffice to state that the RS-232 transmission for the keyboard uses a rate of 300 bit/s, 8 bits without parity check, and 1 stop bit.

(2) An interrupt handler is declared in Oberon as a parameterless procedure marked with a plus sign. The keyboard interrupt handler *KBINT* receives a single character. If it is the *abort character* (cntl-shift-delete), a trap is induced by the statement HALT(24). This enables the operator to interrupt a computation when it appears to be non-terminating.

Abort character

(3) The keyboard buffer is designed as a circular buffer. When full, incoming characters are ignored (except abort).

Timer

(4) The UART's timer (counter) has 16 bits and is accessed in two steps, reading the high and low half respectively. A 32 bit extension is provided in the form of variable T, which is incremented by 2^{16} upon each timer interrupt, which occurs when the UART-counter t has reached zero. Since the UART counter is decremented every 1/300 s, the value delivered by procedure *Time* is computed as $T - t$.

Enabling interrupts

(5) Before an interrupt channel can be active, three conditions must be satisfied:

(i) the processor interrupt must be enabled – it normally is;

(ii) the interrupt mechanism of the device must be enabled;

(iii) the interrupt control unit (ICU) lying between devices and processor must let the respective interrupt signal pass.

The third condition is established by the last two statements of the module's initialization sequence, one instruction being necessary for the keyboard's interrupt, one for the timer's.

(6) The mouse counter values serve as coordinates for the cursor to be displayed on the screen. For this reason, they are confined to the ranges $0 \leq x < MW$ and $0 \leq y < MH$. The limit values can be set by procedure *SetMouseLimits* according to the dimension (resolution) of the available display.

RS-232

Channel B of the UART leads to an external RS-232 (V24) connector. This serial line is not employed by the Oberon system and hence is freely available to the user. Its software interface is module *V24*.

```
DEFINITION V24;
    IMPORT SYSTEM;
    PROCEDURE Start(CSR, MR1, MR2: CHAR);
    PROCEDURE SetOP(s: SET);
    PROCEDURE ClearOP(s: SET);
    PROCEDURE IP(n: INTEGER): BOOLEAN;
    PROCEDURE SR(n: INTEGER): BOOLEAN;
    PROCEDURE Available(): INTEGER;
    PROCEDURE Receive(VAR x: SYSTEM.BYTE);
    PROCEDURE Send(x: SYSTEM.BYTE);
    PROCEDURE Break;
    PROCEDURE Stop;
END V24.
```

Available
Receive
Send

The channel's receiver and transmitter are started by calling procedure *Start*. It has three parameters, whose values are codes for the transmission clock rate, the parity mode, the number of bits per byte and for the number of stop bits. Procedure *Available* denotes the number of bytes available (received) in the input buffer. *Receive* delivers the next byte of the sequence, and *Send* dispatches the byte specified by the parameter. *SR* yields the value of the specified bit in the status register, and *Stop* serves to turn off both transmitter and receiver.

Input port
Output port

The Signetics 2692 dual UART's exaggerated multipurpose nature becomes apparent at this point: in addition to the two channels and a counter/timer, it also contains an input and an output register (7 and 8 bits respectively) with external connections (pins). On the Ceres computer, these signals are used in various ways and must not be used by the programmer, except the following:

Modem
signals

input:	0	DCD	(data carrier detected)
	1	CTS	(clear to send)
	2	DSR	(data set ready)
output:	0	DTR	(data terminal ready)
	1	RTS	(request to send)

The meaning of these bits is derived from their use in connection with modems. Procedures *SetOP* and *ClearOP* serve to set and clear those

Table 9.1   UART Registers

RHRA/B	receiver holding register	received data
THRA/B	transmitter holding reg.	data to be transmitted
MR1A/B	mode register 1	Rx control, parity mode and type, no. of bits per byte
MR2A/B	mode register 2	channel mode, Tx control, stop bit length
CRA/B	command register	
CSRA/B	clock select register	receiver and transmitter clock rates
SRA/B	status register	RxRdy, TxRdy; overrun, parity, framing errors
OPCR	output port configuration register	
IPCR	input port change register	
ISR	interrupt status register	
IMR	interrupt mask register	
CTUR	counter/timer upper byte value	
CTLR	counter/timer lower byte value	

bits of the UART's output register (OP) that are specified in their set parameter. Function procedure *IP* serves to test the specified bit in the UART's input register (IP). And finally, procedure *Break* serves to apply a break signal (0 value during at least 20 ms) to the serial line. Table 9.1 lists the principal registers of the UART.

```
MODULE V24; (*NW 18.3.89 / 19.1.91*)
   (*interrupt-driven UART channel B*)
   IMPORT SYSTEM, Kernel;

   CONST BufLen = 512;
      UART = 0FFFFC000H; ICU = 0FFFF9000H;

   VAR in, out: INTEGER;
      buf: ARRAY BufLen OF SYSTEM.BYTE;

   PROCEDURE+ Int;
   BEGIN SYSTEM.GET(UART+44, buf[in]); in := (in+1) MOD BufLen
   END Int;

   PROCEDURE Start*(CSR, MR1, MR2: CHAR);
   BEGIN in := 0; out := 0; Kernel.InstallIP(Int, 2);
      SYSTEM.PUT(UART+40, 30X); (*CRB reset transmitter*)
      SYSTEM.PUT(UART+40, 20X); (*CRB reset receiver*)
      SYSTEM.PUT(UART+36, CSR); (*CSRB clock rate*)
      SYSTEM.PUT(UART+40, 15X); (*CRB enable Tx and Rx, pointer to MR1*)
      SYSTEM.PUT(UART+32, MR1); (*MR1B, parity, nof bits*)
      SYSTEM.PUT(UART+32, MR2); (*MR2B stop bits*)
      SYSTEM.PUT(UART+20, 20X); (*IMR RxRdy Int enable*)
      SYSTEM.PUT(ICU + 4, 1AX); (*ICU IMR and IRR bit 2*)
   END Start;
```

```
PROCEDURE SetOP*(s: SET);
BEGIN SYSTEM.PUT(UART+56, s)
END SetOP;

PROCEDURE ClearOP*(s: SET);
BEGIN SYSTEM.PUT(UART+60, s)
END ClearOP;

PROCEDURE IP*(n: INTEGER): BOOLEAN;
BEGIN RETURN SYSTEM.BIT(UART+52, n)
END IP;

PROCEDURE SR*(n: INTEGER): BOOLEAN;
BEGIN RETURN SYSTEM.BIT(UART+36, n)
END SR;

PROCEDURE Available*(): INTEGER;
BEGIN RETURN (in − out) MOD BufLen
END Available;

PROCEDURE Receive*(VAR x: SYSTEM.BYTE);
BEGIN
   REPEAT UNTIL in # out;
   x := buf[out]; out := (out+1) MOD BufLen
END Receive;

PROCEDURE Send*(x: SYSTEM.BYTE);
BEGIN
   REPEAT UNTIL SYSTEM.BIT(UART+36, 2);
   SYSTEM.PUT(UART+44, x)
END Send;

PROCEDURE Break*;
   VAR i: LONGINT;
BEGIN SYSTEM.PUT(UART+40, 60X); i := 500000;
   REPEAT DEC(i) UNTIL i = 0;
   SYSTEM.PUT(UART+40, 70X)
END Break;

PROCEDURE Stop*;
BEGIN SYSTEM.PUT(UART+20, 0); (*IMR disable Rx-Int*)
   SYSTEM.PUT(ICU + 4, 3AX) (*ICU chan 2*)
END Stop;

END V24.
```

9.3 The RS-485 SDLC Standard for a network

The Ceres–Oberon System also features a network connection. The principal differences between the RS-232 line and the network connection are that of a point-to-point line versus a bus with multiple taps, and that of asynchronous versus synchronous transmission. Asynchronous transmission as described in the preceding section is uneconomical if transmission speeds beyond 20 Kbit/s are desired, because too much time is wasted between consecutive bytes. Synchronous transmission improves performance, and it is used by the Ceres computers for interconnection in a local area network.

Strictly speaking, the difference between so-called asynchronous and synchronous transmission lies in the packet length only, because the former uses synchronicity during the transmission of each byte, too. The price for longer packets lies in the need for more accurate clocks; clock accuracy limits packet length, unless some encoding scheme is used to transmit the clock together with data. The RS-485 and SDLC Standards do not specify such an encoding; the clock is not transmitted.

Transmission rate
It is fixed here to 230 Kbit/s, yielding about 30 Kbyte/s.

A direct consequence is that computation of the byte sequence and transmission of the packet cannot be interleaved due to the strict timing constraints. Since one byte must be sent every 30 μs, the data of the entire packet must be ready before transmission is initiated.

Packet format
The SDLC (Synchronous Data Link Control) standard specifies a fixed *packet format* of variable length. The role of the start bit is taken by a start byte, a so-called *flag*. It is followed by the data bytes, and the packet is terminated by another flag. The flag consists of 6 consecutive '1's. Hence, any occurrence of 6 consecutive '1's must not occur within the data section. The problem is solved by the transmitter

Zero insertion
automatically inserting and the receiver removing a zero bit after every occurrence of five consecutive ones. If the bit following the 5 ones is not a zero, a flag was received. This zero insertion (and deletion), as well as the pre- and postfixing of a flag, is performed automatically by the interface hardware component SCC (Zilog 8530).

Redundancy check
In order to detect transmission errors, the transmitter computes a cyclic redundancy code (CRC) over the data and appends it to the data stream, just before the terminating flag. The receiver computes the same code and compares it with the received code. If the difference is not zero, a status bit is set that must be inspected for each received packet.

Destination address
The SDLC Standard also requires that the first byte of the packet – the one after the flag – specify the receiver's address. This is necessary, because in a network the recipient is not automatically determined like in a point-to-point connection. Every station is therefore given a unique identification. Beyond this, we postulate some additional properties of packets. Each packet consist of a header followed by the data. The first 9 bytes constitute the header, of which the first is the destination

Packet type
address, the second denotes the sender's address, and the third a packet type. It is followed by two bytes indicating the packet length (in bytes).

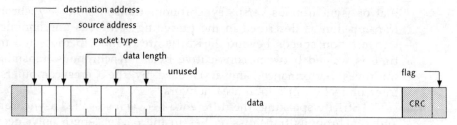

Figure 9.2 Ceres-net packet format.

(The remaining four bytes are currently not used.) The resulting packet format is shown in Figure 9.2, and it is reflected by the data type *Header*.

```
DEFINITION SCC;
  TYPE Header =
    RECORD valid: BOOLEAN; dadr, sadr, typ: SHORTINT;
      len: INTEGER; (*of data following header*)
      destLink, srcLink: INTEGER (*unused*)
    END;

  PROCEDURE Start(filter: BOOLEAN);
  PROCEDURE Send(VAR head: Header; VAR buf: ARRAY
    OF SYSTEM.BYTE);
  PROCEDURE Available(): INTEGER;
  PROCEDURE ReceiveHead(VAR head: Header);
  PROCEDURE Receive(VAR x: SYSTEM.BYTE);
  PROCEDURE Skip(m: INTEGER);
  PROCEDURE Stop;
END SCC.
```

Receive

Available

As in the case of the V24 interface, the receiver buffers the incoming data stream (without flags and CRC). Procedure *Receive* picks consecutive bytes from the buffer. The number of buffered bytes is given by procedure *Available*. The task of receiving is simplified by procedure *ReceiveHead*. It is called when a next packet is expected. The field *valid* has the meaning 'packet has been received and header is valid'.

Address filter

Transmitter and receiver can be switched on and off by calls to procedures *Start* and *Stop*. The former features a Boolean parameter *filter* with the meaning 'filter out packets that are not addressed to this station'. The interface chip is capable of comparing the first header byte (destination address) with its own station's address (stored in a register), and to discard a packet upon mismatch. An active filter is of course the

Table 9.2 SCC Registers

Write registers

0	Command register
1	Transmit/receive interrupt and data transfer mode definition
2	Interrupt vector
3	Receive parameters and control
4	Transmit/receive miscellaneous parameters and modes
5	Transmit parameter and control
6	Sync characters or SDLC address field (filter)
7	Sync character or SDLC flag
8	Transmit buffer (data)
9	Master interrupt control
10	Miscellaneous transmitter/receiver control bits
11	Clock mode control
12	Baud rate generator time constant (low byte)
13	Baud rate generator time constant (high byte)
14	Miscellaneous control bits
15	External/Status interrupt control

Read registers

0	Transmit/receive buffer status
1	Status register (errors, end of frame)
2	Interrupt vector
3	Interrupts pending
8	Received data buffer
10	Status bits

normal mode of operation, because in this mode discarded packets do not require interaction with the computer's processor.

The SCC-driver program is, as one expects, dominated by accesses to the device's registers. The primary function of these registers is indicated in Table 9.2; for further details, we refer to the controller's data sheets. It must suffice to say that registers (except the data register) are accessed in two steps. First, the register's number is sent to the control port, and thereafter its value is transferred. (Register number and value are time-multiplexed; see procedure PUT.) Table 9.2 gives an overview of the available device registers.

```
MODULE SCC; (*NW 13.11.87 / 22.8.90 Ceres-2*)
  IMPORT SYSTEM, Kernel;

  CONST BufLen = 2048;
    com = 0FFFFD008H; (*commands and status, SCC channel A*)
    dat = 0FFFFD00CH;
    DIPS = 0FFFFFC00H;
    ICU = 0FFFF9004H;
    RxCA = 0; (*R0: Rx Char Available*)
    TxBE = 2; (*R0: Tx Buffer Empty*)
```

```
        Hunt = 4; (*R0: Sync/Hunt*)
        TxUR = 6; (*R0: Tx UnderRun*)
        RxOR = 5; (*R1: Rx OverRun*)
        CRC = 6; (*R1: CRC error*)
        EOF = 7; (*R1: End Of Frame*)


TYPE Header* =
    RECORD valid*: BOOLEAN;
        dadr*, sadr*, typ*: SHORTINT;
        len*: INTEGER; (*of data following header*)
        destLink*, srcLink*: INTEGER (*link numbers*)
    END;


VAR in, out: INTEGER;
    Adr: SHORTINT;
    SCCR3: CHAR;
    buf: ARRAY BufLen OF CHAR;

PROCEDURE PUT(r: SHORTINT; x: SYSTEM.BYTE);
BEGIN SYSTEM.PUT(com, r); SYSTEM.PUT(com, x)
END PUT;


PROCEDURE+ Int1;
    VAR del, oldin: INTEGER; stat: SET; dmy: CHAR;
BEGIN SYSTEM.GET(dat, buf[in]);
    PUT(1, 0X); (*disable interrupts*)
    oldin := in; in := (in+1) MOD BufLen; del := 16;
    LOOP
        IF SYSTEM.BIT(com, RxCA) THEN del := 16;
            IF in # out THEN SYSTEM.GET(dat, buf[in]); in := (in+1) MOD BufLen
            ELSE SYSTEM.GET(dat, dmy)
            END
        ELSE SYSTEM.PUT(com, 1X); DEC(del);
            IF SYSTEM.BIT(com, EOF) & (del <= 0) OR (del <= -16) THEN EXIT END
        END
    END;
    SYSTEM.PUT(com, 1X); SYSTEM.GET(com, stat);
    IF (RxOR IN stat) OR (CRC IN stat) OR (in = out) THEN
        in := oldin (*reset buffer*)
    ELSE in := (in-2) MOD BufLen (*remove CRC*)
    END;
    SYSTEM.PUT(com, 30X); (*error reset*)
    SYSTEM.PUT(com, 10X); (*reset ext/stat interrupts*)
    PUT( 1, 8X); (*enable Rx-Int on 1st char*)
    SYSTEM.PUT(com, 20X); (*enable Rx-Int on next char*)
    PUT( 3, SCCR3); (*enter hunt mode*)
END Int1;


PROCEDURE Start*(filter: BOOLEAN);
BEGIN in := 0; out := 0;
    IF filter THEN SCCR3 := 0DDX ELSE SCCR3 := 0D9X END;
    SYSTEM.GET(DIPS, Adr); Adr := Adr MOD 40H;
    Kernel.InstallIP(Int1, 1);
    PUT( 9, 80X); (*reset A, disable all interrupts*)
    PUT( 4, 20X); (*SDLC mode*)
    PUT( 1, 0X); (*disable all interrupts*)
    PUT( 2, 0X); (*interrupt vector*)
```

```
    PUT( 3, SCCR3); (*8bit, hunt mode, Rx-CRC on, adr search, Rx off*)
    PUT( 5, 0E1X); (*8bit, SDLC, Tx-CRC on, Tx off*)
    PUT( 6, Adr); (*SDLC-address*)
    PUT( 7, 7EX); (*SDLC flag*)
    PUT( 9, 6X); (*master int on, no vector*)
    PUT(10, 0E0X); (*FM0*)
    PUT(11, 0F7X); (*Xtal, RxC = DPLL TxC = rate genL*)
    PUT(12, 6X); (*lo byte of rate gen: Xtal DIV 16*)
    PUT(13, 0X); (*hi byte of rate gen*)
    PUT(14, 0A0X); (*DPLL = Xtal*)
    PUT(14, 0C0X); (*FM mode*)
    PUT( 3, SCCR3); (*Rx enable, enter hunt mode*)
    SYSTEM.PUT(com, 80X); (*TxCRC reset*)
    PUT(15, 0X); (*mask ext interrupts*)
    SYSTEM.PUT(com, 10X);
    SYSTEM.PUT(com, 10X); (*reset ext/status*)
    PUT( 1, 0X); (*Rx-Int on 1st char off*)
    PUT( 9, 0EX); (*no A reset, enable int, disable daisy chain*)
    PUT( 1, 8X); (*enable Rx Int*)
    PUT(14, 21X); (*enter search mode*)
    SYSTEM.PUT(ICU, 19X); (*clear IRR and IMR bits, channel 1*)
END Start;


PROCEDURE SendPacket*(VAR head, buf: ARRAY OF SYSTEM.BYTE);
    VAR i, len: INTEGER;
BEGIN head[2] := Adr;
    len := ORD(head[5])*100H + ORD(head[4]);
    LOOP (*sample line*) i := 60;
        REPEAT DEC(i) UNTIL SYSTEM.BIT(com, Hunt) OR (i = 0);
        IF i > 0 THEN (*line idle*) EXIT END;
        i := LONG(Adr)*128 + 800; (*delay*)
        REPEAT DEC(i) UNTIL i = 0
    END;
    Kernel.SetICU(0A2X); (*disable interrupts!*)
    PUT( 5, 63X); (*RTS, send 1s*)
    PUT( 5, 6BX); (*RTS, Tx enable*)
    SYSTEM.PUT(com, 80X); (*reset Tx-CRC*)
    SYSTEM.PUT(dat, ORD(head[1])); (*send dest*)
    SYSTEM.PUT(com, 0C0X); (*reset underrun/EOM flag*)
    REPEAT UNTIL SYSTEM.BIT(com, TxBE);
    i := 2;
    REPEAT SYSTEM.PUT(dat, head[i]); INC(i);
        REPEAT UNTIL SYSTEM.BIT(com, TxBE)
    UNTIL i = 10;
    i := 0;
    WHILE i < len DO
        SYSTEM.PUT(dat, buf[i]); INC(i); (*send data*)
        REPEAT UNTIL SYSTEM.BIT(com, TxBE)
    END;
    REPEAT UNTIL SYSTEM.BIT(com, TxUR) & SYSTEM.BIT(com, TxBE);
    PUT( 5, 63X); (*RTS, Tx disable, send 1s*)
    i := 300;
    REPEAT DEC(i) UNTIL i = 0;
    PUT( 5, 0E1X); (*~RTS*)
    PUT( 1, 8X); (*enable Rx-Int on 1st char*)
    PUT(14, 21X); (*enter search mode*)
    SYSTEM.PUT(com, 20X); (*enable Rx-Int on next char*)
    PUT( 3, SCCR3); (*enter hunt mode*)
```

```
        SYSTEM.PUT(ICU, 0A1X) (*enable interrupts*)
    END SendPacket;

    PROCEDURE Available*(): INTEGER;
    BEGIN RETURN (in − out) MOD BufLen
    END Available;

    PROCEDURE Receive*(VAR x: SYSTEM.BYTE);
    BEGIN
        REPEAT UNTIL in # out;
        x := buf[out]; out := (out+1) MOD BufLen
    END Receive;

    PROCEDURE ReceiveHead*(VAR head: ARRAY OF SYSTEM.BYTE);
        VAR i: INTEGER;
    BEGIN
        IF (in − out) MOD BufLen >= 9 THEN head[0] := 1; i := 1;
            REPEAT Receive(head[i]); INC(i) UNTIL i = 10
        ELSE head[0] := 0
        END
    END ReceiveHead;

    PROCEDURE Skip*(m: INTEGER);
    BEGIN
        IF m <= (in − out) MOD BufLen THEN
            out := (out+m) MOD BufLen ELSE out := in
        END
    END Skip;

    PROCEDURE Stop*;
    BEGIN PUT(9, 80X); (*reset SCCA*)
        SYSTEM.PUT(ICU, 39X); SYSTEM.PUT(ICU, 59X); (*reset IMR and IRR*)
    END Stop;

BEGIN Start(TRUE)
END SCC.
```

Comments

(1) The sequence in which individual registers are initialized is essential for correct functioning. The lack of its specification in the part's documentation was a source of serious difficulties and headaches.

Timing considerations

(2) Some sections of the driver are very time-critical (particularly for Ceres-1). For example, after receiving an interrupt, the first byte must be read immediately. A queue of 3 bytes in the receiver hardware allows for enough time to disable interrupts, store the byte and copy the buffer index (*oldin*), which is used as a reset point in case of a transmission error.

(3) Before sending a packet, it must be verified that the line is free by testing the so-called hunt bit. If the line is busy, the line is

Collision detection

polled again after a delay. The delay is influenced by the station's address, causing all stations to have a slightly different delay. Actual collisions can only be detected by the receiver through the CRC check at the end of the packet.

(4) After transmitting the last data byte, the line must be kept busy for transmitting CRC and flag, and for the receiver to terminate (stop bits!). This time span is of order 200 µs, which is too short for the timers' resolution, and hence must be programmed as a tight delay loop. The delay constant depends on the computer's clock rate and model. This is rather unfortunate.

(5) The end of a packet is indicated by the EOF bit in the SCC's status register. Unfortunately, it is not reliable. It sometimes signals the end prematurely. The situation is saved by testing a number of times while no further data bytes arrive. The resulting program section does not appear to be very neatly conceived – but software that fixes a hardware deficiency never does.

(6) Procedure *Skip* serves to discard received data, namely the next m bytes. m is compared with the stored number of bytes given by $n = (in\text{-}out)\ MOD\ BufLen$, in order not to 'overshoot'. We leave any reader so inclined to discover why the guard $m \leqslant n$ is correct, whereas $m < n$ would be wrong.

9.4 A disk driver using the SCSI interface

The Oberon System's procedural interface to the disk is represented by the two procedures *Kernel.GetSector* and *Kernel.PutSector*. Their details intimately depend on the disk controller used. Several standards have recently emerged for disk interfaces, and we therefore present one of them, namely the *Small Computer Systems Interface* (*SCSI*), which is designed with sufficient generality to be also usable for devices other than disks, and even for fast data exchange between computers.

The Ceres-3 computer is equipped with this interface, and hence disks (or other devices) can be connected externally. We emphasize that SCSI constitutes a bus, and not only a point-to-point connection. However, at most 8 partners may be interconnected.

Control signals

The SCSI signal bus consist of 8 data lines (plus parity) and several control lines (namely SEL, BSY, REQ, ACK, C/D, MSG, I/O, RST, and ATN). Hence, the 8 (or 9) bits composing a byte are transmitted in parallel. Bytes are transmitted asynchronously, that is, without any timing dependencies within their sequence. This is possible with the

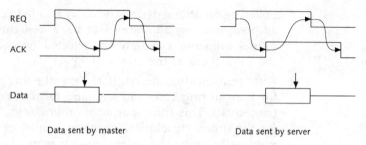

Data sent by master   Data sent by server

Figure 9.3   The SCSI 'handshake'.

aid of the two control signals REQ and ACK, which are used in the following way.

REQ, ACK

In order to transmit a byte from a master to a server, the latter first waits until the master applies the byte to the data lines and signals availability of the byte by asserting the REQ signal. The server then samples (reads) the data lines, asserts the ACK signal, and waits until the master deasserts (resets) the REQ signal. Finally, the server deasserts the ACK signal. The REQ signal is driven (determined) by the master and inspected by the server, the ACK signal is driven by the server

Handshake

and polled by the master. This sequence of actions is called a *handshake*, and is used when transmitting a byte in either direction (see Figure 9.3). In the program listed subsequently, this transmission protocol is

**Send
Receive**

implemented by the two procedures *Send* (a sequence of n bytes) and *Receive* (a single byte).

In order to perform an entire transaction, such as the reading or writing of a disk sector, the SCSI Standard prescribes six phases (apart from *neutral*, or *bus free*). The agent starting the transaction, usually the

**Initiator
Target**

computer, is called *initiator*, and the addressee is called the *target*. In systems where only one agent has the ability to act as initiator, the first action is to select a target. We recall that the SCSI Standard defines not a line, but rather a *bus*; hence the targeted partner must first be notified

**Selection
phase
SEL, BSY**

(selected). This *selection phase* is characterized by the control signal SEL being asserted, concurrently with *one* of the 8 data lines. The addressed device responds by asserting the control signal BSY. In the program listed below, the selection phase is described by procedure *Select*, which includes a timeout for the case that the addressed device does not respond (or does not exist). From this point onwards, the target acts as master, and the initiator as server.

**Command
phase**

The second phase is the *command phase*, in which the selected target requests, and the initiator replies by sending a command encoded as a sequence of bytes. This phase is identified by the C/D

C/D, MSG

(command/data) signal being asserted and the MSG signal being deasserted. The command consists of a sequence of (at least 6) bytes.

Command byte The first byte is the operation code, or *command byte*, the remaining ones its parameters. In the case of the target being a disk controller, the first byte is followed by 3 bytes specifying the sector address (most significant byte first), a byte specifying the number of disk sectors involved and a device-specific byte.

Data phase   If the command is acceptable to the target, the third phase is entered. This is the *data phase*, identified by both C/D and MSG signals being deasserted. Hence the initiator waits for the REQ signal being asserted, and then tests the C/D signal. If it is not deasserted, the data phase is skipped. Otherwise, the specified number of data bytes are transmitted.

Status phase   Then follows the *status phase*, in which the target sends status information, typically a single byte. Zero indicates that the requested command had been completed.

Message phase   The last phase is called the *message phase*, identified by both the C/D and MSG signals being asserted. In this phase, a message is transmitted from the target to the initiator. It has no significance in our application, but must be received anyway according to the rules of the Standard.

In systems where several agents have the capability to act as initiators, the danger exists that some of them may enter the selection phase at the very same moment. The consequences would be unpredictable. In order to avoid this unacceptable possibility, selection must be preceded by the arbitration phase. It is noteworthy that no single, central agency is required for granting bus access to one of the concurrent competitors. Arbitration is called *distributed* and proceeds as follows:

Arbitration phase   First, the initiator asserts the BSY signal and, at the same time, the data line corresponding to the initiator's address. If within a certain time span (arbitration delay 200 ns) no data line with higher number is asserted (by a competitor), the initiator is allowed to enter the selection phase by asserting SEL. Otherwise BSY is deasserted to give priority to the higher ranking competitor. We now understand the reason why only 8 instead of 2^8 devices can be connected to the SCSI bus; each data line must be associated with exactly one device.

The values of the signals characterizing the various phases are given in Table 9.3.

The principal interface registers and their bit assignments are **Interface registers** shown in Figure 9.4. The full standard specifies further registers and facilities that are not relevant for our purpose.

(1) When applying data to the bus, the ODR is connected to the bus only if the following conditions are met: Bit 0 (DB) in the ICR is asserted, and the phases of initiator and target match.

(2) A phase match exists if the phase signals on the bus (I/O, C/D, MSG), as determined by the target, have the same values as are stored in the initiator's target command register. A phase mismatch is indicated in the BSR (PHM).

Table 9.3 SCSI phase signals

Phase	SEL	BSY	C/D	MSG	I/O
Neutral	0	0	x	x	x
Arbitration	0	1	0	0	0
Selection	1	0	0	0	0
Command	0	1	1	0	0
Data	0	1	0	0	0/1
Status	0	1	1	0	1
Message	0	1	1	1	0/1

(3) RST is the reset signal, DP the data bus parity, PCK indicates a parity check, and TAR specifies the target mode of operation.

In the case of a disk drive as device (target), many commands are usually available. Those of concern to us are a read and a write sector command. As explained above, the first byte always specifies the operation. It is followed by three bytes giving the sector number, one byte indicating the number of consecutive sectors to be transmitted, and a zero byte.

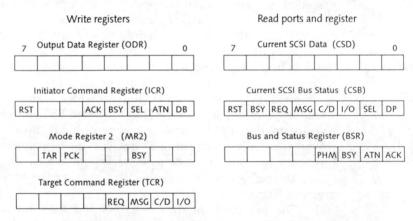

Figure 9.4 Principal SCSI registers and bit assignments.

```
MODULE Disk; (*NW 12.4.90 / 2.10.90*)
  IMPORT SYSTEM, Kernel;

  CONST SS = 1024; devno = 0; maxSector = 102432;
    SCSI = 0FFFF8000H;
    ODR = SCSI; (*output data register*)
```

```
    CSD = SCSI; (*current SCSI data*)
    ICR = SCSI + 4; (*initiator command register*)
    MR2 = SCSI + 8; (*mode register*)
    TCR = SCSI + 12; (*target command register*)
    SER = SCSI + 16; (*select enable register*)
    CSB = SCSI + 16; (*current SCSI bus status*)
    BSR = SCSI + 20; (*bus status*)
    RPI = SCSI + 28; (*reset parity and interrupts*)


TYPE DiskAdr = LONGINT;
    Buffer = ARRAY 256 OF LONGINT;


VAR stat*, msg: CHAR;


PROCEDURE Select(n: LONGINT);
BEGIN
    REPEAT UNTIL ~SYSTEM.BIT(CSB, 6); (*~BSY*)
    REPEAT UNTIL ~SYSTEM.BIT(CSB, 1); (*~SEL*)
    SYSTEM.PUT(ODR, n ); SYSTEM.PUT(ICR, 5); (*SEL*)
    REPEAT UNTIL SYSTEM.BIT(CSB, 6) (*BSY*)
END Select;


PROCEDURE Receive(VAR x: CHAR);
BEGIN
    REPEAT UNTIL SYSTEM.BIT(CSB, 5); (*REQ*)
    SYSTEM.GET(CSD, x);
    SYSTEM.PUT(ICR, 10H); (*assert ACK*)
    REPEAT UNTIL ~SYSTEM.BIT(CSB, 5); (*~REQ*)
    SYSTEM.PUT(ICR, 0); (*deassert ACK*)
END Receive;


PROCEDURE Send(x: CHAR);
BEGIN
    REPEAT UNTIL SYSTEM.BIT(CSB, 5); (*REQ*)
    SYSTEM.PUT(ODR, x);
    SYSTEM.PUT(ICR, 11H); (*assert ACK*)
    REPEAT UNTIL ~SYSTEM.BIT(CSB, 5); (*REQ*)
    SYSTEM.PUT(ICR, 1) (*deassert ACK*)
END Send;


PROCEDURE Reset*;
BEGIN SYSTEM.PUT(ICR, 80X); SYSTEM.PUT(TCR, 0); SYSTEM.PUT(ICR, 0);
    SYSTEM.PUT(MR2, 20X); SYSTEM.GET(RPI, stat)
END Reset;


PROCEDURE GetSector*(src: DiskAdr; VAR dest: Kernel.Sector);
    VAR adr, limit: LONGINT; x: CHAR;
BEGIN INC(src, src);
    SYSTEM.GET(RPI, x); (*reset parity*) Select(devno);
    SYSTEM.PUT(TCR, 2); SYSTEM.PUT(ICR, 1);
    Send(8X); Send(CHR(src DIV 10000H)); Send(CHR(src DIV 100H)); Send(CHR(src));
    Send(2X); Send(0X);
    SYSTEM.PUT(TCR, 1); SYSTEM.PUT(ICR, 0);
    adr := SYSTEM.ADR(dest); limit := adr + SS;
    LOOP Receive(x);
```

```
        IF ~SYSTEM.BIT(CSB, 3) THEN
            SYSTEM.PUT(adr, x); INC(adr) ELSE stat := x; EXIT
        END;
        IF adr = limit THEN Receive(stat); EXIT END
    END;
    Receive(msg); SYSTEM.PUT(TCR, 0); SYSTEM.PUT(ICR, 0)
END GetSector;


PROCEDURE PutSector*(dest: DiskAdr;VAR src: Kernel.Sector);
    VAR adr, limit: LONGINT; x: CHAR;
BEGIN INC(dest, dest); Select(devno);
    SYSTEM.PUT(TCR, 2); SYSTEM.PUT(ICR, 1);
    Send(0AX); Send(CHR(dest DIV 10000H)); Send(CHR(dest DIV 100H)); Send(CHR(dest));
    Send(2X); Send(0X);
    SYSTEM.PUT(TCR, 0); adr := SYSTEM.ADR(src); limit := adr + SS;
    REPEAT SYSTEM.GET(adr, x); Send(x); INC(adr)UNTIL adr = limit;
    Receive(stat); Receive(msg);
    SYSTEM.PUT(TCR, 0); SYSTEM.PUT(ICR, 0)
END PutSector;


PROCEDURE Sense*;
    VAR x: CHAR;
BEGIN Select(devno); SYSTEM.PUT(TCR, 2); SYSTEM.PUT(ICR, 1);
    Send(3X); Send(0X); Send(0X); Send(0X); Send(0X); Send(0X);
    REPEAT Receive(stat) UNTIL SYSTEM.BIT(CSB, 3);
    Receive(msg); SYSTEM.PUT(TCR, 0); SYSTEM.PUT(ICR, 0)
END Sense;


END Disk.
```

10 The network

10.1 Introduction

Workstations are typically, but not always, connected in a local environment by a network. There exist two basically different views of the architecture of such nets. The more demanding view is that all connected stations constitute a single, unified workspace (also called address-space), in which the individual processors operate. It implies the demand that the 'thin' connections between processors are hidden from the users. At worst, they might become apparent through slower data access rates between the machines. To hide the difference between access within a computer and access between computers is regarded primarily as a challenge to implementors.

The second, more conservative view, assumes that individual workstations are, although connected, essentially autonomous units, which exchange data infrequently. Therefore access of data on partner stations is initiated by explicit transfer commands. Commands handling external access are not part of the basic system, but rather are implemented in modules that might be regarded as applications.

In the Oberon System, we adhere to this second view, and in this chapter, we describe the module *Net*, which is an autonomous command module based on the network driver SCC presented in Section 9.3. It can be activated on any station connected in a network, and all of them are treated as equals. Such a set of loosely coupled stations may well operate in networks with moderate transmission rates and therefore with low-cost hardware interfaces and twisted-pair wires.

An obvious choice for the unit of transferred data is the file. The central theme of this chapter is therefore file transfer over a network. Some additional facilities offered by a dedicated server station will be the subject of Chapter 11. The commands to be presented here are a few only: *SendFiles*, *ReceiveFiles* and *SendMsg*.

As explained in Chapter 2, Oberon is a single-process system where every command monopolizes the processor until termination.

When a command involves communication over a network, (at least) two processors are engaged in the action at the same time. The Oberon paradigm therefore appears to exclude such cooperation; but fortunately it does not, and the solution to the problem is quite simple.

Master
Server

Every command is initiated by a user operating on a workstation. For the moment, we call it the *master* (of the command under consideration). The addressed station – obviously called the *server* – must be in a state where it recognizes the command in order to engage in its execution. Since the command – called a *request* – arrives in encoded form over the network, an Oberon task represented by a handler procedure must be inserted into the event polling loop of the system. Such a handler must have the general form

Request
Network
task

IF event present THEN handle event END

The guard, in this case, must imply that a request was received from the network. We emphasize that the event is sensed by the server only after the command currently under execution, if any, has terminated. However, data arrive at the receiver immediately after they are sent by the master. Hence any sizeable delay is inherently inadmissible, and the Oberon metaphor once again appears to fail. It does not, however, because the unavoidable, genuine concurrency of sender and receiver action is handled within the driver module, which places the data into a buffer. The driver is activated by an interrupt, and its receiver buffer effectively decouples the partners and removes the stringent timing constraints. All this remains completely hidden within the driver module.

Interrupt

10.2 The protocol

Protocol

If more than a single agent participates in the execution of a command, a convention must be established and obeyed. It defines the set of requests, their encoding, and the sequence of data exchanges that follow. Such a convention is called a *protocol*. Since, in our metaphor, actions initiated by the master and the server strictly follow each other in alternation, the protocol can be defined using EBNF (extended Backus–Naur formalism), well known from the syntax specification of languages. Items originating from the master will be written with normal font, those originating from the server appear in italics.

ReceiveFile

A simple form of the *ReceiveFile* request is defined as follows and will be refined subsequently:

ReceiveFile = SND filename (*ACK data* | *NAK*).

Here the symbol SND represents the encoded request that the server send the file specified by the file name. ACK signals that the request is honoured and the requested data follow. The NAK symbol indicates that the requested file cannot be delivered. The transaction clearly consists of two parts, the request and the reply, one from each partner.

This simple-minded scheme fails because of the limitation of the size of each transmitted portion imposed by the network driver. We recall that module SCC restricts the data of each packet to 512 bytes. Evidently, files must be broken up and transmitted as a sequence of packets. The reason for this restriction is transmission reliability. The break-up allows the partner to confirm correct receipt of a packet by returning a short acknowledgement. Each acknowledgement also serves as request for the next packet. An exception is the last acknowledgement following the last data portion, which is characterized by its length being less than the admitted maximum. The revised protocol is defined as

> ReceiveFile = SND filename (*DAT data* ACK {*DAT data* ACK} | *NAK*).

We now recall that each packet as defined in Section 9.3 is characterized by a type in its header. The symbols SND, DAT, ACK

Packet type and NAK indicate this *packet type*. The data portions of ACK and NAK packets are empty.

The revised protocol fails to cope with transmission errors. Correct transmission is checked by the driver through a cyclic redundancy check (CRC), and an erroneous packet is simply discarded. This implies that a receiver must impose a timing constraint. If an expected packet

Retransmission fails to arrive within a given time period (timeout), the request must be repeated. In our case, a request is implied by an acknowledgement. Hence the acknowledgement must specify whether the next (normal case) or the previously requested (error case) packet must be sent. The solution is to attach a sequence number to each acknowledgement and

Sequence number to each data packet. These numbers are taken modulo 8, although in principle modulo 2 would suffice.

With the addition of a user identification and a password to every request, and of an alternative reply code NPR for 'no permission', the protocol reaches its final form:

> ReceiveFile = SND username password filename (*datastream* | *NAK* | *NPR*).
> datastream = DAT_0 *data* ACK_1 {DAT_i *data* ACK_{i+1}}.

The protocol for file transmission from the master to the server is defined similarly:

> SendFile = REC username password filename (ACK_0 datastream | *NAK* | *NPR*).

datastream = DAT_0 data ACK_1 {DAT_i data ACK_{i+1}}.

The third request listed above, *SendMsg*, does not refer to any file, but merely transmits and displays a short message. It is included here for testing the link between two partners and perhaps for visibly acknowledging a rendered service by the message 'done', or 'thank you'.

SendMsg = MSG message ACK.

10.3 Station addressing

Every packet must carry a destination address as well as the sender's address. Addresses are station numbers. It would certainly be inconvenient for a user to remember the station number of a desired partner. Instead, the use of symbolic names is preferred. We have become accustomed to use the partner's initials for this purpose.

The source address is inserted automatically into packet headers by the driver. It is obtained from a dip switch set when a computer is installed and connected. But where should the destination address come from? From the start, we reject the solution of an address table in every workstation because of the potential inconsistencies. The concept of a centralized authority holding a name/address dictionary is equally unattractive, because of the updates required whenever a person uses a different computer. Also, we have started from the premise of keeping all participants in the network equal.

Decentralized name service

Broadcast

The most attractive solution lies in a decentralized name service. It is based on the broadcast facility, that is, the possibility to send a packet to all connected stations, bypassing their address filters with a special destination address (-1). The broadcast is used for emitting a name request containing the desired partner's symbolic name. A station receiving the request returns a reply to the requester, if that name matches its own symbolic name. The requester then obtains the desired partner's address from the source address field of the received reply. The corresponding simple protocol is

NameRequest = NRQ partnername [*NRS*].

Here the timeout facility already mentioned is indispensible. The following summarizes the protocol developed so far:

protocol = {request}.
request = ReceiveFile | SendFile | SendMsg | NameRequest.

The overhead incurred by name requests may be reduced by using a local address dictionary. In practice, a single entry is satisfactory. A name request is then needed whenever the partner changes.

10.4 The implementation

Module *Net* is an implementation of the facilities outlined above. The program is listed below. It starts with a number of auxiliary, local procedures. They are followed by procedure *Serve*, which is to be installed as an Oberon task, and the commands *SendFiles*, *ReceiveFiles* and *SendMsg*, each of which has its counterpart within procedure *Serve*. At the end are the commands for starting and stopping the server facility.

For a more detailed presentation, we select procedure *ReceiveFiles*. It starts out by reading the first parameter, which designates the partner station from the command line. Procedure *FindPartner* issues the name request, unless the partner's address has already been determined by a previous command. The global variable *partner* records a symbolic name (id) whose address is stored in the destination field of the global variable *head0*, which is used as header in every packet sent by procedure *SCC.SendPacket*. The variable *partner* may be regarded as a

Name cache name cache with a single entry and with the purpose of reducing the number of issued name requests.

If the partner has been identified, the next parameter is read from the command line. It is the name of the file to be transmitted. If the parameter has the form *name0:name1*, the file stored on the server as *name0.name1* is fetched and stored locally as *name1*. Hence *name0* serves as a prefix of the file name on the server station.

Thereafter, the request parameters are concatenated in the local buffer variable *buf*. They are the user's name and password followed by the file name. (The user's name and password remain unused by the server presented here.) The command package is dispatched by the

Send call *Send(SND, k, buf)*, where k denotes the length of the command parameter string. Then the reply packet is awaited by calling *ReceiveHead*. If the received packet's type is DAT with sequence number 0, a new

Receive file is established. Procedure *ReceiveData* receives the data and stores them in the new file, obeying the protocol defined in Section 10.2. This process is repeated for each file specified in the list of file names in the command line.

Receive head Procedure *ReceiveHead(T)* receives packets and discards them until one arrives from the partner from which it is expected. The procedure represents an input filter in addition to the one provided by the hardware. It discriminates on the basis of the packets' source address, whereas the hardware filter discriminates on the basis of the destination address. If no packet arrives within the allotted time T, a type code −1 is returned, signifying a timeout.

Receive data

Procedure *ReceiveData* checks the sequence numbers of incoming data packets (type 0–7). If an incorrect number is detected, an ACK packet with the previous sequence number is returned (type 16–23), requesting a retransmission. At most, two retries are undertaken. This seems to suffice considering that also the server does not accept any other requests while being engaged in the transmission of a file.

The part corresponding to *ReceiveFiles* within procedure Serve is guarded by the condition *head1.typ* = *SND*. Variable *head1* is the recipient of headers whenever a packet is received by *ReceiveHead*. First, the request's parameters are scanned. *Id* and *pw* are ignored. Then the requested file is opened. If it exists, the transmission is handled by

Timeout

ReceiveData's counterpart, procedure *SendData*. The time limit for receiving the next request is T1, whereas the limit of *ReceiveData* for receiving the next data packet is T0. T1 is roughly T0 multiplied by the maximum number of possible (re)transmissions. Before disengaging itself from a transaction, the sender of data waits until no further retransmission requests can be expected to arrive. The value T0 (300) corresponds to 1 s; the time for transmission of a packet of maximum length is about 16 ms.

Procedure *SendFiles* is designed analogously; its counterpart in the server is guarded by the condition *head1.typ* = *REC*. The server

Write protection

accepts the request only if its state is unprotected (global variable *protected*). Otherwise, the request is negatively acknowledged with an NPR packet. We draw attention to the fact that procedures *SendData* and *ReceiveData* are both used by command procedures as well as by the server.

```
MODULE Net; (*NW 3.7.88 / 25.8.91*)
  IMPORT SCC, Files, Viewers, Texts, TextFrames, MenuViewers, Oberon;

    CONST PakSize = 512;
    T0 = 300; T1 = 1000; (*timeouts*)

    ACK = 10H; NAK = 25H; NPR = 26H; (*acknowledgements*)
    NRQ = 34H; NRS = 35H; (*name request, response*)
    SND = 41H; REC = 42H; MSG = 44H;

  VAR W: Texts.Writer;
    Server: Oberon.Task;
    head0, head1: SCC.Header;
    partner, dmy: ARRAY 8 OF CHAR;
    protected: BOOLEAN; (*write-protection*)

  PROCEDURE SetPartner(VAR name: ARRAY OF CHAR);
```

```
BEGIN head0.dadr := head1.sadr; COPY(name, partner)
END SetPartner;


PROCEDURE Send(t: SHORTINT; L: INTEGER; VAR data: ARRAY OF CHAR);
BEGIN head0.typ := t; head0.len := L; SCC.SendPacket(head0, data)
END Send;


PROCEDURE ReceiveHead(timeout: LONGINT);
    VAR time: LONGINT;
BEGIN time := Oberon.Time() + timeout;
    LOOP SCC.ReceiveHead(head1);
        IF head1.valid THEN
            IF head1.sadr = head0.dadr THEN EXIT ELSE SCC.Skip(head1.len) END
        ELSIF Oberon.Time() >= time THEN head1.typ := -1; EXIT
        END
    END
END ReceiveHead;


PROCEDURE FindPartner(VAR name: ARRAY OF CHAR; VAR res: INTEGER);
    VAR time: LONGINT; k: INTEGER;
BEGIN SCC.Skip(SCC.Available()); res := 0;
    IF name # partner THEN k := 0;
        WHILE name[k] > 0X DO INC(k) END;
        head0.dadr := -1; Send(NRQ, k+1, name); time := Oberon.Time() + T1;
        LOOP SCC.ReceiveHead(head1);
            IF head1.valid THEN
                IF head1.typ = NRS THEN SetPartner(name); EXIT
                ELSE SCC.Skip(head1.len)
                END
            ELSIF Oberon.Time() >= time THEN res := 1; partner[0] := 0X; EXIT
            END
        END
    END
END FindPartner;


PROCEDURE AppendS(VAR s, d: ARRAY OF CHAR; VAR k: INTEGER);
    VAR i: INTEGER; ch: CHAR;
BEGIN i := 0;
    REPEAT ch := s[i]; d[k] := ch; INC(i); INC(k) UNTIL ch = 0X
END AppendS;


PROCEDURE AppendW(s: LONGINT; VAR d: ARRAY OF CHAR; n: INTEGER; VAR k:
        INTEGER);
    VAR i: INTEGER;
BEGIN i := 0;
    REPEAT d[k] := CHR(s); s := s DIV 100H; INC(i); INC(k) UNTIL i = n
END AppendW;


PROCEDURE PickS(VAR s: ARRAY OF CHAR);
    VAR i: INTEGER; ch: CHAR;
BEGIN i := 0;
    REPEAT SCC.Receive(ch); s[i] := ch; INC(i) UNTIL ch = 0X
END PickS;


PROCEDURE PickQ(VAR w: LONGINT);
    VAR c0, c1, c2: CHAR; s: SHORTINT;
```

```
BEGIN SCC.Receive(c0); SCC.Receive(c1); SCC.Receive(c2); SCC.Receive(s);
   w := s; w := ((w * 100H + LONG(c2)) * 100H + LONG(c1)) * 100H + LONG(c0)
END PickQ;


PROCEDURE SendData(F: Files.File);
   VAR k: INTEGER;
      seqno: SHORTINT; x: CHAR;
      len: LONGINT;
      R: Files.Rider;
      buf: ARRAY PakSize OF CHAR;
BEGIN Files.Set(R, F, 0); len := 0; seqno := 0;
   LOOP k := 0;
      LOOP Files.Read(R, x);
         IF R.eof THEN EXIT END;
         buf[k] := x; INC(k);
         IF k = PakSize THEN EXIT END
      END;
      REPEAT Send(seqno, k, buf); ReceiveHead(T1)
      UNTIL head1.typ # seqno + ACK;
      seqno := (seqno + 1) MOD 8; len := len + k;
      IF head1.typ # seqno + ACK THEN
         Texts.WriteString(W, "failed"); EXIT
      END;
      IF k < PakSize THEN EXIT END
   END;
   Texts.WriteInt(W, len, 7)
END SendData;


PROCEDURE ReceiveData(F: Files.File; VAR done: BOOLEAN);
   VAR k, retry: INTEGER;
      seqno: SHORTINT; x: CHAR;
      len: LONGINT;
      R: Files.Rider;
BEGIN Files.Set(R, F, 0); seqno := 0; len := 0; retry := 2;
   LOOP
      IF head1.typ = seqno THEN
         seqno := (seqno + 1) MOD 8; len := len + head1.len; retry := 2;
         Send(seqno + ACK, 0, dmy); k := 0;
         WHILE k < head1.len DO
            SCC.Receive(x); Files.Write(R, x); INC(k)
         END;
         IF k < PakSize THEN done := TRUE; EXIT END
      ELSE DEC(retry);
         IF retry = 0 THEN
            Texts.WriteString(W, "failed"); done := FALSE; EXIT
         END;
         Send(seqno + ACK, 0, dmy)
      END;
      ReceiveHead(T0)
   END;
   Texts.WriteInt(W, len, 7)
END ReceiveData;


PROCEDURE reply(msg: INTEGER);
BEGIN
   CASE msg OF
      0:
```

```
        | 1: Texts.WriteString(W, "no link")
        | 2: Texts.WriteString(W, "no permission")
        | 3: Texts.WriteString(W, "not done")
        | 4: Texts.WriteString(W, "not found")
        | 5: Texts.WriteString(W, "no response")
    END;
    Texts.WriteLn(W); Texts.Append(Oberon.Log, W.buf)
END reply;


PROCEDURE* Serve;
    VAR i: INTEGER;
        done: BOOLEAN; ch: CHAR;
        F: Files.File;
        pw: LONGINT;
        Id: ARRAY 10 OF CHAR;
        FileName: ARRAY 32 OF CHAR;
BEGIN SCC.ReceiveHead(head1);
IF head1.valid THEN
    IF head1.typ = SND THEN
        PickS(Id); PickQ(pw); PickS(FileName);
        Texts.WriteString(W, Id); Texts.Write(W, " "); Texts.WriteString(W, FileName);
        F := Files.Old(FileName);
        IF F # NIL THEN
            Texts.WriteString(W, "sending"); SetPartner(Id);
            Texts.Append(Oberon.Log, W.buf); SendData(F)
        ELSE Send(NAK, 0, dmy); Texts.Write(W, "~")
        END;
        reply(0)
    ELSIF head1.typ = REC THEN
        PickS(Id); PickQ(pw); PickS(FileName);
        IF ~protected THEN
            Texts.WriteString(W, Id); Texts.Write(W, " "); Texts.WriteString(W, FileName);
            F := Files.New(FileName);
            IF F # NIL THEN
                Texts.WriteString(W, "receiving"); SetPartner(Id);
                Texts.Append(Oberon.Log, W.buf);
                Send(ACK, 0, dmy); ReceiveHead(T0); ReceiveData(F, done);
                IF done THEN Files.Register(F) END
            ELSE Send(NAK, 0, dmy); Texts.Write(W, "~")
            END;
            reply(0)
        ELSE Send(NPR, 0, dmy)
        END
    ELSIF head1.typ = MSG THEN i := 0;
        WHILE i < head1.len DO SCC.Receive(ch); Texts.Write(W, ch); INC(i) END;
        Send(ACK, 0, dmy); reply(0)
    ELSIF head1.typ = NRQ THEN i := 0;
        LOOP SCC.Receive(ch); Id[i] := ch; INC(i);
            IF ch = 0X THEN EXIT END;
            IF i = 7 THEN Id[7] := 0X; EXIT END
        END;
        WHILE i < head1.len DO SCC.Receive(ch); INC(i) END;
        IF Id = Oberon.User THEN SetPartner(Id); Send(NRS, 0, dmy) END
    ELSE SCC.Skip(head1.len)
    END
END
END Serve;
```

```
PROCEDURE GetPar1(VAR S: Texts.Scanner);
BEGIN Texts.OpenScanner(S, Oberon.Par.text, Oberon.Par.pos); Texts.Scan(S)
END GetPar1;


PROCEDURE GetPar(VAR S: Texts.Scanner; VAR end: LONGINT);
    VAR T: Texts.Text; beg, tm: LONGINT;
BEGIN Texts.Scan(S);
    IF (S.class = Texts.Char) & (S.c = " ↑ ") THEN
        Oberon.GetSelection(T, beg, end, tm);
        IF tm >= 0 THEN Texts.OpenScanner(S, T, beg); Texts.Scan(S) END
    ELSE end := Oberon.Par.text.len
    END
END GetPar;


PROCEDURE SendFiles*;
    VAR k: INTEGER;
        end: LONGINT;
        S: Texts.Scanner;
        F: Files.File;
        name: ARRAY 32 OF CHAR;
        buf: ARRAY 64 OF CHAR;
BEGIN GetPar1(S);
    IF S.class = Texts.Name THEN
        FindPartner(S.s, k);
        IF k = 0 THEN
            GetPar(S, end);
            LOOP
                IF S.class # Texts.Name THEN EXIT END;
                Texts.WriteString(W, S.s); k := 0; AppendS(S.s, name, k);
                IF S.nextCh = ":" THEN (*prefix*)
                    Texts.Scan(S); Texts.Scan(S);
                    IF S.class = Texts.Name THEN
                        name[k−1] := "."; AppendS(S.s, name, k);
                        Texts.Write(W, ":"); Texts.WriteString(W, S.s)
                    END
                END;
                F := Files.Old(S.s);
                IF F # NIL THEN k := 0;
                    AppendS(Oberon.User, buf, k); AppendW(Oberon.Password, buf, 4, k);
                    AppendS(name, buf, k); Send(REC, k, buf); ReceiveHead(T0);
                    IF head1.typ = ACK THEN
                        Texts.WriteString(W, "sending"); Texts.Append(Oberon.Log, W.buf);
                        SendData(F); reply(0)
                    ELSIF head1.typ = NPR THEN reply(2); EXIT
                    ELSIF head1.typ = NAK THEN reply(3); EXIT
                    ELSE reply(5); EXIT
                    END
                ELSE reply(4)
                END;
                IF Texts.Pos(S) >= end THEN EXIT END;
                Texts.Scan(S)
            END
        ELSE reply(1)
        END
    END
END SendFiles;
```

```
PROCEDURE ReceiveFiles*;
    VAR k: INTEGER; done: BOOLEAN;
        end: LONGINT;
        S: Texts.Scanner;
        F: Files.File;
        name: ARRAY 32 OF CHAR;
        buf: ARRAY 64 OF CHAR;
BEGIN GetPar1(S);
    IF S.class = Texts.Name THEN
        FindPartner(S.s, k);
        IF k = 0 THEN
            GetPar(S, end);
            LOOP
                IF S.class # Texts.Name THEN EXIT END;
                Texts.WriteString(W, S.s); k := 0; AppendS(S.s, name, k);
                IF S.nextCh = ":" THEN (*prefix*)
                    Texts.Scan(S); Texts.Scan(S);
                    IF S.class = Texts.Name THEN
                        name[k−1] := "."; AppendS(S.s, name, k);
                        Texts.Write(W, ":"); Texts.WriteString(W, S.s)
                    END
                END;
                k := 0; AppendS(Oberon.User, buf, k); AppendW(Oberon.Password, buf, 4, k);
                AppendS(name, buf, k); Send(SND, k, buf);
                Texts.WriteString(W, "receiving"); Texts.Append(Oberon.Log, W.buf);
                ReceiveHead(T1);
                IF head1.typ = 0 THEN
                    F := Files.New(S.s);
                    IF F # NIL THEN
                        ReceiveData(F, done);
                        IF done THEN Files.Register(F); reply(0) ELSE EXIT END
                    ELSE reply(3); Send(NAK, 0, dmy)
                    END
                ELSIF head1.typ = NAK THEN reply(4)
                ELSIF head1.typ = NPR THEN reply(2); EXIT
                ELSE reply(5); EXIT
                END;
                IF Texts.Pos(S) >= end THEN EXIT END;
                Texts.Scan(S)
            END
        ELSE reply(1)
        END
    END
END ReceiveFiles;


PROCEDURE SendMsg*;
    VAR i: INTEGER; ch: CHAR;
        S: Texts.Scanner;
        msg: ARRAY 64 OF CHAR;
BEGIN GetPar1(S);
    IF S.class = Texts.Name THEN
        FindPartner(S.s, i);
        IF i = 0 THEN
            Texts.Read(S, ch);
            WHILE (ch >= " ") & (i < 64) DO
                msg[i] := ch; INC(i); Texts.Read(S, ch)
            END;
            Send(MSG, i, msg); ReceiveHead(T0);
```

```
                  IF head1.typ # ACK THEN reply(3) END
          ELSE reply(1)
          END
      END
  END SendMsg;

  PROCEDURE StartServer*;
  BEGIN protected := TRUE; SCC.Start(TRUE);
      Oberon.Remove(Server); Oberon.Install(Server);
      Texts.WriteString(W, "Server started");
      Texts.WriteLn(W); Texts.Append(Oberon.Log, W.buf)
  END StartServer;

  PROCEDURE Unprotect*;
  BEGIN protected := FALSE
  END Unprotect;

  PROCEDURE WProtect*;
  BEGIN protected := TRUE
  END WProtect;

  PROCEDURE Reset*;
  BEGIN SCC.Start(TRUE)
  END Reset;

  PROCEDURE StopServer*;
  BEGIN Oberon.Remove(Server); Texts.WriteString(W, "Server stopped");
      Texts.WriteLn(W); Texts.Append(Oberon.Log, W.buf)
  END StopServer;

BEGIN Texts.OpenWriter(W); NEW(Server); Server.handle := Serve
END Net.
```

11 A dedicated file-distribution, mail, and printer server

11.1 Concept and structure

In a system of loosely coupled workstations, it is desirable to centralize certain services. A first example is a common file store. Even if every station is equipped with a disk for permanent data storage, a common file service is beneficial, for example for storing the most recent versions of system files, reference documents and reports. A common repository avoids inconsistencies that are inevitable when local copies are created.

File distribution We call this a *file distribution service*.

A centralized service is also desirable if it requires equipment whose cost and service would not warrant its acquisition for every workstation, particularly if the service is infrequently used. A prime
Printing example of this case is a *printing service*.

The third case is a communication facility in the form of *electronic*
Electronic *mail*. The repository of messages must inherently be centralized. We
mail imagine it to have the form of a set of mailboxes, one for each user in the system. A mailbox needs to be accessible at all times, that is, also when its owner's workstation has been switched off.

Central A last example of a centralized service is a *time server*. It allows
time a station's real time clock to be synchronized with a central clock.

In passing, we point out that every user has full control over his or her station, including the right to switch it on and off at any time. In contrast, the central server is continuously operational.

In this chapter, we present a set of server modules providing all above mentioned services. They rest on the basic Oberon System without module *Net* (see Chapter 10). In contrast to *Net*, module
NetServer *NetServer*, which handles all network communication, contains no command procedures (apart from those for starting and stopping it). This is because it never acts as a master. The counterparts of its server routines reside in other modules, including (an extended version of) *Net*, on the individual workstations.

Routines for the file distribution service are the same as those

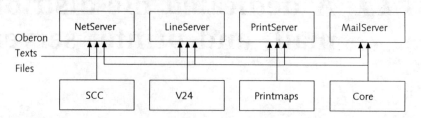

Figure 11.1   Module structure of server system.

contained in module *Net*, with the addition of permission checks based on the received user names and passwords. Routines for printing and mail service could in principle also be included in *NetServer* in the same way. But considerations of reliability and timing made this simple solution appear unattractive. A weaker coupling in time of data transmission and data consumption is indeed highly desirable. Therefore data received for printing or for dispatching into mailboxes are stored (by *NetServer*) into temporary files and thereafter 'handed over' to the appropriate agent, namely the print server or the mail server.

Task queues as interfaces between servers

This data-centered interface between servers – in contrast to procedural interfaces – has the advantage that the individual servers are independent in the sense that none imports any other. Therefore their development could proceed autonomously. Their connection is instead a module that defines a data structure and associated operators for passing temporary files from one server to another. The data structure used for this purpose is the first-in first-out queue. We call its elements tasks, because each one carries an objective and an object, the file to be processed. The module containing the FIFOs is called *Core*. The resulting structure of the involved modules is shown in Figure 11.1.

LineServer

This figure includes yet another server, *LineServer*, and shows the ease with which additional servers may be inserted in this scheme. They act as further sources and/or sinks for tasks, feeding or consuming the queues contained in *Core*. *LineServer* indeed produces and consumes tasks like *NetServer*. Instead of the RS-485 bus, it handles the RS-232, line which, connected to a modem, allows access to the server over telephone lines. We refrain from describing this module in further detail, because in many ways it is a mirror of *NetServer*.

Protection

A centralized, open server calls for certain protection measures against unauthorized use. We recall that requests always carry a user identification and a password as parameters. The server checks their validity by examining a table of users. The respective routines and the table are contained in module *Core* (see Section 11.5).

Book.Server.Text | System.Close System.Copy System.Grow Write.Search Write.Replace All Write.Parcs Write.Store   Copyright N.Wirth, 27.8.91 / 15.11.91

Chapter 11

A Dedicated File–distribution, Mail, and Printer Server

11.1. Concept and Structure

In a system of loosely coupled workstations it is desirable to centralize certain services. A first example is a common file store. Even if every station is equipped with a disk for permanent data storage, a common file service is beneficial, e.g. for storing the most recent versions of system files, reference documents, reports, etc. A common repository avoids inconsistencies which are inevitable when local copies are created. We call this a *file distribution service*.

Message.Text | System.Close System.Copy System.Grow Edit.Store

From: Ludwig
At: 02.11.91 10:37:50
To: all
Re: Sort and Split modules on Pluto

I installed two modules on Pluto: Sort.Obj/Tool and Split.Obj/Tool
Sort sorts CR terminated lines and displays them in a viewer. Fonts and Elements are lost.
Split divides a large file into smaller subfiles.
Source code for ports is available upon request.
shml

Net.ReceiveFiles Pluto shml:Sort.Obj shml:Sort.Tool~
Net.ReceiveFiles Pluto shml:Split.Obj shml:Split.Tool~

Edit.Show | System.Close System.Copy System.Grow Edit.Search Edit.Store

To: Gutknecht
cc: Wirth
I have just finished writing the book
Will now take a vacation. NW

Message.Text | System.Close System.Copy System.Grow Edit.Store

From: eberle@Pa.dec.com
To: wirth@inf.ethz.ch (Niklaus Wirth)
Re:
Submission: 27.11.91 17:24:00

Digital – Opens up its computer designs
(The Boston Globe, 26-Nov-91, p.37)
  Digital provided more details yesterday about a new generation of computers
it is betting on to jumpstart sales and preserve its dominant position in the
computer industry.
  The Maynard company hopes the new machines, code-named Alpha and set for
introduction in April, will finally let it shed its image as a provider of
proprietary, or exclusive design, hardware and software and establish it as
the leader in so-called "open systems" in the 1990s and beyond.
  "If there is a radical change at DEC, the biggest change is really

---

System.Log | System.Close System.Copy System.Grow Edit.Locate Edit.Store

CALL 1213,1

Calling...Press ↑C to stop
Session<1> Call to 1213 completed

OK
Echo

OK
Utility.Snapshot

System.Tool | System.Close System.Copy System.Grow Edit.Search Edit.Store

Edit.Open
Edit.Show
Edit.Search
Edit.Store
Edit.Recall
Edit.Print Pluto % *
Write.SysOpen Button.Tool

Compiler.Compile *
Compiler.Compile ~
Assembler.Assemble *

System.Recall
System.OpenLog
System.SetFont Syntax10.Scn.Fnt

Net.Tool | System.Close System.Copy System.Grow Edit.Search Edit.Store

System.SetUser

Edit.Print Pluto % *
Edit.Print Pluto % ~

Net.Mailbox Pluto   Net.SendMail Pluto

Net.ReceiveFiles Pluto ~
Net.SendFiles Pluto ~
Net.DeleteFiles Pluto Net~
Net.Directory Pluto Net

Net.SendMsg Pluto Hello
Net.GetTime Pluto

Line.Tool | System.Close System.Copy System.Grow Edit.Search Edit.Store

System.SetUser (type user/password)
Line.Start 2400
Line.SendMsg ATDT2512002
Line.SendMsg CALL 1213,1

Line.OpenLink   Line.Mailbox   Line.SendMail

Mailbox.Text | System.Close Line.ReceiveMail Line.DeleteMail

8 28.11.91 10:37:54 Ludwig 457
4 28.11.91 02:35:58 eberle@Pa.dec.com 3150
1 27.11.91 18:07:56 zehnder@orion.inf.s 970
6 02.11.91 15:45:06 pomberger@ws.uni-l 699
5 22.11.91 13:55:14 zehnder@orion.inf.s 2994
3 19.11.91 11:12:34 Wirth 926
2 05.11.91 17:57:34 Mossenboeck 427

Figure 11.2   Viewer with mail directory and messages received and to be sent.

11.2 Electronic mail service

The heart of an e-mail service is the set of mailboxes stored on the dedicated, central server. Each registered user owns a mailbox. The evidently necessary operations are the insertion of a message and its retrieval. In contrast to customary letter boxes, however, a retrieved message need not necessarily be removed from the box; its retrieval produces a copy. The box thereby automatically becomes a repository, and messages can be retrieved many times. This scheme calls for an additional command which removes a message from the box. Also, a command is needed for delivering a table of contents, in which presumably each message is represented by an indication of its sender and time of arrival.

The mail scheme suggested above results in the following commands:

Mailbox inspection

- *Net.Mailbox ServerName.* This command fetches a table of contents of the current user's mailbox from the specified server and displays it in a new viewer. The user's name and password must have been registered previously by the command *System.SetUser.*

Sending a message

- *Net.SendMail ServerName.* The text in the marked viewer is sent to the specified server. In order to be accepted, the text must begin with at least one line beginning with 'To:' and containing at least one recipient. An example is shown in Figure 11.2.

Receiving a message

- *Net.ReceiveMail.* This command is contained in the title bar (menu) of the viewer obtained when requesting the table of contents. Prior to issuing the command, the message to be read must have been specified by selecting a line in the table of contents in this viewer.

Deleting a message

- *Net.DeleteMail.* This command is also contained in the mailbox viewer's title bar. The message to be deleted must be selected before issuing the command.

The mail system presented here is primarily intended to serve as an exchange for short messages, which are typically sent, received, read and discarded. Mailboxes are not intended to serve as long-term archives for a large and ever growing number of long pieces of text. This restrictiveness of purpose allows to choose a reasonably simple implementation and results in an efficient, practically instantaneous access to messages when the serve is idle.

External mail

The Oberon mail server used at ETH also provides communication with external correspondents. It connects to an external mail server, which is treated as a source and a sink for messages (almost) like other customers. Additionally, messages sent to that server need to be encoded

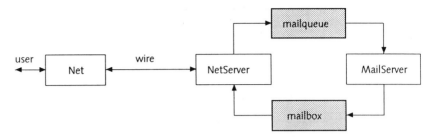

Figure 11.3 Path of messages to and from mailbox.

into a standardized format, and those received need to be decoded accordingly. The parts of module *MailServer* for encoding and decoding are not described in this book. We merely divulge the fact that its design and implementation took a multiple of the time spent on the fast, local message exchange, to which we confine this presentation.

From the structures explained in Section 11.1, it follows that three agents are involved in the transfer of messages from the user into a mailbox. Therefore additions to the server system distribute over three modules. New commands are added to module *Net* (see Section 10.4); these procedures will be listed below. Their counterparts reside in module *NetServer* on the dedicated computer. The third agent is module **MailServer** *MailServer*; both are listed below in this section. The latter handles the insertion of arriving messages into mailboxes. The path which a message traverses for insertion and retrieval is shown in Figure 11.3. Rectangles with bold edges mark storage.

Communication between the master station and the dedicated server runs over the network and therefore calls for an extension of its **Protocol** protocol (see Section 10.2). The additions correspond directly to the four commands given above.

MailBox	= MDIR username password (*datastream* | *NAK* | *NPR*).
SendMail	= RML username password (*ACK* datastream | *NAK* | *NPR*).
ReceiveMail	= SML username password msgno (*datastream* | *NAK* | *NPR*).
DeleteMail	= DML username password msgno (*ACK* | *NAK* | *NPR*).

The message number is taken from the selected line in the mailbox viewer. The data transmitted are taken as (unformatted) texts. This is in contrast to file transfers, where they are taken as any sequence of bytes. The four command procedures listed below belong into module

Net; they are listed together with the auxiliary procedures *SendText* and *ReceiveText*, which correspond closely to *SendData* and *ReceiveData* (see Section 10.4).

```
CONST MDIR = 4AH; SML = 4BH; RML = 4CH; DML = 4DH;

    PROCEDURE SendText(T: Texts.Text);
        VAR k: INTEGER;
            seqno: SHORTINT; x: CHAR;
            R: Texts.Reader;
            buf: ARRAY PakSize OF CHAR;
    BEGIN Texts.OpenReader(R, T, 0); seqno := 0;
        LOOP k := 0;
            LOOP Texts.Read(R, x);
                IF R.eot THEN EXIT END;
                buf[k] := x; INC(k);
                IF k = PakSize THEN EXIT END
            END;
            REPEAT Send(seqno, k, buf); ReceiveHead(T1)
            UNTIL head1.typ # seqno + ACK;
            seqno := (seqno + 1) MOD 8;
            IF head1.typ # seqno + ACK THEN
                Texts.WriteString(W, "failed"); EXIT
            END;
            IF k < PakSize THEN EXIT END
        END
    END SendText;

    PROCEDURE ReceiveText(T: Texts.Text);
        VAR k, retry: INTEGER;
            seqno: SHORTINT; x: CHAR;
    BEGIN seqno := 0; retry := 2;
        LOOP
            IF head1.typ = seqno THEN
                seqno := (seqno + 1) MOD 8; retry := 2;
                Send(seqno + 10H, 0, dmy); k := 0;
                WHILE k < head1.len DO
                    SCC.Receive(x); Texts.Write(W, x); INC(k)
                END;
                Texts.Append(T, W.buf);
                IF k < PakSize THEN EXIT END
            ELSE DEC(retry);
                IF retry = 0 THEN
                    Texts.WriteString(W, "failed"); Texts.WriteLn(W);
                    Texts.Append(Oberon.Log, W.buf); EXIT
                END;
                Send(seqno + 10H, 0, dmy)
            END;
            ReceiveHead(T0)
        END
    END ReceiveText;

    PROCEDURE Mailbox*;
        VAR k, X, Y: INTEGER;
            T: Texts.Text;
            V: Viewers.Viewer;
```

```
        S: Texts.Scanner;
        buf: ARRAY 32 OF CHAR;
BEGIN GetPar1(S);
    IF S.class = Texts.Name THEN
        FindPartner(S.s, k);
        IF k = 0 THEN
            AppendS(Oberon.User, buf, k); AppendW(Oberon.Password, buf, 4, k);
            Send(MDIR, k, buf); ReceiveHead(T1);
            IF head1.typ = 0 THEN
                T := TextFrames.Text("");
                Oberon.AllocateSystemViewer(Oberon.Par.frame.X, X, Y);
                V := MenuViewers.New(
                    TextFrames.NewMenu(S.s, "System.Close  Net.ReceiveMail  Net.DeleteMail"),
                    TextFrames.NewText(T, 0), TextFrames.menuH, X, Y);
                ReceiveText(T)
            ELSIF head1.typ = NAK THEN reply(4)
            ELSIF head1.typ = NPR THEN reply(2)
            ELSE  reply(5)
            END
        ELSE reply(1)
        END
    END
END Mailbox;

PROCEDURE ReceiveMail*;
    VAR k, X, Y: INTEGER;
        T: Texts.Text;
        F: TextFrames.Frame;
        S: Texts.Scanner;
        V: Viewers.Viewer;
        buf: ARRAY 32 OF CHAR;
BEGIN F := Oberon.Par.frame(TextFrames.Frame);
    Texts.OpenScanner(S, F.text, 0); Texts.Scan(S); FindPartner(S.s, k);
    IF k = 0 THEN
        F := F.next(TextFrames.Frame);
        IF F.sel > 0 THEN
            Texts.OpenScanner(S, F.text, F.selbeg.pos); Texts.Scan(S);
            IF S.class = Texts.Int THEN
                k := 0; AppendS(Oberon.User, buf, k); AppendW(Oberon.Password, buf, 4, k);
                AppendW(S.i, buf, 2, k); Send(SML, k, buf); ReceiveHead(T1);
                IF head1.typ = 0 THEN
                    T := TextFrames.Text("");
                    Oberon.AllocateUserViewer(Oberon.Par.frame.X, X, Y);
                    V := MenuViewers.New(
                        TextFrames.NewMenu("Message.Text",
                            "System.Close  System.Copy  System.Grow  Edit.Store"),
                        TextFrames.NewText(T, 0), TextFrames.menuH, X, Y);
                    ReceiveText(T)
                ELSIF head1.typ = NAK THEN reply(4)
                ELSIF head1.typ = NPR THEN reply(2)
                ELSE  reply(5)
                END
            END
        END
    ELSE reply(1)
    END
END ReceiveMail;

PROCEDURE SendMail*;
```

```
        VAR k: INTEGER;
          S: Texts.Scanner;
          T, M: Texts.Text;
          v: Viewers.Viewer;
          buf: ARRAY 64 OF CHAR;
      BEGIN GetPar1(S);
          IF S.class = Texts.Name THEN
              FindPartner(S.s, k);
              IF k = 0 THEN
                  v := Oberon.MarkedViewer();
                  IF (v.dsc # NIL) & (v.dsc.next IS TextFrames.Frame) THEN
                      T := v.dsc.next(TextFrames.Frame).text;
                      IF T.len < 60000 THEN
                          Texts.OpenScanner(S, T, 0); Texts.Scan(S);
                          IF (S.class = Texts.Name) & (S.s = "To") THEN
                              M := v.dsc(TextFrames.Frame).text; Texts.OpenScanner(S, M, 0);
                                  Texts.Scan(S);
                              IF S.class = Texts.Name THEN
                                  Texts.WriteString(W, S.s);
                                  AppendS(Oberon.User, buf, k); AppendW(Oberon.Password, buf, 4,
                                      k);
                                  Send(RML, k, buf); ReceiveHead(T1);
                                  IF head1.typ = ACK THEN
                                      Texts.WriteString(W, "mailing"); Texts.Append(Oberon.Log,
                                          W.buf);
                                      SendText(T); reply(0)
                                  ELSIF head1.typ = NPR THEN reply(2)
                                  ELSIF head1.typ = NAK THEN reply(3)
                                  ELSE reply(5)
                                  END
                              END
                          ELSE reply(8)
                          END
                      ELSE reply(9)
                      END
                  END
              ELSE reply(1)
              END
          END
      END SendMail;


      PROCEDURE DeleteMail*;
          VAR k: INTEGER; ch: CHAR;
          T: Texts.Text;
          F: TextFrames.Frame;
          S: Texts.Scanner;
          buf: ARRAY 32 OF CHAR;
      BEGIN F := Oberon.Par.frame(TextFrames.Frame);
          Texts.OpenScanner(S, F.text, 0); Texts.Scan(S); FindPartner(S.s, k);
          IF k = 0 THEN
              F := F.next(TextFrames.Frame);
              IF F.sel > 0 THEN
                  Texts.OpenScanner(S, F.text, F.selbeg.pos); Texts.Scan(S);
                  IF S.class = Texts.Int THEN
                      k := 0; AppendS(Oberon.User, buf, k); AppendW(Oberon.Password, buf, 4, k);
                      AppendW(S.i, buf, 2, k); Send(DML, k, buf); ReceiveHead(T1);
                      IF head1.typ = ACK THEN
                          REPEAT Texts.Read(S, ch) UNTIL ch < " ";
```

```
                Texts.Delete(F.text, F.selbeg.pos, Texts.Pos(S))
            ELSIF head1.typ = NAK THEN reply(3)
            ELSIF head1.typ = NPR THEN reply(2)
            ELSE reply(5)
            END
          END
        END
      ELSE reply(1)
      END
    END DeleteMail;
```

We now turn our attention to the command procedures' counterparts in module *NetServer* listed in this section. In order to explain these routines, a description of their interface with the mail server and a definition of the structure of mailboxes must precede. We begin with the simplest case, the counterpart of *SendMail*. It is the part of procedure *NetServer.Serve* that is guarded by the condition *typ = RML*, indicating a request to receive mail. As in all other services, the parameters *username* and *password* are read and the admissibility of the request is checked. The check is performed by procedure *Core.UserNo*, which yields a negative number if service is to be refused. In the affirmative case, procedure *ReceiveData* obtains the message and stores it on a file, which is thereafter inserted into the mail queue as a task to be handled by the mail server at a later time. This may involve distribution of the message into several mailboxes.

Core   Module *Core* is listed in Section 11.5. As mentioned before, it serves as link between the various server modules, defining the data types of the linking queues and also of mailboxes. Task queues are represented as FIFO lists. The descriptor of type *Queue* contains a pointer to the first list element used for retrieval and a pointer to the last element used for insertion (see Figure 11.4.). These pointers are not exported; instead, the next task is obtained by calling procedure *Core.GetTask*, and it is deleted by *Core.RemoveTask*. There exist two

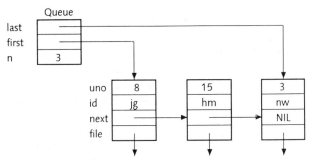

Figure 11.4   Structure of task queue.

exported variables of type *Queue*: *MailQueue* consumed by *MailServer*, and *PrintQueue* consumed by *PrintServer* (see Section 11.3.). (In fact, we use a third queue: *LineQueue* consumed by *LineServer*.) Elements of queues are of type *TaskDesc*, which specifies the file representing the data to be consumed. Additionally, it specifies the user number and identification of the task's originator. Three procedures are provided by module *Core* for handling task queues:

```
PROCEDURE InsertTask(VAR q: Queue; F: Files.File;
        VAR id: ARRAY OF CHAR; uno: INTEGER);
PROCEDURE GetTask(VAR q: Queue; VAR F: Files.File;
        VAR id: ARRAY OF CHAR; VAR uno: INTEGER);
PROCEDURE RemoveTask(VAR q: Queue);
```

The server's counterparts of the remaining mail commands access mailboxes directly. The simplicity of the required actions – a result of a carefully chosen mailbox representation – and considerations of efficiency do not warrant a detour via task queue and mail server.

Mailbox representation
Every mailbox is represented as a file. This solution has the tremendous advantage that no special administration has to be introduced to handle a reserved partition of disk store for mail purposes. A mailbox file is partitioned into three parts: the *block reservation* part, the *directory* part and the *message* part. Each part is quickly locatable, because the first two have a fixed length (32 and $31 \times 32 = 992$ bytes). The message part is regarded as a sequence of blocks (of 256 bytes), and each message occupies an integral number of adjacent blocks. Corresponding to each block, the block reservation part contains a single bit indicating whether or not the block is occupied by a message. Since the block reservation part is 32 bytes long, the message part contains at most 256 blocks, that is, 64 Kbytes. The block length was chosen after an analysis of messages that revealed that the average message is less than 500 bytes long.

Directory representation
The directory part consists of an array of 31 elements of type *MailEntry*, a record with the following fields: *pos* and *len* indicate the index of the message's first block and the message's number of bytes; *time* and *date* indicate the message's time of insertion; and originator indicates the message's source. The entries are linked (field *next*) in chronological order of their arrival, and entry 0 serves as the list's header. It follows that a mailbox contains at most 30 messages. An example of a mailbox state is shown in Figure 11.5.

```
MailEntry = RECORD
            pos, next: INTEGER;
            len: LONGINT;
            time, date: INTEGER;
```

originator: ARRAY 20 OF CHAR
END;
MResTab = ARRAY 8 OF SET;
MailDir = ARRAY 31 OF MailEntry;

Mailbox cache

We are now in a position to inspect the handler for requests for message retrieval. It is guarded by the condition *typ* = *SML*. After a validity check, the respective requestor's mailbox file is opened. The last mailbox opened is retained by the global variable MF, which acts as a single-entry cache. The associated user number is given by the global variable *mailuno*. Since typically several requests involving the same mailbox follow, this measure avoids the repeated reopening of the same file. Thereafter, a rider is directly positioned at the respective directory entry for reading the message's length and position in the message part. The rider is repositioned accordingly, and transmission of the message is handled by procedure *SendMail*.

Requests for the mailbox directory are handled by the routine guarded by the condition *typ* = *MDIR*. The directory part must be read and converted into a text. This task is supported by various auxiliary procedures (Append), which concatenate supplied data in a buffer for latter transmission. We emphasize that this request does not require the reading of any other part of the file, and therefore is very swift.

The last of the four mail service requests (DML) deletes a specified message. Removal from the directory requires a relinking of the entries.

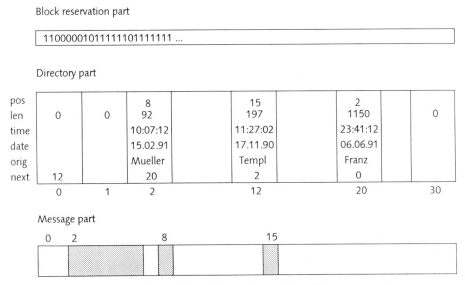

Block reservation part

```
11000001011111101111111 ...
```

Directory part

			8		15		2		
pos			8		15		2		
len	0	0	92		197		1150		0
time			10:07:12		11:27:02		23:41:12		
date			15.02.91		17.11.90		06.06.91		
orig			Mueller		Templ		Franz		
next	12		20		2		0		
	0	1	2		12		20		30

Message part

0   2   8   15

Figure 11.5 State of a mailbox file.

Unused entries are marked by their *len* field having value 0. Also, the blocks occupied by the message become free. The block reservation part must be updated accordingly. Further details can be examined in the following program listing:

```
MODULE NetServer; (*NW 15.2.90 / 22.11.91*)
  IMPORT SCC, Core, FileDir, Files, Texts, Oberon;

  CONST PakSize = 512; GCInterval = 50;
    T0 = 300; T1 = 1000; (*timeouts*)
    maxFileLen = 100000H;


    ACK = 10H; NAK = 25H; NPR = 26H; (*acknowledgements*)
    NRQ = 34H; NRS = 35H; (*name request, response*)
    SND = 41H; REC = 42H; (*send / receive request*)
    FDIR = 45H; DEL = 49H; (*directory and delete file requests*)
    PRT = 43H; (*receive to print request*)
    TRQ = 46H; TIM = 47H; (*time requests*)
    MSG = 44H; NPW = 48H; (*new password request*)
    TOT = 7FH; (*timeout*)
    MDIR = 4AH; SML = 4BH; RML = 4CH; DML = 4DH;


  VAR W: Texts.Writer;
    handler: Oberon.Task;


    head0, head1: SCC.Header;
    partner: Core.ShortName;
    seqno: SHORTINT;


    K, reqcnt, mailuno: INTEGER;
    protected: BOOLEAN;
    MF: Files.File; (*last mail file accessed*)
    buf: ARRAY 1024 OF CHAR; (*used by FDIR and MDIR*)
    dmy: ARRAY 4 OF CHAR;


  PROCEDURE EOL;
  BEGIN Texts.WriteLn(W); Texts.Append(Oberon.Log, W.buf)
  END EOL;


  PROCEDURE SetPartner(VAR name: ARRAY OF CHAR);
  BEGIN head0.dadr := head1.sadr; head0.destLink := head1.srcLink;
    COPY(name, partner)
  END SetPartner;


  PROCEDURE Send(t: SHORTINT; L: INTEGER; VAR data: ARRAY OF CHAR);
  BEGIN head0.typ := t; head0.len := L; SCC.SendPacket(head0, data)
  END Send;


  PROCEDURE ReceiveHead(timeout: LONGINT);
    VAR time: LONGINT;
  BEGIN time := Oberon.Time() + timeout;
    LOOP SCC.ReceiveHead(head1);
      IF head1.valid THEN
        IF head1.sadr = head0.dadr THEN EXIT
```

```
            ELSE SCC.Skip(head1.len)
            END
         ELSIF Oberon.Time() >= time THEN head1.typ := TOT; EXIT
         END
      END
   END ReceiveHead;


   PROCEDURE AppendS(VAR s, d: ARRAY OF CHAR; VAR k: INTEGER);
      VAR i: INTEGER; ch: CHAR;
   BEGIN i := 0;
      REPEAT ch := s[i]; d[k] := ch; INC(i); INC(k) UNTIL ch = 0X
   END AppendS;


   PROCEDURE AppendW(s: LONGINT; VAR d: ARRAY OF CHAR; n: INTEGER; VAR k:
         INTEGER);
      VAR i: INTEGER;
   BEGIN i := 0;
      REPEAT d[k] := CHR(s); s := s DIV 100H; INC(i); INC(k) UNTIL i = n
   END AppendW;


   PROCEDURE AppendN(x: LONGINT; VAR d: ARRAY OF CHAR; VAR k: INTEGER);
      VAR i: INTEGER; u: ARRAY 8 OF CHAR;
   BEGIN i := 0;
      REPEAT u[i] := CHR(x MOD 10 + 30H); INC(i); x := x DIV 10 UNTIL x = 0;
      REPEAT DEC(i); d[k] := u[i]; INC(k) UNTIL i = 0
   END AppendN;


   PROCEDURE AppendDate(t, d: INTEGER; VAR buf: ARRAY OF CHAR; VAR k: INTEGER);

      PROCEDURE Pair(ch: CHAR; x: LONGINT);
      BEGIN buf[k] := ch; INC(k);
         buf[k] := CHR(x DIV 10 + 30H); INC(k); buf[k] := CHR(x MOD 10 + 30H); INC(k)
      END Pair;

   BEGIN
      Pair(" ", d MOD 20H); Pair(".", d DIV 20H MOD 10H); Pair(".", d DIV 200H MOD 80H);
      Pair(" ", t DIV 800H MOD 20H); Pair(":", t DIV 20H MOD 40H); Pair(":", t MOD 20H * 2)
   END AppendDate;


   PROCEDURE SendBuffer(len: INTEGER; VAR done: BOOLEAN);
   VAR i, kd, ks: INTEGER; ch: CHAR;
   BEGIN
      REPEAT Send(seqno, len, buf); ReceiveHead(T1)
      UNTIL head1.typ # seqno + 10H;
      seqno := (seqno+1) MOD 8; kd := 0; ks := PakSize;
      WHILE ks < K DO buf[kd] := buf[ks]; INC(kd); INC(ks) END;
      K := kd; done := head1.typ = seqno + 10H
   END SendBuffer;


   PROCEDURE* AppendDirEntry(name: FileDir.FileName; adr: LONGINT; VAR done:
         BOOLEAN);
      VAR i, kd, ks: INTEGER; ch: CHAR;
   BEGIN i := 0; ch := name[0];
      WHILE ch > 0X DO buf[K] := ch; INC(i); INC(K); ch := name[i] END;
      buf[K] := 0DX; INC(K);
      IF K >= PakSize THEN SendBuffer(PakSize, done) END
```

```
    END AppendDirEntry;

    PROCEDURE PickS(VAR s: ARRAY OF CHAR);
      VAR i, n: INTEGER; ch: CHAR;
    BEGIN i := 0; n := SHORT(LEN(s))-1; SCC.Receive(ch);
      WHILE ch > 0X DO
        IF i < n THEN s[i] := ch; INC(i) END;
        SCC.Receive(ch)
      END;
      s[i] := 0X
    END PickS;

    PROCEDURE PickQ(VAR w: LONGINT);
      VAR c0, c1, c2: CHAR; s: SHORTINT;
    BEGIN SCC.Receive(c0); SCC.Receive(c1); SCC.Receive(c2); SCC.Receive(s);
      w := s; w := ((w * 100H + LONG(c2)) * 100H + LONG(c1)) * 100H + LONG(c0)
    END PickQ;

    PROCEDURE PickW(VAR w: INTEGER);
      VAR c0: CHAR; s: SHORTINT;
    BEGIN SCC.Receive(c0); SCC.Receive(s); w := s; w := w * 100H + ORD(c0)
    END PickW;

    PROCEDURE SendData(F: Files.File);
      VAR k: INTEGER;
        x: CHAR;
        len: LONGINT;
        R: Files.Rider;
    BEGIN Files.Set(R, F, 0); len := 0; seqno := 0;
      LOOP k := 0;
        LOOP Files.Read(R, x);
          IF R.eof THEN EXIT END;
          buf[k] := x; INC(k);
          IF k = PakSize THEN EXIT END
        END;
        REPEAT Send(seqno, k, buf); ReceiveHead(T1)
        UNTIL head1.typ # seqno + 10H;
        seqno := (seqno + 1) MOD 8; len := len + k;
        IF head1.typ # seqno + 10H THEN EXIT END;
        IF k < PakSize THEN EXIT END
      END
    END SendData;

    PROCEDURE ReceiveData(F: Files.File; VAR done: BOOLEAN);
      VAR k, retry: INTEGER;
        x: CHAR;
        len: LONGINT;
        R: Files.Rider;
    BEGIN Files.Set(R, F, 0); seqno := 0; len := 0; retry := 4;
      LOOP
        IF head1.typ = seqno THEN
          seqno := (seqno + 1) MOD 8; len := len + head1.len;
          IF len > maxFileLen THEN
            Send(NAK, 0, dmy); done := FALSE; Files.Close(F); Files.Purge(F); EXIT
          END;
          retry := 4; Send(seqno + 10H, 0, dmy); k := 0;
          WHILE k < head1.len DO
```

```
            SCC.Receive(x); Files.Write(R, x); INC(k)
        END;
        IF k < PakSize THEN done := TRUE; EXIT END
      ELSE DEC(retry);
        IF retry = 0 THEN done := FALSE; EXIT END;
        Send(seqno + 10H, 0, dmy)
      END;
      ReceiveHead(T0)
    END
END ReceiveData;


PROCEDURE SendMail(VAR R: Files.Rider; len: LONGINT);
    VAR k: INTEGER; x: CHAR;
        buf: ARRAY PakSize OF CHAR;
BEGIN seqno := 0;
    LOOP k := 0;
        LOOP Files.Read(R, x);
            IF k = len THEN EXIT END;
            buf[k] := x; INC(k);
            IF k = PakSize THEN EXIT END
        END;
        REPEAT Send(seqno, k, buf); ReceiveHead(T1)
        UNTIL head1.typ # seqno + 10H;
        seqno := (seqno + 1) MOD 8; len := len - k;
        IF head1.typ # seqno + 10H THEN EXIT END;
        IF k < PakSize THEN EXIT END
    END
END SendMail;


    PROCEDURE* Serve;
    VAR i, j, k0, k1, n, uno: INTEGER;
        ch: CHAR; typ: SHORTINT;
        done: BOOLEAN;
        F: Files.File;
        R: Files.Rider;
        t, d, pw, npw, pos, len: LONGINT;
        Id: Core.ShortName;
        fname: Core.Name;
        mdir: Core.MailDir;
        mrtab: Core.MResTab;
    BEGIN SCC.ReceiveHead(head1);
        IF ~head1.valid THEN RETURN END;
        typ := head1.typ;
        IF typ = SND THEN
            PickS(Id); PickQ(pw); PickS(fname); SetPartner(Id);
            IF Core.UserNo(Id, pw) >= 0 THEN
                F := Files.Old(fname);
                IF F # NIL THEN SendData(F)
                ELSE Send(NAK, 0, dmy)
                END
            ELSE Send(NPR, 0, dmy)
            END
        ELSIF typ = REC THEN
            PickS(Id); PickQ(pw); PickS(fname); SetPartner(Id);
            IF ~protected & (Core.UserNo(Id, pw) >= 0) THEN
                F := Files.New(fname);
                Send(ACK, 0, dmy); ReceiveHead(T0);
                IF head1.valid THEN
```

```
                  ReceiveData(F, done);
                  IF done THEN Files.Register(F) END
               END
            ELSE Send(NPR, 0, dmy)
            END
         ELSIF typ = PRT THEN
            PickS(Id); PickQ(pw); SetPartner(Id); uno := Core.UserNo(Id, pw);
            IF uno >= 0 THEN
               F := Files.New("");
               Send(ACK, 0, dmy); ReceiveHead(T0);
               IF head1.valid THEN
                  ReceiveData(F, done);
                  IF done THEN
                     Files.Close(F); Core.InsertTask(Core.PrintQueue, F, Id, uno) END
                  END
               ELSE Send(NPR, 0, dmy)
               END
         ELSIF typ = DEL THEN
            PickS(Id); PickQ(pw); PickS(fname); SetPartner(Id);
            IF ~protected & (Core.UserNo(Id, pw) >= 0) THEN
               Files.Delete(fname, k);
               IF k = 0 THEN Send(ACK, 0, dmy) ELSE Send(NAK, 0, dmy) END
            ELSE Send(NPR, 0, dmy)
            END
         ELSIF typ = FDIR THEN
            PickS(Id); PickQ(pw); PickS(fname); SetPartner(Id); uno := Core.UserNo(Id, pw);
            IF uno >= 0 THEN
               K := 0; seqno := 0; FileDir.Enumerate(fname, AppendDirEntry);
               SendBuffer(K, done)
            ELSE Send(NPR, 0, dmy)
            END
         ELSIF typ = MDIR THEN
            PickS(Id); PickQ(pw); SetPartner(Id); uno := Core.UserNo(Id, pw);
            IF uno >= 0 THEN
               IF uno # mailuno THEN
                  Core.GetFileName(uno, fname); MF := Files.Old(fname); mailuno := uno
               END;
               K := 0; seqno := 0;
               IF MF # NIL THEN
                  Files.Set(R, MF, 32); Files.ReadBytes(R, mdir, SIZE(Core.MailDir));
                  i := mdir[0].next; j := 30; done := TRUE;
                  WHILE (i # 0) & (j > 0) & done DO
                     AppendN(i, buf, K); AppendDate(mdir[i].time, mdir[i].date, buf, K);
                     buf[K] := " "; INC(K); AppendS(mdir[i].originator, buf, K);
                     buf[K-1] := " "; AppendN(mdir[i].len, buf, K); buf[K] := 0DX; INC(K);
                     IF K >= PakSize THEN SendBuffer(PakSize, done) END;
                     i := mdir[i].next; DEC(j)
                  END
               END;
               SendBuffer(K, done)
            ELSE Send(NPR, 0, dmy)
            END
         ELSIF typ = SML THEN (*send mail*)
            PickS(Id); PickQ(pw); PickW(n); SetPartner(Id); uno := Core.UserNo(Id, pw);
            IF uno >= 0 THEN
               IF uno # mailuno THEN
                  Core.GetFileName(uno, fname); MF := Files.Old(fname); mailuno := uno
               END;
```

```
            IF (MF # NIL) & (n > 0) & (n < 31) THEN
                Files.Set(R, MF, (n+1)*32);
                Files.ReadBytes(R, i, 2); Files.ReadBytes(R, j, 2); pos := LONG(i) * 100H;
                Files.ReadBytes(R, len, 4);
                IF len > 0 THEN Files.Set(R, MF, pos); SendMail(R, len)
                ELSE Send(NAK, 0, dmy)
                END
            ELSE Send(NAK, 0, dmy)
            END
        ELSE Send(NPR, 0, dmy)
        END
    ELSIF typ = RML THEN (*receive mail*)
        PickS(Id); PickQ(pw); SetPartner(Id); uno := Core.UserNo(Id, pw);
        IF uno >= 0 THEN
            F := Files.New("");
            Send(ACK, 0, dmy); ReceiveHead(T0);
            IF head1.valid THEN
                ReceiveData(F, done);
                IF done THEN Files.Close(F); Core.InsertTask(Core.MailQueue, F, Id, uno)
                    END
            END
        ELSE Send(NPR, 0, dmy)
        END
    ELSIF typ = DML THEN (*delete mail*)
        PickS(Id); PickQ(pw); PickW(n); SetPartner(Id); uno := Core.UserNo(Id, pw);
        IF uno >= 0 THEN
            IF uno # mailuno THEN
                Core.GetFileName(uno, fname); MF := Files.Old(fname); mailuno := uno
            END;
            IF (MF # NIL) & (n > 0) & (n < 31) THEN
                Files.Set(R, MF, 0);
                Files.ReadBytes(R, mrtab, 32); Files.ReadBytes(R, mdir, SIZE(Core.MailDir));
                i := 0; ks := 30;
                LOOP k := mdir[i].next; DEC(ks);
                    IF (k = 0) OR (ks = 0) THEN Send(NAK, 0, buf); EXIT END;
                    IF k = n THEN
                        j := mdir[n].pos;
                        k := SHORT((mdir[n].len + LONG(j)*100H) DIV 100H) + 1;
                        REPEAT INCL(mrtab[j DIV 32], j MOD 32); INC(j) UNTIL j = k;
                        mdir[n].len := 0; mdir[i].next := mdir[n].next;
                        Files.Set(R, MF, 0); Files.WriteBytes(R, mrtab, 32);
                        Files.WriteBytes(R, mdir, SIZE(Core.MailDir)); Files.Close(MF);
                        Send(ACK, 0, dmy); EXIT
                    END;
                    i := k
                END
            ELSE Send(NAK, 0, dmy)
            END
        ELSE Send(NPR, 0, dmy)
        END
    ELSIF typ = TRQ THEN
        Oberon.GetClock(t, d); SetPartner(Id); i := 0;
        AppendW(t, fname, 4, i); AppendW(d, fname, 4, i); Send(TIM, 8, fname)
    ELSIF typ = NRQ THEN i := 0;
        LOOP SCC.Receive(ch); Id[i] := ch; INC(i);
            IF ch = 0X THEN EXIT END;
            IF i = 7 THEN Id[7] := 0X; EXIT END
        END;
```

```
          WHILE i < head1.len DO SCC.Receive(ch); INC(i) END;
          IF Id = Oberon.User THEN SetPartner(Id); Send(NRS, 0, dmy) END
      ELSIF typ = MSG THEN i := 0;
          WHILE i < head1.len DO SCC.Receive(ch); Texts.Write(W, ch); INC(i) END;
          SetPartner(Id); Send(ACK, 0, dmy); EOL
      ELSIF typ = NPW THEN
          PickS(Id); PickQ(pw); uno := Core.UserNo(Id, pw);
          IF uno >= 0 THEN
              SetPartner(Id); Send(ACK, 0, dmy); ReceiveHead(T0);
              IF head1.typ = 0 THEN
                  PickQ(npw); Core.SetPassword(uno, npw); Send(ACK, 0, dmy)
              ELSE Send(NAK, 0, dmy)
              END
          ELSE Send(NPR, 0, dmy)
          END
      ELSE SCC.Skip(head1.len)
      END;
      Core.Collect
END Serve;


(*———————————— Commands ————————————*)


PROCEDURE Start*;
    VAR password: ARRAY 4 OF CHAR;
        S: Texts.Scanner;
BEGIN Texts.OpenScanner(S, Oberon.Par.text, Oberon.Par.pos); Texts.Scan(S);
    IF S.class = Texts.Name THEN
        Oberon.Remove(handler); Oberon.Install(handler);
        reqcnt := 0; MF := NIL; mailuno := −2;
        password[0] := 0X; Oberon.SetUser(S.s, password);
        Texts.WriteString(W, "Net started (NW 22.11.91)"); EOL
    END
END Start;


PROCEDURE Reset*;
BEGIN SCC.Start(TRUE)
END Reset;


PROCEDURE Stop*;
BEGIN Oberon.Remove(handler); Texts.WriteString(W, "Net stopped"); EOL
END Stop;


PROCEDURE Protect*;
BEGIN protected := TRUE
END Protect;


PROCEDURE Unprotect*;
BEGIN protected := FALSE
END Unprotect;


BEGIN Texts.OpenWriter(W); NEW(handler); handler.handle := Serve
END NetServer.
```

In passing, we note that the use of files for representing mailboxes,
in combination with the file distribution services residing on the same

server station, allows anyone to access (and inspect) any mailbox. Although we do not claim that this system provides secure protection against snooping, a minimal effort for protection was undertaken by a simple encoding of messages in mailbox files. This encoding is not shown in the program listings contained in this book.

Interpretation of message header

One operation remains to be explained in more detail: the processing of tasks inserted into the mail queue. It consists of the insertion of the message represented by the task's file into one or several mailboxes. It involves the interpretation of the message's header, that is, lines containing addresses, and the construction of a new header containing the name of the originator and the date of insertion into the mailbox. These actions are performed by procedures in module *MailServer*. Its procedure *Serve* is installed as an Oberon task, and it is guarded by the condition *Core.MailQueue.n* > 0, indicating that at least one message needs to be dispatched.

The originator's name is obtained from *Core.GetUserName(uno)*, where *uno* is the user number obtained from the queue entry. The actual time is obtained from *Oberon.GetClock*. The form of the new header is shown by the following example:

From: Gutknecht
At: 12.08.91 09:34:15

Message dispatching

The received message's header is then searched for recipients. Their names are listed in header lines starting with "To" (or "cc"). After a name has been read, the corresponding user number is obtained by calling *Core.UserNum*. Then the message is inserted into the designated mailbox by procedure *Dispatch*. The search for recipients continues, until a line is encountered that does not begin with "To" (or "cc"). A negative user number indicates that the given name is not registered. In this case, the message is returned to the sender, that is, it is inserted into the mailbox of the sender. An exception is the recipient "all", which indicates a broadcast to all registered users.

Postmaster

Procedure *Dispatch* first opens the mailbox file of the user specified by the recipient number *rno*. If a mailbox exists, its block reservation part (mrtab) and its directory part (mdir) are read. Otherwise, a new, empty box is created. Then follows the search for a free slot in the directory and, if found, the search for a sufficient number of free, adjacent blocks in the message part. The number of required blocks is given by the message length. If either no free slot exists, or there is no sufficiently large free space for the message part, the message is returned to the sender (identified by *sno*). If this attempt also fails, the message is redirected to the postmaster (with user number 0). The postmaster is expected to inspect his mailbox sufficiently often that no overflow occurs. If the postmaster's mailbox also overflows, the message is lost.

Only if all conditions for a successful completion are satisfied, is insertion begun. It starts with the marking of blocks in the reservation table and with the insertion of the new directory information. Table and directory are then updated on the file. Thereafter, the message with the constructed new header is written into the message part.

```
MODULE MailServer; (*NW 17.4.89 / 25.8.91*)
  IMPORT Core, Files, Texts, Oberon;

  VAR W: Texts.Writer;
    handler: Oberon.Task;

  PROCEDURE Dispatch(F: Files.File; rno, sno, hdlen: INTEGER; VAR orig, head: ARRAY OF
      CHAR);
  (*insert external message (from msg) in recipient rno's mail file*)
    VAR i, j, k, h: INTEGER;
      ch: CHAR; ok: BOOLEAN;
      pos, L, bdylen, tm, dt: LONGINT;
      fname: Core.Name;
      MF: Files.File; (*destination*)
      R, Q: Files.Rider;
      mrtab: Core.MResTab;
      mdir: Core.MailDir;
  BEGIN Core.GetFileName(rno, fname); MF := Files.Old(fname);
    IF MF # NIL THEN
      Files.Set(Q, MF, 0); Files.ReadBytes(Q, mrtab, 32);
      Files.ReadBytes(Q, mdir, SIZE(Core.MailDir))
    ELSE (*create new mailbox file*)
      MF := Files.New(fname); Files.Set(Q, MF, 0); Files.Register(MF);
      mdir[0].next := 0; mrtab[0] := {4 .. 31}; i := 1;
      REPEAT mrtab[i] := {0 .. 31}; INC(i) UNTIL i = 7;
      mrtab[7] := {0 .. 29}; i := 0;
      REPEAT mdir[i].len := 0; INC(i) UNTIL i = 31
    END;
    Files.Set(R, F, 0); bdylen := Files.Length(F);
    ok := FALSE; i := 0;
    REPEAT INC(i) UNTIL (i = 31) OR (mdir[i].len = 0);
    IF i < 31 THEN (*free slot found, now find free blocks in file*)
      j := -1;
      REPEAT INC(j);
        IF j MOD 32 IN mrtab[j DIV 32] THEN
          h := j; k := SHORT((bdylen + hdlen + 255) DIV 256) + j;
          LOOP INC(h);
            IF h = k THEN ok := TRUE; EXIT END;
            IF (h = 256) OR ~(h MOD 32 IN mrtab[h DIV 32]) THEN j := h; EXIT END
          END
        END
      UNTIL ok OR (j >= 255)
    END;
    IF ok THEN (*insert msg in blocks j .. k-1*)
      pos := LONG(j) * 256; mdir[i].pos := j;
      REPEAT EXCL(mrtab[j DIV 32], j MOD 32); INC(j) UNTIL j = k;
      mdir[i].len := bdylen + hdlen;
      Oberon.GetClock(tm, dt);
      mdir[i].time := SHORT(tm DIV 2); mdir[i].date := SHORT(dt);
      j := 0;
```

```
          WHILE (j < 19) & (orig[j] > " ") DO mdir[i].originator[j] := orig[j]; INC(j) END;
          mdir[i].originator[j] := 0X;
          mdir[i].next := mdir[0].next; mdir[0].next := i;
          Files.Set(Q, MF, 0); Files.WriteBytes(Q, mrtab, 32);
          Files.WriteBytes(Q, mdir, SIZE(Core.MailDir)); Files.Set(Q, MF, pos);
          j := 0;
          WHILE j < hdlen DO
            Files.Write(Q, head[j]); INC(j)
          END;
          L := bdylen;
          WHILE L > 0 DO
            Files.Read(R, ch); Files.Write(Q, ch); DEC(L)
          END;
          L := (−Files.Pos(Q)) MOD 256;
          WHILE L > 0 DO Files.Write(Q, 0); DEC(L) END;
          Files.Close(MF)
      ELSIF (rno # sno) & (sno > 0) & (rno > 0) THEN (*return to sender*)
          Dispatch(F, sno, sno, hdlen, orig, head)
      ELSIF (rno # 0) & (sno # 0) THEN (*send to postmaster*)
          Dispatch(F, 0, sno, hdlen, orig, head)
      END
  END Dispatch;


  PROCEDURE* Serve;
      VAR i, j, sno, rno, hdlen: INTEGER;
          ch: CHAR;
          pos, dt, tm: LONGINT;
          F: Files.File; R: Files.Rider;
          Id: Core.ShortName;
          orig: Core.LongName;
          head, recip: ARRAY 64 OF CHAR;


      PROCEDURE Pair(ch: CHAR; x: LONGINT);
      BEGIN head[j] := ch; INC(j);
          head[j] := CHR(x DIV 10 + 30H); INC(j); head[j] := CHR(x MOD 10 + 30H); INC(j)
      END Pair;


      IF Core.MailQueue.n > 0 THEN
          Core.GetTask(Core.MailQueue, F, Id, sno);
            Core.GetUserName(sno, orig); Oberon.GetClock(tm, dt);
            COPY("From: ", head); i := 0; j := 6;
            WHILE orig[i] > 0X DO head[j] := orig[i]; INC(i); INC(j) END;
            head[j] := 0DX; INC(j); head[j] := "A"; INC(j); head[j] := "t"; INC(j); head[j] := ":";
            INC(j); Pair(" ", dt MOD 20H); Pair(".", dt DIV 20H MOD 10H);
            Pair(".", dt DIV 200H MOD 80H); Pair(" ", tm DIV 1000H MOD 20H);
            Pair(":", tm DIV 40H MOD 40H); Pair(":", tm MOD 40H);
            head[j] := 0DX; hdlen := j+1;
            Files.Set(R, F, 0);
            LOOP (*next line*) pos := Files.Pos(R);
                REPEAT Files.Read(R, ch) UNTIL (ch > " ") OR R.eof;
                IF R.eof THEN EXIT END;
                i := 0;
                REPEAT recip[i] := ch; INC(i); Files.Read(R, ch) UNTIL ch <= ":";
                recip[i] := 0X;
                IF (recip # "To") & (recip # "cc") THEN EXIT END;
                LOOP (*next recipient*)
                    WHILE " " <= ch DO Files.Read(R, ch) END;
```

```
                    IF ch < " " THEN EXIT END;
                    i := 0;
                    WHILE ch > " " DO recip[i] := ch; INC(i); Files.Read(R, ch) END;
                    recip[i] := 0X;
                    IF recip = "all" THEN rno := Core.NofUsers();
                        WHILE rno > 1 DO (*exclude postmaster*)
                            DEC(rno); Dispatch(F, rno, 0, hdlen, orig, head)
                        END
                    ELSE rno := Core.UserNum(recip);
                        IF rno < 0 THEN rno := sno END;
                        Dispatch(F, rno, sno, hdlen, orig, head)
                    END;
                    IF ch = "," THEN Files.Read(R, ch) END
                END
            END;
        Core.RemoveTask(Core.MailQueue)
    END
END Serve;


(*------------- Commands -------------*)


PROCEDURE Start*;
BEGIN Oberon.Install(handler);
    Texts.WriteString(W, "Mailer started (NW 25.8.91)");
    Texts.WriteLn(W); Texts.Append(Oberon.Log, W.buf)
END Start;


PROCEDURE State*;
BEGIN Texts.WriteString(W, "Mail queue:"); Texts.WriteInt(W, Core.MailQueue.n, 3);
    Texts.WriteLn(W); Texts.Append(Oberon.Log, W.buf)
END State;


PROCEDURE Stop*;
BEGIN Oberon.Remove(handler); Texts.WriteString(W, "Mailer stopped");
    Texts.WriteLn(W); Texts.Append(Oberon.Log, W.buf)
END Stop;


BEGIN Texts.OpenWriter(W); NEW(handler); handler.handle := Serve
END MailServer.
```

Perhaps it may seem to the reader that the addition of a separate module *MailServer*, together with a new Oberon task and the machinery of the mail queue, is not warranted by the relative simplicity of the insertion operation, and that it could have been incorporated into module *NetServer* just as well as message extraction. The picture changes, however, if handling of external mail is to be added, and if access to mailboxes via other channels, such as the RS-232 line, is to be provided. The presented solution is based on a modular structure that facilitates such extensions without change of existing parts. External mail routines inevitably have to cope with message formats imposed by standards. Format transformations, encoding before sending to an external server and decoding before dispatching, become necessary. Indeed, these operations have inflated module *MailServer* to a surprising degree. And lastly, the queuing machinery supports the easy insertion of additional message sources and provides a welcome decoupling and relaxation of timing constraints, particularly in the case of low-speed transmission media such as telephone lines.

11.3 Printing service

The dedicated server machine is also used as the central printing facility for all workstations connected by the network. On workstations, print commands are part of various tool modules of editing systems. Examples are *Edit.Print* (Chapter 5) and *Draw.Print* (Chapter 13). Documents to be printed typically consist of various elements such as strings of characters, lines and circles. The print commands enumerate these elements and for each element issue a call to the appropriate procedure in module *Printer*, whose interface is listed in Chapter 5. These procedures then concatenate the received information and send it to the printer server in an encoded form. The syntax of this data stream is as follows:

Format of print stream

PrintStream	= Tag {element}.
element	= string | continuation | line | xline | circle | ellipse | area | font | page.
string	= 0 fno x y {char}.
continuation	= 1 fno {char}.
line	= 2 0 x y w h.
xline	= 6 0 x0 y0 x1 y1.
circle	= 9 0 x y r.
ellipse	= 7 0 x y a b.
area	= 5 patno x y w h.
font	= 3 fno fontname.
page	= 4 copies.

x, y, w, h, r, a, b are position coordinates, width, height, radius, all encoded in 2 bytes. *fno* is a font number and *patno* is the number of the dot pattern by which the rectangular area is to be filled. The page command signals that the preceding elements form a page, and *copies* indicates the number of copies to be printed.

The print stream is transmitted to the server as a sequence of packets. The data received by calls of the print procedures are stored in a local buffer until the size of a packet is reached. Every print command must first establish the connection with the server by a call of *Printer.Open*. Furthermore, it must indicate page breaks by calling

Printer.Page, and it must terminate with a call of *Printer.Close*. Evidently, the formatting of the document to be printed is the duty of the respective editor's print command. Module *Printer*, listed below, merely handles the encoding, buffering, and transmission:

```
MODULE Printer; (*NW 27.6.88 / 11.3.91*)
   IMPORT SYSTEM, Input, SCC;
   CONST maxfonts = 16;
      PakSize = 512; Broadcast = -1;
      T0 = 300; T1 = 1200;
      ACK = 10H; NAK = 25H;
      NRQ = 34H; NRS = 35H;
      PRT = 43H; NPR = 26H; TOT = 7FH;

   VAR res*: INTEGER; (*0 = done, 1 = not done*)
      PageWidth*, PageHeight*: INTEGER;
      nofonts: INTEGER;
      seqno: SHORTINT;
      head0: SCC.Header; (*sender*)
      head1: SCC.Header; (*receiver*)
      in: INTEGER;
      PrinterName: ARRAY 10 OF CHAR;
      fontname: ARRAY maxfonts, 32 OF CHAR;
      buf: ARRAY PakSize OF SYSTEM.BYTE;


   PROCEDURE ReceiveHead;
      VAR time: LONGINT;
   BEGIN time := Input.Time() + T0;
      LOOP SCC.ReceiveHead(head1);
         IF head1.valid THEN
            IF head1.sadr = head0.dadr THEN EXIT ELSE SCC.Skip(head1.len) END
         ELSIF Input.Time() >= time THEN head1.typ := TOT; EXIT
         END
      END
   END ReceiveHead;


   PROCEDURE FindPrinter(VAR name: ARRAY OF CHAR);
      VAR time: LONGINT;
         id: ARRAY 10 OF CHAR;
   BEGIN head0.typ := NRQ; head0.dadr := Broadcast; head0.len := 10;
      head0.destLink := 0; COPY(name, id); id[8] := 6X; id[9] := 0X;
      SCC.Skip(SCC.Available()); SCC.SendPacket(head0, id); time := Input.Time() + T1;
      LOOP SCC.ReceiveHead(head1);
         IF head1.valid THEN
            IF head1.typ = NRS THEN head0.dadr := head1.sadr; res := 0; EXIT
            ELSE SCC.Skip(head1.len)
            END
         ELSIF Input.Time() >= time THEN res := 1; EXIT
         END
      END
   END FindPrinter;


   PROCEDURE SendPacket;
   BEGIN head0.typ := seqno; head0.len := in;
      REPEAT SCC.SendPacket(head0, buf); ReceiveHead;
```

```
        UNTIL head1.typ # seqno + ACK;
        seqno := (seqno+1) MOD 8;
        IF head1.typ # seqno + ACK THEN res := 1 END
    END SendPacket;


    PROCEDURE Send(x: SYSTEM.BYTE);
    BEGIN buf[in] := x; INC(in);
        IF in = PakSize THEN SendPacket; in := 0 END
    END Send;


    PROCEDURE SendInt(k: INTEGER);
    BEGIN Send(SHORT(k MOD 100H)); Send(SHORT(k DIV 100H))
    END SendInt;


    PROCEDURE SendBytes(VAR x: ARRAY OF SYSTEM.BYTE; n: INTEGER);
        VAR i: INTEGER;
    BEGIN i := 0;
        WHILE i < n DO Send(x[i]); INC(i) END
    END SendBytes;


    PROCEDURE SendString(VAR s: ARRAY OF CHAR);
        VAR i: INTEGER;
    BEGIN i := 0;
        WHILE s[i] > 0X DO Send(s[i]); INC(i) END;
        Send(0)
    END SendString;


    PROCEDURE Open*(VAR name, user: ARRAY OF CHAR; password: LONGINT);
    BEGIN nofonts := 0; in := 0; seqno := 0; SCC.Skip(SCC.Available());
        IF name # PrinterName THEN FindPrinter(name) ELSE res := 0 END;
        IF res = 0 THEN
            SendString(user); SendBytes(password, 4);
            head0.typ := PRT; head0.len := in; SCC.SendPacket(head0, buf); in := 0;
            ReceiveHead;
            IF head1.typ = ACK THEN Send(0FCX) (*printfileid*)
            ELSIF head1.typ = NPR THEN res := 4 (*no permission*)
            ELSE res := 2 (*no printer*)
            END
        END
    END Open;


    PROCEDURE ReplConst*(x, y, w, h: INTEGER);
    BEGIN Send(2); Send(0);
        SendInt(x); SendInt(y); SendInt(w); SendInt(h)
    END ReplConst;


    PROCEDURE fontno(VAR name: ARRAY OF CHAR): SHORTINT;
        VAR i, j: INTEGER;
    BEGIN i := 0;
        WHILE (i < nofonts) & (fontname[i] # name) DO INC(i) END;
        IF i = nofonts THEN
            IF nofonts < maxfonts THEN
                COPY(name, fontname[i]); INC(nofonts);
                Send(3); Send(SHORT(i)); j := 0;
                WHILE name[j] >= "0" DO Send(name[j]); INC(j) END;
                Send(0)
```

```
        ELSE i := 0
        END
    END;
    RETURN SHORT(i)
END fontno;


PROCEDURE UseListFont*(VAR name: ARRAY OF CHAR);
    VAR i: INTEGER;
        listfont: ARRAY 10 OF CHAR;
BEGIN listfont := "Gacha10l"; i := 0;
    WHILE (i < nofonts) & (fontname[i] # name) DO INC(i) END;
    IF i = nofonts THEN
        COPY(name, fontname[i]); INC(nofonts);
        Send(3); Send(SHORT(i)); SendBytes(listfont, 9)
    END;
END UseListFont;


PROCEDURE String*(x, y: INTEGER; VAR s, fname: ARRAY OF CHAR);
    VAR fno: SHORTINT;
BEGIN fno := fontno(fname); Send(1); Send(fno); SendInt(x); SendInt(y); SendString(s)
END String;


PROCEDURE ContString*(VAR s, fname: ARRAY OF CHAR);
    VAR fno: SHORTINT;
BEGIN fno := fontno(fname); Send(0); Send(fno); SendString(s)
END ContString;


PROCEDURE ReplPattern*(x, y, w, h, col: INTEGER);
BEGIN Send(5); Send(SHORT(col)); SendInt(x); SendInt(y); SendInt(w); SendInt(h)
END ReplPattern;


PROCEDURE Line*(x0, y0, x1, y1: INTEGER);
BEGIN Send(6); Send(0); SendInt(x0); SendInt(y0); SendInt(x1); SendInt(y1)
END Line;


PROCEDURE Circle*(x0, y0, r: INTEGER);
BEGIN Send(9); Send(0); SendInt(x0); SendInt(y0); SendInt(r)
END Circle;


PROCEDURE Ellipse*(x0, y0, a, b: INTEGER);
BEGIN Send(7); Send(0); SendInt(x0); SendInt(y0); SendInt(a); SendInt(b)
END Ellipse;


PROCEDURE Picture*(x, y, w, h, mode: INTEGER; adr: LONGINT);
    VAR a0, a1: LONGINT; b: SHORTINT;
BEGIN Send(8); Send(SHORT(mode));
    SendInt(x); SendInt(y); SendInt(w); SendInt(h);
    a0 := adr; a1 := LONG((w+7) DIV 8) * h + a0;
    WHILE (a0 < a1) & (res = 0) DO SYSTEM.GET(a0, b); Send(b); INC(a0) END
END Picture;


PROCEDURE Page*(nofcopies: INTEGER);
BEGIN Send(4); Send(SHORT(nofcopies))
END Page;
```

```
PROCEDURE Close*;
BEGIN SendPacket;
    WHILE nofonts > 0 DO DEC(nofonts); fontname[nofonts, 0] := " " END
END Close;


BEGIN PageWidth := 2336; PageHeight := 3425; in := 0; PrinterName[0] := 0X
END Printer.
```

Module *Printer* acts as master of the communication. Its partner is module *NetServer*. The syntax of a print request is almost identical to that for sending a file:

Protocol

PrintStream	$=$ PRT username password (*ACK datastream* | *NAK* | *NPR*).
datastream	$=$ DAT_0 data ACK_1 $\{DAT_i$ data $ACK_{i+1}\}$.

The server routine handling the print request is guarded by the condition $typ = PRT$ (see *NetServer* above), and it is almost the same as that for handling requests to receive a file. But, instead of registering the received file, the file is inserted into *Core.PrintQueue*.

The printing tasks are extracted from the queue by a handler in module *PrintServer*, which constitutes an Oberon task guarded by the condition *Core.PrintQueue.n* > 0, which becomes active if the queue of print tasks is not empty. The server to be described here operates a laser printer capable of printing about 10 pages per minute. The shortest printing task therefore takes at least 6 seconds. Since every command in the Oberon System is inherently non-interruptible, a printing task must evidently be broken up into parts, if unacceptably long suspension of all other services is to be avoided. This is achieved by breaking up the printing process into phases and by returning control to the Oberon scheduler after each phase.

Timing considerations

Breaking up the printing task

The processing of a page consists of two parts. First, the elements of the print stream are read and interpreted, resulting in their representation as a dot raster in a page map. Then the raster is transmitted to the printer while the page is printed. During the second part, the computer's processor is disengaged; the transfer is handled by direct memory access under printer control. Only the first part, which is typically much less time-consuming, requires the processor, which therefore is available to accept and interpret other requests during the second part. The printing process of a document is described by four phases, whose possible sequencing is shown by a control flow diagram in Figure 11.6.

Each of the four phases is represented by a handler procedure, one of which is installed as Oberon task at any time. Whenever a phase terminates, the handler installs its selected successor. The raster is

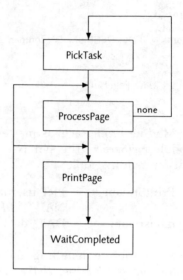

Figure 11.6   Phases of printing process.

generated in the *ProcessPage* phase by procedures defined in module *Printmaps*, whose interface is

Printmaps

```
DEFINITION Printmaps; (*NW 9.7.89 / 17.11.90*)
  VAR Pat: ARRAY 10 OF LONGINT;
  PROCEDURE Map(): LONGINT;
  PROCEDURE ClearPage;
  PROCEDURE CopyPattern(pat: LONGINT; X, Y: INTEGER);
  PROCEDURE ReplPattern(pat: LONGINT;
      X, Y, W, H: INTEGER);
  PROCEDURE ReplConst(X, Y, W, H: INTEGER);
  PROCEDURE Dot(x, y: LONGINT);
END Printmaps.
```

These raster operations are very similar to those of module *Display* (see Chapter 4). They refer to the printer's bitmap rather than the display's, and they feature neither a mode nor a color parameter. For rastering characters, the same font file format is used as for the display.

```
MODULE PrintServer; (*NW 17.4.89 / 25.8.91*)
  IMPORT SYSTEM, Core, Display, Printmaps, Files, Fonts, Texts, Oberon;

  CONST maxFnt = 32; N = 20; (*max dim of splines*)
    PR0 = 0FFF600H;
    proff = 0; prdy = 1; sbusy = 2; end = 3; (*printer status*)
    BMwidth = 2336; BMheight = 3425;
```

```
TYPE RealVector = ARRAY N OF REAL;
    Poly = RECORD a, b, c, d, t: REAL END;
    PolyVector = ARRAY N OF Poly;


VAR W: Texts.Writer;
    handler: Oberon.Task;
    uno, nofcopies, nofpages: INTEGER;
    PR: Files.Rider; (*print rider*)
    font: ARRAY maxFnt OF Fonts.Font;

PROCEDURE circle(x0, y0, r: LONGINT);
    VAR x, y, u: LONGINT;
BEGIN u := 1 − r; x := r; y := 0;
    WHILE y <= x DO
        Printmaps.Dot(x0+x, y0+y); Printmaps.Dot(x0+y, y0+x);
        Printmaps.Dot(x0−y, y0+x); Printmaps.Dot(x0−x, y0+y);
        Printmaps.Dot(x0−x, y0−y); Printmaps.Dot(x0−y, y0−x);
        Printmaps.Dot(x0+y, y0−x); Printmaps.Dot(x0+x, y0−y);
        IF u < 0 THEN INC(u, 2*y+3) ELSE INC(u, 2*(y−x)+5); DEC(x) END;
        INC(y)
    END
END circle;


PROCEDURE ellipse(x0, y0, a, b: LONGINT);
BEGIN ...
END ellipse;


PROCEDURE ↑ ProcessPage;
PROCEDURE ↑ PrintPage;
PROCEDURE ↑ WaitForCompletion;


PROCEDURE Terminate;
    VAR i: INTEGER;
BEGIN Core.RemoveTask(Core.PrintQueue); i := 0;
    REPEAT font[i] := NIL; INC(i) UNTIL i = maxFnt (*release fonts*)
END Terminate;


PROCEDURE Append(src: ARRAY OF CHAR; VAR dst: ARRAY OF SYSTEM.BYTE;
    VAR k: INTEGER);
    VAR i: INTEGER; ch: CHAR;
BEGIN i := 0;
    REPEAT ch := src[i]; dst[k] := ch; INC(i); INC(k) UNTIL ch = 0X
END Append;


PROCEDURE* PickTask;
    VAR F: Files.File;
        Id: Core.ShortName;
        tag: CHAR;
    BEGIN
        IF (Core.PrintQueue.n > 0) & ~SYSTEM.BIT(PR0, proff) & SYSTEM.BIT(PR0, prdy)
            THEN
        Core.GetTask(Core.PrintQueue, F, Id, uno); nofpages := 0;
        Files.Set(PR, F, 0); Files.Read(PR, tag);
        IF tag = 0FCX THEN handler.handle := ProcessPage
        ELSE Texts.WriteString(W, Id); Texts.WriteString(W, "not a print file");
            Texts.WriteLn(W); Texts.Append(Oberon.Log, W.buf); Terminate
```

```
                END
        END
    END PickTask;


    PROCEDURE ProcessPage;
        VAR i, x, y, w, h, x0, x1, y0, y1: INTEGER;
            a, a0, a1: LONGINT;
            d, u: INTEGER;
            typ, sp: SHORTINT;
            ch: CHAR;
            fnt: Fonts.Font;
            fname: Core.Name;


        PROCEDURE String;
            VAR ch: CHAR;
                dx, x0, y0, w, h: INTEGER;
                fnt: Fonts.Font;
                pat: LONGINT;
            BEGIN fnt := font[sp MOD maxFnt];
                IF (x >= 0) & (y >= 0) & (fnt # NIL) & (y + fnt.height < BMheight) THEN
                    LOOP Files.Read(PR, ch);
                        IF ch = 0X THEN EXIT END;
                        Display.GetChar(fnt.raster, ch, dx, x0, y0, w, h, pat);
                        IF (x + x0 + w <= BMwidth) & (h > 0) THEN
                            Printmaps.CopyPattern(pat, x+x0, y+y0)
                        END;
                        INC(x, dx)
                    END
                END
            END String;


        BEGIN Printmaps.ClearPage;
            LOOP Files.Read(PR, typ);
                IF PR.eof THEN
                    Core.IncPageCount(uno, nofpages); Terminate; handler.handle := PickTask;
                    EXIT
                END;
                Files.Read(PR, sp);
                IF typ = 0 THEN String
                ELSIF typ = 1 THEN
                    Files.ReadBytes(PR, x, 2); Files.ReadBytes(PR, y, 2); String
                ELSIF typ = 2 THEN
                    Files.ReadBytes(PR, x, 2); Files.ReadBytes(PR, y, 2);
                    Files.ReadBytes(PR, w, 2); Files.ReadBytes(PR, h, 2);
                    IF x < 0 THEN INC(w, x); x := 0 END;
                    IF x+w > BMwidth THEN w := BMwidth − x END;
                    IF y < 0 THEN INC(h, y); y := 0 END;
                    IF y+h > BMheight THEN h := BMheight − y END;
                    Printmaps.ReplConst(x, y, w, h)
                ELSIF typ = 3 THEN
                    i := 0;
                    REPEAT Files.Read(PR, fname[i]); INC(i) UNTIL fname[i−1] < "0";
                    DEC(i); Append(".Pr3.Fnt", fname, i);
                    fnt := Fonts.This(fname);
                    IF fnt = Fonts.Default THEN fnt := Fonts.This("Syntax10.Pr3.Fnt") END;
                    font[sp MOD maxFnt] := fnt
                ELSIF typ = 4 THEN
```

```
        nofcopies := sp; handler.handle := PrintPage; EXIT
      ELSIF typ = 5 THEN (*shaded area*)
        IF (sp < 0) OR (sp > 9) THEN sp := 2 END;
        Files.ReadBytes(PR, x, 2); Files.ReadBytes(PR, y, 2);
        Files.ReadBytes(PR, w, 2); Files.ReadBytes(PR, h, 2);
        IF x < 0 THEN INC(w, x); x := 0 END;
        IF x+w > BMwidth THEN w := BMwidth − x END;
        IF y < 0 THEN INC(h, y); y := 0 END;
        IF y+h > BMheight THEN h := BMheight − y END;
        Printmaps.ReplPattern(Printmaps.Pat[sp], x, y, w, h)
      ELSIF typ = 6 THEN (*line*)
        Files.ReadBytes(PR, x0, 2); Files.ReadBytes(PR, y0, 2);
        Files.ReadBytes(PR, x1, 2); Files.ReadBytes(PR, y1, 2);
        w := ABS(x1−x0); h := ABS(y1−y0);
        IF h <= w THEN
          IF x1 < x0 THEN u := x0; x0 := x1; x1 := u; u := y0; y0 := y1; y1 := u
          END;
          IF y0 <= y1 THEN d := 1 ELSE d := −1 END;
          u := (h−w) DIV 2;
          WHILE x0 < x1 DO
            Printmaps.Dot(x0, y0); INC(x0);
            IF u < 0 THEN INC(u, h) ELSE INC(u, h−w); INC(y0, d) END
          END
        ELSE
          IF y1 < y0 THEN
            u := x0; x0 := x1; x1 := u; u := y0; y0 := y1; y1 := u END;
          IF x0 <= x1 THEN d := 1 ELSE d := −1
          END;
          u := (w−h) DIV 2;
          WHILE y0 < y1 DO
            Printmaps.Dot(x0, y0); INC(y0);
            IF u < 0 THEN INC(u, w) ELSE INC(u, w−h); INC(x0, d) END
          END
        END
      ELSIF typ = 7 THEN (*ellipse*)
        Files.ReadBytes(PR, x, 2); Files.ReadBytes(PR, y, 2);
        Files.ReadBytes(PR, w, 2); Files.ReadBytes(PR, h, 2);
        ellipse(x, y, w, h)
      ELSIF typ = 8 THEN (*picture*)
        Files.ReadBytes(PR, x, 2); Files.ReadBytes(PR, y, 2);
        Files.ReadBytes(PR, w, 2); Files.ReadBytes(PR, h, 2);
        . . .
      ELSIF typ = 9 THEN (*circle*)
        Files.ReadBytes(PR, x, 2); Files.ReadBytes(PR, y, 2);
        Files.ReadBytes(PR, w, 2); circle(x, y, w)
      ELSE Texts.WriteString(W, "error in print file at");
        Texts.WriteInt(W, Files.Pos(PR), 6); Texts.WriteInt(W, typ, 5);
        Texts.WriteLn(W); Texts.Append(Oberon.Log, W.buf);
        Terminate; handler.handle := PickTask; EXIT
      END
    END
  END
END ProcessPage;


PROCEDURE PrintPage;
BEGIN
  IF SYSTEM.BIT(PR0, prdy) THEN
    SYSTEM.PUT(PR0, Printmaps.Map()); handler.handle := WaitForCompletion;
    REPEAT UNTIL SYSTEM.BIT(PR0, end)
```

```
        END
    END PrintPage;

    PROCEDURE WaitForCompletion;
    BEGIN
        IF ~SYSTEM.BIT(PR0, end) THEN
            DEC(nofcopies); INC(nofpages);
            IF nofcopies > 0 THEN handler.handle := PrintPage; DEC(nofcopies)
            ELSE handler.handle := ProcessPage
            END
        END
    END WaitForCompletion;
    (*-------------- Commands --------------*)

    PROCEDURE Start*;
    BEGIN
        IF ~SYSTEM.BIT(PR0, proff) THEN
            handler.handle := PickTask;
            Oberon.Remove(handler); Oberon.Install(handler);
            Texts.WriteString(W, "Printer started (NW 25.8.91)")
        ELSE Texts.WriteString(W, "Printer off")
        END;
        Texts.WriteLn(W); Texts.Append(Oberon.Log, W.buf)
    END Start;

    PROCEDURE State*;
        VAR s: SHORTINT;
    BEGIN Texts.WriteString(W, "Printer Queue:");
        Texts.WriteInt(W, Core.PrintQueue.n, 4); Texts.WriteLn(W);
            Texts.Append(Oberon.Log, W.buf)
    END State;

    PROCEDURE Reset*;
    BEGIN; handler.handle := PickTask;
    END Reset;

    PROCEDURE Stop*;
    BEGIN Oberon.Remove(handler); Texts.WriteString(W, "Printer stopped");
        Texts.WriteLn(W); Texts.Append(Oberon.Log, W.buf)
    END Stop;

BEGIN Texts.OpenWriter(W); NEW(handler)
END PrintServer.
```

11.4 Miscellaneous services

There exist a few additional services that are quite desirable under the presence of a central facility, and at the same time easy to include. They are briefly described in this section.

Remote directory inspection

The set of commands of the file distribution service is augmented by *Net.DeleteFiles* and *Net.Directory*, allowing the remote deletion of files and inspection of the server's directory. The command procedures are listed below and must be regarded as part of module *Net* (Section 10.4). They communicate with their counterparts in module *NetServer* (Section 11.2) according to the following protocol:

DeleteFile = DEL username password filename (*ACK* | *NAK* | *NPR*).
Directory = FDIR username password prefix (*datastream* | *NAK* | *NPR*).

The directory request carries a prefix; it uses procedure *FileDir.Enumerate* to obtain all file names starting with the specified prefix. Thereby the search can be limited to the relevant section of the directory.

```
PROCEDURE DeleteFiles*;
    VAR k: INTEGER;
        S: Texts.Scanner;
        buf: ARRAY 64 OF CHAR;
BEGIN GetPar1(S);
    IF S.class = Texts.Name THEN
        FindPartner(S.s, k);
        IF k = 0 THEN
            LOOP Texts.Scan(S);
                IF S.class # Texts.Name THEN EXIT END;
                k := 0; AppendS(Oberon.User, buf, k); AppendW(Oberon.Password, buf, 4, k);
                AppendS(S.s, buf, k); Send(DEL, k, buf);
                Texts.WriteString(W, S.s); Texts.WriteString(W, "remote deleting");
                ReceiveHead(T1);
                IF head1.typ = ACK THEN reply(0)
                ELSIF head1.typ = NAK THEN reply(3)
                ELSIF head1.typ = NPR THEN reply(2); EXIT
                ELSE reply(5); EXIT
                END
            END
        ELSE reply(1)
        END
    END
END DeleteFiles;


PROCEDURE Directory*;
    VAR k, X, Y: INTEGER;
        T: Texts.Text;
        V: Viewers.Viewer;
        buf: ARRAY 32 OF CHAR;
        S: Texts.Scanner;
BEGIN GetPar1(S);
    IF S.class = Texts.Name THEN
        FindPartner(S.s, k);
        IF k = 0 THEN
            Texts.Scan(S);
            IF S.class = Texts.Name THEN (*prefix*)
                AppendS(Oberon.User, buf, k); AppendW(Oberon.Password, buf, 4, k);
                AppendS(S.s, buf, k); Send(FDIR, k, buf); ReceiveHead(T1);
                IF head1.typ = 0 THEN
                    T := TextFrames.Text("");
                    Oberon.AllocateSystemViewer(Oberon.Par.frame.X, X, Y);
                    V := MenuViewers.New(
                        TextFrames.NewMenu("Net.Directory", "System.Close Edit.Store"),
```

```
                    TextFrames.NewText(T, 0), TextFrames.menuH, X, Y);
                ReceiveText(T)
            ELSIF head1.typ = NAK THEN reply(4)
            ELSIF head1.typ = NPR THEN reply(2)
            ELSE  reply(5)
            END
        END
    ELSE reply(1)
    END
  END
END Directory;
```

**Set
password**

Since requests to the server are always guarded by a password, a facility is necessary to set and change the password stored by the server. The respective command is *Net.SetPassword*, and its handler in the server is guarded by the condition *typ = NPW*. The corresponding protocol is

$$NewPassword = NPW\ username\ oldpassword$$
$$(ACK\ DAT\ newpassword$$
$$(ACK\ |\ NAK)\ |\ NAK\ |\ NPR).$$

```
PROCEDURE SetPassword*;
    VAR k: INTEGER; oldpw: LONGINT;
        S: Texts.Scanner;
        buf: ARRAY 64 OF CHAR;
BEGIN GetPar1(S);
    IF S.class = Texts.Name THEN
        FindPartner(S.s, k);
        IF k = 0 THEN Texts.Scan(S);
            IF S.class = Texts.String THEN
                AppendS(Oberon.User, buf, k);
                AppendW(Oberon.Password, buf, 4, k);
                Send(NPW, k, buf); ReceiveHead(T1);
                IF head1.typ = ACK THEN
                    k         :=       0;        Oberon.SetUser(Oberon.User,        S.s);
                    AppendW(Oberon.Password, buf, 4, k);
                    Send(0, 4, buf); ReceiveHead(T0);
                    IF head1.typ = ACK THEN reply(7) ELSE reply(3) END
                ELSIF head1.typ = NPR THEN reply(2)
                ELSE reply(3)
                END
            END
        ELSE reply(1)
        END
    END
END SetPassword;
```

Central time   Finally, procedure *Net.GetTime* allows the workstation's real time clock to be adjusted to that of the central server. The protocol is

GetTime = TRQ *TIM time date.*

```
PROCEDURE GetTime*;
    VAR t, d: LONGINT; res: INTEGER;
        S: Texts.Scanner;
BEGIN GetPar1(S);
    IF S.class = Texts.Name THEN
        FindPartner(S.s, res);
        IF res = 0 THEN
            Send(TRQ, 0, dmy); ReceiveHead(T1);
            IF head1.typ = TIM THEN
                PickQ(t); PickQ(d); Oberon.SetClock(t, d); reply(6)
            END
        ELSE reply(1)
        END
    END
END GetTime;
```

In concluding, we summarize the entire protocol specification below. The combined server facility, comprising file distribution, electronic mail, printing and time services is operating on a Ceres-1 computer (1 Mips) with a 2 MByte store, half of which is used by the printer's bitmap.

Summary of protocol

protocol	= {request}.
request	= ReceiveFile | SendFile | DeleteFile | Directory | MailBox | SendMail | ReceiveMail | DeleteMail | PrintStream | SendMsg | NameRequest | NewPassword | GetTime.
ReceiveFile	= SND username password filename (*datastream* | *NAK* | *NPR*).
datastream	= DAT_0 *data* ACK_1 {DAT_i *data* ACK_{i+1}}.
SendFile	= REC username password filename (ACK_0 datastream | NAK | NPR).
datastream	= DAT_0 data ACK_1 {DAT_i data ACK_{i+1}}.
DeleteFile	= DEL username password filename (*ACK* | *NAK* | *NPR*).
Directory	= FDIR username password prefix (*datastream* | *NAK* | *NPR*).
MailBox	= MDIR username password (*datastream* | *NAK* | *NPR*).

SendMail   = RML username password (*ACK* datastream |
                    NAK | *NPR*).
ReceiveMail   = SML username password msgno (*datastream* |
                    NAK | *NPR*).
DeleteMail   = DML username password msgno (*ACK* | *NAK*
                    | *NPR*).
PrintStream   = PRT username password (*ACK* datastream |
                    NAK | *NPR*).
SendMsg   = MSG message *ACK*.
NameRequest   = NRQ partnername [*NRS*].
NewPassword   = NPW username oldpassword (*ACK* DAT
                    newpassword (*ACK* | *NAK*) | *NAK* | *NPR*).
GetTime   = TRQ *TIM time date.*

11.5 User administration

It appears to be a universal law that centralization inevitably calls for an administration. The centralized mail and printing services make no exception. The typical duties of an administration are accounting and protection against misuse. It has to ensure that rendered services are counted and that no unauthorized user is taking advantage of the server. An additional duty is often the gathering of statistical data. In our case, accounting plays a very minor role, and the reason for the existence of the administration presented here is primarily protection.

Authorization Protection We distinguish between two kinds of protection. The first is protection of the server's resources in general, the second is prevention of individual users' resources from being accessed by others. Whereas in the first case some validation of a user's identification might suffice, the second requires the association of personal resources with user names. In any case, the central server must store data for each member of the set of *registered* users. Specifically, it must be able to check the admissibility of a user's request on the basis of stored information.

Evidently, a protection administration is similar in purpose and function to a lock. Quite regularly, locks are subjected to attempts to break them, and locksmiths are subjected to attempts to outwit them. The race between techniques of breaking locks and better countermeasures is well known, and we do not even try to make a contribution to it. Our design is based on the premise that the Oberon server operates in a harmonious environment. Nevertheless, a minimal amount of protection machinery was included. It raises the amount of effort required for breaking protection to a level that is not reached when curiosity alone is the motivation.

The data about users is held in a table in module *Core*. As mentioned earlier, *Core* acts as connector between the various servers by means of task queues. Its second purpose is to provide the necessary access to user data via appropriate procedures.

User table
In the simplest solution, each table entry would contain a user name only. For each request, the administration would merely test for the presence of the request's user name in the table. A significant step towards safe protection is the introduction of a *password* in addition to the user name. In order that a request be honoured, not only must the name be registered, but also the delivered and the stored password must match. Evidently, abusive attempts would aim at recovering the stored passwords. Our solution lies in storing an encoded password. The command *System.SetUser*, which asks for a user identification and a password, immediately encodes the password, and the original is stored nowhere. The encoding algorithm is such that it is difficult to construct a corresponding decoder.

The mail service requires a third attribute in addition to identification and encoded password: the user's name as it is used for addressing messages. Identification typically consists of the user's initials; for the name, we suggest the full last name of the user and discourage cryptic abbreviations.

Accounting
The printing service makes an accounting facility desirable. A fourth field in each user table entry serves as a count for the number of printed pages. As a result, there are four fields: *id*, *name*, *password* and *count*. The table is not exported, but is only accessible via procedures. *Core* is a good example of a resource-hiding module. The program is listed below, and a few additional comments follow here.

Procedures *UserNo(id)* and *UserNum(name)* yield the table index of the identified user; it is called *user number* and is used as a short encoding for recipients and senders within the mail server. In other servers, the number is merely used to check a request's validity ($\geqslant 0$).

The user information must certainly survive any intermission of server operation, be it due to software, hardware or power failure. This requires that a copy of the user information be held on backup store (disk). The simplest solution would be to use a file for this purpose. But this would indeed make protection too vulnerable: files can be accessed easily, and we have refrained from introducing a file protection facility. Instead, the backup of the user information is held on a few permanently reserved sectors on the server machine, which are inaccessible to the file system.

```
MODULE Core; (*NW 17.4.89 / 6.1.90*)
   IMPORT Kernel, Files;

   CONST
      UTsize = 64; (*max nof registered users*)
```

```
            UTsec0 =; (*adr of user table on disk*)
            UTsec1 =;

      TYPE
            ShortName* = ARRAY 8 OF CHAR;
            LongName* = ARRAY 16 OF CHAR;
            Name* = ARRAY 32 OF CHAR;

            MailEntry* = RECORD
                        pos*, next*: INTEGER;
                        len*: LONGINT;
                        time*, date*: INTEGER;
                        originator*: ARRAY 20 OF CHAR
                  END;

            MResTab* = ARRAY 8 OF SET;
            MailDir* = ARRAY 31 OF MailEntry;

            User = RECORD
                  id: ShortName;
                  name: LongName;
                  password, count: LONGINT
            END;

      SectorBuf = RECORD (Kernel.Sector)
                  u: ARRAY 32 OF User
            END;

      Task = POINTER TO TaskDesc;

      TaskDesc = RECORD
                  file: Files.File;
                  uno, class: INTEGER;
                  name: ShortName;
                  next: Task
            END;

      Queue = RECORD n*: INTEGER;
                  first, last: Task
            END;

VAR PrintQueue*, MailQueue*: Queue;
      NUsers: INTEGER;
      UT: ARRAY UTsize OF User;

PROCEDURE RestoreUsers*;
      VAR i: INTEGER; SB: SectorBuf;
BEGIN i := 0; Kernel.GetSector(UTsec0, SB);
      WHILE (i < 32) & (SB.u[i].id[0] > 0X) DO UT[i] := SB.u[i]; INC(i) END;
      IF i = 32 THEN
            Kernel.GetSector(UTsec1, SB);
            WHILE (i < 64) & (SB.u[i−32].id[0] > 0X) DO UT[i] := SB.u[i−32]; INC(i) END
      END;
      NUsers := i
END RestoreUsers;
```

```
PROCEDURE BackupUsers*;
   VAR i: INTEGER; SB: SectorBuf;
BEGIN i := NUsers;
   IF i >= 32 THEN
      IF i < 64 THEN SB.u[i−32].id[0] := 0X END;
      WHILE i > 32 DO DEC(i); SB.u[i−32] := UT[i] END;
      Kernel.PutSector(UTsec1, SB)
   END;
   IF i < 32 THEN SB.u[i].id[0] := 0X END;
   WHILE i > 0 DO DEC(i); SB.u[i] := UT[i] END;
   Kernel.PutSector(UTsec0, SB)
END BackupUsers;


PROCEDURE Uno(VAR id: ShortName): INTEGER;
   VAR i: INTEGER;
BEGIN i := 0;
   WHILE (i < NUsers) & (UT[i].id # id) DO INC(i) END;
   RETURN i
END Uno;


PROCEDURE NofUsers*(): INTEGER;
BEGIN RETURN NUsers
END NofUsers;


PROCEDURE UserNo*(VAR id: ShortName; pw: LONGINT): INTEGER;
   VAR i: INTEGER; (* −1 = user is protected or not registered*)
BEGIN i := Uno(id);
   IF (i = NUsers) OR (UT[i].password # pw) & (UT[i].password # 0) THEN i := −1 END;
   RETURN i
END UserNo;


PROCEDURE UserNum*(VAR name: ARRAY OF CHAR): INTEGER;
   VAR i, j: INTEGER;
BEGIN i := 0;
   LOOP
      IF i = UTsize THEN i := −1; EXIT END;
      j := 0;
      WHILE (j < 4) & (CAP(name[j]) = CAP(UT[i].name[j])) DO INC(j) END;
      IF j = 4 THEN EXIT END;
      INC(i)
   END;
   RETURN i
END UserNum;


PROCEDURE GetUserName*(uno: INTEGER; VAR name: LongName);
BEGIN name := UT[uno].name
END GetUserName;


PROCEDURE GetFileName*(uno: INTEGER; VAR name: ARRAY OF CHAR);
   VAR i: INTEGER; ch: CHAR;
BEGIN i := 0;
   LOOP ch := UT[uno].name[i];
      IF ch = 0X THEN EXIT END;
      name[i] := ch; INC(i)
   END;
   name[i] := "."; name[i+1] := "M"; name[i+2] := "a"; name[i+3] := "i"; name[i+4] := "l";
```

```
      name[i+5] := 0X
  END GetFileName;


  PROCEDURE GetUser*(uno: INTEGER; VAR id: ShortName; VAR name: LongName;
      VAR count: LONGINT; VAR protected: BOOLEAN);
  BEGIN id := UT[uno].id; name := UT[uno].name; count := UT[uno].count;
      protected := UT[uno].password # 0
  END GetUser;


  PROCEDURE InsertUser*(VAR id: ShortName; VAR name: LongName);
      VAR i: INTEGER;
  BEGIN i := Uno(id);
      IF (i = NUsers) & (i < UTsize-1) THEN
          UT[i].id := id; UT[i].name := name; INC(NUsers)
      END
  END InsertUser;


  PROCEDURE DeleteUser*(VAR id: ShortName);
      VAR i: INTEGER;
  BEGIN i := Uno(id);
      IF i < NUsers THEN DEC(NUsers);
          WHILE i < NUsers DO UT[i] := UT[i+1]; INC(i) END
      END
  END DeleteUser;


  PROCEDURE ClearPassword*(VAR id: ShortName);
  BEGIN UT[Uno(id)].password := 0
  END ClearPassword;


  PROCEDURE SetPassword*(uno: INTEGER; npw: LONGINT);
  BEGIN UT[uno].password := npw; BackupUsers
  END SetPassword;


  PROCEDURE IncPageCount*(uno: INTEGER; n: LONGINT);
  BEGIN INC(UT[uno].count, n); BackupUsers
  END IncPageCount;


  PROCEDURE SetCounts*(n: LONGINT);
      VAR i: INTEGER;
  BEGIN i := 0;
      WHILE i < NUsers DO UT[i].count := n; INC(i) END
  END SetCounts;


  PROCEDURE PurgeUsers*(n: INTEGER);
  BEGIN NUsers := 0
  END PurgeUsers;


  PROCEDURE InsertTask*(VAR Q: Queue; F: Files.File; VAR id: ARRAY OF CHAR;
        uno: INTEGER);
      VAR T: Task;
  BEGIN NEW(T); T.file := F; COPY(id, T.name); T.uno := uno; T.next := NIL;
      IF Q.last # NIL THEN Q.last.next := T ELSE Q.first := T END;
      Q.last := T; INC(Q.n)
  END InsertTask;
```

```
PROCEDURE GetTask*(VAR Q: Queue; VAR F: Files.File; VAR id: ShortName;
    VAR uno: INTEGER);
BEGIN (*Q.first # NIL*)
    F := Q.first.file; id := Q.first.name; uno := Q.first.uno
END GetTask;


PROCEDURE RemoveTask*(VAR Q: Queue);
BEGIN (*Q.first # NIL*)
    Files.Purge(Q.first.file); Q.first := Q.first.next; DEC(Q.n);
    IF Q.first = NIL THEN Q.last := NIL END
END RemoveTask;


PROCEDURE Reset(VAR Q: Queue);
BEGIN Q.n := 0; Q.first := NIL; Q.last := NIL
END Reset;


PROCEDURE Collect*;
    VAR n: LONGINT;
BEGIN
    IF Kernel.allocated > 300000 THEN Kernel.GC END
END Collect;


BEGIN RestoreUsers; Reset(PrintQueue); Reset(MailQueue); Reset(LineQueue)
END Core.
```

User administration Apart from procedures and variables constituting the queuing mechanism for tasks, the procedures exported from module *Core* all belong to the administration, and they can be divided into two categories. The first contains the procedures used by the three servers presented in this chapter; they are *UserNo, UserNum, IncPageCount, SetPassword, GetUserName* and *GetFileName*. The second category consists of the procedures *NofUsers* and *GetUser* for inspecting table entries, and *InsertUser, DeleteUser, ClearPassword, ClearCounts* and *Init* for making changes to the table.

The client of the latter category is a module *Users*, which is needed by the human administrator of the server facility.

```
MODULE Users; (*NW 2.2.89 / 25.8.91*)
    IMPORT Texts, Viewers, Oberon, MenuViewers, TextFrames, Core;

    CONST TAB = 9X;
    VAR W: Texts.Writer;

    PROCEDURE List*;
        VAR x, y, i: INTEGER;
            protected: BOOLEAN;
            count: LONGINT;
            T: Texts.Text;
            V: Viewers.Viewer;
            id: Core.ShortName; name: Core.LongName;
    BEGIN i := 0; T := TextFrames.Text("");
        Oberon.AllocateUserViewer(Oberon.Par.frame.X, x, y);
```

```
        V := MenuViewers.New(
            TextFrames.NewMenu("Users.Text", "System.Close Edit.Store"),
            TextFrames.NewText(T, 0), TextFrames.menuH, x, y);
        WHILE i < Core.NofUsers() DO
            Core.GetUser(i, id, name, count, protected);
            Texts.WriteInt(W, i, 4); Texts.Write(W, TAB);
            IF protected THEN Texts.Write(W, "#") END;
            Texts.WriteString(W, id); Texts.Write(W, TAB); Texts.WriteString(W, name);
            Texts.WriteInt(W, count, 8); Texts.WriteLn(W); INC(i)
        END;
        Texts.Append(T, W.buf)
    END List;


    PROCEDURE Insert*;
        VAR id: Core.ShortName; name: Core.LongName; S: Texts.Scanner;
    BEGIN Texts.OpenScanner(S, Oberon.Par.text, Oberon.Par.pos); Texts.Scan(S);
        IF S.class = Texts.Name THEN
            COPY(S.s, id); Texts.Scan(S);
            IF S.class = Texts.Name THEN
                COPY(S.s, name); Core.InsertUser(id, name); Core.BackupUsers
            END
        END
    END Insert;


    PROCEDURE Delete*;
        VAR id: Core.ShortName; S: Texts.Scanner;
    BEGIN Texts.OpenScanner(S, Oberon.Par.text, Oberon.Par.pos); Texts.Scan(S);
        IF S.class = Texts.Name THEN
            COPY(S.s, id); Core.DeleteUser(id); Core.BackupUsers
        END
    END Delete;


    PROCEDURE ClearPassword*;
        VAR id: Core.ShortName; S: Texts.Scanner;
    BEGIN Texts.OpenScanner(S, Oberon.Par.text, Oberon.Par.pos); Texts.Scan(S);
        IF S.class = Texts.Name THEN
            COPY(S.s, id); Core.ClearPassword(id); Core.BackupUsers
        END
    END ClearPassword;


    PROCEDURE ClearCounts*;
    BEGIN Core.SetCounts(0); Core.BackupUsers
    END ClearCounts;


    PROCEDURE Init*;
        VAR id: Core.ShortName; name: Core.LongName; S: Texts.Scanner;
    BEGIN Texts.OpenScanner(S, Oberon.Par.text, Oberon.Par.pos);
        Core.PurgeUsers(0);
        LOOP Texts.Scan(S);
            IF S.class # Texts.Name THEN EXIT END;
            COPY(S.s, id); Texts.Scan(S);
            IF S.class # Texts.Name THEN EXIT END;
            COPY(S.s, name); Core.InsertUser(id, name)
        END;
        Core.BackupUsers
    END Init;
```

```
BEGIN Texts.OpenWriter(W)
END Users.
```

The reader may at this point wonder why a more advanced concept of administration has not been chosen, which would allow the human administrator to operate the server remotely. A quick analysis of the consequences of this widely used approach reveals that a substantial number of additions to our system would be required. The issue of security and protection would become inflated to dimensions that are hardly justified for our local system. The first consequence would be a differentiation among levels of protection. The administrator would become a so-called super-user with extra privileges, such as changing the user table. And so the game of trying to break the protection measures starts to become an interesting challenge.

We have resisted the temptation to introduce additional complexity. Instead, we assume that physical access to the server station is reserved to the administrator. Naturally, module *Users*, and in particular the symbol file of *Core*, do not belong to the public domain. In concluding, we may point out that the impossibility of activating users' programs on the server station significantly reduces the possibilities for inflicting damage from the exterior.

12 The compiler

12.1 Introduction

The compiler is the primary tool of the system builder. It therefore plays a prominent role in the Oberon System, although it is not part of the basic system. Instead, it constitutes a tool module – an application – with a single command: *Compile*. It translates program texts into machine code. Therefore it is as a program inherently machine-dependent; it acts as the interface between source language and target computer.

In order to understand the process of compilation, the reader needs to be familiar with the source language Oberon and with the target computer, the NS-32000 processor architecture. For both, the reader is referred to the literature.

The language is defined as an infinite set of sequences of symbols taken from the language's vocabulary. It is described by a set of equations called syntax. Each equation defines a syntactic construct, or, more precisely, the set of sequences of symbols belonging to the latter. It specifies how that construct is composed of other syntactic constructs. The meaning of programs is defined in terms of semantic rules governing each such construct.

Parsing

Compilation of a program text proceeds by analyzing the text and thereby decomposing it recursively into its constructs according to the syntax. When a construct is identified, code is generated according to the semantic rule associated with it. The components of the identified construct supply parameters for the generated code.

It follows that we distinguish between two kinds of actions: analyzing steps and code generating steps. As a rough approximation, we may say that the former are source-language dependent and target-computer independent, whereas the latter are source-language independent and target-computer dependent. Although reality is somewhat more complex, the module structure of this compiler clearly reflects this division. The tool module *Compiler* is primarily dedicated to syntactic analysis. Upon recognition of a syntactic construct, an appropriate procedure is called from one of the code generator modules.

Symbols vs. characters

Oberon program texts are regarded as sequences of symbols rather than sequences of characters. Symbols themselves, however, are sequences of characters. We refrain from explaining the reasons for this distinction, but mention that, apart from special characters and pairs such as $+$, $\&$ and $<=$, identifiers, numbers and strings are also classified as symbols. Furthermore, certain capital letter sequences are symbols, such as IF and END. Each time the syntax analyzer (parser) proceeds to read the next symbol, it does this by calling procedure *Get*, which

Scanner

constitutes the so-called *scanner* residing in module OCS (Oberon compiler scanner). It reads from the source text as many characters as are needed to recognize the next symbol.

In passing, we note that the scanner alone reflects the definition of symbols in terms of characters, whereas the parser is based on the notion of symbols only. The scanner implements the abstraction of symbols. The recognition of symbols within a character sequence is

Lexical analysis

called *lexical analysis*.

Ideally, the recognition of any syntactic construct, say A, consisting of subconstructs, say B_1, B_2, ... , B_n, leads to the generation of code that depends only on (1) the semantic rules associated with A and (2) (attributes of) B_1, B_2, ... , B_n. If this condition is satisfied, the construct

Context-free

is said to be *context-free*, and if all constructs of a language are context-free then the language is also context-free. Syntax and semantics of Oberon adhere to this rule, although with a significant exception. This exception is embodied by the notion of declarations. The declaration of an identifier, say x, attaches permanent properties to x, such as the fact that x denotes a variable and that its type is T. These properties are 'invisible' when parsing a statement containing x, because the

Context-dependence

declaration of x is not also part of the statement. The 'meaning' of identifiers is thus inherently *context-dependent*.

Context dependence due to declarations is the immediate reason for the use of a global data structure that represents the declared identifiers and their properties (attributes). Since this concept stems from early assemblers where identifiers (then called symbols) were

Symbol table

registered in a linear table, the term *symbol table* tends to persist for this structure, although in this compiler it is considerably more complex than an array. Basically, it grows during the processing of declarations, and it is searched while expressions and statements are processed. Procedures for building and for searching are contained in module OCT.

Export

A complication arises from the notion of exports and imports in

Oberon. Its consequence is that the declaration of an identifier x may be in a module, say M, different from that where x is referenced. If x is exported, the compiler includes x together with its attributes in the *symbol file* of the compiled module M. When compiling another module that imports M, that symbol file is read and its data are incorporated into the symbol table. Procedures for reading and writing symbol files are contained in module OCT, and no other module relies on information about the structure of symbol files.

Symbol files

The syntax is precisely and rigorously defined by a small set of syntactic equations. As a result, the parser is a reasonably perspicuous and short program. Unfortunately, the target computer's instruction set is complex, and as a result the program for generating code is much longer and more difficult to comprehend. This is particularly pronounced in the case of a CISC computer such as the NS-32000. Nevertheless, its instruction set is comparatively regular.

Unlike the parser, which is fully contained in a single module, code generating procedures are distributed over three modules with the goal of keeping their sizes within reasonable limits (1000 lines). Procedures within module OCE are called mainly when parsing expressions. Apart from generating the corresponding code, the procedures perform the checks for type consistency of operands, and they compute the attributes of the processed construct. As they select the appropriate instructions, they directly reflect the *instruction set* of the target computer. Procedures in module OCH are of the same nature; they are primarily called when parsing statements instead of expressions.

Instruction selection

The final production of code is performed by procedures in module OCC. They are typically called from OCE and OCH. In analogy with the scanner transforming character sequences into symbols, OCC procedures transform (abstract) instructions into sequences of bits. Hence this module reflects the binary encoding of instructions, that is, the target computer's *instruction formats*.

Instruction generation

The resulting module structure of the compiler is shown in Figure 12.1 in a slightly simplified manner. In reality, OCS is imported by all other modules due to their need for procedure *OCS.Mark*. This, however, will be explained later.

12.2 Code patterns

Before it is possible to understand *how* code is generated, we need to know *which* code is generated. In other words, we need to know the goal before we find the way leading to the goal. A fairly concise description of this goal is possible due to the structure of the language. As explained before, semantics are attached to each individual syntactic

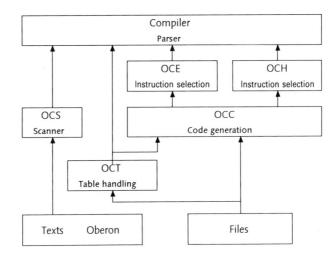

Figure 12.1   Compiler's module structure.

construct, independent of its context. Therefore it suffices to list the expected code – instead of an abstract semantic rule – for each syntactic construct.

As a prerequisite to understanding the resulting instructions and in particular their parameters, we need to know where declared variables are stored, that is, which are their addresses. This compiler uses the straightforward scheme of sequential allocation of consecutively declared variables. An address is a pair consisting of a base address (in a register) and an offset. Global variables are allocated in the module's data section and the respective base address register is SB (see Chapter 6). Local variables are allocated in a procedure activation record on the stack; the respective base register is FP. Offsets are negative integers.

Addressing variables

The amount of storage needed for a variable (called its *size*) is determined by the variable's type. The sizes of basic types are prescribed by the target computer's data representation. Table 12.1 shows these for the NS processor.

Type and size

Table 12.1

Type	Number of bytes
SHORTINT, CHAR, BOOLEAN	1
INTEGER	2
LONGINT, REAL, SET, POINTER, PROCEDURE	4
LONGREAL	8

VAR ch: CHAR; k: INTEGER; b: BOOLEAN; x: REAL

ch   −1
k   −3 => −4
b   −5
x   −9 => −12

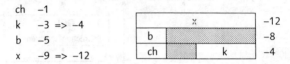

Figure 12.2   Alignment of variables.

VAR ch: CHAR; b: BOOLEAN; k: INTEGER; x: REAL

ch   −1
b   −2
k   −4
x   −8

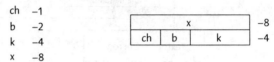

Figure 12.3   Improved order of variables.

The size of an array is the size of the element type multiplied by the number of elements. The size of a record is the sum of the sizes of its fields.

Address alignment   A complication arises due to so-called *alignment*. By alignment is meant the adjustment of an address to a multiple of the variable's size. Alignment is performed for variable addresses as well as for record field offsets. The motivation for alignment is the avoidance of double memory references for variables being 'distributed' over two adjacent words. Proper alignment enhances processing speed quite significantly. Variable allocation using alignment is shown by the example in Figure 12.2.

We note in passing that a reordering of the four variables avoids the occurrence of unused bytes, as shown in Figure 12.3.

Before embarking on a discussion of various code patterns, we briefly present the most important addressing modes of the processor. d0 and d1 are integers, so-called *displacements* or *offsets*. Rn denotes a general purpose register ($0 \leq n < 8$), SB the register holding the Static Base address of global data, and FP the register holding the Frame Pointer, that is, the base address of data local to procedures. Parameters of branch instructions denote jump distances from the instruction's own location (PC-relative).

addressing mode	assembler notation	resulting address
register indirect	d0(Rn)	R[n] + d0
	d0(FP)	FP + d0
	d0(SB)	SB + d0

memory indirect	d1(d0(FP))	Mem[FP + d0] + d1
	d1(d0(SB))	Mem[SB + d0] + d1
indexed	adr[Rx:W]	adr + 2*Rx
top of stack	TOS	SP, represents push and pop operations
immediate	n	n = operand

Pattern 1:
Assignment
of constants

The variables used in this example are global; their base register is SB. Each assignment results in a single instruction. The constant is embedded within the instruction and uses the immediate addressing mode. If the destination operand occupies more bytes than the source operand, sign extension is included (MOVX). For integers in the range −8, ... 7, special instructions with shorter encoding are used (MOVQ).

```
MODULE Pattern1;
    VAR ch: CHAR;           −1
        i: SHORTINT;        −2
        j: INTEGER;         −4
        k: LONGINT;         −8
        x: REAL;            −12
        s: SET;             −16
    BEGIN                   0    ENTER    00 0
        ch := "0";          3    MOVB     48 −1(SB)
        i := 10;            7    MOVB     10 −2(SB)
        j := 1000;          11   MOVW     1000 −4(SB)
        k := 0;             16   MOVQD    0 −8(SB)
        x := 1.5;           19   MOVF     3FC00000 −12(SB)
        s := {0, 5, 8};     27   MOVD     00000121 −16(SB)
        j := j;             34   MOVW     −4(SB) −4(SB)
        k := i;             38   MOVXBD   −2(SB) −8(SB)
        k := j;             43   MOVXWD   −4(SB) −8(SB)
        x := j              48   MOVWF    −4(SB) −12(SB)
    END Pattern1.           53   EXIT     00
                            55   RXP      0
```

Pattern 2:
Simple
expressions

The result of an expression containing operators is always stored in a register before it is assigned to a variable or used in another operation. This is necessary in the general case for machines with two-operand instructions. It follows furthermore from the concept of context-free processing: the code for x+y, for example, is the same regardless of whether x := x+y or z := x+y is parsed, although the former could be represented by a single instruction on a two-address machine, whereas the latter cannot.

Registers for intermediate results are allocated sequentially in the orders R7, R6, ... , R0, and F6, F4, F2, F0, the latter for floating-point operands. Integer multiplication and division by powers of 2 are represented by fast, arithmetic shifts (ASH). Similarly, the modulus by a power of 2 is obtained by masking off leading bits (BIC). The operations of set union, difference and intersection are represented by logical operations (OR, BIC, AND).

```
MODULE Pattern2;
    VAR i, j: INTEGER;        -2, -4
        k, n: LONGINT;        -8, -12
        x, y: REAL;           -16, -20
        s, t, u: SET;         -24, -28, -32
BEGIN                         0      ENTER      00 0
    i := (i + 1) * (i - 1);   3      MOVW       -2(SB) R7
                              6      ADDQW      1 R7
                              8      MOVW       -2(SB) R6
                              11     ADDQW      -1 R6
                              13     MULW       R6 R7
                              16     MOVW       R7 -2(SB)
    k := ABS(k) DIV 17;       19     ABSD       -8(SB) R7
                              23     DIVD       17 R7
                              30     MOVD       R7 -8(SB)
    k := 8*n;                 33     MOVD       -12(SB) R7
                              36     ASHD       3 R7
                              40     MOVD       R7 -8(SB)
    k := n DIV 2;             43     MOVD       -12(SB) R7
                              46     ASHD       -1 R7
                              50     MOVD       R7 -8(SB)
    k := n MOD 16;            53     MOVD       -12(SB) R7
                              56     BICD       FFFFFFF0 R7
                              62     MOVD       R7 -8(SB)
    x := -y / (x-1.5);        65     MOVF       -16(SB) F6
                              69     SUBF       3FC00000 F6
                              76     MOVF       -20(SB) F4
                              80     DIVF       F6 F4
                              83     NEGF       F4 F2
                              86     MOVF       F2 -16(SB)
    k := ENTIER(x);           90     FLOORFD    -16(SB) R7
                              94     MOVD       R7 -8(SB)
    s := s + t * u            97     MOVD       -28(SB) R7
                              100    ANDD       -32(SB) R7
                              103    MOVD       -24(SB) R6
                              106    ORD        R7 R6
                              108    MOVD       R6 -24(SB)
END Pattern2.                 111    EXIT       00
                              113    RXP        0
```


Pattern 3: Indexed variables
References to elements of arrays make use of the indexed addressing mode. The index must be present in a register. It is loaded by a CHECK instruction that, apart from transferring the index value (with sign extension), also checks whether the index is within the bounds specified in the array's declaration. The subsequent flag instruction causes a trap if the index lies outside the bounds. The bounding values are stored

in the module's constant area and are addressed with base SB and with a positive offset.

If the reference is to an element of a multidimensional array (matrix), its address computation involves the INDEX instruction. The address of an element $A[i_{k-1}, \ldots, i_1, i_0]$ of a k-dimensional array A with lengths $n_{k-1}, \ldots, n_1, n_0$ is

$$\text{adr}(A) + ((\ldots ((i_{k-1} * n_{k-2}) + i_{k-2}) * n_{k-3} + \ldots) * n_1 + i_1) * n_0 + i_0$$

The instruction *INDEX r, a, b* computes $r := r*(a-1) + b$. The address of a designator with k indices can therefore be computed by $k-1$ successive INDEX instructions. If all indices are constants, the above polynomial is evaluated by the compiler. The resulting code then consists of a single instruction only.

```
MODULE Pattern3;
    VAR i, j, k, n: INTEGER;              -2, -4, -6, -8
        a: ARRAY 10 OF INTEGER;           -28
        b: ARRAY 10 OF LONGINT;           -68
        x: ARRAY 10, 10 OF INTEGER;       -268
        y: ARRAY 10, 10, 10 OF            -2268
            INTEGER;
BEGIN                              0    ENTER     00 0
    k := a[i];                     3    CHECKW    R7 0(SB) -2(SB)
                                   8    FLAG
                                   9    MOVW      -28(SB)[R7:W] -6(SB)
    n := a[5];                     14   MOVW      -18(SB) -8(SB)
    b[i] := 0;                     18   CHECKW    R7 4(SB) -2(SB)
                                   23   FLAG
                                   24   MOVQD     0 -68(SB)[R7:D]
    x[i, j] := 2;                  29   CHECKW    R7 8(SB) -2(SB)
                                   34   FLAG
                                   35   CHECKW    R6 12(SB) -4(SB)
                                   40   FLAG
                                   41   INDEXW    R7 9 R6
                                   46   MOVQW     2 -268(SB)[R7:W]
    y[i, j, k] := 3;               51   CHECKW    R7 16(SB) -2(SB)
                                   56   FLAG
                                   57   CHECKW    R6 20(SB) -4(SB)
                                   62   FLAG
                                   63   INDEXW    R7 9 R6
                                   68   CHECKW    R5 24(SB) -6(SB)
                                   73   FLAG
                                   74   INDEXW    R7 9 R5
                                   79   MOVQW     3 -2268(SB)[R7:W]
    y[3, 4, 5] := 6               84   MOVQW     6 -1578(SB)
END Pattern3.                     88   EXIT      00
                                   90   RXP       0

    index bounds:                  0   0, 9; 0, 9; 0, 9; 0, 9; 0, 9; 0, 9; 0, 9
```

Pattern 4:
Record fields
and pointers

Fields of records are accessed by computing the sum of the record's (base) address and the field's offset. If the record variable is statically declared, the sum is computed by the compiler. In the case of a dynamically allocated variable, the base is given by the pointer through which the variable is referenced, and the addition is included in the indirect addressing mode. (An operand of the form d1(d0(SB)) denotes the address Mem[SB+d0] + d1.) Dynamic allocation, expressed by the statement NEW(p), is represented by the three instructions

```
ADDR        p, R0
MOVD        dsc, R1
SVC         0
```

where *dsc* denotes the descriptor of the variable's type (see Pattern 13). The supervisor call assigns the address of the allocated variable to p. NIL is represented by 0.

```
MODULE Pattern4;
    TYPE Ptr = POINTER TO Node;
        Node = RECORD num:
            INTEGER;                    0
            name: ARRAY 8 OF CHAR;      2
            next: Ptr                   12
        END ;
    VAR p, q: Ptr;          -4, -8
BEGIN                           0    ENTER    00 0
    NEW(p);                     3    ADDRD    -4(SB) R0
                                6    MOVD     4(SB) R1
                                9    SVC      0
    NEW(q);                    11    ADDRD    -8(SB) R0
                               14    MOVD     4(SB) R1
                               17    SVC      0
    p.num := 6;                19    MOVQW    6 0(-4(SB))
    p.name[7] := "0";          23    MOVB     48 9(-4(SB))
    p.next := q;               28    MOVD     -8(SB) 12(-4(SB))
    p.next.next := NIL         33    MOVD     12(-4(SB)) R7
                               37    MOVQD    0 12(R7)
END Pattern4.                  40    EXIT     00
                               42    RXP      0
```

Pattern 5:
If statements
and Boolean
expressions

Conditional statements imply that parts of them are skipped. This is done by the use of branch instructions whose operand specifies the distance of the branch. The instructions refer to the condition register as an implicit operand. Its value is determined by a preceding instruction, typically a compare or a bit-test instruction.

The Boolean operators & and OR are purposely not defined as total functions, but rather by the equations

```
p & q  = if p then q else FALSE
p OR q = if p then TRUE else q
```

Consequently, Boolean operators must be translated into branches too. Evidently, branches stemming from if statements and branches stemming from Boolean operators should be merged, if possible. The resulting code therefore does not necessarily mirror the structure of the if statement directly, as can be seen from the code in *Pattern5*. We must conclude that code generation for Boolean expressions differs in some aspects from that for arithmetic expressions.

The example of *Pattern5* is also used to exhibit the code resulting from the standard procedures INC, DEC, INCL and EXCL. These procedures provide an opportunity to use shorter code in those cases where a single two-operand instruction suffices, that is, when one of the arguments is identical with the destination.

```
MODULE Pattern5;
    VAR x: INTEGER; s: SET;              -2, -8
BEGIN                            0      ENTER    00 0
    IF x = 0 THEN                3      CMPQW    0 -2(SB)
                                 6      BNE      6
        INC(x)                   9      ADDQW    1 -2(SB)
    END ;
    IF (x >= 0) & (x < 100) THEN 12     CMPQW    0 -2(SB)
                                 15     BGT      14
                                 18     CMPW     100 -2(SB)
                                 23     BLE      6
        DEC(x)                   26     ADDQW    -1 -2(SB)
    END ;
    IF ODD(x) OR (x IN s) THEN   29     TBITB    0 -2(SB)
                                 33     BFS      10
                                 36     TBITW    -2(SB) -8(SB)
                                 40     BFC      10
        INCL(s, 4)               43     ORD      00000010 -8(SB)
    END ;
    IF x < 0 THEN                50     CMPQW    0 -2(SB)
                                 53     BLE      13
        EXCL(s, 0)               56     BICD     00000001 -8(SB)
                                 63     BR       46
    ELSIF x < 10 THEN            66     CMPW     10 -2(SB)
                                 71     BLE      13
        EXCL(s, 1)               74     BICD     00000002 -8(SB)
                                 81     BR       28
    ELSIF x < 100 THEN           84     CMPW     100 -2(SB)
                                 89     BLE      13
        EXCL(s, 2)               92     BICD     00000004 -8(SB)
    ELSE                         99     BR       10
        EXCL(s, 3)               102    BICD     00000008 -8(SB)
    END                                 00
END Pattern5.                    109    EXIT
                                 111    RXP      0
```

Pattern 6:
Repetitive
statements

```
MODULE Pattern6;                    0    ENTER    00 0
   VAR i: INTEGER;
BEGIN
   i := 0;                          3    MOVQW    0 −2(SB)
   WHILE i < 10 DO                  6    CMPW     10 −2(SB)
                                   11    BLE      8
      INC(i)                       14    ADDQW    1 −2(SB)
   END ;                           17    BR       −11
   REPEAT DEC(i)                   19    ADDQW    −1 −2(SB)
   UNTIL i = 0                     22    CMPQW    0 −2(SB)
                                   25    BNE      −6
END Pattern6.                      27    EXIT     00
                                   29    RXP      0
```

Pattern 7:
Case
statements

Case statements serve to select a statement sequence from a set of cases according to an index value. Selection is represented by a direct branch to the selected case; the CASE instruction takes the branch distance from a table using the indexed addressing mode. We conclude from the following code that missing cases yield a table entry leading to a trap instruction (BPT 16). The table of offsets is located in the module's area for constants.

```
MODULE Pattern7;
   VAR i: INTEGER; s: SET;        −2, −8
BEGIN                              0    ENTER    00 0
   CASE i OF                       3    CHECKW   R7 0(SB) −2(SB)
                                   9    BFS      58
                                  12    CASEW    4(SB)[R7:W]
   0: s := {0, 31}                17    MOVD     80000001 −8(SB)
                                  24    BR       45
   | 1: s := {1, 30}              27    MOVD     40000002 −8(SB)
                                  34    BR       35
   | 2: s := {2, 29}              37    MOVD     20000004 −8(SB)
                                  44    BR       25
   | 4: s := {4, 27}              47    MOVD     08000010 −8(SB)
                                  54    BR       15
   | 5: s := {5, 26}              57    MOVD     04000020 −8(SB)
                                  64    BR       5
                                  67    BPT      16
   END
END Pattern7.                     69    EXIT     00
                                  71    RXP      0
index bounds:                      0    0, 5
branch offset array:               4    5, 15, 25, 55, 35, 45
```

Pattern 8:
Procedure
calls

Procedure bodies are surrounded by an ENTER and an EXIT instruction. They set and reset the values of the SP and FP registers (see Chapter 6). The latter holds the address of the procedure activation record on the stack. The (second) parameter of the ENTER instruction indicates the space taken by variables local to the procedure, rounded up to the next multiple of 4. Procedures (which are not exported) end with a RET instruction; its parameter indicates the space taken by parameters, which are addressed with positive offsets relative to the FP register.

Calls (within a module) use the BSR instruction. Parameters are pushed onto the stack prior to the BSR using the TOS addressing mode. Every parameter occupies at least 4 bytes (or a multiple thereof). In the case of value parameters, the value is loaded, while in the case of VAR parameters, the variable's address is loaded.

```
MODULE Pattern8;                         0     ENTER    00 0
    VAR i: INTEGER;                      3     BR       22

PROCEDURE P(x: INTEGER; VAR y: INTEGER);
    VAR z: INTEGER;
    BEGIN                                8     ENTER    00 4
        z := x;                         12     MOVW     12(FP) −2(FP)
        y := z                          16     MOVW     −2(FP) 0(8(FP))
    END P;                              21     EXIT     00
                                        23     RET      8

BEGIN P(5, i)                           25     MOVQD    5 TOS
                                        27     ADDRD    −2(SB) TOS
                                        30     BSR      −22
END Pattern8.                           32     EXIT     00
                                        34     RXP      0
```

Pattern 9:
Function
procedures

Function procedures are handled in exactly the same manner as proper procedures, except that a result specified by a RETURN statement is returned in register R0 or F0. If the function is called in an expression at a place where intermediate results are held in registers, these values are put onto the stack before the call, and they are restored after it, using SAVE and RESTORE instructions. (The BPT 17 instruction occurs at the end of each function procedure and guards against erroneous functions without executed RETURN statement.)

```
MODULE Pattern9;                         0     ENTER    00 0
    VAR x: REAL;                        3     BR       39
```

```
         PROCEDURE F(x: REAL): REAL;
         BEGIN                            8    ENTER    00 0
            x := F(x * 0.5);             12    MOVF     8(FP) F6
                                         16    MULF     3F000000 F6
                                         23    MOVF     F6 TOS
                                         26    BSR      −18
                                         28    MOVF     F0 8(FP)
            RETURN x                     32    MOVF     8(FP) F0
         END F;                          36    EXIT     00
                                         38    RET      4
                                         40    BPT      17

         BEGIN x := F(F(10.0))           42    MOVF     41200000 TOS
                                         49    BSR      −41
                                         51    MOVF     R0 TOS
                                         54    BSR      −46
                                         56    MOVF     F0 −4(SB)
         END Pattern9.                   60    EXIT     00
                                         62    RXP      0
```

Pattern 10:
Dynamic
array
parameters

Dynamic array parameters are passed by loading a descriptor on the stack, regardless of whether they are value or VAR parameters. The descriptor consists of the actual variable's address and its index bounds (the lower bound always being 0). In the case of n-dimensional arrays, n bound pairs are required.

   If the dynamic array is called by value, a copy of its value is made after procedure entry. The length is computed by incrementing the upper bound and dividing the sum by the array element size using a shift instruction, yielding the number of elements to be copied (R7). The copies are pushed onto the stack in a tight loop using the ACB instruction (Add, Compare, Branch). Thereafter, the address of the array in the descriptor is replaced by the address of the copy (SP).

   Elements of dynamic arrays are accessed like those of static arrays, using the CHECK instruction for loading the index into a register. Even when the index is a constant, the check cannot be performed by the compiler. The LEN function obtains the length from the upper bound, and by adding 1 to it.

```
         MODULE Pattern10;                0    ENTER    00 0
                                          3    BR       94
         VAR a: ARRAY 10 OF CHAR;       −10
             b: ARRAY 4, 8 OF INTEGER;  −76


         PROCEDURE P0(x: ARRAY OF
                 CHAR);
             VAR k: LONGINT;
```

BEGIN	8	ENTER	00 4
	12	MOVD	12(FP) R7
	15	ADDQD	4 R7
	17	ASHD	−2 R7
	21	MOVD	8(FP) R6
	24	MOVD	−4(R6)[R7:D] TOS
	28	ACBD	−1 R7 −4
	31	ADDRD	0(SP) 8(FP)
k := LEN(x)	35	MOVD	12(FP) R7
	38	ADDQD	1 R7
	40	MOVD	R7 24(FP)
END P0;	43	EXIT	00
	45	RET	8

PROCEDURE P1(VAR x: ARRAY OF CHAR);
BEGIN

	47	ENTER	00 0
x[1] := "0"	51	CHECKW	R7 12(FP) 0001
	57	FLAG	
	58	MOVB	48 0(8(FP))[R7:B]
END P1;	64	EXIT	00
	66	RET	8

PROCEDURE P2(VAR x: ARRAY OF ARRAY OF INTEGER);
  VAR i, j: INTEGER;

BEGIN	68	ENTER	00 4
x[i, j] := 3	72	CHECKW	R7 16(FP) −2(FP)
	77	FLAG	
	78	CHECKW	R6 12(FP) −4(FP)
	83	FLAG	
	84	INDEXW	R7 12(FP) R6
	88	MOVQW	3 0(8(FP))[R7:W]
END P2;	93	EXIT	00
	95	RET	12

BEGIN P0(a);	97	MOVD	0(SB) TOS
	100	ADDRD	−10(SB) TOS
	103	BSR	−95
P1(a);	106	MOVD	0(SB) TOS
	109	ADDRD	−10(SB) TOS
	112	BSR	−65
P0("ABCDE")	115	MOVQD	5 TOS
	117	ADDRD	12(SB) TOS
	120	BSR	−112
P2(b)	123	MOVD	4(SB) TOS
	126	MOVD	8(SB) TOS
	129	ADDRD	−76(SB) TOS
	133	BSR	−65
END Pattern10.	136	EXIT	00
	138	RXP	0

index bounds and constants:	0	0, 9; 0, 3; 0, 7	
	12	"ABCDE"	

Pattern 11: Nested procedures

Whereas global and local variables are addressed using SB and FP as bases, the variables at intermediate levels are addressed by descending along the static chain in the stack. This is the case if a variable x is referenced from a procedure Q that is local to another procedure P with local x. An element of the static chain is established when a local procedure is called; it denotes the address of the activation record of the procedure in which the calling procedure is declared locally. It is omitted if the calling procedure is global, because then the environment is based on SB. The SB register may be regarded as an optimization feature for access of global variables built into the processor architecture.

Access to a variable local to the procedure immediately surrounding the procedure accessing the variable uses the indirect addressing mode. When the level difference between accessed variable and accessor is greater than 1, several instructions are required for descending along the chain. This, however, rarely occurs.

MODULE Pattern11;	0	ENTER	00 0
VAR u: INTEGER;	3	BR	62
PROCEDURE P;	8	ENTER	00 4
VAR x: INTEGER;	12	BR	44
PROCEDURE Q;	15	ENTER	00 4
VAR y: INTEGER;	19	BR	28
PROCEDURE R;	22	ENTER	00
VAR z: INTEGER;			
BEGIN u := z + y + x	26	MOVW	−2(FP) R7
	29	ADDW	−2(8(FP)) R7
	33	MOVD	8(8(FP)) R6
	37	ADDW	−2(R6) R7
	40	MOVW	R7 −2(SB)
END R;	43	EXIT	00
	45	RET	4
BEGIN R	47	ADDRD	0(FP) TOS static chain
	50	BSR	−28
END Q;	52	EXIT	00
	54	RET	4
BEGIN Q	56	ADDRD	0(FP) TOS static chain
	59	BSR	−44
END P;	61	EXIT	00
	63	RET	0

BEGIN P	65	BSR	−57
END Pattern11.	67	EXIT	00
	69	RXP	0

Pattern 12: External variables and procedures

When a procedure is imported from another module, its address is unavailable to the compiler. Instead, the procedure is identified by a number obtained from the imported module's symbol file. For calling an external procedure, the CXP instruction is generated instead of BSR (see Chapter 6). Its parameter is an index to the calling module's link table. The table entry contains the base address of the referenced module's descriptor and the procedure's offset in the module's code. These values are computed by the loader from a module number and the procedure's number, which are supplied by the compiler in the header of the object file (see Chapter 6). An RXP instruction instead of RET terminates exported procedures.

Imported variables are referenced using the external addressing mode. Their offset is added to the base address of the data area of the imported module that is contained in the link table. If n modules are imported, the first n entries of the table contain the respective base addresses. Hence the first parameter of an external address is the module number, the second the offset.

In the following example, modules *Pattern12a* and *Pattern12b* both export a procedure and a variable. They are referenced from the importing module *Pattern12c*. The first two entries of the link table are data entries (indicated by the special value 255), the remaining entries refer to external procedures, and their indices appear as parameters of CXP instructions.

MODULE Pattern12a;	0	ENTER	00 0
VAR k*: INTEGER;	3	BR	16
PROCEDURE P*;	8	ENTER	00 0
BEGIN k := 1	12	MOVQW	1 −2(SB)
END P;	15	EXIT	00
	17	RXP	0
END Pattern12a.	19	EXIT	00
	21	RXP	0
entry:	1	8	
MODULE Pattern12b;	0	ENTER	00 0
VAR x*: REAL;	3	BR	18
PROCEDURE P*;	8	ENTER	00 0
BEGIN x := 1	12	MOVBF	1 −4(SB)

END P;	17	EXIT	00
	19	RXP	0
END Pattern12b.	21	EXIT	00
	23	RXP	0
entry:	1	8	

MODULE Pattern12c;
    IMPORT Pattern12a, Pattern12b;

VAR i: INTEGER; x: REAL;			
BEGIN 0		ENTER	00 0
i := Pattern12a.k;	3	MOVW	EXT(1)−2 −2(SB)
x := Pattern12b.x;	8	MOVF	EXT(2)−4 −8(SB)
Pattern12a.P;	14	CXP	3
Pattern12b.P	16	CXP	4
END Pattern12c.	18	EXIT	00
	20	RXP	0

imports:	0	Pattern12a
	1	Pattern12b

links (data: mno, 255):	1	1, 255
	2	2, 255
(proc: mno, pno):	3	1, 1
	4	2, 1

Pattern 13:
Record
extensions
with pointers

Fields of a record type R1, which is declared as an extension of a type R0, are simply appended to the fields of R0, that is, their offsets are greater than those of the fields of R0. When a record is statically declared, its type is known by the compiler. If the record is referenced via a pointer, however, this is not the case. A pointer bound to a base type R0 may well refer to a record of an extension R1 of R0. Type tests (and type guards) allow testing for the actual type. This requires that a type can be identified at the time of program execution. Because the language defines name equivalence instead of structural equivalence of types, a type may be identified by a number. We use the address of a unique *type descriptor* for this purpose. Therefore type tests consist of a simple address comparison that is very fast. Type descriptors are generated by the loader, and their address, called *type tag*, is stored in the module's area for constants. The type of a (dynamically allocated) variable is stored as a prefix to the record (with offset −4).

A type descriptor contains (in addition to information stored for use by the garbage collector) a table of tags of all base types. If, for instance, a type R2 is an extension of R1, which is an extension of R0,

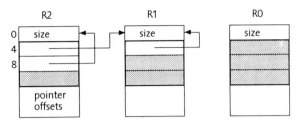

Figure 12.4 Type descriptors.

the descriptor of R2 contains the tags of R2 and R1 as shown in Figure 12.4. The table has a fixed number of 7 entries.

A type guard p(T) is equivalent to the statement

IF ~(p IS T) THEN HALT(18) END

but appears within variable designators. (Evidently, a single-byte instruction similar to FLAG, trapping on inequality would be useful in place of the instruction pair BEQ 4, BPT 18.)

```
MODULE Pattern13;              0      ENTER     00 0
  TYPE
    P0 = POINTER TO R0;
    P1 = POINTER TO R1;
    P2 = POINTER TO R2;
    R0 = RECORD x: INTEGER END ;
    R1 = RECORD (R0) y: INTEGER END ;
    R2 = RECORD (R1) z: INTEGER END ;
  VAR
    p0: P0;                   -4
    p1: P1;                   -8
    p2: P2;                  -12
  BEGIN                        3      MOVD      4(SB) 4(4(SB))
                               8      MOVD      8(SB) 8(8(SB))
                              13      MOVD      4(SB) 4(8(SB))
    p0.x := 0;                18      MOVQW     0  0(-4(SB))
    p1.y := 1;                22      MOVQW     1 4(-8(SB))
    p0(P1).y := 2;            26      MOVD      -4(-4(SB)) R7
                              30      CMPD      4( R7) 4(SB)
                              34      BEQ       4
                              36      BPT       18
                              38      MOVQW     2 4(-4(SB))
    p0(P2).z := 3;            42      MOVD      -4(-4(SB)) R7
                              46      CMPD      8( R7) 8(SB)
                              50      BEQ       4
                              52      BPT       18
                              54      MOVQW     3 8(-4(SB))
    IF p1 IS P2 THEN          58      MOVD      -4(-8(SB)) R7
```

62	CMPD	8(R7) 8(SB)
66	BNE	7
69	MOVD	−12(SB) −4(SB

p0 := p2
END
END Pattern13.

73	EXIT	00
75	RXP	0

Type tags at 0, 4, 8 (SB)

Pattern 14:
Record
extensions as
VAR
parameters

Records occurring as VAR parameters may also require a type test at program execution time. This is because VAR parameters effectively constitute hidden pointers. Type tests and type guards on VAR parameters are handled in the same way as for variables referenced via pointers, with a slight difference, however. Statically declared record variables may be used as actual parameters, and they are not prefixed by a type tag. Therefore the tag has to be supplied together with the variable's address when the procedure is called, that is, when the actual parameter is established. Record-structured VAR parameters therefore consist of address and type tag. This is similar to dynamic array descriptors consisting of address and bounds.

The following example also exhibits a record assignment – in fact, a projection of R1 onto R0. It is represented by a single instruction that moves multiple bytes (MOVM). Its last parameter is the number of bytes to be copied minus 1.

MODULE Pattern14;	0	ENTER	00 0
TYPE	3	BR	30
R0 = RECORD a, b, c: LONGINT END ;			
R1 = RECORD (R0) x, y: LONGINT END ;			
VAR			
r0: R0;	−12		
r1: R1;	−32		
PROCEDURE P(VAR r: R0);	8	ENTER	00 0
BEGIN r.a := 1;	12	MOVQD	1 0(8(FP))
r(R1).x := 2	16	CMPD	4(12(FP)) 4(SB)
	21	BEQ	4
	23	BPT	18
	25	MOVQD	2 12(8(FP))
END P;	29	EXIT	00
	31	RET	8
BEGIN	33	MOVD	4(SB) 4(4(SB))
r0 := r1;	38	MOVMB	−32(SB) −12(SB) 11
P(r1)	44	MOVD	4(SB) TOS
	47	ADDRD	−32(SB) TOS
	50	BSR	−42

END Pattern14.			52	EXIT	00
			54	RXP	0

Type tags at 0, 4 (SB)

Pattern 15:
Set elements

This last code pattern exhibits the construction of sets. If the specified elements are constants, the set value is computed by the compiler (see Pattern 7). Otherwise, sequences of move and shift instructions are used. Since shift instructions do not check whether the shift count is within sensible bounds, the results are unpredictable if elements outside the range 0, ..., 31 are involved.

MODULE Pattern15;				
VAR s: SET; i, j: INTEGER;		$-4, -6, -8$		
BEGIN		0	ENTER	00 0
s := {i};		3	MOVQD	1 R7
		5	LSHD	-6(SB) R7
		9	MOVD	R7 -4(SB)
s := {0 .. i};		12	MOVQD	-2 R7
		14	LSHD	-6(SB) R7
		18	COMD	R7 R7
		21	MOVD	R7 -4(SB)
s := {i .. 27};		24	MOVQD	-1 R7
		26	LSHD	-6(SB) R7
		30	BICD	F0000000 R7
		36	MOVD	R7 -4(SB)
s := {i .. j};		39	MOVQD	-1 R7
		41	LSHD	-6(SB) R7
		45	MOVQD	-2 R6
		47	LSHD	-8(SB) R6
		51	BICD	R6 R7
		53	MOVD	R7 -4(SB)
INCL(s, i)		56	MOVQD	1 R7
		58	LSHD	-6(SB) R7
		62	ORD	R7 -4(SB)
END Pattern15.		65	EXIT	00
		67	RXP	0

12.3 Internal data structures and interfaces

In Section 12.1, it was explained that declarations inherently constitute context dependence of the translation process. Although parsing still proceeds on the basis of a context-free syntax and relies on contextual information only in a few isolated instances, information provided by declarations affects the generated code significantly. During the processing of declarations, their information is transferred into the 'symbol table', a data structure of considerable complexity, from where it is retrieved for the generation of code.

This dynamic data structure is defined in module OCT in terms of two record types called *Object* and *Struct* (see the definition of OCT). These types pervade all other modules with the exception of the scanner. They are therefore explained before further details of the compiler are discussed.

Object

For each declared identifier, an instance of type *Object* is generated. The record holds the identifier and the properties associated with the identifier given in its declaration. Since Oberon is a strongly typed language, every object has a type. It is represented in the record by its *typ* field, which is a pointer to a record of type *Struct*. Since many objects may be of the same type, it is appropriate to record the type's attributes only once and to refer to them via a pointer. The properties of type *Struct* will be discussed below.

Object mode

The kind of object that a table entry represents is indicated by the field *mode*. Its values are denoted by declared integer constants: *Var* indicates that the entry describes a variable, *Con* a constant, *Fld* a record field, *Ind* a VAR parameter and *xProc* a procedure. Different kinds of entries carry different attributes. A variable or a parameter carries an address, a constant has a value, a record field has an offset, and a procedure has an entry address, a list of parameters and a result type. For each kind, the introduction of an extended record type would seem advisable. This was not done, however, for three reasons. First, the compiler was first formulated in (a subset of) Modula-2, which does not feature type extension. Secondly, not making use of type extensions would make it simpler to translate the compiler into other languages for porting the language to other computers. And thirdly, all extensions were known at the time the compiler was planned. Hence extensibility provided no argument for the introduction of a considerable variety of types. The simplest solution lies in using the multipurpose fields *a0*, *a1*, *a2* and *dsc* for variant-specific attributes. For example, *a0* holds an address for variables, parameters and procedures, an offset for record fields, and a value for constants.

Struct

The definition of a type yields a record of type *Struct*, regardless of whether it occurs within a type declaration, in which case also a record of type *Object* (mode = *Typ*) is generated, or in a variable declaration, in which case the type remains anonymous. All types are characterized by a form and a size. A type is either a basic type or a constructed type. In the latter case, it refers to one or more other types. Constructed types are arrays, records, pointers and procedural types. The attribute *form* refers to this classification. Its value is an integer allowing the use of case statements for an efficient discrimination.

Just as different object kinds are characterized by different

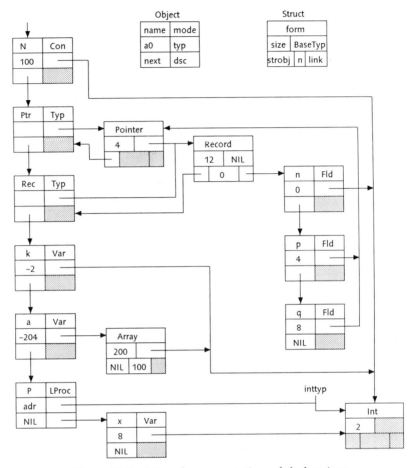

Figure 12.5 Internal representation of declarations.

attributes, different forms have different attributes. Again, the introduction of extensions of type *Struct* was avoided. Instead, some of the fields of type *Struct* remain unused in some cases, such as for basic types, and others are used for form-specific attributes. For example, the attribute *BaseTyp* refers to the element type in the case of an array, to the result type in the case of a procedural type, to the type to which a pointer is bound, or to the base type of a (extended) record type. The attribute *link* refers to the parameter list in the case of a procedural type, or to the list of fields in the case of a record type.

Base type

As an example, consider the following declarations. The corresponding data structure is shown in Figure 12.5. For details, the reader is referred to the program listing of module OCT and the respective explanations.

```
CONST       N = 100;
TYPE        Ptr = POINTER TO Rec;
            Rec = RECORD n: INTEGER; p, q: Ptr END ;
VAR         k: INTEGER;
            a: ARRAY N OF INTEGER;
PROCEDURE P(x: INTEGER): INTEGER;
```

Structure form

Only entries representing constructed types are generated during a compilation. An entry for each basic type is established by the compiler's initialization. It consists of an *Object* holding the standard type's identifier and a *Struct* indicating its form, denoted by one of the values *Byte, Bool, Char, SInt, Int, LInt, Real, LReal* or *Set*. The object records of the basic types are anchored in global pointer variables (which actually should be regarded as constants).

Entries are created not only upon initialization for basic types, but also for all standard procedures. Therefore every compilation starts out with a symbol table reflecting all standard, pervasive identifiers and the objects they stand for.

Basic object modes

We now return to the subject of *Objects*. Whereas objects of basic modes (*Con, Var, Ind, Fld, Typ, xProc* and *Mod*) directly reflect declared identifiers and constitute the context in which statements and expressions are compiled, compilations of expressions typically generate anonymous entities of additional, non-basic modes. Such entities reflect selectors, factors, terms and so on, that is, constituents of expressions and statements. As such, they are of a transitory nature and hence are not represented by records allocated on the heap. Instead, they are represented by record variables local to the processing procedures and are therefore allocated on the stack. Their type is called *Item* and is a slight variation of the type *Object*.

Non-basic modes

Item

Let us assume, for instance, that a term x∗y is parsed. This implies that the operator and both factors have been parsed already. The factors x and y are represented by two variables of type *Item* of *Var* mode. The resulting term is again described by an item, and, since the product is transitory, that is, has significance only within the expression of which the term is a constituent, it is to be held in a temporary location, in a register. In order to express that an item is located in a register, a new, non-basic mode *Reg* is introduced.

Effectively, all non-basic modes reflect the target computer's architecture, in particular its addressing modes. The more addressing modes a computer offers, the more item modes are needed to represent them. The additional item modes and their corresponding addressing modes used in the compiler of the NS-32000 processor are

```
VarX        indexed mode
IndX        indirect, indexed mode
```

Reg	direct register mode
RegI	indirect register mode
RegX	indirect, indexed register mode
Stk	stack mode (TOS)
Coc	condition code mode
Abs	absolute mode

Table 12.2

	Objects				**Items**					
	mode	a0	a1	dsc	lev	a0	a1	a2	obj	
0	Undef									
1	Var	adr			lev	adr	obj			
2	VarX				lev	adr		RX		
3	Ind	adr			lev	adr	off			
4	IndX				lev	adr	off	RX		
5	RegI					R	off			
6	RegX					R	off	RX		
7	Abs					adr				
8	Con	val				val	val			
						sadr	leng			(strings)
9	Stk									(stack)
10	Coc					CC	Tjmp	Fjmp		(condition code)
11	Reg					R				
12	Fld	off					off		obj	
13	Typ				mno	tadr			obj	
14	LProc	adr		pars		adr			obj	(local procedure)
15	XProc	pno	Ladr	pars	mno	pno	Ladr		obj	(external procedure)
16	SProc	fno				fno				(standard procedure)
17	CProc	cno	pars			cno			obj	(code procedure)
18	IProc	pno	Ladr			adr	Ladr		obj	(interrupt procedure)
19	Mod	mno	key			mno			obj	
20	Head	lev	psize							

	Structures					
	form	BaseTyp	link	mno	n	adr
13	Pointer	PBaseTyp				
14	rocTyp	ResTyp	param			
15	Array	ElemTyp		mno	nofel	bounds
16	DynArr	ElemTyp				
17	Record	BaseTyp	fields	mno		descr

The use of the types *Object, Item*, and *Struct* for the various modes and forms, and the meaning of their attributes are explained in Table 12.2.

Items have an attribute called *lev* that is part of the address of the item. Positive values denote the level of nesting of the procedure in which the item is declared; *lev* = 0 implies a global object. Negative values indicate that the object is imported from the module with number $-lev$.

Nesting level

Module number

The three types *Object, Item* and *Struct* are defined in the interface of module OCT, which also contains procedures for accessing the symbol table. *Insert* serves to register a new identifier, and it returns a pointer to the allocated record. *Find* returns the pointer to the object whose name equals the global scanner variable *OCS.name* and the level of the identified object.

Table search

Procedure *Import* serves to read the specified symbol file and to enter its identifier in the symbol table (mode = *Mod*). *FindImport* retrieves an object with a name given by *OCS.name* from a previously imported module. Finally, *Export* generates the symbol file of the compiled module, containing descriptions of all objects and structures marked for export.

```
DEFINITION OCT; (*Table handler*)
  TYPE
    Object = POINTER TO ObjDesc;
    Struct = POINTER TO StrDesc;
    ObjDesc = RECORD
      dsc, next: Object;
      typ: Struct;
      a0, a1: LONGINT;
      a2: INTEGER;
      mode: SHORTINT;
      marked: BOOLEAN;
      name: ARRAY 32 OF CHAR;
    END ;

    StrDesc = RECORD
      form, n, mno, ref: INTEGER;
      size, adr: LONGINT;
      BaseTyp: Struct;
      link, strobj: Object;
    END ;

    Item = RECORD
      mode, lev: INTEGER;
      a0, a1, a2: LONGINT;
      typ: Struct;
```

```
          obj: Object;
      END ;
  VAR topScope: Object;
      undftyp, bytetyp, booltyp, chartyp, sinttyp, inttyp, linttyp,
          realtyp, lrltyp,
      settyp, stringtyp, niltyp, notyp: Struct;
      nofGmod: INTEGER;
      GlbMod: ARRAY 24 OF Object;

  PROCEDURE Init;
  PROCEDURE Close;
  PROCEDURE FindImport (mod: Object; VAR res: Object);
  PROCEDURE Find (VAR res: Object; VAR level: INTEGER);
  PROCEDURE FindField (typ: Struct; VAR res: Object);
  PROCEDURE Insert (VAR name: ARRAY OF CHAR;
          VAR res: Object);
  PROCEDURE OpenScope (level: INTEGER);
  PROCEDURE CloseScope;
  PROCEDURE Import (VAR name, self, FileName: ARRAY
      OF CHAR);
  PROCEDURE Export (VAR name, FileName:
      ARRAY OF CHAR;
      VAR newSF: BOOLEAN; VAR key: LONGINT);
  END OCT.
```

Before embarking on a presentation of the compiler's main module, the parser, an overview of its remaining modules is given in the form of their interfaces. The reader is invited to refer to them when studying the parser.

Scanner interface

The interface of the scanner (OCS) is simple; its chief constituent is procedure *Get*. Each call yields the next symbol from the source text, identified by an integer. Global variables represent attributes of the read symbol in certain cases. If a number was read, *numtyp* indicates its type, and *intval, realval* or *lrlval* specify the numeric value. If an identifier or a string was read, *name* holds the ASCII values of the characters read.

Procedure *Mark* serves to generate a diagnostic output indicating an error number and the scanner's current position in the source text. The procedure is located in the scanner, because only the scanner has access to its current position. *Mark* is called from all other modules.

```
  DEFINITION OCS; (*Scanner*)
  IMPORT Texts;
  VAR numtyp: INTEGER;
      intval: LONGINT;
```

```
                realval: REAL;
                lrlval: LONGREAL;
                scanerr: BOOLEAN;
                name: ARRAY 128 OF CHAR;

            PROCEDURE Mark (n: INTEGER);
            PROCEDURE Get (VAR sym: INTEGER);
            PROCEDURE Init (source: Texts.Text; pos: LONGINT);
        END OCS.
```

Code selection
interface

Module OCE contains the procedures for code selection and type consistency checking for expressions. The names of these procedures clearly indicate the respective constructs for which code is to be selected; a few additional explanations may nevertheless be helpful.

SetIntType is called to identify the exact numeric type of an item denoting a constant; the type depends on the value's magnitude. *TypeTest* is called to process a type test or a type guard. *Set0* constructs a singleton set item consisting of the element specified by the second parameter y, and *Set1* constructs a set with elements y to z. *MOp* and *Op* process constituents of expressions with monadic and dyadic operators respectively. And finally, *StPar1*, *StPar2*, *StPar3*, and *StFct* process calls of standard procedures and functions generating in-line code.

```
    DEFINITION OCE;
        IMPORT OCT;
        VAR inxchk: BOOLEAN;

        PROCEDURE SetIntType (VAR x: OCT.Item);
        PROCEDURE AssReal (VAR x: OCT.Item; y: REAL);
        PROCEDURE AssLReal (VAR x: OCT.Item; y: LONGREAL);
        PROCEDURE Index (VAR x, y: OCT.Item);
        PROCEDURE Field (VAR x: OCT.Item; y: OCT.Object);
        PROCEDURE DeRef (VAR x: OCT.Item);
        PROCEDURE TypTest (VAR x, y: OCT.Item;
            test: BOOLEAN);
        PROCEDURE In (VAR x, y: OCT.Item);
        PROCEDURE Set0 (VAR x, y: OCT.Item);
        PROCEDURE Set1 (VAR x, y, z: OCT.Item);
        PROCEDURE MOp (op: INTEGER; VAR x: OCT.Item);
        PROCEDURE Op (op: INTEGER; VAR x, y: OCT.Item);
        PROCEDURE StPar1 (VAR x: OCT.Item; fctno: INTEGER);
        PROCEDURE StPar2 (VAR p, x: OCT.Item; fctno: INTEGER);
        PROCEDURE StPar3 (VAR p, x: OCT.Item; fctno: INTEGER);
```

```
      PROCEDURE StFct (VAR p: OCT.Item;
          fctno, parno: INTEGER);
   END OCE.
```

Procedures for processing statements are contained in module OCH. Assignments and procedure calls are processed by procedures *Assign, PrepCall, Call* and *Param*. Procedures *Enter, Result* and *Return* generate the code at the beginning and the end of procedure bodies.

If, while, repeat and loop statements involve branches around the code of their constituents. Procedures FJ (forward jump), CFJ (conditional forward jump), BJ (backward jump), CBJ (conditional backward jump) and LFJ (long forward jump) serve to issue such branches. Finally, *CaseIn* and *CaseOut* generate code for case statements. *CaseIn* emits an indexed branch instruction using an address table generated by *CaseOut*.

```
      DEFINITION OCH;
         IMPORT OCT;
         TYPE LabelRange = RECORD low, high, label: INTEGER
            END ;

         PROCEDURE Trap (n: INTEGER);
         PROCEDURE CompareParLists (x, y: OCT.Object);
         PROCEDURE Assign (VAR x, y: OCT.Item;
            param: BOOLEAN);
         PROCEDURE FJ (VAR loc: INTEGER);
         PROCEDURE CFJ (VAR x: OCT.Item; VAR loc: INTEGER);
         PROCEDURE BJ (loc: INTEGER);
         PROCEDURE CBJ (VAR x: OCT.Item; loc: INTEGER);
         PROCEDURE LFJ (VAR loc: INTEGER);
         PROCEDURE PrepCall (VAR x: OCT.Item;
            VAR fpar: OCT.Object);
         PROCEDURE Param (VAR ap: OCT.Item; f: OCT.Object);
         PROCEDURE Call (VAR x: OCT.Item);
         PROCEDURE Enter (mode: SHORTINT; pno: LONGINT;
            VAR L: INTEGER);
         PROCEDURE CopyDynArray (adr: LONGINT;
            typ: OCT.Struct);
         PROCEDURE Result (VAR x: OCT.Item; typ: OCT.Struct);
         PROCEDURE Return (mode: INTEGER; psize: LONGINT);
         PROCEDURE CaseIn (VAR x: OCT.Item;
            VAR L0, L1: INTEGER);
         PROCEDURE CaseOut (L0, L1, L2, L3, n: INTEGER;
            VAR tab: ARRAY OF LabelRange);
      END OCH.
```

12.4 **The parser**

The main module, *Compiler*, constitutes the parser. Its single command *Compile* – at the end of the program listing – identifies the source text according to the Oberon command conventions. It then calls procedure *CompilationUnit* with the identified source text as parameter. The command forms are

Compiler.Compile *	The source text is contained in the marked viewer.
Compiler.Compile ↑	The most recent selection identifies the name of the source file.
Compiler.Compile @	The most recent selection identifies the beginning of the source text.
Compiler.Compile f0 f1 . . . ~	f0, f1, . . . are the names of source files.

Compiler options

Note that file names and the characters * ↑ and @ may be followed by an option specification /s, /x, /t. Option s enables the compiler to overwrite an existing symbol file, thereby invalidating clients. Option x suppresses index checks, and option t suppresses type guards.

Recursive descent

The parser is designed according to the proven method of top-down, recursive descent parsing with a look-ahead of a single symbol. The last symbol read is represented by the global variable *sym*. Syntactic entities are mirrored by procedures of the same name. Their goal is to recognize the specified construct in the source text. The start symbol and corresponding procedure is *CompilationUnit*. The principal parser procedures are shown in Figure 12.6, which also exhibits their calling hierarchy. Loops in the diagram indicate recursion in the syntactic definition. (Procedure *qualident* is omitted; it is called from many other procedures.)

Lookahead violations

The rule of parsing strictly based on a single-symbol look-ahead and without reference to context is violated in three places. The prominent violation occurs in statements. If the first symbol of a statement is an identifier, the decision as to whether an assignment or a procedure call is to be recognized is based on contextual information, namely the mode of the object denoted by the identifier. The second violation occurs in *qualident*; if the identifier x preceding the period denotes a module, it is recognized together with the subsequent identifier as a qualified identifier. Otherwise, x supposedly denotes a record variable. The third violation is made in procedure *selector*; if an identifier is followed by a left parenthesis, the decision of whether a procedure call or a type guard is to be recognized is again made on the basis of contextual information, namely the mode of the identified object.

A fairly large part of the program is devoted to the discovery of errors. They should not only be properly diagnosed – a much more

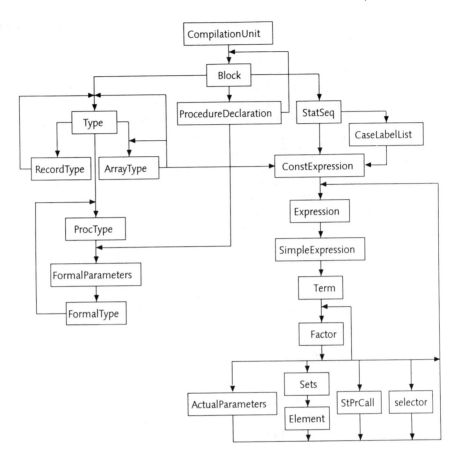

Figure 12.6 Parser procedure hierarchy.

<table>
<tr><td>**Error
diagnostic
and
recovery**</td><td>difficult requirement is that the parsing process should continue on the basis of a good guess about the structure that the text should most likely have. The parsing process must continue with some assumption and possibly after skipping a short piece of the source text. Hence this aspect of the parser is mostly based on heuristics. Incorrect assumptions about the nature of a syntactic error lead to secondary error diagnostics. There is no way to avoid them. A reasonably good result is obtained by the fact that procedure *OCS.Mark* inhibits an error report if it lies less than 10 characters ahead of the last one. Also, the language Oberon is designed with the property that most large constructs begin with a unique symbol, such as IF, WHILE, CASE or RECORD. These symbols</td></tr>
</table>

facilitate the recovery of the parsing process in the erroneous text. More problematic are open constructs that neither begin nor end with key symbols, such as types, factors and expressions. Relying on heuristics, the source text is skipped up to the first occurrence of a symbol that may begin a construct that follows the one being parsed. The scheme employed may not be the best possible, but it yields quite acceptable results and keeps the amount of program devoted to the handling of erroneous texts within justifiable bounds.

Type checking

Whereas the parser delegates type consistency checking and code generation to procedures mainly encapsulated in modules OCE and OCH, the processing of declarations is mostly handled by the routines that parse. Thereby an unjustifiably large number of very short procedures is avoided. However, the strict target-computer independence of the parser is lost. Information about variable allocation strategy including alignment and about the sizes of basic types is used in the parser module. Whereas the former violation is harmless, because the allocation strategy is hardly controversial, the latter case constitutes a genuine target dependence embodied in a number of explicitly declared constants. Mostly these constants are contained in the respective type definitions, represented by records of type *Struct* initialized by OCT. The following procedures allocate objects and generate elements of the symbol table:

Block	Object(Con), Object(Typ), Object(Var)
ProcedureDeclaration	Object(xProc)
FormalParameters	Object(Var), Object(Ind)
OCT.Import	Object(Mod)
RecordType	Object(Fld), Struct(Record)
ArrayType	Struct(Array)
ProcType	Struct(ProcTyp)
Type	Struct(Pointer)
FormalType	Struct(DynArr)

Procedure variants

The language Oberon proper specifies only one kind of procedure. This compiler provides some variants, partly for reasons provided by the computer's instruction set. The compiler requests a specifier in the form of a single character following the symbol PROCEDURE for these variants, similar to the arrow (↑) in the case of forward declarations. The variants are denoted by different modes in their descriptors:

(1) Procedures that are to be assigned to variables must be marked with an asterisk (unless they are exported). This causes the compiler to treat them like external procedures (RXP at the end), such that they can be called uniformly with a CXPD instruction. Here mode = XProc.

(2) The specifier '−' indicates that the procedure is called by an SVC instruction. (Note that supervisor calls are exclusively handled by the kernel. Hence the Oberon text declares a procedure heading only, followed by an empty body.) Here mode = CProc.

(3) The specifier '+' indicates that the parameterless procedure is to be used as an interrupt handler. Its last instruction is RETT. Here mode = IProc.

Forward references

An inherently difficult subject is the treatment of forward references in a single-pass compiler. In Oberon, there are two such cases:

to procedures

(1) Forward declarations of procedures. They are explicitly specified by ↑ following the symbol PROCEDURE. The compiler processes the heading in the normal way and as an external procedure, assuming its body to be missing. When later in the text the full declaration is encountered, it must be properly associated with the already existing entry in the symbol table. Therefore, for every procedure declaration, the table is first searched. If the given identifier is found and denotes a procedure (with address 0), the association is established and the parameter lists are compared by procedure *OCH.CompareParameters*. Otherwise, a multiple definition of the same identifier is present.

to types

(2) Forward declarations of pointer types present a more difficult case, because there exists no explicit indication that a forward reference is present and that no undefined identifier should be diagnosed. If in a pointer declaration the base type (to which the pointer is bound) is not found in the symbol table, a forward reference is therefore assumed automatically. Entries for both the pointer type and its base type are generated (see procedure *Type*). The premature entry of type *Object* containing the name of the base type and with mode = *Undef* is connected with the pointer type through its *link* field. When later in the text a declaration of a record or an array type is encountered with the same identifier, the forward entry is recognized and the proper link is established (see procedure *Block*).

For both cases, the compiler checks for undefined forward references when the current declaration scope is closed. For procedures, this occurs at the end of compilation (procedure *OCC.OutCode*), because only global procedures can be declared forward. For pointer types, the check is performed at the end of the declaration sequence; procedure *Block* invokes *CheckUndefPointerTypes*.

With statement

A with statement

WITH x: T1 DO StatSeq END

states that within the statement sequence, x is to be considered to be
of type T1, which is presumably some extension of the type T0 of which
x is declared. Compilation of the with statement results in a regional
type guard that verifies this assertion, that is, whether x indeed refers
to an object of type T1. The with statement represents the singular case
where a symbol table entry – the type of x – is modified during
compilation. When the end of the with statement is reached, the change
must be reverted.

```
MODULE Compiler; (*NW 7.6.87 / 16.3.91*)
  IMPORT Texts, Files, TextFrames, Viewers, Oberon, OCS, OCT, OCC, OCE, OCH;

  CONST NofCases = 128; MaxEntry = 64; ModNameLen = 20;
    RecDescSize = 8; AdrSize = 4; ProcSize = 4; PtrSize = 4;
    XParOrg = 12; LParOrg = 8; LDataSize = 2000H;

    (*symbol values*)
      times = 1; slash = 2; div = 3; mod = 4;
      and = 5; plus = 6; minus = 7; or = 8; eql = 9;
      neq = 10; lss = 11; leq = 12; gtr = 13; geq = 14;
      in = 15; is = 16; arrow = 17; period = 18; comma = 19;
      colon = 20; upto = 21; rparen = 22; rbrak = 23; rbrace = 24;
      of = 25; then = 26; do = 27; to = 28; lparen = 29;
      lbrak = 30; lbrace = 31; not = 32; becomes = 33; number = 34;
      nil = 35; string = 36; ident = 37; semicolon = 38; bar = 39;
      end = 40; else = 41; elsif = 42; until = 43; if = 44;
      case = 45; while = 46; repeat = 47; loop = 48; with = 49;
      exit = 50; return = 51; array = 52; record = 53; pointer = 54;
      begin = 55; const = 56; type = 57; var = 58; procedure = 59;
      import = 60; module = 61;

    (*object and item modes*)
      Var = 1; Ind = 3; Con = 8; Fld = 12; Typ = 13;
      LProc = 14; XProc = 15; SProc = 16; CProc = 17; IProc = 18; Mod = 19;

    (*structure forms*)
      Undef = 0; Pointer = 13; ProcTyp = 14; Array = 15; DynArr = 16; Record = 17;
      intSet = {4 .. 6}; labeltyps = {3 .. 6};

  VAR W: Texts.Writer;
      sym, entno: INTEGER;
      newSF:    BOOLEAN;
      LoopLevel, ExitNo: INTEGER;
      LoopExit: ARRAY 16 OF INTEGER;

  PROCEDURE ↑ Type(VAR typ: OCT.Struct);
  PROCEDURE ↑ FormalType(VAR typ: OCT.Struct);
  PROCEDURE ↑ Expression(VAR x: OCT.Item);
  PROCEDURE ↑ Block(VAR dsize: LONGINT);

  PROCEDURE CheckSym(s: INTEGER);
  BEGIN
    IF sym = s THEN OCS.Get(sym) ELSE OCS.Mark(s) END
```

END CheckSym;

```
PROCEDURE qualident(VAR x: OCT.Item);
   VAR mnolev: INTEGER; obj: OCT.Object;
BEGIN (*sym = ident*)
   OCT.Find(obj, mnolev); OCS.Get(sym);
   IF (sym = period) & (obj # NIL) & (obj.mode = Mod) THEN
      OCS.Get(sym); mnolev := SHORT(-obj.a0);
      IF sym = ident THEN
         OCT.FindImport(obj, obj); OCS.Get(sym)
      ELSE OCS.Mark(10); obj := NIL
      END
   END ;
   x.lev := mnolev; x.obj := obj;
   IF obj # NIL THEN
      x.mode := obj.mode; x.typ := obj.typ; x.a0 := obj.a0; x.a1 := obj.a1
   ELSE OCS.Mark(0); x.mode := Var;
      x.typ := OCT.undftyp; x.a0 := 0; x.obj := NIL
   END
END qualident;


PROCEDURE ConstExpression(VAR x: OCT.Item);
BEGIN Expression(x);
   IF x.mode # Con THEN
      OCS.Mark(50); x.mode := Con; x.typ := OCT.inttyp; x.a0 := 1
   END
END ConstExpression;


PROCEDURE NewStr(form: INTEGER): OCT.Struct;
   VAR typ: OCT.Struct;
BEGIN NEW(typ);
   typ.form := form; typ.mno := 0; typ.size := 4; typ.ref := 0;
   typ.BaseTyp := OCT.undftyp; typ.strobj := NIL; RETURN typ
END NewStr;


PROCEDURE CheckMark(VAR mk: BOOLEAN);
BEGIN OCS.Get(sym);
   IF sym = times THEN
      IF OCC.level = 0 THEN mk := TRUE ELSE mk := FALSE; OCS.Mark(47) END ;
      OCS.Get(sym)
   ELSE mk := FALSE
   END
END CheckMark;


PROCEDURE CheckUndefPointerTypes;
   VAR obj: OCT.Object;
BEGIN obj := OCT.topScope.next;
   WHILE obj # NIL DO
      IF obj.mode = Undef THEN OCS.Mark(48) END ;
      obj := obj.next
   END
END CheckUndefPointerTypes;


PROCEDURE RecordType(VAR typ: OCT.Struct);
   VAR adr, size: LONGINT;
      fld, fld0, fld1: OCT.Object;
```

```
            ftyp, btyp: OCT.Struct;
            base: OCT.Item;

   BEGIN adr := 0; typ := NewStr(Record); typ.BaseTyp := NIL; typ.n := 0;
      IF sym = lparen THEN
         OCS.Get(sym); (*record extension*)
         IF sym = ident THEN
            qualident(base);
            IF (base.mode = Typ) & (base.typ.form = Record) THEN
               typ.BaseTyp := base.typ; typ.n := base.typ.n + 1; adr := base.typ.size
            ELSE OCS.Mark(52)
            END
         ELSE OCS.Mark(10)
         END ;
         CheckSym(rparen)
      END ;
      OCT.OpenScope(0); fld := NIL; fld1 := OCT.topScope;
      LOOP
         IF sym = ident THEN
            LOOP
               IF sym = ident THEN
                  IF typ.BaseTyp # NIL THEN
                     OCT.FindField(typ.BaseTyp, fld0);
                     IF fld0 # NIL THEN OCS.Mark(1) END
                  END ;
                  OCT.Insert(OCS.name, fld); CheckMark(fld.marked); fld.mode := Fld
               ELSE OCS.Mark(10)
               END ;
               IF sym = comma THEN OCS.Get(sym)
               ELSIF sym = ident THEN OCS.Mark(19)
               ELSE EXIT
               END
            END ;
            CheckSym(colon); Type(ftyp); size := ftyp.size; btyp := ftyp;
            WHILE btyp.form = Array DO btyp := btyp.BaseTyp END ;
            IF btyp.size >= 4 THEN INC(adr, (−adr) MOD 4)
            ELSIF btyp.size = 2 THEN INC(adr, adr MOD 2)
            END ;
            WHILE fld1.next # NIL DO
               fld1 := fld1.next; fld1.typ := ftyp; fld1.a0 := adr; INC(adr, size)
            END
         END ;
         IF sym = semicolon THEN OCS.Get(sym)
         ELSIF sym = ident THEN OCS.Mark(38)
         ELSE EXIT
         END
      END ;
      typ.size := (−adr) MOD 4 + adr; typ.link := OCT.topScope.next;
      CheckUndefPointerTypes; OCT.CloseScope
   END RecordType;


   PROCEDURE ArrayType(VAR typ: OCT.Struct);
      VAR x: OCT.Item; f, n: INTEGER;
   BEGIN typ := NewStr(Array); ConstExpression(x); f := x.typ.form;
      IF f IN intSet THEN
         IF (x.a0 > 0) & (x.a0 <= MAX(INTEGER)) THEN n := SHORT(x.a0)
         ELSE n := 1; OCS.Mark(63)
         END
```

```
        ELSE OCS.Mark(51); n := 1
        END ;
        typ.n := n; OCC.AllocBounds(0, n-1, typ.adr);
        IF sym = of THEN
            OCS.Get(sym); Type(typ.BaseTyp)
        ELSIF sym = comma THEN
            OCS.Get(sym); ArrayType(typ.BaseTyp)
        ELSE OCS.Mark(34)
        END ;
        typ.size := n * typ.BaseTyp.size
    END ArrayType;


    PROCEDURE FormalParameters(VAR resTyp: OCT.Struct; VAR psize: LONGINT);
        VAR mode: SHORTINT;
            adr, size: LONGINT; res: OCT.Item;
            par, par1: OCT.Object; typ: OCT.Struct;
        BEGIN par1 := OCT.topScope; adr := 0;
            IF (sym = ident) OR (sym = var) THEN
                LOOP
                    IF sym = var THEN OCS.Get(sym); mode := Ind ELSE mode := Var END ;
                    LOOP
                        IF sym = ident THEN
                            OCT.Insert(OCS.name, par); OCS.Get(sym); par.mode := mode
                        ELSE OCS.Mark(10)
                        END ;
                        IF sym = comma THEN OCS.Get(sym)
                        ELSIF sym = ident THEN OCS.Mark(19)
                        ELSIF sym = var THEN OCS.Mark(19); OCS.Get(sym)
                        ELSE EXIT
                        END
                    END ;
                    CheckSym(colon); FormalType(typ);
                    IF mode = Ind THEN (*VAR param*)
                        IF typ.form = Record THEN size := RecDescSize
                        ELSIF typ.form = DynArr THEN size := typ.size
                        ELSE size := AdrSize
                        END
                    ELSE size := (-typ.size) MOD 4 + typ.size
                    END ;
                    WHILE par1.next # NIL DO
                        par1 := par1.next; par1.typ := typ; DEC(adr, size); par1.a0 := adr
                    END ;
                    IF sym = semicolon THEN OCS.Get(sym)
                    ELSIF sym = ident THEN OCS.Mark(38)
                    ELSE EXIT
                    END
                END
            END ;
            psize := psize - adr; par := OCT.topScope.next;
            WHILE par # NIL DO INC(par.a0, psize); par := par.next END ;
            CheckSym(rparen);
            IF sym = colon THEN
                OCS.Get(sym); resTyp := OCT.undftyp;
                IF sym = ident THEN qualident(res);
                    IF res.mode = Typ THEN
                        IF res.typ.form <= ProcTyp THEN resTyp := res.typ ELSE OCS.Mark(54) END
                    ELSE OCS.Mark(52)
                    END
```

```
            ELSE OCS.Mark(10)
            END
          ELSE resTyp := OCT.notyp
        END
      END FormalParameters;


      PROCEDURE ProcType(VAR typ: OCT.Struct);
        VAR psize: LONGINT;
      BEGIN typ := NewStr(ProcTyp); typ.size := ProcSize;
        IF sym = lparen THEN
            OCS.Get(sym); OCT.OpenScope(OCC.level); psize := XParOrg;
            FormalParameters(typ.BaseTyp, psize); typ.link := OCT.topScope.next;
            OCT.CloseScope
        ELSE typ.BaseTyp := OCT.notyp; typ.link := NIL
        END
      END ProcType;


      PROCEDURE HasPtr(typ: OCT.Struct): BOOLEAN;
        VAR fld: OCT.Object;
      BEGIN
        IF typ.form = Pointer THEN RETURN TRUE
        ELSIF typ.form = Array THEN RETURN HasPtr(typ.BaseTyp)
        ELSIF typ.form = Record THEN
            IF (typ.BaseTyp # NIL) & HasPtr(typ.BaseTyp) THEN RETURN TRUE END ;
            fld := typ.link;
            WHILE fld # NIL DO
              IF (fld.name = "") OR HasPtr(fld.typ) THEN RETURN TRUE END ;
              fld := fld.next
            END
        END ;
        RETURN FALSE
      END HasPtr;


      PROCEDURE SetPtrBase(ptyp, btyp: OCT.Struct);
      BEGIN
        IF (btyp.form = Record) OR (btyp.form = Array) & ~ HasPtr(btyp.BaseTyp) THEN
            ptyp.BaseTyp := btyp
        ELSE ptyp.BaseTyp := OCT.undftyp; OCS.Mark(57)
        END
      END SetPtrBase;


      PROCEDURE Type(VAR typ: OCT.Struct);
        VAR lev: INTEGER; obj: OCT.Object; x: OCT.Item;
      BEGIN typ := OCT.undftyp;
        IF sym < lparen THEN OCS.Mark(12);
            REPEAT OCS.Get(sym) UNTIL sym >= lparen
        END ;
        IF sym = ident THEN qualident(x);
            IF x.mode = Typ THEN typ := x.typ;
                IF typ = OCT.notyp THEN OCS.Mark(58) END
            ELSE OCS.Mark(52)
            END
        ELSIF sym = array THEN
            OCS.Get(sym); ArrayType(typ)
        ELSIF sym = record THEN
            OCS.Get(sym); RecordType(typ); OCC.AllocTypDesc(typ); CheckSym(end)
        ELSIF sym = pointer THEN
```

```
      OCS.Get(sym); typ := NewStr(Pointer); typ.link := NIL; typ.size := PtrSize;
      CheckSym(to);
      IF sym = ident THEN OCT.Find(obj, lev);
        IF obj = NIL THEN (*forward ref*)
          OCT.Insert(OCS.name, obj); typ.BaseTyp := OCT.undftyp;
          obj.mode := Undef; obj.typ := typ; OCS.Get(sym)
        ELSE qualident(x);
          IF x.mode = Typ THEN SetPtrBase(typ, x.typ)
          ELSE typ.BaseTyp := OCT.undftyp; OCS.Mark(52)
          END
        END
      ELSE Type(x.typ); SetPtrBase(typ, x.typ)
      END
    ELSIF sym = procedure THEN
      OCS.Get(sym); ProcType(typ)
    ELSE OCS.Mark(12)
    END ;
    IF (sym < semicolon) OR (else < sym) THEN OCS.Mark(15);
      WHILE (sym < ident) OR (else < sym) & (sym < begin) DO
        OCS.Get(sym)
      END
    END
END Type;


PROCEDURE FormalType(VAR typ: OCT.Struct);
  VAR x: OCT.Item; typ0: OCT.Struct; a, s: LONGINT;
BEGIN typ := OCT.undftyp; a := 0;
  WHILE sym = array DO
    OCS.Get(sym); CheckSym(of); INC(a, 4)
  END ;
  IF sym = ident THEN qualident(x);
    IF x.mode = Typ THEN typ := x.typ;
      IF typ = OCT.notyp THEN OCS.Mark(58) END
    ELSE OCS.Mark(52)
    END
  ELSIF sym = procedure THEN OCS.Get(sym); ProcType(typ)
  ELSE OCS.Mark(10)
  END ;
  s := a + 8;
  WHILE a > 0 DO
    typ0 := NewStr(DynArr); typ0.BaseTyp := typ;
    typ0.size := s−a; typ0.adr := typ0.size−4; typ0.mno := 0; typ := typ0; DEC(a, 4)
  END
END FormalType;


PROCEDURE selector(VAR x: OCT.Item);
  VAR fld: OCT.Object; y: OCT.Item;
BEGIN
  LOOP
    IF sym = lbrak THEN OCS.Get(sym);
      LOOP
        IF (x.typ # NIL) & (x.typ.form = Pointer) THEN OCE.DeRef(x) END ;
        Expression(y); OCE.Index(x, y);
        IF sym = comma THEN OCS.Get(sym) ELSE EXIT END
      END ;
      CheckSym(rbrak)
    ELSIF sym = period THEN OCS.Get(sym);
      IF sym = ident THEN
```

```
                    IF x.typ # NIL THEN
                        IF x.typ.form = Pointer THEN OCE.DeRef(x) END ;
                        IF x.typ.form = Record THEN
                            OCT.FindField(x.typ, fld); OCE.Field(x, fld)
                        ELSE OCS.Mark(53)
                        END
                    ELSE OCS.Mark(52)
                    END ;
                    OCS.Get(sym)
                ELSE OCS.Mark(10)
                END
            ELSIF sym = arrow THEN
                OCS.Get(sym); OCE.DeRef(x)
            ELSIF (sym = lparen) & (x.mode < Typ) & (x.typ.form # ProcTyp) THEN
                OCS.Get(sym);
                IF sym = ident THEN
                    qualident(y);
                    IF y.mode = Typ THEN OCE.TypTest(x, y, FALSE)
                    ELSE OCS.Mark(52)
                    END
                ELSE OCS.Mark(10)
                END ;
                CheckSym(rparen)
            ELSE EXIT
            END
        END
    END selector;


    PROCEDURE IsParam(obj: OCT.Object): BOOLEAN;
    BEGIN RETURN (obj # NIL) & (obj.mode <= Ind) & (obj.a0 > 0)
    END IsParam;


    PROCEDURE ActualParameters(VAR x: OCT.Item; fpar: OCT.Object);
        VAR apar: OCT.Item; R: SET;
    BEGIN
        IF sym # rparen THEN
            R := OCC.RegSet;
            LOOP Expression(apar);
                IF IsParam(fpar) THEN
                    OCH.Param(apar, fpar); fpar := fpar.next
                ELSE OCS.Mark(64)
                END ;
                OCC.FreeRegs(R);
                IF sym = comma THEN OCS.Get(sym)
                ELSIF (lparen <= sym) & (sym <= ident) THEN OCS.Mark(19)
                ELSE EXIT
                END
            END
        END ;
        IF IsParam(fpar) THEN OCS.Mark(65) END
    END ActualParameters;


    PROCEDURE StandProcCall(VAR x: OCT.Item);
        VAR y: OCT.Item; m, n: INTEGER;
    BEGIN m := SHORT(x.a0); n := 0;
        IF sym = lparen THEN OCS.Get(sym);
            IF sym # rparen THEN
```

```
        LOOP
          IF n = 0 THEN Expression(x); OCE.StPar1(x, m); n := 1
          ELSIF n = 1 THEN Expression(y); OCE.StPar2(x, y, m); n := 2
          ELSIF n = 2 THEN Expression(y); OCE.StPar3(x, y, m); n := 3
          ELSE OCS.Mark(64); Expression(y)
          END ;
          IF sym = comma THEN OCS.Get(sym)
          ELSIF (lparen <= sym) & (sym <= ident) THEN OCS.Mark(19)
          ELSE EXIT
          END
        END ;
        CheckSym(rparen)
      ELSE OCS.Get(sym)
      END ;
      OCE.StFct(x, m, n)
    ELSE OCS.Mark(29)
    END
END StandProcCall;


PROCEDURE Element(VAR x: OCT.Item);
    VAR e1, e2: OCT.Item;
BEGIN Expression(e1);
    IF sym = upto THEN
        OCS.Get(sym); Expression(e2); OCE.Set1(x, e1, e2)
    ELSE OCE.Set0(x, e1)
    END ;
END Element;


PROCEDURE Sets(VAR x: OCT.Item);
    VAR y: OCT.Item;
BEGIN x.typ := OCT.settyp; y.typ := OCT.settyp;
    IF sym # rbrace THEN
        Element(x);
        LOOP
            IF sym = comma THEN OCS.Get(sym)
            ELSIF (lparen <= sym) & (sym <= ident) THEN OCS.Mark(19)
            ELSE EXIT
            END ;
            Element(y); OCE.Op(plus, x, y) (*x := x+y*)
        END
    ELSE x.mode := Con; x.a0 := 0
    END ;
    CheckSym(rbrace)
END Sets;


PROCEDURE Factor(VAR x: OCT.Item);
    VAR fpar: OCT.Object; gR, fR: SET;
BEGIN
    IF sym < lparen THEN OCS.Mark(13);
        REPEAT OCS.Get(sym) UNTIL sym >= lparen
    END ;
    IF sym = ident THEN
        qualident(x); selector(x);
        IF x.mode = SProc THEN StandProcCall(x)
        ELSIF sym = lparen THEN
            OCS.Get(sym); OCH.PrepCall(x, fpar);
            OCC.SaveRegisters(gR, fR, x); ActualParameters(x, fpar);
```

```
            OCH.Call(x); OCC.RestoreRegisters(gR, fR, x);
            CheckSym(rparen)
        END
    ELSIF sym = number THEN
        OCS.Get(sym); x.mode := Con;
        CASE OCS.numtyp OF
            1: x.typ := OCT.chartyp; x.a0 := OCS.intval
          | 2: x.a0 := OCS.intval; OCE.SetIntType(x)
          | 3: x.typ := OCT.realtyp; OCE.AssReal(x, OCS.realval)
          | 4: x.typ := OCT.lrltyp; OCE.AssLReal(x, OCS.lrlval)
        END
    ELSIF sym = string THEN
        x.typ := OCT.stringtyp; x.mode := Con;
        OCC.AllocString(OCS.name, x); OCS.Get(sym)
    ELSIF sym = nil THEN
        OCS.Get(sym); x.typ := OCT.niltyp; x.mode := Con; x.a0 := 0
    ELSIF sym = lparen THEN
        OCS.Get(sym); Expression(x); CheckSym(rparen)
    ELSIF sym = lbrak THEN
        OCS.Get(sym); OCS.Mark(29); Expression(x); CheckSym(rparen)
    ELSIF sym = lbrace THEN OCS.Get(sym); Sets(x)
    ELSIF sym = not THEN
        OCS.Get(sym); Factor(x); OCE.MOp(not, x)
    ELSE OCS.Mark(13); OCS.Get(sym); x.typ := OCT.undftyp; x.mode := Var; x.a0 := 0
    END
END Factor;


PROCEDURE Term(VAR x: OCT.Item);
    VAR y: OCT.Item; mulop: INTEGER;
BEGIN Factor(x);
    WHILE (times <= sym) & (sym <= and) DO
        mulop := sym; OCS.Get(sym);
        IF mulop = and THEN OCE.MOp(and, x) END ;
        Factor(y); OCE.Op(mulop, x, y)
    END
END Term;


PROCEDURE SimpleExpression(VAR x: OCT.Item);
    VAR y: OCT.Item; addop: INTEGER;
BEGIN
    IF sym = minus THEN OCS.Get(sym); Term(x); OCE.MOp(minus, x)
    ELSIF sym = plus THEN OCS.Get(sym); Term(x); OCE.MOp(plus, x)
    ELSE Term(x)
    END ;
    WHILE (plus <= sym) & (sym <= or) DO
        addop := sym; OCS.Get(sym);
        IF addop = or THEN OCE.MOp(or, x) END ;
        Term(y); OCE.Op(addop, x, y)
    END
END SimpleExpression;


PROCEDURE Expression(VAR x: OCT.Item);
    VAR y: OCT.Item; relation: INTEGER;
BEGIN SimpleExpression(x);
    IF (eql <= sym) & (sym <= geq) THEN
        relation := sym; OCS.Get(sym);
        IF x.typ = OCT.booltyp THEN OCE.MOp(relation, x) END ;
```

```
        SimpleExpression(y); OCE.Op(relation, x, y)
      ELSIF sym = in THEN
        OCS.Get(sym); SimpleExpression(y); OCE.In(x, y)
      ELSIF sym = is THEN
        IF x.mode >= Typ THEN OCS.Mark(112) END ;
        OCS.Get(sym);
        IF sym = ident THEN
          qualident(y);
          IF y.mode = Typ THEN OCE.TypTest(x, y, TRUE) ELSE OCS.Mark(52) END
        ELSE OCS.Mark(10)
        END
      END
  END Expression;


  PROCEDURE ProcedureDeclaration;
    VAR proc, proc1, par: OCT.Object;
      L1: INTEGER;
      mode: SHORTINT; body: BOOLEAN;
      psize, dsize: LONGINT;
  BEGIN dsize := 0; proc := NIL; body := TRUE;
    IF (sym # ident) & (OCC.level = 0) THEN
      IF sym = times THEN mode := XProc
      ELSIF sym = arrow THEN (*forward*) mode := XProc; body := FALSE
      ELSIF sym = plus THEN mode := IProc
      ELSIF sym = minus THEN mode := CProc; body := FALSE
      ELSE mode := LProc; OCS.Mark(10)
      END ;
      OCS.Get(sym)
    ELSE mode := LProc
    END ;
    IF sym = ident THEN
      IF OCC.level = 0 THEN OCT.Find(proc1, L1) ELSE proc1 := NIL END;
      IF (proc1 # NIL) & (proc1.mode = XProc) & (OCC.Entry(SHORT(proc1.a0)) = 0)
        THEN (*there exists a corresponding forward declaration*)
        IF mode = LProc THEN mode := XProc END ;
        NEW(proc); CheckMark(proc.marked)
      ELSE
        IF proc1 # NIL THEN OCS.Mark(1); proc1 := NIL END ;
        OCT.Insert(OCS.name, proc); CheckMark(proc.marked);
        IF proc.marked & (mode = LProc) THEN mode := XProc END ;
        IF mode = LProc THEN proc.a0 := OCC.pc
        ELSIF mode # CProc THEN
          IF entno < MaxEntry THEN
            proc.a0 := entno; INC(entno) ELSE proc.a0 := 1; OCS.Mark(226)
          END
        END
      END ;
      proc.mode := mode; proc.typ := OCT.notyp; proc.dsc := NIL; proc.a1 := 0;
      INC(OCC.level); OCT.OpenScope(OCC.level);
      IF (mode = LProc) & (OCC.level = 1) THEN psize := LParOrg
      ELSE psize := XParOrg
      END ;
      IF sym = lparen THEN
        OCS.Get(sym); FormalParameters(proc.typ, psize);
        proc.dsc := OCT.topScope.next
      END ;
      IF proc1 # NIL THEN (*forward*)
        OCH.CompareParLists(proc.dsc, proc1.dsc);
```

```
                        IF proc.typ # proc1.typ THEN OCS.Mark(118) END ;
                        proc := proc1; proc.dsc := OCT.topScope.next
                    END ;
                    IF mode = CProc THEN
                        IF sym = number THEN proc.a0 := OCS.intval; OCS.Get(sym)
                        ELSE OCS.Mark(17)
                        END
                    END ;
                    IF body THEN
                        CheckSym(semicolon); OCT.topScope.typ := proc.typ;
                        OCT.topScope.a1 := mode*10000H + psize; (*for RETURN statements*)
                        OCH.Enter(mode, proc.a0, L1); par := proc.dsc;
                        WHILE par # NIL DO
                            (*code for dynamic array value parameters*)
                            IF (par.typ.form = DynArr) & (par.mode = Var) THEN
                                OCH.CopyDynArray(par.a0, par.typ)
                            END ;
                            par := par.next
                        END ;
                        Block(dsize); proc.dsc := OCT.topScope.next; (*update*)
                        IF proc.typ = OCT.notyp THEN OCH.Return(proc.mode, psize)
                        ELSE OCH.Trap(17)
                        END ;
                        IF dsize >= LDataSize THEN OCS.Mark(209); dsize := 0 END ;
                        OCC.FixupWith(L1, dsize); proc.a2 := OCC.pc;
                        IF sym = ident THEN
                            IF OCS.name # proc.name THEN OCS.Mark(4) END ;
                            OCS.Get(sym)
                        ELSE OCS.Mark(10)
                        END
                    END ;
                    DEC(OCC.level); OCT.CloseScope
                END
            END ProcedureDeclaration;


PROCEDURE CaseLabelList(LabelForm: INTEGER;
            VAR n: INTEGER; VAR tab: ARRAY OF OCH.LabelRange);
    VAR x, y: OCT.Item; i, f: INTEGER;
BEGIN
    IF ~(LabelForm IN labeltyps) THEN OCS.Mark(61) END ;
    LOOP ConstExpression(x); f := x.typ.form;
        IF f IN intSet THEN
            IF LabelForm < f THEN OCS.Mark(60) END
        ELSIF f # LabelForm THEN OCS.Mark(60)
        END ;
        IF sym = upto THEN
            OCS.Get(sym); ConstExpression(y);
            IF (y.typ.form # f) & ~((f IN intSet) & (y.typ.form IN intSet)) THEN
                OCS.Mark(60) END ;
            IF y.a0 < x.a0 THEN OCS.Mark(63); y.a0 := x.a0 END
        ELSE y := x
        END ;
        (*enter label range into ordered table*) i := n;
        IF i < NofCases THEN
            LOOP
                IF i = 0 THEN EXIT END ;
                IF tab[i-1].low <= y.a0 THEN
                    IF tab[i-1].high >= x.a0 THEN OCS.Mark(62) END ;
```

```
                    EXIT
                END ;
                tab[i] := tab[i-1]; DEC(i)
            END ;
            tab[i].low := SHORT(x.a0); tab[i].high := SHORT(y.a0);
            tab[i].label := OCC.pc; INC(n)
        ELSE OCS.Mark(213)
        END ;
        IF sym = comma THEN OCS.Get(sym)
        ELSIF (sym = number) OR (sym = ident) THEN OCS.Mark(19)
        ELSE EXIT
        END
    END
END CaseLabelList;


PROCEDURE StatSeq;
    VAR fpar: OCT.Object; xtyp: OCT.Struct;
        x, y: OCT.Item; L0, L1, ExitIndex: INTEGER;

    PROCEDURE CasePart;
        VAR x: OCT.Item; n, L0, L1, L2, L3: INTEGER;
            tab: ARRAY NofCases OF OCH.LabelRange;
    BEGIN n := 0; L3 := 0;
        Expression(x); OCH.CaseIn(x, L0, L1); OCC.FreeRegs({});
        CheckSym(of);
        LOOP
            IF sym < bar THEN
                CaseLabelList(x.typ.form, n, tab);
                CheckSym(colon); StatSeq; OCH.FJ(L3)
            END ;
            IF sym = bar THEN OCS.Get(sym) ELSE EXIT END
        END ;
        L2 := OCC.pc;
        IF sym = else THEN
            OCS.Get(sym); StatSeq; OCH.FJ(L3)
        ELSE OCH.Trap(16)
        END ;
        OCH.CaseOut(L0, L1, L2, L3, n, tab)
    END CasePart;

BEGIN
    LOOP
        IF sym < ident THEN OCS.Mark(14);
            REPEAT OCS.Get(sym) UNTIL sym >= ident
        END ;
        IF sym = ident THEN
            qualident(x); selector(x);
            IF sym = becomes THEN
                OCS.Get(sym); Expression(y); OCH.Assign(x, y, FALSE)
            ELSIF sym = eql THEN
                OCS.Mark(33); OCS.Get(sym); Expression(y); OCH.Assign(x, y, FALSE)
            ELSIF x.mode = SProc THEN
                StandProcCall(x);
                IF x.typ # OCT.notyp THEN OCS.Mark(55) END
            ELSE OCH.PrepCall(x, fpar);
                IF sym = lparen THEN
                    OCS.Get(sym); ActualParameters(x, fpar); CheckSym(rparen)
                ELSIF IsParam(fpar) THEN OCS.Mark(65)
```

```
                    END ;
                    OCH.Call(x);
                    IF x.typ # OCT.notyp THEN OCS.Mark(55) END
               END
          ELSIF sym = if THEN
               OCS.Get(sym); Expression(x); OCH.CFJ(x, L0); OCC.FreeRegs({});
               CheckSym(then); StatSeq; L1 := 0;
               WHILE sym = elsif DO
                    OCS.Get(sym); OCH.FJ(L1); OCC.FixLink(L0);
                    Expression(x); OCH.CFJ(x, L0); OCC.FreeRegs({});
                    CheckSym(then); StatSeq
               END ;
               IF sym = else THEN
                    OCS.Get(sym); OCH.FJ(L1); OCC.FixLink(L0); StatSeq
               ELSE OCC.FixLink(L0)
               END ;
               OCC.FixLink(L1); CheckSym(end)
          ELSIF sym = case THEN
               OCS.Get(sym); CasePart; CheckSym(end)
          ELSIF sym = while THEN
               OCS.Get(sym); L1 := OCC.pc;
               Expression(x); OCH.CFJ(x, L0); OCC.FreeRegs({});
               CheckSym(do); StatSeq; OCH.BJ(L1); OCC.FixLink(L0);
               CheckSym(end)
          ELSIF sym = repeat THEN
               OCS.Get(sym); L0 := OCC.pc; StatSeq;
               IF sym = until THEN
                    OCS.Get(sym); Expression(x); OCH.CBJ(x, L0)
               ELSE OCS.Mark(43)
               END
          ELSIF sym = loop THEN
               OCS.Get(sym); ExitIndex := ExitNo; INC(LoopLevel);
               L0 := OCC.pc; StatSeq; OCH.BJ(L0); DEC(LoopLevel);
               WHILE ExitNo > ExitIndex DO
                    DEC(ExitNo); OCC.fixup(LoopExit[ExitNo])
               END ;
               CheckSym(end)
          ELSIF sym = with THEN
               OCS.Get(sym); x.obj := NIL; xtyp := NIL;
               IF sym = ident THEN
                    qualident(x); CheckSym(colon);
                    IF sym = ident THEN qualident(y);
                         IF y.mode = Typ THEN
                              IF x.obj # NIL THEN
                                   xtyp := x.typ; OCE.TypTest(x, y, FALSE); x.obj.typ := x.typ
                              ELSE OCS.Mark(130)
                              END
                         ELSE OCS.Mark(52)
                         END
                    ELSE OCS.Mark(10)
                    END
               ELSE OCS.Mark(10)
               END ;
               CheckSym(do); OCC.FreeRegs({}); StatSeq; CheckSym(end);
               IF xtyp # NIL THEN x.obj.typ := xtyp END
          ELSIF sym = exit THEN
               OCS.Get(sym); OCH.FJ(L0);
               IF LoopLevel = 0 THEN OCS.Mark(45)
               ELSIF ExitNo < 16 THEN LoopExit[ExitNo] := L0; INC(ExitNo)
```

```
                    ELSE OCS.Mark(214)
                    END
                ELSIF sym = return THEN OCS.Get(sym);
                    IF OCC.level > 0 THEN
                        IF sym < semicolon THEN
                            Expression(x); OCH.Result(x, OCT.topScope.typ)
                        ELSIF OCT.topScope.typ # OCT.notyp THEN OCS.Mark(124)
                        END ;
                        OCH.Return(SHORT(OCT.topScope.a1 DIV 10000H),
                                SHORT(OCT.topScope.a1))
                    ELSE (*return from module body*)
                        IF sym < semicolon THEN Expression(x); OCS.Mark(124) END ;
                        OCH.Return(XProc, XParOrg)
                    END
                END ;
                OCC.FreeRegs({});
                IF sym = semicolon THEN OCS.Get(sym)
                ELSIF (sym <= ident) OR (if <= sym) & (sym <= return) THEN OCS.Mark(38)
                ELSE EXIT
                END
            END
    END StatSeq;


    PROCEDURE Block(VAR dsize: LONGINT);
        VAR typ, forward: OCT.Struct;
            obj, first: OCT.Object;
            x: OCT.Item;
            L0: INTEGER;
            adr, size: LONGINT;
            mk: BOOLEAN;
            id0: ARRAY 32 OF CHAR;
    BEGIN adr := -dsize; obj := OCT.topScope;
        WHILE obj.next # NIL DO obj := obj.next END ;
        LOOP
            IF sym = const THEN
                OCS.Get(sym);
                WHILE sym = ident DO
                    COPY(OCS.name, id0); CheckMark(mk);
                    IF sym = eql THEN OCS.Get(sym); ConstExpression(x)
                    ELSIF sym = becomes THEN OCS.Mark(9); OCS.Get(sym);
                            ConstExpression(x)
                    ELSE OCS.Mark(9)
                    END ;
                    OCT.Insert(id0, obj); obj.mode := SHORT(x.mode);
                    obj.typ := x.typ; obj.a0 := x.a0; obj.a1 := x.a1; obj.marked := mk;
                    CheckSym(semicolon)
                END
            END ;
            IF sym = type THEN
                OCS.Get(sym);
                WHILE sym = ident DO
                    typ := OCT.undftyp; OCT.Insert(OCS.name, obj); forward := obj.typ;
                    obj.mode := Typ; obj.typ := OCT.notyp; CheckMark(obj.marked);
                    IF sym = eql THEN OCS.Get(sym); Type(typ)
                    ELSIF (sym = becomes) OR (sym = colon) THEN OCS.Mark(9);
                            OCS.Get(sym); Type(typ)
                    ELSE OCS.Mark(9)
                    END ;
                    obj.typ := typ;
```

```
                    IF typ.strobj = NIL THEN typ.strobj := obj END ;
                    IF forward # NIL THEN (*fixup*) SetPtrBase(forward, typ) END ;
                    CheckSym(semicolon)
                END
            END ;
            IF sym = var THEN
                OCS.Get(sym);
                WHILE sym = ident DO
                    OCT.Insert(OCS.name, obj); first := obj;
                    CheckMark(obj.marked); obj.mode := Var;
                    LOOP
                        IF sym = comma THEN OCS.Get(sym)
                        ELSIF sym = ident THEN OCS.Mark(19)
                        ELSE EXIT
                        END ;
                        IF sym = ident THEN
                            OCT.Insert(OCS.name, obj); CheckMark(obj.marked); obj.mode := Var
                    ELSE OCS.Mark(10)
                    END
                END ;
                CheckSym(colon); Type(typ); size := typ.size;
                IF size >= 4 THEN DEC(adr, adr MOD 4)
                ELSIF size = 2 THEN DEC(adr, adr MOD 2)
                END ;
                WHILE first # NIL DO
                    first.typ := typ; DEC(adr, size); first.a0 := adr; first := first.next
                END ;
                CheckSym(semicolon)
            END
        END ;
        IF (sym < const) OR (sym > var) THEN EXIT END ;
    END ;
    CheckUndefPointerTypes;
    IF OCC.level = 0 THEN OCH.LFJ(L0) ELSE OCH.FJ(L0) END ;
    WHILE sym = procedure DO
        OCS.Get(sym); ProcedureDeclaration; CheckSym(semicolon)
    END ;
    IF OCC.level = 0 THEN OCC.fixupL(L0); OCC.InitTypDescs ELSE OCC.fixupC(L0) END ;
    IF sym = begin THEN OCS.Get(sym); StatSeq END ;
    dsize := (adr MOD 4) − adr; CheckSym(end)
END Block;


PROCEDURE CompilationUnit(source: Texts.Text; pos: LONGINT);
    VAR L0: INTEGER; ch: CHAR;
        time, date, key, dsize: LONGINT;
        modid, impid, FName: ARRAY 32 OF CHAR;


    PROCEDURE MakeFileName(VAR name, FName: ARRAY OF CHAR;
            ext: ARRAY OF CHAR);
        VAR i, j: INTEGER; ch: CHAR;
    BEGIN i := 0;
        LOOP ch := name[i];
            IF ch = 0X THEN EXIT END ;
            FName[i] := ch; INC(i)
        END ;
        j := 0;
        REPEAT ch := ext[j]; FName[i] := ch; INC(i); INC(j)
```

```
        UNTIL ch = 0X
   END MakeFileName;



BEGIN entno := 1; dsize := 0; LoopLevel := 0; ExitNo := 0;
   OCC.Init; OCT.Init; OCS.Init(source, pos); OCS.Get(sym);
   Texts.WriteString(W, " compiling ");
   IF sym = module THEN OCS.Get(sym) ELSE OCS.Mark(16) END ;
   IF sym = ident THEN
       Texts.WriteString(W, OCS.name); Texts.Append(Oberon.Log, W.buf);
       L0 := 0; ch := OCS.name[0];
       WHILE (ch # 0X) & (L0 < ModNameLen−1) DO
           modid[L0] := ch; INC(L0); ch := OCS.name[L0]
       END ;
       modid[L0] := 0X;
       IF ch # 0X THEN OCS.Mark(228) END ;
       OCT.OpenScope(0); OCS.Get(sym);
       CheckSym(semicolon); OCH.Enter(Mod, 0, L0);
       IF sym = ihport THEN
           OCS.Get(sym);
           LOOP
              IF sym = ident THEN
                  COPY(OCS.name, impid); OCS.Get(sym);
                  MakeFileName(impid, FName, ".Sym");
                  IF sym = becomes THEN OCS.Get(sym);
                      IF sym = ident THEN
                          MakeFileName(OCS.name, FName, ".Sym"); OCS.Get(sym)
                      ELSE OCS.Mark(10)
                      END
                  END ;
                  OCT.Import(impid, modid, FName)
              ELSE OCS.Mark(10)
              END ;
              IF sym = comma THEN OCS.Get(sym)
              ELSIF sym = ident THEN OCS.Mark(19)
              ELSE EXIT
              END
           END ;
           CheckSym(semicolon)
       END ;
       IF ~OCS.scanerr THEN
           OCC.SetLinkTable(OCT.nofGmod+1);
           Block(dsize); OCH.Return(XProc, 12);
           IF sym = ident THEN
               IF OCS.name # modid THEN OCS.Mark(4) END ;
               OCS.Get(sym)
           ELSE OCS.Mark(10)
           END ;
           IF sym # period THEN OCS.Mark(18) END ;
           IF ~OCS.scanerr THEN
               Oberon.GetClock(time, date); key := (date MOD 4000H) * 20000H + time;
               MakeFileName(modid, FName, ".Sym");
               OCT.Export(modid, FName, newSF, key);
               IF newSF THEN Texts.WriteString(W, " new symbol file") END ;
               IF ~OCS.scanerr THEN
                   MakeFileName(modid, FName, ".Obj");
                   OCC.OutCode(FName, modid, key, entno, dsize);
                   Texts.WriteInt(W, OCC.pc, 6); Texts.WriteInt(W, dsize, 6)
```

```
                        END
                    END
                END ;
                OCT.CloseScope
            ELSE OCS.Mark(10)
        END;
        OCC.Close; OCT.Close;
        Texts.WriteLn(W); Texts.Append(Oberon.Log, W.buf)
    END CompilationUnit;


    PROCEDURE Compile*;
        VAR beg, end, time: LONGINT;
            T: Texts.Text;
            S: Texts.Scanner;
            v: Viewers.Viewer;


        PROCEDURE Options;
            VAR ch: CHAR;
        BEGIN
            IF S.nextCh = "/" THEN
                LOOP Texts.Read(S, ch);
                    IF ch = "x" THEN OCE.inxchk := FALSE
                    ELSIF ch = "t" THEN OCC.typchk := FALSE
                    ELSIF ch = "s" THEN newSF := TRUE
                    ELSE S.nextCh := ch; EXIT
                    END
                END
            END
        END Options;


    BEGIN OCE.inxchk := TRUE; OCC.typchk := TRUE; newSF := FALSE;
        Texts.OpenScanner(S, Oberon.Par.text, Oberon.Par.pos); Texts.Scan(S);
        IF S.class = Texts.Char THEN
            IF S.c = "*" THEN
                v := Oberon.MarkedViewer();
                IF (v.dsc # NIL) & (v.dsc.next IS TextFrames.Frame) THEN
                    Options; CompilationUnit(v.dsc.next(TextFrames.Frame).text, 0)
                END
            ELSIF S.c = " ↑ " THEN
                Oberon.GetSelection(T, beg, end, time);
                IF time >= 0 THEN
                    Texts.OpenScanner(S, T, beg); Texts.Scan(S);
                    IF S.class = Texts.Name THEN
                        Options; Texts.WriteString(W, S.s); NEW(T); Texts.Open(T, S.s);
                        IF T.len # 0 THEN CompilationUnit(T, 0)
                        ELSE Texts.WriteString(W, " not found");
                            Texts.WriteLn(W); Texts.Append(Oberon.Log, W.buf)
                        END
                    END
                END
            ELSIF S.c = "@" THEN
                Oberon.GetSelection(T, beg, end, time);
                IF time >= 0 THEN Options; CompilationUnit(T, beg) END
            END
        ELSE NEW(T);
            WHILE S.class = Texts.Name DO
                Options; Texts.WriteString(W, S.s); Texts.Open(T, S.s);
```

```
        IF T.len # 0 THEN CompilationUnit(T, 0)
        ELSE Texts.WriteString(W, " not found");
            Texts.WriteLn(W); Texts.Append(Oberon.Log, W.buf)
        END ;
        Texts.Scan(S)
      END
    END ;
    Oberon.Collect(0)
  END Compile;

BEGIN Texts.OpenWriter(W);
    Texts.WriteString(W, "Compiler NW 1.8.91"); Texts.WriteLn(W);
    Texts.Append(Oberon.Log, W.buf)
END Compiler.
```

12.5 The scanner

The scanner embodies the lexicographic definitions of the language, that is, the definition of abstract symbols in terms of characters. The scanner's substance is procedure *Get*, which scans the source text and, for each call, identifies the next symbol. It is most important that this process be as efficient as possible. Therefore use of a case statement is made to discriminate the various classes of characters, and to recognize letters indicating the presence of an identifier (or reserved word), and digits signalling the presence of a number. Also, the scanner recognizes comments and skips them. The global variable *ch* stands for the last character read.

A sequence of letters and digits may denote either an identifier or a key word. In order to determine which is the case, a search is made in a table containing all key words for each would-be identifier. This table is organized as a hash table for reasons of efficiency. The hash function is the sum of all characters' ordinal numbers plus their number, modulo the table size. At most, two comparisons suffice to detect the presence of a key word. The hash table is initialized when the compiler is loaded.

The presence of a digit signals a number. Procedure *Number* first scans the subsequent digits (and letters) and stores them in a buffer. This is necessary because hexadecimal numbers are denoted by the postfix letter H (rather than a prefix character). The postfix letter X specifies that the digits denote a character.

There exists a single case where a look-ahead of a single character does not suffice to identify the next symbol. When a sequence of digits is followed by a period, this period may either be the decimal point of a real number, or it may be the first element of a range symbol (..). Fortunately, the problem can be solved locally as follows: If, after reading digits and a period, a second period is present, the number symbol is returned, and the look-ahead variable *ch* is assigned the special value 7FX. A subsequent call of *Get* then delivers the range symbol. Otherwise, the period after the digit sequence belongs to the (real) number.

```
MODULE OCS; (*NW 7.6.87 / 20.12.90*)
   IMPORT Files, Reals, Texts, Oberon;
   (* symbols:
```

	0	1	2	3	4
0	null	*	/	DIV	MOD
5	&	+	–	OR	=
10	#	<	<=	>	>=
15	IN	IS	↑	.	,
20	:	..	)	]	}
25	OF	THEN	DO	TO	(
30	[	{	~	:=	number
35	NIL	string	ident	;	|
40	END	ELSE	ELSIF	UNTIL	IF
45	CASE	WHILE	REPEAT	LOOP	WITH
50	EXIT	RETURN	ARRAY	RECORD	POINTER
55	BEGIN	CONST	TYPE	VAR	PROCEDURE
60	IMPORT	MODULE	eof *)		

```
CONST KW = 43;    (*size of hash table*)
        maxDig = 32;
        maxInt = 7FFFH;
        maxShInt = 7FH;
        maxExp = 38; maxLExp = 308;
        maxStrLen = 128;
(*name, numtyp, intval, realval, lrlval are implicit results of Get*)


VAR numtyp* : INTEGER; (* 1 = char, 2 = integer, 3 = real, 4 = longreal*)
    intval* : LONGINT;
    realval*: REAL;
    lrlval* : LONGREAL;
    scanerr*: BOOLEAN;
    name* : ARRAY maxStrLen OF CHAR;
    R: Texts.Reader;
    W: Texts.Writer;
    ch: CHAR; (*current character*)
    lastpos: LONGINT; (*error position in source file*)
    i: INTEGER;
    keyTab : ARRAY KW OF
                RECORD symb, alt: INTEGER; id: ARRAY 12 OF CHAR END;


PROCEDURE Mark*(n: INTEGER);
    VAR pos: LONGINT;
BEGIN scanerr := TRUE; pos := Texts.Pos(R);
    IF lastpos + 10 < pos THEN
        Texts.WriteLn(W); Texts.WriteString(W, " pos");
        Texts.WriteInt(W, pos, 6); Texts.WriteString(W, " err");
```

```
        Texts.WriteInt(W, n, 4); Texts.Append(Oberon.Log, W.buf); lastpos := pos
    END
END Mark;

PROCEDURE String(VAR sym: INTEGER);
    VAR i: INTEGER;
BEGIN i := 0;
    LOOP Texts.Read(R, ch);
        IF ch = 22X THEN EXIT END ;
        IF ch < " " THEN Mark(3); EXIT END ;
        IF i < maxStrLen−1 THEN name[i] := ch; INC(i) ELSE Mark(212); i := 0 END
    END ;
    Texts.Read(R, ch);
    IF i = 1 THEN sym := 34; numtyp := 1; intval := ORD(name[0])
    ELSE sym := 36; name[i] := 0X (*string*)
    END
END String;

PROCEDURE Identifier(VAR sym: INTEGER);
    VAR i, k: INTEGER;
BEGIN i := 0; k := 0;
    REPEAT
        IF i < 31 THEN name[i] := ch; INC(i); INC(k, ORD(ch)) END ;
        Texts.Read(R, ch)
    UNTIL (ch < "0") OR ("9" < ch) & (CAP(ch) < "A") OR ("Z" < CAP(ch));
    name[i] := 0X;
    k := (k+i) MOD KW; (*hash function*)
    IF (keyTab[k].symb # 0) & (keyTab[k].id = name) THEN sym := keyTab[k].symb
    ELSE k := keyTab[k].alt;
        IF (keyTab[k].symb # 0) & (keyTab[k].id = name) THEN sym := keyTab[k].symb
        ELSE sym := 37 (*ident*)
        END
    END
END Identifier;

PROCEDURE Hval(ch: CHAR): INTEGER;
    VAR d: INTEGER;
BEGIN d := ORD(ch) − 30H; (*d >= 0*)
    IF d >= 10 THEN
        IF (d >= 17) & (d < 23) THEN DEC(d, 7) ELSE d := 0; Mark(2) END
    END ;
    RETURN d
END Hval;

PROCEDURE Number;
    VAR i, j, h, d, e, n: INTEGER;
    x, f: REAL;
    y, g: LONGREAL;
    lastCh: CHAR; neg: BOOLEAN;
    dig: ARRAY maxDig OF CHAR;

    PROCEDURE ReadScaleFactor;
    BEGIN Texts.Read(R, ch);
        IF ch = "−" THEN neg := TRUE; Texts.Read(R, ch)
        ELSE neg := FALSE;
            IF ch = "+" THEN Texts.Read(R, ch) END
        END ;
```

```
            IF ("0" <= ch) & (ch <= "9") THEN
                REPEAT e := e*10 + ORD(ch)-30H; Texts.Read(R, ch)
                UNTIL (ch < "0") OR (ch <"9")
            ELSE Mark(2)
            END
        END ReadScaleFactor;


    BEGIN i := 0;
        REPEAT dig[i] := ch; INC(i); Texts.Read(R, ch)
        UNTIL (ch < "0") OR ("9" < ch) & (CAP(ch) < "A") OR ("Z" < CAP(ch));
        lastCh := ch; j := 0;
        WHILE (j < i-1) & (dig[j] = "0") DO INC(j) END ;
        IF ch = "." THEN Texts.Read(R, ch);
            IF ch = "." THEN lastCh := 0X; ch := 7FX END
        END ;
        IF lastCh = "." THEN (*decimal point*)
            h := i;
            WHILE ("0" <= ch) & (ch <= "9") DO (*read fraction*)
                IF i < maxDig THEN dig[i] := ch; INC(i) END ;
                Texts.Read(R, ch)
            END ;
            IF ch = "D" THEN
                y := 0; g := 1; e := 0;
                WHILE j < h DO y := y*10 + (ORD(dig[j])-30H); INC(j) END ;
                WHILE j < i DO g := g/10; y := (ORD(dig[j])-30H)*g + y; INC(j) END ;
                ReadScaleFactor;
                IF neg THEN
                    IF e <= maxLExp THEN y := y / Reals.TenL(e) ELSE y := 0 END
                ELSIF e > 0 THEN
                    IF e <= maxLExp THEN y := Reals.TenL(e) * y ELSE y := 0; Mark(203) END
                END ;
                numtyp := 4; lrlval := y
            ELSE x := 0; f := 1; e := 0;
                WHILE j < h DO x := x*10 + (ORD(dig[j])-30H); INC(j) END ;
                WHILE j < i DO f := f/10; x := (ORD(dig[j])-30H)*f + x; INC(j) END ;
                IF ch = "E" THEN ReadScaleFactor END ;
                IF neg THEN
                    IF e <= maxExp THEN x := x / Reals.Ten(e) ELSE x := 0 END
                ELSIF e > 0 THEN
                    IF e <= maxExp THEN x := Reals.Ten(e) * x ELSE x := 0; Mark(203) END
                END ;
                numtyp := 3; realval := x
            END
        ELSE (*integer*)
            lastCh := dig[i-1]; intval := 0;
            IF lastCh = "H" THEN
                IF j < i THEN
                    DEC(i); intval := Hval(dig[j]); INC(j);
                    IF i-j <= 7 THEN
                        IF (i-j = 7) & (intval >= 8) THEN DEC(intval, 16) END ;
                        WHILE j < i DO intval := Hval(dig[j]) + intval * 10H; INC(j) END
                    ELSE Mark(203)
                    END
                END
            ELSIF lastCh = "X" THEN
                DEC(i);
                WHILE j < i DO
                    intval := Hval(dig[j]) + intval*10H; INC(j);
```

```
                IF intval > 0FFH THEN Mark(203); intval := 0 END
            END
        ELSE (*decimal*)
            WHILE j < i DO
                d := ORD(dig[j]) − 30H;
                IF d < 10 THEN
                    IF intval <= (MAX(LONGINT) − d) DIV 10 THEN intval := intval*10 + d
                    ELSE Mark(203); intval := 0
                    END
                ELSE Mark(2); intval := 0
                END ;
                INC(j)
            END
        END ;
        IF lastCh = "X" THEN numtyp := 1 ELSE numtyp := 2 END
    END
END Number;


PROCEDURE Get*(VAR sym: INTEGER);
    VAR s: INTEGER; xch: CHAR;


    PROCEDURE Comment; (* do not read after end of file *)
    BEGIN Texts.Read(R, ch);
        LOOP
            LOOP
                WHILE ch = "(" DO Texts.Read(R, ch);
                    IF ch = "*" THEN Comment END
                END ;
                IF ch = "*" THEN Texts.Read(R, ch); EXIT END ;
                IF ch = 0X THEN EXIT END ;
                Texts.Read(R, ch)
            END ;
            IF ch = ")" THEN Texts.Read(R, ch); EXIT END ;
            IF ch = 0X THEN Mark(5); EXIT END
        END
    END Comment;


BEGIN
    LOOP (*ignore control characters*)
        IF ch <= " " THEN
            IF ch = 0X THEN ch := " "; EXIT
            ELSE Texts.Read(R, ch)
            END
        ELSIF ch > 7FX THEN Texts.Read(R, ch)
        ELSE EXIT
        END
    END ;
    CASE ch OF (* " " <= ch <= 7FX *)
        " " : s := 62; ch := 0X (*eof*)
      | "!", "$", "%", "'", "?", "@", "σ", "−", "'": s := 0; Texts.Read(R, ch)
      | 22X : String(s)
      | "#" : s := 10; Texts.Read(R, ch)
      | "&" : s := 5; Texts.Read(R, ch)
      | "(" : Texts.Read(R, ch);
            IF ch = "*" THEN Comment; Get(s) ELSE s := 29 END
```

```
         | ")" :   s := 22; Texts.Read(R, ch)
         | "*" :   s := 1; Texts.Read(R, ch)
         | "+" :   s := 6; Texts.Read(R, ch)
         | "," :   s := 19; Texts.Read(R, ch)
         | "−" :   s := 7; Texts.Read(R, ch)
         | "." :   Texts.Read(R, ch);
                       IF ch = "." THEN Texts.Read(R, ch); s := 21 ELSE s := 18 END
         | "/" :   s := 2; Texts.Read(R, ch)
         | "0".. "9": Number; s := 34
         | ":" :   Texts.Read(R, ch);
                       IF ch = "=" THEN Texts.Read(R, ch); s := 33 ELSE s := 20 END
         | ";" :   s := 38; Texts.Read(R, ch)
         | "<" :   Texts.Read(R, ch);
                       IF ch = "=" THEN Texts.Read(R, ch); s := 12 ELSE s := 11 END
         | "=" :   s := 9; Texts.Read(R, ch);
         | ">" :   Texts.Read(R, ch);
                       IF ch = "=" THEN Texts.Read(R, ch); s := 14 ELSE s := 13 END
         | "A".. "Z": Identifier(s)
         | "[" :   s := 30; Texts.Read(R, ch)
         | "]" :   s := 23; Texts.Read(R, ch)
         | "↑" :   s := 17; Texts.Read(R, ch)
         | "a".. "z": Identifier(s)
         | "{" :   s := 31; Texts.Read(R, ch)
         | "|" :   s := 39; Texts.Read(R, ch)
         | "}" :   s := 24; Texts.Read(R, ch)
         | "~" :   s := 32; Texts.Read(R, ch)
         | 7FX :   s := 21; Texts.Read(R, ch)
    END ;
    sym := s
END Get;


PROCEDURE Init*(source: Texts.Text; pos: LONGINT);
BEGIN
    ch := " "; scanerr := FALSE; lastpos := −8;
    Texts.OpenReader(R, source, pos)
END Init;


PROCEDURE EnterKW(sym: INTEGER; name: ARRAY OF CHAR);
    VAR j, k: INTEGER;
BEGIN j := 0; k := 0;
    REPEAT INC(k, ORD(name[j])); INC(j)
    UNTIL name[j] = 0X;
    k := (k+j) MOD KW; (*hash function*)
    IF keyTab[k].symb # 0 THEN
        j := k;
        REPEAT INC(k) UNTIL keyTab[k].symb = 0;
        keyTab[j].alt := k
    END ;
    keyTab[k].symb := sym; COPY(name, keyTab[k].id)
END EnterKW;


BEGIN i := KW;
    WHILE i > 0 DO
        DEC(i); keyTab[i].symb := 0; keyTab[i].alt := 0
    END ;
    keyTab[0].id := "";
    EnterKW(27, "DO"); EnterKW(44, "IF"); EnterKW(15, "IN"); EnterKW(16, "IS");
```

EnterKW(25, "OF"); EnterKW(8, "OR"); EnterKW(40, "END"); EnterKW(4, "MOD");
EnterKW(35, "NIL"); EnterKW(58, "VAR"); EnterKW(41, "ELSE"); EnterKW(50, "EXIT");
EnterKW(26, "THEN"); EnterKW(49, "WITH"); EnterKW(52, "ARRAY"); EnterKW(55, "BEGIN");
EnterKW(56, "CONST"); EnterKW(42, "ELSIF"); EnterKW(43, "UNTIL"); EnterKW(46, "WHILE");
EnterKW(53, "RECORD"); EnterKW(47, "REPEAT"); EnterKW(51, "RETURN");
EnterKW(59, "PROCEDURE"); EnterKW(28, "TO"); EnterKW(3, "DIV"); EnterKW(48, "LOOP");
EnterKW(57, "TYPE"); EnterKW(60, "IMPORT"); EnterKW(61, "MODULE");
EnterKW(54, "POINTER");
    Texts.OpenWriter(W)
END OCS.

12.6 Searching the symbol table, and symbol files

The symbol table constitutes the context in which statements and expressions are parsed. Each procedure establishes a scope of visibility of local identifiers. The records registering identifiers belonging to a scope are linked as a linear list. Procedures for generating and searching the lists are contained in module OCT. If a new identifier is to be added, procedure *Insert* first searches the list, and if the identifier is already present, a double definition is diagnosed. Otherwise, the new element is appended, thereby preserving the order given by the source text.

Scopes   Procedures, and therefore also scopes, may be nested. Each scope is represented by the list of its declared identifiers, and the list of the currently visible scopes are again connected as a list. Procedure *OpenScope* appends an element and procedure *CloseScope* removes it. The list of scopes is anchored in the global variable *topScope*, and it is treated like a stack. It consists of elements of type *Object*, each being the header (mode = *Head*) of the list of declared entities. A snapshot of a symbol table is shown in Figure 12.7. It is taken when the following declarations are parsed and when the statement S is reached:

    VAR x: INTEGER;

    PROCEDURE P(u: INTEGER);
    BEGIN ... END P;

    PROCEDURE Q(v: INTEGER);
        PROCEDURE R(w: INTEGER);
        BEGIN S END R;
    BEGIN ... END Q;

A search of an identifier proceeds first through the scope list, and for each header its list of object records is scanned. This mirrors the scope rule of the language and guarantees that if several entities carry the same identifier then the most local one is selected. The linear

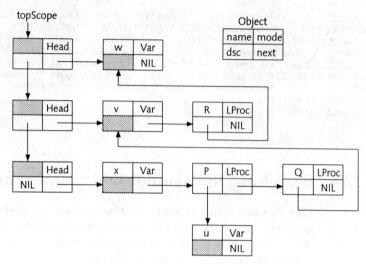

Figure 12.7   Snapshot of a symbol table.

list of objects represents the simplest implementation by far. A tree structure would in many cases be more efficient for searching, and would therefore seem more recommendable. Experiments have shown, however, that the gain in speed is marginal. The reason is that the lists are typically quite short. The superiority of a tree structure becomes manifest only when a large number of global objects is declared. We emphasize that when a tree structure is used for each scope, the linear lists must still be present, because the order of declarations is sometimes relevant in interpretation, for example in parameter lists.

Record scope

Not only procedures, but also record types establish their own local scope. The list of record fields is anchored in the type record's field *link*, and it is searched by procedure *FindField*. If a record type R1 is an extension of R0 then R1's field list contains only the fields of the extension proper. The base type R0 is referenced by the *BaseTyp* field of R1. Hence a search for a field may have to proceed through the field lists of an entire sequence of record base types.

Symbol file

The major part of module OCT is devoted to input and output of symbol files. A symbol file is a linearized form of an excerpt of the symbol table containing descriptions of all exported (marked) objects. All exports are declared in the global scope. Procedure *Export* traverses the list of global objects and transfers them into the symbol file.

The major problem is to find an appropriate representation of pointers, which must be converted to a form that is free of absolute addresses. The only pointers of relevance here are those referring to types, that is, records of type *Struct*. The solution lies in assigning a unique reference number to each occurring type. Since efficiency of importing has priority over efficiency of exporting, these reference numbers should never constitute forward references, that is, the definition of a reference must precede its occurence in the file. This consideration determines the method employed when exporting an object's type.

Reference number

A type's reference number is recorded in the field *ref*. Its initial value 0 signals that the type has not yet been exported. When an identifier is to be exported and its type's reference is 0, the export of the type (*Struct*) precedes that of the identifier (*Object*), which therefore always refers to its type by a backward reference (see procedures *OutObjs* and *OutStr*). The first byte of every object's description in the file indicates its mode, and the first byte of every type's description indicates its form. The second byte is in both cases the type's reference number. Mode and form numbers are disjoint, thereby allowing an efficient identification of the next element in the file.

The structure of a symbol file is defined by the following syntax. Terminal symbols take one byte, unless specified otherwise by ": len". The following terminal symbols are mode and form specifiers or reference numbers for basic types with fixed values:

Syntax of symbol files

Con =1, Typ = 2, Var = 4, XProc = 5, CProc = 7, Pointer = 8, ProcTyp = 9, Array = 10, DynArr = 11, Record = 12, ParList = 13, ValPar = 14, VarPar = 15, FldList = 16, Fld = 17, HPtr = 18, Fixup = 19, Mod = 22, Byte = 1, Bool = 2, Char = 3, SInt = 4, Int = 5, LInt = 6, Real =7, LReal = 8, Set = 9, String = 10, Nil = 11, NoTyp = 12.

SymbolFile = SymTag modAnchor {element}.
modAnchor =Mod key:4 name.

element =   Con constant
            | Typ ref modno name
            | (Var | Fld) ref offset:2 name
            | (ValPar | VarPar) ref offset:4 name
            | ParList {element} (XProc ref pno | CProc ref len
                 code) name
            | Pointer ref mno
            | ParList {element} ProcTyp ref mno
            | Array ref mno size:4 bndadr:2 nofel:4
            | DynArr ref mno size:4 lenoff:2
            | FldList {element} Record ref mno size:4
                 dscadr:2
            | HPtr offset:4
            | Fixup ref ref
            | modAnchor.

constant =	(Byte | Bool | Char | SInt) val name
	| Int val:2 name
	| (LInt | Real | Set) val:4 name
	| LReal val:8 name
	| String name name
	| Nil name.

name =	{char} 0X.

A procedure description with mode specifier *XProc* (or *CProc*) and a procedural type description with form specifier *ProcTyp* are preceded by a parameter list. The list is headed by the specifier *ParList*. Similarly, a record type description with form specifier *Record* is preceded by the list of field descriptions. This list is headed by the specifier *FldList*.

The specifier *HPtr* (in a field list) denotes a field with a pointer type. The field name itself is not exported; it is hidden. The reason for its occurrence in the symbol file is the following. If an extension of this record type is declared, a corresponding type descriptor is constructed. This descriptor must contain the offsets of all pointer fields for use by the garbage collector. Pointers inherited from the base type must not be missing.

The specifier *Fixup* mirrors a forward reference in a pointer type declaration. When reading a symbol file, it triggers a fixup of the base type in the respective pointer type (see procedure *Import*).

Objects exported from some module M0 may refer in their declaration to some other module M1 imported by M0. It would be unacceptable if the import of M0 then also required the import of M1, that is, implied the automatic reading of M1's symbol file. It would trigger a chain reaction of imports that must be avoided. Fortunately, such a chain reaction can be avoided by making symbol files self-contained, that is, by including in every symbol file the description of entities that stem from other modules. Such entities are always types.

Self-contained symbol file

The inclusion of types imported from other modules seems simple enough to handle: type descriptions must include a reference to the module from which the type was imported. This reference is a module number (*mno*); the name and key of the respective module is given by its anchor, which, when read, causes a new entry in the array *LocMod* of imported modules (see procedure *Import*). However, there exists one additional complication that cannot be ignored. Consider a module M0 importing a variable x from a module M1. Let the type T of x be defined in module M2. Also, assume M0 to contain a variable y of type M2.T. Evidently, x and y are of the same type, and the compiler must recognize this fact. Hence, when importing M1 during compilation of M0, not only must the imported element T be registered in the symbol table,

Detecting type identity

but it must also be recognized as being identical to the T already imported from M2 directly. It is rather fortunate that the language definition specifies equivalence of types on the basis of names rather than structure, because it allows type tests at execution time to be implemented by a simple address comparison.

The measures to be taken to satisfy the new requirements are as follows:

(1) Every type element in a symbol file is given a module number referring to a module anchor. Before a type description is emitted to the file, its module anchor is emitted, unless this had been done previously on another occasion.

(2) If a type to be exported has a name and stems from another, imported module then an element with specifier *Typ* is also emitted. The name is obtained from the respective *Object* in the symbol table accessed via the type descriptor's *strobj* field. (This is the only reason for the presence of this field. Anonymous types are characterized by *strobj* = NIL.)

(3) When importing a module, it must be checked whether or not the module is already present, either in full or in part. And when a type is imported, its presence must also be checked. If it already exists, the new structure entry is made to refer to the already-existing type entry (struct[s] := ob0.next.typ, see procedure *Import*).

There is yet another hurdle to be overcome. Types may be given several names; consider a (exported) type T1 to be declared as T1 = T0. In this case, a type element named T1 must be emitted referring by its reference number to the structural element associated with T0 and emitted before (see procedure *OutObjs*). The following sample program may help the reader to understand the structure of symbol files and the way they are generated. It is followed by a listing of the corresponding symbol file in a decoded form.

```
MODULE Sample;
  CONST N* = 100;
  TYPE Ptr0* = POINTER TO Rec0;
    Rec0* = RECORD x, y: INTEGER END ;
    Rec1* = RECORD (Rec0) z: LONGINT END ;
    Ptr1* = Ptr0;
  VAR a*: ARRAY N OF Rec0;

  PROCEDURE P*(x: REAL; p: Ptr1): INTEGER;
  BEGIN END P;

END Sample.
```

Mod	key = 6E08D9E9		name = Sample	
Con	ref = 4	val = 100	name = N	
Pointer	ref = 16	base ref = 0	mno = 0	
Typ	ref = 16	mno = 0	name = Ptr0	

Record	ref = 17	base ref = 12	mno = 0	size = 4	adr = 0
Typ	ref = 17	mno = 0	name = Rec0		

Record	ref = 18	base ref = 17	mno = 0	size = 8	adr = 4
Typ	ref = 18	mno = 0	name = Rec1		
Typ	ref = 16	mno = 0	name = Ptr1		
Array	ref = 19	elem ref = 17	mno = 0	size = 400	adr = 8
Var	ref = 19	adr = −400	name = a		

ValPar	ref = 7	adr = 16	name = x
ValPar	ref = 16	adr = 12	name = p
XProc	ref = 5	pno = 1	name = P
Fixup	ref = 16	ref = 17	

Comparing symbol files   After a symbol file has been generated, it is compared with the file from a previous compilation of the same module, if one exists. Only if the two files differ and if the compiler's s-option is enabled, is the old file replaced by the new version. The comparison is made by comparing byte after byte without consideration of the file's structure. This somewhat crude approach was chosen because of its simplicity, and yielded good results in practice.

```
MODULE OCT; (*NW 28.5.87 / 5.3.91*)
  IMPORT Files, OCS;


  CONST maxImps = 24; SFtag = 0FAX; firstStr = 16;
      maxStr = 80; maxUDP = 16; maxMod = 24; maxParLev = 6;
      PtrSize = 4; ProcSize = 4; NotYetExp = 0;
    (*object modes*)
      Var = 1; Ind = 3; Con = 8; Fld = 12; Typ = 13;
      XProc = 15; SProc = 16; CProc = 17; Mod = 19; Head = 20;
    (*structure forms*)
      Undef = 0; Byte = 1; Bool = 2; Char = 3; SInt = 4; Int = 5; LInt = 6;
      Real = 7; LReal = 8; Set = 9; String = 10; NilTyp = 11; NoTyp = 12;
      Pointer = 13; ProcTyp = 14; Array = 15; DynArr = 16; Record = 17;


  TYPE
    Object* = POINTER TO ObjDesc;
    Struct* = POINTER TO StrDesc;


    ObjDesc* = RECORD
                  dsc*, next*: Object;
```

```
                        typ*: Struct;
                        a0*, a1*: LONGINT; `
                        a2*: INTEGER;
                        mode*: SHORTINT;
                        marked*: BOOLEAN;
                        name*: ARRAY 32 OF CHAR;
                END ;

    StrDesc* = RECORD
                        form*, n*, mno*, ref*: INTEGER;
                        size*, adr*: LONGINT;
                        BaseTyp*: Struct;
                        link*, strobj*: Object
                END ;
    Item* = RECORD
                mode*, lev*: INTEGER;
                a0*, a1*, a2*: LONGINT;
                typ*: Struct;
                obj*: Object
            END ;
VAR topScope*: Object;
    undftyp*, bytetyp*, booltyp*, chartyp*, sinttyp*, inttyp*, linttyp*,
    realtyp*, lrltyp*, settyp*, stringtyp*, niltyp*, notyp*: Struct;
    nofGmod*: INTEGER; (*nof imports*)
    GlbMod*: ARRAY maxImps OF Object;


    universe, syslink: Object;
    strno, udpinx: INTEGER; (*for export*)
    nofExp: SHORTINT;
    SR: Files.Rider;
    undPtr: ARRAY maxUDP OF Struct;


PROCEDURE Init*;
BEGIN topScope := universe; strno := 0; udpinx := 0; nofGmod := 0
END Init;


PROCEDURE Close*;
    VAR i: INTEGER;
BEGIN Files.Set(SR, NIL, 0); i := 0;
    WHILE i < maxImps DO GlbMod[i] := NIL; INC(i) END
END Close;


PROCEDURE FindImport*(mod: Object; VAR res: Object);
    VAR obj: Object;
BEGIN obj := mod.dsc;
    WHILE (obj # NIL) & (obj.name # OCS.name) DO obj := obj.next END ;
    IF (obj # NIL) & (obj.mode = Typ) & obj.marked THEN obj := NIL END ;
    res := obj
END FindImport;


PROCEDURE Find*(VAR res: Object; VAR level: INTEGER);
    VAR obj, head: Object;
BEGIN head := topScope;
    LOOP obj := head.next;
        WHILE (obj # NIL) & (obj.name # OCS.name) DO obj := obj.next END ;
        IF obj # NIL THEN level := SHORT(head.a0); EXIT END ;
```

```
            head := head.dsc;
            IF head = NIL THEN level := 0; EXIT END
        END ;
        res := obj
    END Find;


    PROCEDURE FindField*(typ: Struct; VAR res: Object);
        VAR obj: Object;
    BEGIN (*typ.form = Record*)
        LOOP obj := typ.link;
            WHILE (obj # NIL) & (obj.name # OCS.name) DO obj := obj.next END ;
            IF obj # NIL THEN EXIT END ;
            typ := typ.BaseTyp;
            IF typ = NIL THEN EXIT END
        END ;
        res := obj
    END FindField;


    PROCEDURE Insert*(VAR name: ARRAY OF CHAR; VAR res: Object);
        VAR obj, new: Object;
    BEGIN obj := topScope;
        WHILE (obj.next # NIL) & (obj.next.name # name) DO obj := obj.next END ;
        IF obj.next = NIL THEN NEW(new);
            new.dsc := NIL; new.next := NIL; COPY(name, new.name); obj.next := new; res :=
                new
        ELSE res := obj.next;
            IF obj.next.mode # Undef THEN OCS.Mark(1) END
        END
    END Insert;


    PROCEDURE OpenScope*(level: INTEGER);
        VAR head: Object;
    BEGIN NEW(head);
        head.mode := Head; head.a0 := level; head.typ := NIL;
        head.dsc := topScope; head.next := NIL; topScope := head
    END OpenScope;


    PROCEDURE CloseScope*;
    BEGIN topScope := topScope.dsc
    END CloseScope;


    (*----------------------- import ----------------------*)


    PROCEDURE ReadInt(VAR i: INTEGER);
    BEGIN Files.ReadBytes(SR, i, 2)
    END ReadInt;


    PROCEDURE ReadXInt(VAR k: LONGINT);
        VAR i: INTEGER;
    BEGIN Files.ReadBytes(SR, i, 2); k := i
    END ReadXInt;


    PROCEDURE ReadLInt(VAR k: LONGINT);
    BEGIN Files.ReadBytes(SR, k, 4)
    END ReadLInt;
```

```
PROCEDURE ReadId(VAR id: ARRAY OF CHAR);
    VAR i: INTEGER; ch: CHAR;
BEGIN i := 0;
    REPEAT Files.Read(SR, ch); id[i] := ch; INC(i)
    UNTIL ch = 0X
END ReadId;


PROCEDURE Import*(VAR name, self, FileName: ARRAY OF CHAR);
    VAR i, j, m, s, class: INTEGER; k: LONGINT;
        nofLmod, strno, parlev, fldlev: INTEGER;
        obj, ob0: Object;
        typ: Struct;
        ch, ch1, ch2: CHAR;
        si: SHORTINT;
        xval: REAL; yval: LONGREAL;
        SymFile: Files.File;
        modname: ARRAY 32 OF CHAR;
        LocMod: ARRAY maxMod OF Object;
        struct: ARRAY maxStr OF Struct;
        lastpar, lastfld: ARRAY maxParLev OF Object;


    PROCEDURE reversedList(p: Object): Object;
        VAR q, r: Object;
    BEGIN q := NIL;
        WHILE p # NIL DO
            r := p.next; p.next := q; q := p; p := r
        END ;
        RETURN q
    END reversedList;


BEGIN nofLmod := 0; strno := firstStr;
parlev := -1; fldlev := -1;
IF FileName = "SYSTEM.Sym" THEN
    Insert(name, obj); obj.mode := Mod; obj.dsc := syslink;
    obj.a0 := 0; obj.typ := notyp
ELSE SymFile := Files.Old(FileName);
    IF SymFile # NIL THEN
        Files.Set(SR, SymFile, 0); Files.Read(SR, ch);
        IF ch = SFtag THEN
            struct[Undef] := undftyp; struct[Byte] := bytetyp;
            struct[Bool] := booltyp; struct[Char] := chartyp;
            struct[SInt] := sinttyp; struct[Int] := inttyp;
            struct[LInt] := linttyp; struct[Real] := realtyp;
            struct[LReal] := lrltyp; struct[Set] := settyp;
            struct[String] := stringtyp; struct[NilTyp] := niltyp; struct[NoTyp] := notyp;
            LOOP (*read next item from symbol file*)
                Files.Read(SR, ch); class := ORD(ch);
                IF SR.eof THEN EXIT END ;
                CASE class OF
                    0: OCS.Mark(151)
                  | 1..7: (*object*) NEW(obj); m := 0;
                    Files.Read(SR, ch); s := ORD(ch); obj.typ := struct[s];
                    CASE class OF
                        1: obj.mode := Con;
                            CASE obj.typ.form OF
                                2,4: Files.Read(SR, si); obj.a0 := si
                              | 1,3: Files.Read(SR, ch); obj.a0 := ORD(ch)
```

```
                         |  5: ReadXInt(obj.a0)
                         |  6,7,9: ReadLInt(obj.a0)
                         |  8: ReadLInt(obj.a0); ReadLInt(obj.a1)
                         |  10: ReadId(obj.name); OCS.Mark(151)
                         |  11: (*NIL*)
                         END
                 |2,3: obj.mode := Typ; Files.Read(SR, ch); m := ORD(ch);.5
                      IF obj.typ.strobj = NIL THEN obj.typ.strobj := obj END;
                      obj.marked := class = 2
                 |4:   obj.mode := Var; ReadLInt(obj.a0)
                 |5,6,7: IF class # 7 THEN obj.mode := XProc; Files.Read(SR, ch)
                         ELSE obj.mode := CProc;
                             Files.Read(SR, ch); Files.Read(SR, ch); Files.Read(SR, ch)
                         END ;
                         obj.a0 := ORD(ch); obj.a1 := 0; (*link adr*)
                         obj.dsc := reversedList(lastpar[parlev]); DEC(parlev)
                 END ;
                 ReadId(obj.name); ob0 := LocMod[m];
                 WHILE (ob0.next # NIL) & (ob0.next.name # obj.name) DO ob0 := ob0.next END ;
                 IF ob0.next = NIL THEN ob0.next := obj; obj.next := NIL (*insert object*)
                 ELSIF obj.mode = Typ THEN struct[s] := ob0.next.typ
                 END
         | 8..12: (*structure*)
             NEW(typ); typ.strobj := NIL; typ.ref := 0;
             Files.Read(SR, ch); typ.BaseTyp := struct[ORD(ch)];
             Files.Read(SR, ch); typ.mno := SHORT(LocMod[ORD(ch)].a0);
             CASE class OF
                 8: typ.form := Pointer; typ.size := PtrSize; typ.n := 0
               | 9: typ.form := ProcTyp; typ.size := ProcSize;
                       typ.link := reversedList(lastpar[parlev]); DEC(parlev)
               | 10: typ.form := Array; ReadLInt(typ.size);
                       ReadXInt(typ.adr); ReadLInt(k); typ.n := SHORT(k)
               | 11: typ.form := DynArr; ReadLInt(typ.size); ReadXInt(typ.adr)
               | 12: typ.form := Record; ReadLInt(typ.size); typ.n := 0;
                   typ.link := reversedList(lastfld[fldlev]); DEC(fldlev);
                   IF typ.BaseTyp = notyp THEN typ.BaseTyp := NIL; typ.n := 0
                   ELSE typ.n := typ.BaseTyp.n + 1
                   END ;
                   ReadXInt(typ.adr) (*of descriptor*)
             END ;
             struct[strno] := typ; INC(strno)
         | 13: (*parameter list start*)
             IF parlev < maxParLev-1 THEN INC(parlev); lastpar[parlev] := NIL
             ELSE OCS.Mark(229)
             END
       | 14, 15: (*parameter*)
           NEW(obj);
           IF class = 14 THEN obj.mode := Var ELSE obj.mode := Ind END ;
           Files.Read(SR, ch); obj.typ := struct[ORD(ch)];
           ReadXInt(obj.a0); ReadId(obj.name);
           obj.dsc := NIL; obj.next := lastpar[parlev]; lastpar[parlev] := obj
       | 16: (*start field list*)
           IF fldlev < maxParLev-1 THEN INC(fldlev); lastfld[fldlev] := NIL
           ELSE OCS.Mark(229)
           END
       | 17: (*field*)
           NEW(obj); obj.mode := Fld; Files.Read(SR, ch);
           obj.typ := struct[ORD(ch)]; ReadLInt(obj.a0);
```

```
            ReadId(obj.name); obj.marked := TRUE;
            obj.dsc := NIL; obj.next := lastfld[fldlev]; lastfld[fldlev] := obj
        | 18: (*hidden pointer field*)
            NEW(obj); obj.mode := Fld; ReadLInt(obj.a0);
            obj.name := ""; obj.typ := notyp; obj.marked := FALSE;
            obj.dsc := NIL; obj.next := lastfld[fldlev]; lastfld[fldlev] := obj
        | 19: (*hidden procedure field*)
            ReadLInt(k)
        | 20: (*fixup pointer typ*)
            Files.Read(SR, ch); typ := struct[ORD(ch)];
            Files.Read(SR, ch1);
            IF typ.BaseTyp = undftyp THEN typ.BaseTyp := struct[ORD(ch1)] END
        | 21, 23, 24: OCS.Mark(151); EXIT
        | 22: (*module anchor*)
            ReadLInt(k); ReadId(modname);
            IF modname = self THEN OCS.Mark(49) END;
            i := 0;
            WHILE (i < nofGmod) & (modname # GlbMod[i].name) DO INC(i) END ;
            IF i < nofGmod THEN (*module already present*)
                IF k # GlbMod[i].a1 THEN OCS.Mark(150) END ;
                obj := GlbMod[i]
            ELSE NEW(obj);
                IF nofGmod < maxImps THEN GlbMod[nofGmod] := obj; INC(nofGmod)
                ELSE OCS.Mark(227)
                END ;
                obj.mode := NotYetExp; COPY(modname, obj.name);
                obj.a1 := k; obj.a0 := nofGmod; obj.next := NIL
            END ;
            IF nofLmod < maxMod THEN LocMod[nofLmod] := obj; INC(nofLmod)
            ELSE OCS.Mark(227)
            END
        END
    END (*LOOP*) ;
    Insert(name, obj);
    obj.mode := Mod; obj.dsc := LocMod[0].next;
    obj.a0 := LocMod[0].a0; obj.typ := notyp
  ELSE OCS.Mark(151)
  END
ELSE OCS.Mark(152) (*sym file not found*)
END
END
END Import;


(*----------------------- export ------------------------*)


PROCEDURE WriteByte(i: INTEGER);
BEGIN Files.Write(SR, CHR(i))
END WriteByte;


PROCEDURE WriteInt(i: LONGINT);
BEGIN Files.WriteBytes(SR, i, 2)
END WriteInt;


PROCEDURE WriteLInt(k: LONGINT);
BEGIN Files.WriteBytes(SR, k, 4)
END WriteLInt;


PROCEDURE WriteId(VAR name: ARRAY OF CHAR);
```

```
VAR ch: CHAR; i: INTEGER;
BEGIN i := 0;
REPEAT ch := name[i]; Files.Write(SR, ch); INC(i)
UNTIL ch = 0X
END WriteId;


PROCEDURE ↑ OutStr(typ: Struct);
PROCEDURE OutPars(par: Object);
BEGIN WriteByte(13);
WHILE (par # NIL) & (par.mode <= Ind) & (par.a0 > 0) DO
   OutStr(par.typ);
   IF par.mode = Var THEN WriteByte(14) ELSE WriteByte(15) END ;
   WriteByte(par.typ.ref); WriteInt(par.a0); WriteId(par.name); par := par.next
END
END OutPars;


PROCEDURE OutFlds(fld: Object; adr: LONGINT; visible: BOOLEAN);
BEGIN
IF visible THEN WriteByte(16) END ;
WHILE fld # NIL DO
   IF fld.marked & visible THEN
      OutStr(fld.typ); WriteByte(17); WriteByte(fld.typ.ref);
      WriteLInt(fld.a0); WriteId(fld.name)
   ELSIF fld.typ.form = Record THEN OutFlds(fld.typ.link, fld.a0 + adr, FALSE)
   ELSIF (fld.typ.form = Pointer) OR (fld.name = "") THEN
      WriteByte(18); WriteLInt(fld.a0 + adr)
   END ;
   fld := fld.next
END
END OutFlds;


PROCEDURE OutStr(typ: Struct);
VAR m, em, r: INTEGER; btyp: Struct; mod: Object;
BEGIN
IF typ.ref = 0 THEN
   m := typ.mno; btyp := typ.BaseTyp;
   IF m > 0 THEN mod := GlbMod[m−1]; em := mod.mode;
      IF em = NotYetExp THEN
         GlbMod[m−1].mode := nofExp; m := nofExp; INC(nofExp);
         WriteByte(22); WriteLInt(mod.a1); WriteId(mod.name)
      ELSE m := em
      END
   END;
   CASE typ.form OF
      Undef .. NoTyp:
   | Pointer: WriteByte(8);
            IF btyp.ref > 0 THEN WriteByte(btyp.ref)
            ELSE WriteByte(Undef);
               IF udpinx < maxUDP THEN undPtr[udpinx] := typ; INC(udpinx)
               ELSE OCS.Mark(224)
               END
            END ;
            WriteByte(m)
   | ProcTyp: OutStr(btyp); OutPars(typ.link);
            WriteByte(9); WriteByte(btyp.ref); WriteByte(m)
   | Array: OutStr(btyp);
            WriteByte(10); WriteByte(btyp.ref); WriteByte(m);
```

```
                        WriteLInt(typ.size); WriteInt(typ.adr); WriteLInt(typ.n)
            | DynArr: OutStr(btyp);
                        WriteByte(11); WriteByte(btyp.ref); WriteByte(m);
                        WriteLInt(typ.size); WriteInt(typ.adr)
            | Record:
                        IF btyp = NIL THEN r := NoTyp
                        ELSE OutStr(btyp); r := btyp.ref
                        END ;
                        OutFlds(typ.link, 0, TRUE); WriteByte(12); WriteByte(r); WriteByte(m);
                        WriteLInt(typ.size); WriteInt(typ.adr)
            END ;
            IF typ.strobj # NIL THEN
                IF typ.strobj.marked THEN WriteByte(2) ELSE WriteByte(3) END;
                WriteByte(strno); WriteByte(m); WriteId(typ.strobj.name)
            END ;
            typ.ref := strno; INC(strno);
            IF strno > maxStr THEN OCS.Mark(228) END
    END
END OutStr;


PROCEDURE OutObjs;
VAR obj: Object;
    f: INTEGER; xval: REAL; yval: LONGREAL;
BEGIN obj := topScope.next;
    WHILE obj # NIL DO
        IF obj.marked THEN
            IF obj.mode = Con THEN
                WriteByte(1); f := obj.typ.form; WriteByte(f);
                CASE f OF
                    Undef:
                | Byte, Bool, Char, SInt: WriteByte(SHORT(obj.a0))
                | Int: WriteInt(SHORT(obj.a0))
                | LInt, Real, Set: WriteLInt(obj.a0)
                | LReal: WriteLInt(obj.a0); WriteLInt(obj.a1)
                | String: WriteByte(0); OCS.Mark(221)
                | NilTyp:
                END;
                WriteId(obj.name)
            ELSIF obj.mode = Typ THEN
                OutStr(obj.typ);
                IF (obj.typ.strobj # obj) & (obj.typ.strobj # NIL) THEN
                    WriteByte(2); WriteByte(obj.typ.ref); WriteByte(0); WriteId(obj.name)
                END
            ELSIF obj.mode = Var THEN
                OutStr(obj.typ); WriteByte(4);
                WriteByte(obj.typ.ref); WriteLInt(obj.a0); WriteId(obj.name)
            ELSIF obj.mode = XProc THEN
                OutStr(obj.typ); OutPars(obj.dsc); WriteByte(5);
                WriteByte(obj.typ.ref); WriteByte(SHORT(obj.a0)); WriteId(obj.name)
            ELSIF obj.mode = CProc THEN
                OutStr(obj.typ); OutPars(obj.dsc); WriteByte(7);
                WriteByte(obj.typ.ref); WriteByte(2); WriteByte(226);
                WriteByte(SHORT(obj.a0)); WriteId(obj.name)
            END
        END ;
        obj := obj.next
    END
END OutObjs;
```

```
PROCEDURE Export*(VAR name, FileName: ARRAY OF CHAR;
        VAR newSF: BOOLEAN; VAR key: LONGINT);
    VAR i: INTEGER;
        ch0, ch1: CHAR;
        oldkey: LONGINT;
        typ: Struct;
        oldFile, newFile: Files.File;
        oldSR: Files.Rider;
BEGIN newFile := Files.New(FileName);
    IF newFile # NIL THEN
        Files.Set(SR, newFile, 0); Files.Write(SR, SFtag); strno := firstStr;
        WriteByte(22); WriteLInt(key); WriteId(name); nofExp := 1;
        OutObjs; i := 0;
        WHILE i < udpinx DO
            typ := undPtr[i]; OutStr(typ.BaseTyp); undPtr[i] := NIL; INC(i);
            WriteByte(20); (*fixup*)
            WriteByte(typ.ref); WriteByte(typ.BaseTyp.ref)
        END ;
        IF ~OCS.scanerr THEN
            oldFile := Files.Old(FileName);
            IF oldFile # NIL THEN (*compare*)
                Files.Set(oldSR, oldFile, 2); Files.ReadBytes(oldSR, oldkey, 4); Files.Set(SR, newFile, 6);
                REPEAT Files.Read(oldSR, ch0); Files.Read(SR, ch1)
                UNTIL (ch0 # ch1) OR SR.eof;
                IF oldSR.eof & SR.eof THEN (*equal*) newSF := FALSE; key := oldkey
                ELSIF newSF THEN Files.Register(newFile)
                ELSE OCS.Mark(155)
                END
            ELSE Files.Register(newFile); newSF := TRUE
            END
        ELSE newSF := FALSE
        END
    ELSE OCS.Mark(153)
    END
END Export;


(*----------------------- initialization -----------------------*)


PROCEDURE InitStruct(VAR typ: Struct; f: INTEGER);
BEGIN NEW(typ); typ.form := f; typ.ref := f; typ.size := 1
END InitStruct;


PROCEDURE EnterConst(name: ARRAY OF CHAR; value: INTEGER);
    VAR obj: Object;
BEGIN Insert(name, obj); obj.mode := Con; obj.typ := booltyp; obj.a0 := value
END EnterConst;


PROCEDURE EnterTyp(name: ARRAY OF CHAR; form, size: INTEGER; VAR res: Struct);
    VAR obj: Object; typ: Struct;
BEGIN Insert(name, obj);
    NEW(typ); obj.mode := Typ; obj.typ := typ; obj.marked := TRUE;
    typ.form := form; typ.strobj := obj; typ.size := size;
    typ.mno := 0; typ.ref := form; res := typ
END EnterTyp;


PROCEDURE EnterProc(name: ARRAY OF CHAR; num: INTEGER);
    VAR obj: Object;
```

BEGIN Insert(name, obj); obj.mode := SProc; obj.typ := notyp; obj.a0 := num
END EnterProc;

BEGIN topScope := NIL; InitStruct(undftyp, Undef); InitStruct(notyp, NoTyp);
    InitStruct(stringtyp, String); InitStruct(niltyp, NilTyp); OpenScope(0);
    (*initialization of module SYSTEM*)
    EnterProc("LSH", 22); EnterProc("ROT", 23); EnterProc("ADR", 9); EnterProc("OVFL",15);
    EnterProc("GET", 24); EnterProc("PUT", 25); EnterProc("BIT", 26); EnterProc("VAL", 27);
    EnterProc("NEW", 28); EnterProc("MOVE",30); EnterProc("CC", 2);
    EnterTyp("BYTE", Byte, 1, bytetyp);
    syslink := topScope.next; universe := topScope; topScope.next := NIL;
    EnterTyp("CHAR", Char, 1, chartyp); EnterTyp("SET", Set, 4, settyp);
    EnterTyp("REAL", Real, 4, realtyp); EnterTyp("INTEGER", Int, 2, inttyp);
    EnterTyp("LONGINT", LInt, 4, linttyp); EnterTyp("LONGREAL", LReal, 8, lrltyp);
    EnterTyp("SHORTINT", SInt, 1, sinttyp); EnterTyp("BOOLEAN", Bool, 1, booltyp);
    EnterProc("INC", 16); EnterProc("DEC", 17); EnterConst("FALSE", 0);
    EnterConst("TRUE", 1); EnterProc("HALT", 0); EnterProc("NEW", 1);
    EnterProc("ABS", 3); EnterProc("CAP", 4); EnterProc("ORD", 5);
    EnterProc("ENTIER", 6); EnterProc("SIZE", 7); EnterProc("ODD", 8);
    EnterProc("MIN", 10); EnterProc("MAX", 11); EnterProc("CHR", 12);
    EnterProc("SHORT", 13); EnterProc("LONG", 14); EnterProc("INCL", 18);
    EnterProc("EXCL", 19); EnterProc("LEN", 20); EnterProc("ASH", 21); EnterProc("COPY", 29)
END OCT.

12.7 Code selection

The procedures that determine the selection of instructions corresponding to the various syntactic constructs are contained in modules OCE
and OCH. They reflect the two-address nature of the target computer's
architecture. If, for example, a simple expression consisting of two terms
and an add operator is recognized, procedure *Op* is invoked, the first
parameter specifying addition and the other two denoting the operands.
The sum, representing the simple expression, is assigned to and thereby
replaces the first argument (x := x+y), mirroring the computer's two-
address instruction (ADDW y, x).

By *code selection* we understand the determination of operation
codes, of operand length codes and of addressing modes. The actual
code generation is delegated to module OCC. For example, the
instruction ADDW y, x is selected in procedure *OCE.Op*, which calls
the generating procedure OCC.PutF4(0+1, x, y), where 0 is the opcode
for ADDi, 1 is the length code for integers, and x and y are parameters
of type *Item* describing the operands. *Op* would, for example, select
another instruction, if y denoted a small constant, say 3, instead of a
variable; its selection would be ADDQW 3, x. Actual generation is then
achieved by calling OCC.PutF2(12+1, y.a0, x), where 12 is the opcode
of ADDQi and *y.a0* has the value 3.

Let us dwell somewhat longer on the above example. As explained before, during the evaluation of an expression, no declared variable may change its value. Therefore the sum cannot be stored in the location of variable x. In order to prevent this from happening, the destination operand is chosen to be a temporary, auxiliary variable allocated in a register. Because the first argument and the result are the same in a two-address instruction, the argument must be transferred into the register before addition. Hence the resulting code sequence is

```
MOVW x, r
ADDW y, r
```

Register allocation

where r stands for the mentioned register. Register allocation is done by procedure *OCC.GetReg*, which selects a free register and returns an *Item* with mode = *Reg*, which is one of the intermediate modes generated only during evaluation of expressions.

If the operands of an expression are integer constants, the specified operation is performed by the compiler, the result is represented by the result item, and no instructions are generated. This feature concerns all arithmetic operations in procedure *Op* and sign inversion in procedure *MOp*.

Constant folding

Note that overflow tests are not included in the program listing, but merely indicated by a comment. They can be programmed in a computer-independent form as shown here for addition:

IF x < 0 THEN
    IF (y < 0) & (x < min−y) THEN overflow ELSE sum := x+y END
ELSE
    IF (y > 0) & (x > max−y) THEN overflow ELSE sum := x+y END
END

Direct evaluation of expressions is also performed for negation of Boolean operands and for set union. The latter is implicitly invoked in the construction of sets. For instance, the constant set {0, 2} is computed as {0}+{2}. Constant expressions are not evaluated for real values. One reason is that this rare and avoidable case hardly justifies the additional complexity of the compiler, the other that overflow traps for floating-point operations cannot be suppressed.

The principal code selection procedures for expressions are listed below together with an abstract notation for their action:

Code selection procedures

Index(x, y)	x := x[y]
Field(x, y)	x := x.y
DeRef(x)	x := x ↑
TypTest(x, y, TRUE)	x := x IS y

TypTest(x, y, FALSE) x := x(y)
In(x, y)   x := x IN y
Set0(x, y)   x := {y}
Set1(x, y, z)   x := {y .. z}
MOp(op, x)   x := op y
Op(op, x, y)   x := x op y

Some of these procedures generate items with intermediate modes other than the Reg mode mentioned above. Before we explain the various mode transitions that items may undergo, we list in Table 12.3 the additional item modes, indicating how the resulting operand address is specified by the item-record's attributes a0, a1, and a2.

Item attributes

It is the goal of a good compiler to make use of all addressing modes offered by the computer, thereby avoiding the emission of unnecessary instructions for address computation. This requires that applicability of complex addressing modes be detected, and that instructions for address computations not be emitted before it is established that the situation cannot be handled with one of the available addressing modes. Procedures *Index*, *Field* and *DeRef* contain the necessary case analyses. The mode transitions performed are listed in Tables 12.4–12.7.

Mode transitions

Procedure *Index* also emits an index bound check (CHECKW, FLAG) if the compiler's index checking option is enabled. If the index y denotes a constant, the indexed variable's address is computed and no mode transition takes place.

Array indexing

Dynamic array parameters are treated similarly. Indirect addressing via descriptor is necessary even if the array is called by value. Bound checks cannot be performed by the compiler, even if the index is a constant.

Dynamic arrays

Table 12.3

Mode	Resulting address	Addressing mode
Var	a0	Direct mode
VarX	a0 + s*Reg[a2]	Indexed mode
Ind	Mem[a0] + a1	Indirect mode
IndX	Mem[a0] + a1 + s*Reg[a2]	Indexed indirect mode
RegI	Reg[a0] + a1	Register indirect mode
RegX	Reg[a0] + a1 + s*Reg[a2]	Indexed register indirect mode

s denotes a scale factor selected according to the type of operands (s = 1, 2, 4 or 8).

Table 12.4   Index(x, y), x is static array

Mode transition of x	Instruction emitted	Construct
Var → VarX		Array variable
Ind → IndX		Array, VAR parameter
RegI → RegX		Dereferenced array
VarX → VarX	INDEX	Indexed array (matrix)
IndX → IndX	INDEX	Indexed matrix parameter
RegX → RegX	INDEX	Dereferenced array (matrix)

Table 12.5   Index (x, y), x is dynamic array

Mode transition of x	Instruction emitted	Construct
Var → IndX		Dynamic array
Ind → IndX		Dynamic array, VAR parameter
RegI → RegX		Dereferenced array
IndX → IndX	INDEX	Indexed matrix VAR parameter
RegX → RegX	INDEX	Dereferenced array (matrix)

Table 12.6   Field(x, y)

Mode transition of x	Instruction emitted	Construct
Var → Var		Add field offset to record adr
Ind → Ind		Add field offset to record adr
RegI → RegI		Increment field offset
Others → RegI	ADDR	Offset becomes field offset

Table 12.7   DeRef(x)

Mode transition of x	Instruction emitted	Construct
Var → Ind		Reference via pointer
Others → RegI	ADDR	offset := 0

The *DeRef* procedure is called from *Compiler.selector*. The call may be due to an explicit dereferencing operator (↑), or it may be due to a field designator *p.f* or an array designator *p[i]*, if p denotes a pointer. Note that the transition Var → Ind is inapplicable in the case of external access, because the processor lacks an indirect external addressing mode.

Coc mode

Boolean expressions, and in particular comparisons, give rise to yet another intermediate item mode: the condition code mode *Coc*. This mode signifies that the operand's value is held in the condition code register in encoded form. Consider, for example, the expression x < y, which is translated into the single instruction CMPi y, x. The resulting Boolean item assumes the Coc mode, and its attribute a0 indicates that the value FALSE is obtained by an *Scond* (or *Bcond*) instruction with a0 as its condition mask. The a0 attribute depends on the relation (<) specified.

Compiling AND and OR

The cases of Boolean conjunction and disjunction are more intricate. As mentioned before, these operations must be represented by conditional jumps rather than explicit AND and OR instructions. For example, the expression

$$(x <= y) \ \& \ (y < z)$$

yields the instruction sequence

```
      CMPi     y, x
   L  BLT      ?
      CMPi     z, y
```

and the result item with Coc mode and a0 reflecting the relation < . In addition to the attribute a0, the attribute a1 identifies the location L of the BLT instruction, which performs a branch, if y < x, that is, ~(x <= y). The first two instructions are emitted by procedure *MOp* called from *Compiler.Term*, the last one by *Op* (also called from *Term*).

Similarly, the expression

$$(x = 1) \ \text{OR} \ (y = 3)$$

yields the instruction sequence

```
          CMPQi    1, x
     L    BEQ      ?
          CMPQi    3, y
```

and the result item with Coc mode and a0 reflecting the relation = .
The branch location L is specified by attribute a2 (instead of a1), because
the branch is taken when the first comparison yields TRUE (instead of
FALSE).

The more general cases of expressions p & q & ... & z and p
OR q OR ... OR z yield sets of conditional branches that are to be
taken if the expression value is FALSE or TRUE respectively. The
Fixup lists   locations of these branches are recorded in a list, the so-called *F list* or
T list respectively; its head is recorded by the attribute a1 (or a2), and
the links are embedded in the code in place of the branch addresses,
which will be inserted when the jump destinations are known.

The most general case requires the presence of both the F list
and the T list simultaneously. It is exemplified by the expression

(a < b) & (c < d) OR (e < f) & (g < h)

which is represented by the instructions

```
          CMPi     b, a
          BLE      L1
          CMPi     d, c
     L0   BGT      ?
     L1   CMPi     f, e
     L2   BLE      ?
          CMPi     h, g
```

The F list of the resulting item contains the single element L2,
and the T list the single element L0. For more details, the reader is
referred to the listing of module OCE below; the construction of the
lists and the substitution of links by the branch offsets is handled by
procedures in module OCC. In passing, we note that Boolean expressions
also occur in if, while and repeat statements, where the branch targets
are known only after the entire statement has been processed.

A fairly sizeable amount of program is devoted to the seemingly
Type inclusion   harmless concept of type inclusion. It is a relaxation of the strict
requirement of type equality of operands in an expression. However,
because the computer's instructions strictly require that both operands

Mixed expressions

be of the same type, they have to be preceded by conversion instructions in cases of 'mixed expressions'. We refrain from going into details, and merely mention that implicit conversions of integers are handled by MOVXij instructions implying sign extension, and those involving floating-point operands by MOVif and MOVFL instructions.

Standard functions

An even much larger part of module OCE is devoted to standard procedures and functions. Calls of them do not generate subroutine instructions, but rather in-line code. Therefore each standard procedure represents an individual case, and they have little in common. Some procedures, namely SIZE, ADR, MIN, MAX, CHR, SHORT, LEN, CC and VAL may not even generate any instructions. The three procedures *StPar1*, *StPar2* and *StPar3* are each devoted to the handling of one parameter. Typically, instructions are emitted after the last parameter is recognized.

```
MODULE OCE; (*NW 7.6.87 / 5.3.91*)
  IMPORT SYSTEM, OCS, OCT, OCC;

  CONST (*instruction format prefixes*)
    F6 = 4EH; F7 = 0CEH; F9 = 3EH; F11 = 0BEH;
    (*frequent operation codes: 5C, 5D, 5F = MOVQi, 14, 15, 17 = MOVi, 27 = ADDR*)

    (*object and item modes*)
    Var = 1; VarX = 2; Ind = 3; IndX = 4; RegI = 5;
    RegX = 6; Abs = 7; Con = 8; Stk = 9; Coc = 10;
    Reg = 11; Fld = 12; Typ = 13;

    (*structure forms*)
    Undef = 0; Byte = 1; Bool = 2; Char = 3; SInt = 4; Int = 5; LInt = 6;
    Real = 7; LReal = 8; Set = 9; String = 10; NilTyp = 11; NoTyp = 12;
    Pointer = 13; ProcTyp = 14; Array = 15; DynArr = 16; Record = 17;

  VAR inxchk*: BOOLEAN;
    log: INTEGER; (*side effect of mant*)
    lengcode: ARRAY 18 OF INTEGER;
    intSet, realSet: SET;

  PROCEDURE inverted(x: LONGINT): LONGINT;
  BEGIN (*inverted sense of condition code*)
    IF ODD(x) THEN RETURN x-1 ELSE RETURN x+1 END
  END inverted;

  PROCEDURE load(VAR x: OCT.Item);
    VAR y: OCT.Item;
  BEGIN
    IF x.mode < Reg THEN
      y := x; OCC.GetReg(x);
      IF (y.mode = Con) & (-8 <= y.a0) & (y.a0 <= 7) THEN
        OCC.PutF2(lengcode[x.typ.form] + 5CH, y.a0, x)
      ELSE OCC.PutF4(lengcode[x.typ.form] + 14H, x, y)
      END
```

```
      ELSIF x.mode > Reg THEN OCS.Mark(126)
      END
   END load;


   PROCEDURE loadX(VAR x: OCT.Item);
      VAR y: OCT.Item;
   BEGIN
      IF x.mode <= Reg THEN
         y := x; OCC.GetReg(x);IF (y.mode = Con) & (−8 <= y.a0) & (y.a0 <= 7) THEN
            OCC.PutF2(5FH, y.a0, x)
         ELSE OCC.Put(F7, lengcode[x.typ.form] + 1CH, x, y) (*MOVXiD*)
         END
      ELSIF x.mode > Reg THEN OCS.Mark(126)
      END
   END loadX;


   PROCEDURE loadF(VAR x: OCT.Item);
      VAR y: OCT.Item;
   BEGIN
      IF x.mode < Reg THEN
         y := x; OCC.GetFReg(x); OCC.Put(F11, lengcode[x.typ.form] + 4, x, y) (*MOVf*)
      ELSIF x.mode > Reg THEN OCS.Mark(126)
      END
   END loadF;


   PROCEDURE loadB(VAR x: OCT.Item); (*Coc−Mode*)
      VAR L0, L1: LONGINT;
   BEGIN
      IF (x.a1 = 0) & (x.a2 = 0) THEN
         L0 := x.a0; OCC.GetReg(x); OCC.PutF2(3CH, L0, x)
      ELSE OCC.PutF0(inverted(x.a0)); OCC.PutWord(x.a2); L0 := OCC.pc − 2;
         OCC.FixLink(x.a1); OCC.GetReg(x); OCC.PutF2(5CH, 1, x);
         OCC.PutF0(14); L1 := OCC.pc; OCC.PutWord(0);
         OCC.FixLink(L0); OCC.PutF2(5CH, 0, x); OCC.fixup(L1)
      END
   END loadB;


   PROCEDURE loadAdr(VAR x: OCT.Item);
      VAR y: OCT.Item;
   BEGIN
      IF x.mode < Con THEN
         y := x; OCC.GetReg(x);
         IF (y.mode = Ind) & (y.a1 = 0) THEN y.mode := Var; OCC.PutF4(17H, x, y)
         ELSE OCC.PutF4(27H, x, y); x.a1 := 0
         END ;
         x.mode := RegI; x.obj := NIL
      ELSE OCS.Mark(127)
      END
   END loadAdr;


   PROCEDURE setCC(VAR x: OCT.Item; cc: LONGINT);
   BEGIN
      x.typ := OCT.booltyp; x.mode := Coc; x.a0 := cc; x.a1 := 0; x.a2 := 0
   END setCC;


   PROCEDURE cmp(L: INTEGER; VAR x, y: OCT.Item);
```

```
BEGIN
   IF (y.mode = Con) & (y.a0 <= 7) & (y.a0 >= -8) THEN
      OCC.PutF2(L+1CH, y.a0, x) (*CMPQi*)
   ELSE OCC.PutF4(L+4, x, y) (*CMPi*)
   END
END cmp;

PROCEDURE add(L: INTEGER; VAR x, y: OCT.Item);
BEGIN
   IF (y.mode = Con) & (y.a0 <= 7) & (y.a0 >= -8) THEN
      OCC.PutF2(L+0CH, y.a0, x) (*ADDQi*)
   ELSE OCC.PutF4(L, x, y) (*ADDi*)
   END
END add;

PROCEDURE sub(L: INTEGER; VAR x, y: OCT.Item);
BEGIN
   IF (y.mode = Con) & (y.a0 <= 8) & (y.a0 >= -7) THEN
      OCC.PutF2(L+0CH, -y.a0, x) (*ADDQi*)
   ELSE OCC.PutF4(L+20H, x, y) (*SUBi*)
   END
END sub;

PROCEDURE mant(x: LONGINT): LONGINT; (*x DIV 2 ↑ log*)
BEGIN log := 0;
   IF x > 0 THEN
      WHILE ~ODD(x) DO x := x DIV 2; INC(log) END
   END ;
   RETURN x
END mant;

PROCEDURE SetIntType*(VAR x: OCT.Item);
   VAR v: LONGINT;
BEGIN v := x.a0;
   IF (-80H <= v) & (v <= 7FH) THEN x.typ := OCT.sinttyp
   ELSIF (-8000H <= v) & (v <= 7FFFH) THEN x.typ := OCT.inttyp
   ELSE x.typ := OCT.linttyp
   END
END SetIntType;

PROCEDURE AssReal*(VAR x: OCT.Item; y: REAL);
BEGIN SYSTEM.PUT(SYSTEM.ADR(x.a0), y)
END AssReal;

PROCEDURE AssLReal*(VAR x: OCT.Item; y: LONGREAL);
BEGIN SYSTEM.PUT(SYSTEM.ADR(x.a0), y)
END AssLReal;

PROCEDURE Index*(VAR x, y: OCT.Item);
   VAR f, n: INTEGER; i: LONGINT;
      eltyp: OCT.Struct; y1, z: OCT.Item;
   BEGIN f := y.typ.form;
      IF ~(f IN intSet) THEN OCS.Mark(80); y.typ := OCT.inttyp END ;
      IF x.typ = NIL THEN HALT(80) END ;
      IF x.typ.form = Array THEN
         eltyp := x.typ.BaseTyp; n := x.typ.n;
```

```
      IF eltyp = NIL THEN HALT(81) END ;
      IF y.mode = Con THEN
        IF (0 <= y.a0) & (y.a0 < n) THEN i := y.a0 * eltyp.size
        ELSE OCS.Mark(81); i := 0
        END ;
        IF x.mode = Var THEN INC(x.a0, i)
        ELSIF (x.mode = Ind) OR (x.mode = RegI) THEN INC(x.a1, i); x.obj := NIL
        ELSE loadAdr(x); x.a1 := i
        END
      ELSE
        IF inxchk THEN (*z = bound descr*)
          z.mode := Var; z.a0 := x.typ.adr; z.lev := -x.typ.mno;
          IF y.mode = Reg THEN y1 := y ELSE OCC.GetReg(y1) END ;
          IF f = SInt THEN OCC.Put(F7, 10H, y1, y); y := y1 END ; (*MOVXBW*)
          OCC.Put(0EEH, SHORT(y1.a0)*8+1, y, z); OCC.PutF1(0D2H) (*CHECK, FLAG*)
        ELSE
          IF f = LInt THEN load(y) ELSE loadX(y) END ;
          y1 := y
        END ;
        f := x.mode;
        IF x.mode = Var THEN x.mode := VarX; x.a2 := y1.a0
        ELSIF x.mode = Ind THEN x.mode := IndX; x.a2 := y1.a0
        ELSIF x.mode = RegI THEN x.mode := RegX; x.a2 := y1.a0
        ELSIF x.mode IN {VarX, IndX, RegX} THEN
          z.mode := Con; z.typ := OCT.inttyp;
          z.a0 := (x.typ.size DIV eltyp.size) - 1;
          OCC.Put(2EH, SHORT(x.a2)*8+5, y1, z) (*INDEX*)
        ELSE loadAdr(x); x.mode := RegX; x.a1 := 0; x.a2 := y1.a0
        END
      END ;
      x.typ := eltyp
    ELSIF x.typ.form = DynArr THEN
      IF inxchk THEN
        z.mode := Var; z.a0 := x.a0 + x.typ.adr; z.lev := x.lev;
        IF y.mode = Reg THEN y1 := y ELSE OCC.GetReg(y1) END ;
        IF f = SInt THEN
          IF y.mode = Con THEN y.typ := OCT.inttyp
          ELSE OCC.Put(F7, 10H, y1, y); y := y1
          END
        END ;
        OCC.Put(0EEH, SHORT(y1.a0)*8+1, y, z); OCC.PutF1(0D2H) (*CHECK, FLAG*)
      ELSE
        IF f = LInt THEN load(y) ELSE loadX(y) END ;
        y1 := y
      END ;
      IF x.mode IN {Var, Ind} THEN x.mode := IndX; x.a2 := y1.a0
      ELSIF x.mode = RegI THEN x.mode := RegX; x.a2 := y1.a0
      ELSIF x.mode IN {IndX, RegX} THEN
        z.mode := Var; z.a0 := x.a0 + x.typ.adr; z.lev := x.lev;
        OCC.Put(2EH, SHORT(x.a2)*8+5, y1, z) (*INDEX*)
      ELSE loadAdr(x); x.mode := RegX; x.a1 := 0; x.a2 := y1.a0
      END ;
      x.typ := x.typ.BaseTyp
    ELSE OCS.Mark(82)
    END
  END Index;


  PROCEDURE Field*(VAR x: OCT.Item; y: OCT.Object);
```

```
BEGIN (*x.typ.form = Record*)
    IF (y # NIL) & (y.mode = Fld) THEN
        IF x.mode = Var THEN INC(x.a0, y.a0)
        ELSIF (x.mode = Ind) OR (x.mode = RegI) THEN INC(x.a1, y.a0)
        ELSE loadAdr(x); x.mode := RegI; x.a1 := y.a0
        END ;
        x.typ := y.typ; x.obj := NIL
    ELSE OCS.Mark(83); x.typ := OCT.undftyp; x.mode := Var
    END
END Field;


PROCEDURE DeRef*(VAR x: OCT.Item);
BEGIN
    IF x.typ.form = Pointer THEN
        IF (x.mode = Var) & (x.lev >= 0) THEN x.mode := Ind
        ELSE load(x); x.mode := RegI
        END ;
        x.typ := x.typ.BaseTyp; x.obj := OCC.wasderef
    ELSE OCS.Mark(84)
    END ;
    x.a1 := 0
END DeRef;


PROCEDURE TypTest*(VAR x, y: OCT.Item; test: BOOLEAN);

    PROCEDURE GTT(t0, t1: OCT.Struct; varpar: BOOLEAN);
    VAR t: OCT.Struct; xt, tdes, p: OCT.Item;
    BEGIN
        IF t0 # t1 THEN t := t1;
            REPEAT t := t.BaseTyp UNTIL (t = NIL) OR (t = t0);
            IF t # NIL THEN x.typ := y.typ;
                IF OCC.typchk OR test THEN xt := x;
                    IF varpar THEN xt.mode := Ind; xt.a0 := x.a0+4
                    ELSIF (x.mode = Var) & (x.lev >= 0) THEN
                        xt.mode := Ind; xt.a1 := -4; load(xt); xt.mode := RegI
                    ELSE load(xt); p := xt; p.mode := RegI; p.a1 := -4;
                        OCC.PutF4(17H, xt, p); (*MOVD -4(xt), xt *) xt.mode := RegI
                    END ;
                    xt.a1 := t1.n * 4; tdes.mode := Var; tdes.lev := -t1.mno; tdes.a0 := t1.adr;
                    OCC.PutF4(7, tdes, xt); (*CMPD*)
                    IF ~test THEN
                        OCC.PutF0(0); OCC.PutDisp(4); OCC.PutF1(0F2H); OCC.PutByte(18)
                            (*BPT*)
                    ELSE setCC(x, 0)
                    END
                END
            ELSE OCS.Mark(85);
                IF test THEN x.typ := OCT.booltyp END
            END
        ELSIF test THEN setCC(x, 14)
        END
    END GTT;

BEGIN
    IF x.typ.form = Pointer THEN
        IF y.typ.form = Pointer THEN
            GTT(x.typ.BaseTyp, y.typ.BaseTyp, FALSE)
```

```
        ELSE OCS.Mark(86)
        END
    ELSIF (x.typ.form = Record) & (x.mode = Ind) & (x.obj # NIL) &
        (x.obj # OCC.wasderef) & (y.typ.form = Record) THEN
        GTT(x.typ, y.typ, TRUE)
    ELSE OCS.Mark(87)
    END
END TypTest;


PROCEDURE In*(VAR x, y: OCT.Item);
    VAR f: INTEGER;
BEGIN f := x.typ.form;
    IF (f IN intSet) & (y.typ.form = Set) THEN
        IF y.mode = Con THEN load(y) END ;
        OCC.PutF4(lengcode[f]+34H, y, x); setCC(x, 8) (*TBITi*)
    ELSE OCS.Mark(92); x.mode := Reg
    END ;
    x.typ := OCT.booltyp
END In;


PROCEDURE Set0*(VAR x, y: OCT.Item);
    VAR one: LONGINT;
BEGIN x.mode := Reg; x.a0 := 0; x.typ := OCT.settyp;
    IF y.typ.form IN intSet THEN
        IF y.mode = Con THEN x.mode := Con;
            IF (0 <= y.a0) & (y.a0 < 32) THEN one := 1; x.a0 := SYSTEM.LSH(one, y.a0)
            ELSE OCS.Mark(202)
            END
        ELSE OCC.GetReg(x); OCC.PutF2(5FH, 1, x); OCC.Put(F6, 17H, x, y) (*LSHD*)
        END
    ELSE OCS.Mark(93)
    END
END Set0;


PROCEDURE Set1*(VAR x, y, z: OCT.Item);
    VAR s: LONGINT;
BEGIN x.mode := Reg; x.a0 := 0; x.typ := OCT.settyp;
    IF (y.typ.form IN intSet) & (z.typ.form IN intSet) THEN
        IF y.mode = Con THEN
            IF (0 <= y.a0) & (y.a0 < 32) THEN
                y.typ := OCT.settyp; s := -1; y.a0 := SYSTEM.LSH(s, y.a0);
            IF z.mode = Con THEN
                x.mode := Con;
                IF (y.a0 <= z.a0) & (z.a0 < 32) THEN s := -2;
                    x.a0 := y.a0 - SYSTEM.LSH(s, z.a0)
                ELSE OCS.Mark(202); x.a0 := 0
                END
            ELSIF y.a0 = -1 THEN
                OCC.GetReg(x); OCC.PutF2(5FH, -2, x); OCC.Put(F6, 17H, x, z);
                OCC.Put(F6, 37H, x, x) (*LSHD, COMD*)
            ELSE OCC.GetReg(x); OCC.PutF4(17H, x, y); OCC.GetReg(y);
                OCC.PutF2(5FH, -2, y); OCC.Put(F6, 17H, y, z);
                OCC.PutF4(0BH, x, y) (*BICD*)
            END
        ELSE OCS.Mark(202)
        END
    ELSE OCC.GetReg(x); OCC.PutF2(5FH, -1, x); OCC.Put(F6, 17H, x, y);
```

```
          IF z.mode = Con THEN
             IF (0 <= z.a0) & (z.a0 < 32) THEN
                y.typ := OCT.settyp; y.mode := Con; s := -2;
                y.a0 := SYSTEM.LSH(s, z.a0)
             ELSE OCS.Mark(202)
             END
          ELSE OCC.GetReg(y); OCC.PutF2(5FH, -2, y); OCC.Put(F6, 17H, y, z) (*LSHD*)
          END ;
          OCC.PutF4(0BH, x, y) (*BICD*)
       END
    ELSE OCS.Mark(93)
    END
END Set1;


PROCEDURE MOp*(op: INTEGER; VAR x: OCT.Item);
    VAR f, L: INTEGER; a: LONGINT; y: OCT.Item;
BEGIN f := x.typ.form;
    CASE op OF
    5: (*&*)
       IF x.mode = Coc THEN
          OCC.PutF0(inverted(x.a0)); OCC.PutWord(x.a2);
          x.a2 := OCC.pc-2; OCC.FixLink(x.a1)
       ELSIF (x.typ.form = Bool) & (x.mode # Con) THEN
          OCC.PutF2(1CH, 1, x); setCC(x, 0);
          OCC.PutF0(1); OCC.PutWord(x.a2); x.a2 := OCC.pc-2; OCC.FixLink(x.a1)
       ELSIF x.typ.form # Bool THEN
          OCS.Mark(94); x.mode := Con; x.typ := OCT.booltyp; x.a0 := 0
       END
    | 6: (*+*)
       IF ~(f IN intSet + realSet) THEN OCS.Mark(96) END
    | 7: (*-*)
       y := x; L := lengcode[f];
       IF f IN intSet THEN
          IF x.mode = Con THEN x.a0 := -x.a0; SetIntType(x)
          ELSE OCC.GetReg(x); OCC.Put(F6, L+20H, x, y) (*NEGi*)
          END
       ELSIF f IN realSet THEN
          OCC.GetFReg(x); OCC.Put(F11, L+14H, x, y) (*NEGf*)
       ELSIF f = Set THEN OCC.GetReg(x); OCC.Put(F6, 37H, x, y) (*COMD*)
       ELSE OCS.Mark(97)
       END
    | 8: (*OR*)
       IF x.mode = Coc THEN
          OCC.PutF0(x.a0); OCC.PutWord(x.a1); x.a1 := OCC.pc-2;
          OCC.FixLink(x.a2)
       ELSIF (x.typ.form = Bool) & (x.mode # Con) THEN
          OCC.PutF2(1CH, 1, x); setCC(x, 0);
          OCC.PutF0(0); OCC.PutWord(x.a1); x.a1 := OCC.pc-2; OCC.FixLink(x.a2)
       ELSIF x.typ.form # Bool THEN
          OCS.Mark(95); x.mode := Con; x.typ := OCT.booltyp; x.a0 := 1
       END
    | 9 .. 14: (*relations*)
       IF x.mode = Coc THEN loadB(x) END
    | 32: (*~*)
       IF x.typ.form = Bool THEN
          IF x.mode = Coc THEN x.a0 := inverted(x.a0);
             a := x.a1; x.a1 := x.a2; x.a2 := a
          ELSE OCC.PutF2(1CH, 0, x); setCC(x, 0)
```

```
                END
            ELSE OCS.Mark(98)
            END
        END
    END MOp;


    PROCEDURE convert1(VAR x: OCT.Item; typ: OCT.Struct);
        VAR y: OCT.Item; op: INTEGER;
    BEGIN
        IF x.mode # Con THEN
            y := x;
            IF typ.form = Int THEN op := 10H
            ELSE op := lengcode[x.typ.form] + 1CH
            END;
            IF x.mode < Reg THEN OCC.GetReg(x) END ;
            OCC.Put(F7, op, x, y) (*MOVij*)
        END ;
        x.typ := typ
    END convert1;


    PROCEDURE convert2(VAR x: OCT.Item; typ: OCT.Struct);
        VAR y: OCT.Item;
    BEGIN y := x; OCC.GetFReg(x); (*MOVif*)
        OCC.Put(F9, lengcode[typ.form]*4 + lengcode[x.typ.form], x, y); x.typ := typ
    END convert2;


    PROCEDURE convert3(VAR x: OCT.Item);
        VAR y: OCT.Item;
    BEGIN y := x;
        IF x.mode < Reg THEN OCC.GetFReg(x) END ;
        OCC.Put(F9, 1BH, x, y); x.typ := OCT.lrltyp (*MOVFL*)
    END convert3;


    PROCEDURE Op*(op: INTEGER; VAR x, y: OCT.Item);
        VAR f, g, L: INTEGER; p, q, r: OCT.Struct;


        PROCEDURE strings(): BOOLEAN;
        BEGIN RETURN
            ((((f=Array) OR (f=DynArr)) & (x.typ.BaseTyp.form=Char)) OR (f=String)) &
            ((((g=Array) OR (g=DynArr)) & (y.typ.BaseTyp.form=Char)) OR (g=String))
        END strings;


        PROCEDURE CompStrings(cc: INTEGER; Q: BOOLEAN);
            VAR z: OCT.Item;
        BEGIN z.mode := Reg; z.a0 := 2;
            IF f = DynArr THEN OCC.DynArrAdr(z, x)
            ELSE OCC.PutF4(27H, z, x)
            END ;
            z.a0 := 1;
            IF g = DynArr THEN OCC.DynArrAdr(z, y)
            ELSE OCC.PutF4(27H, z, y)
            END ;
            z.a0 := 0; OCC.PutF2(5FH, −1, z); (*MOVQD −1, R0*)
            z.a0 := 4; OCC.PutF2(5FH, 0, z); (*MOVQD 0, R4*)
            OCC.PutF1(14); OCC.PutF1(4); OCC.PutF1(6); (*CMPSB 6*)
            IF Q THEN (*compare also with zero byte*)
```

```
            OCC.PutF0(9); OCC.PutDisp(5); (*BFC*)
            z.mode := RegI; z.a0 := 2; z.a1 := 0; OCC.PutF2(1CH, 0, z) (*CMPQB*)
        END ;
        setCC(x, cc)
    END CompStrings;

    PROCEDURE CompBool(cc: INTEGER);
    BEGIN
        IF y.mode = Coc THEN loadB(y) END ;
        OCC.PutF4(4, x, y); setCC(x, cc)
    END CompBool;

BEGIN
    IF x.typ # y.typ THEN
        g := y.typ.form;
        CASE x.typ.form OF
                    Undef:
        | SInt:     IF g = Int THEN convert1(x, y.typ)
                    ELSIF g = LInt THEN convert1(x, y.typ)
                    ELSIF g = Real THEN convert2(x, y.typ)
                    ELSIF g = LReal THEN convert2(x, y.typ)
                    ELSE OCS.Mark(100)
                    END
        | Int:      IF g = SInt THEN convert1(y, x.typ)
                    ELSIF g = LInt THEN convert1(x, y.typ)
                    ELSIF g = Real THEN convert2(x, y.typ)
                    ELSIF g = LReal THEN convert2(x, y.typ)
                    ELSE OCS.Mark(100)
                    END
        | LInt:     IF g = SInt THEN convert1(y, x.typ)
                    ELSIF g = Int THEN convert1(y, x.typ)
                    ELSIF g = Real THEN convert2(x, y.typ)
                    ELSIF g = LReal THEN convert2(x, y.typ)
                    ELSE OCS.Mark(100)
                    END
        | Real:   IF g = SInt THEN convert2(y, x.typ)
                    ELSIF g = Int THEN convert2(y, x.typ)
                    ELSIF g = LInt THEN convert2(y, x.typ)
                    ELSIF g = LReal THEN convert3(x)
                    ELSE OCS.Mark(100)
                    END
        | LReal:    IF g = SInt THEN convert2(y, x.typ)
                    ELSIF g = Int THEN convert2(y, x.typ)
                    ELSIF g = LInt THEN convert2(y, x.typ)
                    ELSIF g = Real THEN convert3(y)
                    ELSE OCS.Mark(100)
                    END
        | NilTyp:   IF g # Pointer THEN OCS.Mark(100) END
        | Pointer:  IF g = Pointer THEN
                        p := x.typ.BaseTyp; q := y.typ.BaseTyp;
                        IF (p.form = Record) & (q.form = Record) THEN
                            IF p.n < q.n THEN r := p; p := q; q := r END;
                            WHILE (p # q) & (p # NIL) DO p := p.BaseTyp END;
                            IF p = NIL THEN OCS.Mark(100) END
                        ELSE OCS.Mark(100)
                        END
                    ELSIF g # NilTyp THEN OCS.Mark(100)
                    END
```

```
      | ProcTyp:   IF g # NilTyp THEN OCS.Mark(100) END
      | Array, DynArr, String:
      | Byte, Bool, Char, Set, NoTyp, Record: OCS.Mark(100)
      END
    END ;
    f := x.typ.form; g := y.typ.form; L := lengcode[f];


    CASE op OF
      1:IF f IN intSet THEN (***)
          IF (x.mode = Con) & (y.mode = Con) THEN (*ovfl test missing*)
              x.a0 := x.a0 * y.a0; SetIntType(x)
          ELSIF (x.mode = Con) & (mant(x.a0) = 1) THEN
              x.a0 := log; x.typ := OCT.sinttyp;
              load(y); OCC.Put(F6, L+4, y, x); (*ASHi*) x := y
          ELSIF (y.mode = Con) & (mant(y.a0) = 1) THEN
              y.a0 := log; y.typ := OCT.sinttyp;
              load(x); OCC.Put(F6, L+4, x, y) (*ASHi*)
          ELSE load(x); OCC.Put(F7, L+20H, x, y) (*MULi*)
          END
        ELSIF f IN realSet THEN
          loadF(x); OCC.Put(F11, 30H+L, x, y) (*MULf*)
        ELSIF f = Set THEN
          load(x); OCC.PutF4(2BH, x, y) (*ANDD*)
        ELSIF f # Undef THEN OCS.Mark(101)
        END
      | 2:IF f IN realSet THEN (*/*)
          loadF(x); OCC.Put(F11, 20H+L, x, y) (*DIVf*)
        ELSIF f IN intSet THEN
          convert2(x, OCT.realtyp); convert2(y, OCT.realtyp);
          OCC.Put(F11, 21H, x, y) (*DIVF*)
        ELSIF f = Set THEN
          load(x); OCC.PutF4(3BH, x, y) (*XORD*)
              ELSIF f # Undef THEN OCS.Mark(102)
        END
      | 3:IF f IN intSet THEN (*DIV*)
          IF (x.mode = Con) & (y.mode = Con) THEN
              IF y.a0 # 0 THEN x.a0 := x.a0 DIV y.a0; SetIntType(x)
              ELSE OCS.Mark(205)
              END
          ELSIF (y.mode = Con) & (mant(y.a0) = 1) THEN
              y.a0 := −log; y.typ := OCT.sinttyp;
              load(x); OCC.Put(F6, L+4, x, y) (*ASHi*)
          ELSE load(x); OCC.Put(F7, L+3CH, x, y) (*DIVi*)
          END
        ELSIF f # Undef THEN OCS.Mark(103)
        END
      | 4:IF f IN intSet THEN (*MOD*)
          IF (x.mode = Con) & (y.mode = Con) THEN
              IF y.a0 # 0 THEN x.a0 := x.a0 MOD y.a0; x.typ := y.typ
              ELSE OCS.Mark(205)
                  END
              ELSIF (y.mode = Con) & (mant(y.a0) = 1) THEN
                  y.a0 := ASH(−1, log); load(x); OCC.PutF4(L+8, x, y) (*BICi*)
              ELSE load(x); OCC.Put(F7, L+38H, x, y) (*MODi*)
              END
          ELSIF f # Undef THEN OCS.Mark(104)
          END
        | 5:IF y.mode # Coc THEN (*&*)
```

```
          IF y.mode = Con THEN
              IF y.a0 = 1 THEN setCC(y, 14) ELSE setCC(y, 15) END
          ELSIF y.mode <= Reg THEN OCC.PutF2(1CH, 1, y); setCC(y, 0)
          ELSE OCS.Mark(94); setCC(y, 0)
          END
        END ;
        IF x.mode = Con THEN
            IF x.a0 = 0 THEN OCC.FixLink(y.a1); OCC.FixLink(y.a2); setCC(y, 15) END ;
            setCC(x, 0)
        END;
        IF y.a2 # 0 THEN x.a2 := OCC.MergedLinks(x.a2, y.a2) END ;
        x.a0 := y.a0; x.a1 := y.a1
| 6:IF f IN intSet THEN (*+*)
        IF (x.mode = Con) & (y.mode = Con) THEN
            INC(x.a0, y.a0); SetIntType(x) (*ovfl test missing*)
        ELSE load(x); add(L, x, y)
        END
      ELSIF f IN realSet THEN
        loadF(x); OCC.Put(F11, L, x, y) (*ADDf*)
      ELSIF f = Set THEN
        IF (x.mode = Con) & (y.mode = Con) THEN x.a0 := SYSTEM.VAL (LONGINT,
              SYSTEM.VAL(SET, x.a0) + SYSTEM.VAL(SET, y.a0))
        ELSE load(x); OCC.PutF4(1BH, x, y) (*ORD*)
        END
      ELSIF f # Undef THEN OCS.Mark(105)
      END
| 7:IF f IN intSet THEN (*-*)
        IF (x.mode = Con) & (y.mode = Con) THEN
            DEC(x.a0, y.a0); SetIntType(x) (*ovfl test missing*)
        ELSE load(x); sub(L, x, y)
        END
      ELSIF f IN realSet THEN
        loadF(x); OCC.Put(F11, 10H+L, x, y) (*SUBf*)
      ELSIF f = Set THEN load(x); OCC.PutF4(0BH, x, y) (*BICD*)
      ELSIF f # Undef THEN OCS.Mark(106)
      END
| 8:IF y.mode # Coc THEN (*OR*)
        IF y.mode = Con THEN
            IF y.a0 = 1 THEN setCC(y, 14) ELSE setCC(y, 15) END
        ELSIF y.mode <= Reg THEN OCC.PutF2(1CH, 1, y); setCC(y, 0)
        ELSE OCS.Mark(95); setCC(y, 0)
        END
      END ;
      IF x.mode = Con THEN
          IF x.a0 = 1 THEN OCC.FixLink(y.a1); OCC.FixLink(y.a2); setCC(y, 14) END ;
          setCC(x, 0)
      END ;
      IF y.a1 # 0 THEN x.a1 := OCC.MergedLinks(x.a1, y.a1) END ;
      x.a0 := y.a0; x.a2 := y.a2
| 9:IF f IN {Undef, Char..LInt, Set, NilTyp, Pointer, ProcTyp} THEN
        cmp(L, x, y); setCC(x, 0)
      ELSIF f IN realSet THEN OCC.Put(F11, 8+L, x, y); setCC(x, 0)
      ELSIF f = Bool THEN CompBool(0)
      ELSIF strings() THEN CompStrings(0, TRUE)
      ELSE OCS.Mark(107)
      END
|10:IF f IN {Undef, Char..LInt, Set, NilTyp, Pointer, ProcTyp} THEN
        cmp(L, x, y); setCC(x, 1)
```

```
                    ELSIF f IN realSet THEN OCC.Put(F11, 8+L, x, y); setCC(x, 1)
                    ELSIF f = Bool THEN CompBool(1)
                    ELSIF strings() THEN CompStrings(1, TRUE)
                    ELSE OCS.Mark(107)
                    END
               |11:IF f IN intSet THEN cmp(L, x, y); setCC(x, 6)
                    ELSIF f = Char THEN cmp(0, x, y); setCC(x, 4)
                    ELSIF f IN realSet THEN OCC.Put(F11, 8+L, x, y); setCC(x, 6)
                    ELSIF strings() THEN CompStrings(4, FALSE)
                    ELSE OCS.Mark(108)
                    END
               |12:IF f IN intSet THEN cmp(L, x, y); setCC(x, 13)
                    ELSIF f = Char THEN cmp(0, x, y); setCC(x, 11)
                    ELSIF f IN realSet THEN OCC.Put(F11, 8+L, x, y); setCC(x, 13)
                    ELSIF strings() THEN CompStrings(11, TRUE)
                    ELSE OCS.Mark(108)
                    END
               |13:IF f IN intSet THEN cmp(L, x, y); setCC(x, 12)
                    ELSIF f = Char THEN cmp(0, x, y); setCC(x, 10)
                    ELSIF f IN realSet THEN OCC.Put(F11, 8+L, x, y); setCC(x, 12)
                    ELSIF strings() THEN CompStrings(10, TRUE)
                    ELSE OCS.Mark(108)
                    END
               |14:IF f IN intSet THEN cmp(L, x, y); setCC(x, 7)
                    ELSIF f = Char THEN cmp(0, x, y); setCC(x, 5)
                    ELSIF f IN realSet THEN OCC.Put(F11, 8+L, x, y); setCC(x, 7)
                    ELSIF strings() THEN CompStrings(5, FALSE)
                    ELSE OCS.Mark(108)
                    END
          END
     END Op;


     PROCEDURE StPar1*(VAR x: OCT.Item; fctno: INTEGER);
          VAR f, L: INTEGER; s: LONGINT; y: OCT.Item;
     BEGIN f := x.typ.form;
          CASE fctno OF
               0: (*HALT*)
                    IF (f = SInt) & (x.mode = Con) THEN
                         IF x.a0 >= 20 THEN OCC.PutF1(0F2H); OCC.PutByte(x.a0) (*BPT*)
                         ELSE OCS.Mark(218)
                         END
                    ELSE OCS.Mark(217)
                    END ;
                    x.typ := OCT.notyp
             | 1: (*NEW*) y.mode := Reg;
                    IF f = Pointer THEN
                         y.a0 := 0; OCC.PutF4(27H, y, x);
                         x.typ := x.typ.BaseTyp; f := x.typ.form;
                         IF x.typ.size > 7FFF80H THEN OCS.Mark(227)
                    ELSIF f = Record THEN
                         y.a0 := 1; x.mode := Var; x.lev := −x.typ.mno;
                         x.a0 := x.typ.adr; OCC.PutF4(17H, y, x);
                         OCC.PutF1(0E2H); OCC.PutByte(0) (*SVC 0*)
                    ELSIF f = Array THEN
                         y.a0 := 2; x.a0 := x.typ.size; x.mode := Con; x.typ := OCT.linttyp;
                         OCC.PutF4(17H, y, x); OCC.PutF1(0E2H); OCC.PutByte(1) (*SVC 1*)
                    ELSE OCS.Mark(111)
                    END
```

```
      ELSE OCS.Mark(111)
      END ;
      x.typ := OCT.notyp
  | 2: (*CC*)
      IF (f = SInt) & (x.mode = Con) THEN
          IF (0 <= x.a0) & (x.a0 < 16) THEN setCC(x, x.a0)
          ELSE OCS.Mark(219)
          END
      ELSE OCS.Mark(217)
      END
  | 3: (*ABS*) y := x; L := lengcode[f]; IF f IN intSet THEN
          OCC.GetReg(x); OCC.Put(F6, 30H+L, x, y) (*ABSi*)
      ELSIF f IN realSet THEN
          OCC.GetFReg(x); OCC.Put(F11, 34H+L, x, y) (*ABSf*)
      ELSE OCS.Mark(111)
      END
  | 4: (*CAP*) y.mode := Con; y.typ := OCT.chartyp; y.a0 := 5FH;
      IF f = Char THEN load(x); OCC.PutF4(28H, x, y) (*ANDB*)
      ELSE OCS.Mark(111); x.typ := OCT.chartyp
      END
  | 5: (*ORD*) IF (f = Char) OR (f = Byte) THEN
          IF x.mode # Con THEN
              y := x; OCC.GetReg(x); OCC.Put(F7, 14H, x, y) (*MOVZBW*)
          END
      ELSE OCS.Mark(111)
      END ;
      x.typ := OCT.inttyp
  | 6: (*ENTIER*)
      IF f IN realSet THEN
          y := x; OCC.GetReg(x); OCC.Put(F9, lengcode[f]*4 + 3BH, x, y)
              (*FLOORfD*)
      ELSE OCS.Mark(111)
      END ;
      x.typ := OCT.linttyp
  | 7: (*SIZE*)
      IF x.mode = Typ THEN x.a0 := x.typ.size
      ELSE OCS.Mark(110); x.a0 := 1
      END ;
      x.mode := Con; SetIntType(x)
  | 8: (*ODD*)
      IF f IN intSet THEN
          y.mode := Con; y.typ := OCT.sinttyp; y.a0 := 0; OCC.PutF4(34H, x, y)
              (*TBITB 0*)
      ELSE OCS.Mark(111)
      END ;
      setCC(x, 8)
  | 9: (*ADR*)
      IF f = DynArr THEN y := x; OCC.GetReg(x); OCC.DynArrAdr(x, y)
      ELSE loadAdr(x); x.mode := Reg
      END ;
      x.typ := OCT.linttyp
  | 10: (*MIN*)
      IF x.mode = Typ THEN x.mode := Con;
          CASE f OF
              Bool, Char: x.a0 := 0
          | SInt: x.a0 := -80H
          | Int: x.a0 := -8000H
          | LInt: x.a0 := 80000000H
```

```
                        | Real: x.a0 := 0FF7FFFFFH
                        | LReal: x.a0 := 0FFFFFFFFH; x.a1 := 0FFEFFFFFH
                        | Set: x.a0 := 0; x.typ := OCT.inttyp
                        | Undef, NilTyp .. Record: OCS.Mark(111)
                    END
                ELSE OCS.Mark(110)
                END
          | 11: (*MAX*)
                IF x.mode = Typ THEN x.mode := Con;
                    CASE f OF
                        Bool: x.a0 := 1
                        | Char: x.a0 := 0FFH
                        | SInt: x.a0 := 7FH
                        | Int: x.a0 := 7FFFH
                        | LInt: x.a0 := 7FFFFFFFH
                        | Real: x.a0 := 7F7FFFFFH
                        | LReal: x.a0 := 0FFFFFFFFH; x.a1 := 7FEFFFFFH
                        | Set: x.a0 := 31; x.typ := OCT.inttyp
                        | Undef, NilTyp .. Record: OCS.Mark(111)
                    END
                ELSE OCS.Mark(110)
                END |
        | 12: (*CHR*)
            IF ~(f IN {Undef, Byte, SInt, Int, LInt}) THEN OCS.Mark(111) END ;
            IF (x.mode = VarX) OR (x.mode = IndX) THEN load(x) END ;
            x.typ := OCT.chartyp
        | 13: (*SHORT*)
            IF f = LInt THEN (*range test missing*)
                IF (x.mode = VarX) OR (x.mode = IndX) THEN load(x)
                ELSIF x.mode = Con THEN SetIntType(x);
                    IF x.typ.form = LInt THEN OCS.Mark(203) END
                END ;
                x.typ := OCT.inttyp
            ELSIF f = LReal THEN (*MOVLF*)
                y := x; OCC.GetFReg(x); OCC.Put(F9, 16H, x, y); x.typ := OCT.realtyp
            ELSIF f = Int THEN (*range test missing*)
                IF (x.mode = VarX) OR (x.mode = IndX) THEN load(x)
                ELSIF x.mode = Con THEN SetIntType(x);
                    IF x.typ.form # SInt THEN OCS.Mark(203) END
                END ;
                x.typ := OCT.sinttyp
            ELSE OCS.Mark(111)
            END
        | 14: (*LONG*)
            IF f = Int THEN convert1(x, OCT.linttyp)
            ELSIF f = Real THEN convert3(x)
            ELSIF f = SInt THEN convert1(x, OCT.inttyp)
            ELSIF f = Char THEN
                y := x; OCC.GetReg(x); OCC.Put(F7, 18H, x, y); x.typ := OCT.linttyp
                    (*MOVZBD*)
            ELSE OCS.Mark(111)
            END
        | 15: (*OVFL*)
            IF (f = Bool) & (x.mode = Con) THEN (*BICPSRB 10H*)
                OCC.PutF1(7CH); OCC.PutF1(SHORT(x.a0)*2 + 0A1H); OCC.PutF1(10H)
            ELSE OCS.Mark(111)
            END ;
            x.typ := OCT.notyp
```

```
    | 16,17: (*INC DEC*)
        IF x.mode >= Con THEN OCS.Mark(112)
        ELSIF ~(f IN intSet) THEN OCS.Mark(111)
        END
    | 18,19: (*INCL EXCL*)
        IF x.mode >= Con THEN OCS.Mark(112)
        ELSIF x.typ # OCT.settyp THEN OCS.Mark(111); x.typ := OCT.settyp
        END
    | 20: (*LEN*)
        IF (f # DynArr) & (f # Array) THEN OCS.Mark(131) END
    | 21: (*ASH*)
        IF f = LInt THEN load(x)
        ELSIF f IN intSet THEN loadX(x); x.typ := OCT.linttyp
        ELSE OCS.Mark(111)
        END
    | 22, 23: (*LSH ROT*)
        IF f IN {Char, SInt, Int, LInt, Set} THEN load(x)
        ELSE OCS.Mark(111)
        END
    | 24,25,26: (*GET, PUT, BIT*)
        IF (f IN intSet) & (x.mode = Con) THEN x.mode := Abs
        ELSIF f = LInt THEN
            IF (x.mode = Var) & (x.lev >= 0) THEN x.mode := Ind; x.a1 := 0
            ELSE load(x); x.mode := RegI; x.a1 := 0
            END
        ELSE OCS.Mark(111)
        END
    | 27: (*VAL*)
        IF x.mode # Typ THEN OCS.Mark(110) END
    | 28: (*SYSTEM.NEW*)
        IF (f = Pointer) & (x.mode < Con) THEN
            y.mode := Reg; y.a0 := 0; OCC.PutF4(27H, y, x);
        ELSE OCS.Mark(111)
        END
    | 29: (*COPY*)
        IF (((f=Array) OR (f=DynArr)) & (x.typ.BaseTyp.form = Char))
            OR (f = String) THEN
        y.mode := Reg; y.a0 := 1;
        IF f = DynArr THEN OCC.DynArrAdr(y, x)
        ELSE OCC.PutF4(27H, y, x)
        END
        ELSE OCS.Mark(111)
        END
    | 30: (*MOVE*)
        IF f = LInt THEN y.mode := Reg; y.a0 := 1; OCC.PutF4(17H, y, x)
        ELSE OCS.Mark(111)
        END
    END
END StPar1;


PROCEDURE StPar2*(VAR p, x: OCT.Item; fctno: INTEGER);
    VAR f, L: INTEGER; y, z: OCT.Item; typ: OCT.Struct;
BEGIN f := x.typ.form;
    IF fctno < 16 THEN OCS.Mark(64); RETURN END ;
    CASE fctno OF
    16, 17: (*INC DEC*)
        IF x.typ # p.typ THEN
            IF (x.mode = Con) & (x.typ.form IN intSet) THEN x.typ := p.typ
```

```
            ELSE OCS.Mark(111)
            END
          END ;
        L := lengcode[p.typ.form];
        IF fctno = 16 THEN add(L, p, x) ELSE sub(L, p, x) END ;
        p.typ := OCT.notyp
    | 18: (*INCL*)
        Set0(y, x); OCC.PutF4(1BH, p, y); p.typ := OCT.notyp (*ORD*)
    | 19: (*EXCL*)
        Set0(y, x); OCC.PutF4(0BH, p, y); p.typ := OCT.notyp (*BICD*)
    | 20: (*LEN*)
        IF (x.mode = Con) & (f = SInt) THEN
          L := SHORT(x.a0); typ := p.typ;
          WHILE (L > 0) & (typ.form IN {DynArr, Array}) DO
            typ := typ.BaseTyp; DEC(L)
          END;
          IF (L # 0) OR ~(typ.form IN {DynArr, Array}) THEN OCS.Mark(132)
          ELSE
            IF typ.form = DynArr THEN
              p.mode := Var; p.typ := OCT.linttyp; INC(p.a0, typ.adr);
              load(p); OCC.PutF2(0FH, 1, p) (* ADDQD 1, p *)
            ELSE p := x; p.a0 := typ.n; SetIntType(p)
            END
          END
        ELSE OCS.Mark(111)
        END
    | 21, 22, 23: (*ASH LSH ROT*)
        IF f IN intSet THEN
          IF fctno = 21 THEN L := 4 ELSIF fctno = 22 THEN L := 14H ELSE L := 0 END ;
          IF (x.mode = VarX) OR (x.mode = IndX) THEN load(x) END ;
          x.typ := OCT.sinttyp; OCC.Put(F6, lengcode[p.typ.form]+L, p, x)
        ELSE OCS.Mark(111)
        END
    | 24: (*GET*)
        IF x.mode >= Con THEN OCS.Mark(112)
        ELSIF f IN {Undef..LInt, Set, Pointer, ProcTyp} THEN
          OCC.PutF4(lengcode[f]+14H, x, p)
        ELSIF f IN realSet THEN OCC.Put(F11, lengcode[f]+4, x, p) (*MOVf*)
        END ;
        p.typ := OCT.notyp
    | 25: (*PUT*)
        IF f IN {Undef..LInt, Set, Pointer, ProcTyp} THEN OCC.PutF4(lengcode[f]+14H, p, x)
        ELSIF f IN realSet THEN OCC.Put(F11, lengcode[f]+4, p, x) (*MOVf*)
        END ;
        p.typ := OCT.notyp
    | 26: (*BIT*)
        IF f IN intSet THEN OCC.PutF4(lengcode[f] + 34H, p, x) (*TBITi*)
        ELSE OCS.Mark(111)
        END ;
        setCC(p, 8)
    | 27: (*VAL*)
        x.typ := p.typ; p := x
    | 28: (*SYSTEM.NEW*)
        y.mode := Reg; y.a0 := 2;
        IF f = LInt THEN OCC.PutF4(17H, y, x)
        ELSIF f = Int THEN OCC.Put(F7, 1DH, y, x) (*MOVXWD*)
        ELSIF f = SInt THEN OCC.Put(F7, 1CH, y, x) (*MOVXBD*)
        ELSE OCS.Mark(111)
```

```
            END ;
        OCC.PutF1(0E2H); OCC.PutByte(1); (*SVC 1*)
        p.typ := OCT.notyp
    | 29: (*COPY*)
        IF ((f = Array) OR (f = DynArr)) & (x.typ.BaseTyp.form = Char) THEN
            y.mode := Reg; y.a0 := 2; y.a1 := 0;
            IF f = DynArr THEN p := x; OCC.DynArrAdr(y, x); y.a0 := 0;
                p.mode := Var; INC(p.a0, p.typ.adr); OCC.PutF4(17H, y, p)
            ELSE OCC.PutF4(27H, y, x); y.a0 := 0;
                p.mode := Con; p.typ := OCT.inttyp; p.a0:= x.typ.size−1;
                OCC.Put(F7, 19H, y, p); (*MOVZWD*)
            END;
            y.a0 := 4; OCC.PutF2(5FH, 0, y);      (*MOVQD*)
            OCC.PutF1(14); OCC.PutF1(0); OCC.PutF1(6); (*MOVSB*)
            y.mode := RegI; y.a0 := 2; OCC.PutF2(5CH, 0, y) (*MOVQB*)
        ELSE OCS.Mark(111)
        END ;
        p.typ := OCT.notyp
    | 30: (*MOVE*)
        IF f = LInt THEN y.mode := Reg; y.a0 := 2; OCC.PutF4(17H, y, x)
        ELSE OCS.Mark(111)
        END
    END
END StPar2;


PROCEDURE StPar3*(VAR p, x: OCT.Item; fctno: INTEGER);
    VAR f: INTEGER; y: OCT.Item;
BEGIN f := x.typ.form;
    IF fctno = 30 THEN (*MOVE*)
        y.mode := Reg; y.a0 := 0;
        IF f = Int THEN OCC.Put(F7, 1DH, y, x)
        ELSIF f = SInt THEN OCC.Put(F7, 1CH, y, x)
        ELSIF f = LInt THEN OCC.PutF4(17H, y, x)
        ELSE OCS.Mark(111)
        END ;
        OCC.PutF1(14); OCC.PutF1(0); OCC.PutF1(0); p.typ := OCT.notyp (*MOVSB*)
    ELSE OCS.Mark(64)
    END
END StPar3;


PROCEDURE StFct*(VAR p: OCT.Item; fctno, parno: INTEGER);
BEGIN
    IF fctno >= 16 THEN
        IF (fctno = 16) & (parno = 1) THEN (*INC*)
            OCC.PutF2(lengcode[p.typ.form]+0CH, 1, p); p.typ := OCT.notyp
        ELSIF (fctno = 17) & (parno = 1) THEN (*DEC*)
            OCC.PutF2(lengcode[p.typ.form]+0CH, −1, p); p.typ := OCT.notyp
        ELSIF (fctno = 20) & (parno = 1) THEN (*LEN*)
            IF p.typ.form = DynArr THEN
                p.mode := Var; INC(p.a0, p.typ.adr); p.typ := OCT.linttyp;
                load(p); OCC.PutF2(0FH, 1, p) (*ADDQD 1 p*)
            ELSE p.mode := Con; p.a0 := p.typ.n; SetIntType(p)
            END
        ELSIF (parno < 2) OR (fctno = 30) & (parno < 3) THEN OCS.Mark(65)
        END
    ELSIF parno < 1 THEN OCS.Mark(65)
    END
END StFct;
```

BEGIN intSet := {SInt, Int, LInt}; realSet := {Real, LReal}; lengcode[Undef] := 0;
    lengcode[Byte] := 0; lengcode[Bool] := 0; lengcode[Char] := 0; lengcode[SInt] := 0;
    lengcode[Int] := 1; lengcode[LInt] := 3; lengcode[Real] := 1; lengcode[LReal] := 0;
    lengcode[Set] := 3; lengcode[String] := 0; lengcode[NilTyp] := 3; lengcode[ProcTyp] := 3;
    lengcode[Pointer] := 3; lengcode[Array] := 1; lengcode[DynArr] := 1; lengcode[Record] := 1
END OCE.

Assignments

**Passing
parameters**

Module OCH contains the procedures for code selection and type consistency checking corresponding to statements: assignment, procedure calls and structured control statements. Procedure *Assign* discriminates between the various types of the destination variable with a case statement. It is called both for proper assignments (~*param*) and for the passing of value parameters (*param*). In the latter case, the addressing mode of the destination is TOS; the parameter is pushed onto the stack. Automatic length extension is used if the operand length is 1 or 2, resulting in proper alignment for all parameters.

Assignments of arrays and records is achieved by a block move instruction (MOVMB if the size is at most 16, MOVSB otherwise, see procedure *MoveBlock*). If the destination is an indirectly referenced record, that is, if it is either a VAR parameter or a dereferenced variable, an implicit type guard is necessary. Consider a record type R0 and its extension R1. Let the destination be either a VAR parameter r0 of type R0, or p↑, where p is a pointer bound to R0, and let variable r1 be of type R1. Then the assignment r0 := r1 is acceptable only if the *actual* destination is of type R0, but not if it happens to be some extension of R0 (not necessarily R1). This condition must be guarded by an implicitly inserted guard. This is an example of a case where an apparently simple and basic concept such as type extension produces unexpected side-effects and complications.

Assignments to dynamic arrays as a whole are not permitted by the rules of the language. However, actual parameters corresponding to a formal parameter declared as a dynamic array called by value may be arrays, dynamic arrays or strings. Since this implicit assignment is handled by procedure *Assign*, it must handle the case by constructing an appropriate array descriptor. The descriptor consists of the actual parameter's address and its index bounds. The latter is pushed onto the stack first. In the case of a string, its length minus 1 yields the upper bound, and the lower bound of 0 is implied by extending the upper bound to 4 bytes (see procedure *DynArrBnd*).

Assignment of procedures to variables (and parameters) of a procedural type is handled by constructing a procedure descriptor and assigning it to the destination. The descriptor consists of a module descriptor address and an entry offset. Also, the check for type compatibility is fairly complex in this case, because the language admits structural equivalence instead of name equivalence, which is necessary because the type of a declared procedure bears no name. Therefore both result type and parameter types must be checked for compatibility. This is done by procedure *CompareParameters* and involves the parameters' types and mode. This procedure is also invoked in the case of forward declarations (see *Compiler.ProcedureDeclaration*).

Procedure calls

Procedures *PrepCall*, *Param* and *Call* are used to select code for procedure calls. The first checks that the item properly denotes a procedure and delivers its formal parameter list. *Param* scans the parameters, one per invocation, and delegates its handling to *Assign* in the case of value parameters; otherwise, the address of the actual parameter is pushed onto the stack. In the case of dynamic arrays and records, a descriptor is formed containing, in addition to the address, the array's length or the record's base type tag. The latter is used by type guards and type tests. And finally, procedure *Call* selects the appropriate branch instruction, namely BSR for local, CXP for external, CXPD for indirectly called and SVC for code procedures.

The CXP instruction requires as parameter an index to the module's link table. The indexed entry holds a descriptor identifying the procedure (see Chapter 6). The table entry is established when the compiler encounters a call of the procedure for the first time, and the index is then stored as *a1* attribute in the procedure's symbol table entry by procedure *OCC.LinkAdr*.

Prolog and epilog

Procedures *Enter*, *CopyDynArray*, *Result* and *Return* select the instructions for the prolog and epilog of procedure bodies. The prolog typically consists of an ENTER instruction, the epilog of an EXIT instruction followed by RET for local and RXP for external procedures (see code patterns).

Jumps

Procedures FJ, CFJ, BJ, CBJ and LFJ are called for conditional and repetitive constructs, and generate jumps. F stands for forward, B for backward, C for conditional and L for long jump. FJ, CFJ and LFJ assign the location of the generated branch to their *loc* parameter to be used for a later address fixup.

Case statements

Procedures *CaseIn* and *CaseOut* process case statements. A case statement represents, in contrast to a cascaded conditional statement, a single, indexed branch. *CaseIn* generates this indexed branch instruction together with an instruction to test the index bounds. *CaseOut* is called when the end of the case statement is reached and the addresses of the individual cases are known and therefore the branch table can be constructed. A fixup of the indexed branch instruction is unavoidable. The address of the trap instruction is assigned to cases that remained undefined.

```
MODULE OCH; (*NW 7.6.87 / 15.2.91*)
  IMPORT OCS, OCT, OCC;

  CONST (*instruction format prefixes*)
```

```
          F6 = 4EH; F7 = 0CEH; F9 = 3EH; F11 = 0BEH;

    (*object and item modes*)
        Var = 1; VarX = 2; Ind = 3; IndX = 4; RegI = 5;
        RegX = 6; Abs = 7; Con = 8; Stk = 9; Coc = 10;
        Reg = 11; Fld = 12; LProc = 14; XProc = 15;
        CProc = 17; IProc = 18; Mod = 19;
    (*structure forms*)
        Undef = 0; Byte = 1; Bool = 2; Char = 3; SInt = 4; Int = 5; LInt = 6;
        Real = 7; LReal = 8; Set = 9; String = 10; NilTyp = 11; NoTyp = 12;
        Pointer = 13; ProcTyp = 14; Array = 15; DynArr = 16; Record = 17;


TYPE LabelRange* = RECORD low*, high*: INTEGER; label*: INTEGER END ;
VAR lengcode: ARRAY 18 OF INTEGER;


PROCEDURE setCC(VAR x: OCT.Item; cc: LONGINT);
BEGIN x.typ := OCT.booltyp; x.mode := Coc; x.a0 := cc; x.a1 := 0; x.a2 := 0
END setCC;


PROCEDURE AdjustSP(n: LONGINT);
BEGIN (*ADJSPB n*)
    IF n <= 127 THEN OCC.PutF3(−5A84H); OCC.PutByte(n)
    ELSE OCC.PutF3(−5A83H); OCC.PutWord(n)
    END
END AdjustSP;


PROCEDURE move(L: INTEGER; VAR x, y: OCT.Item);
BEGIN
    IF (y.mode = Con) & (y.a0 <= 7) & (y.a0 >= −8) THEN
        OCC.PutF2(L+5CH, y.a0, x) (*MOVQi*)
    ELSE OCC.PutF4(L+14H, x, y) (*MOVi*)
    END
END move;


PROCEDURE load(VAR x: OCT.Item);
    VAR y: OCT.Item;
BEGIN IF x.mode # Reg THEN y := x; OCC.GetReg(x); move(lengcode[x.typ.form], x, y) END
END load;


PROCEDURE moveBW(VAR x, y: OCT.Item);
BEGIN
    IF (y.mode = Con) & (y.a0 <= 7) & (y.a0 >= −8) THEN
        OCC.PutF2(5DH, y.a0, x)
    ELSE OCC.Put(F7, 10H, x, y) (*MOVXBW*)
    END
END moveBW;


PROCEDURE moveBD(VAR x, y: OCT.Item);
BEGIN
    IF (y.mode = Con) & (y.a0 <= 7) & (y.a0 >= −8) THEN
        OCC.PutF2(5FH, y.a0, x)
    ELSE OCC.Put(F7, 1CH, x, y) (*MOVXBD*)
    END
END moveBD;
```

```
PROCEDURE moveWD(VAR x, y: OCT.Item);
BEGIN
   IF (y.mode = Con) & (y.a0 <= 7) & (y.a0 >= −8) THEN
      OCC.PutF2(5FH, y.a0, x)
   ELSE OCC.Put(F7, 1DH, x, y) (*MOVXWD*)
   END
END moveWD;


PROCEDURE Leng(VAR x: OCT.Item; L: LONGINT);
   VAR y: OCT.Item;
BEGIN
   IF L <= 7 THEN OCC.PutF2(5FH, L, x) (*MOVQD*)
   ELSE y.mode := Con; y.a0 := L; (*MOVZBD*)
      IF L <= 255 THEN y.typ := OCT.sinttyp; OCC.Put(F7, 18H, x, y)
      ELSE y.typ := OCT.inttyp; OCC.Put(F7, 19H, x, y)
      END
   END
END Leng;


PROCEDURE MoveBlock(VAR x, y: OCT.Item; s: LONGINT; param: BOOLEAN);
   VAR L: INTEGER; z: OCT.Item;
BEGIN
   IF s > 0 THEN
      IF param THEN
         s := (s+3) DIV 4 * 4; AdjustSP(s)
      END ;
      IF s <= 16 THEN
         OCC.Put(F7, 0, x, y); OCC.PutDisp(s−1) (*MOVMB*)
      ELSE
         z.mode := Reg; z.a0 := 1; OCC.PutF4(27H, z, y); (*ADDR y,R1*)
         z.a0 := 2; OCC.PutF4(27H, z, x); z.a0 := 0; (*ADDR x,R2*)
         IF s MOD 4 = 0 THEN L := 3; s := s DIV 4
         ELSIF s MOD 2 = 0 THEN L := 1; s := s DIV 2
         ELSE L := 0
         END ;
         Leng(z, s);
         OCC.PutF1(14); OCC.PutByte(L); OCC.PutByte(0) (*MOVS*)
      END
   END
END MoveBlock;


PROCEDURE DynArrBnd(ftyp, atyp: OCT.Struct; lev: INTEGER; adr: LONGINT;
      varpar: BOOLEAN);
   VAR f, s: INTEGER; x, y, z: OCT.Item;
BEGIN (* ftyp.form = DynArr *)
   x.mode := Stk; y.mode := Var;
   IF varpar & (ftyp.BaseTyp = OCT.bytetyp) THEN
      IF atyp.form # DynArr THEN Leng(x, atyp.size−1)
      ELSE y.lev := lev; y.a0 := adr + atyp.adr; y.typ := OCT.linttyp;
         atyp := atyp.BaseTyp;
         IF atyp.form # DynArr THEN
            IF atyp.size > 1 THEN
               z.mode := Con; z.typ := OCT.linttyp; z.a0 := atyp.size;
               load(y); OCC.Put(F7, 23H, y, z); (* MULD z, Ry *)
               z.mode := Con; z.typ := OCT.linttyp; z.a0 := atyp.size−1;
               IF z.a0 < 8 THEN OCC.PutF2(0FH, z.a0, y) (* ADDQD size−1, Ry *)
               ELSE OCC.PutF4(3, y, z) (* ADDD size−1, Ry *)
```

```
                              END
                          END
                      ELSE load(y); OCC.PutF2(0FH, 1, y);
                          REPEAT z.mode := Var; z.lev := lev; z.a0 := atyp.adr + adr;
                              z.typ := OCT.linttyp;
                              load(z); OCC.PutF2(0FH, 1, z); (* ADDQD 1, Rz *)
                              OCC.Put(F7, 23H, y, z); (* MULD Rz, Ry *)
                              atyp := atyp.BaseTyp
                          UNTIL atyp.form # DynArr;
                          IF atyp.size > 1 THEN
                              z.mode := Con; z.typ := OCT.linttyp; z.a0 := atyp.size;
                              OCC.Put(F7, 23H, y, z) (* MULD z, Ry *)
                          END ;
                          OCC.PutF2(0FH, −1, y) (* ADDQD −1, Ry *)
                      END ;
                      OCC.PutF4(17H, x, y) (* MOVD apdynarrlen−1, TOS *)
                  END
              ELSE
                  LOOP f := atyp.form;
                      IF f = Array THEN y.lev := −atyp.mno; y.a0 := atyp.adr
                      ELSIF f = DynArr THEN y.lev := lev; y.a0 := atyp.adr + adr
                      ELSE OCS.Mark(66); EXIT
                      END ;
                      OCC.PutF4(17H, x, y); ftyp := ftyp.BaseTyp; atyp := atyp.BaseTyp;
                      IF ftyp.form # DynArr THEN
                          IF ftyp # atyp THEN OCS.Mark(67) END ;
                          EXIT
                      END
                  END
              END
          END DynArrBnd;


          PROCEDURE Trap*(n: INTEGER);
          BEGIN OCC.PutF1(0F2H); OCC.PutByte(n) (*BPT n*)
          END Trap;


          PROCEDURE CompareParLists*(x, y: OCT.Object);
              VAR xt, yt: OCT.Struct;
          BEGIN
              WHILE x # NIL DO
                  IF y # NIL THEN
                      xt := x.typ; yt := y.typ;
                      WHILE (xt.form = DynArr) & (yt.form = DynArr) DO
                          xt := xt.BaseTyp; yt := yt.BaseTyp
                      END ;
                      IF x.mode # y.mode THEN OCS.Mark(115)
                      ELSIF xt # yt THEN
                          IF (xt.form = ProcTyp) & (yt.form = ProcTyp) THEN
                              CompareParLists(xt.link, yt.link)
                          ELSE OCS.Mark(115)
                          END
                      END ;
                      y := y.next
                  ELSE OCS.Mark(116)
                  END ;
                  x := x.next
              END ;
              IF (y # NIL) & (y.mode <= Ind) & (y.a0 > 0) THEN OCS.Mark(117) END
```

END CompareParLists;

PROCEDURE **Assign***(VAR x, y: OCT.Item; param: BOOLEAN);
   VAR f, g, L, u: INTEGER; s, vsz: LONGINT;
      p, q: OCT.Struct;
      xp, yp: OCT.Object;
      tag, tdes: OCT.Item;
   BEGIN f := x.typ.form; g := y.typ.form;
      IF x.mode = Con THEN OCS.Mark(56) END ;
      CASE f OF
      Undef, String:
   | Byte: IF g IN {Undef, Byte, Char, SInt} THEN
         IF param THEN moveBD(x, y) ELSE move(0, x, y) END
      ELSE OCS.Mark(113)
      END
   | Bool: IF param THEN u := 3 ELSE u := 0 END ;
      IF y.mode = Coc THEN
         IF (y.a1 = 0) & (y.a2 = 0) THEN OCC.PutF2(u+3CH, y.a0, x)
         ELSE
            IF ODD(y.a0) THEN OCC.PutF0(y.a0−1) ELSE OCC.PutF0(y.a0+1) END ;
            OCC.PutWord(y.a2); y.a2 := OCC.pc−2;
            OCC.FixLink(y.a1); OCC.PutF2(u+5CH, 1, x);
            OCC.PutF0(14); L := OCC.pc; OCC.PutWord(0);
            OCC.FixLink(y.a2); OCC.PutF2(u+5CH, 0, x); OCC.fixup(L)
         END
      ELSIF g = Bool THEN
         IF y.mode = Con THEN OCC.PutF2(u+5CH, y.a0, x)
         ELSIF param THEN OCC.Put(F7, 18H, x, y) (*MOVZBD*)
         ELSE OCC.PutF4(14H, x, y)
         END
      ELSE OCS.Mark(113)
      END
   | Char, SInt:
     IF g = f THEN
         IF param THEN moveBD(x, y) ELSE move(0, x, y) END
      ELSE OCS.Mark(113)
      END
   | Int: IF g = Int THEN
         IF param THEN moveWD(x, y) ELSE move(1, x, y) END
      ELSIF g = SInt THEN
         IF param THEN moveBD(x, y) ELSE moveBW(x, y) END
      ELSE OCS.Mark(113)
      END
   | LInt: IF g = LInt THEN move(3, x, y)
      ELSIF g = Int THEN moveWD(x, y)
      ELSIF g = SInt THEN moveBD(x, y)
      ELSE OCS.Mark(113)
      END
   | Real: IF g = Real THEN OCC.Put(F11, 5, x, y)
      ELSIF (SInt <= g) & (g <= LInt) THEN OCC.Put(F9, lengcode[g]+4, x, y)
      ELSE OCS.Mark(113)
      END
   | LReal: IF g = LReal THEN OCC.Put(F11, 4, x, y)
      ELSIF g = Real THEN OCC.Put(F9, 1BH, x, y)
      ELSIF (SInt <= g) & (g <= LInt) THEN OCC.Put(F9, lengcode[g], x, y)
      ELSE OCS.Mark(113)
      END
   | Set: IF g = f THEN move(3, x, y) ELSE OCS.Mark(113) END

```
| Pointer:
   IF x.typ = y.typ THEN move(3, x, y)
   ELSIF g = NilTyp THEN OCC.PutF2(5FH, 0, x)
   ELSIF g = Pointer THEN
      p := x.typ.BaseTyp; q := y.typ.BaseTyp;
      IF (p.form = Record) & (q.form = Record) THEN
         WHILE (q # p) & (q # NIL) DO q := q.BaseTyp END ;
         IF q # NIL THEN move(3, x, y) ELSE OCS.Mark(113) END
      ELSE OCS.Mark(113)
      END
   ELSE OCS.Mark(113)
   END
| Array: s := x.typ.size;
   IF x.typ = y.typ THEN MoveBlock(x, y, s, param)
   ELSIF (g = String) & (x.typ.BaseTyp = OCT.chartyp) THEN
      s := y.a1; vsz := x.typ.n; (*check length of string*)
      IF s > vsz THEN OCS.Mark(114) END ;
         IF param THEN
            vsz := (vsz+3) DIV 4 − (s+3) DIV 4;
            IF vsz > 0 THEN AdjustSP(vsz*4) END
         END ;
         MoveBlock(x, y, s, param)
   ELSE OCS.Mark(113)
   END
| DynArr: s := x.typ.size;
   IF param THEN (*formal parameter is open array*)
      IF (g = String) & (x.typ.BaseTyp.form = Char) THEN Leng(x, y.a1−1)
      ELSIF y.mode >= Abs THEN OCS.Mark(59)
      ELSE DynArrBnd(x.typ, y.typ, y.lev, y.a0, FALSE)
      END ;
      IF g = DynArr THEN OCC.DynArrAdr(x, y)
      ELSE OCC.PutF4(27H, x, y)
      END
   ELSE OCS.Mark(113)
   END
| Record: s := x.typ.size;
   IF x.typ # y.typ THEN
      IF g = Record THEN
         q := y.typ.BaseTyp;
         WHILE (q # NIL) & (q # x.typ) DO q := q.BaseTyp END ;
         IF q = NIL THEN OCS.Mark(113) END
      ELSE OCS.Mark(113)
      END
   END ;
   IF OCC.typchk & ~param &
      ( ((x.mode = Ind) OR (x.mode = RegI)) & (x.obj = OCC.wasderef) (* p ↑ := *)
         OR (x.mode = Ind) & (x.obj # NIL) & (x.obj # OCC.wasderef) ) (* varpar := *)
   THEN
      tag := x; tdes.mode := Var; tdes.lev := −x.typ.mno; tdes.a0 := x.typ.adr;
      IF x.obj = OCC.wasderef THEN tag.a1 := − 4
      ELSE tag.mode := Var; INC(tag.a0, 4)
      END;
      OCC.PutF4(7, tdes, tag); (* CMPD tag, tdes *)
      OCC.PutF0(0); OCC.PutDisp(4); (* BEQ continue *)
      OCC.PutF1(0F2H); OCC.PutByte(19) (* BPT 19 *)
   END ;
   MoveBlock(x, y, s, param)
| ProcTyp:
```

```
      IF (x.typ = y.typ) OR (y.typ = OCT.niltyp) THEN OCC.PutF4(17H, x, y)
      ELSIF (y.mode = XProc) OR (y.mode = IProc) THEN
         (*procedure y to proc. variable x; check compatibility*)
         IF x.typ.BaseTyp = y.typ THEN
            CompareParLists(x.typ.link, y.obj.dsc);
            IF y.a1 = 0 THEN
               y.a1 := OCC.LinkAdr(−y.lev, y.a0); y.obj.a1 := y.a1
            END ;
            y.mode := Var; y.lev := SHORT(−y.a1); y.a0 := 0;
            OCC.PutF4(27H, x, y) (*LXPD*)
         ELSE OCS.Mark(118)
         END
      ELSIF y.mode = LProc THEN OCS.Mark(119)
      ELSE OCS.Mark(111)
      END
 | NoTyp, NilTyp: OCS.Mark(111)
   END
END Assign;


PROCEDURE FJ*(VAR loc: INTEGER);
BEGIN OCC.PutF0(14); OCC.PutWord(loc); loc := OCC.pc−2
END FJ;


PROCEDURE CFJ*(VAR x: OCT.Item; VAR loc: INTEGER);
BEGIN
   IF x.typ.form = Bool THEN
      IF x.mode # Coc THEN OCC.PutF2(1CH, 1, x); setCC(x, 0) END
   ELSE OCS.Mark(120); setCC(x, 0)
   END ;
   IF ODD(x.a0) THEN OCC.PutF0(x.a0−1) ELSE OCC.PutF0(x.a0+1) END ;
   loc := OCC.pc; OCC.PutWord(x.a2); OCC.FixLink(x.a1)
END CFJ;


PROCEDURE BJ*(loc: INTEGER);
BEGIN OCC.PutF0(14); OCC.PutDisp(loc − OCC.pc + 1)
END BJ;


PROCEDURE CBJ*(VAR x: OCT.Item; loc: INTEGER);
BEGIN
   IF x.typ.form = Bool THEN
      IF x.mode # Coc THEN OCC.PutF2(1CH, 1, x); setCC(x,0) END
   ELSE OCS.Mark(120); setCC(x, 0)
   END ;
   IF ODD(x.a0) THEN OCC.PutF0(x.a0−1) ELSE OCC.PutF0(x.a0+1) END ;
   OCC.PutDisp(loc − OCC.pc + 1);
   OCC.FixLinkWith(x.a2, loc); OCC.FixLink(x.a1)
END CBJ;


PROCEDURE LFJ*(VAR loc: INTEGER);
BEGIN OCC.PutF0(14); OCC.PutWord(−4000H); OCC.PutWord(0); loc := OCC.pc−4
END LFJ;


PROCEDURE PrepCall*(VAR x: OCT.Item; VAR fpar: OCT.Object);
BEGIN
   IF (x.mode = LProc) OR (x.mode = XProc) OR (x.mode = CProc) THEN
      fpar := x.obj.dsc
```

```
      ELSIF (x.typ # NIL) & (x.typ.form = ProcTyp) THEN
         fpar := x.typ.link
      ELSE OCS.Mark(121); fpar := NIL; x.typ := OCT.undftyp
      END
   END PrepCall;


   PROCEDURE Param*(VAR ap: OCT.Item; f: OCT.Object);
      VAR q: OCT.Struct; fp, tag: OCT.Item;
   BEGIN fp.mode := Stk; fp.typ := f.typ;
      IF f.mode = Ind THEN (*VAR parameter*)
         IF ap.mode >= Con THEN OCS.Mark(122) END ;
         IF fp.typ.form = DynArr THEN
            DynArrBnd(fp.typ, ap.typ, ap.lev, ap.a0, TRUE);
            IF ap.typ.form = DynArr THEN OCC.DynArrAdr(fp, ap)
            ELSE OCC.PutF4(27H, fp, ap)
            END
         ELSIF (fp.typ.form = Record) & (ap.typ.form = Record) THEN
            q := ap.typ;
            WHILE (q # fp.typ) & (q # NIL) DO q := q.BaseTyp END ;
            IF q # NIL THEN
               IF (ap.mode = Ind) & (ap.obj # NIL) & (ap.obj # OCC.wasderef) THEN
                  (*actual par is VAR−par*) ap.mode := Var; ap.a0 := ap.a0 + 4;
                  OCC.PutF4(17H, fp, ap); ap.a0 := ap.a0 − 4; OCC.PutF4(17H, fp, ap)
               ELSIF ((ap.mode = Ind) OR (ap.mode = RegI)) & (ap.obj = OCC.wasderef)
                  THEN (*actual par is p ↑ *) ap.a1 := − 4; OCC.PutF4(17H, fp, ap);
                  IF ap.mode = Ind THEN ap.mode := Var ELSE ap.mode := Reg END;
                  OCC.PutF4(17H, fp, ap)
               ELSE
                  tag.mode := Var; tag.lev := −ap.typ.mno; tag.a0 := ap.typ.adr;
                  OCC.PutF4(17H, fp, tag); OCC.PutF4(27H, fp, ap)
               END
            ELSE OCS.Mark(111)
            END
         ELSIF (ap.typ = fp.typ) OR ((fp.typ.form = Byte) & (ap.typ.form IN {Char, SInt}))
            THEN
            IF (ap.mode = Ind) & (ap.a1 = 0) THEN (*actual var par*)
               ap.mode := Var; OCC.PutF4(17H, fp, ap)
            ELSE OCC.PutF4(27H, fp, ap)
            END
         ELSE OCS.Mark(123)
         END
      ELSE Assign(fp, ap, TRUE)
      END
   END Param;


   PROCEDURE Call*(VAR x: OCT.Item);
      VAR stk, sL: OCT.Item;
   BEGIN
      IF x.mode = LProc THEN
         IF x.lev > 0 THEN
            sL.mode := Var; sL.typ := OCT.linttyp; sL.lev := x.lev; sL.a0 := 0;
            stk.mode := Stk; OCC.PutF4(27H, stk, sL) (*static link*)
         END ;
         OCC.PutF1(2); OCC.PutDisp(x.a0 − OCC.pc + 1) (*BSR*)
      ELSIF x.mode = XProc THEN
         IF x.a1 = 0 THEN
            x.a1 := OCC.LinkAdr(−x.lev, x.a0); x.obj.a1 := x.a1
         END ;
```

```
            OCC.PutF1(22H); OCC.PutDisp(SHORT(x.a1)) (*CXP*)
         ELSIF (x.mode < Con) & (x.typ # OCT.undftyp) THEN (*CXPD*)
            OCC.PutF2(7FH, 0, x); x.typ := x.typ.BaseTyp
         ELSIF x.mode = CProc THEN
            OCC.PutF1(0E2H); OCC.PutByte(x.a0) (*SVC n*)
         ELSE OCS.Mark(121)
         END
         (*function result is marked when restoring registers*)
      END Call;


   PROCEDURE Enter*(mode: SHORTINT; pno: LONGINT; VAR L: INTEGER);
   BEGIN
      IF mode # LProc THEN OCC.SetEntry(SHORT(pno)) END ;
      OCC.PutF1(82H); (*ENTER*)
      IF mode = IProc THEN OCC.PutByte(0C0H) ELSE OCC.PutByte(0) END ;
      IF mode # Mod THEN L := OCC.pc; OCC.PutWord(0) ELSE OCC.PutByte(0) END
   END Enter;


   PROCEDURE CopyDynArray*(adr: LONGINT; typ: OCT.Struct);
      VAR size, ptr, m2, tos: OCT.Item; add: SHORTINT;


      PROCEDURE DynArrSize(typ: OCT.Struct);
         VAR len: OCT.Item;
      BEGIN
         IF typ.form = DynArr THEN DynArrSize(typ.BaseTyp);
            len.mode := Var; len.lev := OCC.level; len.typ := OCT.linttyp;
            len.a0 := adr + typ.adr; load(len);
            IF (size.mode # Con) OR (size.a0 # 1) THEN
               IF add = 4 THEN OCC.PutF2(0FH, 1, size) END; (* ADDQD 1, size *)
               OCC.PutF2(0FH, 1, len); add := 3; (* ADDQD 1, len *)
               OCC.Put(F7, 23H, len, size) (* MULD size, len *)
            ELSE add := 4
            END;
            size := len
         ELSE size.mode := Con; size.typ := OCT.linttyp; size.a0 := typ.size
         END
      END DynArrSize;

   BEGIN add := 3;
      DynArrSize(typ); (* load total byte size of dyn array *)
      OCC.PutF2(0FH, add, size); (* ADDQD 3 or 4, size *)
      m2.mode := Con; m2.typ := OCT.sinttyp;
      m2.a0 := -2; OCC.Put(F6, 7, size, m2); (* ASHD -2, size *)
      ptr.mode := Var; ptr.lev := OCC.level; ptr.typ := OCT.linttyp;
      ptr.a0 := adr; load(ptr);
      ptr.mode := RegX; ptr.a1 := -4; ptr.a2 := size.a0; tos.mode := Stk;
      OCC.PutF4(17H, tos, ptr); (* loop: MOVD -4(ptr)[size:D], TOS *)
      OCC.PutF2(4FH, -1, size); OCC.PutDisp(-4); (* ACBD -1, size, loop *)
      OCC.PutF3(-31D9H); OCC.PutDisp(0); OCC.PutDisp(adr); (* ADDR 0(SP), adr(FP) *)
      OCC.FreeRegs({})
   END CopyDynArray;



   PROCEDURE Result*(VAR x: OCT.Item; typ: OCT.Struct);
   VAR res: OCT.Item;
   BEGIN res.mode := Reg; res.typ := typ; res.a0 := 0;
```

```
      Assign(res, x, FALSE)
END Result;


PROCEDURE Return*(mode: INTEGER; psize: LONGINT);
BEGIN OCC.PutF1(92H);        (*EXIT*)
   IF mode = LProc THEN
      OCC.PutByte(0); OCC.PutF1(12H); OCC.PutDisp(psize-8) (*RET*)
   ELSIF mode = XProc THEN
      OCC.PutByte(0); OCC.PutF1(32H); OCC.PutDisp(psize-12) (*RXP*)
   ELSIF mode = IProc THEN
      OCC.PutByte(3); OCC.PutF1(42H); OCC.PutDisp(0) (*RETT 0*)
   END
END Return;


PROCEDURE CaseIn*(VAR x: OCT.Item; VAR L0, L1: INTEGER);
   VAR f: INTEGER; r, x0, lim: OCT.Item;
BEGIN f := x.typ.form;
   IF f # Int THEN
      IF f = Char THEN
         x0 := x; OCC.GetReg(x); OCC.Put(F7, 14H, x, x0) (*MOVZBW*)
      ELSIF f = SInt THEN
         x0 := x; OCC.GetReg(x); OCC.Put(F7, 10H, x, x0) (*MOVXBW*)
      ELSIF f # LInt THEN OCS.Mark(125)
      END ;
      f := Int
   END ;
   IF (x.mode IN {VarX, IndX, RegX}) OR (x.mode # Reg) & (x.lev > 0)
      & (x.lev < OCC.level) THEN
      x0 := x; OCC.GetReg(x); OCC.PutF4(15H, x, x0) (*MOVW*)
   END ;
   L0 := OCC.pc+3; (*fixup loc for bounds adr*)
   lim.mode := Var; lim.typ := OCT.inttyp; lim.lev := 0; lim.a0 := 100H;
   OCC.GetReg(r); OCC.Put(0EEH, SHORT(r.a0)*8 + 1, x, lim); (*CHECK*)
   OCC.PutF0(8); OCC.PutWord(0); L1 := OCC.pc; (*BFS*)
   lim.mode := VarX; lim.a2 := r.a0; OCC.PutF2(7DH, 14, lim) (*CASE*)
END CaseIn;


PROCEDURE CaseOut*(L0, L1, L2, L3, n: INTEGER;
                   VAR tab: ARRAY OF LabelRange);
   VAR i, j, lim: INTEGER; k: LONGINT;
BEGIN (*generate jump table*)
   IF n > 0 THEN OCC.AllocBounds(tab[0].low, tab[n-1].high, k)
   ELSE (*no cases*) OCC.AllocBounds(1, 0, k)
   END ;
   j := SHORT(k);
   OCC.FixupWith(L0, j); (*bounds address in check*)
   OCC.FixupWith(L1-2, L2-L1+3); (*out of bounds jump addr*)
   OCC.FixupWith(L1+3, j+4); (*jump address to table*)
   i := 0; j := tab[0].low;
   WHILE i < n DO
      lim := tab[i].high;
      WHILE j < tab[i].low DO
         OCC.AllocInt(L2-L1); INC(j) (*else*)
      END ;
      WHILE j <= lim DO
         OCC.AllocInt(tab[i].label-L1); INC(j)
      END ;
```

```
            INC(i)
        END ;
        OCC.FixLink(L3)
    END CaseOut;


BEGIN lengcode[Undef] := 0;
    lengcode[Byte] := 0; lengcode[Bool] := 0; lengcode[Char] := 0; lengcode[SInt] := 0;
    lengcode[Int] := 1; lengcode[LInt] := 3; lengcode[Real] := 1; lengcode[LReal] := 0;
    lengcode[Set] := 3; lengcode[String] := 0; lengcode[NilTyp] := 3; lengcode[ProcTyp] := 3;
    lengcode[Pointer] := 3; lengcode[Array] := 1; lengcode[DynArr] := 1; lengcode[Record] := 1
END OCH.
```

12.8 Code generation

The subject of this section is module OCC, which generates code in binary form. Its procedures are inherently target-architecture dependent. The details are of much less general interest than the parts of the compiler presented so far, and we therefore keep explanations reasonably short. Nevertheless, a brief summary of the NS-32000 architecture's instruction formats will be given below in order to enable the reader to understand the principal routines of OCC. The presented architecture is of the CISC class, with a fairly elaborate set of instructions (of which only a part is used by the compiler) and addressing modes. However, it features a commendable regularity. For example, all addressing modes are equally applicable independent of the particular instruction.

The NS-32000 instruction stream is byte-oriented, that is, every instruction consists of a number of bytes. The first 1, 2 or 3 bytes constitute the instruction code, including address mode specifiers. They are followed by additional bytes depending on the addressing modes used. These bytes specify addresses (called displacements, because they are relative to a base address held in a register), constants or index registers. We first present the various formats of the leading instruction bytes, the so-called basic instruction. The fields *dst* and *src* are the address mode specifiers for destination and source operands, and they will be explained below.

```
                4        0
Format 0   | cond | 1010 |     Bcond

Format 1   |  op  | 0010 |     0  BSR      3  RXP      7  RESTORE   D  FLAG
                                1  RET      4  RETT     8  ENTER     E  SVC
                                2  CXP      6  SAVE     9  EXIT      F  BPT
```

Format 2   `dst | val | op | 11 | i`   (bits 11 7 4 2 0)

0 ADDQi	3 Scand	5 MOVQi	
1 CMPQi	4 ACBi		

Format 3   `dst | op | 11111 i`

0 CXPD	A ADISPi	E CASE

Format 4   `dst | src | op | i`   (bits 11 6 2 0)

0 ADDi	6 ORi	A ANDi
1 CMPi	8 SUBi	D TBITi
2 BICi	9 ADDR	E XORi
5 MOVi		

Format 6   `dst | src | op | i | 4E`

0	ROTi	8 NEGi
1	ASHi	C ABSi
5	LSHi	D COMi

Format 7   `dst | src | op | i | CE`

0	MOVMi	8 MULi
4	MOVXBW	E MODi
5	MOVZBW	F DIVi
7	MOVXiD	

Format 8   `dst | src | reg | 001 | EE`   CHECKW

`dst | src | reg | 101 | 2E`   INDEXW

Format 9   `dst | src | op | fi | 3E`

0	MOVif	3 MOVFL
2	MOVLF	7 FLOORfi

Format 11   `dst | src | op | 0f | BE`

0	ADDf	5 NEGf
1	MOVf	8 DIVf
2	CMPf	C MULf
4	SUBf	D ABSf

The *dst* and *src* fields specify an addressing mode m as follows; *d0* and *d1* are displacements:

m	operand address	mode
0-7	operand = R[m]	register direct
8-15	R[m-8]	register indirect
16	Mem[FP+d0]+d1	indirect, base FP
18	Mem[SB+d0]+d1	indirect, base SB
20		immediate
21	d0	absolute
22	EXT(d0)+d1	external
23	SP	TOS
24	FP+d0	base FP
26	SB+d0	base SB
28-31		indexed, scale factor 1, 2, 4, 8

The basic instruction bytes containing the opcode and the address specifiers are followed by the operand bytes in the order shown below from right to left. The operand fields may contain one or two displacement values, or an immediate value, or they may be missing alltogether.

implied	dst disp/imm	src disp/imm	dst index	src index	src	dst	op

Index bytes are present only if an indexed mode is specified. They indicate the register holding the index value, and the mode to be used in the basic address computation. Some instructions contain additional, implied operands.

3	0
mode	reg

Displacements are length-encoded as follows (the values are stored as signed integers in most-significant byte first order, contrary to the little-endian representation of integers used by this processor):

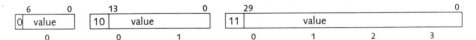

Instructions are generated by procedures *PutF0*, *PutF1*, *PutF2*, *PutF3*, *PutF4* and *Put(F)*, depending on the format required. Procedures *PutByte* and *PutWord* are used to append immediate operands, and *PutDisp* to encode and insert displacements. Instructions, immediate values and displacements are inserted in the array *code*, a global variable. This solution strictly limits the size of modules, but allows for easy fixup of (branch) addresses and is very efficient, because it avoids the use of dynamic allocation.

Similarly, the global arrays *constant, entry* and *link* hold constants, entry addresses of exported procedures, and links for imports. Constants are inserted by procedures *AllocInt*, *AllocString*, *AllocTypDesc*, and *AllocBounds*. Entry addresses are recorded by procedure *SetEntry*, and links are inserted by procedure *LinkAdr*. Various fixup procedures handle the insertion of branch displacements for forward jumps. *SaveRegisters* and *RestoreRegisters* are called for saving and restoring registers (holding intermediate results) before and after a call of a function procedure within an expression.

Generating object file   An object file is generated at the end of a module's compilation by procedure *OutCode*. For a description of the object file format, the reader is referred to Chapter 6. First, the symbol table's global scope is scanned for pointer variables and command procedures. Then the header is written and the various tables used by the loader, containing entry addresses, commands, pointers, imports and links. Then follows the table of global constants, then the code, and finally type descriptor information used by the loader to generate and allocate type descriptors on the heap.

Reference block

After the actual object file data, a part is appended called the *reference block*. It is ignored by the loader, but is used in the case of traps during execution of a program for generating a 'post-mortem dump' in symbolic form (see Section 12.9). For this purpose, the reference block contains the names of variables and procedures together with their addresses. The information is obtained by a full traversal of the symbol table. (Note that only variables of basic, unstructured type and short character arrays are included.)

At least one detail about the implementation of module OCC is worth mentioning. It concerns the generation of code for two-address instructions (procedure *PutF4* and *Put*). Due to the rather complicated ordering of operand fields following a basic instruction, it is impossible to first emit an operation code and then to let it be followed by the two operands. Not only are the address specifiers of both operands contained in the basic instruction bytes, but both index bytes (if any) precede all displacements. Therefore all parts of both operand's specifications must be available before any emission can take place. The

Type Argument

solution chosen is to use two local variables *dst* and *src* of type *Argument* representing the encoded forms of operands, which is computed by procedure *Operand* from a given *Item*. After this computation, the basic instruction bytes are emitted, followed by the operand bytes. The latter is done by procedure *PutArg*. One cannot help but feel that the prescribed instruction format is not exactly the optimal choice.

```
MODULE OCC; (*NW 30.5.87 / 16.3.91*)
   IMPORT Files, OCS, OCT;

   CONST CodeLength = 18000; LinkLength = 250;
           ConstLength = 3500; EntryLength = 64;
           CodeLim = CodeLength - 100;
           MaxPtrs = 64; MaxRecs = 32; MaxComs = 40; MaxExts = 7;
       (*instruction format prefixes*)
       F6 = 4EH; F7 = 0CEH; F9 = 3EH; F11 = 0BEH;

   (*object and item modes*)
       Var  = 1;  VarX = 2;  Ind  = 3;  IndX = 4;  RegI = 5;
       RegX = 6;  Abs  = 7;  Con  = 8;  Stk  = 9;  Coc  = 10;
       Reg  = 11; Fld  = 12; Typ  = 13; LProc = 14; XProc = 15;
       SProc = 16; CProc = 17; IProc = 18; Mod = 19; Head = 20;
```

```
(*structure forms*)
    Undef = 0; Byte = 1; Bool = 2; Char = 3; SInt = 4; Int = 5; LInt = 6;
    Real = 7; LReal = 8; Set = 9; String = 10; NilTyp = 11; NoTyp = 12;
    Pointer = 13; ProcTyp = 14; Array = 15; DynArr = 16; Record = 17;

TYPE Argument =
    RECORD form, gen, inx: INTEGER;
        d1, d2: LONGINT
    END ;

VAR pc*, level*: INTEGER;
    wasderef*: OCT.Object;
    typchk*: BOOLEAN;
    RegSet*, FRegSet: SET;
    lnkx, conx, nofptrs, nofrec: INTEGER;
    PtrTab: ARRAY MaxPtrs OF LONGINT;
    RecTab: ARRAY MaxRecs OF OCT.Struct;
    constant: ARRAY ConstLength OF CHAR;
    code: ARRAY CodeLength OF CHAR;
    link: ARRAY LinkLength OF INTEGER;
    entry: ARRAY EntryLength OF INTEGER;

PROCEDURE GetReg*(VAR x: OCT.Item);
    VAR i: INTEGER;
BEGIN i := 7; x.mode := Reg;
    LOOP IF ~(i IN RegSet) THEN x.a0 := i; INCL(RegSet,i); EXIT END ;
        IF i = 0 THEN x.a0 := 0; OCS.Mark(215); EXIT ELSE DEC(i) END ;
    END
END GetReg;

PROCEDURE GetFReg*(VAR x: OCT.Item);
    VAR i: INTEGER;
BEGIN i := 6; x.mode := Reg;
    LOOP IF ~(i IN FRegSet) THEN x.a0 := i; INCL(FRegSet,i); EXIT END ;
        IF i = 0 THEN x.a0 := 0; OCS.Mark(216); EXIT ELSE i := i−2 END
    END
END GetFReg;

PROCEDURE FreeRegs*(r: SET);
BEGIN RegSet := r; FRegSet := {}
END FreeRegs;

PROCEDURE AllocInt*(k: INTEGER);
BEGIN
    IF conx < ConstLength−1 THEN
        constant[conx] := CHR(k); INC(conx);
        constant[conx] := CHR(k DIV 100H); INC(conx)
    ELSE OCS.Mark(230); conx := 0
    END
END AllocInt;

PROCEDURE AllocString*(VAR s: ARRAY OF CHAR; VAR x: OCT.Item);
    VAR i: INTEGER; ch: CHAR;
BEGIN INC(conx, (−conx) MOD 4); i := 0;
    REPEAT ch := s[i]; INC(i);
        IF conx >= ConstLength THEN OCS.Mark(230); conx := 0 END ;
        constant[conx] := ch; INC(conx)
```

```
      UNTIL ch = 0X;
      x.lev := 0; x.a0 := conx − i; x.a1 := i
   END AllocString;


   PROCEDURE AllocBounds*(min, max: INTEGER; VAR adr: LONGINT);
   BEGIN INC(conx, (−conx) MOD 4); adr := conx;
      AllocInt(max); AllocInt(min)
   END AllocBounds;


   PROCEDURE PutByte*(x: LONGINT);
   BEGIN code[pc] := CHR(x); INC(pc)
   END PutByte;


   PROCEDURE PutWord*(x: LONGINT);
   BEGIN code[pc] := CHR(x DIV 100H); INC(pc); code[pc] := CHR(x); INC(pc)
   END PutWord;


   PROCEDURE PutDbl(x: LONGINT);
      VAR i: INTEGER;
   BEGIN i := −32;
      REPEAT INC(i, 8); code[pc] := CHR(ASH(x, i)); INC(pc) UNTIL i = 0
   END PutDbl;


   PROCEDURE PutDisp*(x: LONGINT);
   BEGIN
      IF x < 0 THEN
         IF x >= −40H THEN code[pc] := CHR(x+80H); INC(pc)
         ELSIF x >= −2000H THEN PutWord(x+0C000H)
         ELSE PutDbl(x)
         END
      ELSIF x < 40H THEN code[pc] := CHR(x); INC(pc)
      ELSIF x < 2000H THEN PutWord(x+8000H)
      ELSE PutDbl(x − 40000000H)
      END
   END PutDisp;


   PROCEDURE PutArg(VAR z: Argument);
   BEGIN
      CASE z.form OF
         0: IF z.inx = 1 THEN code[pc] := CHR(z.d1); INC(pc)
            ELSIF z.inx = 2 THEN PutWord(z.d1)
            ELSIF z.inx = 4 THEN PutDbl(z.d1)
            ELSE PutDbl(z.d2); PutDbl(z.d1)
            END
       | 1: PutDisp(z.d1)
       | 2, 5:
       | 3, 6: PutDisp(z.d1)
       | 4, 7: PutDisp(z.d1); PutDisp(z.d2)
       END
   END PutArg;


   PROCEDURE PutF3*(op: INTEGER);
   BEGIN code[pc] := CHR(op); INC(pc); code[pc] := CHR(op DIV 100H); INC(pc)
   END PutF3;


   PROCEDURE Operand(VAR x: OCT.Item; VAR z: Argument);
```

```
VAR F: INTEGER;

PROCEDURE downlevel(VAR gen: INTEGER);
    VAR n, op: INTEGER; b: OCT.Item;
BEGIN GetReg(b); n := level − x.lev; gen := SHORT(b.a0) + 8;
    op := SHORT(b.a0)*40H − 3FE9H;
    IF n = 1 THEN PutF3(op); PutDisp(8); (*MOVD 8(FP) Rb*)
    ELSE PutF3(op − 4000H); PutDisp(8); PutDisp(8); (*MOVD 8(8(FP)) Rb*)
        WHILE n > 2 DO DEC(n);
            PutF3((SHORT(b.a0)*20H + SHORT(b.a0))*40H + 4017H); PutDisp(8)
        END
    END ;
END downlevel;


PROCEDURE index;
    VAR s: LONGINT;
BEGIN s := x.typ.size;
    IF s = 1 THEN z.gen := 1CH
    ELSIF s = 2 THEN z.gen := 1DH
    ELSIF s = 4 THEN z.gen := 1EH
    ELSIF s = 8 THEN z.gen := 1FH
    ELSE z.gen := 1CH; PutByte(F7); PutByte(x.a2 MOD 4 * 40H + 23H);
        PutByte(x.a2 DIV 4 + 0A0H); PutWord(0); PutWord(s) (*MUL r s*)
    END ;
END index;


BEGIN F := x.mode;
    CASE x.mode OF
    Var:   IF x.lev = 0 THEN
                z.gen := 1AH; z.d1 := x.a0; z.form := 3
            ELSIF x.lev < 0 THEN (*EXT*)
                z.gen := 16H; z.d1 := −x.lev; z.d2 := x.a0; z.form := 4
            ELSIF x.lev = level THEN
                z.gen := 18H; z.d1 := x.a0; z.form := 3
            ELSIF x.lev+1 = level THEN
                z.gen := 10H; z.d1 := 8; z.d2 := x.a0; z.form := 4
            ELSE downlevel(z.gen); z.d1 := x.a0; z.form := 3
            END
    | Ind: IF x.lev = 0 THEN
                z.gen := 12H; z.d1 := x.a0; z.d2 := x.a1; z.form := 4
            ELSIF x.lev = level THEN
                z.gen := 10H; z.d1 := x.a0; z.d2 := x.a1; z.form := 4
            ELSE downlevel(z.gen);
                PutF3((z.gen*20H + z.gen−8)*40H + 17H); PutDisp(x.a0);
                z.d1 := x.a1; z.form := 3
            END
    | RegI:z.gen := SHORT(x.a0)+8; z.d1 := x.a1; z.form := 3
    | VarXindex;
            IF x.lev = 0 THEN
                z.inx := 1AH; z.d1 := x.a0; z.form := 6
            ELSIF x.lev < 0 THEN (*EXT*)
                z.inx := 16H; z.d1 := −x.lev; z.d2 := x.a0; z.form := 7
            ELSIF x.lev = level THEN
                z.inx := 18H; z.d1 := x.a0; z.form := 6
            ELSIF x.lev+1 = level THEN
                z.inx := 10H; z.d1 := 8; z.d2 := x.a0; z.form := 7
            ELSE downlevel(z.inx); z.d1 := x.a0; z.form := 6
```

```
                                END ;
                                z.inx := z.inx*8 + SHORT(x.a2)
                  | IndXindex;
                                IF x.lev = 0 THEN
                                    z.inx := 12H; z.d1 := x.a0; z.d2 := x.a1; z.form := 7
                                ELSIF x.lev = level THEN
                                    z.inx := 10H; z.d1 := x.a0; z.d2 := x.a1; z.form := 7
                                ELSE downlevel(z.inx);
                                    PutF3((z.inx*20H + z.inx-8)*40H + 17H); PutDisp(x.a0);
                                    z.d1 := x.a1; z.form := 6
                                END ;
                                z.inx := z.inx * 8 + SHORT(x.a2)
                  | RegXindex; z.inx := SHORT((x.a0+8)*8 + x.a2); z.d1 := x.a1; z.form := 6
                  | Con: CASE x.typ.form OF
                                Undef, Byte, Bool, Char, SInt:
                                    z.gen := 14H; z.inx := 1; z.d1 := x.a0; z.form := 0
                                | Int: z.gen := 14H; z.inx := 2; z.d1 := x.a0; z.form := 0
                                | LInt, Real, Set, Pointer, ProcTyp, NilTyp:
                                    z.gen := 14H; z.inx := 4; z.d1 := x.a0; z.form := 0
                                | LReal:
                                    z.gen := 14H; z.inx := 8; z.d1 := x.a0; z.d2 := x.a1; z.form := 0
                                | String:
                                    z.gen := 1AH; z.d1 := x.a0; z.form := 3
                                END
                  | Reg: z.gen := SHORT(x.a0); z.form := 2
                  | Stk: z.gen := 17H; z.form := 2
                  | Abs: z.gen := 15H; z.form := 1; z.d1 := x.a0
                  | Coc, Fld .. Head: OCS.Mark(126); x.mode := Var; z.form := 0
                  END
      END Operand;


      PROCEDURE PutF0*(cond: LONGINT);
      BEGIN code[pc] := CHR(cond*10H + 10); INC(pc)
      END PutF0;


      PROCEDURE PutF1*(op: INTEGER);
      BEGIN code[pc] := CHR(op); INC(pc)
      END PutF1;


      PROCEDURE PutF2*(op: INTEGER; short: LONGINT; VAR x: OCT.Item);
          VAR dst: Argument;
      BEGIN Operand(x, dst);
          code[pc] := CHR(SHORT(short) MOD 2 * 80H + op); INC(pc);
          code[pc] := CHR(dst.gen*8 + SHORT(short) MOD 10H DIV 2);
          INC(pc);
          IF dst.form > 4 THEN code[pc] := CHR(dst.inx); INC(pc) END ;
          PutArg(dst)
      END PutF2;


      PROCEDURE PutF4*(op: INTEGER; VAR x, y: OCT.Item);
          VAR dst, src: Argument;
      BEGIN Operand(x, dst); Operand(y, src);
          code[pc] := CHR(dst.gen MOD 4 * 40H + op); INC(pc);
          code[pc] := CHR(src.gen*8 + dst.gen DIV 4); INC(pc);
          IF src.form > 4 THEN code[pc] := CHR(src.inx); INC(pc) END ;
          IF dst.form > 4 THEN code[pc] := CHR(dst.inx); INC(pc) END ;
          PutArg(src); PutArg(dst)
```

```
END PutF4;


PROCEDURE Put*(F, op: INTEGER; VAR x, y: OCT.Item);
    VAR dst, src: Argument;
BEGIN Operand(x, dst); Operand(y, src); code[pc] := CHR(F); INC(pc);
    code[pc] := CHR(dst.gen MOD 4 * 40H + op); INC(pc);
    code[pc] := CHR(src.gen*8 + dst.gen DIV 4); INC(pc);
    IF src.form > 4 THEN code[pc] := CHR(src.inx); INC(pc) END ;
    IF dst.form > 4 THEN code[pc] := CHR(dst.inx); INC(pc) END ;
    PutArg(src); PutArg(dst)
END Put;


PROCEDURE AllocTypDesc*(typ: OCT.Struct); (* typ.form = Record *)
BEGIN INC(conx, (−conx) MOD 4); typ.mno := 0; typ.adr := conx;
    IF typ.n > MaxExts THEN OCS.Mark(233)
    ELSIF nofrec < MaxRecs THEN
        PtrTab[nofptrs] := conx; INC(nofptrs);
        RecTab[nofrec] := typ; INC(nofrec);
        AllocInt(0); AllocInt(0)
    ELSE OCS.Mark(223)
    END
END AllocTypDesc;


PROCEDURE InitTypDescs*;
    VAR x, y: OCT.Item; i: INTEGER; typ: OCT.Struct;
BEGIN
    x.mode := Ind; x.lev := 0; y.mode := Var; i := 0;
    WHILE i < nofrec DO typ := RecTab[i]; INC(i); x.a0 := typ.adr;
        WHILE typ.BaseTyp # NIL DO (*initialization of base tag fields*)
            x.a1 := typ.n * 4; y.lev := −typ.mno; y.a0 := typ.adr; PutF4(17H, x, y);
            typ := typ.BaseTyp
        END
    END
END InitTypDescs;


PROCEDURE SaveRegisters*(VAR gR, fR: SET; VAR x: OCT.Item);
    VAR i, r, m: INTEGER; t: SET;
BEGIN t := RegSet;
    IF x.mode IN {Reg, RegI, RegX} THEN EXCL(RegSet, x.a0) END ;
    IF x.mode IN {VarX, IndX, RegX} THEN EXCL(RegSet, x.a2) END ;
    gR := RegSet; fR := FRegSet;
    IF RegSet # {} THEN
        i := 0; r := 1; m := 0;
        REPEAT
            IF i IN RegSet THEN INC(m, r) END ;
            INC(r, r); INC(i)
        UNTIL i = 8;
        PutF1(62H); PutByte(m)
    END ;
    RegSet := t − RegSet; i := 0;
    WHILE FRegSet # {} DO
        IF i IN FRegSet THEN
            PutF1(F11); PutF3(i*800H + 5C4H); EXCL(FRegSet, i)
        END ;
        INC(i, 2)
    END
END SaveRegisters;
```

```
PROCEDURE RestoreRegisters*(gR, fR: SET; VAR x: OCT.Item);
    VAR i, r, m: INTEGER; y: OCT.Item;
BEGIN RegSet := gR; FRegSet := fR; i := 8;
    (*set result mode*) x.mode := Reg; x.a0 := 0;
    IF (x.typ.form = Real) OR (x.typ.form = LReal) THEN
        IF 0 IN fR THEN GetFReg(y); Put(F11, 4, y, x); x.a0 := y.a0 END ;
        INCL(FRegSet, 0)
    ELSE
        IF 0 IN gR THEN GetReg(y); PutF4(17H, y, x); x.a0 := y.a0 END ;
        INCL(RegSet, 0)
    END ;
    WHILE fR # {} DO
        DEC(i, 2);
        IF i IN fR THEN
            PutF1(F11); PutF3(i*40H − 47FCH); EXCL(fR, i)
        END
    END ;
    IF gR # {} THEN
        i := 8; r := 1; m := 0;
        REPEAT DEC(i);
            IF i IN gR THEN INC(m, r) END ;
            INC(r, r)
        UNTIL i = 0;
        PutF1(72H); PutF1(m)
    END
END RestoreRegisters;


PROCEDURE DynArrAdr*(VAR x, y: OCT.Item); (* x := ADR(y) *)
    VAR l, z: OCT.Item;
BEGIN
    WHILE y.typ.form = DynArr DO (* index with 0 *)
        IF y.mode = IndX THENl.mode := Var; l.a0 := y.a0 + y.typ.adr; l.lev := y.lev;
            (* l = actual dimension length − 1 *)
            z.mode := Con; z.a0 := 0; z.typ := OCT.inttyp;
            Put(2EH, SHORT(y.a2)*8+5, z, l) (* INDEXW inxreg, l, 0 *)
        END;
        y.typ := y.typ.BaseTyp
    END;
    IF (y.mode = Var) OR (y.mode = Ind) & (y.a1 = 0) THEN
        y.mode := Var; PutF4(17H, x, y) (* MOVD *)
    ELSE PutF4(27H, x, y); x.a1 := 0 (* ADDR *)
    END
END DynArrAdr;


PROCEDURE Entry*(i: INTEGER): INTEGER;
BEGIN RETURN entry[i]
END Entry;


PROCEDURE SetEntry*(i: INTEGER);
BEGIN entry[i] := pc
END SetEntry;


PROCEDURE LinkAdr*(m: INTEGER; n: LONGINT): INTEGER;
BEGIN
    IF lnkx >= LinkLength THEN OCS.Mark(231); lnkx := 0 END ;
    link[lnkx] := m*100H + SHORT(n); INC(lnkx); RETURN lnkx−1
END LinkAdr;
```

```
PROCEDURE SetLinkTable*(n: INTEGER);
BEGIN (*base addresses of imported modules*) lnkx := 0;
    WHILE lnkx < n DO link[lnkx] := lnkx*100H + 255; INC(lnkx) END
END SetLinkTable;


PROCEDURE fixup*(loc: LONGINT); (*enter pc at loc*)
    VAR x: LONGINT;
BEGIN x := pc − loc + 8001H;
    code[loc] := CHR(x DIV 100H); code[loc+1] := CHR(x)
END fixup;


PROCEDURE fixupC*(loc: LONGINT);
    VAR x: LONGINT;
BEGIN x := pc+1 − loc;
    IF x > 3 THEN
        IF x < 2000H THEN
            code[loc] := CHR(x DIV 100H + 80H); code[loc+1] := CHR(x)
        ELSE OCS.Mark(211)
        END
    ELSE DEC(pc, 3)
    END
END fixupC;


PROCEDURE fixupL*(loc: LONGINT);
    VAR x: LONGINT;
BEGIN x := pc+1 − loc;
    IF x > 5 THEN
        code[loc+2] := CHR(x DIV 100H); code[loc+3] := CHR(x)
    ELSE DEC(pc, 5)
    END
END fixupL;


PROCEDURE FixLink*(L: LONGINT);
    VAR L1: LONGINT;
BEGIN
    WHILE L # 0 DO
        L1 := ORD(code[L])*100H + ORD(code[L+1]);
        fixup(L); L := L1
    END
END FixLink;


PROCEDURE FixupWith*(L, val: LONGINT);
    VAR x: LONGINT;
BEGIN x := val MOD 4000H + 8000H;
    IF ABS(val) >= 2000H THEN OCS.Mark(208) END ;
    code[L] := CHR(x DIV 100H); code[L+1] := CHR(x)
END FixupWith;


PROCEDURE FixLinkWith*(L, val: LONGINT);
    VAR L1: LONGINT;
BEGIN
    WHILE L # 0 DO
        L1 := ORD(code[L])*100H + ORD(code[L+1]);
        FixupWith(L, val+1 − L); L := L1
    END
END FixLinkWith;
```

```
PROCEDURE MergedLinks*(L0, L1: LONGINT): LONGINT;
    VAR L2, L3: LONGINT;
BEGIN (*merge chains of the two operands of AND and OR *)
    IF L0 # 0 THEN L2 := L0;
        LOOP L3 := ORD(code[L2])*100H + ORD(code[L2+1]);
            IF L3 = 0 THEN EXIT END ;
            L2 := L3
        END ;
        code[L2] := CHR(L1 DIV 100H); code[L2+1] := CHR(L1);
        RETURN L0
    ELSE RETURN L1
    END
END MergedLinks;


PROCEDURE Init*;
    VAR i: INTEGER;
BEGIN pc := 0; level := 0; lnkx := 0; conx := 0; nofptrs := 0; nofrec := 0;
    RegSet := {}; FRegSet := {}; i := 0;
    REPEAT entry[i] := 0; INC(i) UNTIL i = EntryLength
END Init;


PROCEDURE OutCode*(VAR name, progid: ARRAY OF CHAR;
        key: LONGINT; entno: INTEGER; datasize: LONGINT);
    CONST ObjMark = 0F8X;
    VAR ch: CHAR; f, i, m: INTEGER;
        K, s, s0, refpos: LONGINT;
        nofcom, comsize, align: INTEGER;
        obj:     OCT.Object;
        typ:     OCT.Struct;
        ObjFile:  Files.File;
        out:     Files.Rider;
        ComTab: ARRAY MaxComs OF OCT.Object;


PROCEDURE W(n: INTEGER);
BEGIN Files.Write(out, CHR(n)); Files.Write(out, CHR(n DIV 100H))
END W;


PROCEDURE WriteName(VAR name: ARRAY OF CHAR; n: INTEGER);
    VAR i: INTEGER; ch: CHAR;
BEGIN i := 0;
    REPEAT ch := name[i]; Files.Write(out, ch); INC(i) UNTIL ch = 0X;
    WHILE i < n DO Files.Write(out, 0X); INC(i) END
END WriteName;


PROCEDURE FindPtrs(typ: OCT.Struct; adr: LONGINT);
    VAR fld: OCT.Object; btyp: OCT.Struct;
        i, n, s: LONGINT;
BEGIN
    IF typ.form = Pointer THEN
        IF nofptrs < MaxPtrs THEN PtrTab[nofptrs] := adr; INC(nofptrs) ELSE
            OCS.Mark(222) END
    ELSIF typ.form = Record THEN
        btyp := typ.BaseTyp;
        IF btyp # NIL THEN FindPtrs(btyp, adr) END ;
        fld := typ.link;
        WHILE fld # NIL DO
            IF fld.name # "" THEN FindPtrs(fld.typ, fld.a0 + adr)
```

```
            ELSIF nofptrs < MaxPtrs THEN PtrTab[nofptrs] := fld.a0 + adr; INC(nofptrs)
            ELSE OCS.Mark(222)
            END ;
            fld := fld.next
        END
    ELSIF typ.form = Array THEN
        btyp := typ.BaseTyp; n := typ.n;
        WHILE btyp.form = Array DO n := btyp.n * n; btyp := btyp.BaseTyp END ;
        IF (btyp.form = Pointer) OR (btyp.form = Record) THEN
            i := 0; s := btyp.size;
            WHILE i < n DO FindPtrs(btyp, i*s + adr); INC(i) END
        END
    END
END FindPtrs;


PROCEDURE PtrsAndComs;
    VAR obj, par: OCT.Object; u: INTEGER;
BEGIN obj := OCT.topScope.next;
    WHILE obj # NIL DO
        IF obj.mode = XProc THEN par := obj.dsc;
            IF entry[SHORT(obj.a0)] = 0 THEN OCS.Mark(129)
            ELSIF (obj.marked) & (obj.typ = OCT.notyp) &
                ((par = NIL) OR (par.mode > 3) OR (par.a0 < 0)) THEN (*command*)
                u := 0;
                WHILE obj.name[u] > 0X DO INC(comsize); INC(u) END ;
                INC(comsize, 3);
                IF nofcom < MaxComs THEN ComTab[nofcom] := obj; INC(nofcom)
                ELSE OCS.Mark(232); nofcom := 0; comsize := 0
                END
            END
        ELSIF obj.mode = Var THEN
            FindPtrs(obj.typ, obj.a0)
        END ;
        obj := obj.next
    END
END PtrsAndComs;


PROCEDURE OutRefBlk(first: OCT.Object; pc: INTEGER; name: ARRAY OF CHAR);
    VAR obj: OCT.Object;
BEGIN obj := first;
    WHILE obj # NIL DO
        IF obj.mode IN {LProc, XProc, IProc} THEN
            OutRefBlk(obj.dsc, obj.a2, obj.name)
        END ;
        obj := obj.next
    END ;
    Files.Write(out, 0F8X); Files.WriteBytes(out, pc, 2); WriteName(name, 0);
    obj := first;
    WHILE obj # NIL DO
        IF (obj.mode = Var) OR (obj.mode = Ind) THEN
            f := obj.typ.form;
            IF (f IN {Byte .. Set, Pointer})
                OR (f = Array) & (obj.typ.BaseTyp.form = Char) THEN
                Files.Write(out, CHR(obj.mode)); Files.Write(out, CHR(f));
                Files.WriteBytes(out, obj.a0, 4); WriteName(obj.name, 0)
            END
        END ;
        obj:= obj.next
```

```
            END
        END OutRefBlk;


BEGIN (*OutCode*) ObjFile := Files.New(name);
    IF ObjFile # NIL THEN
        Files.Set(out, ObjFile, 0);
        WHILE pc MOD 4 # 0 DO PutF1(0A2H) END ; (*NOP*)
        INC(conx, (-conx) MOD 4);
        nofcom := 0; comsize := 1;
        PtrsAndComs; align := comsize MOD 2; INC(comsize, align);
    (*header block*)
        Files.Write(out, ObjMark); Files.Write(out, "6"); W(0); W(0);
        W(entno); W(comsize); W(nofptrs); W(OCT.nofGmod);
        W(lnkx); Files.WriteBytes(out, datasize, 4); W(conx); W(pc);
        Files.WriteBytes(out, key, 4); WriteName(progid, 20);
    (*entry block*)
        Files.Write(out, 82X); Files.WriteBytes(out, entry, 2*entno);
    (*command block*)
        Files.Write(out, 83X);
        i := 0; (*write command names and entry addresses*)
        WHILE i < nofcom DO
            obj := ComTab[i]; WriteName(obj.name, 0); W(entry[obj.a0]); INC(i)
        END ;
        Files.Write(out, 0X);
        IF align > 0 THEN Files.Write(out, 0FFX) END ;
    (*pointer block*)
        Files.Write(out, 84X); i := 0;
        WHILE i < nofptrs DO
            IF PtrTab[i] < -4000H THEN OCS.Mark(225) END ;
            Files.WriteBytes(out, PtrTab[i], 2); INC(i)
        END ;
    (*import block*)
        Files.Write(out, 85X); i := 0;
        WHILE i < OCT.nofGmod DO
            obj := OCT.GlbMod[i];
            Files.WriteBytes(out, obj.a1, 4); WriteName(obj.name, 0); Files.Write(out, 0X);
            INC(i)
        END ;
    (*link block*)
        Files.Write(out, 86X); Files.WriteBytes(out, link, 2*lnkx);
    (*data block*)
        Files.Write(out, 87X); Files.WriteBytes(out, constant, conx);
    (*code block*)
        Files.Write(out, 88X); Files.WriteBytes(out, code, pc);
    (*type block*)
        Files.Write(out, 89X); i := 0;
        WHILE i < nofrec DO
            typ := RecTab[i]; s := typ.size + 4; m := 4; s0 := 16;
            WHILE (m > 0) & (s > s0) DO INC(s0, s0); DEC(m) END ;
            IF s > s0 THEN s0 := (s+127) DIV 128 * 128 END ;
            nofptrs := 0; FindPtrs(typ, 0);
            s := nofptrs*2 + (MaxExts+1)*4; Files.WriteBytes(out, s, 2); (*td size*)
            Files.WriteBytes(out, typ.adr, 2);      (*td adr*)
            K := LONG(nofptrs)*1000000H + s0; Files.WriteBytes(out, K, 4);
            K := 0; m := 0;
            REPEAT Files.WriteBytes(out, K, 4); INC(m) UNTIL m = MaxExts;
            m := 0;
            WHILE m < nofptrs DO
```

```
                    Files.WriteBytes(out, PtrTab[m], 2); INC(m)
                END ;
                INC(i)
            END ;
        (*ref block*)
            refpos := Files.Pos(out); Files.Write(out, 8AX);
            OutRefBlk(OCT.topScope.next, pc, "$$");
            Files.Set(out, ObjFile, 2); Files.WriteBytes(out, refpos, 4);
            IF ~OCS.scanerr THEN Files.Register(ObjFile) END
        ELSE OCS.Mark(153)
        END
    END OutCode;

    PROCEDURE Close*;
        VAR i: INTEGER;
    BEGIN i := 0;
        WHILE i < MaxRecs DO RecTab[i] := NIL; INC(i) END
    END Close;


BEGIN NEW(wasderef)
END OCC.
```

12.9 A facility for symbolic debugging

Debugger

The facility described in this section is in fact not part of the compiler, but it is nevertheless intimately coupled with it through the definition of storage layout. This facility is used in the case of an abnormal command termination to generate a text displaying the state of the computation. The state is represented by the chain of activated procedures and by their local variables at the time of the termination. Because the current values of the variables are displayed in the same form as used in the source program (that is, in symbolic rather than encoded form), such a facility is usually called a *symbolic debugger*. It is present in the form of a command procedure *Trap*, which, however, is not available as a user-activatable command, but rather is invoked by the system whenever an abnormal program condition occurs. Specifically, the procedure is defined in module *System* and is installed in a procedure variable of module *Kernel*.

When a trap occurs, various register values are stored in exported variables of the kernel. *Kernel.err* indicates the trap number (as defined by the processor). Here we list only the more frequently occurring traps:

2	Address trap	typically reference via NIL pointer
3	Floating−point trap	overflow
6	Division by zero	

    7 Flag trap   invalid index
  13 Integer trap or invalid index
  18 Type guard failure

As an example, let us consider the following command:

```
PROCEDURE Q(multiplier, count: INTEGER);
    VAR sum: LONGINT; ch: CHAR;
BEGIN sum := 1234567; ch := "Q"; Q(m*100, count+1)
END Q;


PROCEDURE Trap*;
    VAR s: ARRAY 32 OF CHAR;
BEGIN s := "This command should never terminate!"); Q(1, 0)
END Trap;
```

The following is the text generated and displayed in a trap viewer after an attempt to multiply caused arithmetic overflow:

```
TRAP 13 FP = 002FFDD0 PC = 00443053
Demo.Q
    multiplier = 10000
    count = 2
    sum = 1234567
    ch = Q
Demo.Q
    multiplier = 100
    count = 1
    sum = 1234567
    ch = Q
Demo.Q
    multiplier = 1
    count = 0
    sum = 1234567
    ch = Q
Demo.Trap
    msg = "This command never terminates!"
Oberon.Call
TextFrames.Call
TextFrames.Edit
TextFrames.Handle
MenuViewers.Handle
Oberon.Loop
Modules.$$
```

In order to identify the currently activated procedures and to list their local variables and current values, the trap routine must not only have free access to the stack, where these values are allocated, but must be able to rely on information about the mapping of source program to stored code. In fact, this mapping has to be reversed. The relevant information is contained in the *reference part* of each module's object file. It is the last part of an object file and is ignored by the loader. In order to enable quick access, bytes 2–5 indicate the position of the reference part.

The reference part is generated by procedure *OutRefBlk*, which is local to *OCC.OutCode*. It generates an entry in the reference part of the object file for each procedure and some of its local variables. Since procedures may be nested, *OutRefBlk* is recursive. For procedures, their name and offset in the code section of the module's block are indicated; for variables, their name, offset address and type (form) are indicated. The syntax of the reference part is

Format of reference block

ReferencePart = {procedure}.
procedure = 0F8X offset:2 name {procedure | variable}.
variable = form:1 mode:1 offset:4 name.
name = {character} 0X.

Module bodies are treated like procedures; in place of a name stands '$$'. Markers with value F8X serve to distinguish procedure entries from those of variables. *form* stands for one of the following values:

2	BOOLEAN	6	LONGINT	13	POINTER
3	CHAR	7	REAL	14	Procedure type
4	SHORTINT	8	LONGREAL	15	Character array type
5	INTEGER	9	SET		

Structured variables are not included, with the exception of short character arrays, which take the form of strings. *mode* assumes one of the values

1	directly addressed
3	indirectly addressed (VAR parameter)

The implementation of the process of generating the desired information can be studied in detail in the subsequent program listing. Procedure *System.Trap* first identifies the head of the dynamic chain of procedure activation records. This value is held in register FP and is now indicated by *Kernel.fp*. The location of the trap is specified by *Kernel.pc*, and the module containing the malfunctioning procedure is specified by *Kernel.mod*. Now this procedure needs to be identified. This is accomplished by accessing the respective module's object file, whose name is found in the module descriptor. The file's reference part is scanned until a procedure is found in whose range the indicated value pc (the trap location) lies. If found, the procedure name is listed and its list of local variables is scanned. For each one of them, the name is read from the reference part and listed in the trap text, and its offset is read in order to obtain its current value from the stack and to list it in the format appropriate for the indicated form.

Trap then proceeds through the chain of procedure activation records, and for each record repeats this process. The scanning of local variables is performed by procedure *Locals*, whose parameter specifies the base address of the respective activation record.

```
PROCEDURE Locals(VAR R: Files.Rider; base: LONGINT);
    VAR adr, val: LONGINT;
        sval, form: SHORTINT;
        ch, mode: CHAR;
        ival, i: INTEGER;
        rval: REAL;
        lrval: LONGREAL;
    BEGIN Texts.WriteLn(W); Files.Read(R, mode);
        WHILE ~R.eof & (mode < 0F8X) DO
            Files.Read(R, form); Files.ReadBytes(R, adr, 4);
            Texts.WriteString(W, " "); Files.Read(R, ch);
            WHILE ch > 0X DO Texts.Write(W, ch); Files.Read(R, ch) END ;
            Texts.WriteString(W, " = "); INC(adr, base);
            IF mode = 3X THEN SYSTEM.GET(adr, adr) (*indirect*) END ;
            CASE form OF
                2: (*BOOL*) SYSTEM.GET(adr, sval);
                    IF sval = 0 THEN Texts.WriteString(W, "FALSE")
                        ELSE Texts.WriteString(W, "TRUE")
                    END
              | 1,3: (*CHAR*) SYSTEM.GET(adr, ch);
                    IF (" " <= ch) & (ch <= "~") THEN Texts.Write(W, ch)
                        ELSE Texts.WriteHex(W, ORD(ch)); Texts.Write(W, "X")
                    END
              | 4: (*SINT*) SYSTEM.GET(adr, sval); Texts.WriteInt(W, sval, 1)
              | 5: (*INT*) SYSTEM.GET(adr, ival); Texts.WriteInt(W, ival, 1)
              | 6: (*LINT*) SYSTEM.GET(adr, val); Texts.WriteInt(W, val, 1)
              | 7: (*REAL*) SYSTEM.GET(adr, rval); Texts.WriteReal(W, rval, 14)
              | 8: (*LREAL*) SYSTEM.GET(adr, lrval); Texts.WriteLongReal(W, lrval, 21)
              | 9, 13, 14: (*SET, POINTER*)
                    SYSTEM.GET(adr, val); Texts.WriteHex(W, val); Texts.Write(W, "H")
              | 15: (*String*) i := 0; Texts.Write(W, 22X);
                    LOOP SYSTEM.GET(adr, ch);
                        IF (ch < " ") OR (ch >= 90X) OR (i = 32) THEN EXIT END ;
                        Texts.Write(W, ch); INC(i); INC(adr)
                    END ;
                    Texts.Write(W, 22X)
            END;
            Texts.WriteLn(W); Files.Read(R, mode)
        END
    END Locals;


PROCEDURE* Trap;
```

```
        VAR V: Viewers.Viewer;
            RefFile: Files.File;
            R: Files.Rider;
            fp, pc, refpos, dmy: LONGINT;
            ch, mode: CHAR;
            X, Y, i: INTEGER;
            mod, curmod: Modules.Module;
            name: Modules.ModuleName;
    BEGIN
        IF ~trapped THEN (*global variable as guard against recursive traps*)
            trapped := TRUE; T := TextFrames.Text("");
            Oberon.AllocateSystemViewer(0, X, Y);
            V := MenuViewers.New(TextFrames.NewMenu("System.Trap", StandardMenu),
                    TextFrames.NewText(T, 0), TextFrames.menuH, X, Y);
            IF V.state > 0 THEN
                fp := Kernel.fp; pc := Kernel.pc; curmod := NIL;
                mod := SYSTEM.VAL(Modules.Module, Kernel.mod MOD 10000H);
                Texts.WriteString(W, "TRAP "); Texts.WriteInt(W, Kernel.err, 1);
                Texts.WriteString(W, " FP ="); Texts.WriteHex(W, fp);
                Texts.WriteString(W, " PC ="); Texts.WriteHex(W, pc);
                IF Kernel.err = 2 THEN
                    Texts.WriteString(W, " EIA ="); Texts.WriteHex(W, Kernel.eia)
                ELSIF Kernel.err = 20 THEN
                    Texts.WriteString(W, " sect ="); Texts.WriteHex(W, Kernel.SectNo)
                END ;
                Texts.WriteLn(W);
                LOOP Texts.WriteString(W, mod.name); Texts.Append(T, W.buf);
                    IF mod # curmod THEN
                        (*load obj file*) i := 0;
                        WHILE mod.name[i] > 0X DO name[i] := mod.name[i]; INC(i) END ;
                        name[i] := "."; name[i+1] := "O"; name[i+2] := "b"; name[i+3] := "j";
                        name[i+4] := 0X;
                        RefFile := Files.Old(name);
                        IF RefFile = NIL THEN curmod := NIL; Texts.WriteLn(W)
                        ELSE curmod := mod; Files.Set(R, RefFile, 2);
                            Files.ReadBytes(R, refpos, 4);
                            Files.Set(R, RefFile, refpos); Files.Read(R, ch);
                            IF ch = 8AX THEN INC(refpos)
                            ELSE curmod := NIL; Texts.WriteInt(W, pc − mod.PB, 7);
                                Texts.WriteLn(W)
                            END
                        END
                    END ;
                    IF curmod # NIL THEN (*find procedure*)
                        Files.Set(R, RefFile, refpos);LOOP Files.Read(R, ch);
                            IF R.eof THEN EXIT END ;
                            IF ch = 0F8X THEN (*start proc*)
                                Files.ReadBytes(R, i, 2);
                                IF pc < mod.PB + i THEN EXIT END;
                                REPEAT Files.Read(R, ch) UNTIL ch = 0X; (*skip name*)
                            ELSIF ch < 0F8X THEN (*skip object*)
                                Files.Read(R, ch); Files.ReadBytes(R, dmy, 4);
                                REPEAT Files.Read(R, ch) UNTIL ch = 0X; (*skip name*)
                            END
                        END ;
                        IF ~R.eof THEN
                            Texts.Write(W, "."); Files.Read(R, ch);
                            WHILE ch > 0X DO Texts.Write(W, ch); Files.Read(R, ch) END ;
```

```
            Texts.Append(T, W.buf); Locals(R, fp)
        END
      END ;
      SYSTEM.GET(fp+4, pc); SYSTEM.GET(fp, fp);
      IF fp >= Kernel.StackOrg THEN EXIT END ;
      mod := SYSTEM.VAL(Modules.Module, Kernel.ModList);
      (*find module of next procedure*)
      WHILE (mod # NIL) &
          ((pc < mod.PB) OR (mod.size + mod.BB <= pc)) DO
          mod := mod.link
      END ;
      IF mod = NIL THEN EXIT END
    END ;
    Texts.Append(T, W.buf)
  END ;
  trapped := FALSE
END
END Trap;
```

The trap routine is operating in the supervisor mode and uses the supervisor stack. Therefore it also operates correctly in the case of a stack overflow. We assume that it does itself not cause another trap, except if it causes heap overflow due to its output operations. The global state variable *trapped* prevents the occurrence of a recursive trap. After termination of the trap handler, control returns to the kernel and the stack is reset.

A fringe benefit of having procedure *Locals* available is that also global variables of a module can be listed in the same way. Command procedure *System. State* serves precisely this purpose. The name of the module to be inspected is provided as parameter, and the relevant module descriptor is obtained by searching the list of module descriptors headed by *Kernel.ModList*. The base address of the area representing the global variables is given by the module's static base *mod.SB*.

```
PROCEDURE OutState (VAR name: ARRAY OF CHAR; t: Texts.Text);
    VAR mod: Modules.Module;
    refpos: LONGINT;
    ch: CHAR; X, Y, i: INTEGER;
    F: Files.File; R: Files.Rider;
BEGIN
    Texts.WriteString(W, name); mod := SYSTEM.VAL(Modules.Module, Kernel.ModList);
    WHILE (mod # NIL) & (mod.name # name) DO mod := mod.link END ;
    IF mod # NIL THEN
      i := 0;
      WHILE (i < 28) & (name[i] > 0X) DO INC(i) END ;
      name[i] := "."; name[i+1] := "O"; name[i+2] := "b"; name[i+3] := "j"; name[i+4] := 0X;
      F := Files.Old(name);
      IF F # NIL THEN
        Texts.WriteString(W, " SB ="); Texts.WriteHex(W, mod.SB);
        Files.Set(R, F, 2); Files.ReadBytes(R, refpos, 4); Files.Set(R, F, refpos+1);
        LOOP Files.Read(R, ch);
          IF R.eof THEN EXIT END ;
          IF ch = 0F8X THEN
```

```
                Files.ReadBytes(R, i, 2); Files.Read(R, ch);
                IF ch = "$" THEN Files.Read(R, ch); Files.Read(R, ch); EXIT END ;
                REPEAT Files.Read(R, ch) UNTIL ch = 0X (*skip name*)
              ELSIF ch < 0F8X THEN (*skip object*)
                Files.Read(R, ch); Files.Read(R, ch); Files.Read(R, ch);
                REPEAT Files.Read(R, ch) UNTIL ch = 0X; (*skip name*)
            END
          END ;
          IF ~R.eof THEN Locals(R, mod.SB) END
        ELSE Texts.WriteString(W, ".Obj not found")
        END
      ELSE Texts.WriteString(W, " not loaded")
      END ;
      Texts.WriteLn(W); Texts.Append(t, W.buf)
  END OutState;


  PROCEDURE State*;
    VAR T: Texts.Text;
        S: Texts.Scanner;
        V: Viewers.Viewer;
        beg, end, time: LONGINT;
    BEGIN Texts.OpenScanner(S, Oberon.Par.text, Oberon.Par.pos); Texts.Scan(S);
      IF S.class = Texts.Name THEN
          Oberon.AllocateSystemViewer(Oberon.Par.vwr.X, X, Y);
          T := TextFrames.Text("");
          V := MenuViewers.New(TextFrames.NewMenu("System.State", StandardMenu),
              TextFrames.NewText(T, 0), TextFrames.menuH, X, Y);
          OutState(S.s, T)
      END
    END State;
```

13 A graphics editor

13.1 History and goal

The origin of current graphics systems was intimately tied to the advent of the high-resolution bit-mapped display and of the mouse as pointing device. The author's first contact with such equipment dates back to 1976. The Alto computer at the Xerox Palo Alto Research Center is justly termed the first workstation featuring those characteristics. The designer of its first graphics package was Ch. Thacker, who perceived the usefulness of the high-resolution screen for drawing and processing schematics of electronic circuits. This system was cleverly tailored to the needs encountered in this activity, and it was remarkable in its compactness and effectiveness due to the lack of unnecessary facilities. Indeed, its acronym was SIL, for Simple ILlustrator.

After careful study of the techniques used, the author designed a variant, programmed in Modula-2 (instead of BCPL) for the PDP-11 computer, thereby ordering and exhibiting the involved data structures more explicitly. In intervals of about two years, that system was revised and grew gradually into the present *Draw* system. The general goal remained a simple line drawing system: emphasis was placed on a clear structure and increase of flexibility through generalization of existing rather than indiscriminate addition of new features.

In the history of this evolution, three major transitions can be observed. The first was the move from a single 'window', the screen, to multiple windows including windows showing different excerpts of the same graphic. This step was performed on the Lilith computer which resembled the Alto in many ways. The second major transition was the application of the object-oriented style of programming, which allowed the addition of new element types to the basic system, making it extensible. The third step concerned the proper integration of the Draw system with Oberon's text system. The last two steps were performed using Oberon and the Ceres computer.

We refrain from exhibiting this evolution and merely present the outcome, although the history might be an interesting reflection of the evolution of programming techniques in general, containing many useful lessons. We stress the fact, however, that the present system rests on a long history of development, during which many features and techniques were introduced and later discarded or revised. The size of the system's description is a poor measure of the effort that went into its construction; deletion of program text sometimes marks bigger progress than addition.

The goal of the original SIL program was to support the design of electronic circuit diagrams. Primarily, SIL was a line drawing system. This implies that the drawings remain uninterpreted. However, in a properly integrated system, the addition of modules containing operators that interpret the drawings is a reasonably straight-forward proposition. In fact, the Oberon system is ideally suited for such steps, particularly due to its command facility.

At first, we shall ignore features specially tailored to circuit design. The primary one is a macro facility to be discussed in a later section.

The basic system consists of the modules *Draw*, *GraphicFrames* and *Graphics*. These contain the facilities to generate and handle horizontal and vertical lines, text captions and macros. Additional modules serve to introduce other elements, such as rectangles and circles, and the system is extensible, that is, further modules may be introduced to handle further types of elements.

13.2 A brief guide to Oberon's line drawing system

In order to provide the necessary background for the subsequent description of the Draw system's implementation, a brief overview is provided in the style of a user's guide. It summarizes the facilities offered by the system and gives an impression of its versatility.

The system called *Draw* serves to prepare line drawings. They contain lines, text captions, and other items, and are displayed in graphic viewers (more precisely, in menu viewers' graphic frames). A graphic viewer shows an excerpt of the drawing plane, and several viewers may show different parts of a drawing. The most frequently used commands are built-in as mouse clicks and combinations of clicks. Additional commands are selectable from texts, either in viewer menus (title bars) or in the text called *Draw.Tool*. Figure 13.1 shows the display with two graphic viewers at the left and the draw tool text at the right. The mouse buttons have the following principal functions whenever the cursor lies in a graphic frame:

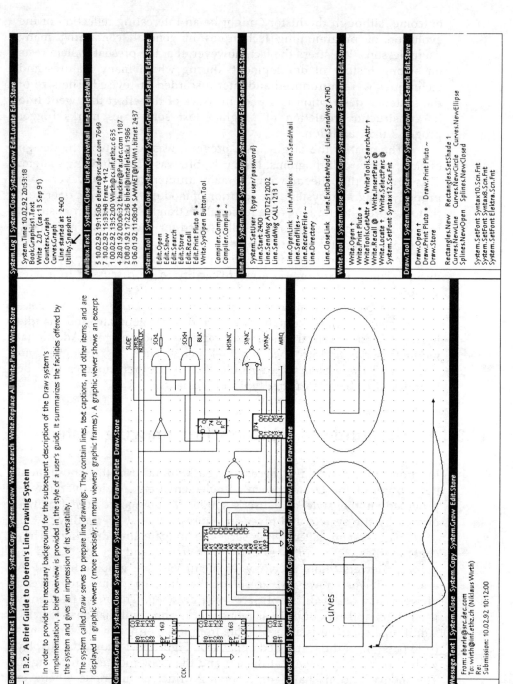

Figure 13.1 Display containing graphics.

left: draw / set caret   middle: move / copy   right: select

A mouse command is identified (1) by the key k0 pressed initially, (2) by the initial position P0 of the cursor, (3) by the set of pressed keys k1 until the last one is released and (4) the cursor position P1 at the time of release.

13.2.1 Basic commands

The command *Draw.Open* opens a new viewer and displays the graph with the name given as parameter. We suggest that file names use the extension *Graph*.

Drawing a line In order to draw a horizontal or vertical line from P0 to P1, the left key is pressed with the cursor at P0 and, while the key is held, the mouse and cursor is moved to P1. Then the key is released. If P0 and P1 differ in both their x and y coordinates, the end point is adjusted so that the line is either horizontal or vertical.

Writing a caption First the cursor is positioned where the caption is to appear. Then the left key is clicked, causing a crosshair to appear. It is called the *caret*. Then the text is typed. Only single lines of texts are accepted. The DEL key may be used to retract characters (backspace).

Selecting Most commands require the specification of operands, and many implicitly assume the previously selected elements – the *selection* – to be their operands. A single element is selected by pointing at it with the cursor and then clicking the right mouse button. This also causes previously selected elements to be deselected. If the left key is also clicked, their selection is retained. This action is called an *interclick*. To select several elements at once, the cursor is moved from P0 to P1 while the right key is held. Then all elements lying within the rectangle with diagonally opposite corners at P0 and P1 are selected. Selected lines are displayed as dotted lines, selected captions (and macros) by inverse video mode. A macro is selected by pointing at its lower left corner. The corner is called the *sensitive area*.

Moving To move (displace) a set of elements, the elements are first selected and then the cursor is moved from P0 to P1 while the middle key is held. The vector from P0 to P1 specifies the movement and is called the *displacement vector*. P0 and P1 may lie in different viewers displaying the same graph. Small displacements may be achieved by using the keyboard's cursor keys.

Copying   Similarly, the selected elements may be copied (duplicated). In addition to pressing the middle key while indicating the displacement vector, the left key is interclicked. The copy command may also be used to copy elements from one graph into another graph by moving the cursor from one viewer into another viewer displaying the destination graph. A text caption may be copied from a text frame into a graphic frame and vice versa. There exist two ways to accomplish this:

(1) First the caret is placed at the destination position, then the text is selected and the middle key is interclicked.

(2) First the text is selected, then the caret is placed at the destination position and the middle key is interclicked.

Shifting the   The entire drawing plane may be shifted behind the viewer by
plane   specifying a displacement vector pressing the middle button (like in a move command) and interclicking the right button.

The following is a summary of the mouse actions:

left	draw line
left (no motion)	set caret
left + middle	copy selected caption to caret
left + right	set secondary caret
middle	move selection
middle + left	copy selection
middle + right	shift drawing plane
right	select area
right (no motion)	select object
right + middle	copy caption to caret
right + left	select without deselection

13.2.2 Menu commands

The following commands are displayed in the menu (title bar) of every graphic viewer. They are activated by being pointed at and by clicking the middle button.

Deleting   Draw.Delete   The selected elements are deleted.
Storing   Draw.Store   The drawing is written as file with the name shown in the title bar. The original file is renamed by appending ".Bak".

13.2.3 Further commands

The following commands are listed in the text *Draw.Tool*, but may appear in any text:

Printing

Draw.Store *name*   The drawing in the marked viewer is stored as a file with the specified name.

Draw.Print *Server **   The drawing in the marked viewer is printed by the named print server.

Draw.Print *Server filename1 filename2 ... ~.*   The named files are printed.

The subsequent commands change attributes of drawing elements, such as line width, text font, and color, and they apply to the most recent selection.

Setting and changing attributes

Draw.SetWidth w   default = 1, 0 < w < 7.
Draw.ChangeFont fontname
Draw.ChangeColor c
Draw.ChangeWidth w   (0 < w < 7)

The *ChangeColor* command either takes a color number in the range 1, ..., 15 or a string as parameter. It serves to copy the color from the selected character (see *Draw.Tool*).

A few actions are initiated by control characters from the keyboard. They apply to the focus viewer.

Control characters

DEL   Selected elements are deleted
Cursor characters   Move selection by 1 unit in the indicated direction
No Scrll   Redraw
Ctrl / No Scrll   Reset origin and redraw

13.2.4 Macros

A macro is a (small) drawing that can be identified as a whole and be used as an element within a (larger) drawing. Macros are typically stored in collections called *libraries*, from where they can be selected and copied individually.

Draw.Macro *lib mac*   The macro *mac* is selected from the library named *lib* and inserted in the drawing at the caret's position.

An example of the use of macros is drawing electronic circuit diagrams. The basic library file containing frequently used TTL components is called *TTL0.Lib*, and a drawing showing its elements is called a *TTL0.Graph* (see Figure 13.2).

13.2.5 Rectangles

Rectangles can be created as individual elements. They are frequently used for framing sets of elements. Rectangles consist of four lines which are selectable as a unit. The attribute commands *Draw.SetWidth*, *System.SetColor*, *Draw.ChangeWidth* and *Draw.ChangeColor* also apply to rectangles. Rectangles are selected by pointing at their lower *left* corner and are created by the following steps:

(1) The caret is placed where a corner of the new rectangle is to lie.

(2) A secondary caret is placed where the opposite corner is to lie (left + right key).

(3) The command *Rectangles.Make* is activated.

Rectangles may be filled with a shade pattern. The shade is specified as a number s ($0 \leq s \leq 9$).

Rectangles.SetShade *s*   default = 0: no shading

By pointing at its lower right corner and clicking the middle button, a rectangle's corner may be dragged, thereby resizing the rectangle.

13.2.6 Oblique lines, circles and ellipses

Further graphic elements are (oblique) lines, circles, and ellipses. The sensitive area of circles and ellipses is at their lowest point. They are created by the following steps:

Lines

(1) The caret is placed where the starting point is to lie.

(2) A secondary caret is placed at the position of the end.

(3) The command *Curves.MakeLine* is activated.

Circles

(1) The caret is placed where the center is to lie.

(2) A secondary caret is placed. Its horizontal distance from the first caret specifies the radius.

(3) The command *Curves.MakeCircle* is activated.

Ellipses

(1) The caret is placed where the center is to lie.

(2) A second caret is placed. Its horizontal distance from the first caret specifies one axis.

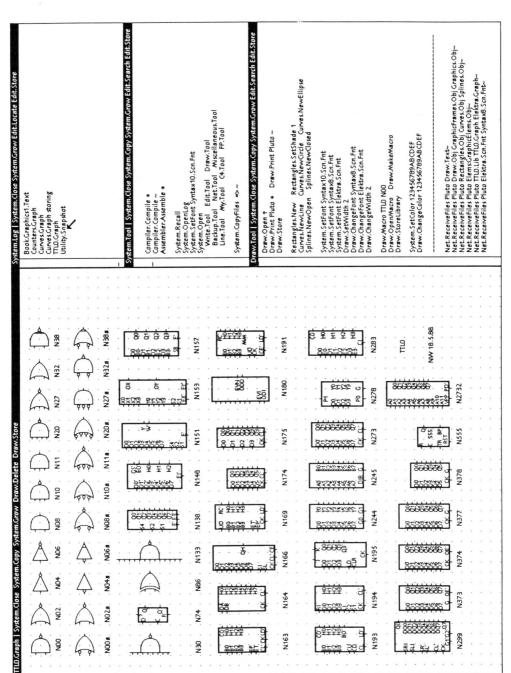

Figure 13.2 Display with electronic circuit macros of TTL library.

(3) A third caret is placed. Its vertical distance from the first caret specifies the other axis.

(4) The command *Curves.MakeEllipse* is activated.

13.2.7   Spline curves

Spline curves are created by the following steps:

(1) The caret is placed where the starting point is to lie.

(2) Secondary carets are placed at the spline's fixed points (at most 20).

(3) The command *Splines.MakeOpen* or *Splines.MakeClosed* is activated.

13.2.8   Constructing new macros

A new macro is constructed and inserted in the library *lib* under the name *mac* as follows:

(1) All elements that belong to the new macro are selected.

(2) The caret is placed at the lower left corner of the area to be spanned by the macro.

(3) A secondary caret is placed at the upper right corner of the area to be spanned by the macro.

Make macro   (4) The command *Draw.MakeMacro lib mac* is activated.

An existing macro can be decomposed (opened) into its parts as follows:

(1) The macro is selected.

(2) The caret is placed at the position where the decomposition is to appear.

Open macro   (3) The command *Draw.OpenMacro* is activated.

The command *Draw.StoreLibrary lib file* stores the library *lib* on the specified file. Only the macros presently loaded are considered as belonging to the library. If one wishes to add some macros to an existing library file, all of its elements must first be loaded. This is best done by opening a graph containing all macros of the desired library file.

13.3 The core and its structure

Like a text, a graphic consists of elements, subsequently to be called *objects*. Unlike a text, which is a *sequence* of elements, a graphic is an *unordered set* of objects. In a text, the *position* of an element need not be explicitly indicated (stored); it is recomputed from the position of its predecessor each time it is needed, for example for displaying or selecting an element. In a graphic, each object must carry its position explicitly, since it is independent of any other object in the set. This is an essential difference, requiring a different treatment and much more storage space for an equal number of objects.

Although this is an important consideration in the choice of a representation of a data structure, the primary determinants are the *kind of objects* to be included and the *set of operations* to be applied to them. Here SIL set a sensible starting point. To begin with, there exist **Objects:** only two kinds of objects, namely straight, horizontal and vertical *lines*, **lines and** and short texts for labelling lines, called *captions*. It is surprising how **captions** many useful tasks can be fulfilled with only these two types of objects.

The typical operations to be performed on objects are creating, drawing, moving, copying and erasing. Those performed on a graphic are inserting, searching for and deleting an object. For the operations on objects, data indicating an object's position (and possibly color), its length and width in the case of lines, and the character string in the case of captions suffice. For the operations on the graphic, some data structure representing the *set* of objects must be chosen. Without question, a dynamic structure is most appropriate, and it requires the **Representation** addition of some linking fields to the record representing an object. **of graphics** Without further deliberation, and with the idea that graphics to be handled with this system contain hundreds rather than tens of thousands of objects, we chose the simplest solution, the linear list. A proper modularization in connection with information hiding will make it possible to alter this choice without affecting client modules.

Although in general the nature of a user interface should not influence the representation chosen for the abstract data structure, we need to take note of the manner in which parameters of certain **Selection** operations are denoted. It is, for example, customary in interactive graphics systems to select the objects to which an operation is to apply *before* invoking that operation. Their *selection* is reflected in their visual appearance in some way, and gives the user an opportunity to verify the selection (and to change it, if necessary) before applying the operation (such as deletion). For an object to be selectable means that it must record a state (selected/unselected). We note that it is important that this state is reflected by visual appearance.

As a consequence, the property *selected* is added to every object record. We now specify the data types representing lines and captions as follows and note that both types must be extensions of the same base type in order to be members of one and the same data structure:

```
TYPE Object = POINTER TO ObjectDesc;
     ObjectDesc = RECORD
         x, y, w, h, col: INTEGER;
         selected: BOOLEAN;
         next: Object
     END ;

     Line = POINTER TO LineDesc;
     LineDesc = RECORD (Object) END ;

     Caption = POINTER TO CaptionDesc
     CaptionDesc = RECORD (Object)
         pos, len: INTEGER
     END
```

Selection of a single element is typically achieved by pointing at the object with mouse and cursor. Selection of a set of objects is achieved by specifying a rectangular area, implying selection of all objects lying within it. In both cases, the search for selected elements proceeds through the linked list and relies on the position and size stored in each object's descriptor. As a consequence, the rule was adopted that every object must specify not only a position through its coordinates x, y, but also the rectangular area within which it lies (width w, height h). It is thus easy to determine whether a given point identifies an object, as well as whether an object lies fully within a rectangular area.

In principle, each caption descriptor carries the sequence of characters (string) representing the caption. The simplest realization would be an array structured field, limiting the length of captions to some fixed, predetermined value. First, this is highly undesirable (although used in early versions of the system). And second, texts carry attributes (color, font). It is therefore best to use a global 'scratch text', and to record a caption by the position and length of the string in this immutable text.

A procedure *drawGraphic* to draw all objects of a graphic now assumes the following form:

```
PROCEDURE drawObj(obj: Object);
BEGIN
    IF obj IS Line THEN drawLine(obj(Line))
    ELSIF obj IS Caption THEN drawCaption(obj(Caption))
```

```
      ELSE (*other object types, if any*)
      END
END drawObj;

PROCEDRE drawGraphic(first: Object);
   VAR obj: Object;
BEGIN obj := first;
   WHILE obj # NIL DO drawObj(obj); obj := obj.next END
END drawGraphic
```

The two procedures are typically placed in different modules, one containing operations on objects, the other those on graphics. Here the former is the service module, the latter the former's client. Procedures for, for example, copying elements, or determining whether an object is selectable, follow the same pattern as *drawGraphic*.

This solution has the unpleasant property that all object types are anchored in the base module. If any new types are to be added, the base module has to be modified (and all clients are to be – at least – recompiled). The object-oriented paradigm eliminates this difficulty by inverting the roles of the two modules. It rests on binding the operations pertaining to an object type to *each* object individually in the form of procedure-typed record fields as shown in the following sample declaration:

```
ObjectDesc = RECORD
      x, y, w, h, col: INTEGER; selected: BOOLEAN;
      draw: PROCEDURE (obj: Object);
      write: PROCEDURE (obj: Object; VAR R: Files.Rider);
      next: Object
   END
```

The procedure *drawGraphics* is now formulated as follows:

```
PROCEDURE drawGraphic(first: Object);
   VAR obj : Object;
BEGIN obj := first;
   WHILE obj # NIL DO obj.draw(obj); obj := obj.next END
END drawGraphic;
```

The individual procedures – in object-oriented terminology called *methods* – are assigned to the record's fields upon its creation. They need no further discrimination of types, since this role is assumed by the assignment of the procedures upon their installation. We note here that the procedure fields are never changed; they assume the role of *constants* rather than variables associated with each object.

This example exhibits in a nutshell the essence of object-oriented programming: *extensibility* as its purpose and the *procedure-typed* record field as the technique.

The given solution, as it stands, has the drawback that each object (instance, variable) contains several procedures (of which two are listed), and therefore leads to a storage requirement that should be avoided. Furthermore, it defines once and for all the number of operations applicable to objects, and also their parameters and result types. A different approach with the same underlying principle removes these drawbacks. It employs a single installed procedure that itself discriminates among the operations according to different types of parameters. The parameters of the preceding solution are merged into a single record called a *message*. The unified procedure is called a handler, and messages are typically extensions of a single base type (Msg).

```
TYPE Msg = RECORD END;
    DrawMsg = RECORD (Msg) END;
    WriteMsg = RECORD (Msg) R: Files.Rider END ;
    ObjectDesc = RECORD
        x, y, w, h, col: INTEGER; selected: BOOLEAN;
        handle: PROCEDURE (obj: Object; VAR M: Msg);
        next: Object
    END ;

PROCEDURE Handler (obj: Object; VAR M: Msg);
    (*this procedure is assigned to the handle field of every
        line object*)
BEGIN
    IF M IS DrawMsg THEN drawLine(obj(Line))
    ELSIF M IS WriteMsg THEN
        writeLine(obj(Line), M(WriteMsg).R)
    ELSE ...
    END
END ;

PROCEDURE drawGraphic(first: Objec; VAR M: Msg);
    VAR obj: Object;
BEGIN obj := first;
    WHILE obj # NIL DO obj.handle(obj, M); obj := obj.next END
END drawGraphics
```

In the present system, a combination of the two schemes presented so far is used. It eliminates the need for individual method fields in each object record as well as the cascaded IF statement for discriminating among the message types. Yet it allows further addition of new methods for later extensions without the need to change the object's declaration. The technique used is to include a single field (called *do*) in each record (analogous to the handler). This field is a pointer to a method record containing the procedures declared for the base type. At least one of them uses a message parameter, that is, a parameter of record structure that is extensible.

```
TYPE Method = POINTER TO MethodDesc;
     Msg = RECORD END;
     Context = RECORD END;
     Object = POINTER TO ObjectDesc;
```

Object

```
     ObjectDesc = RECORD
          x, y, w, h, col: INTEGER; selected: BOOLEAN;
          do: Method; next: Object
        END;
```

Method

```
     MethodDesc = RECORD
          new: Modules.Command;
          copy: PROCEDURE (obj, to: Object);
          draw, handle: PROCEDURE (obj: Object; VAR M:
              Msg);
          selectable: PROCEDURE (obj: Object; x, y: INTEGER):
              BOOLEAN;
          read: PROCEDURE (obj: Object; VAR R: Files.Rider;
              VAR C: Context);
          write: PROCEDURE (obj: Object; cno: SHORTINT;
              VAR R: Files.Rider; VAR C: Context);
          print: PROCEDURE (obj: Object; x, y: INTEGER)
        END
```

A single method instance is generated when a new object type is created, typically in the initialization sequence of the module concerned. When a new object is created, a pointer to this record is assigned to the *do* field of the new object descriptor. A call then has the form *obj.do.write(obj, R)*. This example exhibits the versatility of Oberon's type extension and procedure variable features very well, and it does so without hiding the data structures involved in a dispensible, built-in run-time mechanism.

The foregoing deliberations suggest the system's modular structure shown in Figure 13.3.

The modules in the top row implement the individual object types' methods, and additionally provide commands, in particular *Make* for creating new objects. The base module specifies the base types and procedures operating on graphics as a whole.

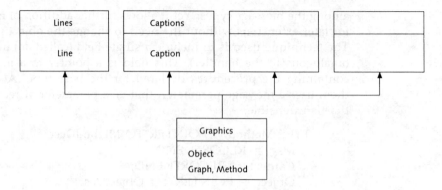

Figure 13.3 Clients of module *Graphics*.

Our system, however, deviates from this scheme somewhat for several reasons:

(i) Implementation of the few methods requires relatively short programs for the basic objects. Although a sensible modularization is desirable, we wish to avoid an atomization, and therefore merge parts that would result in tiny modules with the base module.

(ii) The elements of a graphic refer to fonts used in captions and to libraries used in macros. The writing and reading procedures therefore carry a context consisting of fonts and libraries as an additional parameter. Routines for mapping a font (library) to a number according to a given context on output, and a number to a font (library) on input are contained in module *Graphics*.

(iii) In the design of the Oberon System, a hierarchy of four modules has proven to be most appropriate:

(0) Module with base type handling the abstract data structure.

(1) Module containing procedures for the representation of objects in frames (display handling).

(2) Module containing the primary command interpreter and connecting frames with a viewer.

(3) A command module scanning command lines and invoking the appropriate interpreters.

The module hierarchy of the Draw System is here shown together with its analogy in the Text System:

(3) Command Scanner	Draw	Edit
(2) Viewer Handler	MenuViewers	MenuViewers
(1) Frame Handler	GraphicFrames	TextFrames
(0) Base	Graphics	Texts

As a result, module *Graphics* contains not only the base type *Object*, but also its extensions *Line* and *Caption*. Their methods, however, are defined in *GraphicFrames*, if they refer to frames (for example *draw*), and in *Graphics* otherwise.

So far, we have discussed operations on individual objects and the structure resulting from the desire to be able to add new object types without affecting the base module. We now turn our attention briefly to operations on graphics as a whole. They can be grouped into two kinds, namely operations involving a graphic as a set, and those applying to the selection, that is, to a subset only.

Operations on graphics as a whole   The former kind consists of procedures *Add*, which inserts a new object; *Draw*, which traverses the set of objects and invokes their drawing methods; *ThisObj*, which searches for an object at a given position; *SelectObj*, which marks an object to be selected; *SelectArea*, which identifies all objects lying within a given rectangular area and marks them; *Selectable*, a Boolean function, and *Enumerate*, which applies the parametric procedure *handle* to all objects of a graphic. Furthermore, the procedures *Load*, *Store*, *Print* and *WriteFile* belong to this kind.

Operations on selections   The set of operations applying to selected objects only consist of the following procedures: *Deselect*, *DrawSel* (drawing the selection according to a specified mode), *Change* (changing certain attributes of selected objects like width, font and color), *Move*, *Copy*, *CopyOver* (copying from one graphic into another) and finally *Delete*. Also, there exists the important procedure *Open*, which creates a new graphic, either loading a graphic stored as a file or generating an empty graphic.

The declaration of types and procedures that emerged so far are summarized in the following excerpt of the module's interface definition:

```
DEFINITION Graphics; (*excerpt*)
  IMPORT Files, Fonts, Texts, Modules, Display;
  CONST NameLen = 16;

  TYPE Graph = POINTER TO GraphDesc;
    GraphDesc = RECORD sel: Object; time: LONGINT END ;

    Object = POINTER TO ObjectDesc;
    Method = POINTER TO MethodDesc;

    ObjectDesc = RECORD
      x, y, w, h, col: INTEGER;
```

```
            selected, marked: BOOLEAN;
            do: Method
        END ;

        Name = ARRAY NameLen OF CHAR;
        Msg = RECORD END ;
        Context = RECORD END ;

        MethodDesc = RECORD module, allocator: Name;
            new: Modules.Command;
            copy: PROCEDURE (obj, to: Object);
            draw, handle: PROCEDURE (obj: Object; VAR msg: Msg);
            selectable: PROCEDURE (obj: Object; x, y: INTEGER): BOOLEAN;
            read: PROCEDURE (obj: Object; VAR R: Files.Rider; VAR C: Context);
            write: PROCEDURE (obj: Object; cno: SHORTINT; VAR R: Files.Rider;
                    VAR C: Context);
            print: PROCEDURE (obj: Object; x, y: INTEGER);
        END ;

        Line = POINTER TO LineDesc;
        LineDesc = RECORD (ObjectDesc) END ;

        Caption = POINTER TO CaptionDesc;
        CaptionDesc = RECORD (ObjectDesc) pos, len: INTEGER END ;

        WidMsg = RECORD (Msg) w: INTEGER END ;
        ColorMsg = RECORD (Msg) col: INTEGER END ;
        FontMsg = RECORD (Msg) fnt: Fonts.Font END ;

    VAR new: Object;
        width, res: INTEGER;
        T: Texts.Text;
        LineMethod, CapMethod, MacMethod: Method;

    PROCEDURE Add (G: Graph; obj: Object);
    PROCEDURE Draw (G: Graph; VAR M: Msg);
    PROCEDURE ThisObj (G: Graph; x, y: INTEGER): Object;
    PROCEDURE SelectObj (G: Graph; obj: Object);
    PROCEDURE SelectArea (G: Graph; x0, y0, x1, y1: INTEGER);
    PROCEDURE Enumerate (G: Graph; handle: PROCEDURE (obj: Object; VAR done:
        BOOLEAN));
    PROCEDURE Deselect (G: Graph);
    PROCEDURE DrawSel (G: Graph; VAR M: Msg);
    PROCEDURE Change (G: Graph; VAR M: Msg);
    PROCEDURE Move (G: Graph; dx, dy: INTEGER);
    PROCEDURE Copy (Gs, Gd: Graph; dx, dy: INTEGER);
    PROCEDURE Delete (G: Graph);

    PROCEDURE FontNo (VAR W: Files.Rider; VAR C: Context; fnt: Fonts.Font): SHORTINT;
    PROCEDURE WriteObj (VAR W: Files.Rider; cno: SHORTINT; obj: Object);
    PROCEDURE Store (G: Graph; VAR W: Files.Rider);
    PROCEDURE WriteFile (G: Graph; name: ARRAY OF CHAR);
    PROCEDURE Print (G: Graph; x0, y0: INTEGER);
    PROCEDURE Font (VAR R: Files.Rider; VAR C: Context): Fonts.Font;
    PROCEDURE Load (G: Graph; VAR R: Files.Rider);
    PROCEDURE Open (G: Graph; name: ARRAY OF CHAR);
END Graphics.
```

13.4 Displaying graphics

The base module *Graphics* defines the representation of a set of objects in terms of a data structure. The particulars are hidden and allow the change of structural representation by an exchange of this module without affecting its clients. The problems of displaying a graphic on a screen or a printed page are not handled by this module; they are delegated to the client module *GraphicFrames*, which defines a frame type for graphics which is an extension of *Display.Frame*, just as *TextFrames.Frame* is an extension of *Display.Frame*. In contrast to text frames, however, a graphic instead of a text is associate with it.

Frame

```
FrameDesc = RECORD (Display.Frame)
      graph: Graphics.Graph;
      Xg, Yg, X1, Y1, x, y, col: INTEGER;
      marked, ticked: BOOLEAN;
      mark: LocDesc
   END
```

Every frame specifies its coordinates X, Y within the display area, its size by the attributes W (width) and H (height). Just as a frame represents a (rectangular) section of the entire screen, it also shows an excerpt of the drawing plane of the graphic. The coordinate origin need coincide with neither the rame origin nor the display origin. The frame's position relative to the graphic plane's origin is recorded in the frame descriptor by the coordinates Xg, Yg.

The additional, redundant attributes x, y, X1, Y1 are given by the following invariants, and they are recorded in order to avoid their frequent recomputation.

$$X1 = X + W, \qquad Y1 = Y + H$$
$$x = X + Xg, \qquad y = Y1 + Yg$$

X and Y (and hence also X1 and Y1) are changed when a viewer is modified, that is, when the frame is moved or resized. Xg and Yg are changed when the graph's origin is moved within a frame. The meaning of the various values is illustrated in Figure 13.4.

As a consequence, the display coordinates u, v of an object z of a graph displayed in a frame f are computed as

$$u = z.x + f.x, \qquad v = z.y + f.y$$

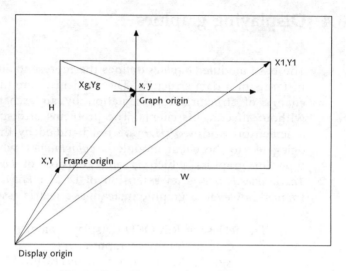

Figure 13.4   Frame and graph coordinates.

Clipping   In order to determine whether an object z lies within a frame f, the following expression must hold:

$$(f.X <= u) \, \& \, (u + z.w <= f.X1) \, \& \, (f.Y <= v) \, \& \, (v + z.h <= f.Y1)$$

The record field *marked* indicates whether or not the frame contains a caret. Its display position is recorded in the field called *mark*. A frame may contain several (secondary) carets; they form a list of location descriptors.

Visualizing selection   When an object is displayed (drawn), its state must be taken into consideration in order to provide visible user feedback. The manner in which selection is indicated, however, may vary among different object types. This can easily be realized, because every object (type) is associated with an individual drawing procedure. The following visualizations of selection have been chosen:

- Selected lines are shown in a grey tone (raster pattern).
- Selected captions are shown with 'inverse video'.

Change of state is a relatively frequent operation, and, if possible, a complete repainting of the involved objects should be avoided for reasons of efficiency. Therefore procedures for drawing an object are given a mode parameter, in addition to the obvious object and frame parameters. The parameters are combined into the message record of type *DrawMsg*:

DrawMsg = RECORD (Graphics.Msg)
  f: Frame;
  mode, x, y, col: INTEGER
 END

Drawing modes

The meaning of the mode parameter's four possible values are the following:

mode = 0: draw object according to its state,
mode = 1: draw reflecting a transition from normal to selected state,
mode = 2: draw reflecting a transition from selected to normal state,
mode = 3: erase.

In the case of captions, for instance, the transitions are indicated by simply inverting the rectangular area covered by the caption. No rewriting of the captions' character patterns is required.

A mode parameter is also necessary for reflecting object deletion. First, the selected objects are drawn with *mode* indicating erasure. Only afterwards are they removed from the graphic's linked list.

Furthermore, the message parameter of the drawing procedure contains two offsets x and y. They are added to the object's coordinates, and their significance will become apparent in connection with macros. The same holds for the color parameter.

The drawing procedures are fairly straightforward and use the four basic raster operations of module *Display*. The only complication arises from the need to clip the drawing at the frame boundaries. In the case of captions, a character is drawn only if it fits into the frame in its entirety. The raster operations do not test (again) whether the indicated position is valid.

At this point, we recall that copies of a viewer (and its frames) can be generated by the *System.Copy* command. Such copies display the same graphic, but possibly different excerpts of them. When a graphic is changed by an insertion, deletion or any other operation, at a place that is visible in several frames, all affected views must reflect the change. A direct call to a drawing procedure indicating a frame and the change therefore does not suffice. Here again, the object-oriented style solves the problem neatly: in place of a direct call a message is broadcast to all frames, the message specifying the nature of the required updates.

The broadcast is performed by the general procedure *Viewers.Broadcast(M)*. It invokes the handlers of all viewers with the parameter M. The viewer handlers either interpret the message or propagate it to the handlers of their subframes. Procedure *obj.handle* is called with a control message as parameter when pointing at the object and clicking the middle mouse button. This allows control to be passed to the handler of an individual object.

The definition of module *GraphicFrames* is summarized by the following interface:

```
DEFINITION GraphicFrames;
    IMPORT Display, Graphics;

    TYPE Frame = POINTER TO FrameDesc;

        Location = POINTER TO LocDesc;LocDesc = RECORD
            x, y: INTEGER;
            next: Location
        END ;

        FrameDesc = RECORD (Display.FrameDesc)
            graph: Graphics.Graph;
            Xg, Yg, X1, Y1, x, y, col: INTEGER;
            marked, ticked: BOOLEAN;
            mark: LocDesc
        END ;

    (*mode = 0: draw according to selected, 1: normal -> selected,
        2: selected -> normal, 3: erase*)

        DrawMsg = RECORD (Graphics.Msg)
            f: Frame;
            x, y, col, mode: INTEGER
        END ;

        CtrlMsg = RECORD (Graphics.Msg)
            f: Frame; res: INTEGER
        END

    PROCEDURE Restore (F: Frame);
    PROCEDURE Focus (): Frame;
    PROCEDURE Selected (): Frame;
    PROCEDURE This(x, y: INTEGER): Frame;
    PROCEDURE Draw (F: Frame);
    PROCEDURE Erase (F: Frame);
    PROCEDURE DrawObj (F: Frame; obj: Graphics.Object);
    PROCEDURE EraseObj (F: Frame; obj: Graphics.Object);
    PROCEDURE Change (F: Frame; VAR msg: Graphics.Msg);
    PROCEDURE Defocus (F: Frame);
    PROCEDURE Deselect (F: Frame);
    PROCEDURE Macro (VAR Lname, Mname: ARRAY OF CHAR);
    PROCEDURE Open (G:Frame; graph: Graphics.Graph; X, Y; col: INTEGER;
        ticked: BOOLEAN);
END GraphicFrames.
```

Focus and *Selected* identify the graphic frame containing the caret, or containing the latest selection. *Draw, Erase* and *Handle* apply to the selection of the specified frame's graphic. And *New* generates a frame displaying the specified graphic with an origin given by coordinates X and Y.

13.5 The User Interface

Although the display is the prime constituent of the interface between the computer and its user, we focus in this section primarily on the computer's input, that is, on its actions instigated by the user's handling of keyboard and mouse, the editing operations. The design of the user interface plays a decisive role in a system's acceptance by users. There is no fixed set of rules determining the optimal choice of an interface. Many issues are a matter of subjective judgement, and all too often convention is being mixed up with convenience. Nevertheless, a few criteria have emerged as fairly generally accepted.

We base our discussion on the premise that input is provided by a keyboard and a mouse, and that keyboard input is essentially to be reserved for textual input. The critical issue is that a mouse – apart from providing a cursor position – allows one to signal actions by the state of its keys. Typically, there are far more actions than there are keys. Some mice feature a single key only, a situation that we deem highly unfortunate. There are, however, several ways to 'enrich' key states:

Position-dependent interpretation
(1) Position. Key states are interpreted depending on the current position of the mouse represented by the cursor. Typically, interpretation occurs by the handler installed in the viewer covering the cursor position, and different handlers are associated with different viewer types. The handler chosen for interpretation may even be associated with an individual (graphic) object and depend on that object's type.

Multiple clicks
(2) Multiple clicks. Interpretation may depend on the number of repeated clicks (of the same key), and/or on the duration of clicks.

Interclicks
(3) Interclicks. Interpretation may depend on the combination of keys depressed until the last one is released. This method is obviously inapplicable for single-key mice.

Apart from position dependence, we have quite successfully used interclicks. A ground rule to be observed is that frequent actions should be triggered by single-key clicks, and only variants of them should be signalled by interclicks. The essential art is to avoid overloading this method.

Less frequent operations may as well be triggered by textual commands, that is, by pointing at the command word and clicking the middle button. Even for this kind of activation, Oberon offers two variants:

(1) The command is listed in a menu (title bar). This solution is favoured when the respective viewer is itself a parameter to the command, and it is recommended when the command is reasonably frequent, because the necessary mouse movement is relatively short.

(2) The command lies elsewhere, typically in a viewer containing a tool text.

Lastly, we note that any package such as *Draw* is integrated within an entire system together with other packages. Hence it is important that the rules governing the user interfaces of the various packages do not differ unnecessarily, but that they display common ground rules and a common design 'philosophy'. *Draw*'s conventions were, as far as possible and sensible, adapted to those of the text system. The right key serves for selection, the left for setting the caret, and the middle key for activating general commands, in this case moving and copying the entire graphic. Inherently, drawing involves certain commands that cannot be dealt with in the same way as for texts. A character is created by typing on the keyboard; a line is created by dragging the mouse while holding the left key. Interclicks left–middle and right–middle are treated in the same way as in the text system (copying a caption from the selection to the caret), and this is not surprising, because text and graphics are properly integrated, that is, captions can be copied from texts into graphics and vice versa. Using different conventions depending on whether the command was activated by pointing at the caption within a text frame or within a graphics frame would be confusing indeed.

13.6 Macros

For many applications, it is indispensible that certain sets of objects may be named and used as objects themselves. Such a named subgraph is called a *macro*. A macro thus closely mirrors the sequence of statements in a program text that is given a name and can be referenced from within other statements: the procedure. The notion of a graphic object becomes recursive, too. The facility of recursive objects is so fundamental that it was incorporated in the base module *Graphics* as the third class of objects.

Representation of macros

Its representation is straightforward: in addition to the attributes

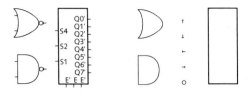

Figure 13.5 Macros and their components.

common to all objects, a field is provided storing the head of the list of elements that constitute the macro. In the present system, a special node is introduced representing the head of the element list. It is of type *MacHeadDesc* and carries also the name of the macro and the width and height of the rectangle covering all elements. These values serve to speed up the selection process, avoiding their recomputation by scanning the entire element list.

The recursive nature of macros manifests itself in recursive calls of display procedures. In order to draw a macro, drawing procedures of the macro's element types are called (which may be macros again). The coordinates of the macro are added to the coordinates of each element, which function as offsets. The color value of the macro, also a field of the parameter of type *DrawMsg*, overrides the colors of the elements. This implies that macros always appear monochrome.

An application of the macro facility is the design of schematics of electronic circuits. Circuit components correspond to macros. Most components are represented by a rectangular frame and by labelled connectors (pins). Some of the most elementary components, such as gates, diodes, transistors, resistors and capacitors are represented by standardized symbols. Such symbols, which may be regarded as forming an alphabet of electronic circuit diagrams, are appropriately provided in the form of a special font, that is, a collection of raster patterns. Three such macros are shown in Figure 13.5, together with the components from which they are assembled. The definitions of the involved data types are

```
Macro = POINTER TO MacroDesc;
MacroDesc = RECORD (ObjectDesc) mac: MacHead END ;

MacHead = POINTER TO MacHeadDesc;
MacHeadDesc = RECORD name: Name;
            w, h: INTEGER; lib: Library
        END ;

Library = POINTER TO LibraryDesc;
LibraryDesc = RECORD name: Name END
```

Procedure *DrawMac(mh, M)* displays the macro with head *mh* according to the draw message parameter M, which specifies a frame, a position within the frame, a display mode and an overriding color.

In the great majority of applications, macros are not created by their user, but are rather provided from another source, in the case of electronic circuits typically by the manufacturer of the components represented by the macros. As a consequence, macros are taken from a collection (inappropriately) called a *library*. In our system, a macro is picked from such a collection by a call to procedure *ThisMac*, which takes a library and a macro name as parameters. The command *Draw.Macro* inserts the specified macro at the place of the caret, as is to be expected.

Macro libraries

Finally, we mention that selection of a macro is visualized by inverting the color over the entire rectangular area covered by the macro. This emphasizes the fact that the macro constitutes an object as a whole.

The design of new macros is a relatively rare activity. They are used rather like characters of a font; the design of new macros and fonts is left to the specialist. Nevertheless, it was decided to incorporate the tools necessary for macro design in the basic system. These tools consist of a few procedures only: *MakeMac* integrates all elements lying within a specified rectangular area into a new macro; *OpenMac* reverses this process by disintegrating the macro into its parts; *InsertMac* inserts a specified macro into a library; *NewLib* creates a new, empty library and *StoreLib* generates a library file containing all macros currently loaded into the specified library. The details of these operations may be examined in the program listings provided later in this chapter.

Constructing macros

13.7 Object classes

Although surprisingly many applications can be covered satisfactorily with the few types of objects and the few facilities described so far, it is nevertheless expected that a modern graphics system allow the addition of further types of objects. The emphasis lies here on addition instead of change. New facilities are to be providable by the inclusion of new modules without requiring any kind of adjustment, not even recompilation of the existing modules. In practice, their source code would quite likely not be available. It is the triumph of the object-oriented programming technique that this is elegantly possible. The means are the extensible record type and the procedure variable, features of the programming language, and the possibility to load modules on demand from statements within a program, a facility provided by the operating environment.

Object class

We call, informally, any extension of the type *Object* a *class*. Hence the types *Line, Caption* and *Macro* constitute classes. Additional classes can be defined in other modules importing the type *Object*. In every such case, a set of methods must be declared and assigned to a variable of type *MethodDesc*. They form a so-called *method suite*. Every such module must also contain a procedure, typically a command, to generate a new instance of the new class. This command, likely to be called *Make*, assigns the method suite to the *do* field of the new object.

This successful decoupling of additions from the system's base suffices almost. Only one further link is unavoidable: when a new graphic, containing objects of a class not defined in the system's core, is loaded from a file then that class must be identified, the corresponding module with its handlers must be loaded – this is called *dynamic loading* – and the object must be generated (allocated). Because the object in question does not already exist at the time when reading the object's attribute values, the generating procedure cannot possibly be installed in the very same object, that is, it cannot be a member of the method suite. We have chosen the following solution to this problem:

Implementation of object classes

(1) Every new class is implemented in the form of a module, and every class is identified by the module name. Every such module contains a command whose effect is to allocate an object of the class, to assign the message suite to it, and to assign the object to the global variable *Graphics.new*.

(2) When a graphics file is read, the class of each object is identified and a call to the respective module's allocation procedure delivers the desired object. The call consists of two parts: a call to *Modules.ThisMod*, which may cause the loading of the respective class module M, and a call of *Modules.ThisCommand*. Then the data of the base type *Object* are read, and lastly the data of the extension are read by a call to the class method *read*.

The following may serve as a template for any module defining a new object class X:

```
MODULE Xs;
    IMPORT Files, Printer, Oberon, Graphics, GraphicFrames;


TYPE X* = POINTER TO XDesc;
    XDesc = RECORD (Graphics.ObjectDesc)
        (*additional data fields*)
        END ;


VAR method: Graphics.Method;
```

```
PROCEDURE New*;
    VAR x: X;
BEGIN NEW(x); x.do := method; Graphics.new := x
END New;


PROCEDURE* Copy(obj, to: Graphics.Object);
BEGIN (*copy X-specific data*)
END Copy;


PROCEDURE* Draw(obj: Graphics.Object; VAR msg: Graphics.Msg);
BEGIN . . .
END Draw;


PROCEDURE* Selectable(obj: Graphics.Object; x, y: INTEGER): BOOLEAN;
BEGIN . . .
END Selectable;


PROCEDURE* Handle(obj: Graphics.Object; VAR msg: Graphics.Msg);
BEGIN
    IF msg IS Graphics.ColorMsg THEN obj.col := msg(Graphics.ColorMsg).col
    ELSIF msg IS . . . THEN . . .
    END
END Handle;


PROCEDURE* Read(obj: Graphics.Object; VAR W: Files.Rider; VAR C: Context);
BEGIN (*read X−specific data*)
END Write;


PROCEDURE* Write(obj: Graphics.Object; cno: SHORTINT; VAR W: Files.Rider;
        VAR C: Context);
BEGIN Graphics.WriteObj(W, cno, obj); (*write X−specific data*)
END Write;


PROCEDURE* Print(obj: Graphics.Object; x, y: INTEGER);
BEGIN (*output object using routines of module Printer*)
END Print;


PROCEDURE  Make*;  (*command*)
    VAR x: X; F: GraphicFrames.Frame;
BEGIN F := GraphicFrames.Focus();
    IF F # NIL THEN
        GraphicFrames.Deselect(F);
        NEW(x); x.x := F.mark.x − F.x; x.y := F.mark.y − F.y; x.w := . . . ; x.h := . . . ;
        x.col := Oberon.CurCol; x.do := method;
        GraphicFrames.Defocus(F); Graphics.Add(F.graph, x); GraphicFrames.DrawObj(F, x)
    END
END Make;


BEGIN NEW(method); method.module := "Xs"; method.allocator := "New";
    method.copy := Copy; method.draw := Draw; method.selectable := Selectable;
    method.handle := Handle; method.read := Read; method.write := Write;
    method.print := Print
END Xs.
```

We wish to point out that the macro and library facilities are also capable of integrating objects of new classes, that is, of types not occurring in the declarations of macro and library facilities. The complete interface definition of module *Graphics* is obtained from its excerpt given in Section 13.3, augmented by the declarations of types and procedures in Sections 13.6. and 13.7.

13.8 The implementation

13.8.1 Module *Draw*

Module *Draw* is a typical command module whose exported procedures are listed in a tool text. Its task is to scan the text containing the command for parameters, to check their validity, and to activate the corresponding procedures, which are primarily contained in modules *Graphics* and *GraphicFrames*. The most prominent among them is the *Open* command. It generates a new viewer containing two frames, namely a text frame serving as menu, and a graphic frame.

We emphasize at this point that graphic frames may also be opened and manipulated by other modules apart from *Draw*. In particular, document editors that integrate texts and graphics – and perhaps also other entities – would refer to *Graphics* and *GraphicFrames* directly, but not make use of *Draw*, which, as a command module, should not have clients.

```
MODULE Draw; (*NW 29.6.88 / 22.11.91*)
    IMPORT Files, Fonts, Viewers, Printer, Texts, Oberon,
        TextFrames, MenuViewers, Graphics, GraphicFrames;

    VAR W: Texts.Writer;

    (*Exported commands:
        Open, Delete,
        SetWidth, ChangeColor, ChangeWidth, ChangeFont,
        Store, Print,
        Macro, OpenMacro, MakeMacro, LoadLibrary, StoreLibrary*)

    PROCEDURE Open*;
        VAR X, Y: INTEGER;
            beg, end, t: LONGINT;
            G: Graphics.Graph;
            F: Graphic Frames.Frame;
            V: Viewers.Viewer;
            text: Texts.Text;
            S: Texts.Scanner;
    BEGIN Texts.OpenScanner(S, Oberon.Par.text, Oberon.Par.pos); Texts.Scan(S);
        IF (S.class = Texts.Char) & (S.c = " ↑ ") THEN
```

```
            Oberon.GetSelection(text, beg, end, t);
            IF t >= 0 THEN Texts.OpenScanner(S, text, beg); Texts.Scan(S) END
        END;
        IF S.class = Texts.Name THEN
            NEW(G); Graphics.Open(G, S.s);
            Oberon.AllocateUserViewer(Oberon.Par.vwr.X, X, Y);
            NEW(F); GraphicFrames.Open(F, G, 0, 0, 0, TRUE);
            V := MenuViewers.New(
                TextFrames.NewMenu(S.s, "System.Close  System.Copy  System.Grow  Draw.Delete
                    Draw.Store"), F, Text
                TextFrames.menuH, X, Y)
        END
END Open;

PROCEDURE Delete*;
    VAR F: GraphicFrames.Frame;
BEGIN
    IF Oberon.Par.frame = Oberon.Par.vwr.dsc THEN
        F := Oberon.Par.vwr.dsc.next(GraphicFrames.Frame);
        GraphicFrames.Erase(F); Graphics.Delete(F.graph)
    END
END Delete;

PROCEDURE SetWidth*;
    VAR S: Texts.Scanner;
BEGIN Texts.OpenScanner(S, Oberon.Par.text, Oberon.Par.pos); Texts.Scan(S);
    IF (S.class = Texts.Int) & (S.i > 0) & (S.i < 7) THEN Graphics.width := SHORT(S.i) END
END SetWidth;

PROCEDURE ChangeColor*;
    VAR ch: CHAR;
        CM: Graphics.ColorMsg;
        S: Texts.Scanner;
BEGIN
    IF Oberon.Par.frame(TextFrames.Frame).sel > 0 THEN
        Texts.OpenScanner(S, Oberon.Par.text, Oberon.Par.frame(TextFrames.Frame).selbeg.pos);
        Texts.Read(S, ch); CM.col := S.col
    ELSE Texts.OpenScanner(S, Oberon.Par.text, Oberon.Par.pos); Texts.Scan(S);
        IF S.class = Texts.Int THEN CM.col := SHORT(S.i) ELSE CM.col := S.col END
    END;
    GraphicFrames.Change(GraphicFrames.Selected(), CM)
END ChangeColor;

PROCEDURE ChangeWidth*;
    VAR WM: Graphics.WidMsg;
        S: Texts.Scanner;
    BEGIN Texts.OpenScanner(S, Oberon.Par.text, Oberon.Par.pos); Texts.Scan(S);
        IF S.class = Texts.Int THEN
            WM.w := SHORT(S.i); GraphicFrames.Change(GraphicFrames.Selected(), WM)
        END
END ChangeWidth;

PROCEDURE ChangeFont*;
    VAR FM: Graphics.FontMsg;
        S: Texts.Scanner;
    BEGIN Texts.OpenScanner(S, Oberon.Par.text, Oberon.Par.pos); Texts.Scan(S);
        IF S.class = Texts.Name THEN
            FM.fnt := Fonts.This(S.s);
```

```
      IF FM.fnt # NIL THEN GraphicFrames.Change(GraphicFrames.Selected(), FM) END
   END
END ChangeFont;


PROCEDURE Backup (VAR name: ARRAY OF CHAR);
   VAR res, i: INTEGER; ch: CHAR;
      bak: ARRAY 32 OF CHAR;
BEGIN i := 0; ch := name[0];
   WHILE ch > 0X DO bak[i] := ch; INC(i); ch := name[i] END;
   IF i < 28 THEN
      bak[i] := "."; bak[i+1] := "B"; bak[i+2] := "a"; bak[i+3] := "k"; bak[i+4] := 0X;
      Files.Rename(name, bak, res)
   END
END Backup;


PROCEDURE Store*;
   VAR par: Oberon.ParList; S: Texts.Scanner;
      Menu: TextFrames.Frame; G: GraphicFrames.Frame;
      v: Viewers.Viewer;
BEGIN par := Oberon.Par;
   IF par.frame = par.vwr. dsc THEN
      Menu := par.vwr.dsc(TextFrames.Frame); G := Menu.next(GraphicFrames.Frame);
      Texts.OpenScanner(S, Menu.text, 0); Texts.Scan(S);
      IF S.class = Texts.Name THEN
         Texts.WriteString(W, S.s); Texts.WriteString(W, "storing");
         Texts.WriteLn(W); Texts.Append(Oberon.Log, W.buf);
         Backup(S.s); Graphics.WriteFile(G.graph, S.s)
      END
   ELSE
      Texts.OpenScanner(S, par.text, par.pos); Texts.Scan(S);
      IF S.class = Texts.Name THEN
         v := Oberon.MarkedViewer();
         IF (v.dsc # NIL) & (v.dsc.next IS GraphicFrames.Frame) THEN
            G := v.dsc.next(GraphicFrames.Frame);
            Texts.WriteString(W, S.s); Texts.WriteString(W, "storing");
            Texts.WriteLn(W); Texts.Append(Oberon.Log, W.buf);
            Backup(S.s); Graphics.WriteFile(G.graph, S.s)
         END
      END
   END
END Store;


PROCEDURE Print*;
   VAR nofcopies: INTEGER;
      S: Texts.Scanner;
      G: Graphics.Graph;
      V: Viewers.Viewer;

   PROCEDURE Copies;
      VAR ch: CHAR;
   BEGIN nofcopies := 1;
      IF S.nextCh = "/" THEN
         Texts.Read(S, ch);
         IF (ch >= "0") & (ch <= "9") THEN nofcopies := ORD(ch) − 30H END;
         WHILE ch > "" DO Texts.Read(S, ch) END;
         S.nextCh := ch
      END
```

```
        END Copies;

    BEGIN Texts.OpenScanner(S, Oberon.Par.text, Oberon.Par.pos); Texts.Scan(S);
        IF S.class = Texts.Name THEN
            Printer.Open(S.s, Oberon.User, Oberon.Password);
            IF Printer.res = 0 THEN
                Texts.Scan(S);
                WHILE S.class = Texts.Name DO
                    Texts.WriteString(W, S.s); Copies; NEW(G); Graphics.Open(G, S.s);
                    IF Graphics.res = 0 THEN
                        Texts.WriteString(W, "printing");
                        Texts.WriteInt(W, nofcopies, 3); Texts.Append(Oberon.Log, W.buf);
                        Graphics.Print(G, 0, Printer.PageHeight−128); Printer.Page(nofcopies)
                    ELSE Texts.WriteString(W, "not found")
                    END;
                    Texts.WriteLn(W); Texts.Append(Oberon.Log, W.buf); Texts.Scan(S)
                END;
                IF (S.class = Texts.Char) & (S.c = "*") THEN
                    Copies; V := Oberon.MarkedViewer();
                    IF (V.dsc # NIL) & (V.dsc.next IS GraphicFrames.Frame) THEN
                        Texts.OpenScanner(S, V.dsc(TextFrames.Frame).text, 0);
                        Texts.Scan(S);
                        IF S.class = Texts.Name THEN
                            Texts.WriteString(W, S.s); Texts.WriteString(W, "printing");
                            Texts.WriteInt(W, nofcopies, 3); Texts.Append(Oberon.Log, W.buf);
                            Graphics.Print(V.dsc.next(GraphicFrames.Frame).graph, 0,
                                    Printer.PageHeight−128);
                            Printer.Page(nofcopies)
                        END
                    END
                END;
                Printer.Close
            ELSIF Printer.res = 1 THEN Texts.WriteString(W, "no printer")
            ELSIF Printer.res = 2 THEN Texts.WriteString(W, "no link")
            ELSIF Printer.res = 3 THEN Texts.WriteString(W, "bad response")
            ELSIF Printer.res = 4 THEN Texts.WriteString(W, "no permission")
            END
        END;
        Texts.WriteLn(W); Texts.Append(Oberon.Log, W.buf)
    END Print;


    PROCEDURE Macro*;
        VAR S: Texts.Scanner;
            T: Texts.Text;
            time, beg, end: LONGINT;
            Lname: ARRAY 32 OF CHAR;
    BEGIN Texts.OpenScanner(S, Oberon.Par.text, Oberon.Par.pos); Texts.Scan(S);
        IF S.class = Texts.Name THEN
            COPY(S.s, Lname); Texts.Scan(S);
            IF (S.class = Texts.Char) & (S.c = " ↑ ") THEN
                Oberon.GetSelection(T, beg, end, time);
                IF time >= 0 THEN Texts.OpenScanner(S, T, beg); Texts.Scan(S) END
            END;
            IF (S.class = Texts.Name) OR (S.class = Texts.String) THEN
                GraphicFrames.Macro(Lname, S.s)
            END
        END
    END Macro;
```

```
PROCEDURE OpenMacro*;
    VAR F: GraphicFrames.Frame; sel: Graphics.Object;
BEGIN F := GraphicFrames.Selected();
    IF F # NIL THEN
        sel := F.graph.sel;
        IF (sel # NIL) & (sel IS Graphics.Macro) THEN
            GraphicFrames.Deselect(F);
            Graphics.OpenMac(sel(Graphics.Macro).mac, F.graph, F.mark.x − F.x,
                F.mark.y − F.y);
            GraphicFrames.Draw(F)
        END
    END
END OpenMacro;


PROCEDURE MakeMacro*;
    VAR new: BOOLEAN;
        F: GraphicFrames.Frame;
        S: Texts.Scanner;
        Lname: ARRAY 32 OF CHAR;


    PROCEDURE MakeMac;
        VAR x0, y0, x1, y1, w, h: INTEGER;
            mh: Graphics.MacHead;
            L: Graphics.Library;
    BEGIN
        L := Graphics.ThisLib(Lname, FALSE);
        IF L = NIL THEN L := Graphics.NewLib(Lname) END;
        x0 := F.mark.x; y0 := F.mark.y; x1 := F.mark.next.x; y1 := F.mark.next.y;
        w := ABS(x1−x0); h := ABS(y1−y0);
        IF x0 < x1 THEN x0 := x0 − F.x ELSE x0 := x1 − F.x END;
        IF y0 < y1 THEN y0 := y0 − F.y ELSE y0 := y1 − F.y END;
        mh := Graphics.MakeMac(F.graph, x0, y0, w, h, S.s);
        Graphics.InsertMac(mh, L, new)
    END MakeMac;


BEGIN Texts.OpenScanner(S, Oberon.Par.text, Oberon.Par.pos); Texts.Scan(S);
    IF S.class = Texts.Name THEN
        COPY(S.s, Lname); Texts.Scan(S);
        IF (S.class = Texts.Name) OR (S.class = Texts.String) & (S.len <= 8) THEN
            F := GraphicFrames.Focus();
            IF (F # NIL) & (F.graph.sel # NIL) THEN
                MakeMac; Texts.WriteString(W, S.s);
                IF new THEN Texts.WriteString(W, "inserted in")
                ELSE Texts.WriteString(W, "replaced in")
                END;
                Texts.WriteString(W, Lname); Texts.WriteLn(W);
                Texts.Append(Oberon.Log, W.buf)
            END
        END
    END
END MakeMacro;


PROCEDURE LoadLibrary*;
    VAR S: Texts.Scanner; L: Graphics.Library;
BEGIN Texts.OpenScanner(S, Oberon.Par.text, Oberon.Par.pos); Texts.Scan(S);
    IF S.class = Texts.Name THEN
        L := Graphics.ThisLib(S.s, TRUE);
```

```
                Texts.WriteString(W, S.s); Texts.WriteString(W, "loaded");
                Texts.WriteLn(W); Texts.Append(Oberon.Log, W.buf)
        END
    END LoadLibrary;

    PROCEDURE StoreLibrary*;
        VAR i: INTEGER; S: Texts.Scanner; L: Graphics.Library;
            Lname: ARRAY 32 OF CHAR;
        BEGIN Texts.OpenScanner(S, Oberon.Par.text, Oberon.Par.pos); Texts.Scan(S);
            IF S.class = Texts.Name THEN i := 0;
                WHILE S.s[i] >= "0" DO Lname[i] := S.s[i]; INC(i) END;
                Lname[i] := 0X; L := Graphics.ThisLib(Lname, FALSE);
                IF L # NIL THEN
                    Texts.WriteString(W, S.s); Texts.WriteString(W, "storing");
                    Texts.WriteLn(W); Texts.Append(Oberon.Log, W.buf); Graphics.StoreLib(L, S.s)
                END
            END
        END StoreLibrary;

    BEGIN Texts.OpenWriter(W)
    END Draw.
```

13.8.2   Module *GraphicFrames*

Module *GraphicFrames* contains all routines concerned with displaying, visualizing graphic frames and their contents, namely graphics. It also contains the routines for creating new objects of the base classes, namely lines, captions and macros. And most importantly, it specifies the appropriate frame handler that interprets input actions and thereby defines the user interface. The handler discriminates among the following message types:

Updating

(1) Update messages. According to the *id* field of the message record, either a specific object or the entire selection of a graphic are drawn according to a mode. The case id = 0 signifies a restoration of the entire frame, including all objects of the graphic.

Queries

(2) Selection, focus and position queries. They serve for the identification of the graphic frame containing the latest selection, containing the caret (mark) or the indicated position. In order to identify the latest selection, the time is recorded in the graph descriptor whenever a new selection is made or when new objects are inserted.

Input messages

(3) Input messages. They originate from the central loop of module *Oberon* and indicate either a mouse action (track message) or a keyboard event (consume message).

Control messages

(4) Control messages from *Oberon*. They indicate that all marks (selection, caret and star) are to be removed (neutralize), or that the focus has to be relinquished (defocus).

Generic Messages

(5) Selection, copy and copy-over messages from *Oberon*. They constitute the interface between the graphics and the text system, and make possible identification and copying of captions between graphic and text frames.

Modify viewer messages

(6) Modify messages from *MenuViewers*. They indicate that a frame has to be adjusted in size and position because a neighbouring viewer had been reshaped or because its own viewer has been repositioned

(7) Display messages. They originate from procedure *InsertChar* and handle the displaying of single characters when a caption is composed (see below).

The frame handler receiving a consume message interprets the request through procedure *InsertChar* (except for cursor and restore characters), and receiving a track message through procedure *Edit*. If no mouse key is depressed, the cursor is simply drawn, and thereby the mouse is tracked. Instead of the regular arrow, a crosshair is used as cursor pattern. Thereby, immediate visual feedback is provided to indicate that now mouse actions are interpreted by the graphics handler (instead of, for example, a text handler). Such feedback is helpful when graphic frames appear not only in a menuviewer, but as subframes of a more highly structured document frame.

Editing graphics

Procedure *Edit* first tracks the mouse while recording further key activities (interclicks) until all keys are released. The subsequent action is determined by the perceived key clicks. The actions are (the second key denotes the interclick):

keys = left	set caret, if mouse was not moved, draw new line otherwise,
keys = left, middle	copy text selection to caret position
keys = left, right	set secondary caret (mark)
keys = middle	move selection
keys = middle, left	copy selection
keys = middle, right	shift origin of graph
keys = right	select (either object, or objects in area)
keys = right, middle	copy selected caption to caret position

When copying or moving a set of selected objects, a distinction must be made between cases where the source and destination graphics are the same and those where they are different. In the former case, source and destination positions may lie in the same or in different frames.

Creating captions

Procedure *InsertChar* handles the creation of new captions. The actual character string is appended to the global text T, and the new object records its position within T and its length.

A complication arises because the input process consists of as many user actions as there are characters, and because other actions may possibly intervene between the typing. It is therefore unavoidable to record an insertion state, which is embodied by the global variable *newcap*. When a character is typed, and *newcap* = NIL, a new caption is created consisting of the single typed character. Subsequent typing results in appending characters to the string (and *newcap*). The variable is reset to NIL, when the caret is repositioned. The DEL character is interpreted as a backspace by procedure *DeleteChar*.

Since the caption being generated may be visible simultaneously in several frames, its display must be handled by a message. For this reason, the special message type *DispMsg* is introduced, and as a result, the process of character insertion turns out to be a rather complex action. To avoid even further complexity, the restriction is adopted that all characters of a caption must use the same attributes (font and color).

```
MODULE GraphicFrames; (*NW 18.4.88 / 22.11.91*)
    IMPORT Display, Viewers, Input, Fonts, Texts, Graphics, Oberon, MenuViewers;

    CONST (*update message ids*)
        restore = 0;
        drawobj = 1; drawobjs = 2; drawobjd = 3;
        drawnorm = 4; drawsel = 5; drawdel = 6;

        markW = 5;


    TYPE
        Frame* = POINTER TO FrameDesc;
        Location* = POINTER TO LocDesc;

        LocDesc* = RECORD
                x*, y*: INTEGER;
                next*: Location
            END;

        FrameDesc* = RECORD (Display.FrameDesc)
                graph*: Graphics.Graph;
                Xg*, Yg*: INTEGER; (*pos rel to graph origin*)
                X1*, Y1*: INTEGER; (*right and upper margins*)
                x*, y*, col*: INTEGER; (*x = X + Xg, y = Y1 + Yg*)
                marked*, ticked*: BOOLEAN;
                mark*: LocDesc
            END;

        DrawMsg* = RECORD (Graphics.Msg)
                f*: Frame;
                x*, y*, col*, mode*: INTEGER
            END;
```

```
CtrlMsg* = RECORD (Graphics.Msg)
        f*: Frame; res*: INTEGER
    END;


UpdateMsg = RECORD (Display.FrameMsg)
        id: INTEGER;
        graph: Graphics.Graph;
        obj: Graphics.Object
    END;


SelQuery = RECORD (Display.FrameMsg)
        f: Frame; time: LONGINT
    END;


FocusQuery = RECORD (Display.FrameMsg)
        f: Frame
    END;


PosQuery = RECORD (Display.FrameMsg)
        f: Frame; x, y: INTEGER
    END;


DispMsg = RECORD (Display.FrameMsg)
        x1, y1, w: INTEGER;
        pat: Display.Pattern;
        graph: Graphics.Graph
    END;


VAR Crosshair*: Oberon.Marker;
    newcap: Graphics.Caption;
    DW, DH, CL: INTEGER;
    W: Texts.Writer;


(*Exported procedures:
    Restore, Focus, Selected, This, Draw, Erase,
    DrawObj, EraseObj, Change, Defocus, Deselect, Macro, Handle, Open*)


PROCEDURE Restore*(F: Frame);
    VAR M: DrawMsg; x, y, col: INTEGER;
BEGIN F.X1 := F.X + F.W; F.Y1 := F.Y + F.H;
    F.x := F.X + F.Xg; F.y := F.Y1 + F.Yg; F.marked := FALSE; F.mark.next := NIL;
    IF F.X < CL THEN col := Display.black ELSE col := F.col END;
    Oberon.RemoveMarks(F.X, F.Y, F.W, F.H);
    Display.ReplConst(col, F.X, F.Y, F.W, F.H, 0);
    IF F.ticked THEN
        y := F.Yg MOD 16 + F.Y1 − 16;
        WHILE y >= F.Y DO (*draw ticks*)
            x := F.Xg MOD 16 + F.X;
            WHILE x < F.X1 DO Display.Dot(Display.white, x, y, 0); INC(x, 16) END;
            DEC(y, 16)
        END
    END;
    M.f := F; M.x := F.x; M.y := F.y; M.col := 0; M.mode := 0; Graphics.Draw(F.graph, M)
END Restore;
```

```
PROCEDURE Focus*(): Frame;
   VAR FQ: FocusQuery;
BEGIN FQ.f := NIL; Viewers.Broadcast(FQ); RETURN FQ.f
END Focus;


PROCEDURE Selected*(): Frame;
   VAR SQ: SelQuery;
BEGIN SQ.f := NIL; SQ.time := 0; Viewers.Broadcast(SQ); RETURN SQ.f
END Selected;


PROCEDURE This*(x, y: INTEGER): Frame;
   VAR PQ: PosQuery;
BEGIN PQ.f := NIL; PQ.x := x; PQ.y := y; Viewers.Broadcast(PQ); RETURN PQ.f
END This;


PROCEDURE Draw*(F: Frame);
   VAR UM: UpdateMsg;
BEGIN UM.id := drawsel; UM.graph := F.graph; Viewers.Broadcast(UM)
END Draw;


PROCEDURE DrawNorm(F: Frame);
   VAR UM: UpdateMsg;
BEGIN UM.id := drawnorm; UM.graph := F.graph; Viewers.Broadcast(UM)
END DrawNorm;


PROCEDURE Erase*(F: Frame);
   VAR UM: UpdateMsg;
BEGIN UM.id := drawdel; UM.graph := F.graph; Viewers.Broadcast(UM)
END Erase;


PROCEDURE DrawObj*(F: Frame; obj: Graphics.Object);
   VAR UM: UpdateMsg;
BEGIN UM.id := drawobj; UM.graph := F.graph; UM.obj := obj; Viewers.Broadcast(UM)
END DrawObj;


PROCEDURE EraseObj*(F: Frame; obj: Graphics.Object);
   VAR UM: UpdateMsg;
BEGIN UM.id := drawobjd; UM.graph := F.graph; UM.obj := obj; Viewers.Broadcast(UM)
END EraseObj;


PROCEDURE Change*(F: Frame; VAR msg: Graphics.Msg);
BEGIN
   IF F # NIL THEN Erase(F); Graphics.Handle(F.graph, msg); Draw(F) END
END Change;


PROCEDURE FlipMark(x, y: INTEGER);
BEGIN
   Display.ReplConst(Display.white, x-7, y, 15, 1, 2);
   Display.ReplConst(Display.white, x, y-7, 1, 15, 2)
END FlipMark;


PROCEDURE Defocus*(F: Frame);
   VAR m: Location;
BEGIN newcap := NIL;
   IF F.marked THEN
```

```
        FlipMark(F.mark.x, F.mark.y); m := F.mark.next;
        WHILE m # NIL DO FlipMark(m.x, m.y); m := m.next END;
        F.marked := FALSE; F.mark.next := NIL
    END
END Defocus;


PROCEDURE Deselect*(F: Frame);
    VAR UM: UpdateMsg;
BEGIN
    IF F # NIL THEN
        UM.id := drawnorm; UM.graph := F.graph; Viewers.Broadcast(UM);
        Graphics.Deselect(F.graph)
    END
END Deselect;


PROCEDURE Macro*(VAR Lname, Mname: ARRAY OF CHAR);
    VAR x, y: INTEGER;
        F: Frame;
        mac: Graphics.Macro; mh: Graphics.MacHead;
        L: Graphics.Library;
BEGIN F := Focus();
    IF F # NIL THEN
        x := F.mark.x − F.x; y := F.mark.y − F.y;
        L := Graphics.ThisLib(Lname, FALSE);
        IF L # NIL THEN
            mh := Graphics.ThisMac(L, Mname);
            IF mh # NIL THEN
                Deselect(F); Defocus(F);
                NEW(mac); mac.x := x; mac.y := y; mac.w := mh.w; mac.h := mh.h;
                mac.mac := mh; mac.do := Graphics.MacMethod; mac.col := Oberon.CurCol;
                Graphics.Add(F.graph, mac); DrawObj(F, mac)
            END
        END
    END
END Macro;


PROCEDURE CaptionCopy(F: Frame;
        x1, y1: INTEGER; T: Texts.Text; beg, end: LONGINT): Graphics.Caption;
    VAR ch: CHAR;
        dx, w, x2, y2, w1, h1: INTEGER;
        cap: Graphics.Caption;
        pat: Display.Pattern;
        R: Texts.Reader;
BEGIN Texts.Write(W, 0DX);
    NEW(cap); cap.len := SHORT(end − beg);
    cap.pos := SHORT(Graphics.T.len)+1; cap.do := Graphics.CapMethod;
    Texts.OpenReader(R, T, beg); Texts.Read(R, ch); W.fnt := R.fnt; W.col := R.col; w := 0;
    cap.x := x1 − F.x; cap.y := y1 − F.y + R.fnt.minY;
    WHILE beg < end DO
        Display.GetChar(R.fnt.raster, ch, dx, x2, y2, w1, h1, pat);
        INC(w, dx); INC(beg); Texts.Write(W, ch); Texts.Read(R, ch)
    END;
    cap.w := w; cap.h := W.fnt.height; cap.col := W.col;
    Texts.Append(Graphics.T, W.buf); Graphics.Add(F.graph, cap); RETURN cap
END CaptionCopy;


PROCEDURE SendCaption(cap: Graphics.Caption);
```

```
                VAR M: Oberon.CopyOverMsg;
        BEGIN
            M. text := Graphics.T; M.beg := cap.pos; M.end := M.beg + cap.len;
            Viewers.Broadcast(M)
        END SendCaption;


        PROCEDURE Edit(F: Frame; x0, y0: INTEGER; k0: SET);
            VAR obj: Graphics.Object;
                x1, y1, w, h, t, pos: INTEGER;
                beg, end, time: LONGINT;
                k1, k2: SET; ch: CHAR;
                mark, newmark: Location;
                T: Texts.Text;
                Fd: Frame;
                G: Graphics.Graph;
                CM: CtrlMsg;
                name: ARRAY 32 OF CHAR;


            PROCEDURE NewLine(x, y, w, h: INTEGER);
                VAR line: Graphics.Line;
            BEGIN NEW(line); line.col := Oberon.CurCol; line.x := x − F.x; line.y := y − F.y;
                line.w := w; line.h := h; line.do := Graphics.LineMethod; Graphics.Add(G, line)
            END NewLine;


        BEGIN k1 := k0; G := F.graph;
            IF k0 = {1} THEN
                obj := Graphics.ThisObj(G, x0 − F.x, y0 − F.y);
                IF (obj # NIL) & ~obj.selected THEN
                    CM.f := F; CM.res := 0; obj.do.handle(obj, CM);
                    IF CM.res # 0 THEN (*done*) k0 := {} END
                END
            END;
            REPEAT Input.Mouse(k2, x1, y1); k1 := k1 + k2;
                DEC(x1, (x1−F.x) MOD 4); DEC(y1, (y1−F.y) MOD 4);
                Oberon.DrawCursor(Oberon.Mouse, Crosshair, x1, y1)
            UNTIL k2 = {};
            Oberon.FadeCursor(Oberon.Mouse);
            IF k0 = {2} THEN (*left key*)
                w := ABS(x1−x0); h := ABS(y1−y0);
                IF k1 = {2} THEN
                    IF (w < 7) & (h < 7) THEN (*set mark*)
                        IF (x1 − markW >= F.X) & (x1 + markW < F.X1) &
                        (y1 − markW >= F.Y) & (y1 + markW < F.Y1) THEN
                        Defocus(F); Oberon.PassFocus(Viewers.This(F.X, F.Y));
                        F.mark.x := x1; F.mark.y := y1; F.marked := TRUE; FlipMark(x1, y1)
                    END
                    ELSE (*draw line*) Deselect(F);
                        IF w < h THEN
                            IF y1 < y0 THEN y0 := y1 END;
                            NewLine(x0, y0, Graphics.width, h)
                        ELSE
                            IF x1 < x0 THEN x0 := x1 END;
                            NewLine(x0, y0, w, Graphics.width)
                        END;
                        Draw(F)
                    END
                ELSIF k1 = {2, 1} THEN (*copy selection to caret mark*)
```

```
            Deselect(F); Oberon.GetSelection(T, beg, end, time);
            IF time >= 0 THEN DrawObj(F, CaptionCopy(F, x1, y1, T, beg, end)) END
        ELSIF k1 = {2, 0} THEN
            IF F.marked THEN (*set secondary mark*)
                NEW(newmark); newmark.x := x1; newmark.y := y1; newmark.next := NIL;
            FlipMark(x1, y1); mark := F.mark.next;
            IF mark = NIL THEN F.mark.next := newmark ELSE
                WHILE mark.next # NIL DO mark := mark.next END;
                mark.next := newmark
            END
        END
    END
ELSIF k0 = {1} THEN (*middle key*)
    IF k1 = {1} THEN (*move*)
        IF (x0 # x1) OR (y0 # y1) THEN
            Fd := This(x1, y1); Erase(F);
            IF Fd = F THEN Graphics.Move(G, x1−x0, y1−y0)
            ELSIF (Fd # NIL) & (Fd.graph = G) THEN
                Graphics.Move(G, (x1−Fd.x−x0+F.x) DIV 4 * 4, (y1−Fd.y−y0+F.y) DIV 4 * 4)
            END;
            Draw(F)
        END
    ELSIF k1 = {1, 2} THEN (*copy*)
        Fd := This(x1, y1);
        IF Fd # NIL THEN DrawNorm(F);
            IF Fd = F THEN Graphics.Copy(G, G, x1−x0, y1−y0)
            ELSE Deselect(Fd);
                Graphics.Copy(G, Fd.graph, (x1−Fd.x−x0+F.x) DIV 4 * 4,
                    (y1−Fd.y−y0+F.y) DIV 4 * 4)
            END;
            Draw(Fd)
        END
    ELSIF k1 = {1, 0} THEN (*shift graph origin*)
        INC(F.Xg, x1−x0); INC(F.Yg, y1−y0); Restore(F)
    END
ELSIF k0 = {0} THEN (*right key: select*)
    newcap := NIL;
    IF (ABS(x0−x1) < 7) & (ABS(y0−y1) < 7) THEN
        IF ~(2 IN k1) THEN Deselect(F) END;
        obj := Graphics.ThisObj(G, x1 − F.x, y1 − F.y);
        IF obj # NIL THEN
            Graphics.SelectObj(G, obj); DrawObj(F, obj);
            IF (k1 = {0, 1}) & (obj IS Graphics.Caption) THEN
                SendCaption(obj(Graphics.Caption))
            END
        END
    ELSE Deselect(F);
        IF x1 < x0 THEN t := x0; x0 := x1; x1 := t END;
        IF y1 < y0 THEN t := y0; y0 := y1; y1 := t END;
        Graphics.SelectArea(G, x0 − F.x, y0 − F.y, x1 − F.x, y1 − F.y); Draw(F)
    END
END
END Edit;


PROCEDURE NewCaption(F: Frame; col: INTEGER; font: Fonts.Font);
BEGIN Texts.Write(W, 0DX);
    NEW(newcap); newcap.x := F.mark.x − F.x; newcap.y := F.mark.y − F.y + font.minY;
    newcap.w := 0; newcap.h := font.height; newcap.col := col;
```

```
        newcap.pos := SHORT(Graphics.T.len + 1); newcap.len := 0;
        newcap.do := Graphics.CapMethod; Graphics.Add(F.graph, newcap); W.fnt := font
    END NewCaption;


    PROCEDURE InsertChar(F: Frame; ch: CHAR);
        VAR w1, h1: INTEGER; DM: DispMsg;
    BEGIN DM.graph := F.graph;
        Display.GetChar(W.fnt.raster, ch, DM.w, DM.x1, DM.y1, w1, h1, DM.pat);
        DEC(DM.y1, W.fnt.minY);
        IF newcap.x + newcap.w + DM.w + F.x < F.X1 THEN
            Viewers.Broadcast(DM); INC(newcap.w, DM.w); INC(newcap.len); Texts.Write(W, ch)
        END;
        Texts.Append(Graphics.T, W.buf)
    END InsertChar;


    PROCEDURE DeleteChar(F: Frame);
        VAR w1, h1: INTEGER; ch: CHAR; pos: LONGINT;
            DM: DispMsg; R: Texts.Reader;
    BEGIN DM.graph := F.graph;
        IF newcap.len > 0 THEN
            pos := Graphics.T.len; Texts.OpenReader(R, Graphics.T, pos−1); (*backspace*)
            Texts.Read(R, ch);
            IF ch >= " " THEN
                Display.GetChar(R.fnt.raster, ch, DM.w, DM.x1, DM.y1, w1, h1, DM.pat);
                DEC(newcap.w, DM.w); DEC(newcap.len); DEC(DM.y1, R.fnt.minY);
                Viewers.Broadcast(DM); Texts.Delete(Graphics.T, pos−1, pos)
            END
        END
    END DeleteChar;


    PROCEDURE GetSelection(F: Frame; VAR text: Texts.Text; VAR beg, end, time: LONGINT);
        VAR obj: Graphics.Object;
    BEGIN obj := F.graph.sel;
        IF (obj # NIL) & (obj IS Graphics.Caption) & (F.graph.time >= time) THEN
            WITH obj: Graphics.Caption DO beg := obj.pos; end := obj.pos + obj.len END;
            text := Graphics.T; time := F.graph.time
        END
    END GetSelection;


    PROCEDURE Handle*(G: Display.Frame; VAR M: Display.FrameMsg);
        VAR i: LONGINT; ch: CHAR;
            x, y: INTEGER;
            DM: DispMsg; dM: DrawMsg;
            G1: Frame;


        PROCEDURE move(G: Frame; dx, dy: INTEGER);
            VAR M: UpdateMsg;
        BEGIN Defocus(G); Oberon.FadeCursor(Oberon.Mouse);
            M.id := drawdel; M.graph := G.graph; Viewers.Broadcast(M);
            Graphics.Move(G.graph, dx, dy); M.id := drawsel; Viewers.Broadcast(M)
        END move;


    BEGIN
        WITH G: Frame DO
            IF M IS Oberon.InputMsg THEN
                WITH M: Oberon.InputMsg DO
```

```
                IF M.id = Oberon.track THEN
                    x := M.X − (M.X − G.x) MOD 4; y := M.Y − (M.Y − G.y) MOD 4;
                    IF M.keys # {} THEN Edit(G, x, y, M.keys)
                    ELSE Oberon.DrawCursor(Oberon.Mouse, Crosshair, x, y)
                    END
                ELSIF M.id = Oberon.consume THEN
                    IF M.ch = 7FX THEN
                        IF newcap # NIL THEN DeleteChar(G)
                        ELSE Oberon.FadeCursor(Oberon.Mouse); Defocus(G); Erase(G);
                            Graphics.Delete(G.graph)
                        END
                    ELSIF M.ch = 91X THEN Restore(G)
                    ELSIF M.ch = 93X THEN G.Xg := −1; G.Yg := 0; Restore(G) (*reset*)
                    ELSIF M.ch = 0C1X THEN move(G, 0, 1)
                    ELSIF M.ch = 0C2X THEN move(G, 0, −1)
                    ELSIF M.ch = 0C3X THEN move(G, 1, 0)
                    ELSIF M.ch = 0C4X THEN move(G, −1, 0)
                    ELSIF (M.ch >= 20X) & (M.ch <= 86X) THEN
                        IF newcap # NIL THEN InsertChar(G, M.ch)
                        ELSIF G.marked THEN
                            Defocus(G); Deselect(G); NewCaption(G, M.col, M.fnt);
                            InsertChar(G, M.ch)
                        END
                    END
                END
            END
        ELSIF M IS UpdateMsg THEN
            WITH M: UpdateMsg DO
                IF M.graph = G.graph THEN
                    dM.f := G; dM.x := G.x; dM.y := G.y; dM.col := 0;
                    CASE M.id OF
                      restore: Restore(G)
                    | drawobj: dM.mode := 0; M.obj.do.draw(M.obj, dM)
                    | drawobjs: dM.mode := 1; M.obj.do.draw(M.obj, dM)
                    | drawobjd: dM.mode := 3; M.obj.do.draw(M.obj, dM)
                    | drawsel: dM.mode := 0; Graphics.DrawSel(G.graph, dM)
                    | drawnorm: dM.mode := 2; Graphics.DrawSel(G.graph, dM)
                    | drawdel: dM.mode := 3; Graphics.DrawSel(G.graph, dM)
                    END
                END
            END
        ELSIF M IS SelQuery THEN
            WITH M: SelQuery DO
                IF (G.graph.sel # NIL) & (M.time < G.graph.time) THEN
                    M.f := G; M.time := G.graph.time
                END
            END
        ELSIF M IS FocusQuery THEN
            IF G.marked THEN M(FocusQuery).f := G END
        ELSIF M IS PosQuery THEN
            WITH M: PosQuery DO
                IF (G.X <= M.x) & (M.x < G.X1) & (G.Y <= M.y) & (M.y < G.Y1) THEN
                    M.f := G
                END
            END
        ELSIF M IS DispMsg THEN
            DM := M(DispMsg);
            x := G.x + newcap.x + newcap.w; y := G.y + newcap.y;
```

```
            IF (DM.graph = G.graph) & (x >= G.X) & (x + DM.w < G.X1) & (y >= G.Y) &
            (y < G.Y1) THEN
                Display.CopyPattern(Oberon.CurCol, DM.pat, x + DM.x1, y + DM.y1, 2);
                Display.ReplConst(Display.white, x, y, DM.w, newcap.h, 2)
            END
        ELSIF M IS Oberon.ControlMsg THEN
            WITH M: Oberon.ControlMsg DO
                IF M.id = Oberon.neutralize THEN
                    Oberon.RemoveMarks(G.X, G.Y, G.W, G.H); Defocus(G);
                    DrawNorm(G); Graphics.Deselect(G.graph)
                ELSIF M.id = Oberon.defocus THEN Defocus(G)
                END
            END
        ELSIF M IS Oberon.SelectionMsg THEN
            WITH M: Oberon.SelectionMsg DO
                GetSelection(G, M.text, M.beg, M.end, M.time)
            END
        ELSIF M IS Oberon.CopyMsg THEN
            Oberon.RemoveMarks(G.X, G.Y, G.W, G.H); Defocus(G);
            NEW(G1); G1↑ := G↑; M(Oberon.CopyMsg).F := G1
        ELSIF M IS MenuViewers.ModifyMsg THEN
            WITH M: MenuViewers.ModifyMsg DO G.Y := M.Y; G.H := M.H; Restore(G) END
        ELSIF M IS Oberon.CopyOverMsg THEN
            WITH M: Oberon.CopyOverMsg DO
                IF G.marked THEN
                    DrawObj(G, CaptionCopy(G, G.mark.x, G.mark.y, M.text, M.beg, M.end))
                END
            END
        END
    END
END Handle;


(*–––––––––––––– Methods ––––––––––––––*)


PROCEDURE* DrawLine(obj: Graphics.Object; VAR M: Graphics.Msg);
    (*M.mode = 0: draw according to state,
        = 1: normal –> selected,
        = 2: selected –> normal,
        = 3: erase*)
    VAR x, y, w, h, col: INTEGER; f: Frame;
BEGIN
    WITH M: DrawMsg DO
        x := obj.x + M.x; y := obj.y + M.y; w := obj.w; h := obj.h; f := M.f;
        IF (x+w > f.X) & (x < f.X1) & (y+h > f.Y) & (y < f.Y1) THEN
            IF x < f.X THEN DEC(w, f.X−x); x := f.X END;
            IF x+w > f.X1 THEN w := f.X1−x END;
            IF y < f.Y THEN DEC(h, f.Y−y); y := f.Y END;
            IF y+h > f.Y1 THEN h := f.Y1−y END;
            IF M.col = Display.black THEN col := obj.col ELSE col := M.col (*macro*) END;
            IF (M.mode = 0) & obj.selected OR (M.mode = 1) THEN
                Display.ReplPattern(col, Display.grey2, x, y, w, h, 0)
            ELSIF M.mode = 3 THEN Display.ReplConst(Display.black, x, y, w, h, 0) (*erase*)
            ELSE Display.ReplConst(col, x, y, w, h, 0)
            END
        END
    END
END DrawLine;


PROCEDURE* DrawCaption(obj: Graphics.Object; VAR M: Graphics.Msg);
```

```
        VAR x, y, dx, x0, x1, y0, y1, w, h, w1, h1, col: INTEGER;
          f: Frame;
          ch: CHAR; pat: Display.Pattern; fnt: Fonts.Font;
          R: Texts.Reader;
   BEGIN
      WITH M: DrawMsg DO
         x := obj.x + M.x; y := obj.y + M.y; w := obj.w; h := obj.h; f := M.f;
         IF (f.X <= x) & (x <= f.X1) & (f.Y <= y) & (y+h <= f.Y1) THEN
            IF x+w > f.X1 THEN w := f.X1−x END;
            Texts.OpenReader(R, Graphics.T, obj(Graphics.Caption).pos); Texts.Read(R, ch);
            IF M.mode = 0 THEN
               IF ch >= "" THEN
                  IF M.col = Display.black THEN col := obj.col ELSE col := M.col (*macro*)
                     END;
                  fnt := R.fnt; x0 := x; y0 := y − fnt.minY;
                  LOOP
                     Display.GetChar(fnt.raster, ch, dx, x1, y1, w1, h1, pat);
                     IF x0+x1+w1 <= f.X1 THEN
                        Display.CopyPattern(col, pat, x0+x1, y0+y1, 1)
                     ELSE EXIT
                     END;
                     INC(x0, dx); Texts.Read(R, ch);
                     IF ch < "" THEN EXIT END
                  END;
                  IF obj.selected THEN Display.ReplConst(Display.white, x, y, w, h, 2) END
               END
            ELSIF M.mode < 3 THEN Display.ReplConst(Display.white, x, y, w, h, 2)
            ELSE Display.ReplConst(Display.black, x, y, w, h, 0)
            END
         END
      END
   END DrawCaption;

   PROCEDURE* DrawMacro(obj: Graphics.Object; VAR M: Graphics.Msg);
      VAR x, y, w, h: INTEGER;
          f: Frame; M1: DrawMsg;
   BEGIN
      WITH M: DrawMsg DO
         x := obj.x + M.x; y := obj.y + M.y; w := obj.w; h := obj.h; f := M.f;
         IF (x+w > f.X) & (x < f.X1) & (y+h > f.Y) & (y < f.Y1) THEN
            M1.x := x; M1.y := y;
            IF x < f.X THEN DEC(w, f.X−x); x := f.X END;
            IF x+w > f.X1 THEN w := f.X1−x END;
            IF y < f.Y THEN DEC(h, f.Y−y); y := f.Y END;
            IF y+h > f.Y1 THEN h := f.Y1−y END;
            IF M.mode = 0 THEN
               M1.f := f; M1.col := obj.col; M1.mode := 0;
                  Graphics.DrawMac(obj(Graphics.Macro).mac, M1);
               IF obj.selected THEN Display.ReplConst(Display.white, x, y, w, h, 2) END
            ELSIF M.mode < 3 THEN Display.ReplConst(Display.white, x, y, w, h, 2)
            ELSE Display.ReplConst(Display.black, x, y, w, h, 0)
            END
         END
      END
   END DrawMacro;

   PROCEDURE Open*(G: Frame; graph: Graphics.Graph; X, Y, col: INTEGER; ticked:
         BOOLEAN):
      VAR G: Frame;
   BEGIN G.graph := graph; G.Xg := X; G.Yg := Y; G.col := col; G.marked := FALSE;
```

```
            G.mark.next := NIL; G.ticked := ticked; G.handle := Handle; RETURN G
        END Open;


    PROCEDURE* DrawCrosshair(x, y: INTEGER);
    BEGIN
        IF x < CL THEN
            IF x < markW THEN x := markW
            ELSIF x > DW THEN x := DW − markW
            END
        ELSE
            IF x < CL + markW THEN x := CL + markW
            ELSIF x > CL + DW THEN x := CL + DW − markW
            END
        END;
        IF y < markW THEN y := markW ELSIF y > DH THEN y := DH − markW END;
        Display.CopyPattern(Display.white, Display.cross, x − markW, y − markW, 2)
    END DrawCrosshair;


BEGIN DW := Display.Width − 8; DH := Display.Height − 8; CL := Display.ColLeft;
    Crosshair.Draw := DrawCrosshair; Crosshair.Fade := DrawCrosshair; Texts.OpenWriter(W);
    Graphics.LineMethod.draw := DrawLine; Graphics.CapMethod.draw := DrawCaption;
    Graphics.MacMethod.draw := DrawMacro
END GraphicFrames.
```

13.8.3   Module *Graphics*

The preceding presentations of the interface definitions have explained the framework of the graphics system and set the goals for their implementation. We recall that the core module *Graphics* handles the data structures representing sets of objects without reliance on the specifications of individual objects. Even the structural aspects of the object sets are not fixed by the interface. Several solutions, and hence several implementations, are imaginable.

Here we present the simplest solution for representing an abstract, unordered set: the linear, linked list. It is embodied in the object record's additional, hidden field *next*. Consequently, a graphic is represented by the head of the list, and the type *GraphDesc* obtains the hidden field *first* (see the listing of *Graphics*). In addition, the descriptor contains the exported field *sel* denoting a selected element, and the field *time* indicating the time of its selection. The latter is used to determine the most recent selection in various viewers.

Macros   Additional data structures become necessary through the presence of macros and classes. Macros are represented by the list of their elements, like graphics. Their header is of type *MacHeadDesc*, in analogy to *GraphDesc*. In addition to a macro's name, width and height, it contains the field *first*, pointing to the list's first element, and the field *lib*, referring to the library from which the macro stems.

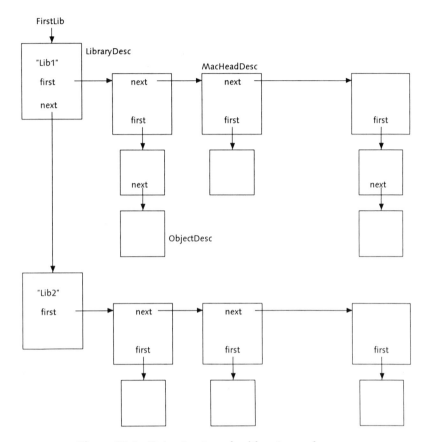

Figure 13.6 Data structure for libraries and macros.

A library descriptor is similarly structured: in addition to its name, the field *first* points to the list of elements (macros) of the library, which are themselves linked through the field *next*. Figure 13.6 shows the data structure containing two libraries. It is anchored in the global variable *FirstLib*.

Libraries Libraries are permanently stored as files. It is evidently unacceptable that file access be required upon every reference to a macro, for example each time a macro is redrawn. Therefore a library is loaded into primary store, when one of its elements is referenced for the first time. Procedure *ThisMac* searches the data structure representing the specified library and locates the header of the requested macro.

We emphasize that the structures employed for macro and library representation remain hidden from clients, just as the structure of graphics remains hidden within module *Graphics*. Thus none of the linkage fields of records (first, next) are exported from the base module.

**Loading
and storing**

This measure retains the possibility to change the structural design decisions without affecting the client modules. But partly it is also responsible for the necessity to include macros in the base module.

A large fraction of module *Graphics* is taken up by procedures for reading and writing files representing graphics and libraries. They convert their internal data structure into a sequential form and vice versa. This would be a rather trivial task, were it not for the presence of pointers referring to macros and classes. These pointers must be converted into descriptions that are position-independent, such as names. The same problem is posed by fonts (which are also represented by pointers).

Evidently, the replacement of every pointer by an explicit name would be an uneconomical solution with respect to storage space as well as speed of reading and writing. Therefore pointers to fonts and libraries – themselves represented as files – are replaced by indices to font and library dictionaries. These dictionaries establish a context and are constructed while a file is read. They are used only during this process and hence are local to procedure *Load* (or *Open*). For classes, a dictionary listing the respective allocation procedures is constructed in order to avoid repeated calls to determine the pertinent allocator.

When a graphics file is generated by procedure *Store*, local dictionaries are constructed of fonts, libraries, and classes of objects that have been written onto the file. Upon encountering a caption, a macro, or any element whose font, library or class is not contained in the respective dictionary, a pair consisting of index and name is emitted to the file, thereby assigning a number to each name. These pairs are interspersed within the sequence of object descriptions.

When the graphic file is read, these pairs trigger insertion of the font, library or class in the respective dictionary, whereby the name is converted into a pointer to the entity, which is obtained by a loading process embodied by procedures *Fonts.This*, *ThisLib* and *ThisClass*. Both the *Load* and *Store* procedures traverse the file only once. The files are self-contained in the sense that all external quantities are represented by their names. The format of a graphics file is defined in Extended BNF syntax as follows:

**Format of
graphics**

file =	tag stretch.
stretch =	{item} −1.
item =	0 0 fontno fontname | 0 1 libno libname |
	0 2 classno classname allocname |
	1 data | 2 data fontno string |
	3 data libno macname |
	classno data extension.
data =	x y w h color.

All class numbers are at least 4; the values 1, 2 and 3 are assigned to lines, captions, and macros. x, y, w, h and *color* are two-byte integer attributes of the base type *Object*.

The same procedures are used for loading and storing a library file. In fact, *Load* and *Store* read and write a file stretch representing a sequence of elements which is terminated by a special value (-1). In a library file each macro corresponds to a stretch, and the terminator is followed by values specifying the macro's overall width, height, and its name. The structure of library files is defined by the following syntax:

Format of
library file

libfile =   libtag {macro}.
macro =   stretch w h name.

The first byte of each element is a class number within the context of the file and identifies the class to which the element belongs. An object of the given class is allocated by calling the class' allocation procedure, which is obtained from the class dictionary in the given context. The class number is used as dictionary index. The presence of the required allocation procedure in the dictionary is guaranteed by the fact that a corresponding index/name pair had preceded the element in the file.

The encounter of such a pair triggers the loading of the module specifying the class and its methods. The name of the pair consists of two parts: the first specifies the module in which the class is defined, and it is taken as the parameter of the call to the loader (see procedure *ThisClass*). The second part is the name of the relevant allocation procedure which returns a fresh object to variable *Graphics.new*. Thereafter, the data defined in the base type *Object* are read.

Data belonging to an extension follow those of the base type, and they are read by the extension's *read* method. This part must always be headed by a byte specifying the number of bytes which follow. This information is used in the case where a requested module is not present; it indicates the number of bytes to be skipped in order to continue reading further elements.

Moving

A last noteworthy detail concerns the *Move* operation, which appears as surprisingly complicated, particularly in comparison with the related copy operation. The reason is our deviation from the principle that a graphics editor must refrain from an interpretation of drawings. Responsible for this deviation was the circumstance that the editor was at first primarily used for the preparation of circuit diagrams. They suggested the view that adjoining, perpendicular lines be connected. Consequently, the horizontal or vertical displacement of a line was to preserve connections. Procedure *Move* must therefore identify all connected lines, and subsequently extend or shorten them.

```
MODULE Graphics; (*NW 21.12.89 / 3.2.92*)
  IMPORT Files, Modules, Display, Fonts, Printer, Texts, Oberon;

  CONST NameLen* = 16; GraphFileId = 0F9X; LibFileId = 0FDX;

  TYPE
    Graph* = POINTER TO GraphDesc;
    Object* = POINTER TO ObjectDesc;
    Method* = POINTER TO MethodDesc;

    Line* = POINTER TO LineDesc;
    Caption* = POINTER TO CaptionDesc;
    Macro* = POINTER TO MacroDesc;

    ObjectDesc* = RECORD
        x*, y*, w*, h*, col*: INTEGER;
        selected*, marked*: BOOLEAN;
        do*: Method;
        next, dmy: Object
      END;

    Msg* = RECORD END;
    WidMsg* = RECORD (Msg) w*: INTEGER END;
    ColorMsg* = RECORD (Msg) col*: INTEGER END;
    FontMsg* = RECORD (Msg) fnt*: Fonts.Font END;
    Name* = ARRAY NameLen OF CHAR;

    GraphDesc* = RECORD
        time*: LONGINT;
        sel*, first: Object
      END;

    MacHead* = POINTER TO MacHeadDesc;
    MacExt* = POINTER TO MacExtDesc;
    Library* = POINTER TO LibraryDesc;

    MacHeadDesc* = RECORD
        name*: Name;
        w*, h*: INTEGER;
        ext*: MacExt;
        lib*: Library;
        first: Object;
        next: MacHead
      END;

    LibraryDesc* = RECORD
        name*: Name;
        first: MacHead;
        next: Library
      END;

    MacExtDesc* = RECORD END;

    Context* = RECORD
        nofonts, noflibs, nofclasses: INTEGER;
        font: ARRAY 10 OF Fonts.Font;
```

```
        lib: ARRAY 4 OF Library;
        class: ARRAY 10 OF Modules.Command
    END;

MethodDesc* = RECORD
        module*, allocator*: Name;
        new*: Modules.Command;
        copy*: PROCEDURE (from, to: Object);
        draw*, handle*: PROCEDURE (obj: Object; VAR msg: Msg);
        selectable*: PROCEDURE (obj: Object; x, y: INTEGER): BOOLEAN;
        read*: PROCEDURE (obj: Object; VAR R: Files.Rider; VAR C: Context);
        write*: PROCEDURE (obj: Object; cno: SHORTINT; VAR R: Files.Rider;
            VAR C: Context);
        print*: PROCEDURE (obj: Object; x, y: INTEGER)
    END;


LineDesc* = RECORD (ObjectDesc)
    END;


CaptionDesc* = RECORD (ObjectDesc)
        pos*, len*: INTEGER
    END;


MacroDesc* = RECORD (ObjectDesc)
        mac*: MacHead
    END;


VAR new*: Object;
    width*, res*: INTEGER;
    T*: Texts.Text; (*captions*)
    LineMethod*, CapMethod*, MacMethod* : Method;


    FirstLib: Library;
    W, TW: Texts.Writer;


PROCEDURE Add*(G: Graph; obj: Object);
BEGIN obj.marked := FALSE; obj.selected := TRUE; obj.next := G.first;
    G.first := obj; G.sel := obj; G.time := Oberon.Time()
END Add;


PROCEDURE Draw*(G: Graph; VAR M: Msg);
    VAR obj: Object;
BEGIN obj := G.first;
    WHILE obj # NIL DO obj.do.draw(obj, M); obj := obj.next END
END Draw;


PROCEDURE ThisObj*(G: Graph; x, y: INTEGER): Object;
    VAR obj: Object;
BEGIN obj := G.first;
    WHILE (obj # NIL) & ~obj.do.selectable(obj, x ,y) DO obj := obj.next END;
    RETURN obj
END ThisObj;


PROCEDURE SelectObj*(G: Graph; obj: Object);
BEGIN
    IF obj # NIL THEN obj.selected := TRUE; G.sel := obj; G.time := Oberon.Time() END
```

```
   END SelectObj;


PROCEDURE SelectArea*(G: Graph; x0, y0, x1, y1: INTEGER);
   VAR obj: Object; t: INTEGER;
BEGIN obj := G.first;
   IF x1 < x0 THEN t := x0; x0 := x1; x1 := t END;
   IF y1 < y0 THEN t := y0; y0 := y1; y1 := t END;
   WHILE obj # NIL DO
      IF (x0 <= obj.x) & (obj.x + obj.w <= x1) & (y0 <= obj.y) & (obj.y + obj.h <= y1)
         THEN
            obj.selected := TRUE; G.sel := obj
      END;
      obj := obj.next
   END;
   IF G.sel # NIL THEN G.time := Oberon.Time() END
END SelectArea;


PROCEDURE Enumerate*(G: Graph;
      handle: PROCEDURE (obj: Object; VAR done: BOOLEAN));
   VAR obj: Object; done: BOOLEAN;
BEGIN done := FALSE; obj := G.first;
   WHILE (obj # NIL) & ~done DO handle(obj, done); obj := obj.next END
END Enumerate;


(*---------procedures operating on selection --------*)


PROCEDURE Deselect*(G: Graph);
   VAR obj: Object;
BEGIN obj := G.first; G.sel := NIL; G.time := 0;
   WHILE obj # NIL DO obj.selected := FALSE; obj := obj.next END
END Deselect;


PROCEDURE DrawSel*(G: Graph; VAR M: Msg);
   VAR obj: Object;
BEGIN obj := G.first;
   WHILE obj # NIL DO
      IF obj.selected THEN obj.do.draw(obj, M) END;
      obj := obj.next
   END
END DrawSel;


PROCEDURE Handle*(G: Graph; VAR M: Msg);
   VAR obj: Object;
BEGIN obj := G.first;
   WHILE obj # NIL DO
      IF obj.selected THEN obj.do.handle(obj, M) END;
      obj := obj.next
   END
END Handle;


PROCEDURE Move*(G: Graph; dx, dy: INTEGER);
   VAR obj, ob0: Object; x0, x1, y0, y1: INTEGER;
BEGIN obj := G.first;
   WHILE obj # NIL DO
      IF obj.selected & ~(obj IS Caption) THEN
         x0 := obj.x; x1 := obj.w + x0; y0 := obj.y; y1 := obj.h + y0;
```

```
        IF dx = 0 THEN (*vertical move*)
            ob0 := G.first;
            WHILE ob0 # NIL DO
                IF ~ob0.selected & (ob0 IS Line) & (x0 <= ob0.x) & (ob0.x <= x1) &
                    (ob0.w < ob0.h) THEN
                    IF (y0 <= ob0.y) & (ob0.y <= y1) THEN
                        INC(ob0.y, dy); DEC(ob0.h, dy); ob0.marked := TRUE
                    ELSIF (y0 <= ob0.y + ob0.h) & (ob0.y + ob0.h <= y1) THEN
                        INC(ob0.h, dy); ob0.marked := TRUE
                    END
                END;
                ob0 := ob0.next
            END
        ELSIF dy = 0 THEN (*horizontal move*)
            ob0 := G.first;
            WHILE ob0 # NIL DO
                IF ~ob0.selected & (ob0 IS Line) & (y0 <= ob0.y) & (ob0.y <= y1) &
                    (ob0.h < ob0.w) THEN
                    IF (x0 <= ob0.x) & (ob0.x <= x1) THEN
                        INC(ob0.x, dx); DEC(ob0.w, dx); ob0.marked := TRUE
                    ELSIF (x0 <= ob0.x + ob0.w) & (ob0.x + ob0.w <= x1) THEN
                        INC(ob0.w, dx); ob0.marked := TRUE
                    END
                END;
                ob0 := ob0.next
            END
        END
    END;
    obj := obj.next
END;
obj := G.first; (*now move*)
WHILE obj # NIL DO
    IF obj.selected THEN INC(obj.x, dx); INC(obj.y, dy) END;
    obj.marked := FALSE; obj := obj.next
END
END Move;


PROCEDURE Copy*(Gs, Gd: Graph; dx, dy: INTEGER);
    VAR obj: Object;
BEGIN obj := Gs.first;
    WHILE obj # NIL DO
        IF obj.selected THEN
            obj.do.new; obj.do.copy(obj, new); INC(new.x, dx); INC(new.y, dy);
            obj.selected := FALSE; Add(Gd, new)
        END;
        obj := obj.next
    END;
    new := NIL
END Copy;


PROCEDURE Delete*(G: Graph);
    VAR obj, pred: Object;
BEGIN G.sel := NIL; obj := G.first;
    WHILE (obj # NIL) & obj.selected DO obj := obj.next END;
    G.first := obj;
    IF obj # NIL THEN
        pred := obj; obj := obj.next;
        WHILE obj # NIL DO
```

```
                    IF obj.selected THEN pred.next := obj.next ELSE pred := obj END;
                    obj := obj.next
              END
        END
END Delete;


(* ----------- File I/O ----------- *)


PROCEDURE ReadInt*(VAR R: Files.Rider; VAR x: INTEGER);
    VAR c0: CHAR; s1: SHORTINT;
BEGIN Files.Read(R, c0); Files.Read(R, s1); x := s1; x := x * 100H + ORD(c0)
END ReadInt;


PROCEDURE ReadLInt*(VAR R: Files.Rider; VAR x: LONGINT);
    VAR c0, c1, c2: CHAR; s3: SHORTINT;
BEGIN Files.Read(R, c0); Files.Read(R, c1); Files.Read(R, c2); Files.Read(R, s3);
    x := s3; x := ((x * 100H + LONG(c2)) * 100H + LONG(c1)) * 100H + LONG(c0)
END ReadLInt;


PROCEDURE ReadString*(VAR R: Files.Rider; VAR s: ARRAY OF CHAR);
    VAR i: INTEGER; ch: CHAR;
BEGIN i := 0;
    REPEAT Files.Read(R, ch); s[i] := ch; INC(i) UNTIL ch = 0X
END ReadString;


PROCEDURE ReadObj(VAR R: Files.Rider; obj: Object);
BEGIN ReadInt(R, obj.x); ReadInt(R, obj.y);
    ReadInt(R, obj.w); ReadInt(R, obj.h); ReadInt(R, obj.col)
END ReadObj;


PROCEDURE WriteInt*(VAR W: Files.Rider; x: INTEGER);
BEGIN Files.Write(W, CHR(x)); Files.Write(W, CHR(x DIV 100H))
END WriteInt;


PROCEDURE WriteLInt*(VAR W: Files.Rider; x: LONGINT);
BEGIN Files.Write(W, CHR(x)); Files.Write(W, CHR(x DIV 100H));
    Files.Write(W, CHR(x DIV 10000H)); Files.Write(W, CHR(x DIV 1000000H))
END WriteLInt;


PROCEDURE WriteString*(VAR W: Files.Rider; VAR s: ARRAY OF CHAR);
    VAR i: INTEGER; ch: CHAR;
BEGIN i := 0;
    REPEAT ch := s[i]; INC(i); Files.Write(W, ch) UNTIL ch = 0X
END WriteString;


PROCEDURE WriteObj*(VAR W: Files.Rider; cno: SHORTINT; obj: Object);
BEGIN Files.Write(W, cno); WriteInt(W, obj.x); WriteInt(W, obj.y);
    WriteInt(W, obj.w); WriteInt(W, obj.h); WriteInt(W, obj.col)
END WriteObj;


(* ----------- Storing ----------- *)


PROCEDURE WMsg(s0, s1: ARRAY OF CHAR);
BEGIN Texts.WriteString(W, s0); Texts.WriteString(W, s1);
    Texts.WriteLn(W); Texts.Append(Oberon.Log, W.buf)
```

END WMsg;

```
PROCEDURE InitContext(VAR C: Context);
BEGIN C.nofonts := 0; C.noflibs := 0; C.nofclasses := 4;
   C.class[1] := LineMethod.new; C.class[2] := CapMethod.new;
   C.class[3] := MacMethod.new
END InitContext;


PROCEDURE FontNo*(VAR W: Files.Rider; VAR C: Context; fnt: Fonts.Font): SHORTINT;
   VAR fno: SHORTINT;
BEGIN fno := 0;
   WHILE (fno < C.nofonts) & (C.font[fno] # fnt) DO INC(fno) END;
   IF fno = C.nofonts THEN
      Files.Write(W, 0); Files.Write(W, 0); Files.Write(W, fno);
      WriteString(W, fnt.name); C.font[fno] := fnt; INC(C.nofonts)
   END;
   RETURN fno
END FontNo;


PROCEDURE StoreElems(VAR W: Files.Rider; VAR C: Context; obj: Object);
   VAR cno: INTEGER;
BEGIN
   WHILE obj # NIL DO
      cno := 1;
      WHILE (cno < C.nofclasses) & (obj.do.new # C.class[cno]) DO INC(cno) END;
      IF cno = C.nofclasses THEN
         Files.Write(W, 0); Files.Write(W, 2); Files.Write(W, SHORT(cno));
         WriteString(W, obj.do.module); WriteString(W, obj.do.allocator);
         C.class[cno] := obj.do.new; INC(C.nofclasses)
      END;
      obj.do.write(obj, SHORT(cno), W, C); obj := obj.next
   END;
   Files.Write(W, −1)
END StoreElems;


PROCEDURE Store*(G: Graph; VAR W: Files.Rider);
   VAR C: Context;
BEGIN InitContext(C); StoreElems(W, C, G.first)
END Store;


PROCEDURE WriteFile*(G: Graph; name: ARRAY OF CHAR);
   VAR F: Files.File; W: Files.Rider; C: Context;
BEGIN F := Files.New(name); Files.Set(W, F, 0); Files.Write(W, GraphFileId);
   InitContext(C); StoreElems(W, C, G.first); Files.Register(F)
END WriteFile;


PROCEDURE Print*(G: Graph; x0, y0: INTEGER);
   VAR obj: Object;
BEGIN obj := G.first;
   WHILE obj # NIL DO obj.do.print(obj, x0, y0); obj := obj.next END
END Print;


(* ––––––––––––– Loading ––––––––––––– *)


PROCEDURE ThisClass*(VAR module, allocator: ARRAY OF CHAR): Modules.Command;
   VAR mod: Modules.Module; com: Modules.Command;
```

```
BEGIN mod := Modules.ThisMod(module);
  IF mod # NIL THEN
    com := Modules.ThisCommand(mod, allocator);
    IF com = NIL THEN WMsg(allocator, "unknown") END
  ELSE WMsg(module, "not available"); com := NIL
  END;
  RETURN com
END ThisClass;


PROCEDURE Font*(VAR R: Files.Rider; VAR C: Context): Fonts.Font;
  VAR fno: SHORTINT;
BEGIN Files.Read(R, fno); RETURN C.font[fno]
END Font;


PROCEDURE ↑ ThisLib*(VAR name: ARRAY OF CHAR; replace: BOOLEAN): Library;


PROCEDURE LoadElems(VAR R: Files.Rider; VAR C: Context; VAR obj: Object);
  VAR cno, k: SHORTINT; len: INTEGER;
    name, name1: ARRAY 32 OF CHAR;
  BEGIN obj := NIL; Files.Read(R, cno);
    WHILE ~R.eof & (cno >= 0) DO
      IF cno = 0 THEN
        Files.Read(R, cno); Files.Read(R, k); ReadString(R, name);
        IF cno = 0 THEN C.font[k] := Fonts.This(name)
        ELSIF cno = 1 THEN C.lib[k] := ThisLib(name, FALSE)
        ELSE ReadString(R, name1); C.class[k] := ThisClass(name, name1)
        END
      ELSIF C.class[cno] # NIL THEN
        C.class[cno]; ReadObj(R, new);
        new.selected := FALSE; new.marked := FALSE; new.next := obj; obj := new;
        new.do.read(new, R, C)
      ELSE Files.Set(R, Files.Base(R), Files.Pos(R) + 10);
        Files.ReadInt(R, len); Files.Set(R, Files.Base(R), Files.Pos(R) + len)
      END;
      Files.Read(R, cno)
    END;
    new := NIL
  END LoadElems;


PROCEDURE Load*(G: Graph; VAR R: Files.Rider);
  VAR C: Context;
BEGIN G.sel := NIL; InitContext(C); LoadElems(R, C, G.first)
END Load;


PROCEDURE Open*(G: Graph; name: ARRAY OF CHAR);
  VAR tag: CHAR;
    F: Files.File; R: Files.Rider; C: Context;
BEGIN G.first := NIL; G.sel := NIL; G.time := 0; F := Files.Old(name);
  IF F # NIL THEN
    Files.Set(R, F, 0); Files.Read(R, tag);
    IF tag = GraphFileId THEN InitContext(C); LoadElems(R, C, G.first); res := 0
      ELSE res := 1
    END
  ELSE res := 2
  END
END Open;


(* –––––––––– Macros / Libraries –––––––––– *)
```

```
PROCEDURE ThisLib*(VAR name: ARRAY OF CHAR; replace: BOOLEAN): Library;
    VAR i, j: INTEGER; ch: CHAR;
        L: Library; mh: MacHead; obj: Object;
        F: Files.File; R: Files.Rider; C: Context;
        Lname, Fname: ARRAY 32 OF CHAR;
BEGIN L := FirstLib; i := 0;
    WHILE name[i] >= "0" DO Lname[i] := name[i]; INC(i) END;
    Lname[i] := 0X;
    WHILE (L # NIL) & (L.name # Lname) DO L := L.next END;
    IF (L = NIL) OR replace THEN
        (*load library*) j := 0;
        WHILE name[j] > 0X DO Fname[j] := name[j]; INC(j) END;
        IF i = j THEN
            Fname[j] := "."; Fname[j+1] := "L"; Fname[j+2] := "i"; Fname[j+3] := "b";
            INC(j, 4)
        END;
        Fname[j] := 0X; F := Files.Old(Fname);
        IF F # NIL THEN
            WMsg("loading", name); Files.Set(R, F, 0); Files.Read(R, ch);
            IF ch = LibFileId THEN
                IF L = NIL THEN
                    NEW(L); COPY(Lname, L.name); L.next := FirstLib; FirstLib := L
                END;
                L.first := NIL; InitContext(C); LoadElems (R, C, obj);
                WHILE obj # NIL DO
                    NEW(mh); mh.first := obj;
                    ReadInt(R, mh.w); ReadInt(R, mh.h); ReadString(R, mh.name);
                    mh.lib := L; mh.next := L.first; L.first := mh; LoadElems (R, C, obj)
                END
            ELSE L := NIL; WMsg(name, "bad library")
            END
        ELSE WMsg(name, "not found")
        END
    END;
    RETURN L
END ThisLib;


PROCEDURE NewLib*(VAR Lname: ARRAY OF CHAR): Library;
    VAR L: Library;
BEGIN NEW(L); COPY(Lname, L.name); L.first := NIL;
    L.next := FirstLib; FirstLib := L; RETURN L
END NewLib;


PROCEDURE StoreLib*(L: Library; VAR Fname: ARRAY OF CHAR);
    VAR mh: MacHead;
        F: Files.File; W: Files.Rider;
        C: Context;
BEGIN F := Files.New(Fname); Files.Set(W, F, 0); Files.Write(W, LibFileId);
    InitContext(C); mh := L.first;
    WHILE mh # NIL DO
        StoreElms(W, C, mh.first); WriteInt(W, mh.w); WriteInt(W, mh.h);
        WriteString(W, mh.name); mh:= mh.next
    END;
    Files.Register(F)
END StoreLib;


PROCEDURE RemoveLibraries*;
```

```
    BEGIN FirstLib := NIL
    END RemoveLibraries;


    PROCEDURE ThisMac*(L: Library; VAR Mname: ARRAY OF CHAR): MacHead;
        VAR mh: MacHead;
    BEGIN mh := L.first;
        WHILE (mh # NIL) & (mh.name # Mname) DO mh := mh.next END;
        RETURN mh
    END ThisMac;


    PROCEDURE OpenMac*(mh: MacHead; G: Graph; x, y: INTEGER);
        VAR obj: Object;
    BEGIN obj := mh.first;
        WHILE obj # NIL DO
            obj.do.new; obj.do.copy(obj, new); INC(new.x, x); INC(new.y, y);
            new.selected := TRUE; Add(G, new); obj := obj.next
        END;
        new := NIL
    END OpenMac;


    PROCEDURE DrawMac*(mh: MacHead; VAR M: Msg);
        VAR elem: Object;
    BEGIN elem := mh.first;
        WHILE elem # NIL DO elem.do.draw(elem, M); elem := elem.next END
    END DrawMac;


    PROCEDURE MakeMac*(G: Graph; x, y, w, h: INTEGER;
            VAR Mname: ARRAY OF CHAR): MacHead;
        VAR obj, last: Object; mh: MacHead;
    BEGIN obj := G.first; last := NIL;
        WHILE obj # NIL DO
            IF obj.selected THEN
                obj.do.new; obj.do.copy(obj, new); new.next := last; new.selected := FALSE;
                DEC(new.x, x); DEC(new.y, y); last := new
            END;
            obj := obj.next
        END;
        NEW(mh); mh.w := w; mh.h := h; mh.first := last; mh.ext := NIL;
        COPY(Mname, mh.name); new := NIL; RETURN mh
    END MakeMac;


    PROCEDURE InsertMac*(mh: MacHead; L: Library; VAR new: BOOLEAN);
        VAR mh1: MacHead;
    BEGIN mh.lib := L; mh1 := L.first;
        WHILE (mh1 # NIL) & (mh1.name # mh.name) DO mh1 := mh1.next END;
        IF mh1 = NIL THEN
            new := TRUE; mh.next := L.first; L.first := mh
        ELSE
            new := FALSE; mh1.w := mh.w; mh1.h := mh.h; mh1.first := mh.first
        END
    END InsertMac;


    (* ----------- Line Methods -----------*)


    PROCEDURE* NewLine;
```

```
      VAR line: Line;
BEGIN NEW(line); new := line; line.do := LineMethod
END NewLine;


PROCEDURE* CopyLine(src, dst: Object);
BEGIN dst.x := src.x; dst.y := src.y; dst.w := src.w; dst.h := src.h; dst.col := src.col
END CopyLine;


PROCEDURE* HandleLine(obj: Object; VAR M: Msg);
BEGIN
   IF M IS WidMsg THEN
      IF obj.w < obj.h THEN
         IF obj.w <= 7 THEN obj.w := M(WidMsg).w END
      ELSIF obj.h <= 7 THEN obj.h := M(WidMsg).w
      END
   ELSIF M IS ColorMsg THEN obj.col := M(ColorMsg).col
   END
END HandleLine;


PROCEDURE* LineSelectable(obj: Object; x, y: INTEGER): BOOLEAN;
BEGIN
   RETURN (obj.x <= x) & (x < obj.x + obj.w) & (obj.y <= y) & (y < obj.y + obj.h)
END LineSelectable;


PROCEDURE* ReadLine(obj: Object; VAR R: Files.Rider; VAR C: Context);
BEGIN
END ReadLine;


PROCEDURE* WriteLine(obj: Object; cno: SHORTINT; VAR W: Files.Rider;
      VAR C: Context);
BEGIN WriteObj(W, cno, obj)
END WriteLine;


PROCEDURE* PrintLine(obj: Object; x, y: INTEGER);
   VAR w, h: INTEGER;
BEGIN w := obj.w * 2; h := obj.h * 2;
   IF w < h THEN h := 2*h ELSE w := 2*w END;
   Printer.ReplConst(obj.x * 4 + x, obj.y *4 + y, w, h)
END PrintLine;


(* ----------- Caption Methods ----------- *)


PROCEDURE* NewCaption;
   VAR cap: Caption;
BEGIN NEW(cap); new := cap; cap.do := CapMethod
END NewCaption;


PROCEDURE* CopyCaption(src, dst: Object);
   VAR ch: CHAR; R: Texts.Reader;
BEGIN
   WITH src: Caption DO
      WITH dst: Caption DO
         dst.x := src.x; dst.y := src.y; dst.w := src.w; dst.h := src.h; dst.col := src.col;
         dst.pos := SHORT(T.len + 1); dst.len := src.len;
         Texts.Write(TW, 0DX); Texts.OpenReader(R, T, src.pos);
```

```
                    Texts.Read(R, ch); TW.fnt := R.fnt;
                    WHILE ch > 0DX DO Texts.Write(TW, ch); Texts.Read(R, ch) END
            END
        END;
        Texts.Append(T, TW.buf)
    END CopyCaption;


    PROCEDURE* HandleCaption(obj: Object; VAR M: Msg);
        VAR dx, x1, dy, y1, w, w1, h1, len: INTEGER;
            pos: LONGINT;
            ch: CHAR; pat: Display.Pattern; fnt: Fonts.Font;
            R: Texts.Reader;
    BEGIN
        IF M IS FontMsg THEN
            fnt := M(FontMsg).fnt; w := 0; len := 0; pos := obj(Caption).pos;
            Texts.OpenReader(R, T, pos); Texts.Read(R, ch); dy := R.fnt.minY;
            WHILE ch > 0DX DO
                Display.GetChar(fnt.raster, ch, dx, x1, y1, w1, h1, pat);
                INC(w, dx); INC(len); Texts.Read(R, ch)
            END;
            INC(obj.y, fnt.minY−dy); obj.w := w; obj.h := fnt.height;
            Texts.ChangeLooks(T, pos, pos+len, {0}, fnt, 0 , 0)
        ELSIF M IS ColorMsg THEN obj.col := M(ColorMsg).col
        END
    END HandleCaption;


    PROCEDURE* CaptionSelectable(obj: Object; x, y: INTEGER): BOOLEAN;
    BEGIN
        RETURN (obj.x <= x) & (x < obj.x + obj.w) & (obj.y <= y) & (y < obj.y + obj.h)
    END CaptionSelectable;


    PROCEDURE* ReadCaption(obj: Object; VAR R: Files.Rider; VAR C: Context);
        VAR ch: CHAR; fno: SHORTINT; len: INTEGER;
    BEGIN obj(Caption).pos := SHORT(T.len + 1); Texts.Write(TW, 0DX);
        Files.Read(R, fno); TW.fnt := C.font[fno]; len := 0; Files.Read(R, ch);
        WHILE ch > 0DX DO Texts.Write(TW, ch); INC(len); Files.Read(R, ch) END;
        obj(Caption).len := len; Texts.Append(T, TW.buf)
    END ReadCaption;


    PROCEDURE* WriteCaption(obj: Object; cno: SHORTINT; VAR W: Files.Rider;
            VAR C: Context);
        VAR ch: CHAR; fno: SHORTINT;
            TR: Texts.Reader;
    BEGIN Texts.OpenReader(TR, T, obj(Caption).pos); Texts.Read(TR, ch);
        fno := FontNo(W, C, TR.fnt);
        WriteObj(W, cno, obj); Files.Write(W, fno);
        WHILE ch > 0DX DO Files.Write(W, ch); Texts.Read(TR, ch) END;
        Files.Write(W, 0X)
    END WriteCaption;


    PROCEDURE* PrintCaption(obj: Object; x, y: INTEGER);
        VAR fnt: Fonts.Font;
            i: INTEGER; ch: CHAR;
            R: Texts.Reader;
            s: ARRAY 128 OF CHAR;
    BEGIN Texts.OpenReader(R, T, obj(Caption).pos); Texts.Read(R, ch);
        fnt := R.fnt; DEC(y, fnt.minY*4); i := 0;
```

```
    WHILE ch >= "" DO s[i] := ch; INC(i); Texts.Read(R, ch) END;
    s[i] := 0X;
    IF i > 0 THEN Printer.String(obj.x*4 + x, obj.y*4 + y, s, fnt.name) END
END PrintCaption;


(* ———————————— Macro Methods ——————————— *)


PROCEDURE* NewMacro;
    VAR mac: Macro;
BEGIN NEW(mac); new := mac; mac.do := MacMethod
END NewMacro;


PROCEDURE* CopyMacro(src, dst: Object);
BEGIN dst.x := src.x; dst.y := src.y; dst.w := src.w; dst.h := src.h;
    dst.col := src.col; dst(Macro).mac := src(Macro).mac
END CopyMacro;


PROCEDURE* HandleMacro(obj: Object; VAR M: Msg);
BEGIN
    IF M IS ColorMsg THEN obj.col := M(ColorMsg).col END
END HandleMacro;


PROCEDURE* MacroSelectable(obj: Object; x, y: INTEGER): BOOLEAN;
BEGIN
    RETURN (obj.x <= x) & (x <= obj.x + 8) & (obj.y <= y) & (y <= obj.y + 8)
END MacroSelectable;


PROCEDURE* ReadMacro(obj: Object; VAR R: Files.Rider; VAR C: Context);
    VAR lno: SHORTINT; name: ARRAY 32 OF CHAR;
BEGIN Files.Read(R, lno);
    ReadString(R, name); obj(Macro).mac := ThisMac(C.lib[lno], name)
END ReadMacro;


PROCEDURE* WriteMacro(obj: Object; cno: SHORTINT; VAR W1: Files.Rider
        VAR C: Context);
    VAR ch: CHAR; lno: SHORTINT; TR: Texts.Reader;
BEGIN lno := 0;
    WITH obj: Macro DO
        WHILE (lno < C.noflibs) & (obj.mac.lib # C.lib[lno]) DO INC(lno) END;
        IF lno = C.noflibs THEN
            Files.Write(W1, 0); Files.Write(W1, 1); Files.Write(W1, lno);
            WriteString(W1, obj.mac.lib.name); C.lib[lno] := obj.mac.lib; INC(C.noflibs)
        END;
        WriteObj(W1, cno, obj); Files.Write(W1, lno); WriteString(W1, obj.mac.name)
    END
END WriteMacro;


PROCEDURE* PrintMacro(obj: Object; x, y: INTEGER);
    VAR elem: Object; mh: MacHead;
BEGIN mh := obj(Macro).mac;
    IF mh # NIL THEN elem := mh.first;
        WHILE elem # NIL DO
            elem.do.print(elem, obj.x*4 + x, obj.y*4 + y); elem := elem.next
        END
    END
END PrintMacro;
```

```
PROCEDURE* Notify(T: Texts.Text; op: INTEGER; beg, end: LONGINT);
BEGIN
END Notify;

BEGIN Texts.OpenWriter(W); Texts.OpenWriter(TW); width := 1;
    NEW(T); Texts.Open(T, ""); T.notify := Notify;
    NEW(LineMethod); LineMethod.new := NewLine; LineMethod.copy := CopyLine;
    LineMethod.selectable := LineSelectable; LineMethod.handle := HandleLine;
    LineMethod.read := ReadLine; LineMethod.write := WriteLine;
    LineMethod.print := PrintLine;
    NEW(CapMethod); CapMethod.new := NewCaption; CapMethod.copy := CopyCaption;
    CapMethod.selectable := CaptionSelectable; CapMethod.handle := HandleCaption;
    CapMethod.read := ReadCaption; CapMethod.write := WriteCaption;
    CapMethod.print := PrintCaption;
    NEW(MacMethod); MacMethod.new := NewMacro; MacMethod.copy := CopyMacro;
    MacMethod.selectable := MacroSelectable; MacMethod.handle := HandleMacro;
    MacMethod.read := ReadMacro; MacMethod.write := WriteMacro;
    MacMethod.print := PrintMacro
END Graphics.
```

13.9 Rectangles and curves

13.9.1 Rectangles

In this section, we present two extensions of the basic graphics system that introduce new classes of objects. The first implements rectangles, which are typically used for framing a set of objects. They are, for example, used in the representation of electronic components (macros, see Figure 13.2). Their implementation follows the scheme presented at the end of Section 13.7 and is reasonably straightforward, considering that each rectangle merely consists of four lines. Additionally, a background raster may be specified.

One of the design decisions occurring for every new class concerns the way to display the selection. In this case we chose, in contrast to the cases of captions and macros, not inverse video, but a small square dot in the lower right corner of the rectangle.

The data type *Rectangle* contains two additional fields: *lw* indicates the line width and *vers* specifies the background pattern.

In spite of the simplicity of the notion of rectangles, their drawing method is more complex than might be expected. The reason is that drawing methods are responsible for appropriate clipping at frame boundaries. In this case, some of the component lines may have to be shortened, and some may disappear altogether.

Procedure *Handle* provides an example of a receiver of a control message. It is activated as soon as the middle mouse button is pressed, in contrast to other actions, which are initiated after the release of all buttons. Therefore, this message allows for the implementation of actions under control of individual handlers interpreting further mouse movements. In this example, the action serves to change the size of the rectangle, namely by moving its lower right corner.

```
MODULE Rectangles; (*NW 25.2.90 / 1.2.92*)
  IMPORT Display, Files, Input, Printer, Texts, Oberon, Graphics, GraphicFrames;

  TYPE Rectangle* = POINTER TO RectDesc;

    RectDesc* = RECORD (Graphics.ObjectDesc)
        lw*, vers*: INTEGER
      END;

  VAR method*: Graphics.Method;
    shade: INTEGER;

  PROCEDURE New*;
    VAR r: Rectangle;
  BEGIN NEW(r); r.do := method; Graphics.new := r
  END New;

  PROCEDURE* Copy(src, dst: Graphics.Object);
  BEGIN
    dst.x := src.x; dst.y := src.y; dst.w := src.w; dst.h := src.h; dist.col := src.col;
    dst(Rectangle).lw := src(Rectangle).lw; dst(Rectangle).vers:= src(Rectangle).vers
  END Copy;

  PROCEDURE mark(col, x, y: INTEGER);
  BEGIN Display.ReplConst(col, x−4, y, 4, 4, 0)
  END mark;

  PROCEDURE* Draw(obj: Graphics.Object; VAR M: Graphics.Msg);
    VAR x, y, w, h, lw, col: INTEGER; s: SET; f: GraphicFrames.Frame;

    PROCEDURE draw(col: INTEGER);
    BEGIN
      IF 0 IN s THEN Display.ReplConst(col, x, y, w, lw, 0) END;
      IF 1 IN s THEN Display.ReplConst(col, x+w−lw, y, lw, h, 0) END;
      IF 2 IN s THEN Display.ReplConst(col, x, y+h−lw, w, lw, 0) END;
      IF 3 IN s THEN Display.ReplConst(col, x, y, lw, h, 0) END
    END draw;
  BEGIN
    WITH M: GraphicFrames.DrawMsg DO
      x := obj.x + M.x; y := obj.y + M.y; w := obj.w; h := obj.h; f := M.f;
      lw := obj(Rectangle).lw; s := {0..3};
      IF x+w < f.X THEN s := {}
      ELSIF x < f.X THEN DEC(w, f.X−x); x := f.X; EXCL(s, 3)
      END;
      IF x >= f.X1 THEN s := {}
      ELSIF x+w > f.X1 THEN w := f.X1−x; EXCL(s, 1)
      END;
      IF y+h < f.Y THEN s := {}
      ELSIF y < f.Y THEN DEC(h, f.Y−y); y := f.Y; EXCL(s, 0)
      END;
```

```
            IF y >= f.Y1 THEN s := {}
            ELSIF y+h > f.Y1 THEN h := f.Y1-y; EXCL(s, 2)
            END;
            IF s # {} THEN
                IF M.col = Display.black THEN col := obj.col ELSE col := M.col END;
                IF M.mode = 0 THEN
                    draw(col);
                    IF obj.selected THEN mark(Display.white, x+w-lw, y+lw) END;
                    IF obj(Rectangle).vers # 0 THEN
                        Display.ReplPattern(col, Display.grey0, x, y, w, h, 1)
                    END
                ELSIF M.mode = 1 THEN mark(Display.white, x+w-lw, y+lw)
                ELSIF M.mode = 2 THEN mark(Display.black, x+w-lw, y+lw)
                ELSIF obj(Rectangle).vers = 0 THEN
                        draw(Display.black); mark(Display.black, x+w-lw, y+lw)
                ELSE Display.ReplConst(Display.black, x, y, w, h, 0)
                END
            END
        END
    END
END Draw;

PROCEDURE* Selectable(obj: Graphics.Object; x, y: INTEGER): BOOLEAN;
BEGIN
    RETURN (obj.x + obj.w − 4 <= x) & (x <= obj.x + obj.w) &
        (obj.y <= y) & (y <= obj.y + 4)
END Selectable;

PROCEDURE* Handle(obj: Graphics.Object; VAR M: Graphics.Msg);
    VAR x0, y0, x1, y1, dx, dy: INTEGER; k: SET;
BEGIN
    IF M IS Graphics.WidMsg THEN obj(Rectangle).lw := M(Graphics.WidMsg).w
    ELSIF M IS Graphics.ColorMsg THEN obj.col := M(Graphics.ColorMsg).col
    ELSIF M IS GraphicFrames.CtrlMsg THEN
        WITH M: GraphicFrames.CtrlMsg DO
            WITH obj: Rectangle DO
                M.res := 1; x0 := obj.x + obj.w + M.f.x; y0 := obj.y + M.f.y;
                mark(Display.white, x0 − obj.lw, y0 + obj.lw);
                REPEAT Input.Mouse(k, x1, y1);
                    DEC(x1, (x1−M.f.x) MOD 4); DEC(y1, (y1−M.f.y) MOD 4);
                    Oberon.DrawCursor(Oberon.Mouse, GraphicFrames.Crosshair, x1, y1)
                UNTIL k = {};
                mark(Display.black, x0 − obj.lw, y0 + obj.lw);
                IF (x0 − obj.w < x1) & (y1 < y0+ obj.h) THEN
                    GraphicFrames.EraseObj(M.f, obj);
                    dx := x1 − x0; dy := y1 − y0;
                    INC(obj.y, dy); INC(obj.w, dx); DEC(obj.h, dy);
                    GraphicFrames.DrawObj(M.f, obj)
                END
            END
        END
    END
END Handle;

PROCEDURE* Read(obj: Graphics.Object; VAR R: Files.Rider;
        VAR C: Graphics.Context);
    VAR w, v: SHORTINT; len: INTEGER
BEGIN Graphics.ReadInt(R, len); Files.Read(R, w); Files.Read(R, v);
    obj(Rectangle).lw := w; obj(Rectangle).vers := v
```

```
END Read;


PROCEDURE* Write(obj: Graphics.Object; cno: SHORTINT; VAR W:
Files.Rider;
VAR C: Graphics.Context);
BEGIN Graphics.WriteObj(W, cno, obj); Graphics.WriteInt(W, 2);
    Files.Write(W, SHORT(obj(Rectangle).lw)); Files.Write(W,
    SHORT(obj(Rectangle).vers))
END Write;


PROCEDURE* Print(obj: Graphics.Object; x, y: INTEGER);
    VAR w, h, lw, s: INTEGER;
BEGIN INC(x, obj.x * 4); INC(y, obj.y * 4); w := obj.w * 4; h := obj.h
* 4;
    lw := obj(Rectangle).lw * 2; s := obj(Rectangle).vers;
    Printer.ReplConst(x, y, w, lw);
    Printer.ReplConst(x+w-lw, y, lw, h);
    Printer.ReplConst(x, y+h-lw, w, lw);
    Printer.ReplConst(x, y, lw, h);
    IF s > 0 THEN Printer.ReplPattern(x, y, w, h, s) END
END Print;


PROCEDURE Make*; (*command*)
    VAR x0, x1, y0, y1: INTEGER;
        R: Rectangle;
        G: GraphicFrames.Frame;
BEGIN G := GraphicFrames.Focus();
    IF (G # NIL) & (G.mark.next # NIL) THEN
        GraphicFrames.Deselect(G);
        x0 := G.mark.x; y0 := G.mark.y; x1 := G.mark.next.x; y1 :=
        G.mark.next.y;
        NEW(R); R.col := Oberon.CurCol;
        R.w := ABS(x1-x0); R.h := ABS(y1-y0);
        IF x1 < x0 THEN x0 := x1 END;
        IF y1 < y0 THEN y0 := y1 END;
        R.x := x0 - G.x; R.y := y0 - G.y;
        R.lw := Graphics.width; R.vers := shade; R.do := method;
        Graphics.Add(G.graph, R);
        GraphicFrames.Defocus(G); GraphicFrames.DrawObj(G, R)
    END
END Make;


PROCEDURE SetShade*;
    VAR S: Texts.Scanner;
BEGIN Texts.OpenScanner(S, Oberon.Par.text, Oberon.Par.pos);
Texts.Scan(S);
    IF S.class = Texts.Int THEN shade := SHORT(S.i) END
END SetShade;

BEGIN shade := 0; NEW(method);
    method.module := "Rectangles"; method.allocator := "New";
    method.new := New; method.copy := Copy; method.draw := Draw;
    method.selectable := Selectable; method.handle := Handle;
    method.read := Read; method.write := Write; method.print := Print
END Rectangles.
```

13.9.2   Oblique lines, circles and ellipses

The second extension is module *Curves*. It introduces three new kinds of objects: lines that are not necessarily horizontal or vertical, circles and ellipses (with horizontal and vertical axes). All are considered to be variants of the same type *Curve*, the variant being specified by the field *kind* of the object record. Selection is again indicated by a small, square dot at the end of a line and at the lowest point of a circle or an ellipse.

In order to avoid computations involving floating-point numbers and to increase efficiency, Bresenham algorithms are used. The algorithm for a line defined by $bx - ay = 0$ (for $b \leq a$) is summarized by the following statements:

```
x := 0; y := 0; h := b - a DIV 2;
WHILE x <= a DO Dot(x, y);
    IF h <= 0 THEN INC(h, b) ELSE INC(h, b-a); INC(y) END;
    INC(x)
END
```

The Bresenham algorithm for a circle given by the equation $x^2 + y^2 = r^2$ is

```
x := r; y := 0; h := 1-r;
WHILE y <= x DO Dot(x, y);
    IF h < 0 THEN INC(h, 2*y + 3)
    ELSE INC(h, 2*(y-x)+5); INC(x)
    END; INC(y)
END
```

```
MODULE Curves; (*NW 8.11.90 / 1.2.91*)
    IMPORT Display, Files, Printer, Oberon, Graphics, GraphicFrames;

    TYPE Curve* = POINTER TO CurveDesc;

    CurveDesc* = RECORD (Graphics.ObjectDesc)
        kind*, lw*: INTEGER
    END;

    (*kind: 0 = up-line, 1 = down-line, 2 = circle, 3 = ellipse*)

    VAR method*: Graphics.Method;

    PROCEDURE dot(f: GraphicFrames.Frame; col: INTEGER; x, y: LONGINT);
    BEGIN
```

```
    IF (f.X <= x) & (x < f.X1) & (f.Y <= y) & (y < f.Y1)
        THEN Display.Dot(col, x, y, 0)
    END
END dot;


PROCEDURE mark(f: GraphicFrames.Frame; col, x, y: INTEGER);
BEGIN
    IF (f.X <= x) & (x+4 < f.X1) & (f.Y <= y) & (y+4 < f.Y1) THEN
        Display.ReplConst(col, x, y, 4, 4, 0)
    END
END mark;


PROCEDURE line(f: GraphicFrames.Frame; col: INTEGER; x, y, w, h, d: LONGINT);
    VAR x1, y1, u: LONGINT;
BEGIN
    IF h < w THEN
        x1 := x+w; u := (h−w) DIV 2;
        IF d = −1 THEN INC(y, h) END;
        WHILE x < x1 DO
            dot(f, col, x, y); INC(x);
            IF u < 0 THEN INC(u, h) ELSE INC(u, h−w); INC(y, d) END
        END
    ELSE y1 := y+h; u := (w−h) DIV 2;
        IF d = −1 THEN INC(x, w) END;
        WHILE y < y1 DO
            dot(f, col, x, y); INC(y);
            IF u < 0 THEN INC(u, w) ELSE INC(u, w−h); INC(x, d) END
        END
    END
END line;


PROCEDURE circle(f: GraphicFrames.Frame; col: INTEGER; x0, y0, r: LONGINT);
    VAR x, y, u: LONGINT;
BEGIN u := 1 − r; x := r; y := 0;
    WHILE y <= x DO
        dot(f, col, x0+x, y0+y); dot(f, col, x0+y, y0+x); dot(f, col, x0−y, y0+x);
        dot(f, col, x0−x, y0+y);
        dot(f, col, x0−x, y0−y); dot(f, col, x0−y, y0−x); dot(f, col, x0+y, y0−x);
        dot(f, col, x0+x, y0−y);
        IF u < 0 THEN INC(u, 2*y+3) ELSE INC(u, 2*(y−x)+5); DEC(x) END;
        INC(y)
    END
END circle;


PROCEDURE ellipse(f: GraphicFrames.Frame; col: INTEGER; x0, y0, a, b: LONGINT);
    VAR x, y, y1, aa, bb, d, g, h: LONGINT;
BEGIN aa := a*a; bb := b*b;
    h := (aa DIV 4) − b*aa + bb; g := (9*aa DIV 4) − 3*b*aa + bb; x := 0; y := b;
    WHILE g < 0 DO
        dot(f, col, x0+x, y0+y); dot(f, col, x0−x, y0+y); dot(f, col, x0−x, y0−y);
        dot(f, col, x0+x, y0−y);
        IF h < 0 THEN d := (2*x+3)*bb; INC(g, d)
        ELSE d := (2*x+3)*bb − 2*(y−1)*aa; INC(g, d + 2*aa); DEC(y)
        END;
        INC(h, d); INC(x)
    END;
    y1 := y; h := (bb DIV 4) − a*bb + aa; x := a; y := 0;
```

```
        WHILE y <= y1 DO
            dot(f, col, x0+x, y0+y); dot(f, col, x0-x, y0+y); dot(f, col, x0-x, y0-y);
            dot(f, col, x0+x, y0-y);
            IF h < 0 THEN INC(h, (2*y+3)*aa)
            ELSE INC(h, (2*y+3)*aa - 2*(x-1)*bb); DEC(x)
            END;
            INC(y)
        END
    END ellipse;


    PROCEDURE New*;
        VAR c: Curve;
    BEGIN NEW(c); c.do := method; Graphics.new := c
    END New;


    PROCEDURE* Copy(src, dst: Graphics.Object);
    BEGIN
        dst.x := src.x; dst.y := src.y; dst.w := src.w; dst.h := src.h; dst.col := src.col;
        dst(Curve).kind := src(Curve).kind; dst(Curve).lw:= src(Curve).lw
    END Copy;


    PROCEDURE* Draw(obj: Graphics.Object; VAR M: Graphics.Msg);
        VAR x, y, w, h, col: INTEGER; f: GraphicFrames.Frame;
    BEGIN
        WITH M: GraphicFrames.DrawMsg DO
            x := obj.x + M.x; y := obj.y + M.y; w := obj.w; h := obj.h; f := M.f;
            IF M.col = Display.black THEN col := obj.col ELSE col := M.col END;
            IF (x < f.X1) & (f.X <= x+w) & (y < f.Y1) & (f.Y <= y+h) THEN
                IF obj(Curve).kind = 0 THEN (*up-line*)
                    IF M.mode = 0 THEN
                        IF obj.selected THEN mark(f, Display.white, x, y) END;
                        line(f, col, x, y, w, h, 1)
                    ELSIF M.mode = 1 THEN mark(f, Display.white, x, y)
                    ELSIF M.mode = 2 THEN mark(f, Display.black, x, y)
                    ELSE mark(f, Display.black, x, y); line(f, Display.black, x, y, w, h, 1)
                    END
                ELSIF obj(Curve).kind = 1 THEN (*down-line*)
                    IF M.mode = 0 THEN
                        IF obj.selected THEN mark(f, Display.white, x, y+h) END;
                        line(f, col, x, y, w, h, -1)
                    ELSIF M.mode = 1 THEN mark(f, Display.white, x, y+h)
                    ELSIF M.mode = 2 THEN mark(f, Display.black, x, y+h)
                    ELSE mark(f, Display.black, x, y+h); line(f, Display.black, x, y, w, h, -1)
                    END
                ELSIF obj(Curve).kind = 2 THEN (*circle*)
                    w := w DIV 2;
                    IF M.mode = 0 THEN
                        IF obj.selected THEN mark(f, Display.white, x+w, y-4) END;
                        circle(f, col, x+w, y+w, w)
                    ELSIF M.mode = 1 THEN mark(f, Display.white, x+w, y-4)
                    ELSIF M.mode = 2 THEN mark(f, Display.black, x+w, y-4)
                    ELSE mark(f, Display.black, x+w, y-4); circle(f, Display.black, x+w, y+w, w)
                    END
                ELSIF obj(Curve).kind = 3 THEN (*ellipse*)
                    w := w DIV 2; h := h DIV 2;
                    IF M.mode = 0 THEN
                        IF obj.selected THEN mark(f, Display.white, x+w, y-4) END;
                        ellipse(f, col, x+w, y+h, w, h)
```

```
                    ELSIF M.mode = 1 THEN mark(f, Display.white, x+w, y−4)
                    ELSIF M.mode = 2 THEN mark(f, Display.black, x+w, y−4)
                    ELSE mark(f, Display.black, x+w, y−4);
                           ellipse(f, Display.black, x+w, y+h, w, h)
                    END
                END
            END
        END
END Draw;


PROCEDURE* Selectable(obj: Graphics.Object; x, y: INTEGER): BOOLEAN;
    VAR xm, y0, w, h: INTEGER;
BEGIN
    IF obj(Curve).kind <= 1 THEN (*line*)
        w := obj.w; h := obj.h;
        IF obj(Curve).kind = 1 THEN y0 := obj.y + h; h := −h ELSE y0 := obj.y END;
        RETURN (obj.x <= x) & (x < obj.x + w) &
            (ABS(LONG(y−y0)*w − LONG(x−obj.x)*h) < w*4)
    ELSE (*circle or ellipse*)
        xm := obj.w DIV 2 + obj.x;
        RETURN (xm − 4 <= x) & (x <= xm + 4) & (obj.y − 4 <= y) & (y <= obj.y + 4)
    END
END Selectable;


PROCEDURE* Handle(obj: Graphics.Object; VAR M: Graphics.Msg);
BEGIN
    IF M IS Graphics.ColorMsg THEN obj.col := M(Graphics.ColorMsg).col END
END Handle;


PROCEDURE* Read(obj: Graphics.Object; VAR R: Files.Rider; VAR C: Graphics.Context);
    VAR len: INTEGER;
BEGIN Graphics.ReadInt(R, len); Graphics.ReadInt(R, obj(Curve).kind);
Graphics.ReadInt(R, obj(Curve).lw)
END Read;


PROCEDURE* Write(obj: Graphics.Object; cno: SHORTINT; VAR W: Files.Rider;
VAR C: Graphics.Context);
BEGIN Graphics.WriteObj(W, cno, obj);
    Graphics.WriteInt(W, 4); Graphics.WriteInt(W, obj(Curve).kind);
    Graphics.WriteInt(W, obj(Curve).lw)
END Write;


PROCEDURE* Print(obj: Graphics.Object; x, y: INTEGER);
    VAR x0, y0: INTEGER;
BEGIN
    IF obj(Curve).kind = 0 THEN
        x0 := obj.x * 4 + x; y0 := obj.y * 4 + y;
        Printer.Line(x0, y0, obj.w * 4 + x0, obj.h * 4 + y0)
    ELSIF obj(Curve).kind = 1 THEN
        x0 := obj.x * 4 + x; y0 := obj.y * 4 + y;
        Printer.Line(x0, obj.h * 4 + y0, obj.w * 4 + x0, y0)
    ELSIF obj(Curve).kind = 2 THEN
        Printer.Circle((obj.x*2 + obj.w)*2 + x, (obj.y*2 + obj.h)*2 + y, obj.w*2)
    ELSE
        Printer.Ellipse((obj.x*2 + obj.w)*2 + x, (obj.y*2 + obj.h)*2 + y, obj.w*2, obj.h*2)
    END
END Print;
```

```
PROCEDURE MakeLine*; (*command*)
  VAR x0, x1, y0, y1: INTEGER;
      c: Curve;
      G: GraphicFrames.Frame;
BEGIN G := GraphicFrames.Focus();
  IF (G # NIL) & (G.mark.next # NIL) THEN
    GraphicFrames.Deselect(G);
    x0 := G.mark.x; y0 := G.mark.y; x1 := G.mark.next.x; y1 := G.mark.next.y;
    NEW(c); c.col := Oberon.CurCol;
    c.w := ABS(x1−x0); c.h := ABS(y1−y0); c.lw := Graphics.width;
    IF x0 <= x1 THEN c.x := x0;
        IF y0 <= y1 THEN c.kind := 0; c.y := y0 ELSE c.kind := 1; c.y := y1 END
    ELSE c.x := x1;
        IF y1 < y0 THEN c.kind := 0; c.y := y1 ELSE c.kind := 1; c.y := y0 END
    END;
    DEC(c.x, G.x); DEC(c.y, G.y); c.do := method;
    Graphics.Add(G.graph, c);
    GraphicFrames.Defocus(G); GraphicFrames.DrawObj(G, c)
  END
END MakeLine;


PROCEDURE MakeCircle*; (*command*)
  VAR x0, y0, r: INTEGER;
      c: Curve;
      G: GraphicFrames.Frame;
  BEGIN G := GraphicFrames.Focus();
    IF (G # NIL) & (G.mark.next # NIL) THEN
      GraphicFrames.Deselect(G);
      x0 := G.mark.x; y0 := G.mark.y; r := ABS(G.mark.next.x−x0);
      IF r > 4 THEN
        NEW(c); c.x := x0 − r − G.x; c.y := y0 − r − G.y; c.w := 2*r+1; c.h := c.w;
        c.kind := 2; c.col := Oberon.CurCol;
        c.lw := Graphics.width; c.do := method;
        Graphics.Add(G.graph, c);
        GraphicFrames.Defocus(G); GraphicFrames.DrawObj(G, c)
      END
    END
  END MakeCircle;


PROCEDURE MakeEllipse*; (*command*)
    VAR x0, y0, a, b: INTEGER;
        c: Curve;
        G: GraphicFrames.Frame;
  BEGIN G := GraphicFrames.Focus();
    IF (G # NIL) & (G.mark.next # NIL) & (G.mark.next.next # NIL) THEN
      GraphicFrames.Deselect(G);
      x0 := G.mark.x; y0 := G.mark.y;
      a := ABS(G.mark.next.x−x0); b := ABS(G.mark.next.next.y − y0);
      IF (a > 4) & (b > 4) THEN
        NEW(c); c.x := x0 − a − G.x; c.y := y0 − b − G.y; c.w := 2*a+1;
        c.h := 2*b+1;
        c.kind := 3; c.col := Oberon.CurCol;
        c.lw := Graphics.width; c.do := method;
        Graphics.Add(G.graph, c);
        GraphicFrames.Defocus(G); GraphicFrames.DrawObj(G, c)
      END
    END
  END MakeEllipse;
```

```
BEGIN NEW(method); method.module := "Curves"; method.allocator := "New";
    method.new := New; method.copy := Copy; method.draw := Draw;
    method.selectable := Selectable; method.handle := Handle;
    method.read := Read; method.write := Write; method.print := Print
END Curves.
```

14 Building and maintenance tools

14.1 The startup process

An aspect usually given little attention in system descriptions is the process of how a system is started. Its choice, however, is itself an interesting and far from trivial design consideration and will be described here in some detail. Moreover, it directly determines the steps in which a system is developed from scratch, mirroring the steps in which it builds itself up from a bare store to an operating body.

The startup process typically proceeds in several stages, each of them bringing further facilities into play, raising the system to a higher level towards completion. The term for this strategy is *bootstrapping* or, **Booting** in modern computer jargon, *booting*.

Boot loader

Stage 1 is initiated when power is switched on or when the reset button is pressed and released. To be precise, power-on issues a reset signal to all parts of the computer and holds it for a certain time. Pushing the reset button therefore appears like a power-on without power having been switched off. Release of the reset signal causes the processor to start the so-called *boot loader*. This program resides in a read-only store (ROM) and hence is always present, even on a 'bare' machine. It loads data into memory, which are interpreted as code in Stage 2. In order to keep the boot loader as simple as possible – remember that it is burnt into ROM on every workstation and therefore cannot be changed without considerable effort – the format of its data must be simple. We have chosen the following structure, which had never to be changed during the entire development effort of the Oberon System because of both its simplicity and generality:

Format of
boot file

```
BootFile    = {block}.
block       = size:4 address:4 {byte}.
```

The address of the last block, distinguished by size = 0, is interpreted as the address of the starting point of Stage 2. The size of the boot loader on Ceres is about 250 bytes.

The source of the boot data is typically a fixed location on the disk. In our case, the data occupy less than a single track, which is therefore called the *boot track* and remains permanently reserved.

Inner core

The data loaded in Stage 1 are interpreted as code in Stage 2, representing modules *Kernel*, *FileDir*, *Files* and *Modules*, which are said to constitute the *inner core* of the system. Control is transferred to module *Kernel's* initialization part. First, the processor's base address registers are initialized, then the chain of free module descriptors is formed. This is followed by the initialization of the required virtual address pages on machines that feature a memory management unit. Interrupt table and interrupt control unit (ICU) are initialized, and finally the initialization parts of the remaining three modules are executed, the last one being *Modules*. Note that only a single device driver is contained in the inner core: the disk driver in module *Kernel*.

Collection of garbage files

The presence of *Modules* implies that the regular loader is available for the further build-up of the system. Module *Files* is present in the inner core, because it is imported by *Modules*, and *FileDir* because it is imported by *Files*. The initialization of module *FileDir* constructs the sector reservation table by recording all files registered in the file directory. This process requires the traversal of the entire directory and the reading of all file headers. It can be regarded as the garbage collection process of disk sectors. The initialization part of *Modules* contains the statement

M := ThisMod("Oberon")

which causes loading of module *Oberon* and with it automatically of all modules imported by *Oberon*. This constitutes Stage 3 of the boot process. In particular, Stage 3 loads and initializes the display, keyboard and mouse drivers, as well as the display, text and font machinery. It terminates with the initialization of module *Oberon* itself, which contains the statement

M := Modules.ThisMod("System")

Outer core

It initiates Stage 4 of the boot process and completes the system by loading the first tool module. The initialization of *System* opens a viewer for the log and one for a tool text. In addition to *System*, modules *MenuViewers* and *TextFrames* are loaded, because they are imported by *System*. The modules loaded so far form the *outer core*. In passing, we note that the default font and the text *System.Tool* are also needed in Stage 4. After completion of Stage 4, control returns to the statements

P := ThisCommand(M, "Loop"); P

in the initialization part of *Modules*. Thereby control enters the central loop of the Oberon System for polling input events. Normal operation has begun.

Let us summarize the prerequisites for the four stages:

(0) The bootloader must reside in the ROM.

(1) The boot file must reside on the boot track of the disk.

(2) The modules of the outer core must reside in the file system.

These conditions are usually met. But they are not satisfied if either a new, bare machine is present or if the disk store is defective. In these cases, the prerequisites must be established with, of course, the aid of suitable tools. The tools needed for the case of the bare machine or the incomplete file store are called *building tools*, and those required in the case of defects are called *maintenance tools*.

14.2 Building tools

Building tools allow one to establish the three preconditions for the boot process on a bare machine. Condition (0) requires an assembler for programming the boot loader, and a so-called ROM programmer, typically an external device connected by an RS-232 (V24) link. We shall not discuss these tools any further. Condition (1) requires a tool to compose the boot file, and one to load it onto the boot track. Condition (2) requires a tool that establishes a file directory and is able to load files. The tool that creates the boot file is called a *boot linker*; this module was given the name *Boot*. The tool that has the capability to load the boot track and to load files is module *Oberon0*.

Oberon0

There remains the important question of how *Oberon0* is loaded onto a bare machine. A partial answer is: by a boot process consisting of Stages 1 and 2 only, using a boot file in which module *Modules* is replaced by *Oberon0*. But this does not suffice. The key facility is a boot loader that admits an exernal source as alternative to the disk's boot track. As alternative source we use (the boot track of) the diskette. The selection of the source is determined by a switch. It makes the use of I/O devices apart from the diskette driver during the boot phase avoidable. The initiation rite for a bare machine then consists of the following steps:

Boot process

(1) Select the alternative boot source by the appropriate switch setting.

(2) Reset. The boot file is read and *Oberon0* is started.

(3) Invoke the command that reads all files from the diskette (which supposedly holds all files needed for the outer core).

(4) Reset the switch and boot again. This initiates the regular boot process.

A more modern solution would be to select the network as alternative boot file source. We rejected this option in order to keep net access routines outside the ROM, in order to keep the startup of a computer independent of the presence of a server, and also in consideration of the fact that there exist machines that operate in a stand-alone mode. As it turns out, the need for the alternative boot file source arises very rarely.

Boot linker   The boot linker is almost identical to the module loader, with the exception that object code is not deposited in newly allocated blocks, but in a fixed buffer that is finally output to form the boot file. Its name is supplied as second parameter to the command *Boot.Link*. The first parameter specifies the module that is the top of the hierarchy forming the inner core

        Boot.Link Modules Ceres2.Boot
        Boot.Link Oberon0 Ceres2.Boot0

The boot file consists of four blocks (see Section 14.1). The first block contains the module descriptors (see Chapter 6) for the modules of the inner core. The second block consists of their code and global data sections. The third block contains the lengths of the first two blocks. The fourth block specifies the start address of *Kernel*. The load addresses of the first three blocks are fixed constants in the *Boot* program (4000H, 8000H, 0).

From the description of the start-up process for a bare machine given above, module *Oberon0* must first initialize the file directory and then load all files contained on a boot diskette. We have chosen to extend *Oberon0* into a much more versatile tool. This was not merely clever foresight, but is due to *Oberon0*'s emergence from the development process of the Oberon System, which, naturally, included a considerable amount of error detection and correction (Wirth, 1989). *Oberon0* therefore contains a genuine command interpreter. There exist commands for inspecting memory areas, disk sectors, for inspecting the file directory, and even for loading modules. The presence of a command interpreter requires input (keyboard) and output (display) facilities. They were kept to a bare minimum and encapsulated in module IO:

```
DEFINITION IO;
    PROCEDURE Read (VAR ch: CHAR);
    PROCEDURE WriteLn;
    PROCEDURE Write (ch: CHAR);
    PROCEDURE WriteString (s: ARRAY OF CHAR);
    PROCEDURE WriteHex (x: LONGINT);
    PROCEDURE WriteInt (x, n: LONGINT);
END IO.
```

The command interpreter is a simple loop, accepting commands specified by a single letter followed by parameters that are either hexadecimal numbers or names. User-friendliness was not given any importance at this point, and it would indeed be unjustified. We refrain from elaborating on further details and concentrate on providing a list of available commands. This should give the reader an impression of the capabilities of this tool module for system initiation and for error searching.

r	name	read file form diskette
w	name	write file to diskette
d	name	delete file form diskette
z		read all files contained on diskette
e		enumerate diskette files
!i		initialize diskette directory
!f		format diskette
E		enumerate file directory
D	name	delete file
N	name0 name1	rename file
M	name	load and initialize module
C	name	call command
O		load Oberon and call Loop
a	address	display memory block (256 bytes) in hex
A	address	display memory block (256 bytes) as characters
k	number	display disk sector in hex
K	number	display disk sector as characters
l		clear display
?		list available commands
t		get time and date from real time clock
T	time date	set real time clock
!B	name	load file onto boot track
!Y		initialize bad sector file
!1		initialize file directory

All these additional commands give *Oberon*0 the character of a maintenance tool. In particular, the possibility to read individual files from the diskette allows recovery when a file required in stages 3 or 4 of the boot process has been corrupted. The O command allows to detect the point at which the process fails. Nevertheless, the original purpose of *Oberon0* is to initiate a bare machine through commands !1, !B and z.

14.3 Maintenance tools

An important prerequisite for Stage 2 (and the following stages) in the boot process has not been mentioned above. Recall that the initialization of module *FileDir* constructs the disk sector reservation table in the *Kernel* from information contained on the disk. Obviously, its prerequisite is an intact, consistent file directory. A single unreadable, corrupted file directory or file header sector lets this process fail, and booting becomes impossible. To cope with this (fortunately rare) situation, a maintenance tool has been designed: **DiskCheck** module *DiskCheck*. It is included in a special boot file generated by the command

> Boot.Link DiskCheck Ceres2.CheckBoot

DiskCheck is organized similarly to *Oberon0* as a simple command interpreter, but it imports only *Kernel* and IO. Hence booting involves only Stages 1 and 2 without any access to the disk. Operating *DiskCheck* requires care and knowledge of the structure of the file system (Chapter 7). The available commands are the following; those that write on the disk are guarded by an exclamation mark:

r	n	read sector n into sector buffer, display hex
R	n	read sector n into sector buffer, display as characters
e	n	read extended index sector n into sector buffer
!W		write sector buffer
d	n	read directory sector n into dir buffer
!D		write dir buffer
h	n	read header sector into Header buffer
!H		write header buffer
x	n	read track containing sector n into track buffer
!Y		format track
!Z		write track buffer

S	m, n	insert sector n as header address of entry m in dir buffer
s	m, n	insert sector n in entry m of sector table in header buffer
L	n	set file length in header buffer to n
i	adr val	insert val at adr in sector buffer
f	name	read header sector of named file into header buffer
q	n	find all files of which sector n is part
c		check consistency of files and directory
b	n	add faulty sector to bad sector table
l		clear display
Q		reset disk drive
?		list available commands
!0	n	clear sector n (write zeroes)
!1		initialize file directory
!2		initialize bad sector table
!?		read all disk sectors and record faulty sectors
!*		format disk

Sectors are always read into a buffer, namely the sector buffer, the directory buffer, the header buffer or the track buffer, and the number of the sector in the respective buffer is retained. Changes are made on the data stored in the respective buffer, which is displayed after each reading or change in an appropriately decoded format. Every change must be confirmed, because only a writing command transfers the buffered data to the disk.

Faulty sectors   The typical handling of the occurence of a corrupted sector in a file consists of the following steps:

(1) The track containing the unreadable sector is read (x).

(2) The track is reformatted (!Y).

(3) The track is restored (!Z) (the faulty sector data are lost).

(4) The track is reread (x) and the steps are repeated, if the condition persists.

(5) If, after several tries, the sector cannot be corrected, the file must be removed. In order to make a directory traversal possible without changing the directory data, the corresponding entry is changed (S). The simplest way is to set it equal to its neighbouring entry, thereby introducing an inconsistency (double reference), which must be corrected by deleting the file as soon as the Oberon System is operational.

(6) An unrecoverably faulty sector must be made unreferenceable. This is done by appending it to a file called *BadSectors*, which is inherently unreadable, but which lets its sectors be marked as used in the initialization process of the sector reservation table in Boot Stage 2. A sector is appended to this file by command b.

(7) When the Oberon System is available again, the recovered files must be either deleted or inspected and, if possible, corrected.

Program *DiskCheck* must be extremely robust. No data read can be assumed to be correct, no index can be assumed to lie within its declared bounds, no sector number can be assumed to be valid, and no directory or header page may be assumed to have the expected format. Guards and error diagnostics take a prominent place. Because any program failure must be prevented, no use is made of disk procedures provided by the *Kernel*. They are reprogrammed with additional guards and status reporting.

Corrupted directory

Whereas a faulty, unreadable sector in a file in the worst case leads to the loss of that file, a fault in a sector carrying a directory page is quite disastrous, because not only the files referenced from that page, but also those referenced from descendant pages, become inaccessible. A fault in the root page even causes the loss of all files. The catastrophe is of such proportions that measures should be taken even if the case is very unlikely. After all, it may happen – and indeed it has occurred.

The only way to recover files that are no longer accessible from the directory is by scanning the entire disk. In order to make a search at all possible, every file header carries a mark field that is given a fixed, constant value. It is very unlikely, but not entirely impossible, that data sectors that happen to have the same value at the location corresponding to that of the mark may be mistaken to be headers.

Scavenger

The tool performing such a scan is called *Scavenger*. It is, like *DiskCheck*, a simple command interpreter, and a boot file is created by

Boot.Link Scavenger Ceres2.ScavBoot

The available commands are

s	n	Scan the first n sectors and collect headers
d		Display names of collected files
W		Build new directory
l		Clear display
?		Show available commands

During the scan, a new directory is gradually built up in primary store. Sectors marked as headers are recorded by their name and creation date. The scavenger is the reason for recording the file name in the header, although it remains unused there by the Oberon System. Recovery of the date is essential, because several files with the same name may be found. If one is found with a newer creation date, the older entry is overwritten.

Command W transfers the new directory to the disk. For this purpose, it is necessary to have free sectors available. These have been collected during the scan: both old directory sectors (identified by a directory mark similar to the header mark) and overwritten headers are used as free locations.

The scavenger has proved its worth on more than one occasion. Its main drawback is that it may rediscover files that had been deleted. The deletion operation by definition affects only the directory, but not the file. Therefore the header carrying the name remains unchanged and is discovered by the scan. All in all, however, it is a small deficiency.

Reference

Wirth, N. (1989). Designing a system from scratch. *Structured Programming*, **1**, 11–19.

Index of Words

abort character 261
abstract data type 33
abstract marker 76
abstract printer 138
accessing text 100
accounting 325
actual parameter 36
address-mapping 241
after-method 100
alignment 336
alphabet 98
arbitration phase 273
Arrow marker 77
ASCII code 98
ASCII files 117
ASCII format 257
assignment 424
at character 40
atomic action 34

B-tree page 218
background color 78, 118
background task 26
base line 134
base type 353
bit block transfer (BitBlk) 80
bitmap 82
block 240
block oriented operation 79
block space 240
boot loader 526
boot linker 529
bootstrapping 526
bound objects 69
box representation of characters 134
Bravo text editor 107
broadcast 66, 280
built-in commands 137
built-in text editor 122

caching pieces 111
caption 459, 465
caret 9, 75, 118, 459

caret tracking 126
Cedar system 54
central loop 13, 31
change looks 109
character 98
character attributes 100, 133
character imaging model 134
character outlines 135
character pattern 134
character run 137
clipping 474
cloning 37, 74
code selection 401
color 100
color table 84
command 9, 10, 26, 34
command interface 38
command interpreter 59
command module 17
command phase 272
command row 54
command table 184
configuring display area 66
constant folding 402
consume message 31
contents region 61
context-dependent 333
context-free 333
continue message 29
control message 488
creating textual output 106
creation of viewers 72
cursor 9, 19, 75
cursor handling 63
customized commands 137
customized parameters 36
cyclic redundancy code 265

data phase 273
debugging aid 449
default font 135
defocus message 31
delegation 74

535

Index of Modules

Index of Global Type and Procedure Identifiers